THE JACOBEAN AND
CAROLINE STAGE

G. C. Moore Smith noted (op. cit.) that the initials and the 'POSTHUMUS VATES' in the dedication were obviously intended to make the reader believe that the play had been written by the famous and recently deceased Thomas Randolph. John Aubrey listed it among Randolph's works. (Andrew Clark, ed., *Aubrey's Brief Lives* [1898], ii. 197.) Whether Randolph really wrote it or not is a different and much discussed matter. Brinsley Nicholson (loc. cit.) doubted it because Randolph's brother, who collected and edited his works, neither published nor mentioned it; because the list of errata and the Latin motto at the end suggest a living author—or at least one alive later than 1634/5, when Randolph died; and because, if Randolph had written it, there would have been nothing to prevent the printers from advertising it with his name and degree on the title-page in 1638, three years after his death. G. C. Moore Smith wanted to think that Randolph had written the comedy, or at least sketched it out before it was finished by Richard Brathwait, and he noted some vague and some very undistinctive parallels to Randolph's other work. He could, however, find no clear references to Cambridge, which occur in most of Randolph's dramatic work, though there is one to 'Oxonia'.

James Crossley (loc. cit.) rejected Randolph's authorship and argued for Richard Brathwait, who frequently used his initials or pseudonyms on his title-pages and four of whose works (according to Black, op. cit., p. 82) were published by Harper, the printer of *Cornelianum Dolium*. Crossley also noted in the comedy rhyming Latin verses in the metre of Brathwait's popular *Barnabee's Journal*, published in the same year and in a Latin style which seemed to him similar. Finally, he pointed out that the play was dedicated to Sir Alexander Radcliffe, to whom Brathwait had dedicated *Whimzies* (1631) and probably *Barnabee's Journal* (1638). His other arguments are not very weighty. Professor Black (loc. cit.) accepts Randolph's original authorship, adding somewhat irrelevantly that the lost *Prodigal Scholar*, which was entered in the Stationers' Register in 1650 as by Randolph and whose title fits the Latin play, may have been Randolph's translation of his own Latin. In general he thinks *Cornelianum Dolium* too clever for Brathwait, but agrees that Brathwait may have touched up the play and prepared it for publication. He notes an influence of the play on Brathwait's later work.

It does not seem to me that the case for either Randolph or Brathwait is very convincing. Either is a possible author, but the acceptance of either leaves too many contradictions. The assignment to Thomas Riley of Trinity College, Cambridge (Hazlitt, *Manual*, p. 50), has only the initials to justify it.

The prologue seems to imply that the play had been acted, but there is no clue as to the time or place. Moore Smith (op. cit., pp. 318–19) noted the large amount of medical material in *Cornelianum Dolium* and thought it might have been presented before the College of Physicians, who are mentioned in the play, but he found no records that plays had ever been presented there.

Moore Smith also vaguely suggested the possibility of an Italian source, but offered no candidates.

The Extravagant Shepherd (written 1654)

As the 1654 title-page indicates, this piece is only a translation, 'Written in French by *T. Corneille*. Englished by *T. R.* 1654.' Apparently T. R. meant to indicate that 1654 was the date at which his translation was made; this date also appears in the imprint. The dedicatory epistle, signed by T. R., alludes to composition after the closing of the theatres.

W. R.

The '*W. R.* Master of Arts' given on the title-page of the 1682 edition as author of *The Christmas Ordinary* (q.v., under Anon.) is evidently derived by the publisher from the preface for the edition, which is signed by W. R. and dated 'Helmdon, Octob. 18. 1682'. The preface indicates that this man was not the author but the sponsor of the manuscript, which '*hath lain Dormant almost half an Age*'. W. R. was apparently William Richards (q.v.), a Trinity College, Oxford, man, who was born at Helmdon in 1643 and instituted rector there in 1675.

THOMAS RANDOLPH (Randal, Randall, Randalle, Randol, Randolf, Randoll, Randolphe, Rondolph)
1605–34/5

Bentley, G. E. 'Randolph's *Praeludium* and the Salisbury Court Theatre', in *Joseph Quincy Adams Memorial Studies* (1948), pp. 775–83.

Bowers, Fredson T. 'A Possible Randolph Holograph', *Library*, Fourth Series, xx (1939), 159–62.

Day, Cyrus L. 'New Poems by Randolph', *R.E.S.* viii (1932), 29–36.

Day, Cyrus L. 'Three Notes on Randolph', *M.L.N.* xlvi (1931), 507–10.

Kottas, Karl. *Thomas Randolph: sein Leben und seine Werke* (1909).

Mills, Laurens J. *Peter Hausted: Playwright, Poet, and Preacher,* Indiana University Publications (1944), pp. 17–37.

Parry, J. J., ed. *The Poems and Amyntas of Thomas Randolph* (1917), pp. 1–30.

Smith, G. C. Moore. 'The Canon of Randolph's Dramatic Works', *R.E.S.* i (1925), 309–23.

—— 'Randolph's *Epithalamium to George Goring*', *R.E.S.* ii (1926), 146–51.

—— 'Some Unpublished Poems of Thomas Randolph (1605–1635)', *Palaestra,* cxlviii (1925), 244–57.

—— *Thomas Randolph.* Warton Lecture, *Proceedings of the British Academy* (1927).

Tannenbaum, Samuel A., and Dorothy R. *Thomas Randolph (A Concise Bibliography)* (1946).

Thorn-Drury, G., ed. *The Poems of Thomas Randolph* (1929), pp. vii–xxviii.

The poet and playwright was the eldest son of William Randolph, steward to Sir George Goring and to Edward, Lord Zouch. His mother was Elizabeth, daughter of Thomas Smith of Newnham-cum-Badby, near Daventry. He was born at or baptized from the house of his maternal grandfather on 15 June 1605. (Parry, pp. 1–6; Thorn-Drury, p. ix.) At an unknown date he entered Westminster School, where he was a schoolfellow of William Cartwright, John Donne the younger, James Duport, and William Heminges (Parry, p. 7; Thorn-Drury, p. x); the latter two wrote verses to him later.

Randolph was a notoriously precocious youth, though some of the stories about him should no doubt be questioned. Aubrey says (Clark ed. ii. 196) that at the age of nine 'he wrot the history of our Saviour's incarnation in English verse, which his brother John haz to shew under his owne handwriting'; Dr. Plume says that at the age of ten he made extempore English verses for Bishop Williams, the Dukes of Buckingham and Richmond, and Sir Fulke Greville (*Essex Review,* xiv [1905], 19); and Richard West, in his verses for the 1638 edition of Randolph's poems, says:

> . . . who truly tells
> His History, must needs write miracles.
> Hee lisp'd Wit worthy th' Presse, as if that hee
> Had us'd his Cradle as a Librarie.

Some of these Fruits had birth, when other Boyes
(His Elders) play'd with Nuts; Books were his Toyes.
Hee had not long of Playes Spectatour beene
But his small Feete wore *Socks* fit for the Scene.

These verses suggest that he began writing plays before he left Westminster School and lend support to the contentions of Tannenbaum and Rollins and Bowers that *The Drinking Academy* may have been prepared for performance by Westminster boys before Randolph went to Cambridge.

In the spring of 1623 he was elected to a scholarship at Trinity College, Cambridge, and admitted 9 April 1624. (Moore Smith, *Thomas Randolph*, p. 84, says that 'it was the rule at Trinity not to admit a Westminster Scholar till a year after his leaving school'.) He was graduated in 1627/8, elected a Fellow of Trinity 22 September 1629, and granted an M.A. in July 1631, a degree in which he was incorporated at Oxford. (*Alumni Cantab.* iii. 420.)

Randolph's career at Cambridge was a notable one. Much of his poetry dates from his Cambridge days, some of it having been published while he was still an undergraduate. Of his plays and shows, 'Thom Randolfs Salting', *Aristippus*, *The Conceited Pedlar*, and possibly early versions of *Hey for Honesty* and *The Muses' Looking Glass*, were written during his undergraduate days for college production. In the spring of 1632 his *Jealous Lovers*, written at the request of the Master of Trinity, was performed by the members of his college before the King and Queen, achieved a glorious triumph over Peter Hausted's *Rival Friends*, which was acted on the same occasion by the members of Queens', and touched off an amusing academic War of the Theatres. (Moore Smith, *Thomas Randolph*, pp. 100–1; L. J. Mills, loc. cit.)

Randolph's academic life seems to have been interrupted by a theatrical career highly unusual for a Fellow of a college. Possibly late in 1629 and certainly in 1630 (during seven months of which time Cambridge was closed because of the plague) he was writing plays for the company of the King's Revels at the Salisbury Court theatre in London. His *Amyntas* and his *Muses' Looking Glass* were licensed for performance by this troupe; there is some evidence that *The Muses' Looking Glass* was the play with which the new Salisbury Court theatre opened, and his *Praeludium* was, I think, written for the reopening of that theatre in November 1630 after the seven months' plague-closing. Such activity suggests that Randolph was the regular playwright for the company and not an occasional contributor, a position which seems to me in accord with certain allusions in his own poems and in references

to him by others. (See above, ii. 537–9, and Bentley, loc. cit.;
see also the evidence of his intimacy with London theatrical
affairs in his verses to Shirley's *The Grateful Servant*, in *Jealous
Lovers*, III. 5, and in his verses, *In Lesbiam, & Histrionem*.)

If Randolph was the regular playwright for the Salisbury Court
theatre—perhaps under contract, as Brome was to this theatre
five years later—he probably had to provide more material for
the King's Revels company than the three pieces we can now
identify. It may be that some of his academic shows and plays
were revised for use at the Salisbury Court, a possibility which
might be profitably investigated. G. C. Moore Smith (*Thomas
Randolph*, pp. 103–5) and Professor J. J. Parry (op. cit., pp. 17–18),
following Fleay, date Randolph's theatrical interlude in the period
1632–4, when it would indeed be less unusual from an academic
point of view, but all the theatrical evidence points to 1630.

Certain undated events in Randolph's life may possibly belong
to this London sojourn in 1630. That he was a 'Son of Ben' is
known from his own poem on his adoption, as well as other poems
to Jonson and reiterated deference to him; the adoption may well
have taken place in this period, though it is often dated earlier.
Both Randolph and several of his friends refer to the loss of his
little finger 'in a fray', the occasion of William Heminges's (q.v.)
theatrically illuminating burlesque, *Elegy on Randolph's Finger*,
another event appropriate to Randolph's metropolitan career.

Just when Randolph deserted the commercial theatre to return
to Cambridge is not known, but it must have been before he was
granted his degree of M.A. in July 1631. He wrote his *Jealous
Lovers*, which he says in the dedication of the 1632 edition to the
Master of Trinity was 'born at your command', for performance
by members of his college before the King and Queen at Trinity
on 22 March 1631/2. At the following Commencement Randolph
was Praevaricator, and his Latin oration includes numerous witty
digs at the rival Cambridge dramatist, Peter Hausted. (Mills,
op. cit., pp. 26–29.)

Randolph apparently left Cambridge some time in the next
year or two, for Aubrey says Captain William Stafford 'gave him
a pension of I Thinke C^{li}. per annum, and he was tutor to his son
and heir'. (Clark ed. ii. 196.) Some confirmation of this assertion
is seen in Randolph's late poem, *The Constant Lovers*, written on
the second marriage of William Stafford of Blatherwick, to Lady
Dorothy Shirley, in 1634, and published from a commonplace
book at the Huntington Library by B. H. Newdigate. (*T.L.S.*, 18
and 25 April 1942.) Further confirmation is afforded by the record

of Randolph's burial, 17 March 1634/5, among the members of
the Stafford family in Blatherwick Church, where a marble tab-
let to his memory was set up by Sir Christopher Hatton, with
an inscription said to have been composed by Randolph's Cambridge rival, Peter Hausted. (Thorn-Drury, pp. xix–xx; Parry,
pp. 19–20; Aubrey, Clark ed. ii. 198.)

Randolph's contemporary reputation was very great. In seventeenth-century commonplace books his poems and anecdotes of
his career are among those most frequently found. He is several
times mentioned as Jonson's rival or heir. In addition to the scores
of manuscript copies of his verses, I have noted nearly a hundred
allusions to him in the seventeenth century, mostly before the
Restoration. Indicative of the position which Randolph held with
his contemporaries are the following lines written by George Lynn
in his commendatory verses prefixed to John Tatham's *Fancies
Theater*, 1640:

> For, when th' inticing pleasure of thy Line,
> And teeming *Fancies* unexhausted Myne
> I view, me thinks the *Genius* of those *Three*
> Admired *Laureats* are ensphear'd in *Thee*,
> Smooth *Shakespeare*, neat *Randolph*, and wittie *Ben*,
> Flow in a mutuall sweetnesse from *Thy* Pen.

Collected Editions

1638. Poems With The Mvses Looking-Glasse: *And* Amyntas. By
Thomas Randolph Master of Arts, and late Fellow of *Trinity*
Colledge in *Cambridge*. Oxford, Printed by Leonard Lichfield
Printer to the Vniversity, for Francis Bowman: M.DC.XXXVIII.

1640. [Another edition, 'The second Edition Enlarged'.]

1643. [Another edition, 'The third Edition inlarged. Whereunto is
added, *The Jealous Lovers*', with separate title-page dated
1640.]

1643. [Another issue, with title-page of *The Jealous Lovers* dated
1646.]

1652. [Another edition, 'The fourth Edition inlarged'.]

1652. [Another issue.]

1664. [Another edition, 'The Fifth Edition, with several Additions
Corrected and Amended'.]

1668. [Another edition, 'The Fifth Edition with several Additions
Corrected and Amended'.]

N.D. [Another edition falsely dated 1668.]

1875. *Poetical and Dramatic Works of Thomas Randolph of Trinity College, Cambridge. Now First Collected and Edited from the early Copies and from MSS. with some Account of the Author and Occasional Notes. By W. Carew Hazlitt.* 2 vols.

Amyntas, or The Impossible Dowry (1630)

Edition: John Jay Parry, ed., *The Poems and Amyntas of Thomas Randolph* (1917), pp. 30–35, 233–352, and 371–3.

Day, Cyrus L. 'Three Notes on Randolph', *M.L.N.* xlvi (1931), 507–8.

Delattre, Floris. *English Fairy Poetry* (1912), pp. 168–72.

Greg, W. W. *Pastoral Poetry & Pastoral Drama* (1906), pp. 282–96.

Jeffery, V. M. 'Sources of Daniel's "Queen's Arcadia" and Randolph's "Amyntas"', *Mod. Lang. Rev.* xix (1924), 435–44.

Smith, G. C. Moore. *Thomas Randolph.* Warton Lecture, *Proceedings of the British Academy* (1927), pp. 94–95.

1630, 26 Nov. '*Amintas* was licensed by Sir Henry Herbert November 26, 1630. It was acted by the Children of the Revels. See his Office Book.' (MS. note by Edmond Malone opposite the account of Randolph in his copy of Langbaine's *Account of the English Dramatick Poets.* See W. J. Lawrence, *T.L.S.*, 29 November 1923, p. 820.)

1638. Amyntas Or The Impossible Dowry. A Pastorall Acted before the King & Queene at *White-Hall*. Written by Thomas Randolph ... Oxford, Printed by *Leonard Lichfield*, for *Francis Bowman*. 1638. (Separate title-page in *Poems With The Mvses Looking-Glasse: And Amyntas* ... 1638.)

1640. Amyntas. Or The Impossible Dowry. A Pastorall Acted before the King & Queene At *White-Hall*. By T. R. ... 1640. (Separate title-page in the second edition of *Poems*, 1640.)

1643. [Separate title-page dated 1640 in the third edition of *Poems*, 1643.]

1652. [Separate title-page in the fourth edition of *Poems*, 1652.]

1664. [Separate title-page dated 1662 in the fifth edition of *Poems*, 1664.]

1668. [Separate title-page in *Poems*, 1668.]

N.D. [Separate title-page in the edition of *Poems* falsely dated 1668.]

Greg (loc. cit.) and Parry (ed. cit., pp. 31–34) note the general indebtedness of the play to Tasso's *Aminta* and Guarini's *Pastor Fido*, and Greg thinks there may be special indebtedness to Bonarelli's *Filli di Sciro*. Parry suggests (p. 33) that Randolph borrowed from Hausted's *Rival Friends*, but, if the relationship is valid, it must have been the other way round, for this play had to be in existence before Herbert licensed it for performance, 26 November 1630, while Hausted's play was prepared for a performance of 19 March 1631/2. (See Hausted.) Miss Jeffery points out the similarity between II. 7 (not II. 6, as she says) of Randolph's play and I. 4 of Luigi Groto's *Pentimento Amoroso*, and between the answer of the oracle (II. 2) and an episode in Giovanni Donato Cuccheti's *La Pazzia*. These similarities are clear enough, but they are found in only a small part of Randolph's play; they do not demonstrate the two Italian pastorals as Randolph's main source or even necessarily indicate any direct knowledge of the two rather obscure Italians on Randolph's part. Pastoral drama is necessarily repetitious, for the suitable episodes are definitely limited; repetition of incident is not so likely to indicate direct borrowing as it is in less restricted dramatic types.

This pastoral of Randolph's is sometimes thought to be too academic to have been originally written for the London dramatic company for which it was licensed, especially since most Randolph scholars have not recognized his connexion with the Salisbury Court theatre. It is possible, of course, that Randolph originally wrote the play for a Cambridge audience, but it is well to remember that pastoral drama was in vogue at the private theatres and at court in the thirties and possibly even earlier, for a second edition of Fletcher's originally unpopular *Faithful Shepherdess* appeared in 1629.

The *terminus ad quem* for the composition of *Amyntas* is Malone's date of 26 November 1630, from Herbert's office-book. This was two weeks after the theatres were reopened following upon the seven months' plague-closing of 1630. (See above, ii. 657–8.) Herbert had licensed Randolph's *Muses' Looking Glass* the day before, saying it had been acted by the company during the previous summer, i.e. when the London theatres were closed, and therefore presumably acted in the provinces. Whether *Amyntas* had the same provincial history is unknown. Since nothing is said of previous performance in Malone's copy of Herbert's licence, it may well be that *Amyntas* was a more recent and untried composition.

The date of the performance at Whitehall before the King and Queen, referred to on the title-page of the 1638 edition, is unknown. Since Herbert licensed the play to the King's Revels company, and since this company presented three unnamed plays at Whitehall in 1631 (see above, i. 284), it is tempting to conjecture that one of the three plays was *Amyntas*.

A revision of *Amyntas* entitled *The Fickle Shepherdess* was printed in 1703 as acted by a cast of women in the new theatre in Lincoln's Inn Fields. Greg (op. cit., p. 296, n. 1) calls it 'a prose rendering, much compressed, of the main action of Randolph's play, the language being for the most part just sufficiently altered to turn good verse into bad prose'. Cyrus L. Day (op. cit.) lists various books which contain John Eccles's music for the songs in this play.

Aristippus, or The Jovial Philosopher (Autumn, 1625 or 1626)

MS.: B.M. MS. Sloane 2531, fols. 124–40*b*.

Bowers, F. T. 'Marriot's Two Editions of Randolph's *Aristippus*', *Library*, Fourth Series, xx (1939), 163–6.

Parry, John J. 'A New Version of Randolph's *Aristippus*', *M.L.N.* xxxii (1917), 351–4.

Smith, G. C. Moore. *Thomas Randolph*. Warton Lecture, *Proceedings of the British Academy* (1927), pp. 89–90.

1630, 26 Mar. S.R. John Marriott entered for his copy 'vnder the handes of Sr Hen: Herbert and mr Bill Arristippus and The Pedler vj^d.' (Greg, *Bibliography*, i. 37.)

1630, 8 Apr. S.R. Robert Allott entered for his copy 'vnder the handes of Sr Hen Herbert and Mr Purfoote A Comedy called The Pedler by R: Davenport'. (Ibid., p. 38.)

1630. Aristippvs, Or The Iouiall Philosopher: Demonstrativelie proouing, That Quartes, Pintes, and Pottles, Are sometimes necessary Authours in a Scholers Library. *Presented in a priuate Shew*. To which is added, The Conceited Pedlar . . . *Thomas Harper*, for *Iohn Marriot* . . . M.DC.XXX.

1630. [Another edition with almost identical title-page. See Greg, *Bibliography*, ii. 581–2.]

N.D. [1630?] [Another edition. 'Dvblin, Printed by the Society of Statio⟨ners⟩.' See ibid.]

1630. [Another edition, 'Printed for Robert Allot, MDCXXX'.]

1631. [Another edition printed for Allott.]

1635. [Another edition printed for Allott.]

1637, 1 July. S.R. Mrs. Allott transferred a long list of titles that
had belonged to Robert Allott, deceased, to Mr. Legatt and
Andrew Crooke; included is '36. Aristippus'. (Greg, *Bibliography*, i. 46.)

1652. [Another edition with separate title-page in *Poems*, 1652.]

1664. [Another edition with separate title-page 'Printed by *T. N.*
1662.' in *Poems*, 1664.]

1668. [Another edition with separate title-page in *Poems*, 1668.]

N.D. [Another edition with separate title-page in edition of *Poems*,
falsely dated 1668.]

Aristippus is not a monologue, as it has several times been
called, for there are more than half a dozen speaking parts in
addition to those in the Praeludium. It must have been prepared
for a college audience at Cambridge, as the many allusions to
academic interests and to Cambridge affairs indicate. The statement with which the Praeludium begins, 'Shewes hauing beene
long intermitted, and *forbidden by Authority for their abuses*', and
the frequent references in the dialogue of the Praeludium to this
revival of shows after a prohibition, do not refer, as has been
sometimes assumed, to a suppression of all plays at Cambridge.
Prologue clearly indicates that comedies are in good standing and
tells *Show* that she too may be in good standing again if she will
hereafter refrain from personal abuse. This admonition seems a bit
odd, considering the treatment of Lichfield and of the butler of
Trinity College that follows in *Aristippus* itself. Halliwell's and
Hazlitt's assertion (*Dictionary of Old English Plays*, p. 23; *Manual*,
p. 18) that this show of Randolph's ridicules the prologue to
Shakespeare's *Troilus and Cressida* is, as Fleay noted (*Biog. Chron.*
ii. 166), pure delusion.

The manuscript version of the play in Sloane MS. 2531 has a
dramatis personae and several passages which do not appear in the
printed texts. Professor Parry thinks (op. cit., p. 353) that the
manuscript represents an earlier version of the piece before it was
revised for publication. The manuscript dramatis personae calls
Medico de Campo a 'vaine glorious Quacksalve personating Dick
Litchfeild a Barber Surgeon in Cambridge', and Wildman 'Buttler
of Trinitie Coll. in Cambridge, & one that keepes a Tipling house'.
Other passages not in the printed texts refer to Ben Jonson,
Gondomar, Don Olivares, and to curing 'England of a Subsidie'.

These additional passages in the manuscript furnish material for
dating this Cambridge show, which must have been written after
Randolph matriculated 8 July 1624. The line, 'If he be not sent

from Gondomar, or employed by Spinola to seduce the King's lawful subjects', was probably written before news of the death of Gondomar reached England, especially since the first clause was suppressed in the printed text. Gondomar died 2 October 1626, and a letter announcing his death and dated London, 4 November 1626, was received by the Reverend Joseph Mead. (Birch, *Charles I*, i. 165.) The same implication of composition before Gondomar's death is found in the line, 'If it had not been treason I had cured Gondomar of his fistula', which appears in the manuscript but not in the printed text. The manuscript line which is added to Medico de Campo's cures, 'And England of a Subsidie', would be especially apt in September or October 1626, when many stories of the attempts to collect the subsidy in London were being told. (Ibid., pp. 149–64.)

Since it does not seem likely that Randolph would have been asked in his freshman year to prepare the first show given at Cambridge after a long suppression, the probable date for performance of *Aristippus* must be some time between the beginning of the academic year on 10 October 1625 (see Masson, *Milton*, rev. ed. [1946], i. 133–4 and 154) and November 1626, the date of the currency in Cambridge of the news of Gondomar's death. Randolph's *Conceited Pedlar*, a show similar to *Aristippus* in its allusions and college character and which was printed with *Aristippus* in 1630, was performed on All Saints' Day 1627. The conjecture that *Aristippus* was also prepared for All Saints' Day in 1626 is tempting.

The number of printings of this play from 1630 to 1635 is evidence of its surprising popularity. No doubt it was an important factor in Randolph's great reputation.

For the entry to Marriott and the publication by both Marriott and Allott, see above, under Robert Davenport, *The Pedlar*.

The Careless Shepherdess (Prologues, Epilogue, and Praeludium)

See Thomas Goffe for a discussion of the play.

The Careless Shepherdess was entered in the Stationers' Register in 1655 as by Thomas Goffe, and it was published in the next year as by 'T. G. Mr. of Arts', with a statement on the title-page that it had been acted before the King and Queen and at the Salisbury Court theatre. Since Goffe, who was a clergyman in Surrey for about the last six years of his life, died before the Salisbury Court theatre was opened, it has been doubted that he wrote the theatrically knowledgeable prologues, epilogue, and Praeludium published with the play. Randolph has been suggested as the author of these pieces.

Professor Moore Smith (*R.E.S.* i [1925], 320–3), following W. J. Lawrence (*T.L.S.*, 24 July 1924, p. 463), takes the references in the epilogue to the '*LAdies*' and '*gentle youths*' in the audience, and the references to the theatre as '*the Orbe*', as evidence of Randolph's authorship, since Randolph uses these same rather unusual phrases in his epilogues for *Amyntas* and *The Muses' Looking Glass*. Professor Moore Smith also concludes, for reasons more obscure, that Randolph wrote the prologue at Whitehall.

There has been too much ill-supported speculation about *The Careless Shepherdess*. It seems probable that the clergyman Goffe was dead when the prologues, epilogue, and Praeludium were written, but there has been no thorough consideration of their authorship. One would expect the author to have been the regular poet for the Salisbury Court theatre at the time of their composition, but—except for Richard Brome—the identity and sequence of the Salisbury Court theatre poets are both uncertain. Randolph, Brome, and Shirley are all possibilities.

The Conceited Pedlar (1 November 1627)

MSS.: B.M. MS. Add. 27406; University of Edinburgh MS. Laing, iii. 493.

Bowers, F. T. 'Marriot's Two Editions of Randolph's *Aristippus*', *Library*, Fourth Series, xx (1939), 163–6.
Wagner, Bernard M. 'Manuscript Plays of the Seventeenth Century', *T.L.S.*, 4 October 1934, p. 675.
—— 'Thomas Randolph's *The Conceited Pedlar*', *T.L.S.*, 9 April 1931, p. 288.

1630, 26 Mar. S.R. John Marriott entered for his copy 'vnder the handes of Sʳ Hen: Herbert and mr Bill Arristippus and The Pedler   vjᵈ.' (Greg, *Bibliography*, i. 37.)
1630, 8 Apr. S.R. Robert Allott entered for his copy 'vnder the handes of Sʳ Hen Herbert and Mʳ Purfoote A Comedy called The Pedler by R: Davenport'. (Ibid., p. 38.)
1630. Aristippvs, Or The Iouiall Philosopher: . . . To which is added, The Conceited Pedlar . . . Printed by *Thomas Harper*, for *Iohn Marriot* . . . M.DC.XXX.
1630. [Another edition with almost identical title-page. See Greg, *Bibliography*, ii. 581–2.]

and Tannenbaum, though it is not impossible, considering the curiously academic character of some of their other plays, that Randolph may have revised it for the use of the boys of the King's Revels company at the Salisbury Court theatre. The date cannot be earlier than 1626 because of the repeated use of material from *The Staple of News*, which was acted after the coronation of 2 February 1625/6. Bowers's contention (*N. & Q.*, loc. cit.) that the First and Third Intermeans of *The Staple of News* refer to Randolph's[?] *Fairy Knight*, and that the prologue of *The Drinking Academy* is a reply in turn to the Intermeans, seems to me far-fetched. There were too many play-producing schoolmasters in and about London for us to identify now the basis of the remarks of the ignorant gossips in the Intermeans of *The Staple of News*—indeed, it would be appropriate to their ignorance if their remarks had no basis in fact. The prologue of *The Drinking Academy* does, however, seem to refer to Randolph's relations with the Tribe of Ben at the Apollo room and his real or pretended disgrace with them because 'since the honoure done him to be listed in the sacred tribe of Apollo he hath bin more a coniurer then a poet and conuersed more with the furies then the muses'. Thus the prologue, though it may postdate the play, seems to have been written after Randolph's admission to the Tribe of Ben. Unfortunately that date is unknown.

Thus we are forced to fall back, for a *terminus ad quem* for *The Drinking Academy*, to the period of Randolph's composition of his comedy *The Jealous Lovers*, a play which was prepared for a performance of 22 March 1631/2, and one whose text shows extensive borrowings by Randolph from his own *Drinking Academy*. (See Day, loc. cit.)

Bowers contends, on the basis of somewhat tenuous evidence, that the Huntington MS. of *The Drinking Academy* was transcribed, like that of *The Fairy Knight*, some time after 1637. (*H.L.Q.* i [1938], 193–8.) The 'Epigramma' on the Synod of Dort, which is found on the page of the manuscript preceding the play and which influenced the dating of Rollins and Tannenbaum and Moore Smith, is irrelevant. It could have been written any time after May 1619, and it has nothing to do with the play. Bowers's discoveries about the manuscript of which *The Drinking Academy* was once a part show that the 'Epigramma' may have been copied into the manuscript quite independently of the play.

Cyrus L. Day suggested (op. cit., pp. 808–9) that the play entered by Humphrey Moseley in the Stationers' Register 29 June 1660, 'The Prodigall Scholar. a Comedy. by Tho: Randall'

(Greg, *Bibliography*, i. 69), may well have been *The Drinking Academy*. He makes a good case, but the evidence is still very tentative.

The Entertainment

An alternate title used at least twice by Randolph's contemporaries for *The Muses' Looking Glass* (q.v.).

The Fairy Knight

See Anon.

Hey for Honesty, Down with Knavery
(1626–8?; revised 1648–9?)

Day, Cyrus L. 'Thomas Randolph's Part in the Authorship of *Hey for Honesty*', *P.M.L.A.* xli (1926), 325–34.

Leech, Clifford. 'Francis Jaques, Author of *The Queene of Corsica*', *Durham University Journal*, xxxix (1947), 111–19.

Smith, G. C. Moore. 'The Canon of Randolph's Dramatic Works', *R.E.S.* i (1925), 310–11.

—— *Thomas Randolph*. Warton Lecture, *Proceedings of the British Academy* (1927), pp. 90–91.

1651. Πλουτοφθαλμία Πλουτογαμία. A Pleasant Comedie, Entituled *Hey For Honesty, Down With Knavery*. Translated out of *Aristophanes* his *Plutus*, By Tho: Randolph. Augmented and Published by *F. J.* . . . 1651.

The play is a free translation, adaptation, and expansion of Aristophanes' *Plutus*. All the characters of the original appear, though about half of them have different names, and about a dozen new characters have been added. *Hey for Honesty* is more than twice as long as *Plutus* and has six and a half new scenes. (See Leech, loc. cit.) The scene is London, and there are copious allusions to London places, customs, and people.

The reliability of the attribution on the title-page of the 1651 edition has been questioned by Fleay, Sir Sidney Lee, A. W. Ward, and others, on the grounds that the play did not appear in the Randolph editions of 1652, 1664, and 1668, and that it contains allusions to events which occurred after Randolph's death. The best discussion of the problem is that of Cyrus L. Day (loc. cit.). He points out that the play has the usual parallels to Randolph's other works, including one quatrain taken verbatim, except for one word, from *Aristippus*. The slapdash style and general hilarity are also very like Randolph in *Aristippus* and *The Muses' Looking Glass*. The principal arguments against Randolph's authorship have been the omission of the piece from the fourth and subsequent editions of the *Poems*, and the numerous Commonwealth allusions in the text. The omission argument was a dubious one in the nineteenth century; now that so much unpublished Randolph work has been discovered in the last two or three decades, it is worth nothing at all. The Commonwealth allusions are a different matter; obviously they could not have been made by Thomas Randolph. The title-page of the first edition points out, however, that the play had been 'Augmented and Published by *F. J.*'. Day (op. cit., p. 328) has worked out a very neat confirmation of this statement:

> The play as it stands is a free translation of the *Plutus* of Aristophanes. Some parts of it, however, are much freer than others, and there are frequent passages which have no counterpart at all in the Greek. Now it is in this last group, in the passages which are entirely modern additions, that all the allusions of later date than Randolph's death occur. Sometimes one or two speeches are slipped in, often lengthy passages are inserted bodily; but invariably it is these additions and interpolations which contain the references to the Civil War. In fact, of the seventy or more allusions to events after Randolph's death, every one shows clear evidence of having been added at a later date to some original form of the translation.

There is no real difficulty, then, about accepting the statement that Randolph made the adaptation of *Plutus* which was 'Augmented and Published by *F. J.*'. F. J. signed the dedication of the play, leaving a blank space for the insertion of the name of the dedicatee—apparently to be filled in as prospects appeared. F. J. also signed the preface, and there is an unsigned commendatory poem, 'To his worthy Friend, F. I. on the setting forth of this excellent Comedy'.

Who was F. J., and when did he make his adaptation? Hazlitt noted (ed. *Works* [1875], ii. 375, n. 1) that the initials are those of Francis Jaques (q.v.), the author of *The Queen of Corsica* (Lansdowne MS. 807), and W. W. Greg, with unaccustomed credulity, affirmed, 'The collaborator was Francis Jaques'. (*A List of English Plays*, p. 88.) There is no reason, beyond the coincidence of the initials, for this identification. Indeed, Dr. Leech says: 'There is such a vast difference in manner between *The Queene of Corsica* and this version of the *Plutus* that no argument from style seems possible. . . . All we can deduce is that, if "F. J." was

Jaques, he could write in a very different style from the one that he had used in 1642.' (Op. cit., pp. 113 and 114.)

The approximate date of F. J.'s augmentations is not difficult to fix. Most of the allusions are to events or attitudes of the forties (Day, op. cit., p. 334); the latest refer to Prince Rupert as commander of a fleet (1648) and, apparently, to the impeachment of Manwaring in 1628 as 'some twenty years now since'. (Ibid., p. 334, n. 29.) F. J. would appear to have made his alterations, then, not earlier than 1648 and not later than the date of publication in 1651, probably in 1648 or 1649, since in such a profusion of Civil War and Commonwealth allusions (seventy to seventy-five), the absence of any reference to events of 1649, 1650, and 1651 suggests that they had not yet occurred.

The date of Randolph's original adaptation is somewhat more obscure. The play contains references to the Gunpowder Plot, Sir Giles Mompesson (fled 1621; Gardiner, iv. 44), the fat Archbishop of Spalatro (in England 1616–22, died 1624; ibid., pp. 284–8), the siege of Breda (1624–5; ibid. v. 275 and 335), Thomas Shelton's shorthand (S.R. 17 April 1626, first edition untraceable, second edition 1630), and, most significantly, the remark on the entrance of the Pope: 'thou, the Devil, Cardinal *Richlieu*, and the French faction at Court, have brought all the wars into *England*' (pointless before 1626 and most valid 1626–8; ibid. vi, *passim*). The number of these references to events of 1621–6 suggests strongly that the play was written very shortly after 1626, perhaps 1626–8. During these years Randolph was an undergraduate at Trinity, Cambridge, and the play has an academic tone not unlike *Aristippus* and *The Conceited Pedlar*. I should not hesitate to call it another of Randolph's productions for a Cambridge audience were it not for the odd fact that there are none of the usual Cambridge allusions in the piece but many London ones. Perhaps the Cambridge allusions were cut out at the time of the revision of 1648–9.

The Jealous Lovers (March 1631/2)

Adams, J. Q. 'Peter Hausted's *The Rivall Friends*, with Some Account of His Other Works', *J.E.G.P.* xi (1912), 433–50.

Cooper, Charles H. *Annals of Cambridge*, 5 vols. (1842–53), iii. 249–50.

Masson, David. *The Life of John Milton: Narrated in Connexion with the Political, Ecclesiastical, and Literary History of His Time*, 7 vols. (1946), i. 251–7.

Mills, Laurens J. *Peter Hausted: Playwright, Poet, and Preacher.*
Indiana University Publications, Humanities Series No. 12
(1944), pp. 17–37.
—— ed. *Peter Hausted's The Rival Friends.* Indiana University
Publications, Humanities Series No. 23 (1951), pp. xi–xvi.
Smith, G. C. Moore. *Thomas Randolph.* Warton Lecture, *Proceedings of the British Academy* (1927), pp. 100–3.
Thorn-Drury, G., ed. *A Little Ark* (1921), pp. 43–46.

1632. The Jealous Lovers. A Comedie presented to their gracious
   Majesties at Cambridge, by the Students of Trinity-Colledge.
   Written by Thomas Randolph, Master of Arts, and Fellow of
   the House . . . *Cambridge.* Ann. Dom. 1632.
1634. [Another Cambridge edition.]
1643. [Another Cambridge edition, with title-page dated 1640,
   found in *Poems*, 1643.]
1643. [Another edition with title-page dated '*London* . . . 1646',
   found in *Poems*, 1643.]
1645, 3 June. S.R. Richard Roiston entered for his copy 'by
   Consent of Richard Ireland bookeseller of Cambridge & M^r
   Daniell Printer there, a Comedie called the Iealous Lovers. by
   Tho: Randall wch sd Copie was formerly printed at Cambridge.
      as by a Note vnder their hands apps wch is putt vpon the
   file.' (Greg, *Bibliography*, i. 55.)
1652. [Another edition with separate title-page in *Poems*, 1652.]
1664. [Another edition with separate title-page dated 1662 in
   Poems, 1664.]
1668. [Another edition with separate title-page dated 1668 in
   Poems, 1668.]
N.D. [Another edition with separate title-page dated 1668 in
   Poems, falsely dated 1668.]

The play was performed by members of Trinity College as part
of the entertainment for the King and Queen during their visit
to Cambridge in March 1631/2. That it was specially prepared for
the occasion is implied in Randolph's dedication of the first edition to Dr. Comber, Master of Trinity and (after April 1632)
Vice-Chancellor of the University, who, like a 'carefull father
disposing of his children to several imployments', assigns serious
tasks to the more learned members of 'our Society . . . while I, the
last of that learned Body, am task'd to these lighter exercises.
Accept, Sir, a thing born at your command, and preserved by
your patronage.'

This comedy and its production and reception were an important part of a notorious academic row at Cambridge, one of the alleged consequences of which was the suicide of Dr. Butts, Vice-Chancellor of the University. (Masson, op. cit., i. 254–7.) In the preparations for the visit of the King and Queen, there seems to have been some rivalry between the men of Queens' and those of Trinity. The Vice-Chancellor, according to one correspondent (ibid., p. 256), intervened to give the precedency to Queens', and their play, Peter Hausted's *Rival Friends* (q.v.), was produced first. It has several times been asserted that this performance took place at Newmarket, but the matter seems to be settled by the direct statement of Sir Simonds D'Ewes in his *Autobiography* (1845 ed., ii. 67):

Friday, March the 16th, I began a journey towards Cambridge, in the afternoon, and came thither the next day. Monday, March the 19th, after dinner, the King and Queen came from Newmarket to Trinity College. Whilst they were at an idle play there, that gave much offence to most of the hearers, I went into Trinity College library, and there viewed divers ancient manuscripts, which afforded me as much content as the sight of the extreme vanity of the Court did sorrow. The royal pair departed from Cambridge, Tuesday, March the 20th, in the afternoon; and the day following, after dinner, I left the University.

That this play was *The Rival Friends* is demonstrated by the statement on the title-page of Hausted's play: 'As it was Acted before the King and Queens Maiesties, when out of their princely favour they were pleased to visite their Vniversitie of *Cambridge*, upon the 19. day of *March*. 1631. Cryed downe by Boyes, Faction, Envie, and confident Ignorance', by his indignant preface and dedication, and by various verses on the reception of the play.

Three days later, on 22 March, Randolph's *Jealous Lovers* was acted in the hall of Trinity College before the royal guests. (Mills, *Peter Hausted*, pp. 19–20.) Numerous sets of verses, both prefixed to the play and found elsewhere, attest its enthusiastic reception, and the chagrin of Hausted and the men of Queens'. It must have been at the performance of either Hausted's play or Randolph's that in the 'great preasse of people' Sir Arthur Gorge with a lady on his arm was jostled by Theodore Kelly. Sir Arthur threatened to cudgel Kelly, and Kelly later sent him a letter which was interpreted as 'provocation to a challenge', (Gardiner, *Reports of Cases in the Courts of Star Chamber and High Commission*, Camden Society, pp. 112–14.)

Perhaps Randolph and the members of Trinity might have

rested content with their glorious triumph before royalty, but Hausted was so ill advised as to rush into print with his play (S.R., 13 June 1632) and to prepare for it a dedication, a title-page, and commendatory verses defending his comedy and belittling his detractors. Randolph and his friends were not forbearing in their replies. *The Jealous Lovers* was published with copious sponsorship. Randolph prepared an epistle to Dr. Comber, Master of Trinity, Vice-Chancellor of the University, and Dean of Carlisle; an address to the reader; verses to Sir Kenelm Digby, Sir Christopher Hatton, Anthony Stafford, Richard Lane, 'Magistro Olboston', and to Thomas Riley, who had acted in the play; commendatory verses were contributed by Edward Hyde, Edward Fraunces, Richard Benfield, James Duport, Thomas Riley, Charles Fotherbie, Francis Meres, Robert Randolph, and Thomas Vincent.

The Jealous Lovers was evidently prepared for the printer after the appearance of *The Rival Friends*, for, though the first edition does not appear in the Stationers' Register (since it was published at Cambridge), Randolph's commenders, Edward Hyde and James Duport, make clear allusions to the jealous attacks in the Hausted volume.

Randolph himself had ridiculed Hausted. Mills points out (*Hausted*, pp. 26–29) that Randolph's *Oratio Praevaricatoria*, which was delivered at Great St. Mary's Church as part of the Commencement of July 1632, concludes with direct ridicule of Hausted and *The Rival Friends* and its publication. Randolph went further. That *The Jealous Lovers* was revised between its performance in March and its publication later in 1632 is indicated by the verses of Edward Fraunces prefixed to the first edition and entitled, '*To his dearest friend the Author, after he had revised his Comedie*'. Adams points out (op. cit., p. 439) that the gravediggers' scene (IV. 3) has clear allusions to Hausted and to the title-page and front matter of *The Rival Friends*.

No cast for the play is known, but when it was published Randolph wrote a commendatory poem to Thomas Riley praising his acting, and concluding, 'I writ this comedy, but 'twas made by thee'. Since Randolph speaks of him once as a lover, he may have played Tyndarus.

Aphra Behn revised *The Jealous Lovers* for a production at Dorset Garden in 1682. Though the play is not extant, there appears in *Miscellany, Being a Collection of Poems by Several Hands*, 1685, p. 263, a set of verses entitled, 'EPILOGUE TO THE Jealous Lovers. By Mrs. *Behn*, in 1682', and in a small folio broadside appears the same epilogue, with half a dozen

additional lines, and a prologue entitled, 'A PROLOGUE By Mrs.
Behn to her New PLAY, CALLED Like Father, like Son, OR THE
Mistaken Brothers.' (Thorn-Drury, loc. cit. See also Summers,
Restoration Theatre, pp. 177–8.)

The Muses' Looking Glass, or The Entertainment (1630)

Bentley, G. E. 'Randolph's *Praeludium* and the Salisbury Court
Theatre', in *Joseph Quincy Adams Memorial Studies* (1948),
pp. 775–83.
Day, Cyrus L. 'Randolph and Prynne', *Mod. Phil.* xxix (1932),
349–50.
—— 'Three Notes on Randolph', *M.L.N.* xlvi (1931), 508–9.
Lawrence, W. J. 'New Facts from Sir Henry Herbert's Office
Book', *T.L.S.*, 29 November 1923, p. 820. Revised in *Speeding
Up Shakespeare* (1937), pp. 167–72.
Smith, G. C. Moore. *Thomas Randolph*. Warton Lecture, *Pro-
ceedings of the British Academy* (1927), p. 94.

1630, 25 Nov. '*The Muses' Looking Glass* was not printed till
1638 (at Oxford by Leonard Lichfield and Francis Bowman),
and the titlepage has only "by T. R.," without any preface or
mention of the theatre where it was acted. But it was acted by
the Children of the Revels under the title of the Entertainment
in the summer of 1630 and licensed by Sir Henry Herbert,
November 25, 1630.' (Edmond Malone's manuscript note opposite the entry for Thomas Randolph in his copy of Langbaine's
Account of the English Dramatick Poets. See W. J. Lawrence,
T.L.S., 29 November 1923, p. 820.)
1630, 25 Nov. 'It was licensed by Sir Henry Herbert under the
name of The Entertainment, November 25, 1630, and it appears
from his office book that it had been acted in the summer of that
year.' (Malone's manuscript note on the fly-leaf of his copy of
the play. Ibid.)
1638. The Mvses Looking-Glasse. By T. R. . . . Oxford, Printed by
Leonard Lichfield, for *Francis Bowman*. 1638. (Separate title-
page in *Poems*, 1638.)
1640. [Another edition with separate title-page in *Poems*, 1640.]
1643. [Another edition with separate title-page in *Poems*, 1643.]
1652. [Another edition with separate title-page in *Poems*, 1652.]
1664. [Another edition with title-page dated 1662 in *Poems*, 1664.]
1668. [Another edition with separate title-page in *Poems*, 1668.]
N.D. [Another edition with separate title-page dated 1668 in
Poems, falsely dated 1668.]

W. J. Lawrence's discovery (loc. cit.) of Malone's note of Sir Henry Herbert's licence of the play to the Children of the Revels 25 November 1630, after they had already acted it in the summer of that year, dates the play earlier than it had been set by Fleay (*Biog. Chron.* ii. 166–7) and other scholars and editors. Malone's repeated statement that the play was acted in the summer before it was licensed suggests that the company first performed it on the road and got it licensed just before it was to be acted for the first time in London. Presumably the licence date comes so late in the season because of the protracted plague-closing of 1630, when Herbert closed the theatres on 17 April and did not allow them to reopen until 12 November. (See above, ii. 657–8.)

This presumed first London performance in November 1630 seems to contradict other evidence that *The Muses' Looking Glass* was the first play performed when the new Salisbury Court theatre—the playhouse of the Children of the Revels—was opened. (See Bentley, op. cit., pp. 778–80.) The play fits objections which Prynne made in his *Histriomastix* against 'the first Play that was acted in the New-erected Play-house'; and the conversation in the first scene between the Puritans, Bird and Mistress Flowerdew, about the building of new playhouses and their own preference for new churches seems appropriate for an opening play. The epilogue by Roscius tells the audience what they will see in plays if they will come to this house.

The difficulty is that the date that Malone gives for the licence —November 1630—seems too late for the opening of the Salisbury Court. The lease for the ground for the new theatre was signed in July 1629, and it has been generally assumed that the play-house would have been in operation in the winter of 1629–30. True, there is no evidence that the theatre had been opened before November 1630, and the plague-closing of April–November 1630 shows that the new building would have had to be completed in eight months or so if there was to be an opening before the long plague-closing. Perhaps the generally assumed opening date for the new Salisbury Court is too early.

The Muses' Looking Glass is an oddly academic play for a London theatre. The way in which the roles of Bird, Flowerdew, and Roscius are joined to the more allegorical parts of the play suggests that Randolph may have taken a Cambridge comedy and reworked it for the London stage. Perhaps some such revision would also account for Roscius' curious address to the audience at the end of Act I, an address that sounds like a modified pro-logue. I am not impressed by the contention of Cyrus Day (*Mod.*

Phil., loc. cit.) that the play was revised after the publication of Prynne's *Histriomastix* because Randolph uses Comedy, Tragedy, Mime, and Satire as the four forms of drama, just as Prynne did. In the first place, this division of drama was by no means peculiar to Prynne, and in the second, such a good rough-and-tumble satirist as Randolph elsewhere proves himself to be would surely not have been so delicate as this in handling a popular butt like Prynne. Day's observation (ibid., p. 349, n. 4) that *Entertainment* would scan much better in the first line of the epilogue than the present *The Muses' Looking Glass* is apt, but it affords no evidence whatever as to the date of the revision.

Fleay's attempt to date the play in 1632 or 1633 (*Biog. Chron.* ii. 166–7) derives from his shrewd but mistaken conclusion that these were the years of Randolph's association with the Salisbury Court. (See above, ii. 537–9.) Fleay's fen-draining evidence is inapplicable, for there were many fen-draining projects which antedated 1632, especially the one of 1629. (See Gardiner, viii. 294–5.) Fleay's suggestion that Randolph was satirizing Inigo Jones in Caunus—a likely suggestion—does not necessarily imply a date following Jonson's quarrel of 1631; even allowing the greatest possible influence of Jonson on Randolph, one must recognize that the Jones–Jonson quarrel had been simmering for years. (See D. J. Gordon, 'Poet and Architect', *Journal of the Warburg and Courtauld Institutes*, xii [1949], 152–78.)

The alternative title for the play, *The Entertainment*, noted by Malone but not found in any of the editions of the piece, is also used by Sir Aston Cokayne in his commendatory poem, '*To my friend Mr.* Thomas Randolph *on his Play called the* Entertainment, *Printed by the name of the* Muses' Looking-Glass', which he included in his *Chayne of Golden Poems*, 1658, pp. 98–99. Sir Aston implies, for what it is worth, that the play was well received. Richard Doddridge alludes to *The Muses' Looking Glass* in his commendatory verses for the 1640 edition of Harding's *Sicily and Naples*. Thomas D'Urfey, after alluding to Randolph's comedy in his *Archerie Reviv'd*, 1676 (Day, *Mod. Phil.*, loc. cit.), makes great use of its didacticism and quotes it in his reply to Jeremy Collier in the preface to *The Campaigners*, 1698.

Mr. John Cutts has pointed out (*N. & Q.*, cxcvii [8 November 1952], 492) that the music for the song in I. 4 beginning 'Say Daunce how shall wee goe' is found in B.M. M.S. Add. 10338, fol. 28*b*, and it may be that the title 'The Masque of Vices' was attached to the dance in this scene that is called in the dialogue 'a rude Dance / Presented by the seven deadly sinnes'. (See Anon.,

The Masque of Vices.) Cutts could find no trace of the music for the corresponding Masque of the Virtues in v. 1 and v. 2 of the play, but he did not notice that the words of the two songs preceding 'Say Daunce' in the B.M. MS. are also by Randolph and are published as independent poems in the edition of 1638. Possibly these songs belonged in v. 1 and v. 2, where, according to the early editions of the play, at least one song is omitted.

Scenes from *The Muses' Looking Glass* were acted as an afterpiece at Covent Garden 14 March 1748 and 9 March 1749. (Cyrus L. Day, *M.L.N.*, loc. cit.)

The Pedlar

See *The Conceited Pedlar.*

Πλουτοφθαλμία Πλουτογαμία

See Randolph, *Hey for Honesty, Down with Knavery.*

Praeludium (November 1630?)

MS.: B.M. Add. MS. 37425, fols. 54–55.
Edition: J. J. Parry, ed., *The Poems and Amyntas of Thomas Randolph* (1917), pp. 226–31 and 370–71.

Bentley, G. E. 'Randolph's *Praeludium* and the Salisbury Court Theatre', *Joseph Quincy Adams Memorial Studies* (1948), pp. 775–83.
Smith, G. C. Moore. 'The Canon of Randolph's Dramatic Works', *R.E.S.* i (1925), 319–20.

This short dialogue of less than two hundred lines is endorsed on the B.M. MS.: 'T. Randall after ye last Plague', in the hand of the Earl of Clarendon, and there is reason to think he knew whereof he spoke. (See Bentley, op. cit., pp. 775–6.) The two characters are Histrio, an actor at the London theatre where the dialogue takes place, and Gentleman, a patron of the theatre, who rallies the actor in friendly terms about the long period during which the theatres have been closed.

There is quite a little evidence—enough to convince me—that Randolph was the regular playwright for the Salisbury Court theatre in 1630. (See above, ii. 537–9, and Bentley, op. cit., pp. 777–80.) If, therefore, *Praeludium* was written by Randolph and for a London theatre, that theatre was presumably the Salisbury Court. If, as Clarendon says and as the dialogue implies, it was

written for performance after a period when the theatres were
closed because of the large number of deaths from the plague in
London, the period should be identifiable. Between Randolph's
majority and his death, the London theatres were closed by plague
three times, in 1625, 1630, and 1631 (see above, ii. 654–9), but
only one of these periods fits the allusions in the dialogue, the
facts of Randolph's career, and the history of the Salisbury Court
theatre. (Bentley, op. cit., pp. 780–2.) That period was the one in
1630, when Sir Henry Herbert was ordered to close the theatres
on 17 April and did not allow them to reopen until 12 November
following. (See above, ii. 657–8.)

Praeludium, therefore, seems to be Randolph's curtain-raiser
for the patrons of the Salisbury Court theatre when that house
reopened after the trying plague-closing of nearly seven months in
1630.

So far as I know, no similar piece for a Jacobean or Caroline
theatre exists, yet they must have been fairly common. Given the
intimacy between actors and audience which a repertory theatre
necessarily develops, and of which prologues and epilogues are
the most familiar exploitation, shrewd theatre people like Heminges and Beeston and Shakespeare and Davenant surely did not
fail to see the advantage of cultivating intimacy with their regular
patrons by short pieces like this *Praeludium* to celebrate reopen-
ings, returns to town, perhaps anniversaries, and surely the opening of new theatres. Such pieces, with only a very ephemeral
interest, would not be attractive to publishers, and doubtless were
not saved even in the playhouses, since they could seldom be used
again.

We probably have the record of a similar piece in the bill for
'An Induction for the Howse' which the King's men presented
5 November 1630. (See above, i. 27–28 and n. 1.) Perhaps another
will show up in some manuscript collection. Some of them must
have been catchy enough to attract young Inns of Court men,
courtiers, or university students, especially those who were keeping commonplace books.

The Prodigal Scholar (?)

(Lost?)

Day, Cyrus L. 'Thomas Randolph and *The Drinking Academy*',
P.M.L.A. xliii (1928), 808–9.

1660, 29 June. S.R. In a long list of plays entered by Humphrey

Moseley as his copies occurs the item: 'The Prodigall Scholar. a
Comedy. by Tho: Randall.' (Greg, *Bibliography*, i. 69.)

Moseley's licensing entry is the only evidence that a play with
this title ever existed. Various attempts to identify the title with
one or another of the extant plays of Randolph have been put
forward. No convincing identification of Moseley's manuscript
can be made without further evidence of the use of the title, but
the suggestion of Cyrus L. Day (loc. cit.), accepted by Tannenbaum
and Rollins, that the play was *The Drinking Academy*, is very
tempting. The title is apt, more apt, Day suggests, than the one
on the manuscript; at least one manuscript of the play (the one
now at the Huntington) was evidently extant when Moseley made
his entry; and *The Drinking Academy*, unlike the printed plays
of Randolph, had not been, so far as we can find, claimed by any
other publisher. These arguments are far from conclusive, but
they do suggest that if Moseley's entry was honest and accurate,
the play either is lost or is *The Drinking Academy*.

'Thom̃ Randolfs Salting' (Autumn 1627)

MS.: Offered for sale by Maggs Brothers, Catalogue 598 (1934),
No. 1488.

Bowers, Fredson. 'Thomas Randolph's *Salting*', *Mod. Phil.* xxxix
(1942), 275–80.

This piece is extant only in a manuscript commonplace book
which was offered for sale by Maggs Brothers of London. It was
examined by Professor F. T. Bowers at Maggs's and described by
him in the *Modern Philology* article.

Professor Bowers says that the commonplace book runs to
three-hundred-odd closely written pages and appears to be the
miscellaneous collection of one or more college students. The
Randolph piece is a monologue of 316 lines of iambic pentameter
couplets, on nine pages, entitled 'Thom̃ Randolfs Salting'. Bowers
says it is not holograph. A salting, he points out, was an initiation
banquet for freshmen, and this one evidently took place in the hall
at Trinity.

A much more complete description of salting is found in J. H.
Marsden's extracts from the diary of Sir Simonds D'Ewes, *College
Life in the Time of James the First As Illustrated by an Unpublished
Diary of Sir Symonds D'Ewes, Baronet and M.P. for Some Time*

a Fellow-Commoner of St. John's College, Cambridge (1851), pp. 14–15:

It appears, from scattered notices in the diary, that when Salting took place, all the undergraduates were assembled in the Hall, and that certain senior Sophisters were selected from them as 'Fathers', to each of whom were assigned a number of freshmen as 'Sons'; and that by these was enacted a sort of burlesque upon the public exercises of the schools: those who 'did ill' being compelled to drink a certain quantity of salted beer. At the salting at Pembroke College, in August, 1620, one of the fathers, and two or three of the sons did 'excellently well'. At Merton College, Oxford, in Anthony Wood's time, the freshman, being stripped of his gown and band, and made to look 'like a scoundrel' as much as possible, was set upon the high table, and required to address the audience in a humorous speech. If he succeeded in tickling their fancy by some 'pretty apothegm, or jest, or eloquent nonsense,' they rewarded him with a cup of caudle from a brass pot which stood by the fire. If his performance was pronounced indifferent, they gave him two drinks, the one of caudle, and the other of salted beer. And if it was 'downright dull', they gave him the salted drink only, 'with some tucks to boot':—the tuck being an abrasion of the skin, from the chin to the upper lip, with the thumb nail. After this, the senior cook administered an oath to each, upon an old shoe, and when the freshman had reverently kissed the old shoe, he was entitled to take his place among his seniors. . . . Symonds tells us, that at Pembroke, 'a great deal of beer, as at all such meetings, was drunk.' . . . The practice was in some degree recognized by the authorities, for Symonds informs us, that they 'exceeded in Hall', on account of the 'salting'. And we find not a few instances of the charge for the 'salting' introduced into the tutor's accounts. Our hero paid the sum of three shillings and four-pence.

In the light of this discussion, Randolph's composition, as Bowers describes it, must have been highly traditional. It begins:

> No salting here these many yeares was seene
> Salt hath wth vs long out of season bene.

Randolph says that there are only two 'Fathers' in the college, of whom he is one. He decides that each of his 'sons' shall be a dish for the table and proceeds with twelve satirical sketches of named students under the guise of dishes. The piece breaks off in the discussion of the twelfth student.

Bowers (op. cit., pp. 278–9) identifies all but two of the twelve named students and finds that all but one matriculated between Michaelmas 1626 and Michaelmas 1627; the remaining one matriculated at Easter 1626. These dates suggest that the Salting must have taken place after, but not long after, Michaelmas 1627.

Moreover, Randolph's matriculation in July 1624 and his B.A. commencement in March 1628 would make him a senior at this time. Several references to the [supposed] English capture of the Salt Islands and to the fact that the English fleet is still at sea indicate a date between the departure of the English fleet on the Rhé expedition in June 1627 and the arrival in England of the news of its disastrous failure, which had occurred 29 October 1627. The Salting must have taken place, therefore, between late September and some time in the first half of November 1627.

Such a monologue as this can add little to Randolph's modern reputation, but it is just the sort of effort, if handled with exceptional cleverness, that would build up his reputation among Cambridge men and help to account for the renown that he enjoyed at the University.

THOMAS RAWLINS
c. 1618–70

D.N.B.

Walpole, Horace. *Anecdotes of Painting in England; with some account of the principal artists; and incidental notes on other arts; collected by the late Mr. George Vertue; digested and published from his original MSS. by the Honourable Horace Walpole; with considerable additions by the Rev. James Dallaway,* 5 vols. (1826–8), ii. 327–9.

Nothing is known of the birth or early life of Thomas Rawlins, though Warwick Wroth says in the *D.N.B.* that he 'appears to have received instruction as a goldsmith and gem engraver, and to have worked under Nicholas Briot at the mint'. The date of his birth is conjectured from his first appearance as the author of *The Rebellion* in 1640. Several of the writers of commendatory verses for this play speak of Rawlins's youth (see below), and 1620 has accordingly been suggested as the date of his birth, but since the play was entered in the Stationers' Register in 1639 and may have been written a year or so earlier, 1618 might be more likely for the birth date.

Rawlins had no professional connexion with the theatre, as he points out rather insolently in his address to the reader in the quarto:

Take no notice of my name, for a second worke of this nature shall hardly beare it. I have no desire to bee knowne by a thread-bare Cloake, having a Calling that will maintaine it woolly. Farewell.

He was an engraver, and his usual productions were coins, medals, seals, and tokens. Wroth (*D.N.B.*) says that his first dated medal is 1641, that he followed the King to Oxford at the outbreak of the Civil War, that he appears in warrants for making badges and medals in 1643, and that his name appears on coins of the Oxford mint 1644–6. Between March 1647 and March 1648 he was formally appointed chief engraver of the mint. He must have been in London in October of 1647, for in this month the minute-book of the Painters' Company records that 'Dr. George Wild, Colonel Richard Lovelace, Thomas Rawlins, Esq., graver of seals to his Majesty, and Mr. Peter Lilly were all made free'. (Rachel Poole, *Walpole Society*, xi [1922–3], 34.)

Warwick Wroth says (*D.N.B.*) that from 1648 to 1652 Rawlins appears to have been in France. Since the second issue of *The Rebellion* was brought out in 1652, it may be that Rawlins himself prompted it at his return from France.

After his return to England Rawlins eked out a living by making tradesmen's tokens and town tokens, but in February 1657/8 he was in prison for debt. In that month he wrote a letter, now at the Folger Shakespeare Library, to John Evelyn from 'the Hole in St Martins' asking for money. Evelyn endorsed the letter, 'Mr Tho Rawlins from prison: 27: ffeb: 1657   Sometime ye Grauer of ye Mint in ye Tower & an Excellent Artist, but debashd fellow'. However, in his *Numismata. A Discourse of Medals, Antient and Modern*, 1697, p. 225, Evelyn called him 'our Industrious *Rawlins*'.

With the return of the King, Rawlins got back his old position as chief engraver of the mint, where, Wroth noted, he had a residence. At an unknown time and place Rawlins was married, for Walpole had seen a print of his wife with the inscription: 'Dorothea Narbona uxor D. Thomae Rawlins supremi sculptoris sigilli Carol. I. et Carol. II.' (Op. cit. ii. 329.)

Winstanley, a friend of Rawlins, said that he died in 1670 (*The Lives of the Most Famous English Poets*, 1687, p. 169), and this death date has been repeated by Walpole and Wroth, but I know of no citation of the evidence.

Though *Tom Essence, or the Modish Wife*, printed anonymously in 1677, and *Tunbridge Wells, or a Day's Courtship*, printed in 1678 as 'Written by a Person of Quality', have been attributed to Thomas Rawlins, his death in 1670 makes it most unlikely that he was responsible for either. Winstanley wrote of him as '*Thomas Rawlins* my old Friend, chief Graver of the Mint to King *Charles* the First, as also to King *Charles* the Second' (loc. cit.), and, though he mentions 'some other small things which he wrote' besides *The Rebellion*, he does not name the two late plays. Possibly the small things Winstanley referred to are the poems in *Calanthe*, by T. R., subjoined to *Good-Friday, being meditations on that day*, 1648; Oldys identified T. R. as Thomas Rawlins. It may be relevant that in his verses for *The Rebellion* 'Jo. Meriell' speaks of a throng of friends '*who oft have read Your learned Poems*'.

Rawlins wrote verses for certain publications of his friends: Robert Chamberlain's *Whimzies*, 1639, and his *Swaggering Damsel*, 1640; John Tatham's *Fancies Theatre*, 1640; Nathanael Richards's *Messalina*, 1640; and Richard Lovelace's *Lucasta*, 1649. Richard Flecknoe published a poem to Rawlins entitled '*On that Excellent* Cymilist, *or Sculptor in Gold and precious Stones*, &c Tho: Rawlins.'(*Miscellania or Poems of all sorts, with divers other Pieces*, 1653, pp. 58–59.)

The Rebellion (1638–9?)

Jones, Fred L. 'Echoes of Shakspere in the Later Elizabethan Drama', *P.M.L.A.* xlv (1930), 801–3.

1639, 20 Nov. S.R. Daniel Frere entered for his copy 'vnder the hand of D^r wykes a Play called The Rebellion by Tho: Rawlins'. (Greg, *Bibliography*, i. 52.)

1640. The Rebellion: A Tragedy: As it was acted ninedayes together, and divers times since with good applause, by his Majesties Company of Revells. Written by *Thomas Rawlins* ... 1640.

1652. The Rebellion. A Tragedie. Written by *T. R.* London, Printed in the Yeare, 1652. (Another issue with cancel A$_1$. See Greg, *Bibliography*, ii. 721.)

The Rebellion, incoherent as it is, has enough scenes of startling melodrama to suggest that it might have appealed for nine successive days—as the title-page asserts—to audiences like those at the Fortune or Red Bull described by Edmund Gayton. (See above, ii. 690–1.) Certain allusions in the scene of the tailors preparing to give a play (v. 2; I$_1$^v–I$_2$^v) suggest production by a Red Bull troupe in rivalry with a Fortune troupe, a rivalry for the vulgar audience in the last decade of the Caroline theatre to which various writers allude. The relevant lines follow:

Old. Now for the credit of Taylors.
3 *Tay.* Nay, Master and we doe not act as they say,

With any Players in the Globe of the world [i.e. the King's men
    of the Globe and Blackfriars, the premier London troupe.]
Let us be baited like a Bull [present theatre?] for a company of
    Strutting Coxecombes: nay we can act I can tell you.

.   .   .   .   .

3 Tay. Play a play a play, ha, ha, ha; O egredious nonsensensicall
    wigeon, thou shame to our crosse-legg'd corporation; thou fellow
    of a sound, play a play; why forty pound golding of the beggars
    Theater [i.e. Fortune] speakes better, yet has a marke for the sage
    audience to exercise their dexterity, in throwing of rotten apples
    whilst my stout Actor pockets, and then eates up the injury:
    play a play, it makes my worship laugh yfaith.

A few lines later the tailors decide to perform *The Spanish
Tragedy*, and they begin casting.

2 Tay. Who shall act *Ieronimo*?
3 Tay. That will I:
    Marke if I doe not gape wider than the widest
    Mouth'd Fowler of them all, hang me:
    'Who calls *Jeronimo* from his naked bed: haugh!
    Now for the passionate part—
    'Alas it is my sonne *Horatio*.

The allusion to Richard Fowler, apparently the best-known actor
at the Fortune in its later days (see above, ii. 439–40), is clear,
and the tailors may even have parodied the Fortune rendition of
bits of *The Spanish Tragedy*.

These sneers at the Fortune and the apparent allusions to a Red
Bull performance are not easy to reconcile with the title-page
statement that the piece was performed 'by his Majesties Company of Revells', for the King's Revels company, which usually
performed at the Salisbury Court theatre, is not known to have
played at the Red Bull, or even to have been in existence after the
plague of 1636–7. (See above, i. 283–96.) Except for the King's
company, Queen Henrietta's company, and Beeston's Boys, however, there is great uncertainty about the London companies and
their theatres after 1636—most of the later allusions refer simply
to 'the Fortune company' or 'the Red Bull company' and leave
the historian to guess at the identity of the troupe. Conceivably a
remnant of the King's Revels company could have been at the
Red Bull after the long plague-closing, as Fleay suggested (*Biog.
Chron.* ii. 168–9); it seems less likely that the episode of the tailors
was a later addition to a text originally written for performance by
the King's Revels company at the Salisbury Court, for the *naïveté*
of *The Rebellion* does not suggest that private theatre.

The precise date of *The Rebellion* is equally uncertain. Presumably it was written after the formation of the company about 1629 (see above, i. 283-5), and certainly it was composed before the Stationers' Register entry of 20 November 1639. The birth date of the author has usually been given as 1620, but since this is only a guess derived from the publication date of the play, it is useless here. It is notable, however, that the front matter of the 1640 quarto contains several references to the youthfulness of the author of the play. Rawlins himself, in his address to the reader, pleads that 'youth hath many faults'; in his verses to the author Robert Davenport speaks of '*your young pen*'; Robert Chamberlain addresses Rawlins as '*a Springot of thy tender age*', notes the '*disproportion 'twixt thy Lines and Yeares*', and admires the dramatic knowledge of '*one so young*'; and I. Knight refers to Rawlins as 'being so yong And teeming yet'. If, then, Rawlins was still notably young at the time the front matter for the 1640 quarto was prepared (presumably about November 1639), it seems likely that *The Rebellion* was written and performed not long before publication. One would very tentatively suggest 1638-9, though this apparently contradicts my previous conclusion (see above, i. 296) that the King's Revels company did not survive the plague of 1636-7.

So far as I know, no comprehensive source for the play has been noted. Langbaine said:

> The Scene of this Play lyes in *Sevile*; but I cannot direct you to any particular History, because I know not in what King of *Spain's* Reign this Action happened: All I can tell you is, That I believe this Taylor was fitted upon *Crispin's* Last; and that Webster's *Shoomaker* gave Birth to our Poet's Don *Sebastiano*. (*An Account of the English Dramatick Poets*, 1691, p. 425.)

I do not know any shoemaker in a play of Webster's which Langbaine might have had in mind. Could he have been referring to Lacy's disguise as Hans the shoemaker in *The Shoemakers' Holiday*, a disguise which is used in somewhat the same way as Sebastiano's tailor's disguise in *The Rebellion*? Langbaine classified *The Shoemakers' Holiday* as an anonymous play, and it is only a desperate guess that he might have written Webster by mistake. Could he have meant William Rowley's *A Shoemaker a Gentleman*?

Evidently Sebastiano's disguise as a tailor was one of the popular appeals of *The Rebellion*, for he is mentioned in the commendatory verses of Davenport, Knight, C. G., and R. W.

Professor Fred L. Jones has pointed out (loc. cit.) that the conference of the tailors about their proposed production in Act v has too many elements in common with the meeting of the Athenian mechanicals in *A Midsummer Night's Dream* to be purely fortuitous. The passages that he thinks imitated from *King Lear* and *Romeo and Juliet* do not seem clear imitations to me.

The quarto of 1640 is elaborately introduced to the reader. Rawlins wrote a dedicatory letter to his kinsman, Robert Ducie of Aston in Staffordshire, and an address to the reader; there are eleven sets of commendatory verses, signed by "Nath." Richards, C. G., Robert Davenport, R. W., Robert Chamberlain, T[homas?] Jordan, I. Gough, E. B., I. Latham [John Tatham?], I. Knight, and Jo[hn?] Meriell. There are suggested relationships in this group of verse writers: Nathanael Richards also had a play, *Messallina*, published by Daniel Frere in 1640 as acted by the King's Revels company, and for it Rawlins and his friends Davenport and Jordan wrote verses, and Jordan had acted a boy's role in the performance. Jordan's most popular play, *The Walks of Islington and Hogsdon*, was written for the Red Bull theatre, as this one appears to have been, and John Tatham, for whose *Fancies Theatre*, 1640, Rawlins wrote verses, was also connected with the Red Bull, as is indicated by three prologues for Red Bull players or the Red Bull theatre in his collections, *Fancies Theatre*, 1640, and *Ostella*, 1650. All this is highly inconclusive, but there seems to be a faint suggestion of a group of young men associated through the Red Bull theatre.

Tom Essence, or The Modish Wife

In the 'Unknown Authours' section of his *Momus Triumphans*, 1688 (p. 32, note h), Langbaine annotates *Tunbridge Wells* with: '*That and* Tom Essence *ascrib'd to Mr.* Rawlins.' He refers to the anonymous play, *Tom Essence*, which was acted at Dorset Garden in 1676 (Allardyce Nicoll, *A History of Restoration Drama*, 3rd ed., p. 371) and published in 1677. But Langbaine omits the attribution in his discussion of Rawlins in *An Account of the English Dramatick Poets*, 1691 (pp. 424–5). Since Thomas Rawlins, the engraver, died in 1670, it is highly improbable that he wrote the play, though it has been attributed to him by various later biographers.

Tunbridge Wells, or A Day's Courtship

Like *Tom Essence*, *Tunbridge Wells*, though published in 1678 as 'Written by a Person of Quality', was annotated '*ascrib'd to*

Mr. Rawlins' by Langbaine in *Momus Triumphans*, 1688 (p. 32, note h). Langbaine did not repeat his attribution in his account of Rawlins in *An Account of the English Dramatick Poets*, 1691, pp. 424–5. There is no good reason for attributing to Rawlins, who died in 1670, a play acted at Dorset Garden in 1677/8. (Allardyce Nicoll, *A History of Restoration Drama*, 3rd ed., p. 371.) The attribution appears, however, in various dramatic histories long after Langbaine.

HENRY (JOHN?) REYNOLDS

Reynolds was not a dramatist, but a translator of Tasso. His translation of *Aminta* was published anonymously in 1628, but the entry in the Stationers' Register, 7 November 1627, says that the piece was 'Englished by Hen: Reynolld[es]'. (Greg, *Bibliography*, i. 35.) Edward Phillips said (*Theatrum Poetarum*, 1675, p. 186) that the translator was John Reynolds, but his authority is slight, and none of the known men named John Reynolds seems a likely candidate. (See *D.N.B.* and W. W. Greg, *Pastoral Poetry & Pastoral Drama* [1908], pp. 238–9 and n. 2.)

Aminta

This play is only a translation, as the title-page of the anonymous edition of 1628 indicates: 'Torqvato Tasso's Aminta Englisht'.

NATHANAEL RICHARDS
fl. 1631–41

D.N.B.

Skemp, A. R. *Nathanael Richards' Tragedy of Messallina The Roman Emperesse, Materialien* (1910), pp. v–vi and 1–27.
Smith, G. C. Moore. 'Nathanael Richards, Dramatist', *N. & Q.*, Tenth Series, xi (1909), 461–2.

For more than a century after the appearance of *Biographia Dramatica* in 1782, the author of *Messallina* was nicely pigeon-holed as the son of Richard Richards, rector of Kentisbury, Devon. This Nathaniel Richards was admitted to the scholars' table at Caius College, Cambridge, 28 February 1628/9, aged seventeen, after four years in school at Torrington, received his LL.B. in 1634, came into his father's living of Kentisbury in 1637/8, had a son baptized there 23 July 1638, and remained rector of Kentisbury until his death in 1660. (*D.N.B.*; John Venn, *Biographical History of Gonville and Caius College, 1349–1897*, i. 287; and G. C. Moore Smith, op. cit.) A clergyman seemed a likely author for the pious poems in *The Celestiall Publican*, and a Cambridge LL.B. a plausible composer of the learnedly footnoted *Messallina*.

Then Professor G. C. Moore Smith noted a number of serious discrepancies between the career of the Caius man and the information and suggestions in *Messallina*, 1640, and in *The Celestiall Publican*, 1630, and in the revision of the latter with alterations and additions called *Poems Sacred and Satyricall*, 1641. Most conclusive is the fact that the arms given above the engraved portrait of Richards prefixed to *Messallina* and partly re-engraved for *Poems Sacred and Satyricall* are those of the Richards family of Rowling, Kent, not of Kentisbury, Devonshire. Equally suggestive is the fact that there are obituary acrostics in *The Celestiall Publican*, which was published in 1630, on four people who died in 1624, 1624/5, and 1625. Such poems are almost always timely, and the Caius man was surely too young to have written them in these years, since he was only twelve or thirteen years old at the time of the deaths and only eighteen when *The Celestiall Publican* was entered in the Stationers' Register on 6 March 1629/30. (Edward Arber, *A Transcript of the Register of the Company of Stationers of London, 1554–1640 A.D.*, [1877], iv. 196.) Professor Moore Smith noted further that one poem in *The Celestiall Publican* refers to the author's experience in Spain, and another in *Poems Sacred and Satyricall* seems to do likewise— a most unlikely experience for a Caius freshman from a Devonshire rectory. Finally, he pointed out that one poem in the 1630 collection celebrates the conception of a child born in 1625, and another the marriage of the child's parents, Sir Thomas Stanley and Mary Hammond. This Mary Hammond was a Hammond of St. Albans, near Dover, in the parish adjacent to that in which lived the family of Richards of Rowling, whose arms appear above the portrait engravings of the author of *Messallina* and *Poems Sacred and Satyricall*. These facts make it most unlikely that the playwright and poet was the Nathaniel Richards who was an undergraduate at Caius when *The Celestiall Publican* was published and a Devonshire clergyman when *Messallina* went through the press. Moore Smith did not note that two of the commendatory verses for *Messallina* were written by actors and two others by playwrights, one of whom John Evelyn later called debauched—rather odd friends for a Devonshire clergyman. Nor did Moore Smith observe the commendatory verses for

Middleton's *Women Beware Women* that were written by Nathanael Richards, saying that he had seen the play and calling Middleton his 'Familiar Acquaintance'; Middleton was buried in July 1627, and could scarcely have been the familiar acquaintance of a Torrington schoolboy.

The Nathanael Richards who wrote *Messallina* has not, then, been identified, but he was probably a Richards of Rowling, Kent, conceivably, as Moore Smith suggested, the third son of Captain William Richards, whose second son, Gabriel, left most of his estate to William Hammond, 'eldest son of my cousin William Hammond of St. Albans, Esq.' This man was probably a London resident, for four of the six sets of verses for *Messallina* were written by London playwrights and actors: Robert Davenport, Thomas Rawlins, John Robinson, and Thomas Jordan. Moreover, as Moore Smith noticed, *Poems Sacred and Satyricall*, 1641, is dedicated to 'Thomas Soame Esquire, Alderman, and one of the Burgesses of Parliament for the Honorable City of London', and the author speaks of '*this Cities approbation*'. J. A. Venn (loc. cit.) says that the Nathaniel Richards of Caius College was 'Master of St Alban's School, London, in 1640', but this seems an odd post for the clergyman who in 1637/8 had been nicely instituted into the rectory formerly held by his father. Could Venn—who did not know that there were two men of the same name—have attributed to the Caius man a record properly appertaining to the author of *Messallina*? I know nothing of St. Alban's School, London.

The author of the play was something of a scholar, as is indicated by the Latin footnotes quoting his sources, and by his general use of Suetonius, Tacitus, Pliny, and Juvenal. His moralizing bent is shown by many of the poems in *The Celestiall Publican*, 1630, and its revision and extension, *Poems Sacred and Satyricall*, 1641. Several poems reflect ideas and interests found in *Messallina*, and various short passages are used in both poems and play. (See Skemp ed., pp. 108, 120, 125, 132, 141–2, and 152–3.)

Nathanael Richards's London friends are presumably represented by the names signed to the commendatory verses for *Messallina*: Stephen Bradwell, Robert Davenport, Thomas Combes, Jo[hn] Robinson, Thomas Jordan, and Thomas Rawlins. It is noteworthy that three of these men are also associated with the King's Revels company as actors or playwrights—John Robinson, Thomas Jordan, and Thomas Rawlins. The association with Rawlins is repeated, for Richards wrote verses for Rawlins's play *The Rebellion*, acted by the King's Revels company, and Rawlins, who was an engraver by trade, is probably the 'T R sculp:' of the portraits in *Messallina* and *Poems Sacred and Satyricall*. In his commendatory verses for *Women Beware Women*, as we have noted, Richards calls Thomas Middleton his 'Familiar Acquaintance'.

Presumably the author of *Messallina* is also the author of two poems published in single sheets: *Truth's Acrostick An Elegie Vpon The most renowned, true, and unparalleld Worthy Knight, Sir Paul Pindar Deceased*, [1650], signed 'N. Richards', and *Upon the Declaration of His Majesty King Charles of England the Second*, 1660, signed 'Nathaniel Richards'.

The Tragedy of Messallina, the Roman Empress (July 1634–May 1636)

Edition: A. R. Skemp, ed., in *Materialien zur Kunde des älteren Englischen Dramas* (1910).

Briggs, William Dinsmore. 'The Influence of Jonson's Tragedy in the Seventeenth Century', *Anglia*, xxxv (1912), 287–91.

1639, 3 Oct. S.R. Daniel Frere entered for his copy 'vnder the hands of Doctor Wykes & M^r ffetherston warden [a *deleted*] The Tragedy of Messalina the Roman Empresse by N: R.' (Greg, *Bibliography*, i. 51.)

1640. The Tragedy Of Messallina The Roman Empresse. As it hath beene Acted With generall applause divers times, by the Company of his Majesties Revells. Written by Nathanael Richards . . . 1640.

This Senecan melodrama on the havoc wreaked by lust is an odd combination of moralizing and spectacle scenes which must have taxed the resources of the King's Revels company in casting and staging. Evidently some of the casting was beyond them, for in the last scene after an elaborate duet between two spirits '*to the Treble Violin and Lute*' comes the stage direction,

After this song (which was left out of the Play in regard there was none could sing in Parts) (F$_6$–F$_6$^{v}).

The author's intent is fairly, if not lucidly, stated in his dedication to John Cary, Viscount Rochford:

. . . the world (unlesse among the crooked conditions of the *Envious*) may (being honestly opinionated) perceive, that the sole Ayme of my discovery herein, no otherwise tends then to separate *Soules* from the discovered *Evill*, the suppression of *Vice*, and the exaltation of *Vertue*, flight from sinne for feare of Iudgement; which seriously considered in a *Noble nature*. The *glorious Strumpet*, sparkling in beautie and destruction can never have power to tempt.

The parenthetical statements in Richards's declaration, as well as the insistence on the moral purpose of the play in most of the commendatory verses, suggest that the piece had been criticized as immoral.

The evidence for dating the play must be derived from the assignment of nine of the thirty-odd parts listed under 'The Actors Names' in the octavo of 1640. (See above, i. 297.) Since this cast includes William Cartwright, senior, who was still a member of another company as late as 18 July 1634 (see above, ii. 688), *Messallina* must have been played later than that date. The 'boy' actor who played the long and trying role of Messallina was John Barrett, who had sons christened at St. Giles', Cripplegate, in November 1637 and November 1638. (See above, ii. 359.) Presumably Barrett would have been unsuited for female roles by 1637, and we can further limit the probable period of first production from the fact that all London theatres were closed by plague from 12 May 1636 to 2 October 1637. (See above, ii. 661–5.) *Messallina* would appear, then, to have been first acted by the cast of King's Revels men given in the 1640 octavo some time after 18 July 1634 and before 12 May 1636.

The principal sources of the play are recorded by the author himself. In his dedication to Viscount Rochford, Richards notes that Messallina is discussed by '*Romes* Historians, (*Tacitus, Suetonous, Pliny, Plutarch* and *Juvenall*)', and in the footnotes to his text he quotes Tacitus, Suetonius, and Pliny. Skemp (op. cit., pp. 33–38) quotes in full the relevant passages, showing what parts of the Messallina material Richards has used for his documentation. This editor's rather full analysis of Richards's use of his sources (pp. 32–51) shows the dramatist's consistent effort to make Messallina a monster of lust, sometimes by extending her crimes and generally by making the other characters more virtuous than he found them in his sources. Skemp's suggestion (op. cit., pp. 39–42) that certain passages and situations in *Messallina* show indebtedness to *Macbeth* and to Marston's *Dutch Courtesan* are tempting, but not wholly convincing. Dean Briggs pointed out influences of Jonson's tragedy on the play (loc. cit.), but he objected to Schelling's assertion (*Elizabethan Drama, 1558–1642*, ii. 48) that *Messallina* 'belongs to the type of *Sejanus*'. Undoubtedly *Messallina* is, as Briggs asserted, far too melodramatic to have pleased Jonson, but the combination of Roman material with a strong and unmistakable moral purpose and the sudden use of the Emperor Claudius in the last act probably remind the modern reader more of *Sejanus* than the laureate would be pleased to know.

The octavo of 1640 has an engraved portrait of the author with his coat of arms. It is inscribed '*Vera, ac viva Effigies* Nathanaelis Richards *Gen:*' and signed 'T R *sculp:*' (See Greg, *Bibliography*, ii, Plate lxxxvi.) There is also an engraved title-page (see ibid., Plate lxxxv), which shows a contemporary stage in a small compartment at the bottom. This engraving, which is one of four known contemporary reproductions of 'Elizabethan' stages, has been much discussed. (See Arthur R. Skemp, 'Some Characteristics of the English Stage before the Restoration', *Shakespeare Jahrbuch*, xlv [1909], 101–25; V. E. Albright, *The Shaksperian Stage* [1909], pp. 44–45; J. Q. Adams, 'Four Pictorial Representations of the Elizabethan Stage', *J.E.G.P.* x [1911], 329–33.)

Tragoedia Miserrima Pyrami et Thisbes Fata Enuncians

See N. R.

WILLIAM RICHARDS
1643–1705

William Richards is probably the '*W. R.* Master of Arts' named as author on the title-page of the 1682 edition of *The Christmas Ordinary* (q.v., under Anon.). He was born at Helmdon, Northamptonshire, in 1643, the son of the rector. He entered Trinity College, Oxford, in 1658, matriculated in 1659, and was granted degrees of B.A. 1663 and M.A. 1666. He was a Fellow of Trinity from 1666 to 1675, when he instituted himself rector of Helmdon. In 1689 he was appointed lecturer of St. Andrew's, Newcastle upon Tyne, where he died and where he was buried in the chancel, 22 August 1705. He published *The English Orator*, 1680, and *Wallography, or the Britton Described*, 1682. (*D.N.B.*)

These facts of Richards's life indicate fairly clearly that he is the '*W. R.*' of *The Christmas Ordinary*, for the preface to that play, signed 'W. R.,' is dated 'Helmdon, Octob. 18, 1682', and Richards, born in this town, was rector there in 1682. Moreover, Moseley's entry of *The Christmas Ordinary* in the Stationers' Register 29 June 1660 calls the play 'a Comedy by Trinity Coll. Oxford'. (See Anon., *The Christmas Ordinary*.) Trinity was Richards's college, and the '*W. R.*' of the preface says of the play:

'Tis the First-Born of a young Academick Head, which since hath been Deliver'd of most excellent Productions. It hath lain Dormant almost half an Age, and hath only crawl'd out in Manuscript into some few hands.

Though these facts and the preface are enough to indicate that William Richards is the 'W. R.' of *The Christmas Ordinary*, they also show that the publisher was in error in taking the initials from the signature to the preface and placing them on the title-page as author. The implication of the preface is clearly that the play was the work of another man and that 'W. R.' was only the preserver of the manuscript. The *'half an Age'* would presumably mean half a century, which would place the play's composition before Richards's birth, a date which would accord with allusions in the text of the play.

Since the above was written, Dr. Greg's contention that William Richards was indeed the author of *The Christmas Ordinary* has appeared. (*Bibliography*, ii. 1007–8.) He thinks that '[W. R. student of]' has been omitted from the Stationers' Register entry, that William Richards, who was something of a wag, was concealing his own identity in the preface, and that the piece dates after the closing of the theatres. I think my own interpretation of the evidence is the more plausible, especially in the light of apparent allusions in the play. (See under Anon.)

JOHN RICKETS

c. 1606– <46

A John Rickets was admitted as pensioner at Emmanuel College, Cambridge, 3 July 1622. He matriculated in 1623 and on 26 March 1625 migrated to Jesus College as a Scholar. He received his degrees of B.A. in 1625/6 and M.A. in 1629. On 14 October 1633 he was instituted rector of All Saints', Worcester, from which parish he was ejected after the reduction of Worcester in 1646. (*Alumni Cantab.* iii. 456, and R. H. Bowers, ed., *Byrsa Basilica* [1939], pp. xiv and xxxvi.) An unidentified John Rickets was examined, 2 January 1645/6, by the Committee of Accounts at Warwick, relative to goods seized by the garrison and taken into Warwick Castle. (Bowers, p. xiv, n. 3.)

Byrsa Basilica, seu Regale Excambium (1633?)

MS.: Bodleian MS. Tanner 207: 'Byrsa Basilica. seu Regale Excambium. A Sereniss: Regina Elizabetha in Persona sua sic insignitum; Año Dom: 1570. Mense Ianuar: 23° die. Monvmentvm Mercvriale D: D: Thomae Greshami Militis & Negotiatoris Regij; Qui suis solius sumptibus e solo erexit, dicavitqve tam Mercatori quam Mercvrio.' The manuscript is inscribed at the end, 'Hoc Meum Vivum I. Rickets'.

Edition: R. H. Bowers, *Byrsa Basilica, seu Regale Excambium . . . Edited from Bodleian MS. Tanner 207, Materials for the Study of the Old English Drama* (1939).

Churchill, George B., and Wolfgang Keller. 'Die lateinischen Universitäts-Dramen Englands in der Zeit der Königin Elisabeth', *Shakespeare-Jahrbuch*, xxxiv (1898), 281–5.

The direct address to an academic audience in the prologue and epilogue and the analogies drawn between commercial activities and academic activities show that, in spite of its subject, *Byrsa Basilica* was prepared for an academic audience. Actually there is much more of the usual Plautine comedy than of the Royal Exchange in the piece, though there is an extended explanation and defence of marine insurance in III. 3 and III. 5.

The play was first dated 1570 by Churchill (op. cit., p. 281) because he was confused by the date of the founding of the Royal Exchange that is given on the title-page of the manuscript. Boas pointed out the error (*University Drama in the Tudor Age*, 132, n. 1) and noted that the letter in I. 7 is dated 'A di: 20: Aug: 1633', and that the three ships mentioned in the marine policy that is read in III. 2 are called 'Charolum', 'Mariam', and 'Iacobum'. Boas went no further than to note that the play must belong to the reign of Charles I, but a somewhat more specific date is suggested by the letter and the ship names. The letter is delivered in London from Venice and may be supposed to have been written some time before it is received. The ship names, though they might honour King Charles, Queen Henrietta Maria, and James I, would be a more graceful compliment if they referred to the three children of Charles and Henrietta, born in 1630, 1631, and 14 October 1633. In III. 5 Rialto reads from a news-letter, 'Hispano Gallus indixit bellum publice'. Though this declaration did not take place until May 1635, it would have been a welcome rumour to many Englishmen in the autumn of 1633 when the French forces in Alsace and Lorraine were a threat to the Spaniards. (Gardiner, vii. 342–84.) All things considered, therefore, the late autumn of 1633 seems a not unlikely date for the performance of *Byrsa Basilica*.

Moore Smith suggests that the play was performed at Jesus

College, Cambridge. (*College Plays*, p. 95.) Though there are no records of performances at this college after 1623 (*Malone Society Collections*, II. ii. 213), the fact that it is the college to which Rickets migrated in 1625 and from which he took his degrees makes it the most likely candidate for place of performance.

The comments of Bowers on the handwriting of the Bodleian MS. are somewhat contradictory. 'Bodleian MS. Tanner 207 . . . is apparently in the same hand as the parish register of All Saints', Worcester, started in 1641 by John Ricketts, who is presumably the author of the play. However the numerous mistakes in the MS. render the possibility of its being holograph slight. It is surely a copy, not a first draft, since no corrections of any importance are to be found.' After stating his evidence that the parish registers must be in the hand of Rickets, he continues: 'It follows that, unless MS Tanner 207 is of a strikingly similar hand, several pages of *Byrsa* were written most carelessly and distractedly, and were not favoured with an attentive re-reading.' (Op. cit., pp. xi and xxxvi.) Dr. Bowers does not consider the possibility that both the registers and the Bodleian MS. might be fair copies of Rickets's originals by a Worcester parish clerk.

W. RIDER
?–?

There seems to be no evidence as to the identity of the '*W. Rider*, Master of Arts', named as author on the title-page of *The Twins*, 1655. There were several men named William Rider at Oxford, but their matriculation dates—1583, 1596, 1641, and 1658—seem either too early or too late for a man whose play was acted at a theatre that opened after 1629 and closed in 1642. The least unlikely is William Rider, of Bristol, who was seventeen in May 1596 and received his B.A. 23 February 1596/7. (*Alumni Oxon.* iii. 1257.) There is no record that he received an M.A., and single plays are more likely to have been produced by a young man than by a man in his fifties. No W. Riders are listed at Cambridge between 1580 and the Restoration.

The William Rider who published *The Rider of the White Horse*, 1643, might be the author of the play, but nothing seems to be known of him.

On the title-page of the copy of Jasper Fisher's *Fuimus Troes*, 1633, in the Huntington Library, the attribution, 'By W. Rider', has been written in a contemporary hand. There seems to be no reason to take it seriously.

The Twins (1630? < > 42?)

1611/12, 1 Jan. 'The Kings players' performed at Court 'On Neweres night A play called the Twiñes Tragedie'. (Chambers, *Eliz. Stage*, iv. 178.)

1611/12, 15 Feb. S.R. Edward Blunt entered for his copy under the hands of 'Sʳ. Geo: Buc & Thwar[dens] A tragedye called, The Twynnes tragedye written by [*blank*] Niccolls'. (Greg, *Bibliography*, i. 27.)

1612–13. John Heminges was paid for performances of fourteen plays at court by the King's company in the season 1612–13, one of which was 'The Twins Tragedie'. (Chambers, *Eliz. Stage*, iv. 180.)

1655, 20 June. S.R. John Sweeting entered for his copy 'a booke entituled The Twinnes a TragiComedy written by W. Rider. Mʳ. A.' (Greg, *Bibliography*, i. 64.)

1655. The Twins. A Tragi-Comedy. *Acted at the Private House at* Salisbury-Court, *with general Applause.* Written By *W. Rider*, Master of Arts . . . 1655.

1662, 16 July. S.R. Robert Horne entered as his copies by virtue of an assignment under the hands of John Sweeting and Clement Punge, executors of John Sweeting deceased, a number of titles, including '[18] The Twinns a Tragi Comedy by Wᵐ: Rider'. (Greg, *Bibliography*, i. 70.)

The identification of Rider's *The Twins* with the play called 'The Twynnes tragedye', licensed as by 'Niccolls' in February 1611/12, and acted at court shortly before and after, was made without reason or comment in *Biographia Dramatica* (ed. 1782, i. 369). Fleay passed on the notion in his account of Rider's play:

> I suspect that it was only a revival of Niccols' play (*q.v.*). The authority of title-pages after 1650 is next to *nil*. (*Biog. Chron.* ii. 170.)

Actually the suggestion is an unlikely one, not only because of the different authors named, but because the early play in each of the three known references is called a tragedy, whereas Rider's play is a tragi-comedy, and because, furthermore, a play belonging to the powerful King's company is not likely to have got into the repertory at Salisbury Court.

Our information about Rider's play extends little beyond that given on the title-page of the 1655 edition. If it was first performed at the Salisbury Court playhouse, that performance could not antedate June 1629, when the ground for the construction of the playhouse was let (see above, i. 283, n. 7) and probably it could not have taken place before 1630. It is possible, of course, that the applauded performances noted on the title-page were not the original ones. The *terminus ad quem* would presumably be the closing of the theatres in 1642, yet the Salisbury Court is one of the theatres in which surreptitious performances are known to have taken place after the wars began. (See Hotson, *The Commonwealth and Restoration Stage* [1928], pp. 24–27.) The years 1630 and 1642 are not, then, unquestionable limits for the first performance of *The Twins*.

The quarto of 1655 has no prologue, epilogue, commendatory verses, dedication, or address to afford clues about author or performance. The dramatis personae is oddly explanatory, e.g. 'Carolo, *Lover of* Julietta, *flyes to the wood, received by* Julio *under the name of* Laberio.' A number of the stage directions are elaborately descriptive.

For most of its existence the Salisbury Court theatre was occupied by either the King's Revels company or Queen Henrietta's men, but Prince Charles's (II) troupe was also there for a time.

THOMAS RILEY
fl. 1632

The Latin comedy, *Cornelianum Dolium*, published in 1638 as by T. R., has been attributed to Thomas Riley by Hazlitt (*Manual*, p. 50), who called him 'of Trinity College, Cambridge'. Presumably he meant the friend of Randolph's who acted the principal role in *The Jealous Lovers*, to whom Randolph wrote a set of verses addressed 'To his deare friend', praising his acting in the play, and who wrote a set of commendatory verses to Randolph for the play. There is no evidence that Thomas Riley wrote *Cornelianum Dolium*. See T. R.

Mr. RIVERS

See James Shirley, *The Traitor*.

SAMUEL ROWLEY
c. 1575?–<1624

Very little is known about Samuel Rowley's career, and that little is puzzling. No record of his birth or parentage has been cited, and none of his life records gives any hint as to his age. Possibly he was the Samuel Rowley married to Alice Coley in 1594 (see above, ii.

555), but the name is not sufficiently uncommon for certainty. It has frequently been said that Samuel was the brother of the actor-dramatist, William Rowley, but no evidence has ever been cited, so far as I know. His name is found most frequently in Henslowe's accounts, where, with other members of the Lord Admiral's company, he was named as a witness on 3 August 1597 and where he appeared as a sharer in the company in 1598, 1600, and 1602. (*Henslowe's Diary*, ii. 307.) He collaborated on *Judas*, wrote *Joshua*, and revised *Doctor Faustus* for Henslowe and the company in 1601 and 1602, and he appears as an actor in the plots for four of the company's plays. (Ibid.) His *When You See Me, You Know Me* was entered in the Stationers' Register and published in 1605 as a production of Prince Henry's company, the old Admiral's troupe with a new patron. (*Eliz. Stage*, iii. 472.) Sykes has seen Rowley's hand in a number of earlier plays, and Sir Edmund Chambers was impressed by Sykes's stylistic parallels.

Rowley appears as a patented member of the company in the official lists of 1603/4, 1606, and 1612/13 (*Eliz. Stage*, ii. 186–8 and 190), but there are no certain records of him from the last date until his compositions for the Palsgrave's men (his old company under a third patron) in 1623 and 1624. If he was the Samuel Rowley, merchant-tailor, buried in 1620 (see above, ii. 555), two playwrights of the same name must have written for the Admiral's–Prince's–Palsgrave's company, but this seems most unlikely. He may have been the 'm^r Rowly' connected with the Leopard's Head tavern in 1620, but we have only the name for evidence. (*Hens. Papers*, pp. 94–95.)

The real puzzle of Rowley's career is his disappearance from all records for a period of ten years. For fifteen years, from 1597 to 1612–13, he is found regularly in the Admiral's–Prince's–Palsgrave's company records, including all the major documents, then for ten years, when the records of the company are fairly numerous (see above, i. 136–49), he is found in none of them, only to appear again in connexion with the same company in 1623 and 1624. He may have been in Germany after 1613 with his old fellow, Richard Jones (see above, ii. 486–7), but there is no evidence. Whatever the reasons for his absence from London, when the company had fallen on hard times and was in desperate need of a repertory (see above, i. 149–51), he returned to his old task as playwright, possibly at the request of Richard Gunnell, who had joined the company about the time Rowley left and who seems to have been acting as manager of the troupe. (See above, ii. 454–6.)

In rapid succession Sir Henry Herbert licensed for the Palsgrave's company three plays by Rowley: *Richard III, or The English Profit* [*Prophet*?], 27 July 1623; *Hardshift for Husbands, or Bilboe's the Best Blade*, 29 October 1623; and *A Match or No Match*, 6 April 1624. Nothing beyond the licence is known of any of these plays, and nothing beyond the plays is known of Samuel Rowley. One is even tempted to wonder if the three plays of 1623 and 1624 which Herbert licensed could have been memorial reconstructions by Gunnell and the other actors of old plays by Rowley which were burned in the Fortune fire of December 1621.

It has several times been said that Rowley had died by 1634, because of the fact that the printer's address to the reader in the 1634 quarto of *The Noble Soldier* speaks of the author as dead. Unfortunately there is much confusion about the authorship of *The Noble Soldier* (q.v.)—even about the printer's opinion as to authorship. Sir Edmund Chambers (*Eliz. Stage*, iii. 472) gives the death date as 1624, without comment, an unaccustomed lapse on Sir Edmund's part. All we know is that after 1624 nothing more is heard of Samuel Rowley.

Such later allusions as there are to a dramatist named Rowley do not give the Christian name and are rather more likely to refer to William (q.v.) than to Samuel. The only certain allusion I have seen is a libellous one directed at Hugh Peters in the frenzied vilification campaign of the late forties. *Mercurius Pragmaticus* says of Peters:

he has a fine wit I can tell you, *Sam Rowley* and he were a *Pylades*, and *Orestes*, when he played a womans part at the Curtaine Playhouse. (Quoted Hotson, *Commonwealth and Restoration Stage*, p. 15.)

Evidently Samuel Rowley was remembered as an actor as late as 1647, and it might be argued, in the light of the obvious intent to defame the hated Independent Peters, that his reputation was not a very savoury one.

Hardshift for Husbands, or Bilboe's the Best Blade (1623)
(Lost)

1623, 29 Oct. 'For the Palsgrave's Players; a new Comedy, called, *Hardshifte for Husbands, or Bilboes the best blade*, Written by Samuel Rowley.' (Adams, *Herbert*, p. 26.)

The play is known only from Sir Henry Herbert's licence, which was granted at a time when the Palsgrave's men, in desperate straits because of the destruction of their repertory in the Fortune fire of 9 December 1621 (see above. i. 141–2 and 149–51).

were licensing an abnormal number of plays, most of which are now lost.

Nothing more is known of the play.

A Match and No Match (1624)
(Lost?)

1624, 6 Apr. 'For the Fortune; a new Comedy, called, *A Match or no Match*: Written by Mr. Rowleye.' (Adams, *Herbert*, p. 27.)
1624, 6 Apr. 'For the Fortune–   1624.

A New Comedy called a Match or no Match written by M[r]. Rowlye this 6th Apr: 1624 – 1[li].' (Halliwell-Phillipps's Scrap-Books, *Fortune*, p. 41, Folger Shakespeare Library.)

There has been much confusion about this play. First, there is the problem of identity: is the play the same as *A Match at Midnight* and therefore presumably written by William Rowley? Second, if the two plays are not the same, there is the problem of authorship: does Herbert's 'Mr. Rowleye' mean William Rowley or Samuel Rowley? Though the identity of one play under two titles is assumed by Hazlitt (*Manual*, p. 153), there is no good reason for identifying them: the title of 1624 would not be appropriate for *A Match at Midnight* and the Fortune company had no connexion with the 'Children of the Revells' who are named on the title-page of the 1633 quarto of *A Match at Midnight* as the actors of that play.

Did Sir Henry Herbert mean William Rowley or Samuel Rowley in his entry for the licence of *A Match and No Match*? The evidence suggests Samuel. He had written two plays for the company at the Fortune in the previous year, and five months had elapsed since the licence for the last, not too short a composition period for an old Henslowe hack, working for a company in desperate need of plays. William Rowley, on the other hand, was a King's man at this time (see above, ii. 555–8), and most of his work was done for that company. It is true that in 1624 William Rowley did have a hand in a play for another company, for in September of that year he was one of the collaborators on *The Late Murder of the Son upon the Mother, or Keep the Widow Waking*. That play appears to have been the property of Prince Charles's company (see above, i. 208–9), the troupe to which William Rowley had belonged for a number of years and with which he seems still to have had some odd sort of connexion. Though the evidence is not conclusive, it makes Samuel a somewhat more likely author of *A Match and No Match* than William.

The two versions of Herbert's licence for the play come from two different transcripts of the original, one made by George Chalmers and reprinted by J. Q. Adams, and the second made by a nineteenth-century hand, perhaps Craven Ord's, and pasted into Halliwell-Phillipps's scrap-books at the Folger Shakespeare Library. They differ only in form and in the notation of Herbert's fee, his usual one for licensing a new play at this time. (Adams, *Herbert*, pp. 17–18.)

The Noble Soldier [The Noble Spanish Soldier], or A Contract Broken Justly Revenged

This play has been commonly listed as Rowley's because the title-page of the 1634 edition says, '*Written by* S. R.' The identification of initials is always hazardous, and in this case the play had been entered in the Stationers' Register in 1631 as by 'Tho: Deckar' and in 1633 as by 'm^r Decker'. The best discussions of the play indicate that the author probably was Dekker (q.v.).

Richard III, or the English Profit [Prophet?] (1623)

(Lost)

1623, 27 July. 'For the Palsgrave's Players, a Tragedy of *Richard the Third, or the English Profit,* with the Reformation, written by Samuel Rowley.' (Adams, *Herbert*, p. 24.)

1623, 27 July. 'The Palsgraves Players—A Tragedy of Richard the thirde or the English Prophett with the reformation contayninge 17 sheetes written by Samuell Rowleye for the companye at the Fortune this 27th. July 1623—1^{li}. o.' (Folger Shakespeare Library, Halliwell-Phillipps's Scrap-Books, *Fortune*, p. 41.)

The play is known only from Sir Henry Herbert's licence to the Palsgrave's men to perform it at the Fortune in 1623. At that time the Palsgrave's company was engaged in a desperate attempt at survival after the destruction of their repertory in the Fortune fire of 9 December 1621. (See above, i. 141–2 and 149–51.) Most of the phenomenal number of plays licensed to the company in this period are now lost, probably an indication of their inferior quality.

The first version of Sir Henry Herbert's licence entry is the familiar one printed by J. Q. Adams from George Chalmers's publication of extracts from Herbert's original manuscript. The

second version comes from an independent transcript in a nineteenth-century hand—perhaps Craven Ord's—which has been cut
up and pasted into appropriate volumes of the Halliwell-Phillipps
scrap-books now at the Folger Shakespeare Library. Both transcripts show that Sir Henry found censorable material in Rowley's
play. The additional information of Halliwell-Phillipps's transcript suggests a rather long play (cf. Bonen, *The Cra. . . Merchant*, and Dekker, *The Late Murder of the Son upon the Mother*),
adds the familiar information that the Palsgrave's men were
acting at the Fortune at this time, and notes the fee, the usual one
for a new play. (See Adams, *Herbert*, pp. 17–18.)

Whether Chalmers or the unknown transcriber was correct in
his spelling of the last word of the title, one cannot tell now. It is
interesting to speculate on what Rowley might have made of
Richard if the spelling 'Prophett' is correct.

The fame of the subject of the play has led to speculations as to
the connexion of Rowley's tragedy with others. I can see no
grounds for any connexion at all with Shakespeare's play. On 22
June 1602 Henslowe paid Ben Jonson £10 'in earneste of a Boocke
called Richard crockbacke & for new adicyons for Jeronymo'.
(*Henslowe's Diary*, i. 168.) The suggestive facts here are that
Jonson wrote—or at least started to write, since there is no evidence of completion—a play about Richard III for Henslowe and
the Admiral's men in 1602 when Rowley was also writing for
them, and that the company for which Rowley's *Richard III* was
licensed by Herbert in 1623 was the same as that for which Jonson
had written. Quite possibly there was no connexion, but Fleay's
conjecture, 'This may have been only an alteration of Jonson's
Richard Crookback of 1602' (*Biog. Chron.* ii. 171), is more cogent
than many of his others.

Whether there could have been any relationship between Rowley's play and the Dutch *De Roode en Witte Roos* is a matter of
pure speculation. Campbell's comparison of the Dutch play with
Shakespeare, Legge, and *The True Tragedie* (*Shakespeare Studies
by Members of the Department of English of the University of
Wisconsin* [1916], pp. 231–52) does not consider Rowley's play.

WILLIAM ROWLEY (Roulle)
c. 1585–1625/6

Dickson, M. J. 'William Rowley', *T.L.S.*, 28 March 1929, p. 260.
Dunkel, Wilbur D. 'Did Not Rowley Merely Revise Middleton?'
P.M.L.A. xlviii (1933), 799–805.

Morris, Edgar Coit. 'On the Date and Composition of *The Old Law*', *P.M.L.A.* xvii (1902), 1–70.
Robb, Dewar M. 'The Canon of William Rowley's Plays', *M.L.R.* xlv (1950), 129–41.
Stork, Charles Wharton. *William Rowley His All's Lost by Lust and A Shoemaker a Gentleman.* Publications of the University of Pennsylvania, Series in Philology and Literature, vol. xiii (1910), pp. 7–68.
Tischner, Friederich. *Die Verfasserschaft der Webster-Rowley Dramen* (1907).
Wiggin, Pauline G. *An Inquiry into the Authorship of the Middleton-Rowley Plays.* Radcliffe College Monograph No. 9 (1897).

There are no known records of the parentage, birth, education, or early life of the actor-dramatist William Rowley. The conjectural date of his birth is a guess derived from the date of publication of his first known work. It has several times been said that he was a brother of Samuel Rowley (q.v.), who appears in dramatic records about ten years before William does, but I know of no evidence of the relationship.

William Rowley's name first appears in 1607. The second issue of the 1607 quarto of *The Travels of the Three English Brothers* has an added epistle to the family of the Shirleys which is signed 'Iohn Day. William Rowley. George Wilkins.' This play was performed by Queen Anne's men, according to the title-page. Since Rowley's *A Shoemaker a Gentleman* and his collaboration with Heywood called *Fortune by Land and Sea* seem also to have been written for this troupe, and probably about the same time (see *Eliz. Stage,* iii. 343 and 473–4), it seems possible that Rowley may have begun his stage career as an actor in Queen Anne's company, but his name appears in none of their records. The first records of Rowley as an actor connect him with the new company of the Duke of York, later Prince Charles's (I) men (see *Eliz. Stage,* ii. 241–6), but the fact that by 8 May 1609 he was acting as one of the responsible leaders of the troupe (see Charles William Wallace, *Globe Theatrical Apparel* [1909], pp. 5, 8, 11) makes it seem likely that he had had previous experience in the theatre.

For at least ten and probably for fourteen years after 1609, Rowley was a leading member of Prince Charles's (I) company, receiving payment for their plays at court, representing them before the Privy Council, writing plays for them, and presumably acting in their daily performances. (See above, i. 198–213.) He was a comedian and the quartos record his performance of the roles of Plumporridge in *The Inner Temple Masque,* Jaques in *All's Lost by Lust,* and perhaps Simplicity in *The World Tossed at Tennis.* (See above, under Middleton.) Probably the fat clown roles in a number of other plays of Prince Charles's (I) company and later of the King's men were written for him. (See above, ii. 556.) His affection for members of Prince Charles's (I) company is recorded in his dedication of *A Search for Money,* 1609, to his fellow actor, Thomas Hobbes, and in his funeral elegy for another of the company, Hugh Attwell. (See above, ii. 352–3.) For this company Rowley wrote, usually in collaboration, *A Fair Quarrel, All's Lost by Lust, The World Tossed at Tennis, The Witch of Edmonton, Hymen's Holiday,* probably *The Late Murder of the Son upon the Mother, or Keep the Widow Waking,* and no doubt several of his plays not now assignable.

In 1622 and 1623 *The Changeling* and *The Spanish Gypsy,* both collaborations of Middleton and Rowley, were licensed for Lady Elizabeth's men, the successors of Prince Charles's (I) company at the Phoenix. It seems odd that Rowley should have written plays for a rival troupe against the best interests of his own company. Could Christopher Beeston have held him to an unfulfilled contract at the Phoenix after the Prince's men left?

By August 1623 Rowley had become a member of the King's company, though he still appeared in the official list of Prince Charles's men prepared for the funeral of King James. (See above, i. 209.) For his new company he performed in *A Game at Chess,* in *The Maid in the Mill,* in which he had collaborated, and probably in various other plays containing his familiar comic role. (See above, ii. 556–7.) His popular standing as an actor at this time is suggested by some manuscript verses in which his name is linked with those of John Lowin, Nicholas Tooley, and Joseph Taylor. (See below, Robert Ward, *Fucus Histriomastix.*)

The actor-dramatist was evidently the 'William Rowley, householder', who was buried at St. James's, Clerkenwell, 11 February 1625/6, and whose widow Grace renounced the administration of his estate five days later. (See Miss M. J. Dickinson, loc. cit.) The papers of the suit about his play, *The Late Murder of the Son upon the Mother, or Keep the Widow Waking,* show that he was alive in 1624 but dead by 24 March 1625/6. (See C. J. Sisson, *Library,* Fourth Series, viii [1927–8], 237.) Ben Jonson refers to his death in *The Staple of News.* (See above, ii. 557.) Obviously the dramatist and actor of the King's company cannot have been the William Rowley who married Isabell Tooley in 1637, though it has often been asserted that he was.

There is little evidence that Rowley received any literary recognition as a dramatist in his own day. None of his plays was published with commendatory verses, and in only one list of contemporary writers, that of John Taylor, the Water Poet, in his *Praise of Hemp Seed*, 1620 (p. 27) is Rowley included. The dates of his activity make it obvious that William Rowley was not the 'Maister *Rowley* once a rare Scholler of learned Pembroke Hall in Cambridge' whom Francis Meres listed in 1598 as one of the best 'for Comedy amongst vs'. (*Palladis Tamia. Wits Treasury*, 1598, Oo₃ᵛ.)

Rowley himself, on the other hand, wrote commendatory verses for John Taylor's *Nipping or Snipping of Abuses*, 1614, and for Webster's *Duchess of Malfi*, 1623; he wrote a series of consolatory verses on the death of Prince Henry which were appended to John Taylor's *Great Britain All in Black*, 1612, and a four-line poem on the death of Prince Henry which concluded William Drummond's collection called *Mavsolevm or, The Choicest Flowres of the Epitaphs, written on the Death of the neuer-too-much lamented Prince Henrie*, Edinburgh, 1613. (See L. E. Kastner, ed., *The Poetical Works of William Drummond of Hawthornden* [1913], i, pp. xlvii–l.) It is not unlikely that William Rowley was the 'W. R.' who wrote the couplet 'Vpon the death of Thomas Greene', the famous comedian of Queen Anne's company, in Joshua Cooke's *Greene's Tu Quoque*, 1614.

For his own plays Rowley joined with Wilkins and Day in an address to the Shirley family for *The Travels of Three English Brothers*, 1607, and he is probably the 'Simplicitie' who wrote the address to the reader for *The World Tossed at Tennis*, 1620 (see under Thomas Middleton), but he composed only one proper dedication, namely that in the 1617 quarto of *A Fair Quarrel*, which is addressed to 'the nobly disposed, vertuous, and faithful-brested Robert Grey Esquire, *one of the Grooms of* his Highnesse Bed-Chamber' and somewhat intimate in tone. Presumably Rowley had had dealings with Grey in their capacity as servants to Prince Charles. Two records of Rowley found by Halliwell-Phillipps and entered, without adequate reference, in his scrap-books refer to the kind of transaction which might have brought Rowley and Grey together:

William Rowley for himselfe & his fellowes the Princes Players for presenting a play before his —— on the xxviij.th of December, 1616.   Treas. Chamb.
(Folger Shakespeare Library, Halliwell-Phillipps's Scrap-Books, *Noble Companies*, p. 114.)

Feby. 17 Iac. 1619–20. 'A message to Roulle one of his highnes players.' (Ibid., p. 119.)

Whatever the occasion of the acquaintance of Rowley and Robert Grey, this single dedication to a not very exalted personage by a dramatist who had a hand in more than twenty plays contrasts sharply with the practice of Rowley's contemporaries, Jonson, Middleton, Massinger, and Ford. Together with the fact that the great majority of Rowley's plays were not published until after his death, if at all, it suggests an indifference to the published text of his plays reminiscent of Shakespeare. Apparently Rowley thought of himself as an actor and assumed none of the literary airs of supervised publication, dedications, and commendatory verses found in many Jacobean and Caroline dramatists.

The fact that the Rowley canon contains a large amount of collaboration, and perhaps also the fact that Rowley, as an actor, was in a good position to touch up old plays and add required comic material to new ones, have made William Rowley a favourite candidate for the disintegrators. There has long been a tendency to suggest that any material, especially comic material, found distasteful to the sensitive critic in plays of Shakespeare, Jonson, Ford, Fletcher, Webster, Middleton, Massinger, or Chapman was probably written by William Rowley. It is not inconceivable that Rowley was a 'play doctor', but the sense of delicacy and propriety of nineteenth- and twentieth-century literary critics is a very poor guide to his work. I have included in the following list only those plays for which there is some external evidence of Rowley's authorship.

All's Lost by Lust (1619 or 1620?)

Editions: Edgar C. Morris, ed., *The Spanish Gipsie, and All's Lost by Lust, by Thomas Middleton and William Rowley*, Belles Lettres Series (1908); Charles Wharton Stork, ed., *William Rowley His All's Lost by Lust, and A Shoemaker, a Gentleman*, Publications of the University of Pennsylvania, Series in Philology and Literature, vol. xiii (1910).

Wiggin, Pauline G. *An Inquiry into the Authorship of the Middleton-Rowley Plays*. Radcliffe College Monograph No. 9 [1897], pp. 15–23.

c. 1619 or 1620. The title 'All's Lost by Lust' appears in a list of plays on waste paper of the Revels Office, probably dating about 1619 or 1620. It has been plausibly suggested that the plays of the list were being considered for performance at court. (See Marcham, *Revels*, p. 15, and E. K. Chambers, *R.E.S.* i [1925], 484.)

1632, 27 Sept. S.R. Thomas Harper entered for his copy under the hands of 'S^r. Henry Herbert & m^r. Weaver warden a Tragedy called All's lost by Lust by Will: Rowley.' (Greg, *Bibliography*, i. 41.)

1633. A Tragedy Called All's Lost By Lvst. Written by *William Rowley. Divers times Acted by the Lady* Elizabeths Servants. And now lately by her Maiesties Servants, with great applause, at the *Phœnix* in *Drury Lane* . . . 1633.

1639. 10 Aug. 'Alls Lost by Lust' is included in the list of plays protected by the Lord Chamberlain for the King and Queen's Young Company at the Cockpit in Drury Lane. (See above, i. 330–1.)

1661, Mar. or Mar.–May. 'All's Loste by Luste' appears in a list of performances of plays by 'the Kings Companie at the Red Bull and the new house in Gibbon's Tennis Court near Clare Market', 1660–2. (Adams, *Herbert*, pp. 116, 117, and n. 1.)

1660/1, 23 Mar. '. . . At last into the pitt [at the Red Bull] where I think there was not above ten more than myself, and not one hundred in the whole house. And the play, which is called "All's lost by Lust," poorly done; and with so much disorder, among others, in the musique-room the boy that was to sing a song, not singing it right, his master fell about his ears and beat him so, that it put the whole house into an uprore.' (Diary of Samuel Pepys.)

1661, 4 July. 'Th. [i.e. Thursday], a play in the morning at the same place [King's Arms, Holywell, Oxford], called "All is lost by lust," 1s.' (Andrew Clark, *The Life and Times of Anthony Wood* [1891], i. 405.)

1661, 9 July. 'T. [Tuesday], "All's lost by lust" in the morning; in the afternoone "The Milkmaids," 6d.' (Ibid., p. 406.)

The title-page of the 1633 quarto records performances by the Lady Elizabeth's company and by their successors at the Phoenix, Queen Henrietta's men, and it has usually been deduced from this statement that Rowley wrote the play for Lady Elizabeth's men during the time of their occupancy of the Phoenix, 1622–5. (See above, i. 183–8.) This deduction is invalidated by the statement in the dramatis personae of the quarto: '*Iaques*, a simple clownish Gentleman, his sonne, personated by the Poet', for Rowley was never a member of the Lady Elizabeth's company or of Queen

Henrietta's (see above, ii. 555–8) ; evidently the play was retained in the repertory at the Phoenix when some earlier company left and was acted at that theatre in the decade before publication by the two companies named. The predecessor of Lady Elizabeth's company at the Phoenix was Prince Charles's (I) men, who played at the Phoenix from the departure of Queen Anne's company, the original occupants, in 1619 (see above, i. 160–5), to the arrival of the Lady Elizabeth's in 1622. (See above, i. 202–5.) William Rowley was a leading member of Prince Charles's (I) troupe, and it is most likely, therefore, that this was the company for which he wrote *All's Lost by Lust* and played Jaques. Since the title appears in a Revels Office list of plays apparently dating about 1619–20, the Prince's men must have performed it before the end of 1620 at the latest. The fact that the play remained in the repertory of the Phoenix to be acted by later companies there and was not taken away with the Prince's men when they left suggests that the manuscript was not the property of the company but of Christopher Beeston, owner and manager of the Phoenix, and therefore that Rowley probably wrote it while the company was at the Phoenix and that Beeston probably paid for it. This date of 1619 or 1620—i.e. after the company came to the Phoenix and before the Revels list—seems to be confirmed by an apparent allusion in III. 2 (F_1^v) to the Declaration of Sports of 1618 (see S. R. Gardiner, *History of England 1603–42*, iii. 247–52) by the clown, who was played by Rowley himself:

> . . . you woud have me be an informer
> Of unlawfull games, as Ticktack, whipper ginny, in & in.

The principal characters and the central action of the play derive from legendary Spanish history, but Charles Wharton Stork, who notes various accounts (op. cit., pp. 69–70), does not cite any which seems a very likely source for Rowley, and he makes no attempt to compare the incidents Rowley used with those in earlier accounts. Langbaine said, 'As to *Margaretta's* Design'd Revenge on her Husband *Antonio*, read the *Unfortunate Lovers*, Novel the 3.' (*An Account of the English Dramatick Poets*, 1691, p. 428.) If, as Stork surmises (op. cit., p. 70), he meant *The Fortunate, the Deceived and the Unfortunate Lovers*, the book was published too late—1632—for Rowley.

The prologue printed in the 1633 quarto was also printed in the 1636 quarto of Dekker's *Wonder of a Kingdom* (q.v.), though the plays were not published, printed, or licensed by the same stationers. The prologue is not particularly applicable to either play. *The*

Wonder of a Kingdom also has the same title-page motto as *All's Lost—Quod non dant Proceres, Dabit Histrio*—a further suggestion of some sort of connexion.

The short and uninformative epilogue printed by Stork evidently does not belong to the play. Dr. Greg found it in only one of the twenty copies of the quarto he recorded, and he says that in this one it is printed on 'a modern leaf signed "K" (verso blank)'. (*Bibliography*, ii. 621).

In the Oxford performances of the play in 1661 the role of 'Dionysia' was performed by Mrs. Anne Gibbs, according to Richard Walden, who seems to have been much taken with her during the engagement. (See his *Io Ruminans*, 1662, A₃.)

The rather surprising number of recorded Restoration performances of *All's Lost* indicate an appeal which probably accounts for the adaptation of the play by W. C. called *The Rape Reveng'd, Or, The Spanish Revolution*, which is found in a manuscript of about 1690 (see W. C. Hazlitt, *A Manual for the Collector and Amateur of Old English Plays* [1892], p. 191) and for the more complete reworking by Mrs. Mary Pix under the title, *The Conquest of Spain*, published 1705. (See Allardyce Nicoll, *A History of Early Eighteenth Century Drama* [1925], p. 97.)

John Cotgrave quoted *All's Lost by Lust* five times in his *English Treasury of Wit and Language*, 1655. (See G. E. Bentley, *Stud. Phil.* xl [1943], 186–203.)

The Birth of Merlin, or The Child Hath Found His Father

See Chambers, *The Elizabethan Stage*, iii. 474–5; William Wells, '*The Birth of Merlin. 1608*', *M.L.R.* xvi (1921), 129–37; E. H. C. Oliphant, *The Plays of Beaumont and Fletcher* (1927), pp. 402–14; R. C. Bald, ed., *Hengist King of Kent; or the Mayor of Queenborough by Thomas Middleton* (1938), pp. xxii–xxiii and xxxiv–xxxv.

The Changeling
with Thomas Middleton
See Middleton.

A Cure for a Cuckold
with John Webster
See Webster.

A Fair Quarrel
with Thomas Middleton

See Middleton.

The Fool without Book
(Lost)

1653, 9 Sept. S.R. In a long list of plays entered as his copies by
Humphrey Moseley occur the titles:

The Foole without Booke⎫
A Knaue in Print, or One for another⎭ by W^m: Rowley

(Greg, *Bibliography*, i. 61.)
Nothing is known of the play save this entry in the Stationers'
Register. A large number of the plays in the list are not otherwise
known, but two or three, never printed by Moseley or by anyone
else in the seventeenth century, have been discovered in manuscript.

Fortune by Land and Sea
with Thomas Heywood

See *The Elizabethan Stage*, iii. 343, and Clark, *Heywood*, pp.
49–50, 180–2, and 213.

The Four Honourable Loves
(Lost)

1660, 29 June. S.R. The second group of plays entered as his
copies on this date by Humphrey Moseley includes eleven
titles, of which the first three are:

The None such. a Comedy.⎫
The booke of ye 4. Hono^ble. Loves. a⎬ by Wiłłm Rowley.
Comedy.⎪
The Parliament of Love.⎭

(Greg, *Bibliography*, i. 69.)
c. 1710–50. 'The Hon^r. Loves by Will. Rowley' appears in Warburton's list of manuscript plays. (W. W. Greg, *Library*,
Third Series, ii [1911], 230.)

Humphrey Moseley's entry in the Stationers' Register is the
only certain record of the existence of this play. Warburton's

listing of it among the plays allegedly burned by his cook is no
assurance that he ever owned the manuscript or even saw more
than the Stationers' Register entry. (See W. W. Greg, *Library*,
Third Series, ii [1911], 225–59.)

Dr. E. Herz noted (*Englische Schauspieler und englisches Schau-
spiel zur Zeit Shakespeares in Deutschland, Theatergeschichtliche
Forschungen*, xviii [1903], p. 68) that about 1660 at the Court of
Count Gustav Adolf of Mecklenburg there was performed a play entitled 'Die 4 bestendigen Liebhabers'. Conceivably the play could
have been a translation or adaptation of Rowley's lost comedy.

Hymen's Holiday, or Cupid's Vagaries (> 1612)
(Lost)

1611/12, 24 Feb. 'Shroue Munday: A play called Himens Haliday.
By the Duck of Yorks players' was performed at court. (Peter
Cunningham, *Extracts from the Accounts of the Revels at Court
in the Reigns of Queen Elizabeth and King James I, Publications
of the Shakespeare Society* [1842], p. 211.)

1633, 15 Aug. 'Received of Biston, for an ould play called *Hymen's
Holliday*, newly revived at their house, being a play given unto
him for my use, this 15 Aug. 1633, 3*l*.o.o. Received of him for
some alterations in it 1*l*.o.o.' (Adams, *Herbert*, p. 35.)

1633, 16 Dec. 'On Monday night the 16 of December, 1633, at
Whitehall was acted before the King and Queen, *Hymens Holliday or Cupids Fegarys*, an ould play of Rowleys. Likte.' (Ibid.,
p. 53.)

1639, 10 Aug. Included in a list of plays protected on this date by
the Lord Chamberlain for the King and Queen's Young Company
at the Cockpit is 'Cupids Vagaries'. (See above, i. 330–1.)

Hymen's Holiday does not fall within the period of our discussion. It is included here because, though mentioned several
times in *The Elizabethan Stage*, it is not separately discussed under
William Rowley, and some of the material concerning the play is
not noticed in that work. Though none of the records of this
piece gives the Christian name of the author, he was probably
William and not Samuel Rowley, for, as Fleay noticed (*Biog. Chron.*
ii. 95–96), William was a leading member of the Duke of York's
company (see above, ii. 555–6), which performed the play at
court in 1611/12, while Samuel Rowley was a member of a rival
troupe. (See above, ii. 555.)

Both of Sir Henry Herbert's records of 1633 note that the play was then an old one. The first record shows that it did not originally belong to the repertory of Queen Henrietta's men—who had then been performing for several years at Christopher Beeston's theatre, the Cockpit or Phoenix in Drury Lane (see above, i. 218–30)—but that Sir Henry somehow owned or controlled the manuscript. The phrases, 'newly revived at their house' and 'given unto him for my use', imply that the £3 which Herbert received from Beeston came from a benefit performance like those the King's company gave for him. (See Adams, *Herbert*, pp. 42–45.) The revisions in the old play that Sir Henry allowed for a fee of £1 would probably have been made by the regular dramatist at the Cockpit, James Shirley (q.v.). One is tempted to conclude that Shirley (?) did very well, since Herbert said that the performance was 'Likte', but a little consideration gives one pause. While Sir Henry made no comment on the reception of most of the court performances he recorded, in the season of 1633–4 he was oddly loquacious: he noted that eleven plays were liked and one not liked; only four were not graded. (Adams, *Herbert*, pp. 53–55.) Was he defending himself against criticism of his choice of plays for court performance?

A Knave in Print, or One for Another
(Lost)

1653, 9 Sept. S.R. In a long list of plays entered as his copies by Humphrey Moseley occur the titles:

> The Foole without Booke.
> A Knaue in Print, or One for another } by Wm.: Rowley.

(Greg, *Bibliography*, i. 61.)

This precise title is not known from any source save the entry in the Stationers' Register, but two plays called *The First Part of the Knaves* and *The Second Part of the Knaves* were performed at court on 2 and 10 March 1612/13. (See *The Elizabethan Stage*, iv. 180.) The plays were performed by the company of Prince Charles (then still Duke of York), and the man who accepted payment for the company's performances was William Rowley. The record does not say that he was author, as Hazlitt asserted (*A Manual for the Collector and Amateur of Old English Plays* [1892], p. 126), and there is no adequate reason for suggesting that the play that Moseley says Rowley wrote is the same as those for whose court performance Rowley represented his company as payee—as he did on both earlier and later occasions. (See *The Elizabethan Stage*, iv. 176 ff.) So far as I know, Fleay had no authority for listing the play as belonging to the King's men 1622–5. (*Biog. Chron.* ii. 107.)

Humphrey Moseley's long Stationers' Register entry of 9 September 1653 is a puzzling and suspicious one. Not only does the list contain an unusually large number of titles never published by Moseley, but a high proportion of the plays are listed with alternative titles. In a few instances the alternative titles are certainly a fraudulent entry of two different plays as one. (See Greg, *Bibliography*, ii. 979–80.) It is quite possible, therefore, that *One for Another* was a play wholly distinct from *A Knave in Print*.

The Late Murder of the Son upon the Mother, or Keep the Widow Waking (1624)
(Lost)
with Ford, Webster, and Dekker

See Thomas Dekker.

The Maid in the Mill
with John Fletcher

See Fletcher.

A Match at Midnight
See *The Elizabethan Stage*, iii. 474.

A New Wonder, A Woman Never Vext
See ibid.

The Nonesuch
(Lost)

1660, 29 June, S.R. The second group of plays entered as his copies on this date by Humphrey Moseley includes eleven titles, of which the first three are:

The None such. a Comedy.
The booke of ye 4. Honoᵇˡᵉ. Loves. a Comedy. } by Willm Rowley.
The Parliament of Love.

(Greg, *Bibliography*, i. 69.)

c. 1710–50. 'The None Such A C. Wᵐ Rowley' appears in Warburton's list of manuscript plays. (W. W. Greg, *Library*, Third Series, ii [1911], 231.)

Nothing is known of *The Nonesuch* except that the great play publisher, Moseley, had a manuscript of it in 1660 which he presumably intended to publish. The fact that the title—with the same classification and author—appears in the list of plays in manuscript that John Warburton, the Somerset herald, says were burnt by his cook, is no assurance that Warburton ever owned a manuscript of Rowley's comedy or had even seen anything more than the Stationer's Register entry. (See W. W. Greg, *Library*, Third Series, ii [1911], 225–59.)

Fleay's classification of *The Nonesuch* as a composition for the King's company, 1622–5 (*Biog. Chron.* ii. 107), is, as far as I can see, only an irresponsible guess.

The Old Law
with Philip Massinger and Thomas Middleton
See Middleton.

The Parliament of Love
See Philip Massinger.

A Shoemaker a Gentleman
See *The Elizabethan Stage*, iii. 473–4.

The Spanish Gypsy
with Thomas Middleton
See Middleton.

The Thracian Wonder
See Anon.

The Travels of Three English Brothers
with John Day and George Wilkins
See *The Elizabethan Stage*, iii. 286–7.

The Witch of Edmonton
with John Ford and Thomas Dekker
See Dekker.

A Woman Never Vext

See *A New Wonder, a Woman Never Vext* in *The Elizabethan Stage*, iii. 474.

The World Tossed at Tennis
with Thomas Middleton

See Middleton.

GEORGE RUGGLE
1575–1621 or 1622

George Ruggle, son of Thomas Ruggle, a clothier, was born in Lavenham, Suffolk, where he was baptized 13 November 1575. He attended the Lavenham Grammar School and matriculated as a pensioner from St. John's College at Cambridge in June 1589. In May 1593 he was admitted to a scholarship at Trinity, whence he graduated B.A. in 1593/4 and M.A. in 1597, incorporated at Oxford, 1605. He was elected Fellow of Clare Hall in 1598 and became one of the two University taxors in 1604. In 1620 he vacated his fellowship, apparently to become tutor to the sons of Toby Palavicino. His will—which shows that he was not a poor man—was made 6 September 1621 and proved 3 November 1622. (Hawkins, ed., *Ignoramus* [1787], pp. i–cxxii; *D.N.B.*; *Alumni Cantab.* iii. 498.)

Ruggle's *Ignoramus* was first performed at Cambridge 8 March 1614/15 before King James, who returned for a second performance about two months later. The play was widely admired and was frequently reprinted. (See *The Elizabethan Stage*, iii. 475–6.)

Club Law

See *The Elizabethan Stage*, iv. 5–6, and below, *Re Vera, or Verily*.

Ignoramus

See *The Elizabethan Stage*, iii. 475–6.

Re Vera, or Verily (?)
(Lost)

The only evidence for the existence of a play of this name is set forth by J. S. Hawkins in his edition of *Ignoramus*, 1787, p. lxxii:

> The evidence on which Mr. *Ruggle's* claim to the above comedies is founded, is a memorandum which I find inserted in manuscript in a copy of *Ignoramus*, which, in 1741, belonged to Mr. *John Hayward*, a master of arts in *Clare* hall, *Cambridge*. In this copy Mr. *Hayward* has inserted, from a manuscript copy at *Clare* hall (as he expressly notices), and from archbishop *Sancroft*'s printed copy, the names of the original performers, after which follow these words:
>> '*N.B.* Mr. *Geo. Ruggle* wrote besides two other comedies, *Revera or Verily*, and *Club Law*, to expose the puritans, not yet printed. MS.'

Since Hawkins wrote his note, the manuscript of *Club Law* (acted at Clare Hall, Cambridge, in 1599 or 1600) has been found, but Ruggle's authorship has been neither confirmed nor disproved. (See Moore Smith, ed., *Club Law*, pp. lv–lvi, and *The Elizabethan Stage*, iv. 5–6.) Nothing more has appeared of *Re Vera*. If it exists, it may not be by Ruggle, or it may have been written before 1616. One might suspect, however, that after the success of *Ignoramus* in March 1614/15, Ruggle would not rest on his laurels.

JOSEPH RUTTER
fl. 1633–40

D.N.B.
Harbage, Alfred. *Cavalier Drama* (1936), pp. 117–18.

Very little has been discovered concerning the life of Joseph Rutter beyond what is found in his publications. His name does not appear in the published lists of Oxford or Cambridge, though his employment as tutor to the son of the Earl of Dorset and his translations suggest that he was probably a university man. No records of his parentage, birth, or death have been noted.

In the thirties he was living in the household of Sir Kenelm Digby, for he says in his dedication to Digby in the volume containing *The Shepherds' Holiday* and '*Thyrsis. A Pastorall Elegie . . . on the Death of . . . the Lady Venetia Digby*' that both were written in Digby's house, and he implies that he was living there both before and after the death of Lady Venetia Digby, which occurred 1 May 1633. (See *The Shepherds' Holiday* below.)

By 1637 Rutter was tutor to the sons of the Earl of Dorset, to whom he dedicated *The Cid* (Part I), translated from Corneille, which was entered in the Stationers' Register 29 January 1637/8. Perhaps Rutter was living in Dorset's household; he says in his

dedication that Dorset had commanded him to make the translation which is in

some places of my Lords your sonnes translation, from whose attendance, if I have borrowed this time, I must account it upon your
Lordships service, from whom I have received all I have.

Apparently Rutter was tutor to the Earl's sons.

Rutter was a friend and disciple of Ben Jonson in his old age
and apparently a member of the Tribe of Ben, for Jonson wrote
highly commendatory verses for *The Shepherds' Holiday*, which
was published in 1635, two years before the laureate's death, and
addressed them '*To my deare Sonne, and right-learned Friend,
Master* Joseph Rvtter'. This relationship may be alluded to in
some of the lines that Rutter wrote for *Jonsonus Virbius*, 1638:

> But *thou* art gon, and *we* like greedy Heires,
> That snatch the fruit of their dead Fathers cares,
> Begin t' enquire what *meanes thou* left'st behind
> For *us* pretended Heires unto *thy* mind.
> And *my-selfe* not the latest 'gan to looke
> And found the Inventory in *thy* Booke.
>
> (*Jonsonus Virbius*, 1638, F_4^v–G_1.)

In Richard Flecknoe's *Miscellania. Or, Poems of all sorts, with
divers other Pieces*, 1653, pp. 55–56, is a versified dinner invitation
entitled, '*To Colonell* Jos. Rutter. *Inviting him to a Feast in* Lisbon'.
The military rank seems a bit exalted for a former nobleman's
tutor, but nothing is known of Rutter's later life.

There are very few allusions to Rutter or his work. Jonson's
poem for *The Shepherds' Holiday* is accompanied by one by Thomas
May; George Daniel simply names 'Rutter' in a list of eighteen
poets called 'names of my own time' in his *A Vindication of
Poesie*. (A. B. Grosart, ed., *The Poems of George Daniel, Esq.*, 4 vols.
[1878], i. 31.) It seems likely that Rutter is the poet referred to as
'little Cid' in Sir John Suckling's 'A Sessions of the Poets':

> During these troubles in the Court was hid
> One that *Apollo* soon mist, little *Cid*;
> And having spied him, call'd him out of the throng,
> And advis'd him in his ear not to write so strong.
>
> (*Fragmenta Aurea*, 1646, A_5^v.)

Fleay asserted (*Biog. Chron.* ii. 260) that the 'I. R.' signed to
commendatory verses for John Tatham's *The Distracted State*,
1651, stood for Joseph Rutter. This is the purest conjecture.
Miss C. Fell Smith in her account of Joseph Rutter (*D.N.B.*) said
that 'Some verses "On a Lady's tempting eye", attributed to a

John Rutter in Harleian MS. 6917., f. 77, may probably be his.'

If there is any substance to the claim on the title-page of the 1650 edition of *The Cid*, Part I, '*The Second Edition Corrected and Amended*', it might suggest that Rutter was still alive in 1650, but I have not collated the two editions, and in any case someone else than the author might have made corrections.

The Cid, Part I (1636/7–1637/8)

Harbage, Alfred. *Cavalier Drama* (1936), pp. 117–18.

1637/8, 12 Jan. 'This Tragicomedy, called, *The Valiant Cid*, translated out of the French, as it was acted before the King and Queene at Court, may be printed. /HENRY HERBERT./ *Janu.* 12. 1637.' (1637 edition D₄ᵛ.)

1637/8, 26 Jan. '*Imprimatur.* Tho. Wykes. *Jan.* 26. 1637.' (1637 edition, D₅.)

1637/8, 29 Jan. S.R. Thomas Walkley entered for his copy under the hands 'of Sʳ. Hen: Herbert. Mʳ. Wykes & Mʳ Aspley warden a Play called The Cid a Tragicomedy translated out of ffrench [Mʳ *deleted*] By Mʳ Rutter'. (Greg, *Bibliography*, i. 47.)

1637[/8]. The Cid, A Tragicomedy, out of French made English: And acted before their Majesties at Court, and on the *Cock-pit* Stage in *Drury*-lane, by the servants to both their Majesties … 1637.

1649, 3 Nov. S.R. Humphrey Moseley had assigned over to him by Thomas Walkley his rights in two books, one of which was: '[2] The Valiant Cid. the first part. TrageComedy. translated by Ios: Rutter genť.' (Greg, *Bibliography*, i. 59.)

1650. The Cid, A Tragicomedy, out of French made English: And acted before their Majesties at Court, and on the *Cock-pit* Stage in *Drury*-lane, by the servants to both their *Majesties. The Second Edition Corrected and Amended* … 1650.

Though *The Cid*, like *The Shepherds' Holiday* before it, was published with no title-page ascription, the author's name, as in the case of the previous play, appears in both Stationers' Register entries and is signed to the dedication. In this dedication to the Earl of Dorset, Lord Chamberlain to the Queen, whom he calls 'my singular good Lord and Master', Rutter says, 'I no sooner was commanded by you to translate this Poem than I went about it', and he adds that bits of the translation are the work of Dorset's sons, to whom Rutter appears to have been tutor. A very wily approach to a patron! Since Rutter says that the translation was suggested by the Lord Chamberlain to the Queen, it is not impossible that Dorset had been prompted by Henrietta Maria, who would certainly have heard of Corneille's current success in her native Paris and perhaps anticipated for it a corresponding London success. (Certainly beyond her anticipation was the Third Programme broadcast of Rutter's translation in 1952.)

Like Rutter's previous play *The Shepherds' Holiday*, *The Cid* was performed at court by the company attached to the Phoenix or Cockpit in Drury Lane, but by the time of the performance of *The Cid* at the Phoenix the former occupants of that theatre and the producers of *The Shepherds' Holiday*, Queen Henrietta's men, had been broken (see above, i. 236–9), and Beeston had formed a new troupe, the King and Queen's Young Company, to which the title-page of *The Cid* attributes performance. Since all theatres were closed because of plague from 12 May 1636—when Queen Henrietta's men were still at the Phoenix—until 24 February 1636/7, and then again from 1 March 1636/7 until 2 October 1637 (see above, ii. 661–5), *The Cid* must have had its first public performance either in the last week of February 1636/7, when the theatres were briefly open, or between 2 October 1637, when they were finally permitted to resume regular performances, and 12 January 1637/8, when Sir Henry Herbert allowed the manuscript for publication.

In the first edition the Sackville crest occupies signatures A_1 and D_5^v. The copy of the edition of 1650 at the Huntington Library contains a number of manuscript alterations for a performance, including a few stage directions. Presumably they were made for a Restoration performance.

The Cid, Part II (written 1637–9)

1639 [1638 in error], 6 Apr. S.R. 'Samuel: Browne. Entred for his Copie vnder the handes of Master Clay and Master Rothwell warden a play called *the Second part of the valiant Cid*. translated out of French by Master Rutter. vj^d.' (Edward Arber, *A Transcript of the Registers of the Company of Stationers of London 1554–1640*, iv. 437. Inadvertently omitted in Greg, *Bibliography*, i. 50, and ii. 595.)

1639, 6 Apr. 'Imprimatur Matth. Clay. Aprilis 6. 1639.' (1640 edition, A_1^v.)

1640. The Second Part of The Cid. London. Printed by *I. Okes*, for *Samuell Browne* . . . M.D.C.XL.

The second part of Rutter's translation of *The Cid*, unlike the first part, carries no statement that it was ever acted, either at court or in public. If it had been, it seems likely that Rutter, who wrote a dedicatory letter for the publication, would have provided the information for the title-page. The translation of Part II is said to have been made at the command of King Charles, but I do not know upon what evidence.

Like Rutter's other two dramatic publications, the second part of *The Cid* appeared with no author's name on the title-page, but, again as in the other instances, the name is supplied in the entry in the Stationers' Register and signed to the dedication 'To the Truley Noble the Ladie, *Theophila Cooke*'.

The Shepherds' Holiday (1633–4?)

Edition: W. C. Hazlitt, ed., *A Select Collection of Old English Plays, Originally Published by Robert Dodsley* (1875), xii. 361–444.

Greg, W. W. *Pastoral Poetry & Pastoral Drama* (1906), pp. 358–61.

Harbage, Alfred. *Cavalier Drama* (1936), p. 118.

Smith, Homer. 'Pastoral Influence in the English Drama', *P.M.L.A.* xii (1897), 423–7.

Townsend, Freda L. 'Ben Jonson's "Censure" of Rutter's *Shepheards* Holy-Day', *Mod. Phil.* xliv (1947), 238–47.

1634/5, 19 Jan. S.R. John Benson entered for his copy under the hands of 'Sʳ. Henry Herbert & both the wardens a TragiComedy called the Sheapards holliday by I: Rutter.' (Greg, *Bibliography*, i. 44.)

1635. The Shepheards Holy-Day. A Pastorall Tragi-Comædie. Acted Before Both Their Maiesties At White-Hall, by the Queenes Servants. *With* An Elegie On The Death of the most noble Lady, the Lady Venetia Digby. Vir. *Nec erubuit Sylvas habitare Thalia. Written By* J. R. .... 1635.

Though the title-page gives only the initials of the author, the Stationers' Register entry gives his family name, and the dedication to Sir Kenelm Digby is signed 'Jos. RVTTER'. This dedication informs Digby that,

'Tis then but reason that these Pöems should of themselves returne to you, by whose influence they were conceived; Both of them being borne in your house: The one whilst I admir'd the serenity, and sweetnesse of your disposition: the other when I kept time with your griefe, which you tooke for the losse of that noble Lady, your deare wife: So that now I doubt whether I may call my selfe the Author, or you.

Rutter's statement suggests the order of composition of the play
and the elegy that were published together in the octavo of 1635.
The poem he calls '*the other*' must have been the elegy on the
death of Lady Venetia Digby, after the text of which he wrote,
'*Obijt* 1. *Maij*, 1633'. The poem called '*the one*' must therefore
have been *The Shepherds' Holiday*, and since it was written in
Digby's house before the elegy was composed and while Sir
Kenelm still displayed the '*serenity, and sweetnesse*' of his disposition, i.e. before the death of his wife on 1 May 1633, we can at
least be sure that the play had been written before that date.

When the play was first performed, nothing indicates clearly.
Though the title-page records only the court performance by
Queen Henrietta's men, and the epilogue is headed 'The Epilogue
to the King and Qveene', there was at least one performance
before the public, for the prologue is headed '*The Prologue for the
Stage*', and it refers to the fact that the audience has paid admission. This performance must have been given at the Phoenix in
Drury Lane, the theatre of the company designated on the title-
page, but there is no record of Sir Henry Herbert's licence for
performance, though the Stationers' Register entry shows that
the play passed through his hands at least for press allowance.
First performance would have antedated the Stationers' Register
entry, and it would therefore have to have taken place in the
period 11 May 1633 < > 19 January 1634/5.

Both the prologue and Ben Jonson's commendatory verses
point out that *The Shepherds' Holiday* was Rutter's first play.
The high praise from Jonson in the commendatory verses and
their heading, '*To my deare Sonne, and right-learned Friend*',
comprise the principal evidence of Rutter's attachment to the
Tribe of Ben. Miss Townsend uses Jonson's praise of *The Shepherds' Holiday* to work out his own theory of the pastoral. (Loc.
cit.) The commendatory verses of Thomas May, an acknowledged
disciple of Jonson, offer another suggestion of Rutter's association with the Tribe of Ben.

Both Homer Smith (loc. cit.) and Dr. Greg, (loc. cit.) note
Rutter's indebtedness to Daniel's *Hymen's Triumph* and to Tasso.

Hazlitt (*A Manual for the Collector and Amateur of Old English
Plays* [1892], p. 207, following ed. cit., p. 362) suggested that one
episode in the play 'has been surmised to allude to the intimacy
between Sir Kenelm Digby and the Queen', as if Rutter were a
madman, or the Master of the Revels and Christopher Beeston
fools! Fleay's notion (*Biog. Chron.* ii. 173) that in v. 1 Stella may
have represented the Lady Venetia Digby and Mirtillus the Earl

of Dorset seems but little more sensible in view of Rutter's dedication of the play to Sir Kenelm.

J. S.

I cannot identify the J. S. whose initials appear on the title-pages of *Andromana* and *The Prince of Prigs' Revels*. There is no similarity between the two to suggest that the same man wrote both. Various dramatists, or alleged dramatists, of the Jacobean and Caroline periods had these initials—John Sadler, John Shank, James Shirley, Jonathan Sidnam, Joseph Simons, John Speed, John Squire, and John Suckling. I have no brief for any of them.

Andromana, or The Merchant's Wife (1642 < > 60)

Reprint: Dodsley's *Old English Plays*, ed. W. C. Hazlittt (1875), xiv. 193–271.

Ewing, S. Blaine. 'Burton, Ford, and *Andromana*', *P.M.L.A.* liv (1939), 1007–17.

Greg, W. W. *Pastoral Poetry & Pastoral Drama* (1906), pp. 330–1.

Herbst, Carl. *Cupid's Revenge by Beaumont and Fletcher und Andromana, or the Merchant's Wife in ihrer Beziehung zu einander und zu ihrer Quelle* (1906).

1660, 19 May. S.R. John Bellinger entered for his copy 'a booke called The Tragedy of Andromana or the fatall & deserved end of Disloyalty and Ambition by Iam: Shirley'. (Greg, *Bibliography*, i. 68.)

1660. Andromana: Or The Merchant's Wife. *The Scæne*, Iberia. By J. S. *London*, Printed for *John Bellinger* . . . 1660.

John Bellinger did not carry the attribution he made to James Shirley in his Stationers' Register entry on to the title-page of the quarto, and it has been generally doubted, for the tragedy is much too clumsily handled for an experienced playwright like Shirley. In the first part of the play there is a marked attention to Burtonian melancholy, a subject of no particular interest to Shirley, and, though it does not dominate the play as Professor Ewing implies (loc. cit.), it is still too obvious a feature to be characteristic of James Shirley.

The precise date of *Andromana* cannot be set, but an allusion in III. 5 makes it clear that it was written after the closing of the theatres. In this scene Libacer says:

> These women are alwayes with their Cannots,
> What cannot be? Have you but read the Sophy?
> You will finde that *Haly* (Oh how I hug that fellow's name)
> Ruin'd great *Mirza* by his father, and his father by his son.
> That great Politician, while all the Court
> Flam'd round about him, sat secure and laught.

Libacer clearly refers to John Denham's play *The Sophy*, printed in 1642 (S.R. 6 August 1642), and he says 'have you but read', not 'seen', thus clearly indicating the printed text and not a performance. There is no evidence that *Andromana* itself was ever performed, and the handling of the material as well as the date suggest that it is closet drama.

The source of *Andromana* is the Plangus story in Sidney's *Arcadia*, a story which had been more effectively used in Beaumont and Fletcher's *Cupid's Revenge*. (See Herbst, op. cit., and Ewing, op. cit.) In both plays it is much more elaborately developed than in the source.

W. R. Chetwood said that the play was revived in 1671 with a prologue containing the lines:

> 'Twas *Shirley's* Muse that laboured for it's Birth,
> Tho' now the Sire rests in the silent Earth.
> (The British Theatre [1752], p. 47.)

As Greg observes (*Bibliography*, ii. 911), the statement 'has only Chetwood's authority', but even if Chetwood was right, a Restoration prologue is of little value in establishing the authorship of an early play.

The Prince of Prigs' Revels (1651)

1651. An Excellent Comedy, Called, The Prince Of Priggs Revels: Or, The Practises of that grand Thief Captain James Hind, Relating Divers of his Pranks and Exploits, never heretofore published by any. *Repleat with various Conceits, and Tarltonian Mirth, suitable to the Subject.* Written by J. S. . . . 1651.

The play was not written until after the closing of the theatres and does not properly belong in this volume. The prologue indicates that the theatres have been suppressed:

> Since that the Apes and Parrots of the Stage,
> Are silenc'd by the Clamours of the Age;
> Like Conies forc'd to feed on Bran and Grass,
>
> .   .   .   .   .   .
>
> You'l (sure) have cause to praise, and thank that man
> Can make each Thief a compleat *Roscian.*

That the play was written in the year of publication is shown
by the reference to the defeat of Charles II, who had become King
of Scotland, at the Battle of Worcester, 3 September 1651, in the
Argument for Act v: '*The Scots King being overthrown at the battel
of* Worcster *accepts of* Hinds *conduct*.' King Charles has a speech
on the fate of kings, and the play ends with Hinds vowing per-
petual loyalty to him. Since the Thomason copy in the British
Museum has had the date 'Nouemb. 11th' added, J. S. must have
written his playlet between 3 September and 11 November 1651.

The piece consists of five very short acts—the entire play is only
thirteen pages.

W. S.

The identity of W. S. is not known. Besides the obvious great
example, the initials would fit William Strode and William Sampson among Jacobean and Caroline dramatists.

The Famous History of Petronius Maximus (> 1619)

1619. The Famouse Historie of Petronius Maximus, with the tragicall deathe of Ætius, the Roman General, and the Misdeeds of
   Valentinian, the Western Emperour, now attempted in blank
   verse, by W. S. London: Printed by William Brent, for Nathaniel Butter, and sold by him at his shop in Paule's Churchyarde,
   1619.

This title is known only from an article in *The Edinburgh
Magazine and Literary Miscellany; A New Series of the Scots
Magazine*, ix (July 1821), 3–8, which is signed 'T.' The author of
the article says that the play is not mentioned in *Biographia
Dramatica* 'or in any of the works of the dramatic bibliographers
with which I am acquainted' and proceeds to quote the title-page
from his copy, which, he says, is 'bound up in a volume of worth-
less tracts, and is in very fine preservation'. He notes that the
story has been handled by Beaumont and Fletcher in *Valentinian* and proceeds to summarize the story in detail, noting the
handling of the character Maximus and concluding that 'W. S.
however, has managed it better than might have been expected in
a *coup d'essai*, as this I imagine to be, from some expressions in the
author's dedication "to his looving uncle, T. S. Gent."' Three
long passages from the play are then given.

It is odd that no one else seems to have seen this play. Could it be a hoax? The phrase on the title-page, 'now attempted in blank verse', sounds curious.

EDWARD and RICHARD SACKVILLE

It has been suggested that Edward Sackville, fourth Earl of Dorset, or his second son, Edward Sackville, wrote *The King and Queen's Entertainment at Richmond*, 1636. Though the son certainly acted and danced in this entertainment and the father may have arranged for the performance, it is unlikely that either wrote it. See under Anon.

For the part of the fourth earl's eldest son, Richard, Lord Buckhurst, who wrote verses for *Jonsonus Virbius*, 1638, and of his second son, Edward, in the translation of Corneille's *The Cid*, see Joseph Rutter.

JOHN SADLER
1615–74

D.N.B.

John Sadler was certainly not a dramatist, and it is not even certain that he was the author of *Masquerade du Ciel*, his only connexion with dramatic history. This piece was published in 1640 with a title-page which said that it was by '*J. S.*' and an epistle to the Queen signed 'I. S.', and it was entered in the Stationers' Register in November of the same year as 'by I: S:' (See below.) The attribution to Sadler comes from the copy of the play in the library of Emmanuel College, Cambridge, where it is bound up with several contemporary publications. To the initials on the title-page, letters have been added in an old hand to make the ascription read 'By Jo. S*adler of E. C.*' In any ordinary copy this ascription would mean little, but the book at Emmanuel belonged to Archbishop Sancroft, who left it with others to the college, and presumably the ascription is his. Surely the designation '*of E. C.*' would mean nothing to any but an Emmanuel man. Now both Archbishop Sancroft and John Sadler were Emmanuel men and must have been acquainted, for Sadler entered the college in 1630 and was elected a Fellow in 1639 (*Alumni Cantab.* iv. 3); Sancroft entered in 1633, received his B.A. in 1637/8 and his M.A. in 1641, and became Master of the College in 1662. (Ibid. iv. 13.) The ascription in the Emmanuel copy, therefore, was made to a Fellow of Emmanuel apparently by another Emmanuel man, his contemporary, who was a member of the college at the time the book was published in 1640.

The ascription of *Masquerade du Ciel* to an Emmanuel man of the late thirties is compatible with the presentation inscription in the copy at the University Library, Cambridge, to Richard Holdsworth, Master of Emmanuel 1637–43—therefore Master when Sadler became a Fellow—and Vice-Chancellor of the University 1640–3. (See below and *Alumni Cantab.* ii. 391.) It seems more likely, under the circumstances, than the identification of J. S. in Thomason's copy at the British Museum as 'Chaplein to yᵉ Ld. Brooks'.

John Sadler was the son of John Sadler, who was incumbent of the parish of Patchem, Sussex, at the time of the birth of his son on 18 August 1615. (*Alumni Cantab.* iv. 3.) The younger John Sadler entered Emmanuel 13 November 1630, three years after his future brother-in-law, John Harvard; he matriculated in 1631, became B.A. in 1634, M.A. in 1638, and Fellow of the College in 1639. (Ibid.) He is said to have been distinguished for his knowledge of Hebrew and Oriental languages. (*D.N.B.*) He entered Lincoln's Inn and became a Master in Ordinary of the Court of Chancery in 1644. In 1649 he was made Town Clerk of London, and in 1650 Master of Magdalen College, Cambridge, upon the removal of Edward Rainbow. In 1653 he was M.P. for Cambridge. At the Restoration he was removed from his offices and deprived of most of his property. He died in April 1674. (Ibid.) A number of non-dramatic works are attributed to him in Donald Wing, *Short-Title Catalogue . . . 1641–1700* (1945), iii. 172, but several of them must surely be the work of other men.

Masquerade du Ciel (1640)

1640, 24 Nov. S.R. Samuel Cartwright entered for his copy 'vnder the hands of Sʳ. Henry Herbert & Mʳ Mʳ [*sic*] Man warden a booke called Masquerade du Ciel. pʳsented to the great queene of the litle world &c by I: S:' (Greg, *Bibliography*, i. 54.)

1640, 24 Nov. 'This *Masquarade Du Ciel* may be printed. Henry Herbert. *Novemb.* 24. 1640.' (In 1640 quarto opposite the title-page.)

1640. Masquarade Du Ciel: Presented to the Great Queene of the Little World. A Celestiall Map, Representing The True Site and Motions of the Heavenly Bodies, through the yeeres 1639, 1640, &c. Shadowing The late Commotions, between Saturn and Mercury, about the Northern Thule. With the Happy Peace and

Union, through the whole Little World, made by the Goodnesse of Phebus and His Royall Phebe. By *J. S.* . . . 1640.

This composition was clearly not intended for production. It is a sort of allegorical, astrological treatise with a central section roughly in the form of a masque, though too elaborate for production, and nearly all descriptive and explanatory. There are several pages of introduction and eighteen pages of notes. Several persons seem to be represented, and the Bishops' Wars appear to be obscurely alluded to. The title-page and repeated references to several months in 1639 and 1640 indicate composition shortly before the date of Sir Henry Herbert's licence.

As noted above, the copy of the piece in the library of Emmanuel College, Cambridge, has been ascribed on the title-page, apparently by Archbishop Sancroft, to John Sadler, while the copy in the Thomason collection at the British Museum identifies J. S. as 'Chaplein to yᵉ Ld. Brooks'. The copy in the University Library at Cambridge has on the fly-leaf an inscription by the author to:

> Viro Dignissimo, Doctissimo;
> Hoc est
> Ricᵈᵒ. Holdsworth, S. T. Dʳⁱ.
> Coll. Emanˡⁱˢ. Magistro,
> Acadᵃᵉ Cantab. Procanᵒ.

The author, unfortunately, does not give his name, but the inscription to the man who was Master of Emmanuel at the time John Sadler was a Fellow there is at least compatible with his authorship.

SIR THOMAS SALUSBURY
c. 1605–43

D.N.B.
Gollancz, Sir Israel. 'Contemporary Lines to Heminge and Condell', *T.L.S.*, 26 January 1922, p. 56.
—— 'Ben Jonson's Ode to "The Phoenix and the Turtle"', *T.L.S.*, 8 October 1925, p. 655.

Thomas Salusbury was the son of Henry, first baronet, of Llewenny, Denbighshire, but his birth date is unknown. The only record of his university career is found in connexion with his degree of D.C.L. at Oxford in 1642, when he is called 'sometimes of Jesus coll. in this university' (*Fasti Oxonienses*, Bliss ed., ii.

42), but there is no record that he took a degree, and his admission to the Inner Temple is recorded in November 1631. (*Students Admitted to the Inner Temple 1547–1660* [1877], p. 266.) He succeeded to the baronetcy on 2 August 1632, and Wood says that 'he retired (after he had seen the vanities of the great city) to his patrimony' (*Athenae Oxon.*, Bliss ed., iii. 56), but one wonders if this retirement from the capital was as final as Wood suggests, for Salusbury seemed to consider himself one of the Sons of Ben, and he wrote an elegy on the death of Jonson. (See Gollancz, *T.L.S.*, 8 October 1925.)

Salusbury became a burgess of Denbigh in September 1632, shortly after the death of his father, and a common councilman in 1633; he served as alderman 1634–8 and 1639. (*D.N.B.*) In 1636 he published *The History of Joseph*, a work which is presumably the basis of Anthony à Wood's statement that Salusbury had 'a natural geny to poetry and romance' and was 'a most noted poet of his time'. (Loc. cit.) I have not found contemporary allusions which bear out Wood's statement.

In March 1640 Salusbury became M.P. for Denbighshire (*D.N.B.*), and in November 1642 the degree of D.C.L. was conferred upon him by Oxford. (*Alumni Oxon.* iv. 1305.) He is said to have been active in the Royalist cause early in the civil wars and to have been ordered impeached. Wood said he was dead before August 1643, leaving a widow, Hester, and 'was, as I suppose, buried in the vault at Whitchurch joining to Leweni before-mentioned, near to the body of his father sir Henry, who died 2 Aug. 1632'. (*Athenae Oxon.*, Bliss ed., iii. 57.)

Sir Thomas Salusbury's only known publication is his *History of Joseph*, 1636, which he dedicated to Lady Middleton, wife of the former Lord Mayor of London, who had cared for him in his youth. The book has six sets of commendatory verses. His only known dramatic composition was prepared for a family entertainment and was never published.

A Masque at Knowsley (6 January 1640/1)

MS.: A Commonplace Book of the Salusbury Family, in the National Library of Wales.

Edition: R. J. Broadbent, ed., 'A Masque at Knowsley', *Transactions of the Historic Society of Lancashire and Cheshire*, New Series, xli (1925), 1–17.

Gollancz, Sir Israel. 'Contemporary Lines to Heminge and Con-
dell', *T.L.S.*, 26 January 1922, p. 56.
—— 'Ben Jonson's Ode to "The Phoenix and the Turtle"',
T.L.S., 8 October 1925, p. 655.

The essential facts about the masque are set forth in the heading in the commonplace book (Broadbent ed., p. 7):

A Masque as it was pʳsented at yᵉ right honᵇˡᵉ
yᵉ Lord Strange his [house] at Knowsley on Twelfth night 1640
Christmas day yᵗ year lighting on friday.

Designed & written in six howres space
by Sʳ Th. Salusbury
The Prologue made to bee spoken by Mr
Abraham L'Anglois
who speaks very broken English.

Sir Thomas has put together a rather pleasing family entertainment which brings in the names, characters, and persons of
more than a dozen members of the Knowsley household. But his
employment of the twelve months of the year as characters was
not an original device, for it had been used, as Broadbent observed
(op. cit., p. 3), in a masque of about 1612. Broadbent calls it a
masque by Inigo Jones, but presumably he means that anonymous masque called *The Masque of the Twelve Months* which Peter
Cunningham published in his *Inigo Jones*. (*Shakespeare Society
Publications*, No. 39 [1848]. See also *The Elizabethan Stage*, iv.
58–59.)

In spite of the similarity between *A Masque at Knowsley* and
The Masque of the Twelve Months, it is improbable that Salusbury
should have seen the earlier work, since it was not printed until
the nineteenth century. Another and later entertainment was,
however, available to him, and Salusbury's title-page boast that
his masque was designed and written in six hours becomes less
impressive when one compares it with Middleton and Rowley's
Inner Temple Masque or Masque of Heroes (q.v.), which was performed at the Inner Temple in 1618/19 and printed in 1619. It was
the Inner Temple of which Salusbury was a member, and only
four or five years before the composition of his masque he had
drawn attention to his connexion on the title-page of his *History
of Joseph*, 1636, in the description of himself as 'Sir Thomas
Salusbury, Barronet, late of the Inner Temple'.

The structure of the two masques is very similar. Salusbury used
the device of Christmas dying at Twelfth Night and leaving a

series of legacies that had been developed before him by Middleton
and Rowley, and similarly both masques open with the entrance
of Dr. Almanac carrying a urinal, though Salusbury had the
Doctor lead Christmas on stage, whereas Middleton and Rowley
had kept him off. For the fancifully named members of the household in *The Inner Temple Masque*—In and In, Gleek, Tickle-Me
Quickly—Salusbury has substituted Knowsley people and has
made the legacies appropriate. Salusbury has used the Fasting-day
idea from the earlier masque in his second ante-masque.

The lines in the Knowsley masque do not, however, appear to
have been derived from Middleton and Rowley, and those in the
legacies show a certain amount of wit and malice.

WILLIAM SAMPSON

c. 1600–<55/6

Godfrey, John T. *William Sampson, A Seventeenth Century Poet
and Dramatist* (1894).

Wallrath, Hans. *William Sampson's Vow-Breaker, Materialien
zur Kunde des älteren Englischen Dramas* (1914), pp. 4–10.

William Sampson identifies himself in his dedication of *The
Vow-Breaker* to Anne Willoughby, daughter of Sir Henry Willoughby of Risley, as a faithful servant of the Willoughbys, and
he says that the play was written in Sir Henry's house. This identification makes it likely that he was the 'William Sampson now
aged about fourty nine Yeeres' who in 1649 testified as to the
precise day and hour of the birth of Sir Henry's daughter Elizabeth, then wife of Sir Simonds d'Ewes. (Wallwrath, op. cit., p. 5,
from B.M. MS. Harleian 99 [18].)

Another document that Wallrath found is a petition of 15
February 1655/6 in which Henry Smith, William Sampson, and
Michael Cowle, all late of Risley, Derby, say that they are the
executors of the will of Sir Henry Willoughby. (Ibid., p. 6, from
B.M. MS. Add. 6688, fol. 142.) It seems likely that the William
Sampson who knew the Willoughby household so well as to testify
to the hour of the birth of Elizabeth Willoughby was probably the
same as Sir Henry's executor. Yet there must have been another
William Sampson in the vicinity, for in December 1637 (1647,
according to Wallrath, loc. cit.), Obadiah Grew married Helen
Vicars, 'widow of William Sampson of South Leverton, Nottinghamshire' (*D.N.B.* under Grew), and this woman is said to be the
mother of Henry Sampson, Fellow of Pembroke Hall and 'son of

Mr. William Sampson of South Leverton, Nottinghamshire'. (Godfrey, loc. cit.) Since Godfrey also notes that Sampsons were landowners in the parish and appeared frequently in the registers after 1658, there may have been more than two William Sampsons in the parish in Caroline times. Sir Henry's executor, therefore, was not necessarily the author of the plays, though composition and publication dates make it seem rather likely that he was. The Hanna Sampson who is charged with trusts in Sir Henry Willoughby's will was apparently the daughter of the dramatist. (Wallrath ed., pp. 8–9.)

In addition to his plays William Sampson published a volume of verse entitled *Virtus Post Funera Vivit, or Honour Triumphing over Death*, 1636, and Wallrath notes a long unpublished poem, 'Loues Metamorphosis or Apollo and Daphne'.

Herod and Antipater
with Gervase Markham
See Markham.

Love's Labour Lost

Edward Archer published 'An Exact and perfect Catalogue of all the Plaies that were ever printed; together, with all the Authors names; and what are Comedies, Histories, Interludes, Masks, Pastorels, Tragedies'. This catalogue was appended to his edition of Massinger, Middleton, and Rowley's *The Old Law*, 1656. Dr. Greg shows that this catalogue of Archer's is derived from the similar list of Rogers and Ley published in the same year. (*Bibliography*, ii. 996.) One title in Archer's list is 'Loves labor lost C Will. Sampson'. This entry almost certainly derives from some confusion with Shakespeare's play. Dr. Greg suggests (*Bibliography*, ii. 998) that Archer may have seen a lost early edition of Shakespeare's play with W. S. on the title-page and wrongly expanded it.

The Vow-Breaker, or The Fair Maid of Clifton (1625?–36)

Edition: Edited by Hans Wallrath in *Materialien* (1914).

Tillotson, Kathleen. 'William Sampson's "Vow-Breaker" (1636) and the Lost Henslowe Play "Black Batman of the North"', *M.L.R.* xxxv (1940), 377–8.

1636. The Vow Breaker. *Or*, The Faire Maide of *Clifton. In* Notinghamshire *as it hath beene diuers times Acted by seuerall Companies with great applause.* By William Sampson . . . 1636.

Sampson's dedication of his play to Anne Willoughby, 'Daughter of . . . *Henry Willoughby* of *Risley*, in the County of *Derby Baronet*', indicates that it was not written in London, and might be interpreted to mean that it had first been acted in Derbyshire. It begins:

> THIS *infant received breath, and being vnder your noble Fathers roofe (my ever honored Master) and therefore, as an Aire-lover belonging to that Hospitable Fabricke, it properly prostrates it selfe to you for a patronnesse.*

Provincial performance is also suggested by the statement on the title-page, '*as it hath bene diuers times Acted by severall Companies*', without mention of any specific London troupe. Such a vague indication of performance by various companies at unspecified places is sometimes found on the title-pages of early plays, but it is practically unknown in the twenties and thirties when the ownership of acting rights was more settled. There is also a strong suggestion of provincial rather than London performance in the last scene of the play, in which Queen Elizabeth appears for the first time and grants the totally irrelevant petition of Nottingham that the Trent be made navigable, and later in the scene she proposes to visit the underground passages of Nottingham Castle. Such irrelevancies might have had a strong appeal in the neighbourhood of Nottingham and Derby, but surely they would have had little or none in London.

It is asserted in the 'Prologue to Censurers' that *The Vow-Breaker* is a true story:

> Truth saies the Author, this Time will be bold
> To tell a Story, truer ne're was told.
> Wherein he boldly vouches all is true
> That this Time's spoke by vs, or heard by you.
> If Chronicle, that ever yet gain'd favour
> May please true Iudgments: his true endeavour
> From serious houres has gaind it: for vs
> He hopes our labours will be prosperous
> And yet me thinkes I here some Criticke say
> That they are much abus'd in this our Play.
> Their Magistracy laught at! as if now
> When Ninty yeeres since dy'd, afresh did grow:
> To those wee answer, that ere they were borne,
> The story that we glaunse at, then was worne
> And held authentick: and the men wee name
> Grounded in Honours Prowesse, Vertues Fame.

Both plots of the play are based on historical facts—or at least what Sampson believed to be facts. One concerns the English-French-Scottish military action around Leith and Edinburgh in 1560, and the other, which gives the play its title, relates Ann Boote's faithlessness to her affianced Bateman, and his suicide and haunting of her. The first plot comes, as Wallrath has shown (ed. cit., pp. 19–27), from Holinshed, often reproducing his words, dates, and figures. The second is derived from the ballad, variously entitled 'A Godly Warning for all Maidens', or 'A Warning for Maidens', or 'Young Bateman'. (See William Chappell, ed., *The Roxburghe Ballads*, iii [1880], 193–7.) This ballad, reprinted by Chappell and by Wallrath (ed. cit., pp. 13–16), was entered in the Stationers' Register in one form or another in 1603, 1624, and 1675. (See Hyder Rollins, 'An Analytical Index to the Ballad-Entries', *Stud. Phil.* xxi [1924], pp. 22, 91, 247.) Miles sings twelve lines of it in v. 2, and calls it 'a very mery lamentable dolefull new Ditty of young *Bateman*, and his *Nan*'. His 'new' might refer to the edition which a group of printers entered in the Stationers' Register with many other ballads under the title of 'Bateman', 14 December 1624 (Arber ed. iv. 93), but there may well have been issues not indicated by Stationers' Register entries.

'The Prologue to Censurers' published in the quarto is a little puzzling. Its insistence on the truth of the story is understandable enough in the light of the ballad and Holinshed, for the numerous additions which Sampson makes to the ballad story may have had a basis in local facts. But why did he say ninety years old? The military action in which appear the only men of the play whose names were '*Grounded in Honours Prowesse, Vertues Fame*' was not ninety years old until 1650, long after Sampson wrote the play. The assertion that the story was ninety years old is associated with the alleged ridicule of magistrates, but there are no magistrates in the play. Puritans are satirized, especially in the episode of Joshua hanging his cat on Monday for killing mice on Sunday (III. 2). Did Sampson mean to date this familiar anecdote? The whole prologue seems a bit devious. What was Sampson afraid of?

In 1598 Henslowe had two plays (Parts I and II) called 'Black Batman of the North' (see W. W. Greg, ed., *Henslowe's Diary*, ii. 193), and it has been suggested that Sampson's piece was a revision of one or both. (See Kathleen Tillotson, loc. cit.) I see no reason to associate the titles; the Young Bateman of this play could certainly not be called black; he is an abused lover. The ballad, the action of the play, the characterization of the principals, and the moralizing verses on the illustrations in the quarto all make Ann the sinner, not Bateman.

The Widow's Prize, or The Woman Captain (1624/5)

(Lost)

1624/5, 25 Jan. 'For the Prince's Company; A new Play, called,
   The Widow's Prize; which containing much abusive matter, was
   allowed of by me, on condition, that my reformations were
   observed.' (Adams, *Herbert*, p. 30.)

1624/5, 25 Jan. 'For the Prin: comp: A new P. call: the Widowes
   prize contayn[ing much abusive] matter was allowed by mee on
   condition my reformations [were observed 25 Jan. 1624].' (Folger Shakespeare Library, MS. Scrap-Books of J. O. Halliwell-
   Phillipps. *Lowin*, p. 131.)

1653, 9 Sept. S.R. Humphrey Moseley entered for his copies a
   long list of plays, including 'The Widdowes Prize. by M^r. W^m.
   Samson'. (Greg, *Bibliography*, i. 60.)

c. 1677–1703. 'the widdows prise or the woman Captain.' (J. Q.
   Adams, 'Hill's List of Early Plays in Manuscript', *Library*,
   Fourth Series, xx [1939], 71–99. See Middleton, *The Conqueror's
   Custom*.)

c. 1710–50. 'The Widows Prise C. Wm Sampson' appears in
   Warburton's list of manuscript plays. (See W. W. Greg, *Library*,
   Third Series, ii [1911], 231.)

The Widow's Prize is one of the better recorded of the lost plays.
The first entry above comes from Chalmers's extract from Sir
Henry Herbert's manuscript office-book. The second comes from
an independent transcript of the office-book in a nineteenth-century hand. This transcript, perhaps that of Craven Ord, has been
cut up and pasted into appropriate sections of Halliwell-Phillipps's
scrap-books, now preserved in the Folger Shakespeare Library.
The bracketed sections indicate passages in a different hand which
replace sections of the original transcript inadvertently clipped
off before pasting.

The third entry, giving the name of the author, comes from the
long list of plays entered by Moseley, more than half of which
were never published. The fifth entry may derive from the third
and does not necessarily indicate a separate record of a play
actually in Warburton's possession. (See Greg, op. cit., pp. 225–
59.)

The fourth entry indicates the presence of the title as the forty-
second in the list of manuscript plays found among the papers of
Abraham Hill. (See Middleton, *The Conqueror's Custom*.) The list
seems to have been Hill's record of some bookseller's stock, set

down between 1677 and 1703, but it is notable that nearly all the identifiable plays and playwrights of the list are Jacobean and Caroline. It seems slightly odd that Hill should be the first to record a sub-title for the play. Moseley recorded a number of sub-titles for other plays licensed at the same time as *The Widow's Prize*, several of them false sub-titles used to cover the entry of two plays. A valid sub-title for *The Widow's Prize* would have helped to cover his peccadillos. Conceivably this omission could indicate that his manuscript had no sub-title and that therefore Hill saw a second one.

At the time Herbert licensed this play for them, the Prince's men had almost reached the end of their existence as a company (see above, i. 208–10), and for the past three or four years they had not been very distinguished. Probably most of their plays were on the market a year or so after this one was licensed to be acted. The fact that under these circumstances *The Widow's Prize* does not appear in the Stationers' Register until 1653 and then was not published suggests that it was a poor thing.

Fleay's confusion about the play (*Biog. Chron.* ii. 175) comes from his oversight in searching Chalmers and his wrong inference about the date.

GEORGE SANDYS
1577/8–1643/4

Dictionary of American Biography.
D.N.B.
Bowers, Fredson T., and Richard B. Davis. 'George Sandys: a bibliographical catalogue of printed editions in England to 1700', *Bulletin of the New York Public Library*, liv (1950).

George Sandys was not a dramatist, but a traveller, translator, and a very influential poet, one of whose works, *Christ's Passion*, translated from the Latin of Hugo Grotius, is in dramatic form, though certainly not intended for performance. He was born in the palace at Bishopthorpe on 2 March 1577/8, the youngest son of Edwin Sandys, Archbishop of York. In December 1589, at the age of eleven, he matriculated at Oxford from St. Mary Hall, but apparently he did not take a degree. (*Alumni Oxon.* iv. 1309.) His *Relation of a Journey Begun Anno Domini 1610* is an account of his extensive travels in Turkey, Egypt, the Holy Land, and Italy.

Sandys was actively interested in colonial affairs from 1611 on, and he spent the years 1621–8 and possibly more in Virginia.

(*D.A.B.*) In 1621 the first five books of his translation of Ovid's *Metamorphoses* appeared, and in 1626 the complete translation. After his return he was made a Gentleman of the Privy Chamber to King Charles. In 1636 he published *A Paraphrase upon the Psalms of David and upon Hymns Dispersed throughout the Old and New Testaments*. Sandys died at Boxley Abbey in Kent in March 1643/4.

Christ's Passion
Translation from Hugo Grotius

1639, 17 Sept. 'September 17. 1639. *Imprimatur: Tho: Wykes.*' (*Christ's Passion*, 1640, a$_4$v.)

1639, 27 Sept. 'September 27. 1639. *Imprimatur. Ioannes Hansley.*' (Ibid., H$_6$v.)

1639, 9 Oct. S.R. John Legatt entered for his copy 'vnder the handes of D^r. wykes M^r. Hansley & m^r Bourne warden a booke called Christs [Chr *altered from* The] Passion. a Tragedy. wth. Annotations by Geo: Sands Esqr.' (Greg, *Bibliography*, i. 51.)

1640. Christs Passion. A Tragedie. With Annotations . . . M.D.C.XL.

1640. [Another issue.]

1640. [A third issue.]

1685. 'Imprimatur. October 8th. 1685. Robert Midgely.' (*Christ's Passion*, 1687, A$_8$v.)

1687. Christ's Passion. A Tragedy; With Annotations. By *George Sandys*, Author of the *Paraphrase* on the *Psalmes*, and *Ovid's Metamorphosis*, &c. *The Second Edition, Illustrated with Sculptvres* . . . 1687.

1698. Christ's Passion. A Tragedy; With Annotations. Dedicated to the King's Most Excellent Majesty . . . M DC XC VIII.

The dedication to the King is signed 'George Sandys'. The second issue has a set of commendatory verses signed 'Falkland'. The translation has no connexion with the theatre.

WILLIAM SHAKESPEARE
1564–1616

Even a dramatic historian can be confident that Shakespeare wrote nothing after his death, but several plays written, or probably written, after 1616, have contemporary attributions to

Shakespeare, and it may be convenient to have them assembled here. They are:

Duke Humphrey (see Anon.).
Henry I (see Robert Davenport).
Henry II (see Robert Davenport).
Iphis and Iantha, or A Marriage without a Man (see Anon.).
The History of King Stephen (see Anon.).

JOHN SHANK (Schanks, Shanck, Shancke, Shanckes, Shancks, Shanke, Shankes, Shanks, Shanucke)

c. 1580?–1635/6

Baldwin, T. W. *The Organization and Personnel of the Shakespearean Company* (1927), *passim*.
Baskervill, C. R. *The Elizabethan Jig and Related Song Drama* (1929), pp. 118–19, 301.

The career of the well-known comedian, John Shank, Sr., is set forth in some detail in the second volume on Players (see above, ii. 562–7) and need be only summarized here.

In 1635 Shank described himself as an old man who had served in the companies of Queen Elizabeth and the Lord Chamberlain in his youth. (*Malone Society Collections*, ii, Part 3, p. 367.) This statement might refer to service as a boy actor, but the fact that Shank in his will called himself 'cittizen and weaver of London' suggests another youthful activity. Since he called himself an old man in this quality in 1635 (ibid.) and had a son buried in 1610 (see above, ii. 564), any birth date between 1570 and 1590 would fit the evidence.

Shank was a member of Prince Henry's–Palsgrave's company from 1610 or earlier until about 1614, and later, at an uncertain date, he joined the King's company. He was in fact a King's man from at least 1619 until his death in 1635/6, and he held shares in both the Globe and the Blackfriars. In addition to his performance of comic roles in the productions of the King's company, Shank seems to have taken care of an unusual number of the boy actors and may have run a sort of boarding-house for them. As a comedian he was well known, and he also had something of a reputation as a jig-dancer—possibly as a jig-maker also.

Shank had a namesake son, also an actor, with whom he can easily be confused.

Shank's Ordinary (1623/4)
(Lost)

Lawrence, W. J. *Pre-Restoration Stage Studies* (1927), pp. 332–3.

1623/4, 16 Mar. '"For the king's company. *Shankes Ordinary*, written by Shankes himself, this 16 March, 1623—1*l. os. od.*" MS. Herbert.' (Adams, *Herbert*, p. 27.)

1623/4, 16 Mar. 'For the Kings company. Shankes Ordinary written by Shankes himself this 16th March 1623. For Lent— Mr. Hemings brought mee for Lent this 1st Apr. 1624—2 ll' (Folger Shakespeare Library, MS. Scrap-Books of J. O. Halliwell-Phillipps, *Kemp*, p. 152.)

The second version of Herbert's entry above has been clipped from a transcript of Herbert's entries in a hand apparently of the nineteenth century—perhaps that of Craven Ord—and pasted into one of his scrap-books by Halliwell-Phillipps.

It has been generally supposed because its author was associated with jigs that *Shankes Ordinary* was a jig, and it may have been, but the evidence for assuming it is at least inadequate. W. J. Lawrence (loc. cit.) said that the piece was shown to be a jig by Herbert's charge of half his regular fee for licensing it, but he is mistaken. Later on, Herbert did charge £2 for licensing new plays, but in the early twenties his usual fee was only £1. (See above, Gunnell, *The Way to Content All Women*; Samuel Rowley, *A Match or No Match* and *Richard III*; Bonen, *Two Kings in a Cottage*; Davenport, *The History of Henry I* and *The City Night-cap*; Massinger, *The Renegado*; Heywood, *The Captive, or The Lost Recovered*; and below, Anon. *The Angel King, The Dutch Painter and the French Branke*, and *The Fair Star of Antwerp*.)

The fee charged by the Master of the Revels for allowing *Shank's Ordinary*, then, was the same as the fee charged in this period for allowing a full-length play. Would he have made the same charge for allowing a short piece, like a jig? (See C. R. Baskervill, *The Elizabethan Jig* [1929], *passim*.) Perhaps the fact that the allowance was made during Lent and that two weeks later John Heminges, Shank's fellow sharer in the King's company and general business manager for the organization (see above, ii. 465–9), paid Herbert £2 for allowing Lenten activities at their house (see Adams, *Herbert*, p. 48) is significant here. Could *Shank's Ordinary* have been a full afternoon's entertainment—a Lenten variety show of some sort—analogous to the fencers and rope dancers at the Red Bull and Fortune—and perhaps including jigs? Was it perhaps given at the Globe in Lent, 1623/4, when we know from Heminges's payment to Herbert that the King's men used their theatre for something? This is pure speculation, but it seems more compatible with the known facts than the assumption that *Shank's Ordinary* was either a play or a simple jig.

LEWIS SHARPE
fl. 1640

Nothing save what can be derived from the edition of his play is known of Lewis Sharpe, whose initials appear on the title-page of *The Noble Stranger*, but whose full name is signed to the dedication to Sir Edmund Williams. In this dedication Sharpe says:

> As for the name of *Poet*, it is a stile I never aimed at, (though afarre off I have admired their sacred Raptures) and therefore will not be injurious to *your Expectation*, to bribe *your Acceptance* with promising *Workes* of a higher *strain* hereafter, this being the only *Issue*, of some vacant houres, which if *you* vouchsafe at like times to smile on, there ends the ambition of him. . . .

The Noble Stranger is called a first play again in the prologue:

> *Faith use our Author well . . .*
> *'Tis the first accent of his tender Muse,*
> *He hopes 'twill please you. . . .*

The Noble Stranger (1638–40)

1640. The Noble Stranger. *As it was Acted at the Private House in* Salisbury Court, by her Maiesties Servants. The Author, *L. S.* . . . 1640.

The Noble Stranger, which does not appear in the Stationers' Register or in the extant records from Sir Henry Herbert's office-book, was presumably first performed by Queen Henrietta's company after their reorganization for the Salisbury Court theatre, to which the opening lines of the prologue appear to refer. The plays written for Queen Henrietta's company before the plague of 1636–7 appear to have been kept in the repertory of the Cockpit theatre by Christopher Beeston, and since, as the title-page shows, this one was not kept at the Cockpit, it seems likely that it was not written for Queen Henrietta's company until after they had left the Cockpit and been re-formed at the Salisbury Court. Such a date—after the autumn of 1637 (see above, i. 236–40) and before publication in 1640—would agree with the apparent allusion to the Scottish Covenant of February and March 1637/8 (see Gardiner, *History of England*, viii. 325–48), and perhaps to the preliminaries of the First Bishops' War in early 1639 (ibid. ix. 1–32) in the prologue:

> *Our Author does beleeve there will not want*
> *Some to subscribe the Factious Covenant*
> *Of your prescitian wits, if such there are,*
> *Proclaime 'hem Rebells, and bid open warre.*

A date of 1638–40, then, seems probable for the first production of *The Noble Stranger*.

Both the author and Richard Woolfall, who wrote commendatory verses for him, assert that the play was popular. The author says in his dedication to Sir Edmund Williams, 'This *Play*, (I dare not say how worthy) was received generally well upon the *Stage*', and Richard Woolfall goes much further in his verses:

> *. . . yet doe not feare the danger*
> *Of Critick Readers, since thy* Noble Stranger,
> *With pleasing strains has smooth'd the rugged Fate*
> *Of oft cram'd Theatres, and prov'd fortunate.*

The opening lines of the prologue seem to indicate some special occasion on which the audience was more distinguished than usual:

> *Blest Fate protect me! what a lustre's here?*
> *How many Starres deck this our little spheare?*

I do not know what such an occasion could have been.

Langbaine admired the school-for-gulls scenes of Mercutio and Pupillus (*An Account of the English Dramatick Poets*, 1691, p. 470), and suggested that Lacy derived from one of them the character-of-the-poets scenes in *Sir Hercules Buffoon, or The Poetical Squire*. The scene in Act IV in which Pupillus is induced to imitate famous poets is quite an amusing one. It would seem to demand a fairly high degree of literary sophistication in the audience, since the poets are not named, but perhaps the spectators at Salisbury Court enjoyed the bombast without recognizing the originals.

SAMUEL SHEPPARD
c. 1624–55?

Rollins, Hyder E. 'Samuel Sheppard and His Praise of Poets', *Stud. Phil.* xxiv (1927), 509–55.

Samuel Sheppard was long thought of as a Jacobean and Caroline poet and general candidate for the authorship of plays attributed to 'S. S.', though he was scarcely old enough to write a play when the theatres were closed. The confusion is based on the statement of E. I. Carlyle in the *D.N.B.* that Sheppard 'commenced his literary career about 1606 as amanuensis to Ben Jonson, but wrote nothing himself till a later period', and this statement seems to have been shakily based on a misreading of stanza 11 in the sixth sestyad of Sheppard's *The Times Displayed*, 1646. Two lines in this stanza read:

> . . . for unto his wit
> My selfe gave personal ayd *I* dictated
> To him when as *Sejanus* fall he writ.

Carlyle—and better scholars than he—assumed that '*I*' was the author, Samuel Sheppard, whereas a little more extended reading in the sixth sestyad makes it quite clear that '*I*' is Apollo, as Professor Rollins pointed out. Even Sir Edmund Chambers (*Elizabethan Stage*, iii. 491) and W. W. Greg (*Edinburgh Bibliographical Society Transactions*, ii, Part 4 [1946], 308) were taken in.

The evidence indicates that Samuel Sheppard was born not earlier than 1624, since his parents were married 10 April 1623. (Rollins, op. cit., pp. 509–10.) His first known publication is in 1646, and for several years he issued newsbooks, pamphlets, and poems, often characterized by extensive plagiarism. (Ibid., pp. 520–38.) Rollins thinks that Sheppard probably died in 1655, since the last of his rather crowded series of publications is dated 1655 (though Thomason bought it 3 November 1654) and the last reference to him is in 1655. (Ibid., p. 537.)

The Committee-Man Curried (1647)

The two parts of the playlet, published 16 July and 14 August 1647, express Sheppard's reactions to events of 1647. (See Rollins, op. cit., p. 521.)

The Honest Lawyer (> 1615)

Chambers's tentative suggestion (*Elizabethan Stage*, iii. 491 and iv. 19) that Samuel Sheppard may have been the 'S. S.' of the 1616 title-page of *The Honest Lawyer* is another example of the chaos deriving from the misunderstanding that Sheppard had said that Jonson dictated *Sejanus* to him. *The Honest Lawyer* was published before Sheppard was born.

The Jovial Crew, or The Devil Turned Ranter (c. 1650)

A pamphlet written in dramatic form in five short acts. The title-page, dated 1651, calls it 'a Character of *The roaring* Ranters *of these Times* . . . a Sect (lately sprung up amongst us) called *Ranters*'. Thomason's copy in the British Museum is dated 'Jan: 6 1650'. (Greg, *Bibliography*, ii. 817.)

SIR EDWARD SHERBURNE
1618–1702

Sir Edward Sherburne was not a dramatist, but a scholar and translator whose translations of classic plays all appeared after the closing of the theatres. He was born in London in 1618 and died there in 1702. In 1641 he became Clerk of the Ordinance and later served the King as commissary-general of artillery. He was knighted in January 1681/2. (*D.N.B.*)

Sherburne's only dramatic publication before the Restoration was 'Medea: A Tragedie. Written in Latine by Lucius Annæus Seneca. Englished by E. S. Esq. . . . 1648.' His name appears in the commendatory verses written for the publication by his friend Thomas Stanley.

ROGER SHIPMAN
c. 1621–<63

The only material I know on the life of Roger Shipman is that in *Alumni Oxon.* iv. 1351:

Shipman, Roger, s. William, of Whaddon, Wilts, sacerd. St. John's Coll., matric. 19 May, 1637, aged 16, B.A. 6 Feb., 1640–1; vicar of Chisledon, Wilts, 1663; father of William 1671.

He was presumably co-author with William Taylor (q.v.) of the St. John's College play, *Grobiana's Nuptials*.

Grobiana's Nuptials (1637?–41?)

MS.: Bodleian MS. 30 (formerly Bodl. 27639).

Edition: Reprinted by Ernst Rühl in *Grobianus in England*, *Palaestra*, xxxviii (1904), 164–91.

Bowers, R. H. 'The Text of *Grobiana's Nuptialls*', *M.L.N.* lv (1940), 109.

Herford, C. H. *Studies in the Literary Relations of England and Germany in the Sixteenth Century* (1886), pp. 389–98.

N[ott], J., ed. *The Gull's Hornbook, Reprinted; with Notes of Illustration by J. N.* (1812), pp. 6–7.

This short play of nine scenes seems to be the only thorough-going exploitation of the Grobianus material in English Renaissance drama. The chief characters are *Grobianus*, his daughter *Grobiana*, her servant *Ungartered*, the members of the Grobian society, *Pamphagus*, *Lorrell*, and *Oyestus*, and the court of assistants, *Vanscop*, *Tantoblin*, and *Ursin*, the bearward. The action consists mostly of the feast and the courtship of *Grobiana*.

Nott, whose note on the play seems to be the first comment on it (op. cit., p. 6, n.), says that the play was

penned, as the ingenious librarian, Mr. Bliss, conjectures, much about Decker's day: it is entitled *Grobiana's Nuptials*; and is such a tissue of obscenity and beastliness, that it is impossible to select a single scene or passage fit for the publick eye. . . . Might there not have existed in Decker's time a society, perhaps of low profligates, who called themselves *Grobians*; and might not this very drama have been written, much about that time, to satirize them?

This dating seems to have been suggested more by the fact that Dekker also used some Grobian material than by any more considerable reason; at least none is offered.

Herford attempts no exact date, but implies a somewhat later one. He notes the Oxford character of the piece implied by the location of the manuscript, the prologue sketch of 'Our Schollers', the allusion to the game of 'Bambery hott cockles', and remarks,

Grobiana's Nuptials is nevertheless as distinctly of Oxford as *Grobianus* is of Wittenberg, and as distinctly of the seventeenth century as this of the sixteenth. (Op. cit., pp. 393, n. 1, and 395.)

The only internal evidence suggestive of a date that I have noted is found in the prologue, which begins:

Had you had a prologue, I had not enter'd, for to say *the* truth I am *old* Grobian; did you ever heare of old Grobian? Thats I, and am he that hate manners worse then Tymon hated man. And *what* did he hate them for? Marrie for their foolish, foppish, apish complements, niceties, lispings, cringes; can't our buisinesse bee done, and *our* Play acted, but a Coxe-combe in a cloke must scrape his lease of leggs to begge *Sir* Tottipate's applause in dogrime verse? And he goe away and swore he understood ne're a worde. I like his stout humour best that [says] twas good, a good fat old Grobian he was.

This last line, especially in context, sounds like an allusion to the frequently noted last line of Ben Jonson's epilogue for *Cynthia's Revels*, '*By* (——) *'tis good, and if you lik't, you may*', and the description of Jonson as 'a good fat old Grobian' would be sufficiently appropriate to raise a laugh. If this interpretation is correct, the use of the past tense would indicate a date after Jonson's death in August 1637. Such a date would correspond well enough with the Oxford residence of William Taylor and Roger Shipman, whose names Rühl noted on the manuscript of the play and whom he assumed to be the authors. (Ed. cit., p. lii.)

These two men are not, however, given as authors in the manuscript, though they may have been. Madan noted that 'At the end (deleted) is 'William Taylor et Roger Shipman,' who perhaps owned the book, or possibly copied into it the second part. Both were of St. John's college.' (Loc. cit.).

If either or both of these men may be taken as the author or authors of *Grobiana's Nuptials*, the play was probably a St. John's play, since both of them belonged to that college and since the only other piece in the Bodleian MS. in which *Grobiana's Nuptials* is found was also written by a St. John's man, Christopher Wren, Sr., and was dedicated to John Buckeridge, president of the college. (Madan, loc. cit.) Though the character of the play does not suggest authorized college presentation to the modern mind, the prologue—nicely conceived for an opening speech—clearly indicates that it was so intended.

The play, if Shipman and Taylor are the authors, probably dates from their St. John's years, beginning with Taylor's matriculation in 1636 and ending with his B.A. in July 1641 (*Alumni Oxon.* iv. 1464), and if the Jonson allusion is not misleading, the play must have been written after August 1637.

R. H. Bowers's article makes a number of corrections in Rühl's transcription of the text.

HENRY SHIRLEY
c. 1594–1627

Fleay, F. G. 'Annals of the Careers of James and Henry Shirley', *Anglia*, viii (1885), 405–14.

Nason, Arthur Huntington. *James Shirley Dramatist* (1915), pp. 11–14.

Shirley, Evelyn Philip. *Stemmata Shirleiana* (1873), pp. 269–70.

—— 'Who Was Henry Shirley, the Author of "The Martyr'd Soldier"?' *N. & Q.* xii (1855), 26–27.

Various guesses about Henry Shirley have been printed, most of them associating him with his better known namesake, James Shirley. Evelyn Philip Shirley, the chief authority on the Shirley family, says they 'could not claim kindred'. (*Stemmata Shirleiana*, p. 270.) He finds Henry to have been the second son of Sir Thomas Shirley, the younger, of Wiston, Sussex—one of the three travelling Shirley brothers—and of Frances (Vavasour), his wife. (Ibid., p. 269.) Henry Shirley must have been born between 1591, when his parents were married (ibid., p. 266), and 1597, when his younger brother was born. (Ibid., p. 271.) In the Caroline genealogy of the Shirley family, Henry Shirley is said to have died without issue. (E. P. Shirley, *N. & Q.*)

In 1622 Henry Shirley was left £40 per annum by his grandmother, Lady Anne, wife of Sir Thomas Shirley, the elder, of Wiston. This sum, according to her will, was to be paid annually by Sir Thomas Bishop from £300 left him by Lady Anne. (*Stemmata Shirleiana*, pp. 263-4.) From this situation grew the only event specifically known in the life of Henry Shirley. It is recorded in a letter of 31 October 1627, from Mr. Beaulieu in London to Sir Thomas Puckering:

> There is a foul murther committed on Friday last by Sr Edward Bishop [son of Sir Thomas], of Sussex, on Mr Henry Shirley of the same shire, whom he run thro' with his sword (having no weapon about him), as he came to him in his lodging in Chancery Lane to demand of him an annuity of 40 *l.*, which the said Sr Edward Bishop was to give him, whose lands (which are reported to be of 1500 *l* or 2000 *l* by the year) were presently begged or given away, but himself not yet found. (Quoted by Shirley, *N. & Q.*)

Later records in the *Calendar of State Papers* record Henry Shirley's debts at the time of his murder and imply that he was hard pressed for money:

> 91. Petition of Ellen Scafe, widow, to the Council. Henry Sherley, at his death, was indebted to petitioner for his diet thirty odd pounds. Sir Edward Bishop, being in arrear of an annuity due to the said Henry Sherley, promised to pay petitioner 20 *l.*, but now refuses, the arrear having been claimed by Thomas Sherley. Prays an order that she may be satisfied the 20 *l.* (*C.S.P., Domestic, 1629–31*, p. 461.)
>
> 141. Petition of Martha Wildman, widow, to the Council. Sir Edward Bishop being required to give petitioner satisfaction of 17 *l.*, due to her husband from Henry Sherley, whom Sir Edward Bishop slew when he came to his chamber by appointment to receive moneys due to him. . . . (*C.S.P., Domestic, 1637-8*, p. 124.)

The murder of Henry Shirley was not soon forgotten. William Prynne, joyfully recording in *Histriomastix* 'the sudden and untimely ends of all these ancient Play-poets', adds for further warning a marginal note of a modern example: 'Witnesse *Sherly*, slaine suddenly by Sir *Edward Bishop*, whiles hee was drunke; as most report.' (William Prynne, *Histrio-Mastix, The Players Scourge, or Actors Tragædie*, 1633, fol. 553^v [Ggg$_1^v$].)

A newsbook for 3–10 January 1644/5 recalls that:

> Sr Edward Bishop some years since embued his wilfull hands in the blood of Master Henry Shirley, kinsman to Mr. James Shirley, the playwright, and who did excel him in that faculty. (Quoted by Shirley, *N. & Q.*)

And in another newsbook for 8–15 January 1644/5 Sir Edward Bishop is identified as one 'who is also stigmatized with blood, *for killing of a man that only demanded his due of him*'. (Quoted Ibid.)

Except for his violent end and his debts, which suggest an impecunious London existence, Henry Shirley's life is a blank. E. P. Shirley notes (*N. & Q.*) that in the Ashmolean there are some verses on an encounter of Sir Ambrose Vaux and 'Glascott, the Bailey of Southwark', which are subscribed 'Henrye Sherley', and he calls attention to verses addressed to 'Henry Sherley, Esquire', in John Davies of Herford's *A Scourge of Folly*, 1611. The latter seems a little early for the dramatist.

The Arcadia

In an article entitled 'The Authorship of the Dramatic *Arcadia*' (*Modern Philology*, xxxv [1938], 233–7) Professor Harbage contended that James Shirley was not the author of the play called *The Arcadia* published with his name on the title-page in 1640. (See below under James Shirley.) He made the passing suggestion that *The Arcadia* might have been written by Henry Shirley, since Francis Egglesfield, one of the publishers of *The Arcadia*, was the publisher of Henry Shirley's *The Martyred Soldier*. The evidence seems inadequate for attribution to Henry Shirley, even if the case against James Shirley is accepted.

The Duke of Guise (> 1627)
(Lost)

1653, 9 Sept. S.R. Humphrey Moseley entered as his copies a long list of plays, including:

The spãnish Duke of Lerma. ⎫
The Duke of Guize   ⎪
The Dumbe Bawd &   ⎬ by Henry Shirley.
Giraldo, the Constant Lover   ⎭

(Greg, *Bibliography*, i. 60–61.)

Nothing is known of *The Duke of Guise* save that a manuscript of it must have been in existence in 1653 for Moseley to license. It might be conjectured that the play had belonged to the King's company, since *The Dumb Bawd* and *The Spanish Duke of Lerma* did, but Moseley could just as well have grouped together manuscripts that he had collected from various sources.

One can only speculate as to whether there was any connexion between this piece and Webster's lost play called *Guise* (q.v.) or with Marlowe's *Massacre at Paris, with the Death of the Duke of Guise*.

The Dumb Bawd of Venice (> 1627)
(Lost)

1628, 15 Apr. 'A Warraunt to yᵉ Trẽr of yᵉ Chamber for yᵉ payment of xˡⁱ vnto Iohn Hemings in yᵉ behalfe of him selfe and yᵉ rest of his fellowes his Matˡᵉˢˡ Comædians for one play called yᵉ Dumbe Baud of Venice by them Acted before his Maᵗʸ on Easter Tuesday. beeing yᵉ 15ᵗʰ of Aprill. signed the 9ᵗʰ of Mya. 1628.' (*Malone Society Collections*, ii, Part 3 [1931], p. 347.)

1653, 9 Sept. S.R. Entered by Moseley with three other Shirley plays in a long list. See *The Duke of Guise*, above.

Since *The Dumb Bawd* is an unusual title, it seems likely that the play that was acted at court under the title of *The Dumb Bawd of Venice* was the same as Henry Shirley's *Dumb Bawd*, which Humphrey Moseley registered twenty-five years later. If so, half the group of Shirley plays in the entry of 1653 had come from the repertory of the King's company, and it may be that all four did.

The Dumb Bawd of Venice was not kept in the active repertory of the company and protected by the Lord Chamberlain in 1641, as *The Spanish Duke of Lerma* was—evidence, probably, that it had outlived its popularity.

Giraldo, the Constant Lover (> 1627)
(Lost)

1653, 9 Sept. S.R. Entered by Moseley with three other Shirley plays in a long list. See *The Duke of Guise*, above.

Nothing is known of *Giraldo, the Constant Lover* beyond Moseley's entry of his manuscript. Two of the four Shirley plays in the entry, *The Dumb Bawd* and *The Spanish Duke of Lerma*, had belonged to the King's company before the closing of the theatres, and it is possible that Moseley had got all four of his manuscripts from the old repertory of the company, but they might have been brought together by chance.

The Martyred Soldier (> 1618/19?)

Edition: A. H. Bullen, ed., *A Collection of Old English Plays* (1882–5), i. 165–256.

Clark, Arthur Melville. *Thomas Heywood, Playwright and Miscellanist* (1931), pp. 295–300.

1637/8, 15 Feb. S.R. John Okes entered for his copy 'a Play called the Martyred Soldiour. [by *deleted*] wth the life & Death of Purser Clinton by H: Shirley vj^d.' (Greg, *Bibliography*, i. 47.)

1638. The Martyr'd Souldier: As it was sundry times Acted with a generall applause at the Private house in Drury lane, and at other publicke Theaters. *By the Queenes Majesties servants*. The Author H. Shirley Gent. . . . 1638.

1673, 30 June. S.R. Thomas Vere and John Wright entered as their copies under an assignment from Anne Oakes, widow and executrix of Edward Oakes, a number of titles, including '[14] A Shoemaker is A gentleman, & the Martyrd soldeir'. (Greg, *Bibliography*, i. 73.)

The Martyred Soldier is another Christian martyr play, somewhat like Massinger and Dekker's *The Virgin Martyr*, to which Clark suggests (op. cit., p. 295), unconvincingly, that it is indebted. Clark's principal contention about the play, however, is that Heywood contributed to or at least revised it. His argument is based mainly on the character of the clown's dialogue, which he finds irrelevant to the rest of the action and reminiscent of Heywood. This dialogue seems to me no more like that of Heywood's clowns than like that of other clowns of the period, most of whom indulge in irrelevant dialogue.

Heywood is, however, curiously involved in the publication of

The Martyred Soldier. As Clark notes (op. cit., pp. 166–7), the publisher, John Okes, had printed much of Heywood's work; the address 'To the Reader of this Play now come in Print', which is oddly placed at the end of the play, just before the epilogue, is the same set of verses, apologizing for the age of the play, which had been called 'The Epilogue to the Reader' when it was printed the year before by Nicholas and John Okes after Heywood's own *Royal King and Loyal Subject*; and, finally, when Okes entered *The Martyred Soldier* in the Stationers' Register he added to the name of the play 'wth the life & Death of Purser Clinton'. Now there is no Purser and no Clinton, or Purser Clinton, in the play; this addition is evidently a surreptitious entry for the pamphlet which Okes published in the next year, 1639, called *A True Relation of the Lives and Deaths of . . . Purser, and Clinton*, and which Clark shows good reason (op. cit., pp. 179–82) for thinking was written by Thomas Heywood.

All these occurrences of Heywood's name may be only the chance conjunctions brought about by a publisher's unscrupulousness, but John Kirke (see above, ii. 492–3) was certainly connected with the publication of *The Martyred Soldier*. The dedication of the quarto to Sir Kenelm Digby is signed 'I. K.' in most copies, but in some, e.g. Harvard, the signature is expanded to 'Io. Kirke', and this dedication seems to show a special knowledge of the play in the line, 'When it first appeared upon the *Stage*, it went off with Applause and favour.' John Kirke's own play, *The Seven Champions of Christendom*, was published in the same year, 1638, by John Okes with only J. K. on the title-page, but with John Kirke's full name in the Stationers' Register entry and signed to the dedication. If it was Kirke who brought the manuscript of *The Martyred Soldier* to John Okes—and it is not easy to see how else he would have had any right to dedicate it—then his own theatrical connexions become relevant. He was long connected with the Red Bull theatre, where his own play was performed, but he is not known to have been associated with Queen Henrietta's men, who are generally taken to be the '*Queenes Majesties servants*' of *The Martyred Soldier* title-page, but who never performed at the Red Bull. (See above, i. 218–48.) May not the Queen's servants of the title-page refer to Queen Anne's men, who were long at the Red Bull and for a short time (see above, i. 160–5) at the Phoenix or Cockpit in Drury Lane, the theatre named on the title-page? If so, the play must have been written and produced before the end of 1618/19, when Queen Anne's company ceased to exist as a London company under that name. (See above, i. 164–5.)

Such a date would be compatible with the address to the reader before the epilogue, which concentrates on the age and old-fashioned character of the play (though these verses may be really appropriate only for *The Royal King and the Loyal Subject* and not for *The Martyred Soldier*); and it would be compatible with the lines in the preliminary address 'To the Courteous Reader':

> ... *but the worke it selfe being now an Orphant, and wanting him to protect that first begot it, it were an iniury to his memory to passe him unspoken of. . . . This worke not the meanest of his labours, has much adorned not only one, but many Stages, with such a generall applause; as it hath drawne even the Rigid Stoickes of the Time.*

A first production of *The Martyred Soldier* by Queen Anne's men not later than 1618/19 is compatible, then, with the repeated statements of the age of the play, with the designation '*Queenes Majesties servants*', with performance at several theatres including the Phoenix, and with the possession of the manuscript by John Kirke, who was long connected with the Red Bull and who, at least in 1642, exercised some sort of managerial function for a company.

No source for the play has been pointed out. Clark says (op. cit., p. 295) that 'it is doubtful if the author . . . had any other source than a very hazy knowledge of the Vandal persecutions under Hunneric (A. D. 477–84) of the African Catholics'.

The Spanish Duke of Lerma (> 1627)
(Lost)

Harbage, Alfred. 'Elizabethan-Restoration Palimpsest', *Modern Language Review*, xxxv (1940), 297–304.

1641, 7 Aug. 'The Duke of Lerma or yᵉ spanish Duke' appears in a list of King's men's plays which the Lord Chamberlain forbade the printers to publish without the company's consent. (See above, i. 65–66.)

1653, 9 Sept. S.R. Humphrey Moseley entered as his copies a long list of plays, including:

> The spãnish Duke of Lerma. ⎫
> The Duke of Guize   ⎪ by Henry Shirley.
> The Dumbe Bawd &   ⎬
> Giraldo, the Constant Lover ⎭

(Greg, *Bibliography*, i. 60–61.)

1668. The Great Favourite, Or the Duke Of Lerma. As it was
Acted at the *Theatre-Royal* By His Majesties Servants. *Written
by the Honourable Sir* Robert Howard . . . 1668.

1668/9, *c.* 12 Jan. In 'A Catalogue of part of His Ma^{tes} Servants
Playes as they were formerly acted at the Blackfryers & now
allowed of to his Ma^{tes} Servants at ye New Theatre' occurs the
title, 'The Duke of Lerma'. (Allardyce Nicoll, *A History of
Restoration Drama 1660–1700*, 3rd ed., pp. 315–16.)

In the repertory of the King's company protected by the Lord
Chamberlain in 1641, all plays are listed without author, but it
seems almost certain that *The Spanish Duke of Lerma* that
Humphrey Moseley registered in 1653 as by Henry Shirley was the
same as the repertory play, in spite of the slight variation in title.
And *The Duke of Lerma* in the list of plays of January 1668/9
must also be the same play, since it was 'formerly acted at Black-
fryers'.

Less certain is the relation of Sir Robert Howard's *The Great
Favourite, or The Duke of Lerma* to the earlier play, but it seems not
unlikely that the two were basically the same. In his address to the
reader Sir Robert made some highly suggestive statements:

. . . For the Subject, I came accidentally to write upon it; for a
Gentleman brought a Play to the Kings Company, call'd *The Duke
of* Lerma; and by them I was desir'd to peruse it, and return my
opinion, whether I thought it fit for the Stage; after I had read it, I
acquainted them, that in my judgment it would not be of much use
for such a design, since the contrivance, scarce would merit the name
of a plot; and some of that, assisted by a disguise; and it ended
abruptly: and on the Person of *Philip* the 3. there was fixt such a
mean Character, and on the Daughter of the Duke of *Lerma*, such a
vitious one, that I cou'd not but judge it unfit to be presented by any
that had a respect, not only to Princes, but indeed to either Man or
Woman; and about that time, being to go into the Countrey, I was
perswaded by Mr. *Hart* to make it my diversion there that so great a
hint might not be lost, as the Duke of *Lerma*, saving himself in his
last extremity, by his unexpected disguise, which is as well in the true
story as the old Play; and besides that and the Names, my altering
the most part of the Characters, and the whole design, made me un-
capable to use much more; though perhaps written with higher Stile
and Thoughts, then I cou'd attain to.

Was Howard really given Shirley's old play? At first he seems
to imply that the play which the 'Gentleman' brought to the
King's company was a new one, but at the end he calls it 'the
old Play'. Of course it is possible that Shirley's manuscript had

not remained in the repertory for forty years or more but had strayed into private hands and was brought in by the 'Gentleman'—Howard's words are capable of this construction. At any event, in January 1668/9 the company did have an old play of the Blackfriars repertory called *The Duke of Lerma*, and this was less than a year after Howard's play was published as theirs; it seems highly unlikely that they would have gone to the trouble of getting the old play allowed if they had a brand-new one on the same subject and with the same sub-title.

It seems to me that Professor Harbage (loc. cit.) has made a good case that Howard's *The Great Favourite or The Duke of Lerma* is a Jacobean or Caroline play slightly revised. His further contention that the old play which Howard revised was not written by Henry Shirley but by John Ford is much less convincing. The dissimilarity of the revised *Great Favourite* to *The Martyred Soldier* is too easily explained away to constitute grounds for denying the play to Shirley, and it is not at all clear, as Harbage suggests, that the original *Duke of Lerma or The Spanish Duke* contained material not known before Henry Shirley's death.

JAMES SHIRLEY (Sharlie, Sherley, Shirly, Shurley)
1596–1666

Anon. 'The Life and Writings of James Shirley', *Quarterly Review*, xlix (1833), 1–29.

Armstrong, Ray Livingstone, ed. *The Poems of James Shirley* (1941), pp. xiii–xxx.

Baugh, Albert C. 'Further Facts about James Shirley', *R.E.S.* vii (1931), 62–66.

—— 'Some New Facts about Shirley', *M.L.R.* xvii (1922), 228–35.

Bentley, G. E. 'James Shirley and a Group of Unnoted Poems on the Wedding of Thomas Stanley', *Huntington Library Quarterly*, ii (1939), 219–31.

Forsythe, Robert Stanley. *The Relations of Shirley's Plays to the Elizabethan Drama* (1914).

Gregory, George M. *Two Studies in James Shirley*. Duke University Library (1935).

Hickerson, William Howard. *The Significance of James Shirley's Realistic Plays in the History of English Comedy*. Unpublished University of Michigan Thesis, 1932.

Howarth, R. G. 'Some Unpublished Poems of James Shirley', *R.E.S.* ix (1933), 24–29.

Nason, Arthur Huntington. *James Shirley, Dramatist* (1915).

Nissen, Peter. *James Shirley. Ein Beitrag zur englischen Litteratur-geschichte* (1901).

Parlin, H. T. *A Study in Shirley's Comedies of London Life. Bulletin of the University of Texas*, No. 371 (1914).

Radtke, Stephen J. *James Shirley: His Catholic Philosophy of Life* (1929).

Ritter, Otto. 'Amor und Tod', *Englische Studien*, xxxii (1903), 157–9.

Schipper, Jakob. *James Shirley: sein Leben und seine Werke, nebst einer Übersetzung seines Dramas 'The Royal Master'* (1911).

Shirley, Evelyn P. *Stemmata Shirleiana*, second edition (1873), pp. 119–20 and 339.

Stevenson, Allan H. 'James Shirley and the Actors at the First Irish Theater', *Mod. Phil.* xl (1942), 147–60.

—— 'New Uses of Watermarks as Bibliographical Evidence', *Papers of the Bibliographical Society, University of Virginia*, i (1948), 149–82.

—— 'Shirley's Dedications and the Date of His Return to England', *M.L.N.* lxi (1946), 79–83.

—— 'Shirley's Publishers: The Partnership of Crooke and Cooke', *Library*, Fourth Series, xxv (1944–5), 140–61.

—— 'Shirley's Years in Ireland', *R.E.S.* xx (1944), 19–28.

Swinburne, A. C. 'James Shirley', *The Fortnightly Review*, N.S., xlvii (1890), 461–78.

Tannenbaum, Samuel A. and Dorothy R. *James Shirley (A Concise Bibliography)* (1946).

James Shirley was baptized in the parish of St. Mary Wool-church, London, as the son of 'James Sharlie', 7 September 1596. (See the facsimile, Nason, op. cit., p. 17.) He was the eldest son of a London family and not of any of the county families with which various early biographers associated him. (See ibid., pp. 8–20.) He was admitted to the Merchant Taylors' School in London 4 October 1608, and there are various records of his standing in the school during the next four years, though the pages of the school register which presumably recorded his departure in 1612 are missing. (Ibid., pp. 16–21 and n. 24.)

There is a puzzling gap in Shirley's career between 1612, when he appears to have left the Merchant Taylors' School, and 1615, when he matriculated at Cambridge. Anthony à Wood, who had a surprising amount of information about Shirley—along with some misinformation—said that he entered St. John's, Oxford, that

Laud esteemed him, but advised him against taking orders because of a large mole on his cheek, and that Shirley left Oxford without a degree and went to Cambridge. No Oxford records to substantiate any of this have been found, but Wood is uncomfortably particular, and he accounts for the three blank years, though he did not know the date of Shirley's matriculation at Cambridge. (*Athenæ Oxonienses*, Bliss ed., iii. 737.) Professor Baugh found the record of Shirley's Cambridge matriculation as a pensioner at St. Catharine's College in Easter term, 1615 (*M.L.R.* xvii [1922], 234), and of his degree of B.A. in 1617. This residence is verified by a poem published by Thomas Bancroft in his *Two Bookes of Epigrammes, and Epitaphs*, 1639 (A₄):

13. *To* Iame Shirley.
Iames, thou and I did spend some precious yeeres
At *Katherine-Hall*; . . .

Bancroft matriculated at St. Catharine's in 1613. (Baugh, loc. cit.)

Perhaps Shirley wrote his narrative poem, '*Ecc[h]o and Narcissus the 2 vnfortunate Louers*', while still at Cambridge. Francis Constable entered this poem, 'written by JEAMES. SHERLEY', in the Stationers' Register (Arber, iii. 618) on 4 January 1617/18. No copy is known now, but Alexander Dyce (*Works*, i, p. vi) found in Sir Samuel Egerton Brydges's *Censura Literaria* (ed. 1815, ii. 381 [1805–9, ii. 382]) a reprint of a manuscript transcription of a title-page: '*Eccho, or The Infortunate Lovers, a poem by James Sherley, Cant. in Art. Bacc. Lond.* 1618, 8vo. *Primum hunc Arethusa mihi concede laborem.*' The rights in the poem were transferred from Constable to Moseley, Stationers' Register, 31 October 1646, and it seems likely, therefore, that the poem entitled 'NARCISSVS, OR, The Self-Lover' in Moseley's edition of *Poems &c.*, 1646, is this poem or Shirley's revision of it.

Wood said that Shirley took orders, went to St. Albans, and taught in the grammar school there, but again it remained for Professor Baugh to establish the facts. That the dramatist was at one time in orders is shown by an extract from a *Schedula Excommunicationis* in an ecclesiastical suit:

Idcirco nos Iacobus Sherley in Artib*us* M*a*gis*ter* presb*yter* auc*tori*tate sufficienti d*ic*ti d*o*mi*ni* Iudicis in hac p*ar*te. . . .

[Subscribed] Lecta per me Iacobum
Sherley Presbyter*um* decimo
die Novembris A*n*no D*o*mini. 1623.
(Baugh, *R.E.S.* vii [1931], 66.)

Another record that Baugh found (*M.L.R.* xvii [1922], 233–4) records Shirley's election in February 1623/4 by the clergy of St. Albans to represent them as proctor. No record of his consecration has been found, but the document in the *Liber Eleccionum* at St. Albans guaranteeing him the reversion of the mastership of the grammar school contains a statement about him which is at least compatible with the assumption that he was already a clergyman by that date, 2 November 1618:

. . . and especiallie having respect to the sufficiency in learning discreete and religious conu*er*sac*ion* of Iames Sherley of the same Burrough Batchelo*r* in Art*es*. . . . (Baugh, *R.E.S.* vii [1931], 64.)

Probably Shirley was recommended for this reversionship by the mayor of St. Albans, for on 1 June 1618 he had married Elizabeth Gilmet of St. Albans, daughter of either Richard Gilmet or Robert Gilmet, both members of a prominent St. Albans family, and both at one time or another mayor of St. Albans; Richard Gilmet was mayor when Shirley's reversion was granted. (Ibid., pp. 62–63.) 'Marie', daughter of this couple, was baptized at St. Albans on 27 December 1619, and their daughter Grace was buried there 20 December 1622. (Baugh, *M.L.R.* xvii [1922], 233.)

Shirley's mastership of the St. Albans Grammar School has been widely alluded to, and there are various contemporary records of his incumbency. Precisely when he succeeded Thomas Gibson is not known, but he was receiving student fees as Master in January 1620/1. He was succeeded by John Westerman in January 1624/5. (Ibid., pp. 230–2.)

This indication of Shirley's departure from St. Albans is verified by the record of the baptism at St. Giles', Cripplegate, on 26 February 1624/5, of 'Mathias, sonne of Mr. James Shurley, gentleman', evidently the 'eldest Son, Mathias Shirley', of Shirley's will. (Nason, pp. 37 and 159.) It has been frequently said that Shirley became a Catholic before he left St. Albans, and his Catholicism has sometimes been given as the reason for his departure. Wood said:

. . . so that soon after entring into holy orders, he became a minister of God's word in, or near to, S. Albans in Hertfordshire. But being then unsetled in his mind, he changed his religion for that of Rome, left his living and taught a grammar school in the said town of S. Albans; which employment also he finding uneasy to him, he retired to the metropolis, lived in Greys-inn, and set up for a play-maker. (*Athenæ Oxonienses*, Bliss ed., iii. 737.)

A. F. Leach, writing in *The Victoria History of the County of*

Hertfordshire (ed. William Page [1908], ii. 63), says, presumably deriving his information from local sources:

> On 1 July, 1624, Shirley left St. Albans, having become a Romanist, and . . . was followed in January, 1625, by John Westerman . . . appointed [*Corporation Minutes*] at St. Albans 1 July, 1624. (Quoted by Nason, pp. 32–33.)

Leach's sequence of events is more probable than that in *Athenæ Oxonienses*, for Wood's chronology is contradicted by the records of Shirley as a clergyman of good standing in November 1623 and February 1623/4. Both agree, however, that Shirley did become a Catholic, and his Catholicism has been generally assumed (see Radtke, op. cit.), but some documentary evidence of it would be welcome.

That Shirley was, as Wood says, associated with Gray's Inn in the course of his London residence we now know from other evidence, but Wood must be wrong about his early residence there, for the parents of the child Mathias were parishioners of St. Giles', Cripplegate.

The first record of Shirley's London play-writing career is the licence of his play, *Love Tricks, or The School of Compliments*, by Sir Henry Herbert on 11 February 1624/5 for the Cockpit company under the management of Christopher Beeston, at that time the Lady Elizabeth's company. (See above, i. 184–7.) Shirley's association with this theatre continued for years, and most of his plays were written for it. The regularity of his composition of plays for the Cockpit suggests that he may have had a contract with Christopher Beeston similar to that of Richard Brome with the Salisbury Court theatre. (See Brome.) Shirley seems normally to have written two plays a year for the troupe, and there is some evidence that he aimed at an autumn play and a spring play each year. (See above, i. 226–7 and n. 3.) This relationship lasted from Shirley's first recorded play in 1624/5 to his departure for Ireland in 1636, with one break in January 1631/2, when he wrote *The Changes* for the Salisbury Court theatre. The prologue and epilogue of this comedy (see above, i. 305–6) indicate that Shirley had left the Phoenix for the Salisbury Court and hoped to continue to write for the new theatre. Why he deserted Beeston at the Cockpit or why he returned after writing one play for the Salisbury Court is unknown.

At an unknown date, probably while he was the principal playwright for Queen Henrietta's players at the Cockpit, Shirley became attached to the household of Charles's Catholic queen.

Dr. Armstrong notes (op. cit., p. xiv) that in the Gray's Inn record of Shirley's admission to membership, 23 January 1633/4, Shirley is called 'one of the Valets of the Chamber of Queen Henrietta Maria'. (Joseph Foster, *Register of Admissions to Gray's Inn, 1521–1889* [1889], p. 202.) No doubt it is this post which is referred to on the title-page of his play *The Bird in a Cage* (S.R., 19 March 1632/3): '*The Author* IAMES SHIRLEY, Servant to Her Majesty.' Perhaps the recency of the honour is indicated by the fact that this designation appears on none of Shirley's earlier or later title-pages. Another unique designation among Shirley title-pages is that for *The Triumph of Peace*, 'Invented and Written, By *James Shirley*, of *Grayes Inne*, Gent.' Perhaps both these honours, almost certainly the second, came to Shirley in recognition of his attack on William Prynne in the dedication of *The Bird in a Cage* and his preparation of *The Triumph of Peace* as a token of the anti-Prynne loyalty of the Queen's subjects at the Inns of Court.

On 12 May 1636 all London theatres were closed as a plague precaution, and except for a one-week intermission, they remained closed for nearly seventeen months. (See above, ii. 661–5.) During this period Shirley went to Dublin and for about four years wrote for the Irish theatre. Dr. Allan H. Stevenson makes the likely suggestion that Shirley went to Dublin in the train of the Lord Deputy in November 1636. ('Shirley's Years in Ireland', loc. cit.) In Ireland Shirley wrote for the company that John Ogilby had organized, that Shirley himself may have helped to recruit, and that, for at least the latter half of Shirley's residence, was acting in the new St. Werburgh Street theatre in Dublin. (See Allan H. Stevenson, 'James Shirley and the Actors at the First Irish Theatre', loc. cit., and La Tourette Stockwell, *Dublin Theatres and Theatre Customs* [1938], p. 4.) For this troupe Shirley wrote *The Royal Master, St. Patrick for Ireland*, presumably *Rosania* (*The Doubtful Heir*), and probably several of his other plays not now certainly associated with the Irish theatre; he revised other plays for them, like Middleton's *No Wit No Help Like a Woman's*; and he wrote prologues and epilogues, nine of which he printed in his *Poems &c.*, 1646. During his Irish exile Shirley probably made two trips back to London, one in the early spring of 1637 and one in the spring of 1638. (Nason, pp. 109–15; Stevenson, *Mod. Phil.* xl [1942], 151–2; Stevenson, *M.L.R.* lxi [1946], 81.)

During these Irish years Shirley clearly had a publishing arrangement with the London publishers, William Cooke and Andrew Crooke, who jointly or individually published sixteen of his plays or revisions in the years 1637–40, many of them with dedications signed by the dramatist. (See Stevenson, 'Shirley's Publishers', loc. cit.)

On his return from Ireland Shirley did not go back to Queen Henrietta's company, then acting at the Salisbury Court theatre, or to the company at his old theatre under the management of Christopher Beeston's son William, the King and Queen's Young Company. He became the dramatist for the King's men at Black-friars, in succession to Philip Massinger (q.v.), who had died in March, just before Shirley returned about the middle of April 1640. (See Stevenson, 'Shirley's Years in Ireland', loc. cit.) It seems likely that Shirley worked under a contract with the King's men, for all his known plays between his return and the closing of the theatres were prepared for this troupe, and they were licensed in a fairly regular sequence of a play in late spring and then another in the autumn. (See above, i. 63.)

With the closing of the theatres at the outbreak of the Civil War, Shirley's occupation was gone. Anthony à Wood's summary of his activities in the next twenty years is verifiable in part. Wood says that Shirley left London and joined Newcastle in the field, and Dr. Armstrong found verification, at least of Shirley's delinquency, among the papers of the Committee on Delinquents. Shirley's petition, dated 4 February 1650/1, acknowledges that he 'did adhere vnto and assist the fforces raysed ag[ains]t the Parl[iamen]t in the Late Warres'. (Armstrong, op. cit., p. xv.)

Wood continues of Shirley that 'After the king's cause declined, he retired obscurely to London, where, among others of his noted friends, he found Tho. Stanley, esq; who exhibited to him for the present'. (*Athenæ Oxonienses*, Bliss ed., iii. 737.) This relation with Stanley is verified by various poems of Shirley and of a group of Stanley's friends. (See Bentley, loc. cit.)

Wood's next statement is that 'Afterwards following his old trade of teaching school, which was mostly in the White-friers, he not only gained a comfortable subsistence (for the acting of plays was then silenced) but educated many ingenious youths, who afterwards proved most eminent in divers faculties'. (Op. cit., pp. 737–8.) That Shirley was fairly prosperous is confirmed by the surprising sums he left in his will, which also gives Whitefriars as his place of residence. (See Nason, pp. 158–60.) The school teaching is probably the background of Shirley's publication of *Via Ad Latinam Linguam Complanata. The Way made plain to the Latine Tongue*, 1649, and of *The Rudiments of Grammar. The Rules Composed in English Verse*, 1656.

During these years when the theatres were closed, Shirley prepared for the press his non-dramatic verse, published under the title, *Poems &c.*, in 1646. It includes a section entitled 'PROLOGVES, AND EPILOGVES; Written to severall Playes Presented in this Kingdom, and else-where'. In 1647 the great first Folio of Beaumont and Fletcher appeared with an address to the reader signed by James Shirley. It has sometimes been said, on this evidence, that Shirley was the editor of the Folio, but it seems more likely that, as the last regular dramatist of the King's company, he was simply assisting with a sort of long commendatory verse in prose.

In these interregnum years Shirley also published a series of masques, *The Triumph of Beauty, Cupid and Death, Honoria and Mammon,* and *The Contention of Ajax and Ulysses for the Armour of Achilles*. All but *Honoria and Mammon* were acted, perhaps by Shirley's schoolboys, but they present occasional analogies to Davenant's interregnum efforts, and one wonders if Shirley had any ideas about reviving dramatic activities similar to Davenant's but lacked the energy to carry them through.

Nothing is known of Shirley's activities from the Restoration until his death. Wood's account of this is circumstantial:

> At length after Mr. Shirley had lived to the age of 72 years at least, in various conditions, and had seen much of the world, he with his second wife Frances were driven by the dismal conflagration that happened in London an. 1666, from their habitation near to Fleet-street, into the parish of S. Giles's in the Fields in Middlesex, where being in a manner overcome with affrightments, disconsolations, and other miseries occasion'd by that fire and their losses, they both died within the compass of a natural day: whereupon their bodies were buried in one grave in the yard belonging to the said church of S. Giles's on the 29th of Octob. in sixteen hundred sixty and six. (*Athenæ Oxonienses*, Bliss ed., iii. 740.)

The burial registers of St. Giles-in-the-Fields verify Wood's statement of date and place, and the bracketed entry for James Shirley and for Frances his wife (see facsimile, Nason, p. 162) at least suggests burial in a common grave.

Shirley's will, discovered and printed by Nason (op. cit., pp. 158–60), shows a sizeable estate for a poet, and names three sons, two daughters, two sons-in-law, a grandson, his wife Frances, and several friends.

Numerous manuscript copies of Shirley's verse have been found, and one manuscript collection entitled 'Verses and Poems, by James Shirley', apparently in the poet's own hand. (See Armstrong, op. cit., pp. xxviii–xxix.)

There is a portrait of Shirley in the Bodleian Library, an

engraving dated 1646 was printed with *Poems &c.*, 1646, and an engraving dated 1658 was printed with *Honoria and Mammon*, n.d. All three are reproduced by Nason.

Perhaps it should be noted here that Wood also said:

> Our author Shirley did also much assist his generous patron William duke of Newcastle in the composure of certain plays, which the duke afterwards published; and was a drudge for John Ogilby in his translation of *Homer's Iliads, and Odysses*, and some of Virgil's works, into English verse, with the writing of annotations on them. (*Athenæ Oxonienses*, Bliss ed., iii. 739–40.)

There is some evidence that Shirley did assist William Cavendish, Earl of Newcastle (q.v.), and he had certainly worked with Ogilby in Ireland.

Shirley's reputation in his own century should perhaps be characterized as sound but not brilliant. There are a fair number of manuscript transcripts of his verses extant; John Cotgrave took eighty-five quotations from his plays (see Bentley, *Stud. Phil.* xl [1943], 186–203); and I have found thirty-odd allusions to the man and his works in seventeenth-century publications, most of them in lists of dramatists or poets. Dryden's familiar use of Shirley and Heywood in *MacFlecknoe* as examples of the dullness of the last age is not unique, but it is a Restoration and not a Caroline opinion. Even in the Restoration it was by no means universal, as the records of Restoration productions of Shirley's plays show.

Collected Editions

1653. Six New Playes. *Viz.*

The
{
Brothers.
Sisters.
Doubtfull Heir.
Imposture.
Cardinall.
Court Secret.
}

The Five first were acted at the Private House in *Black Fryers* with great Applause. The last was never Acted. All Written by James Shirley. *Never printed before. London*, Printed for *Humphrey Robinson* at the Three Pigeons, and *Humphrey Moseley* at the Prince's Armes in St. *Paul's* Curch-yard [sic], 1653.

1833. *The Dramatic Works and Poems of James Shirley, Now First Collected; With Notes by the Late William Gifford, Esq. And*

Additional Notes, And Some Account of Shirley and His Writings,
ed. Alexander Dyce, 6 vols.

Andromana, or The Merchant's Wife

See J. S.

The Antiquary

Shirley's authorship of this play might be suggested by the
ambiguous entry in the Stationers' Register, 11 March 1639/40:
'two Comedies vizt. The Antiquarie. & Looke to the Ladie by
Iames Shirley'. (Greg, *Bibliography*, i. 52.) *The Antiquary* was
published, however, as Marmion's (q.v.), and there is no doubt
that it is his.

Anything for a Quiet Life

Bullen suggested (*The Works of Thomas Middleton*, i, pp.
lxxxvii–lxxxviii) that in its present state *Anything for a Quiet
Life* was a revision of Middleton's work by Shirley. There seems
to be no good reason to think that Shirley ever worked on the
play. (See under Middleton.)

The Arcadia (> 1632?)

Fleay, F. G. 'Annals of the Careers of James and Henry Shirley',
   Anglia, viii (1885), 406–7.
Forsythe, Robert Stanley. *The Relations of Shirley's Plays to the
   Elizabethan Drama* (1914), pp. 268–79.
Greg, W. W. *Pastoral Poetry & Pastoral Drama* (1906), pp. 319–22.
Harbage, Alfred. 'The Authorship of the Dramatic *Arcadia*',
   Mod. Phil. xxxv (1938), 233–7.
Nason, Arthur Huntington. *James Shirley, Dramatist* (1915), pp.
   70–72 and 242–5.

1639, 29 Nov. S.R. John Williams and Francis Egglesfield entered
   for their copies 'Two Playes vizt. A Pastorall called The Arcadia.
   & a Tragedy called Loues Crueltie. by Iames Shirley xij^d.
   [*altered from* vj^d.] [*in margin* Loues Crueltie is Entred before
   to m^r Crooke]'. (Greg, *Bibliography*, i. 52.)
1640. A Pastorall Called The Arcadia. Acted by her Majesties
   Servants at the *Phœnix* in *Drury* Lane. Written by *Iames
   Shirly* Gent. . . . Printed by *I. D.* for *Iohn Williams*, and *F.
   Eglesfeild* . . . 1640.

Professor Harbage (loc. cit.) has raised doubts as to whether *The Arcadia* is really Shirley's play. His principal arguments against Shirley's authorship are: (1) *The Arcadia* is not included in the list of Shirley's works printed after *The Cardinal* in *Six New Playes* of 1653; (2) there is no extant record of Sir Henry Herbert's licence for the play; (3) the play appeared in print when Shirley was in Ireland, and it was published not by his usual publishers, Crooke and Cooke, but by Williams and Egglesfield, publishers whom Harbage suspects because they entered *Love's Cruelty* in the Stationers' Register though it had already been entered as the property of Crooke and Cooke and because they later entered as Shirley's the lost play, *Look to the Lady*, which appears in a Revels Office list that he dates 1612–22 and which therefore cannot, he thinks, have been written by Shirley; and (4) the poetry and dialogue of *The Arcadia* do not sound to Harbage like Shirley's other work.

None of these arguments is conclusive, for the following reasons: (1) *The Young Admiral*, an unquestioned Shirley composition, is also omitted from the list in *Six New Playes*; (2) *The Constant Maid* and *St. Patrick for Ireland* are also missing from Sir Henry Herbert's list of licences; moreover this Herbert argument is never very weighty because the complete office-book of the Master of the Revels is not extant, only those extracts survive that Chalmers and Malone chose to make, and these extracts are demonstrably very incomplete (see above, i. 101–2); (3) the publication of the play by Williams and Egglesfield, considering Shirley's custom at this time (see Allan H. Stevenson, 'Shirley's Publishers: The Partnership of Crooke and Cooke', *Library*, Fourth Series, xxv [1944–45], 140–61), does suggest that Shirley did not himself give them the manuscript, but on the other hand many plays were published with correct ascriptions but no co-operation from the author, and the fact that Williams and Egglesfield were dishonest or mistaken about *Look to the Lady* does not establish their invariable inaccuracy; finally, (4) subjective judgements about the style of a play are notoriously unreliable. Thus Harbage cannot be said to have demonstrated that *The Arcadia* must be excluded from the Shirley canon, but it must be granted that his arguments raise serious doubts about the authorship. In the present state of our knowledge it seems to me better to list the play as 'by Shirley (?)' rather than as anonymous.

The source of the play, as the title suggests, is Sidney's *Arcadia*; indeed, the play was evidently intended to capitalize on the reputation of the romance, for it is a careful dramatization of Sidney's narrative; Greg calls it 'the most full and faithful [of all the] stage rendering[s] of Sidney's work'. (Op. cit., p. 319.)

Fleay had two notions about *The Arcadia*. First he suggested that it was the play in which Queen Henrietta Maria acted and to which William Prynne was alleged to have alluded in *Histrio-mastix*. (*Anglia*, loc. cit.) This play was really Montagu's *Shepherd's Paradise*, and Fleay later contended that *The Arcadia* was first produced on the King's birthday, 19 November 1632. He thought that the piece was a birthday play because of the references to the King's birthday in III. 1 (not III. 2), and he selected 1632 because he had other plays for the birthdays in 1633 and 1634 and because he thought he saw allusions to this play in Nabbes's *Covent Garden*, 1632/3, and Heywood's *Love's Mistress*, 1634. (*Biog. Chron.* ii. 239.) This date of 19 November 1632, often accepted, was shaken by Forsythe when he pointed out (op. cit., pp. 268–70) that the birthday allusion upon which Fleay rested his case is derived from the source, and Fleay's evidence that *The Arcadia* was pre-pared for a performance on 19 November 1632 is therefore worth-less. But the birthday allusion was really only half Fleay's case. The reference to *The Arcadia* in Nabbes's *Covent Garden* (q.v.) does indeed sound like a reference to an actor in a play rather than to a character in a novel. If this interpretation is sound and Nabbes was referring to the performer of Mopsa in the play called *The Arcadia*, then Shirley's play would probably date 1632 or shortly before, and Nabbes would be reminding his audience at a performance by Queen Henrietta's men at the Phoenix of the antics and the make-up of the boy in this company who had played Mopsa recently at this theatre.

It is just possible that a garbled entry in Sir Henry Herbert's office-book records the licensing of this play for the stage. Malone transcribed this entry as follows:

For the king's company. An olde play called The Honest Man's Fortune, the originall being lost, was re-allowed by mee at Mr. Taylor's intreaty, and on condition to give mee a booke [The Arcadia], this 8 Februa. 1624. (*Variorum*, iii. 229.)

George Chalmers, in his transcript (*A Supplemental Apology for the Believers in the Shakspeare-Papers*, 1799, p. 220), omits the name of the book. A third transcript in a nineteenth-century hand—possibly that of Craven Ord—which has been cut up and pasted into Halliwell-Phillipps's scrap-books, now at the Folger Shake-speare Library, gives the entry in this form:

For the Kg̃s comp: An olde P. call: The honests mans fortune the original being lost was reallowed by me att M^r. Taylors intreaty & on condition to give me a booke

8^{++}. Feb: 1624. The Arcadia.

The Cock: comp: A new P. call. Love tricks with comp^{ts}. 11^{++}. Feb: 1624. 1^{li}. (Volume labelled *Lowin*, p. 71.)

Evidently Malone thought that the name of the book Taylor was to give Sir Henry was *The Arcadia*; presumably Chalmers thought it referred to something else and did not copy it. The question is: Does the fourth line in the Folger transcript constitute a separate entry, or is it the conclusion of *The Honest Man's Fortune* entry? The evidence supports the second alternative. It was Herbert's custom to give the date of his entry last, not first, as the Folger transcript and Malone's directly quoted extracts show. Moreover, the date of his reallowance of *The Honest Man's Fortune*, 8 February 1624/5, is confirmed by his statement, which appears on the extant manuscript of the play. (See W. W. Greg, *Dramatic Documents*, p. 288.) Finally, it was Herbert's custom at this time to give the name of the company first in his entries, as demonstrated in both the *Love Tricks* and the *Honest Man's Fortune* records. All in all, it is likely that Malone's interpretation of the entry is correct, though it is barely possible that the transcript from Herbert in Halliwell-Phillipps's scrap-books records two incomplete entries, the second of which refers to the play called *The Arcadia*.

Fleay's suggestion (*Biog. Chron.* ii. 239) that the six songs for an unknown play printed in Carew's *Poems*, 1640, were intended for *The Arcadia* is highly improbable. (See above under Carew, Unknown Play.)

The title of the play in the quarto, *A Pastorall Called The Arcadia*, was probably intended to play up the relation to Sidney, for, as Greg (op. cit., p. 321) and Nason (op. cit., p. 244) have pointed out, the play is not a pastoral but a romance.

The Ball (1632)

Edition: *The Plays and Poems of George Chapman: The Comedies*, edited with Introduction and Notes by Thomas Marc Parrott (1914), pp. 537–605, 869–87.

Forsythe, Robert Stanley. *The Relations of Shirley's Plays to the Elizabethan Drama* (1914), p. 407–14.

Nason, Arthur Huntington. *James Shirley, Dramatist* (1915), pp. 230–7.

Parlin, Hanson T. *A Study in Shirley's Comedies of London Life. Bulletin of the University of Texas*, No. 371 (1914), pp. 39–64.

1632, 16 Nov. '*The Ball*, by James Shirley, licensed.' (Adams, *Herbert*, p. 34.)

1632, 18 Nov. '18 Nov. 1632. In the play of *The Ball*, written by Sherley, and acted by the Queens players, ther were divers personated so naturally, both of lords and others of the court, that I took it ill, and would have forbidden the play, but that Biston [Christopher Beeston, the manager] promiste many things which I found faulte withall should be left out, and that he would not suffer it to be done by the poett any more, who deserves to be punisht; and the first that offends in this kind, of poets or players, shall be sure of publique punishment.' (Ibid., p. 19.)

1638, 24 Oct. S.R. Andrew Crooke and William Cooke entered for their copies 'a Booke called Phillip Chalbott [*sic*] Admirall of ffrance & the Ball. by Iames Shirley   vj^d.' (Greg, *Bibliography*, i. 49.)

1639. The Ball. A Comedy, As it was presented by her Majesties Servants, at the private House in *Drury* Lane. Written by [bracket] *George Chapman*, / and / *James Shirly*. . . . 1639.

There have been discussions in various dramatic histories of the authorship of this comedy, which is attributed on the title-page of the only early edition to George Chapman and James Shirley. Most scholars have found little or no Chapman in the play but have made tentative assignments in deference to the title-page. The best analysis is Parrott's. (Op. cit., pp. 869–75.) He notes that in the Stationers' Register entry only Shirley is named, that the two plays are called 'a Booke', and he might have added that the fee paid is for one publication, not two. This entry indicates that what Crooke and Cooke had was a single manuscript volume containing both *Chabot, Admiral of France* and *The Ball*. Sir Henry Herbert noted that the former was a joint production of Shirley and Chapman, but he made no reference to Chapman in connexion with *The Ball*. Crooke and Cooke had the two printed together by Thomas Cotes, who used the same setting of type for the statement of authorship and the imprint in both quartos. (See Allan H. Stevenson, *Library*, Fourth Series, xxv [1944–5], 148–9, and Greg, *Bibliography*, ii. 690–1.) Apparently the publishers found somehow that *Chabot* was the work of both Shirley and Chapman and jumped to the erroneous but understandable conclusion that both plays in their manuscript volume were collaborations, whereas Chapman really had nothing to do with *The Ball*. Though Shirley had regular dealings with these publishers, he was in Ireland in 1639, and the plays published in his absence—with the exception of *The Maid's Revenge*—do not have his usual dedications and other evidences of an author's supervision. (See Stevenson, op. cit., pp. 140–61.)

Sir Henry Herbert's memorandum of 18 November 1632 shows that Shirley had exploited the tempting appeal of personal satire in *The Ball*. It is a little odd that Herbert's memorandum should be dated the 18th and his licence the 16th. Did he license it and then revoke his licence and consult Beeston after he heard about the first performance, or is the memorandum merely a late recording of actions which took place before the 16th? The former seems more likely, except that it is hard to imagine Beeston going through all his rehearsals and advance publicity before the play was allowed, as he must have done if Herbert wrote of a performance on the 16th, 17th, or even the 18th. Yet the phrases 'acted by the Queens players' and 'personated so naturally' seem to refer to events in the theatre and not to a script, and actors can always give personal point to comparatively innocent lines by recognizable costumes, make-up, and mimicry. But if the actors were chiefly to blame, why did Beeston have to promise that 'he would not suffer it to be done by the poett any more'? Shirley's own reference to the affair three years later in *The Lady of Pleasure* certainly indicates some pride in his accomplishment and some revision of his original lines, though he is pleased to say that the alterations were due to 'bribery' and not to the orders of the Master of the Revels. In the opening scene of *The Lady of Pleasure*, performed by the same actors at the same theatre, he makes Sir Thomas Bornwell scold Lady Bornwell about her social indulgences in these words:

> Another game you have, which consumes more
> Your fame than purse, your revells in the night,
> Your meetings cal'd the Ball, to which appeare [repair?],
> As to the Court of Pleasure, all your gallants,
> And Ladies thither bound by a Subpena
> Of *Venus*, and small *Cupids* high displeasure,
> Tis but the family of love translated
> Into more costly sinne, there was a play on't,
> And had the Poet not beene brib'd to a modest
> Expression of your Anticke gambolls in't,
> Some darkes had been discovered, and the deeds too,
> In time he may repent and make some blush,
> To see the second part danc'd on the Stage.

The Ball belongs to the series of more or less realistic comedies of London high life that Shirley wrote for the Queen's men at the Phoenix, 1632–5: *Hyde Park, The Ball, The Gamester, The Example*, and *The Lady of Pleasure*. All seem to be rather close observations of London life—Sir Henry Herbert evidently thought *The Ball* too closely observed—and all include satiric characterizations, often in the Jonsonian vein. Such plays do not usually have comprehensive sources, and none has been noted for *The Ball*, but Forsythe (loc. cit.) gives a number of analogues to scenes and characters. The allusions to Jonson's *Bartholomew Fair* and *A Tale of a Tub* that Fleay saw (*Biog. Chron.* ii. 239) are imaginary.

Dr. Greg noted (*Bibliography*, ii. 691) that various copies of the quarto show variants in signatures A, C, F, and H, and a number of specific ones are noted in the Rosenbach catalogue, *English Plays to 1700* (1940), pp. 22–23.

Probably the play was popular only so long as the special interest in the new social fad of the Ball lasted, for it is not included in the Phoenix repertory list protected in August 1639 (see above, i. 330–1), though *The Example, Hyde Park*, and *The Lady of Pleasure* from Shirley's series of comedies of London high life were included. There appear to be no records of any performances after the first ones, and no later adaptations. Yet one cannot be quite sure. In the list of Shirley's publications printed after *The Cardinal* in the *Six New Playes* of 1653, this play appears as '*The Ball, or French Dancing Master*'. Samuel Pepys records in his diary under date of 21 May 1662:

> But we went to the Theatre, to 'The French Dancing Master,' and there with much pleasure gazed upon her (Lady Castlemaine). . . . The play pleased us very well; but Lacy's part, the Dancing Master, the best in the world.

This piece has sometimes been taken to be the droll called *The Humours of Monsieur Galliard*, published in *The Wits*, 1662. But as J. J. Elson remarks (*The Wits or Sport upon Sport* [1932], p. 388), it does not seem likely that Pepys would have thought a droll an evening's entertainment, or have praised it, or called it a play. Would Lady Castlemaine have been displaying herself at a droll? Possibly Pepys saw *The Ball* acted under its seldom-used subtitle.

The Beauties

Alternative title for *The Bird in a Cage*, q.v.

The Bird in a Cage (1632/3?)

Edition: *James Shirley's The Bird in a Cage*, edited from the
Quarto of 1633, with Introduction and Notes, by Frances Frazier
Senescu. Unpublished University of Chicago Thesis, 1948.

Forsythe, Robert Stanley. *The Relations of Shirley's Plays to the
Elizabethan Drama* (1914), pp. 286–97.
Nason, Arthur Huntington. *James Shirley, Dramatist* (1915), pp.
76–79, 245–7.

1632/3, 21 Jan. '*The Bewties*, by James Shirley, licensed.' (Adams,
Herbert, p. 34.)

1632/3, 19 Mar. S.R. William Cooke entered for his copy 'vnder
the hands of Sr. Henry Herbert & mr Weaver warden a Comedy
called The Bird in the Cage. by Ia: Shirley.' (Greg, *Bibliography*,
i. 42.)

1633. The Bird In A Cage. *A Comedie*. As it hath beene Presented
at the *Phœnix* in *Drury-Lane. The Author* Iames Shirley, Servant to Her Majesty . . . 1633.

1668, 20 Aug. In the list of plays allotted to Davenant, 'Playes
allowed to be acted by his Royall Highnesse ye Duke of Yorkes
Comoedians', is the title, 'Bird in a Cage'. (Nicoll, *A History
of Restoration Drama*, 3rd ed., p. 315.)

Nearly all scholars have followed Fleay (*Biog. Chron.* ii. 239–
40) in assuming that *The Bird in a Cage* is a new title for Shirley's
The Beauties, which was licensed for performance by Sir Henry
Herbert two months before *The Bird in a Cage* was entered in the
Stationers' Register. *The Beauties* would be an appropriate title
for *The Bird in a Cage* as we have it. Fleay thought that Shirley
had changed the title before the play was printed to make it
appropriate for William Prynne, the theatre-hater, to whom he
wrote an ironic dedication of the play and who was in prison at the
time of printing. This step seems likely enough, for, as Mrs.
Senescu points out (op. cit., p. xlix), Shirley remarks in the dedication on the appropriateness of his title:

> *I had an early desire to congratulate your happy* Retirement, *but no*
> Poeme *could tempt mee with so faire a circumstance as this in the Title,*
> *wherein I take some delight to thinke . . . how aptly I may present you at*
> *this time, with* The Bird in a Cage.

The idea of Fleay and Forsythe (*Relations*, p. 293) that Shirley
hastily introduced the ladies' play-within-the-play in reference to
the performance of the Queen and her attendants in Montagu's

Shepherd's Paradise in January 1632/3 is unlikely, however, since Mrs. Senescu shows (op. cit., pp. xlix–li) how thoroughly the play-within-the-play is integrated into the comedy. She cites allusions which she thinks date the composition of the play 'after January 1629, and before January 1630' (ibid., pp. li–lv), but the allusions do not seem to me definite enough to prove composition such an unusually long time before Herbert's licence of 21 January 1632/3.

The quarto of *The Bird in a Cage* is very much a part of the *Histriomastix* controversy. Shirley's play was entered in the Stationers' Register while William Prynne was in the Tower awaiting trial for his alleged attacks on Queen Henrietta Maria's play-acting in his enormous diatribe against the theatres, *Histriomastix*. As the principal dramatist for the Queen's company and a Valet of the Chamber to the Queen—an honour apparently alluded to in the phrase 'Servant to Her Majesty' on the title-page of this play—Shirley must have felt a particular obligation to castigate the Puritan. He wrote an ironic dedication to Prynne for his play, beginning:

> SIR, THe *fame of your* Candor *and* Innocent-Love *to Learning, especially to that Musicall part of humane knowledge,* Poetry, *and in particular to that which concernes the* Stage *and* Scene (*your selfe as I heare, having lately written a* Tragedie) *doth iustly chalenge from me this* Dedication.

The taunting tone of this dedication offended Gifford and others, in view of the monstrously excessive punishments meted out to Prynne, but they did not observe that Shirley's dedication was written, as Mrs. Senescu points out (op. cit., pp. lv–lxviii), while Prynne was still awaiting trial and before any of his excessive sentence had been pronounced. Possibly the selection of Shirley by the lawyers of the four Inns of Court to compose *The Triumphs of Peace* as a shrill assertion of their loyalty to the slandered Queen and to the drama was in part a result of this ironic dedication, which must have given satisfaction to many indignant cavaliers.

No comprehensive source for *The Bird in a Cage* has been cited, but Forsythe notes (op. cit., p. 288) that a good section of the action seems to derive from Fletcher's *Women Pleased*. Mrs. Senescu compares the differences in the treatments given the material by the two dramatists. (Op. cit., pp. lxix–lxxi.)

Genest (*Some Account of the English Stage*, vi. 399–400) notes that this play with *Money Works Wonders* for a sub-title was performed for Quick's benefit at Covent Garden 24 April 1786. He says that the alterations were slight.

The Brothers [of 1626]
(Lost)

See *The Brothers* [of 1641?], *The Wedding*, and Anon., *Dick of Devonshire*.

The Brothers [1641?]

Forsythe, Robert Stanley. *The Relations of Shirley's Plays to the Elizabethan Drama* (1914), pp. 255–61, 405–7.

Harbage, Alfred. 'Shirley's *The Wedding* and the Marriage of Sir Kenelm Digby', *Phil. Quart.* xvi (1937), 35–40.

Nason, Arthur Huntington. *James Shirley, Dramatist* (1915), pp. 46–68, 336–42.

1626, 4 Nov. '*The Brothers*, by James Shirley, licensed.' (Adams, *Herbert*, p. 31.)

1641, 26 May. '*The Politique Father*, by James Shirley, licensed.' (Ibid., p. 39.)

1641, 7 Aug. In the list of King's men's plays which the Lord Chamberlain forbade the printers to publish without the consent of the company is the title, 'The Brothers'. (See above, i. 65–66.)

1646, [4] Sept. S.R. Humphrey Robinson and Humphrey Moseley entered as their copies a long list of plays, all apparently from the repertory of the King's company. Included is 'Brothers . . . by Mr Shirley.' (Greg, *Bibliography*, i. 57.)

1652. The Brothers, A Comedie, *As* It was Acted at the private House In *Black Fryers*. Written By James Shirley. *Never Printed before* . . . 1652. (Separate title-page in *Six New Playes*, 1653.)

1662, 6 July. 'July 6. 62. The Brothers' appears in a list of performances of plays by 'the Kings Companie at the Red Bull and the new house in Gibbon's Tennis Court near Clare Market', 1660–2. (Adams, *Herbert*, p. 118.)

1662–3. The General Account Book of the Inner Temple, Nov. 1662 to Nov. 1663, records: 'For a play called "The Brothers," which was acted by the King's players, 20*li*.' (F. A. Inderwick, *A Calendar of the Inner Temple Records*, 3 vols. [1896–1901], iii. 16.)

1668/9, *c.* 12 Jan. In 'A Catalogue of part of His Ma^tes Servants Playes as they were formerly acted at the Blackfryers & now allowed of to his Ma^tes Servants at ye New Theatre' occurs the title, 'The Brothers'. (Allardyce Nicoll, *A History of Restoration Drama*, 3rd ed., pp. 315–16.)

There has been much confusion about this play because various scholars who have considered it have concluded that the comedy called *The Brothers* that was protected by the King's company in 1641 and published as theirs in *Six New Playes*, 1653, cannot be the same as the play called *The Brothers* that was licensed by Sir Henry Herbert for an unspecified company in 1626. The case is most cogently and most extensively stated by Nason. (Op. cit., pp. 46–68.)

Shirley dedicated *The Brothers* 'To his truly Noble Friend THO: STANLEY Esq;' with the statement:

Witness this Composition, which after its birth, had in my thoughts a dedication to your name, although it but now took the boldness to wear it in the forehean [sic] both as an Ornament and preserver.

Now at the time of the birth of the first *Brothers*, in 1626, Thomas Stanley, of whose patronage of Shirley there is much evidence (see G. E. Bentley, ' James Shirley and a Group of Un-noted Poems on the Wedding of Thomas Stanley', *Huntington Library Quarterly*, ii [1939], 219–31), was aged one year, and an unlikely patron, but by 1641 Stanley could have been in Shirley's thoughts as a dedicatee. Secondly, there are repeated statements that *The Brothers* belonged to the King's company, a troupe for which Shirley is known to have worked only from his return from Ireland in 1640 to the closing of the theatres in 1642. Finally, Moseley entitled his Shirley collection of 1652–3 *Six New Playes* and says in an advertisement that the six were 'all that ever the Author made for the Private house in Black-Fryers'. (Nason, op. cit., pp. 59–60.) Such a title and statement in a publication with which Shirley himself was associated—witness the signed dedications to each of the six plays—would be appropriate for the six plays Shirley wrote for the King's men to produce at Blackfriars in 1640, 1641, and 1642, but not for five produced then and one written fifteen or sixteen years earlier, probably for another company.

A second aspect of the confusion about the play printed under the title of *The Brothers* in 1652, but which was not the play called *The Brothers* licensed in 1626, is the problem of its licence for performance by the King's company at Blackfriars. We have seen that Moseley claimed that the 1652 collection contained all the plays that Shirley wrote for Blackfriars, and six is about the number of plays Shirley would have been expected to prepare in the twenty-eight months of his connexion with the King's company, from late April or May 1640 to September 1642 (see above, Life), since one of them had already been prepared in some form for production in Ireland under the title *Rosania*. One of these plays, *The Court Secret*, Moseley says on its title-page was prepared for Blackfriars, but never acted, and Shirley explains in his dedication that this was so because it '*happened to receive birth, when the Stage was interdicted*', i.e. it was completed after the theatres were closed by the Long Parliament and therefore was probably never licensed by the Master of the Revels. We should, therefore, expect five plays of Shirley's to have been licensed for performance while the playwright was working for Blackfriars in 1640, 1641, and 1642. And five is the number of Shirley play licences which Malone copied from Herbert's office-book for 1640–2: *Rosania*, licensed 1 June 1640 and published in *Six New Playes* as *The Doubtful Heir*; *The Imposter*, licensed 10 November 1640 and published in *Six New Playes* as *The Imposture*; *The Politique Father*, licensed 26 May 1641 and never published under this title; *The Cardinal*, licensed 25 November 1641 and published in *Six New Playes*; and *The Sisters*, licensed 26 April 1642 and published in *Six New Playes*. Thus the licensing situation for all the plays in the collection except *The Brothers* is accounted for, and the publication of all the plays Herbert licensed except *The Politique Father* is accounted for. Fleay (*Biog. Chron.* ii. 246) made the obvious deduction that *The Brothers* was licensed as *The Politique Father*, but that its title was changed to *The Brothers* before the Blackfriars repertory was protected by the Lord Chamberlain in August 1641, and Nason (op. cit., pp. 336–8) shows that Don Ramires of *The Brothers* is indeed a politic father whose manœuvres might well have given the play its original title.

No comprehensive source for *The Brothers* has been noted, but Forsythe (loc. cit.) finds the usual analogies to characters and situations in earlier plays.

Shirley printed the prologue and epilogue that he wrote for *The Brothers* in his *Poems &c.*, 1646, pp. 156–7 (i.e. 56–57).

Captain Underwit

See William Cavendish, *The Country Captain*.

The Cardinal (1641)

Bowers, Fredson Thayer. *Elizabethan Revenge Tragedy 1587–1642* (1940), pp. 228–34.

Forsythe, Robert Stanley. *The Relations of Shirley's Plays to the Elizabethan Drama* (1914), pp. 185–9.

Nason, Arthur Huntington. *James Shirley, Dramatist* (1915), pp. 344–61.

1641, 25 Nov. '*The Cardinal*, by James Shirley, licensed.' (Adams, *Herbert*, p. 39.)

1646, [4] Sept. S.R. Humphrey Robinson and Humphrey Moseley entered as their copies a long list of plays, all apparently from the repertory of the King's company. Included is 'Cardinall . . . by Mr Shirley'. (Greg, *Bibliography*, i. 57.)

1652. The Cardinal, A Tragedie, As It was acted at the private House In *Black Fryers*, Written By James Shirley. *Not Printed before*. . . . 1652. (Separate title-page in *Six New Playes*, 1653.)

1662, 23 July. In a list of performances of plays by 'the Kings Companie at the Red Bull and the new house in Gibbon's Tennis Court near Clare Market', 1660–2, appears the entry, ' July 23. 62. The Cardinal'. (Adams, *Herbert*, p. 118.)

1662, 2 Oct. '. . . at night . . . hearing that there was a play at the Cockpit [in Whitehall palace] . . . I do go thither . . . Here we saw "The Cardinall," a tragedy I had never seen before, nor is there any great matter in it.' (Diary of Samuel Pepys.)

<1663. Downes lists 'The Cardinal' as one of the plays acted by the King's company after the opening of the new Drury Lane Theatre in 1663. (*Roscius Anglicanus*, ed. Summers, p. 8.)

1667, 24 Aug. 'After dinner to a play, and there saw "The Cardinall" at the King's house, wherewith I am mightily pleased; but, above all, with Becke Marshall.' (Diary of Samuel Pepys.)

1668, 27 Apr. '. . . thence I to the King's playhouse, and there saw most of "The Cardinall," a good play.' (Ibid.)

1668/9, c. 12 Jan. In 'A Catalogue of part of His Mates Servants Playes as they were formerly acted at the Blackfryers & now allowed of to his Mates Servants at ye New Theatre' occurs the title, 'The Cardinall'. (Allardyce Nicoll, *A History of Restoration Drama*, 3rd ed., pp. 315–16.)

1672/3, 30 Jan. S.R. Humphrey Robinson, executor of Humphrey Robinson, assigned to John Martin and Henry Herringman all his rights in a long list of plays, including '[89] Cardinall. halfe'. (Greg, *Bibliography*, i. 72.)

1683, 21 Aug. S.R. Sarah Martin, executrix of John Martin, transferred her rights in a long list of plays to Robert Scott. Included is '[96] Cardinalls [*sic*]' in which one-fourth interest was transferred. (Greg, *Bibliography*, i. 75–76.)

The Cardinal is the first tragedy Shirley wrote for the King's men at Blackfriars, as the actor Thomas Pollard pointed out in the epilogue:

> the Play is a Tragedy,
> The first that ever he compos'd for us.

Shirley himself thought it his best play, saying in his dedication of *The Cardinal* to his friend 'G. B. Esq': '. . . *at this my modesty took full encouragement, to make this offering, which as I conceive to be the best of my flock . . .*'; and in the prologue he makes approximately the same estimate:

> Yet I will tell you e'r you see it plaid,
> What the Author, and he blusht too, when he said
> (Comparing with his own for't had been pride
> He thought, to build his wit a Pyramyde
> Vpon anothers wounded Fame,) this Play
> Might rivall with his best. . . .

Others of the time thought well of it too. Pathericke Jenkyn praised it in his verses, '*To Mr.* James Sherley *on his playes*' (*Amorea* [1661], p. 50):

> Who is not joyed when he seeth the fall,
> And punnishment of vice, thy Cardinall.

'HALL', the author of the commendatory verses for the 1652 edition of the play, substitutes Shirley's name for Shakespeare's in the usual 'triumvirate' (see G. E. Bentley, *Shakespeare and Jonson*, i. 67–68):

> Yet this I dare assert, when men have nam'd
> *Iohnson* (the Nations Laureat,) the fam'd
> *Beaumont*, and *Fletcher*, he, that wo' not see
> *Shirley*, the fourth, must forfeit his best ey.

Edward Howard, in the preface to his *The Women's Conquest*, 1671, lists *The Cardinal* among 'the highest of our English Tragedies', along with *Catiline, The Maid's Tragedy, Rollo*, and *The Traitor*. Most nineteenth- and twentieth-century critics, though not so laudatory as their seventeenth-century predecessors, have thought the play among the best Caroline tragedies, and it has been frequently reprinted.

The date of Sir Henry Herbert's licence shows that *The Cardinal* was Shirley's autumn play for the Blackfriars in 1641 (see above, i. 63), and it was probably composed in the summer and early autumn of 1641. The despondent prologue which Shirley published before *The Sisters* in *Six New Playes*, 1653, was printed in *Poems &c.*, 1646, with minor alterations and eight new lines under the title, '*Prologue to his Tragedy call'd* the Cardinall'. Probably the prologue was first used with *The Sisters*, to whose original performances in late April and early May of 1642 the line 'London is gone to York' is more appropriate than to early performances of *The Cardinal* in late November and December 1641. In the new lines added to the version of the prologue in *Poems &c.*, 1646, is 'We are to have but little Summer here', which suggests that for some revival of *The Cardinal* early in the summer of 1642 Shirley revised his *Sisters* prologue.

No comprehensive source is known, though the play's similarity to Webster's *Duchess of Malfi* has frequently been remarked upon, Dyce going so far as to say that 'There can be little doubt that, while composing this tragedy, Shirley kept his eye on Webster's *Dutchess of Malfy*'. (*The Dramatic Works and Poems of James Shirley* [1833], i, p. xxxix.) If he did, Shirley was remarkably resolute in keeping his hands off the details of Webster's play.

Bowers (loc. cit.) discusses the relation of the play to the revenge tradition.

The records show that the play had more vogue during the Restoration than did most Caroline plays. Possibly the popular Restoration actor, Charles Hart, was in part responsible, for John Wright says:

Hart and *Clun,* were bred up Boys at the *Blackfriers*; and Acted Womens Parts, *Hart* was *Robinson*'s Boy or Apprentice: He Acted the Dutchess in the Tragedy of *the Cardinal*, which was the first Part that gave him Reputation. (*Historia Histrionica*, 1699, p. 3; see above, ii. 692.)

Sophia Lee's tragedy, *Almeyda: Queen of Granada*, acted at Drury Lane in April 1796, and published in the same year (Allardyce Nicoll, *A History of Late Eighteenth Century Drama* [1937] p. 281), is said to be derived in part from *The Cardinal*.

After *The Cardinal* in *Six New Playes* is printed a valuable list of Shirley's publications:

A Catalogue of the Authors Poems already Printed

Tragedies.

The Traytour
   Philip Chabot Admirall of France
Loves Cruelty
The Maids Revenge
Dukes Mistris
The Cardinal.

Comedies and Tragi-comedies.

The School of Complement
The Lady of Pleasure
Hide-parke
The Constant Maid.

*The Coronation   * Falsely ascribed to
                         Jo. Fletcher.

The Changes, or Love in a Maze
The Gratefull Servant
The Patron of Ireland
The Humorous Court
The Wedding
The Ball, or French Dancing Master
The Gamester
The Example
The Bird in a cage
The Royall Master
The Opportunity
The Witty Fair one
The Imposture
The Brothers
The Sisters.

A Masque of the four Honorable Innes of Court, presented before the King and Queens Majesty at Whitehall in the Banqueting house.
Poems.

The Careless Shepherdess

See under Thomas Goffe for Shirley's connexion with the play.

Chabot, Admiral of France (written 1621–21/2? ; revised and acted 1635)

with George Chapman

Editions: *The Tragedie of Chabot Admiral of France, Written by George Chapman and James Shirley*, edited by Ezra Lehman (1906); *The Plays and Poems of George Chapman: The Tragedies*, edited by Thomas Marc Parrott (1910), pp. 273–337 and 631–53.

Ferguson, A. S. 'Chapman, "The Tragedy of Chabot," Act III, Sc. ii, ll. 147–68', *M.L.R.* xxiii (1928), 46.
Forsythe, Robert Stanley. *The Relations of Shirley's Plays to the Elizabethan Drama* (1914), pp. 417–19.
Koeppel, Emil. *Quellen-Studien zu den Dramen George Chapman's, Philip Massinger's und John Ford's* (1897), pp. 52–61.

Nason, Arthur Huntington. *James Shirley, Dramatist* (1915), pp. 83–89.

Schipper, Jakob. *James Shirley: sein Leben und seine Werke* (1911), pp. 177–82.

Solve, Norma Dobie. *Stuart Politics in Chapman's Tragedy of Chabot* (1928).

1635, 29 Apr. '*Chabot, Admiral of France*, by George Chapman and James Shirley, licensed.' (Adams, *Herbert*, p. 36.)

1638, 24 Oct. S.R. Andrew Crooke and William Cooke entered for their copy 'a Booke called Phillip Chalbott [*sic*] Admirall of ffrance & the Ball. by Iames Shirley   vj^d.' (Greg, *Bibliography*, i. 49.)

1639. The Tragedie Of Chabot Admirall Of France: As it was presented by her Majesties Servants, at the private House in *Drury* Lane. Written by [bracket] *George Chapman*, and *James Shirly* . . . 1639.

1639, 10 Aug. Included in the list of plays protected from other companies by the Lord Chamberlain for the King and Queen's Young Company at the Cockpit is 'Philip Chabot Admirall of France'. (See above, i. 330–1.)

Though *Chabot, Admiral of France* was entered with *The Ball*, and though the statement of authorship is the same on each title-page—even from the same setting of type—the relation of the two authors is entirely different in the two plays: Chapman seems to have had nothing to do with *The Ball* (q.v.), but he was clearly the principal author of *Chabot*. Nearly all scholars who have considered the play have found much more of the work of Chapman than of Shirley in the latter play, and the principal editors agree (Lehman, op. cit., pp. 24–28; Parrott, op. cit., pp. 632–3) that most of the structure and style are so characteristic of Chapman as to indicate original composition by Chapman and revision by Shirley. Such a course of events is suggested by the age of the dramatists, for when Sir Henry Herbert licensed the play in 1635, Chapman had died the previous year at the age of about seventy-five, and Shirley was thirty-nine; the last of Chapman's dramatic work had been completed years before. Koeppel pointed out (loc. cit.) that the various historians suggested by Langbaine (*Account* . . ., p. 477) as sources for the play could not have served, and he makes a good case that the principal source of the play is Étienne Pasquier's *Les Recherches de la France*. Parrott (op. cit., pp. 631–2) notes that there were three different editions of this work, in 1607, 1611, and 1621, which carried the story of Chabot. A number of the details which Chapman used are not found in the edition of 1607, but are added in the fuller account in the edition of 1611, Book V, chapter 12, entitled *Du procés extraordinaire fait, premierement à Messire Philippe Chabot Admiral de France, puis à Messire Guillaume Pouyet Chancelier*. This account is repeated almost without change in the 1621 edition. So far as his source is concerned, then, Chapman could have written his original play any time after 1611. Mrs. Solve (op. cit.) points out that many of the parts of the Chabot story as recounted by Pasquier correspond to events in the fall of Robert Carr, Earl of Somerset, and later of his enemy, Lord Chancellor Bacon, and that other material in Chapman's play which corresponds to the Stuart political affair are not found in the French account, but have been added by Chapman. She concludes that Chapman saw in the 1621 edition of Pasquier's history a close analogy to the fall of his patron, Somerset, and the later (1621) fall of Bacon, and that after Bacon's disgrace Chapman wrote *Chabot, Admiral of France* as a political allegory of the career of the Earl of Somerset and a plea for his pardon. Her case is much more reasonable than most such, for there is reason to think that Chapman was interested both in allegory and in the patronage of the Earl of Somerset, even after the Earl's disgrace. Mrs. Solve even shows that the additions apparently made by Shirley weaken the allegory, especially the added wife, who is not in the dramatis personae and who has no resemblance to Carr's wife, Frances Howard.

Parrott accepted Mrs. Solve's case in his review of her book (*J.E.G.P.* xxix [1930], 300–4) and narrowed the period for the composition of the play from her date of between 1621 (Bacon's fall) and 1624 (Somerset's pardon) to 1621 to 18 January 1621/2, the date of Somerset's release from the Tower.

Mrs. Solve (op. cit., pp. 153–6) accounts for the late licence of the play by assuming that it would have been too controversial to produce immediately after composition, and by observing that at a date close to the events Sir Henry Herbert, then Master of the Revels and a member of the family of one of the principal enemies of Somerset, would certainly have refused a licence. By the time the play was finally licensed in 1635, most of the principals were dead, and the Carr scandal largely forgotten. Mrs. Solve agrees with Parrott that in the present text of the play I. 1, II. 3, and v. 2 are Chapman's composition unchanged; that II. 1 and III. 1 are new scenes by Shirley; and that the other scenes are Chapman's, revised by Shirley.

The play seems to have appealed to John Cotgrave, who quoted it eleven times in his *English Treasury of Wit and Language*, 1655 (see G. E. Bentley, 'John Cotgrave's *English Treasury of Wit and Language* and the Elizabethan Drama', *Stud. Phil.* xl [1943], 186–203), but there is no other evidence of any currency of the play after the closing of the theatres.

The Changes, or Love in a Maze (1631/2)

Edition: *James Shirley's Changes, or Love in a Maze*, edited from the quarto of 1632 with introduction and notes by Henrietta Louise Herod. Unpublished University of Chicago Thesis, 1942.

Forsythe, Robert Stanley. *The Relations of Shirley's Plays to the Elizabethan Drama* (1914), pp. 342–9.

1631/2, 10 Jan. '*The Changes*, by James Shirley, licensed.' (Adams, *Herbert*, p. 33.)

1631/2, 9 Feb. S.R. William Cooke entered for his copy 'vnder the hands of S^r. Henry Herbert & m^r Islip warden a Comedy called the Changes or Loue in a Maze by m^r Sherley'. (Greg, *Bibliography*, i. 41.)

1632. Changes: Or, Love in a Maze. *A Comedie*, As it was presented at the Private House in *Salisbury Court*, by the Company of His Majesties Revels. Written by Iames Shirley, Gent. . . . 1632.

1660–82. John Downes, after listing a number of plays in the repertory of the King's company, adds, 'All the foregoing, both Old and Modern Plays being the Principal in their Stock and most taking, yet, they Acted divers others, . . . *As . . . Love in a Maze.*' (*Roscius Anglicanus*, Summers ed., p. 15.)

1662, 17 May. 'Loue In a maze. 17. May' appears in a list of performances of plays by 'the Kings Companie at the Red Bull and the new house in Gibbon's Tennis Court near Clare Market', 1660–2. (Adams, *Herbert*, pp. 116–18.)

1662, 22 May. '. . . we by coach to the Theatre and saw "Love in a Maze." The Play hath little in it but Lacy's part of a country fellow, which he did to admiration.' (Diary of Samuel Pepys.)

1662[–3?] Edward Browne's 'Memorandum Book, 1662' (B.M. MS. Sloane 1900, fols. 65–60 [*sic*]), contains a list of plays and sums which presumably represent plays which Browne saw and the amounts he paid for seats. Under the heading, 'At the New Theatre in Lincolnes Jnne fields', is the entry, 'Love in amaze . . . 1 0.' (W. W. Greg, 'Theatrical Repertories of 1662', *Gentleman's Magazine*, ccci [1906], 69–72.)

1663, 10 June. '... to dinner, and thence to the Royal Theatre by water ... [where] we saw "Love in a Maze." The play is pretty good, but the life of the play is Lacy's part, the clown, which is most admirable; but for the rest, which are counted such old and excellent actors, in my life I never heard both men and women so ill pronounce their parts.' (Diary of Samuel Pepys.)

1664/5, 2 Feb. 'To the King's actors for acting a play called "Love in a Maze," at the Inner Temple Hall on Candlemas Day.' (F. A. Inderwick, *A Calendar of the Inner Temple Records*, 3 vols. [1896–1901], iii. 38.)

1667, 1 May. '... Thence away to the King's playhouse ... and saw "Love in a Maze:" but a sorry play: only Lacy's clowne's part, which he did most admirably indeed; and I am glad to find the rogue at liberty again. Here was but little, and that ordinary, company. ... But here was neither Hart, Nell, nor Knipp; therefore, the play was not likely to please me.' (Diary of Samuel Pepys.)

1667/8, 7 Feb. '... Lord Brouncker, and W. Pen, and I, and with us Sir Arnold Breames, to the King's playhouse, and there saw a piece of "Love in a Maze," a dull, silly play, I think.' (Ibid.)

1668, 28 Apr. '... to the King's house, and there did see "Love in a Maze," wherein very good mirth of Lacy, the clown, and Wintersell, the country-knight, his master.' (Ibid.)

1674, 11 May. In a warrant for payment for performances of plays before royalty at court or at the Theatre Royal occurs the item, 'May 11 Loue in a Maze ... [£]10.' (Nicoll, *A History of Restoration Drama*, 3rd ed., pp. 306–7.)

1674, 24 Nov. In a warrant for payment for performances of plays before royalty at court or at the Theatre Royal occurs the item, '[Nouember] 24 Loue in a Mase ... [£]10.' (Ibid., p. 307.)

Sir Henry Herbert's licence gives an approximate date for the first performance of the play, and it was doubtless written immediately before licensing. The fact that three other Shirley plays were licensed for performance in 1631—*The Traitor, The Duke*, and *Love's Cruelty*—would seem at first glance to postulate too much composition for 1631, but probably one or two of them had been written in 1630 when the theatres were closed by the plague and when Sir Henry Herbert is not known to have licensed any plays at all. (See above, ii. 657–8, and Adams, *Herbert*, p. 33.)

If the play was performed shortly after Sir Henry had licensed it—i.e. some time in January 1631/2—then it was not performed by the King's Revels company at Salisbury Court, as the title-page of the 1632 quarto says, for that company left the Salisbury Court before December 1631. (See above, i. 292–3.) This contradictory statement on the title-page of the quarto of *The Changes* has set quite a puzzle, but it seems to me that the only acceptable solution is the one first suggested by J. Q. Adams (*Shakespearean Playhouses*, pp. 374–8) that the title-page should have indicated presentation at Salisbury Court, not by the King's Revels but by Prince Charles's (II) company. The evidence of theatrical history and of the prologue and epilogue of *The Changes* fits this solution and not any other that I know. (See above, i. 304–7.) It may well be that Shirley did *prepare* this comedy for the King's Revels company at Salisbury Court theatre, probably in the last half of 1631, when that company still performed there. Corroborative evidence is perhaps offered by the unusual prominence and number of the roles for boy actors, which suggest preparation for a children's company. If completion of the comedy, Herbert's licence, and first production were delayed until January 1631/2, as Herbert's entry suggests, then the King's Revels company for which the play was planned would have left the Salisbury Court before they could use it, but the rights in the play would presumably have remained with the manager of the theatre, who would thereupon have had the play performed by the succeeding company, Prince Charles's (II) men. If the manuscript the printers had was Shirley's, and not a playhouse manuscript, as the state of the text suggests, then the title-page would indicate the intent of the author rather than the fact of production and thus explain the contradiction. Such a reconstruction of events is, of course, hypothetical, but whatever the facts, it seems certain that the title-page statement about the production of the play is erroneous.

No source for the play has ever been noted, but—as in most Caroline comedies—there are minor similarities of character and incident to many earlier comedies. (See the notes to Miss Herod's edition, *passim*.)

The large number of Restoration performances of *The Changes* is also witnessed to by Gerard Langbaine, who says of Shirley's plays:

Of these I have seen four since my Remembrance, two of which were acted at the King's House; and the other two presented at the Duke's Theatre, in Little *Lincolns-Inn* Fields: *viz. Court Secret, Chan[g]es, Grateful Servant, School of Compliments:* with what success, I leave it to the Players now in being . . . this Play [*Changes*] has been received with Success (as I said) in our Time; and as I remember, the deceas'd Mr. *Lacy* acted *Jonny Thump*, Sir *Gervase Simple*'s Man, with general Applause. (*An Account of the English Dramatick Poets* [1691], pp. 475 and 477.)

More performances of this play are recorded in the Restoration than of any other play of Shirley's, and Langbaine joins Pepys in suggesting that much of its success was due to Lacy's performance of Thump. Miss Herod notes (op. cit., p. xx) that Thump's role in the quarto of 1632 comprises only forty-one lines and suggests that more lines and business were added for him in the Restoration performances. No record of such additions is known, however, unless a single line added in manuscript to a copy of the quarto in the Aitken collection at the University of Texas can be thought such. (Ibid., pp. xxvi–xxix.) Another testimony to this vogue in the Restoration, or perhaps earlier, is the series of quotations in an Ashmolean manuscript headed '(2.) Witty extracts from a play intitled "Changes, or love in a maze, by JAMES SHIRLY."' (William Henry Black, *Catalogue of the Ashmolean Manuscripts*, Col. 326, No. 420.)

Dion Boucicault's *Love in a Maze*, according to Miss Herod, shows no indebtedness to Shirley's comedy, and she could find no evidence that Proctor's *Changes*, 1876, or Aylmer's *Changes*, 1890, reflected the earlier play of the name. (Op. cit., pp. xxi–xxii.) She likewise found no convincing evidence of indebtedness to Shirley's play in Dryden's *Maiden Queen*, Glapthorne's *Lady's Privilege*, or Howard's *Change of Crowns*, Langbaine, Forsythe, and Hazlitt respectively to the contrary notwithstanding. (Ibid., pp. xxiii–xxv.)

Miss Herod found variants in copies of the quarto in the Huntington Library, Harvard Library, and University of Texas Library which are more significant than ordinary variants and which she suggests were made by the author rather than by a compositor. (Op. cit., pp. xxxi–xxxv.) While these variants are not in themselves important, they do suggest an author's hand and support the hypothesis that the printers had Shirley's own manuscript and that the author made some press corrections.

Shirley dedicated the play to Lady Dorothy Shirley, but he claimed no kinship, and Gifford said (Nason, *James Shirley*, pp. 9–10) that the playwright was not related to the Warwickshire Shirleys, into which family she had married.

In his *Poems &c.*, 1646, Shirley reprinted the prologue for the play under the title, '*A Prologue to his Comedy of the* Changes, *or* Love in a Maze: *First Acted at Salisbury Court*'.

The Conceited Duke

See under Anon.

The Constant Maid (1636–40?)

Forsythe, Robert Stanley. *The Relations of Shirley's Plays to the Elizabethan Drama* (1914), pp. 379–90.

Nason, Arthur Huntington. *James Shirley, Dramatist* (1915), pp. 314–19.

1640, 28 Apr. S.R. Whitaker entered for his copies 'two Playes vizt. S^t. Patrick for Ireland. & The Constant Maide. by Iames Shirley'. (Greg, *Bibliography*, i. 53.)

1640. The Constant Maid. A Comedy. Written by *James Shirley* . . . 1640.

1661. *Love will finde out the Way*. An Excellent Comedy. By *T. B.* As it was Acted with great Applause, by Her Majesties Servants, at the Phœnix in *Drury Lane* . . . 1661.

1667. The Constant Maid: Or, Love will finde out the Way. A Comedy. By *J. S.* As it is now Acted at the new Play-house called *The Nursery*, in Hatton-Garden . . . 1667.

The Constant Maid is one of the very few extant Shirley plays for which we have no licence for performance. Of course the licence may have been in Sir Henry Herbert's office-book but missed by Malone and Chalmers when they examined the manuscript, but the unusually high proportion of Shirley licences which Malone copied implies that he was trying to get them all. This absence of production licence has suggested to various scholars that the play was produced at Ogilby's theatre in Dublin when Shirley worked there but not given a London production, and therefore not licensed. Such a deduction is compatible with the entrance of the play in the Stationers' Register with *St. Patrick for Ireland* (q.v.), a play known to have been prepared for Irish presentation, but it is contradicted by the statement on the title-page of the 1661 edition that the piece was acted by the Queen's men at the Phoenix. 1661, however, is a bit late for accurate information about Caroline productions.

It is notable that the text of this edition is quite different from the 1640 text. A rough collation shows that it is several hundred lines longer and that some pages seem to be completely revised; more of the songs are given in 1661 than in 1640. A more thorough collation might indicate whether this text would seem to have been revised for production at the Phoenix—where the title-page says it was acted but where Shirley did not work after his return from Ireland—or revised for Restoration production. There seem to be objections to either alternative. The T. B. [Theophilus Bird?] who appears as author on the 1661 title-page is unknown. Presumably his initials were carried to the title-page from the epilogue, to which they are signed. If he revised for a Restoration performance, why was not the Restoration performance used for advertising on the title-page?

If the play was written for production in Ireland, it would date 1636–40, the years of Shirley's Dublin residence. Fleay once dated it 1634 (*Anglia*, viii [1885], 407) because of allusions to *The Spanish Tragedy*, reprinted in 1633, and to Perkin Warbeck. Allusions to *The Spanish Tragedy*, however, are very common for fifty years, and they consequently offer no dating evidence. The Perkin Warbeck allusion in Act III (E_2) could refer either to the historic character or to Ford's play, but since Ford's *Perkin Warbeck* (q.v.) is itself of uncertain date, the allusion is of little help.

No comprehensive source for the play has been cited. Resemblances to Glapthorne's *Lady Mother* and to Fletcher's *Noble Gentleman* have been noted, and Forsythe sees a general influence of Brome's comedies as well as the usual series of analogues. (Op. cit., pp. 381 ff.)

A Contention for Honour and Riches (> 1632)

Forsythe, Robert Stanley. *The Relations of Shirley's Plays to the Elizabethan Drama* (1914), pp. 391–2.

1632, 9 Nov. S.R. William Cooke entered for his copy 'vnder the hands of Sr Henry Herbert knight & Mr Aspley warden a booke called a Dialogue of Riches & honor by I: S.' (Greg, *Bibliography*, i. 41.)

1633. A Contention For Honovr And Riches. By *J. S.* . . . 1633.

1646, 12 Dec. S.R. Humphrey Moseley had assigned to him all the rights of William Cooke 'in these two playes or masques vizt. Contention for honor & Riches. & The Triumph of peace. by Mr Iames Shirley'. (Greg, *Bibliography*, i. 58.)

There is no indication on the title-page or elsewhere that this short moral masque was ever acted. It is published with a dedication to Edward Golding signed by James Shirley, and it seems likely that if it had been acted Shirley would have mentioned the fact in the dedication or have given Cooke the information for his title-page.

Fleay's observation (*Biog. Chron.* ii. 238) that Ingenuity 'seems to be Shirley himself' is probably sound enough if interpreted to mean 'sets forth the ideas of Shirley himself'—or of most other gentlemanly Caroline writers. Fleay's further suggestion that the piece was 'probably written during the plague, c. June 1631' is only a guess; there seems to be no evidence for or against.

The ridicule of Lord Mayors' pageants (B_4v–C_1) is fairly general and not likely to be an attack on Heywood, as Fleay suggested.

Forsythe notes (loc. cit.) that Fleay's assertion that this moral play was 'Founded on *Decameron* v. 8' is groundless.

A Contention for Honour and Riches was later revised and expanded by Shirley as the first part of *Honoria and Mammon* (q.v.).

The Contention of Ajax and Ulysses for the Armour of Achilles

(c. 1645?–58)

Forsythe, Robert Stanley. *The Relations of Shirley's Plays to the Elizabethan Drama* (1914), pp. 402–3.

[1658.] The Contention Of Ajax and Ulysses, For The Armor of *Achilles*. As It was nobly represented by young Gentlemen of quality, at a private Entertainment of some persons of Honour. Written By *James Shirley*. . . . [N.D.] (Separate title-page in *Honoria and Mammon*, N.D. [q.v.].)

N.D. [Another issue. See *Honoria and Mammon*.]

1659. [Another issue. See *Honoria and Mammon*.]

As Forsythe noted (loc. cit.), following Langbaine (*Account . . .*, p. 485), *The Contention of Ajax and Ulysses for the Armour of Achilles* is a dramatization of the first section of Book xiii of Ovid's *Metamorphoses*. Shirley has added the two pages and Polybrontes.

Fleay suggested (*Biog. Chron.* ii. 247) that the piece was produced about 1640, and this deduction cannot be disproved, but it seems to me unlikely that Shirley would have been engaged on such a composition while working regularly for the King's men at Blackfriars. The piece is the sort of thing that might have been presented by schoolboys, who might—in the proper school—have been called 'young Gentlemen of quality' and with whom Shirley is known to have been associated in the fifties. His addition of the pages, Lysippus and Didimus, roles traditionally suitable for

schoolboys but not found in Ovid, suggests composition for young-
sters, as does the character '*Polybrontes*, a small Souldier'. The
lines of Lysippus, Didimus, and Polybrontes make much of the
small size of the actors and would have required boys whose
diminutive stature made them conspicuous, as in Lyly's comedies.

The piece concludes with Shirley's best-known verses, the dirge
beginning '*The glories of our blood and state*'. A note in the first
edition shows that this dirge was early separated from its context:
'This was afterwards sung in parts, the Musick excellently composed by Mr. *Ed. Coleman.*' Dyce records (*Works*, vi. 397) Oldys's
manuscript note in a British Museum copy of Langbaine's *Account
of the English Dramatick Poets*, 'In this *Contention* is the fine song
which old Bowman used to sing to king Charles, and which he has
often sung to me, *The glories, &c*'; and he notes (ibid. i, p. liii, n. 4)
Zouch's even more interesting contribution to folk-lore: 'Oliver
Cromwell is said, on the recital of it, to have been seized with
great terror and agitation of mind.' (Izaac Walton, *The Lives*, ed.
1807, p. 342, n.)

The Coronation (1634/5)

Forsythe, Robert Stanley. *The Relations of Shirley's Plays to the
Elizabethan Drama* (1914), pp. 304–13.

Nason, Arthur Huntington. *James Shirley, Dramatist* (1915), pp.
270–4.

Schipper, Jacob. *James Shirley: sein Leben und seine Werke* (1911),
pp. 159–67.

1634/5, 6 Feb. '*The Coronation*, by James Shirley, licensed.'
(Adams, *Herbert*, p. 36.)

1639, 25 Apr. S.R. Andrew Crooke and William Cooke entered as
their copies 'these five playes vidlt Night walters [*sic*],
Oportunity. Loues Cruellty, The Coronation witt without
money. ij^s vj^d.' (Greg, *Bibliography*, i. 50.)

1639, 10 Aug. Included in a list of plays protected from other
companies by the Lord Chamberlain for the King and Queen's
Young Company at the Cockpit is 'The Coronation:' (See
above, i. 330–1.)

1640. The Coronation A Comedy. As it was presented by her
Majesties Servants at the private House in *Drury* Lane.
Written by *John Fletcher*. Gent. . . . 1640.

1653. In *Six New Playes . . . All Written by James Shirley*, 1653,
appears 'A Catalogue of the Authors Poems already Printed'.

One title under 'Comedies and Tragi-comedies' is '*The Coronation   *Falsely ascribed to Jo. Fletcher'.
1679. The forty-first play printed in the second Beaumont and
Fletcher Folio is 'The Coronation. A Comedy.'

The fact that Malone found the play licensed in Sir Henry
Herbert's office-book as Shirley's is reasonable evidence that it
was his; suggestive is the fact that in the repertory list protected
by the Lord Chamberlain for the Cockpit company in 1639 the
title is in the midst of a series of Shirley titles and separated from
the Fletcher titles (see above, i. 330–1); more significant is the
fact that in his Poems &c., 1646, Shirley published 'A Prologue to
his Comedy at the Cock-pit, called the CORONATION, Presented in
the person of a Lady'. This is the prologue from the 1640 quarto,
except for minor variations and the omission of six lines referring
to critics. Under the circumstances it seems to me that the statement in the catalogue of Shirley's plays in Six New Playes—a
volume with the publication of which Shirley was associated, as
shown by his six signed dedications—that The Coronation had
been 'Falsely ascribed to Jo. Fletcher' is fairly conclusive. The
reprinting of the play in the 1679 Beaumont and Fletcher Folio,
and the listing of it under 'Plays written by Francis Beamount,
and John Flecher, printed in Quarto', which was printed as an
advertisement in Andrew Crooke's 1661 edition of Wit without
Money (see Greg, Bibliography, ii. 702 and 710), seem to me much
less significant.

There is no reason for thinking (see Schipper, loc. cit.) that the
licensing of the play by Sir Henry Herbert did not, as usual, come
shortly after the play was ready for the players and not long
before its first production. Forsythe thought (loc. cit.) that The
Coronation was based upon Beaumont and Fletcher's A King and
No King, with the main situation reversed and various character
parallels.

Fleay (Biog. Chron. ii. 241) took the first lines of the prologue:

> SInce tis become the Title of our Play,
> A woman once in a Coronation may
> With pardon, speake the Prologue,

as an indication that the title of the play had been changed, but
Herbert's licence implies the contrary.

The Country Captain

See William Cavendish.

The Court Secret (written 1642 but not acted)

MS.: Worcester College, Oxford, MS. 1200.

Forsythe, Robert Stanley. *The Relations of Shirley's Plays to the Elizabethan Drama* (1914), pp. 248–54.
Howarth, R. G. 'A Manuscript of James Shirley's *Court Secret*', *R.E.S.* vii (1931), 302–13, and viii (1932), 203.
Nason, Arthur Huntington. *James Shirley, Dramatist* (1915), pp. 372–80.
Schipper, Jakob. *James Shirley: sein Leben und seine Werke* (1911), pp. 280–90.

1653, 10 Sept. S.R. After entering a long list of plays on the ninth, Humphrey Moseley on the tenth 'Entred also for his Copie a Play called The Court Secret, Written by Iames Shirley'. (Greg, *Bibliography*, i. 61.)
1653. The Court Secret, A Tragi-Comedy: *Never Acted*, But prepared for the Scene at *Black-Friers*. Written By James Shirley. *Never printed before* . . . 1653. (Separate title-page in *Six New Playes*, 1653.)
1664, 18 Aug. 'Dined alone at home, my wife going to-day to dine with Mrs. Pierce, and thence with her and Mrs. Clerke to see a new play, "The Court Secret". . . . My wife says the play she saw is the worst that ever she saw in her life.' (Diary of Samuel Pepys.)
1682. Listed under Theatre Royal for 1682: 'Court Secret—This T. C. was written by Shirley . . . after the Restoration it was brought out by the King's Company.' (Genest, *Account of the English Stage* [1832], i. 351–2.)
1691. 'Of these [Shirley's plays] I have seen four since my Remembrance, two of which were acted at the King's House; and the other two presented at the Duke's Theatre, in Little *Lincolns-Inn* Fields: *viz. Court Secret, Chan[g]es, Grateful Servant, School of Compliments*: with what success, I leave it to the Players now in being.' (Langbaine, *An Account of the English Dramatick Poets* [1691], p. 475.)

The title-page statement that the play was never acted but written for Blackfriars is in part reiterated by Shirley in his dedication to William, Earl of Strafford, the young son of the executed Earl who had been Lord Deputy when Shirley was in Ireland. Shirley says that the play is

one, that weareth no Ribbands in the forehead; not so much as warranted
by Applause; for it happened to receive birth, when the Stage was
interdicted, and wanted that publique Seal which other Compositions
enjoyed.

Of course, '*interdicted*' could mean that the theatres were
closed because of plague, but Shirley says that the play was never
acted, and had a plague-closing been meant, production would
have been possible after the removal of the ban. Evidently Shirley
means that *The Court Secret* was completed after Parliament had
closed the theatres at the opening of the war. Sir Henry Herbert's
entries show a regular sequence of allowances of Shirley's plays
for the spring and autumn of 1640, 1641, and 1642, except that
there is no autumn play for 1642. (Adams, *Herbert*, p. 39.) Since
the *Six New Playes* by Shirley published in 1653 are said to be
'all that ever the Author made for the Private house in Black-
Fryers' (Nason, op. cit., pp. 59–60), *The Court Secret* is apparently
the piece intended for production at Blackfriars in the autumn
of 1642.

The manuscript of *The Court Secret* in the library of Worcester
College, Oxford, has no title, but the modern binder's title, *Don
Manuel*, has occasionally been attached to the play. This manuscript offers a text of *The Court Secret* different from that published in 1653, written in a hand (A) which Howarth found (*R.E.S.*
viii [1932], 203) to be the same as that of the B.M. MS. of the Earl
of Newcastle's play, *The Country Captain*. It has been revised by
a second hand (B) which Howarth thinks is Shirley's (*R.E.S.* vii
[1931], 302–7); a third hand (C) has added an induction, apparently
intended for a Restoration performance; and a fourth hand (D)
has made minor alterations in pencil.

In the first scene, which Howarth reprints in both versions, the
variants are so numerous and so radical as to make it clear that
1653 was set up from a different version of the play. Howarth adds
that there are in the manuscript scenes and portions of scenes, as
well as six or more characters, not in the printed text. If I follow
Howarth correctly, he thinks that the manuscript in its original
state (hand A) is a copy of Shirley's foul papers for the play;
1653 is a revision, presumably the one intended for production
at Blackfriars; and the revisions in the manuscript (hand A as
revised by B and D, with the induction in hand C) constitute
the text prepared for the Restoration performance seen by
Mrs. Pepys.

That there were Restoration performances of the play we have
ample evidence, and that the Induction at the end of the

Worcester College MS. was prepared for a Restoration production is indicated by the lines:

> . . . wit's as high now as our late Treason was.
> we ha' been swinging rebells, from that sin
> did our Conversion to this wit begin. (*R.E.S.* vii [1931], 304.)

I cannot believe, however, that the differences between the hand A version of I. I and the 1653 version are accounted for by Shirley's revision of his foul papers. A professional Caroline dramatist who had written thirty to forty plays, five of them for the company for which *The Court Secret* was prepared, would not need to rewrite the majority of his lines, as in this scene. Howarth seems also to be assuming that Shirley would have controlled the acting rights in his play, a state of affairs which seems most unlikely. A more complete and elaborate collation of the two texts of *The Court Secret* might produce interesting results.

No comprehensive source has been noted for the complex plot of *The Court Secret*, but Forsythe (loc. cit.) points out the usual analogues to earlier plays.

Cupid and Death (1651?–3; 1653; and 1659)

MSS.: B.M. Add. MS. 17799; Huntington Library MS. HM 601; B.M. Add. MS. 17800.

Forsythe, Robert Stanley. *The Relations of Shirley's Plays to the Elizabethan Drama* (1914), pp. 401–2.
Howarth, R. G. 'Shirley's *Cupid and Death*', *T.L.S.*, 15 November 1934, p. 795.
Ritter, Otto. 'Amor und Tod', *Englische Studien*, xxxii (1903), 157–9.
Welsford, Enid. *The Court Masque* (1927), pp. 261–4.

1653. Cvpid *And* Death. *A Masque.* As it was Presented before his Excellencie, The Embassadour of Portugal, Upon the 26. of *March*, 1653. *Written by J. S.* London, Printed according to the Authors own Copy, by *T. W.* for *J. Crook*, & *J. Baker* . . . 1653.
1659. Cupid And Death, A Private Entertainment, represented with Scenes & Musick, Vocall & Instrumentall. Writen by *J. S.* . . . 1659.
1659. [Perhaps another issue or possibly only a variant setting of the title-page. See Greg, *Bibliography*, ii. 829–30.]

The masque is based on the story of the exchange of weapons by Cupid and Death, a story which Shirley might have found in various places but which Langbaine (*An Account of the English Dramatick Poets* [1691], p. 478) connects with John Ogilby's translation, *The Fables of Æsop, Paraphras'd in Verse*, 1651. The suggestion is apt, since Shirley had been associated with Ogilby for three or four years in Ireland and had written commendatory verses for his translation of Aesop two years before *Cupid and Death* was performed before the Portuguese ambassador. Reference to another publication of 1651 seems intended in Shirley's lines in the masque:

> Some great affairs take up the Devil's time,
> He cannot sure attend these low employments,
> Hee's busie 'bout Leviathans I know not.   (B₃ᵛ.)

The quarto of 1653 seems to have been published immediately after the performance of 26 March 1653, for the British Museum copy in the Thomason collection has the manuscript note, 'march. 28', added to the title-page date. (Greg, *Bibliography*, ii. 829.) Perhaps the reason for the haste was that given by the printer, along with other interesting information, in his address to the reader:

THIS Masque was born without ambition of more, than to make a good privat entertainment, though it found, without any address or design of the Author, an honourable acceptation from his Excellency, the Embassadour of *Portugal*, to whom it was presented by Mr. *Luke Channen*, &c.

It had not so soon been published, for the Author meant all civilities to all persons, but that he heard an imperfect Copy was put to the Press, with an addition before it, of some things, that should be obtruded by another hand, which the Authors judgement could not consent too.

The Scæns wanted no elegance, or curiosity for the delight of the Spectator. The Musical compositions had in them a great soul of Harmony. For the Gentlemen that perform'd the Dances, thus much the Author did affirm, upon sight of their practise, that they shew'd themselves Masters of their quality.

The first paragraph indicates that the masque was not written for the entertainment of the ambassador, but for a more private occasion, now unknown. Possibly it was the text for this earlier private occasion which someone proposed to print after the advertisement of the ambassadorial performance.

The musical compositions praised in the printer's third paragraph were not those written by Matthew Locke and Christopher Gibbons, as asserted in the *D.N.B.* and Grove's *Dictionary of Music and Musicians* (1927 ed., iii. 223). Before the B.M. MS. of the score (Add. MS. 17799) is a description in Locke's hand, headed:

The Instrumentall and Vocall Musique in the Morall representation att the Millitary Ground in Lescester ffields 1659. (See Howarth, loc. cit.)

Evidently, then, the second edition of *Cupid and Death* records a third production of the masque six years after the second, at another place, with new music and presumably new scenes. The 'Millitary Ground', Howarth finds from C. L. Kingsford's *Early History of Piccadilly, Leicester Square, Soho* (1925, pp. 57–64), was a house used by the Military Company, north of Leicester Square. Howarth suggests that the masque may have been presented by or to the Military Company.

The Huntington MS. of the play and the B.M. Add. MS. 17800 are of no value for Shirley. The former is a transcript of the quarto with the note at the end:

M[r] E. Malone obligingly lent me the first Edition of *Cupid* and *Death*, from which I have faithfully transcrib'd this Copy.—I. P. Kemble.

April 19th 1786.

The second B.M. MS. is a nineteenth-century transcript by Edward Jones with score by Sir Henry Rowley Bishop. (Howarth, loc. cit.)

Dick of Devonshire

See Anon.

Don Manuel

See *The Court Secret*.

Double Falsehood, or the Distressed Lovers

Chambers, E. K. *William Shakespeare: A Study of the Facts and Problems* (1930), ii. 538–42.

Forsythe, Robert Stanley. *The Relations of Shirley's Plays to the Elizabethan Drama* (1914), pp. 431–3.

Lewis Theobald published in 1728 a play called *Double Falsehood; or, The Distrest Lovers*. He said that it was his adaptation of a newly discovered manuscript play of Shakespeare's. Most competent scholars have agreed that Theobald's play is an adaptation of an older play, but there has been much disagreement as to what manuscript, or manuscripts, he had. Several have thought that he had a manuscript of a lost play which was licensed by Humphrey Moseley 9 September 1653, 'The History of Cardenio, by M^r. Fletcher. & Shakespeare'. (Greg, *Bibliography*, i. 61.) Richard Farmer (*An Essay on the Learning of Shakespeare*, 2nd ed. [1767], p. 29) thought the original play had been written by Shirley, and Dyce (*Works*, i, p. lix) agreed with him. Actually the evidence for Shirley's authorship of the lost manuscript from which Theobald adapted his *Double Falsehood* is nil.

The Doubtful Heir, or Rosania, or Love's Victory
(c. 1638 Dublin; 1640 London)

Forsythe, Robert Stanley. *The Relations of Shirley's Plays to the Elizabethan Drama* (1914), pp. 213–20.

Nason, Arthur Huntington. *James Shirley, Dramatist* (1915), pp. 321–30.

1640, 1 June. '*Rosania*, by James Shirley, licensed.' (Adams, *Herbert*, p. 39.)

1641, 7 Aug. 'The doubtfull heire' is in a list of King's men's plays which the Lord Chamberlain forbade the printers to publish without the company's consent. (See above, i. 65–66.)

1646, [4] Sept. S.R. Humphrey Robinson and Humphrey Moseley entered as their copies a long list of plays, all apparently from the repertory of the King's company. Included is 'Doubtfull heire ... by Mr Shirley'. (Greg, *Bibliography*, i. 56–57.)

1652. The Doubtful Heir. A Tragi-comedie, As It was Acted at the private House In *Blackfriers*, Written By James Shirley. *Never Printed before* ... 1652. (Separate title-page in *Six New Playes*, 1653.)

1668/9, c. 12 Jan. In 'A Catalogue of part of His Ma^{tes} Servants Playes as they were formerly acted at the Blackfryers & now allowed of to his Ma^{tes} Servants at ye New Theatre' occurs the title, 'The Doubtfull Heire'. (Allardyce Nicoll, *A History of Restoration Drama*, 3rd ed., pp. 315–16.)

1672/3, 30 Jan. S.R. In a long list of plays transferred from Humphrey Robinson, executor of Humphrey Robinson, to John Martin and Henry Herringman is '[86] Doutfull Heire, halfe'. (Greg, *Bibliography*, i. 72.)

1683, 21 Aug. S.R. In a long list of plays transferred from Sarah Martin, executrix of John Martin, to Robert Scott is the title: '[93] doubtfull Heirs. [sic]', in which a one-fourth interest was transferred. (Ibid., p. 75.)

The play was evidently called after its sentimental heroine, Rosania, when first written, but the title was changed to *The Doubtful Heir* between the time of Sir Henry's licence and the protecting of the repertory of the King's company in August 1641. The play was not new, however, when Herbert licensed it. It had been acted by Shirley's company while he was in Ireland (1636–40), as is indicated by the prologue which he published in his *Poems &c.*, 1646, in the section headed 'PROLOGVES, AND EPILOGVES'.

> *To his own Comedy there* [i.e. Ireland], *called* Rosania
> *or* Loves Victory.
>
> *Rosania*? Mee thinks I hear one say,
> What's that? 'Tis a strange title to a Play.
>   .   .   .
> To save this charge of wit, that you might know
> Something i'th Title, which you need not owe
> To anothers understanding, you may see
> In honest English there, *Loves Victory*.

In the same prologue, between these two statements, Shirley provides evidence of the date in his further defence of his title:

> . . . others that have seen,
> And fashionably observ'd the English Scene,
> Say, (but with lesse hope to be understood)
> Such titles unto Playes are now the mood,
> *Aglaura*, *Claricilla*, names that may
> (Being Ladies) grace, and bring guests to the Play.

Killigrew's *Claracilla* (q.v.) was presented by Shirley's old company, Queen Henrietta's men, at the Phoenix in 1636, and Suckling's great court favourite was attracting attention at Black-friars in February 1637/8. (See under Suckling.) Since Shirley was speaking of the fashionable 'mood' at London's two most fashionable theatres, these plays must have been quite recent when he wrote, and a date of about 1638 for the original production of the play in Dublin under the title *Rosania* is suggested.

Apparently Shirley brought the manuscript back to London with him, and the King's men had it licensed as a new play, since it had not been licensed in London before. Shirley assumed that his tragi-comedy would be acted at Blackfriars, a private theatre probably not unlike the Dublin theatre for which the play had been written, but it was licensed too late in the season and acted at the Globe instead, to Shirley's distress, as indicated in the prologue for the London performance, a prologue which Shirley reprinted in *Poems &c.*, 1646, under the title '*A Prologue at the* Globe *to his Comedy call'd* The doubtfull Heire, *which should have been presented at the* Black-Friers'. (See above, i. 30, n. 6.) In the epilogue for the play, also printed in *Poems &c.*, 1646, Shirley implies the popularity of the actor Stephen Hammerton as a romantic lead. (See above, ii. 460–1.)

Forsythe points out (loc. cit.) that Shirley has taken much of his material for this tragi-comedy from his own piece, *The Coronation*, and reflected again the influence of *Philaster* and *A King and No King*, and he points out analogues and possible sources in other earlier plays.

The Duke

See *The Humorous Courtier.*

The Duke's Mistress (1635/6)

Forsythe, Robert Stanley. *The Relations of Shirley's Plays to the Elizabethan Drama* (1914), pp. 199–205.

Nason, Arthur Huntington. *James Shirley, Dramatist* (1915), pp. 280–6.

Schipper, Jakob. *James Shirley: sein Leben und seine Werke* (1911), pp. 182–8.

1635/6, 18 Jan. '*The Duke's Mistress*, by James Shirley, licensed.' (Adams, *Herbert*, p. 37.)

1635/6, 22 [25?] Feb. '*The Dukes Mistres* played at St. James the 22 of Feb. 1635. Made by Sherley.' (Ibid., p. 56. Adams suggests that the date may be a mistake for the 25th.)

1637/8, 13 Mar. S.R. Andrew Crooke and William Cooke entered for their copy 'a Play called The Dukes Mistris. by Ia: Shirley'. (Greg, *Bibliography*, i. 47.)

1638. The Dvkes Mistris, *As* It Was Presented by her *Majesties* Servants, At the private House in *Drury-Lane. Written by* Iames Shirly . . . 1638. (There are two other variant imprints. See ibid. ii. 674.)

The Duke's Mistress appears to be the last of the long series of plays which Shirley wrote for Queen Henrietta's company under Christopher Beeston at the Phoenix. (See above, i. 226–7.) Four months after the play was licensed the theatres were all closed by the protracted plague of 1636–7. (See above, ii. 661–5.) During the plague-closing Shirley went to Dublin (see above, Life), and after his return in 1640 he wrote for the King's men at Blackfriars.

No comprehensive source for the play has been found. Forsythe (loc. cit.) notes its resemblance to Fletcher's *A Wife for a Month* and Brome's *The Queen and Concubine*, but the Brome play is likely to have been written later, rather than earlier, than Shirley's tragi-comedy.

Gifford suggested (Dyce, *Works*, iv. 226, n. 2) that the verses about his preference for ugly women which Horatio reads to Fiametta in Act III (E_3^v) but which are not printed in the quarto, are probably those Shirley entitled, '*One that loved none but deformed Women*' in his *Poems &c.*, 1646. (First part, D_1–D_1^v.)

Nason (loc. cit.) discusses the play as characteristic of Shirley's romantic tragi-comedies.

The Example (1634)

Forsythe, Robert Stanley. *The Relations of Shirley's Plays to the Elizabethan Drama* (1914), pp. 365–71.

Nason, Arthur Huntington. *James Shirley, Dramatist* (1915), pp. 258–62.

Schipper, Jakob. *James Shirley: sein Leben und seine Werke* (1911), pp. 138–47.

Swinburne, A. C. 'James Shirley', *The Fortnightly Review*, N.S. xlvii [1890], 472.

1634, 24 June. '*The Example*, by James Shirley, licensed.' (Adams, *Herbert*, p. 36.)

1637, 18 Oct. S.R. Andrew Crooke and William Cooke entered for their copy 'vnder the hands of M^r. Weekes & Mr Aspley warden a Play called The Example by Mr Shirley'. (Greg, *Bibliography*, i. 47.)

1637. The Example. *As* It Was Presented by her *Majesties* Servants At the private House in *Drury-Lane*. Written by Iames Shirly . . . 1637.

1639, 10 Aug. Included in the list of plays protected by the Lord Chamberlain for the King and Queen's Young Company at the Cockpit is 'The Example'. (See above, i. 330–1.)

<1663. Downes lists 'The Example' as one of the plays acted by the King's company after the opening of the new Drury Lane Theatre in 1663. (*Roscius Anglicanus*, ed. Summers, p. 8.)

The Example belongs to Shirley's series of London comedies, though it makes less use of the realistic details of London life than *Hyde Park*, *The Ball*, *The Gamester*, and *The Lady of Pleasure*.

Actually *The Example* is dominantly romantic and sentimental, with a couple of sub-plots of Jonsonian humours. Sir Solitary Plot is a typical humours figure in the style of Jonson, showing strong resemblances—as has been often noted—to Sir Politic Would-Be of *Volpone*. His action is, however, a minor one, and the play is dominated by the chaste Bellamia, 'the example', and the reformed Lord Fitzavarice.

The approximate date of first performance is set by Sir Henry Herbert's licence, and the references to the ghost of Tilly at the end of Act III (E_4) and the murder of Wallenstein in Act IV ($F_3{}^v$) show that the play had been written very recently indeed, probably in the four or five months after *The Triumph of Peace* was performed, 3 February 1633/4. As Dr. Greg points out (*Bibliography*, ii. 664), there seems to have been some confusion about the licensing of the play for the press, for it is entered in the Stationers' Register 18 October 1637, as licensed by Mr. Weeks, but his imprimatur after the epilogue in the quarto is dated 19 October.

The prologue for the comedy has some interesting references to theatre customs as well as a number of cryptic allusions. The players seem to be talking about recent difficulties in the lines:

> *This is a destiny, to which wee bow,*
> *For all are innocent but the Poets now,*
> *Who suffer for their guilt of truth, and arts,*
> *And we for only speaking of their parts.*

Could this refer to difficulties of Jonson and this company over the satire in *A Tale of a Tub* a year before?

There is another puzzling passage in the prologue:

> *If any meete here, as some men i'th age*
> *Who understand no sense, but from one stage,*
> *And over partiall will entaile like land*
> *Vpon heires male all action, and command*
> *Of voice and gesture, upon whom they love,*
> *These, though cal'd Judges, may delinquent's prove.*

Fleay thought (*Biog. Chron.* ii. 240) that the passage referred to C. Burbage and his attempt to 'monopolize the Drama by right of inheritance from his father'. There is no evidence that any Burbage carried much weight in the London theatre in 1634, and the passage refers to '*men*', not one man. Do the players refer to London gentry who thought the King's men at Blackfriars the only important actors in London? Such an interpretation would fit the context and the reputations of the companies, but some particular event must have given rise to the complaint of the Queen's actor who spoke the prologue.

Shirley reprinted the duet of Sir Solitary and Lady Plot near the end of the play (I₃) in his *Poems &c.*, 1646 (First part, C₂–C₂ᵛ), under the title, '*Melancholy converted*'.

Professor Arthur Ludwig Stiefel said categorically that *The Example* had a Spanish source. ('Die Nachahmung spanischer Komödien in England unter den ersten Stuarts', *Romanische Forschungen*, v [1890], 196, n. 1.) He made an excellent case for *The Opportunity* and *The Young Admiral*, but so far as I know his evidence for the source of *The Example* was never published.

The Faithful Servant

See *The Grateful Servant*.

The French Dancing Master

See *The Ball*.

The Gamester (1633)

Edition: *James Shirley's The Gamester, A Critical Edition of the 1637 Quarto with Introduction and Notes*, by Stephen H. Ronay. Unpublished University of Chicago Thesis, 1948.

Forsythe, Robert Stanley. *The Relations of Shirley's Plays to the Elizabethan Drama* (1914), pp. 357–65.
Nason, Arthur Huntington. *James Shirley, Dramatist* (1915), pp. 254–8.
Schipper, Jakob, *James Shirley: sein Leben und seine Werke* (1911), pp. 112–22.

1633, 11 Nov. '*The Gamester*, by James Shirley, licensed.' (Adams, Herbert, p. 35.)
1633/4, 6 Feb. 'On thursday night the 6 of Febru. 1633, *The Gamester* was acted at Court, made by Sherley, out of a plot of the king's, given him by mee; and well likte. The king sayd it was the best play he had seen for seven years.' (Ibid., pp. 54–55.)
1633/4, 6 Feb. '. . . this nighte I was att Whitehall att the daunce-inge & playe, & laye all nighte wᵗʰ Bor Anth:' (Diary of Sir Humphrey Mildmay. See above, ii. 675.)
1637, 15 Nov. S.R. Andrew Crooke and William Cooke entered as

their copy 'a Play called The Gamester by Ia: Shirley'. (Greg, *Bibliography*, i. 47.)

1637. The Gamester. *As* It Was Presented by her *Majesties* Servants At the private House in *Drury-Lane. Written* By Iames Shirly . . . 1637.

The original production of *The Gamester* probably took place very shortly after Herbert licensed the play, and one would assume that it was mainly composed after Shirley's *Young Admiral* was licensed for performance by the same company on 3 July 1633.

Sir Henry says that the plot was the King's, but it is also found in Malespini's *Ducento Novelle*, Part II, Novella 96, and in the *Heptameron*, i. 8, as Langbaine pointed out (*An Account of the English Dramatick Poets* [1691], p. 479), and Ronay's comparison of the general outlines and certain details (op. cit., pp. viii–xii) make it fairly clear that either King Charles remembered Margaret of Navarre's story or else Shirley had recourse to it. The scenes from London life have numerous parallels, as Forsythe pointed out (loc. cit.), but none could be called a source.

It is surprising that there are no records of performances of *The Gamester* after the one at court in February 1633/4. Certainly the King's high praise would have ensured another court performance, and one would assume that a play so satisfactory to King Charles would have appealed to the loyal audiences at the Phoenix. Probably there were other court and Phoenix performances which have left no record. The play did not lose its appeal for everyone with the closing of the theatres, for John Cotgrave prints seven passages from it in his *English Treasury of Wit and Language*, 1655. (See G. E. Bentley, ' John Cotgrave's *English Treasury of Wit and Language* and the Elizabethan Drama', *Stud. Phil.* xl [1943], 186–203.)

The Gamester provided good material for later audiences, and it was adapted twice in the eighteenth century and once in the nineteenth. In 1712 Charles Johnson published an adaptation in prose entitled *The Wife's Relief: or, The Husband's Cure*, as it had been performed at Drury Lane in November and December 1711. It continued to be acted off and on through the century. (See Nicoll, *A History of Early Eighteenth Century Drama, 1700–1750* [1929], p. 339, and John Genest, *Some Account of the English Stage, 1660–1830* [1832], ii. 490–3, and vi. 226.) Johnson's revision, the usual eighteenth-century sentimentalization, is compared with the original by Ronay. (Op. cit., pp. xvii–xix.) Another eighteenth-century revision entitled *The Gamesters* was published by David

Garrick in 1758. It had an original six-day run in 1757 and was revived in 1772, 1789–90, and 1806. (Genest, op. cit., iv. 512; v. 341; vii. 12 and 708.) Garrick's adaptation was closer to Shirley than Johnson's. A third revision by John Poole called *The Wife's Stratagem: or More Frightened than Hurt* was performed a number of times in London and New York in 1827. (Ibid. ix. 388, and G. C. D. Odell, *Annals of the New York Stage*, iii. 271.) Poole seems to have worked almost entirely from the versions of Johnson and Garrick. (Ronay, op. cit., pp. xxiv–xxvi.)

The General

During his Dublin residence Shirley wrote a number of prologues and epilogues for plays not his own. He published eight of them in his *Poems &c.*, 1646, clearly separating them from the ten following prologues and epilogues for plays he wrote himself. This distinction between the two groups has been missed by several commentators, who have mistakenly attributed *The Irish Gentleman*, *The Toy*, and *The General* to Shirley. Whether *The General* is a lost anonymous play or an early form of Orrery's tragi-comedy called *The General* has not been demonstrated. (See Roger Boyle.)

The Gentleman of Venice (Dublin?, ?; London, 1639)

Forsythe, Robert Stanley. *The Relations of Shirley's Plays to the Elizabethan Drama* (1914), pp. 231–40.

Huberman, Edward. 'Bibliographical Note on James Shirley's *The Polititian*', *Library*, Fourth Series, xviii (1937), 104–8.

Nason, Arthur Huntington. *James Shirley, Dramatist* (1915), pp. 305–7.

Schipper, Jakob. *James Shirley: sein Leben und seine Werke* (1911), pp. 222–30.

1639, 30 Oct. '*The Gentleman of Venise*, by James Shirley, licensed.' (Adams, *Herbert*, p. 38 and n. 5.)

1653, 9 July. S.R. Humphrey Moseley entered for his copy 'a Play called The Gentleman of Venice Written by Iames Shirley'. (Greg, *Bibliography*, i. 60.)

1655. The Gentleman Of Venice A Tragi-Comedie Presented at the Private house in *Salisbury* Court by her Majesties Servants. *Written by* James Shirley . . . 1655.

1655. [Another issue from the same setting of type, but quarto instead of octavo. See Greg, *Bibliography*, ii. 856–7, and Huberman, op. cit.]

The Gentleman of Venice and *The Royal Master* are the only plays of Shirley's that are known to have been licensed for London performance by Sir Henry Herbert while Shirley was absent in Dublin. *The Royal Master* was published in 1638, the year in which Sir Henry licensed it, and the players may, therefore, have secured the piece by simply buying a copy of the quarto, but *The Gentleman of Venice* was not published until 1655, and the players must have had a manuscript to present to Sir Henry. It is not clear how they got it, but Shirley himself seems not to have kept a copy, for in the 1655 dedication to Sir Thomas Nightingale he says of the play:

I must acknowledge many years have past, since it did *Vagire in Cunis*, and when it had gotten strength, and legs to walk, traveling without direction, it lost it self, till it was recovered after much inquisition, and now upon the first return home. . . .

It may be that *The Gentleman of Venice* was produced in Dublin before it was licensed by Sir Henry and performed by the Queen's men at Salisbury Court. When it was licensed Shirley was writing for the Dublin theatre, and he is not known to have visited London in 1639 (see Allan H. Stevenson, 'Shirley's Dedications and the Date of His Return to England', *M.L.N.* lxi [1946], 79–83), yet he speaks in the dedication as if he had seen it performed:

THE Poem that approacheth to kiss your hand, had once a singular grace and lustre from the Scene, when it enjoy'd the life of action; Nor did it want the best hands to applaud it in the Theater.

No comprehensive source for the play is known. Langbaine said:

. . . and the Intrigue between *Florelli*, *Cornari*, and *Claudiana*, is borrowed (as I suppose) from a Novel out of *Gayton's Festivous* Notes on *Don Quixote*: see Book 4. Chap. 6, 7, 8. (*An Account of the English Dramatick Poets* [1691], p. 479.)

But since, as Ward (*H.E.D.L.* iii. 117, n. 3) and Forsythe (loc. cit.) noted, Gayton's book was not published until 1654, Shirley could scarcely have used it in 1639. Forsythe sees little resemblance in the *Don Quixote* story suggested by Dibdin; he lists the usual analogues.

Moseley published the play with *The Politician* in 1655 in both an octavo and a quarto edition, the octavo impressions 'evidently designed to range with the collection of *Six New Playes* of 1653, the quarto with the earlier separate editions of the author's pieces'. (Greg, *Bibliography*, ii. 856.) Both issues were printed from the

same setting of type, with the signatures altered. The octavos of
The Politician and *The Gentleman of Venice* are generally found
bound together. (Greg, *Bibliography*, ii. 856–7, and Huberman,
op. cit.)

The Grateful Servant (1629)

Forsythe, Robert Stanley. *The Relations of Shirley's Plays to the
Elizabethan Drama* (1914), pp. 261–8.
Nason, Arthur Huntington. *James Shirley, Dramatist* (1915), pp.
191–7.
Schipper, Jakob. *James Shirley: sein Leben und seine Werke* (1911),
pp. 37–44.

1629, 3 Nov. '*The Faithful Servant*, by James Shirley, licensed.'
(Adams, *Herbert*, p. 33.)
1629/30, 26 Feb. S.R. John Grove entered for his copy under the
hands of Sir Henry Herbert and Mr. Purfoote, warden, 'A play
Called The gratefull servant by Ia: Sherley'. (Greg, *Bibliography*, i. 37.)
1630. The Gratefvll Servant. *A Comedie.* As it was lately presented with good applause at the priuate House in *Drury-Lane,
By her Majesties Servants*. Written by Iames Shirley Gent. . . .
1630.
1637, 25 Sept. S.R. John Grove assigned to William Leake all his
rights in 'these ffour Playes following (vizt.) The Wedding. The
Tragedie of Hoffman The gratefull Servant. Hollands Leaguer.'
(Greg, *Bibliography*, i. 46.)
1637. The Gratefvll Servant. A Comedie. As it was lately presented with good applause in the private House in *Drury-Lane.
By her Majesties Servants*. Written by James Shirley Gent . . .
1637.
1639, 10 Aug. Included in a list of plays protected against other
companies for the King and Queen's Young Company at the
Cockpit by the Lord Chamberlain is 'The gratefull seruant'.
(See above, i. 330–1.)
1662[–3?]. In Edward Browne's accounts for plays seen in '1662',
under the heading 'At Sr Will Davenants theatre in Lincolnes
Jnne fields', is the entry, 'Gratefull Servant . . . 1 6'. (W. W.
Greg, 'Theatrical Repertories of 1662', *Gentleman's Magazine*,
ccci [1906], 69–72; from B.M. MS. Sloane 1900.)
<1662. The grateful Servant. A Comedy. As it was Presented with
good Applause in the private House in *Drury-Lane. By Her*

Majesties Servants. Written by *James Shirley*, Gent . . . [N.D.] (Greg points out, *Bibliography*, ii. 580, that the advertisement of Leake's books printed with this quarto indicates that it cannot be earlier than 1662.)

1666. 'The first new Play that was Acted in 1666, was: *The Tragedy of* Cambyses. . . . *After this the Company Reviv'd Three Comedies of Mr. Sherly's, viz. The Grateful Servant. The Witty Fair One. The School of Complements. The Woman's a Weather Cock.* These Plays being perfectly well Perform'd; especially *Dulcino* the Grateful Servant, being Acted by Mrs. *Long*; and the first time she appear'd in Man's Habit, prov'd as Beneficial to the Company, as several succeeding new Plays.' (John Downes, *Roscius Anglicanus*, Summers ed., p. 27.)

1668/9, 20 Feb. '. . . after dinner out with my wife and my two girls to the Duke of York's house, and there saw "The Gratefull Servant," a pretty good play, and which I have forgot that ever I did see.' (Diary of Samuel Pepys.)

1691. 'Of these [Shirley's plays] I have seen four since my Remembrance, two of which were acted at the King's House; and the other two presented at the Duke's Theatre, in Little *Lincolns-Inn* Fields: *viz. Court Secret, Chan[g]es, Grateful Servant, School of Complements*: with what success, I leave it to the Players now in being.' (Langbaine, *An Account of the English Dramatick Poets* [1691], p. 475.)

The Grateful Servant was Shirley's autumn play for Queen Henrietta's company in 1629 and was probably first performed at the Cockpit about the time of Herbert's licence on 3 November, under the title of *The Faithful Servant*. Since the 1639 protected list shows that *The Grateful Servant* was kept in the Cockpit repertory when other Shirley plays were dropped, we can assume that it was a success in the theatre.

There appears to have been something unusual about the reception of this tragi-comedy. As a rule, Shirley's plays were not printed until several years after first performance. Those besides *The Grateful Servant* that got immediately into print—*The Changes, The Bird in a Cage*, and *The Royal Master*—all were produced or printed under exceptional circumstances. Moreover, though Shirley frequently prepared dedications for his quartos, comparatively few of them appear with commendatory verses—only *The Wedding, The Grateful Servant, The Royal Master*, and *The Cardinal. The Grateful Servant*, however, has ten sets of commendatory verses, and several of them hint at difficulties. John Fox says:

> PResent thy worke vnto the wiser few
> That can discerne and iudge; . . .
>
> .   .   .   .   .
>
> . . . be therefore boldly wise
> And scorne malicious censures, like flies
> They tickle but not wound, . . .
>
> .   .   .   .   .
>
> Let others barke, keepe thou poeticke lawes
> Deserue their enuy, and command applause.

'Jo. Hall' takes a similar line:

> WHo would writ well for the abused stage
> When only swelling word do please the age
> And malice is thought wit, to make 't appeare
> They iudge they mis-interpret what they heare.
>
> .   .   .   .   .
>
> Let purblind critticks still endure this curse
> To see good playes and euer like the worse.

Charles Aleyn seems to suggest that some particular person has attacked the play:

> Tush I will not beleeue, that iudgements light
> Is fixt but in one spheare, and that dull night,
> Muffles the rest.

Thomas Randolph belittles the obscurity of some other dramatist (the critic?), but indicates that *The Grateful Servant* was successful in the theatre:

> Know I aplaud thy smooth and euen straines
> That will informe and not confound our braines
> Thy Helicon like a smooth streame doth flow
> While others with disturbed channels goe
> And headlong like Nile Cataracts do fall
> With a huge noise, and yet not heard at all.
> When thy intelligence on the Cockpit stage
> Giues it a soule from the immortall rage
> I heare the muses birds with full delight
> Sing where the birds of mars were wont to fight.

Thomas Craford's obscure verses seem to imply that the critic who misunderstood Shirley's play was a dramatist for another company:

> [Thy poem]
> Which grac'd with comely action, did appeare
> The full delight of euery eye and eare,
> And had that stage no other play, it might
> Haue made the critticke blush at cockpit flight

> Who not discouering what pitch it flies
> His wit came downe in pitty to his eyes
> And lent him a discourse of cocke and bull
> To make his other comendations full,
> But let such Momi passe and giue applause
> Among the brood of actors, in whose cause
> As champion he hath sweat let their stale pride
> Find some excuse in being magnified,
>
> .   .   .   .   .
>
> Let 'em vnkennell malice, yet thy praise
> Shall mount secure, hell cannot blast thy bayes.

William Habington seems to be hinting darkly that the unknown maligner was a sycophant:

> My name is free, and my rich clothes commend
> No deformd bounty of a looser friend,
> Nor am I warme i'th Sunshine of great men
> By guilding their darke sinnes . . .
>
> .   .   .   .   .
>
> Go forward still, and when his muse expires
> Whose English, staines the greeke and latine lires
> Diuinest *Ionson*, liue to make vs see
> The glory of the stage reuiu'd in thee.

One would guess from these various hints that *The Grateful Servant* had been attacked by someone who was a dramatist for a rival company, who wrote obscure or bombastic plays himself, and who was a shameless and successful flatterer of the great. Since commendatory verses were contributed by Thomas Randolph, who wrote for the Salisbury Court, and Philip Massinger, who wrote for Blackfriars, the troupes of the two rival private theatres seem to be eliminated. Shirley's own statements in the front matter of the play are in general agreement with these implications of the commendatory verses. In his dedication of the play to Francis, Earl of Rutland, Shirley hints that there have been attacks on his tragi-comedy and on the actors, and he may be relating the attacks to gentlemanly authors of inflated plays:

When the Age declineth from her primitiue vertue, and the Silken witts of the Time, (that I may borrow from our acknowledg'd Master, learned Ionson) *disgracing Nature, & harmonious Poësie, are transported with many illiterate and prodigious births, it is not safe to appeare without Protection.*

And in the address to the reader, Shirley makes a point of praising the actors and defending them from attack. He says that he has not solicited the commendatory verses,

but I must joyne with them that haue written, to do the Comedians
iustice, among whom, some are held comparable With the best that
are, and haue beene in the world, and the most of them deseruing a
name in the file of those that are eminent for gracefull and vnaffected
action. Thus much Reader I thought meet to declare in this place,
and if thou beest ingenuous, thou wilt accuse with me, their bold
seuerity, who for the offence of being modest and not iustling others
for the wall haue most iniuriously thrust so many actors into the
Kennell—now—

Panduntur portæ, Iuvat ire.—

It would be amusing and perhaps illuminating to learn more
about this miniature war of the theatres, but I can wring nothing
more from the evidence at hand.

No comprehensive source for *The Grateful Servant* has been
found, though Forsythe (loc. cit.) notes similarities to *Philaster*,
Twelfth Night, and *The City Night Cap*, as well as analogues to
other plays.

The number of allusions to Restoration performances of the
play, especially John Downes's comment, show that it had a
longer appeal in the theatre than most of Shirley's productions.
That it was also read is shown by the three editions of the play,
by the ten quotations from it in *English Treasury of Wit and
Language*, 1655 (see G. E. Bentley, 'John Cotgrave's *English
Treasury of Wit and Language* and the Elizabethan Drama', *Stud.
Phil.* xl [1943], 186–203), and by the two quotations in Thomas
Blount's *The Academy of Eloquence* (1656), pp. 68 and 106.

Honoria and Mammon (1647 ?–58)

Forsythe, Robert Stanley. *The Relations of Shirley's Plays to the
Elizabethan Drama* (1914), pp. 393–8.

[1658.] Honoria And Mammon. Written By *James Shirley . . . London*, Printed for the use of the Author. [N.D.] [Greg notes, *Bibliography*, ii. 623, that a copy in the Huth sale of 8 July 1918,
No. 6848, bore the inscription: 'This Mr. James Sherley himselfe sent me by his sonn in Law wh. [*sic*] a Letter June 11. 1658.
E libris Rob. Bolley Esq.']

N.D. Honoria And Mammon . . . *London*, Printed by *T. W.* for
John Crook, at the sign of the ship in S. *Pauls* Church-yard.
[N.D.] [Another issue.]

1659. Honoria And Mammon. Written by *James Shirly* Gent.

Scene Metropolis, Or *New-Troy*. Whereunto is added the Contention of *Ajax* and *Ulisses*, for the Armour of *Achilles*. As it was represented by young Gentlemen of quality at a private entertainment of some Persons of Honour . . . 1659. [Another issue.]

Honoria and Mammon is a five-act moral allegory which is an elaboration and expansion of the author's *A Contention for Honour and Riches*, published fifteen years before. Shirley himself notes the relationship in his address 'To THE CANDID READER':

> A Small part of this Subject, many years since had drop'd from my pen: But looking at some opportunities upon the Argument, I thought some things more considerable might be deduced; and applying my self further, at times of recess, I felt it grow and multiply under my imagination: Nor left I it then (the matter being so pregnant in it self) till I form'd it into such limbs and proportions as you now see it. . . . What is now presented, I hope will appear a genuine and unforc'd Moral, which though drest in Drammatique Ornament, may not displease, in the reading, persons of ingenuity, such whose nature is not to create prejudice, where they intend a recreation. . . . I will onely adde, it is like to be the last, for in my resolve, nothing of this nature shall after this, engage either my pen or invention.

I take it that the sentence about 'genuine and unforc'd Moral . . . drest in Drammatique Ornament' is intended to forestall Puritan criticism of the dramatic form and indicates that the piece was never acted, or intended to be.

Apparently the first issue was printed off for Shirley's own use at least as early as June 1658, according to the note on the title-page of the Huth copy noted above. Of the later issues, the Thomason copy of the 1659 issue, the third one, in the British Museum has the date 'march: 27.' added to that on the title-page, and Greg notes: 'Thus nine months after the author's copies had been distributed it appears to have been thought worth while printing a new title to call attention to the complete contents of the volume.' (Op. cit., p. 623.)

The 'times of recess' in which Shirley says he expanded *A Contention for Honour and Riches* into *Honoria and Mammon* were presumably recess from his duties as schoolmaster during the later years of the Interregnum. The last sentence of the quotation seems to indicate that he had resolved to do no more dramatic writing. In 1658 and 1659 Davenant and others were showing that dramatic productions might again be profitable. Had Shirley reformed, or was he despondent?

The Humorous Courtier (The Duke) (1631)

Forsythe, Robert Stanley. *The Relations of Shirley's Plays to the Elizabethan Drama* (1914), pp. 279–86.

Nason, Arthur Huntington. *James Shirley, Dramatist* (1915), pp. 102–3 and 222–3.

Schipper, Jakob. *James Shirley: sein Leben und seine Werke* (1911), pp. 230–40.

1631, 17 May. '*The Duke*, by James Shirley, licensed.' (Adams, *Herbert*, p. 33.)

1639, 29 July. S.R. William Cooke entered for his copy 'a play called The humerous Courtier. by Iames Shirley'. (Greg, *Bibliography*, i. 51.)

1640. The Hvmorovs Covrtier. A Comedy, As it hath been presented with good applause at the private house in *Drury-Lane*. Written by Iames Shirley Gent . . . 1640.

The identification of the play published as *The Humorous Courtier* in 1640 with the one licensed for performance as *The Duke* in 1631 was suggested by Fleay (*Biog. Chron.* ii. 237) and has been generally accepted, for, as Nason observes (op. cit., p. 102), 'the plot turns on the question of who shall become the Duke of Mantua, and . . . the successful suitor proves to be the Duke of Parma in disguise'. Fleay's further identification of *The Humorous Courtier* with *The Conceited Duke* of the Cockpit repertory protected in August 1639 (see above, i. 330–1) is not acceptable, for the Duke of Parma in the play is not conceited. Moreover, this title, *The Conceited Duke*, does not stand with Shirley's fourteen other plays in the 1639 list, but between Rowley's *Cupid's Vagaries* and Webster's *Appius and Virginia* at the end.

The play was presumably acted about the date of Herbert's licence for performance. It seems likely, however, that it was not written immediately before licensing, as usual, but several months previously, during the plague-closing of 1630. (See above, ii. 657–8.) The evidence is that in the calendar years 1631 and 1632 six plays of Shirley's were licensed for production, but in the plague year of 1630 none. As Shirley's normal rate of composition for Queen Henrietta's men appears to have been two plays a year, this distribution of licences suggests that he did write the usual two plays in 1630, but that the company, unable to use them in 1630, held them over and licensed them in 1631, keeping one of the 1631 plays for 1632. The first two Shirley plays licensed in 1631 were *The Traitor* and *The Duke*, on 4 and 17 May respectively, and it seems likely that one or both were compositions of the plague year of 1630.

Professor Arthur Ludwig Stiefel made the categorical statement that *The Humorous Courtier* had a Spanish source. ('Die Nachahmung spanischer Komödien in England unter den ersten Stuarts', *Romanische Forschungen*, v [1890], 196, n. 1.) His evidence, so far as I know, was never presented, but he made such solid cases for similar statements about *The Opportunity* and *The Young Admiral* that one is inclined to respect his assertion.

Forsythe (loc. cit.) notes the usual analogues, especially to the comedies of humours around the turn of the century, which this play resembles in its presentation of the humours of the members of the court as they posture for the hand of the Duchess.

Since one of the Bodleian copies of the play belonged to Robert Burton, who died 25 January 1639/40, Greg suggests (*Bibliography*, ii. 715) that the quarto may well have been issued before the end of 1639.

Printed with the quarto (A₂) is 'A Catalogue of such things as hath beene published by *James Sherley* Gent.':

> TRaytor.
> *Witty Faire one.*
> *Bird in a Cage.*
> *Changes*, or *Love in a Maze.*
> *Gratefull Servant.*
> *Wedding.*
> *Hide Parke.*
> *Young Admirall.*
> *Lady of Pleasure.*
> *Gamster.*
> *Example.*
> *Dukes Mistresse.*
> *Ball.*
> *Chabot Admirall of France.*
> *Royall Master.*
> *Schoole of Complements.*
> *Contention for Honour and Riches.*
> *Triumph of peace, a Masque.*
> *Maides Revenge.*
> *Humorous Courtier.*

Hyde Park (1632)

Edition: *James Shirley's Hyde Park edited from the Quarto of 1637. With Introduction and Notes*, by Theodore Miles. Unpublished University of Chicago Thesis, 1940.

Forsythe, Robert Stanley. *The Relations of Shirley's Plays to the Elizabethan Drama* (1914), pp. 349–56.

Miles, Theodore. 'Place-Realism in a Group of Caroline Plays', *R.E.S.* xviii (1942), 428–40.

Nason, Arthur Huntington. *James Shirley, Dramatist* (1915), pp. 227–30.

1632, 20 Apr. '*Hyde Park*, by James Shirley, licensed.' (Adams, *Herbert*, p. 34.)

1637, 13 Apr. S.R. Andrew Crooke and William Cooke entered for their copy 'vnder the hands of Tho: Herbert deputy to S^r. Hen: Herbert & M^r. Downes warden a Comedy called Hide Parke by Iames Shirley'. (Greg, *Bibliography*, i. 46.)

1637. Hide Parke A Comedie, As it was presented by her Majesties Servants, at the private house in *Drury* Lane. Written by *James Shirly* . . . 1637.

1639, 10 Aug. 'Hide parke' is included in a list of plays protected by the Lord Chamberlain for the King and Queen's Young Company at the Cockpit. (See above, i. 330–1.)

1668, 11 July. '. . . to the King's playhouse, to see an old play of Shirly's, called 'Hide Park;' the first day acted; where horses are brought upon the stage: but it is a very moderate play, only an excellent epilogue spoke by Beck Marshall.' (Diary of Samuel Pepys.)

1668, 14 July. In a warrant for plays presented before royalty at court or at the Theatre Royal appears the entry: 'July 14 Hide Parke at the Theatre . . . [£]10.' (Nicoll, *A History of Restoration Drama*, 3rd ed., pp. 305–6.)

Hyde Park probably had its opening performance by Queen Henrietta's men at the Phoenix about the time of the licence by Sir Henry Herbert, 20 April 1632, and this opening may well have been planned to coincide with the annual opening of the park. Dr. Theodore Miles showed (ed. cit., pp. xxi–xxii) that the park was normally open in the spring and summer months, and he cites allusions to 'Hyde Park time'. References in the third and fourth acts of the play to the spring and to the first appearance of the nightingale would be appropriate for an April opening, and Miles shows very clearly the pains Shirley has taken to present an accurate picture of the park and its activities. (Ibid., pp. xiv–xxxiii.) He has demonstrated that *Hyde Park* belonged to a small group of Caroline plays which exploited London place-realism in the theatre. (*R.E.S.*, loc. cit.)

No source for the plot has been noted, but characters, incidents, and attitudes are reminiscent of numerous earlier plays. (See Forsythe, loc. cit.) It is not likely that Shirley consulted the printed texts, but he was no doubt consciously manipulating familiar theatrical types and situations.

The quarto is dedicated to Henry Rich, first Earl of Holland. The Earl, as Miles noted, was Keeper of the Crown land of Hyde Park, and it is probably to this fact that Shirley refers in his opening sentence:

> THis Comedy in the title, is a part of your Lordships Command, which heretofore grac'd, and made happy by your smile, when it was presented, after a long silence, upon first opening of the Parke, is come abroad to kisse your Lordships hand.

The second half of the sentence is ambiguous, since it could refer either to the printing or to the performance of the play. The 'long silence' reference probably alludes to a plague-closing, and the plague of 1636–7 would be more apt for a publication reference of 1637 than the plague-closing of 1630 for a performance reference of 1632. (See above, ii. 657–8 and 661–5.) The phrase, 'upon first opening of the Parke', refers to a seasonal opening, which Miles found was about April, but since the play was licensed for performance in April 1632, and for printing in April 1637, the ambiguity persists. (See Miles edition, pp. 81–84.)

In his introduction Dr. Miles shows very clearly the position of Hyde Park in the developing comedy of manners, and it was perhaps the very niceness of the allusions to Cavalier London society which discouraged later revivals of the play, though Pepys notes the attempt of the King's players to add a new theatrical feature by bringing horses on the stage. In 1693 George Powell incorporated three scenes from Hyde Park and a number of its character names in his A Very Good Wife. Powell also lifted scenes from Middleton's No Wit No Help like a Woman's and from Brome's City Wit and his Court Beggar for his play. (Ibid., pp. 70–71.)

Shirley reprinted Venture's song in Act IV (G_2–G_2^{v}) in his Poems &c., 1646, under the title, 'A Song in a Play called Hide-Parke'.

Imposture (Impostor) (1640)

Forsythe, Robert Stanley. The Relations of Shirley's Plays to the Elizabethan Drama (1914), pp. 240–8.

Nason, Arthur Huntington. James Shirley, Dramatist (1915), pp. 330–5.

Schipper, Jakob. *James Shirley: sein Leben und seine Werke* (1911), pp. 260–71.

1640, 10 Nov. '*The Impostor*, by James Shirley, licensed.' (Adams, *Herbert*, p. 39.)

1641, 7 Aug. 'The Imposture' is found in a list of King's men's plays which the Lord Chamberlain forbade the printers to publish without the consent of the company. (See above, i. 65–66.)

1646, [4] Sept. S.R. Humphrey Moseley and Humphrey Robinson entered as their copies a long list of plays, all apparently from the repertory of the King's company. Included is 'Imposture . . . by Mr Shirley'. (Greg, *Bibliography*, i. 56–57.)

1652. The Impostvre A Tragi-Comedie, *As* It was Acted at the private House In *Black Fryers*. Written By James Shirley. *Never Printed before* . . . 1652. (Separate title-page in *Six New Playes*, 1653.)

1662[–3?]. In Edward Browne's accounts for plays seen in '1662' under the heading, 'At the New Theatre in Lincolnes Jnne fields' is the entry, 'Jmposture . . . 1 6'. (W. W. Greg, 'Theatrical Repertories of 1662', *Gentleman's Magazine*, ccci [1906], 69–72; from B.M. MS. Sloane 1900.)

1668/9, *c.* 12 Jan. In 'A Catalogue of part of His Mates Servants Playes as they were formerly acted at the Blackfryers & now allowed of to his Mates Servants at ye New Theatre' occurs the title, 'The Impostor'. (Allardyce Nicoll, *A History of Restoration Drama*, 3rd ed., pp. 315–16.)

1672/3, 30 Jan. S.R. In a long list of plays transferred from Humphrey Robinson, executor of Humphrey Robinson, to John Martin and Henry Herringman is '[87] Imposture. halfe'. (Greg, *Bibliography*, i. 72.)

1683, 21 Aug. S.R. In a long list of plays transferred from Sarah Martin, executrix of John Martin, to Robert Scott is the title '[94] Imposture', in which one-fourth interest was transferred. (Ibid., p. 75.)

The Imposture is the second play that Shirley prepared for the King's company at Blackfriars after his return from Ireland; he himself refers to the recency of his return in the prologue:

> He [*our poet*] *has been stranger long to' th' English scene,*
> *Knowes not the mode, nor how with artfull pen*
> *To charm your airy soules.*

He also says in the dedication to Sir Robert Bolles that the play was successful in the theatre, and, in his own estimation, one of his best:

> Sir, this Poem, I may with modesty affirm, had a fair reception, when [it] was personated on the stage, and may march in the first rank of my own compositions.

Forsythe (loc. cit.) found no comprehensive source for the play, but pointed out that Shirley has used elements from his earlier plays, particularly *The Maid's Revenge* and *The Royal Master*. He also notices analogues to numerous earlier plays.

The male chorus sung before the Duke in the first act ($B_3{}^v$–B_4) was printed by Shirley in his *Poems &c.*, 1646, under the title 'Io'.

The Irish Gentleman
(Lost)

Shirley wrote the prologue, not the play. See Anon.

The Lady of Pleasure (1635)

Forsythe, Robert Stanley. *The Relations of Shirley's Plays to the Elizabethan Drama* (1914), pp. 371–9.

Nason, Arthur Huntington. *James Shirley, Dramatist* (1915), pp. 276–80.

Schipper, Jakob. *James Shirley: sein Leben und seine Werke* (1911), pp. 167–77.

1635, 15 Oct. '*The Lady of Pleasure*, by James Shirley, licensed.' (Adams, *Herbert*, p. 37.)

1635, 5 or 6 Nov. '. . . being thursday, my sister Margaret was married to Edward Bysshe. . . . Wee are all ther the 2 days dinner and supper, all the batchelors (?), wee were at a play, some at cockpit, some at blackfriers. The play at cockpit was Lady of pleasure, at blackfriers the conspiracy.' (E. M. Symonds, 'The Diary of John Greene [1635–57]', *English Historical Review*, xliii [1928], 389.)

1635, 8 Dec. 'To the playe Called the La: of pleasure . . . oo–oi–oo.' '. . . dined wth Rob: Dowgill wente to the La: of pleasure & sawe that rare playe came home late Supped.' (Diary and accounts of Sir Humphrey Mildmay. See above, ii. 677.)

1637, 13 Apr. S.R. Andrew Crooke and William Cooke entered for their copies 'vnder the hands of Tho: Herbert Deputy to S^r. Hen: Herbert & M^r. Downes warden two Playes called. The

Lady of pleasure. & The young Admirall. by Iames Shirley'. (Greg, *Bibliography*, i. 46.)

1637. The Lady Of Pleasvre. A Comedie, As it was Acted by her Majesties Servants, at the private House in *Drury* Lane. Written by *James Shirly* . . . 1637.

1639, 10 Aug. Included in a list of plays belonging to the King and Queen's Young Company at the Cockpit and protected against other companies by the Lord Chamberlain is 'The Lady of pleasure'. (See above, i. 330–1.)

The Lady of Pleasure was Shirley's autumn play for 1635 after his spring play, *The Coronation*, which was licensed 6 February 1634/5; probably the piece was composed between February and October 1635, and opened at the Cockpit about the time of Sir Henry's licence. Though one is tempted to cite the two exceedingly rare records of witnesses of performances of the play in its first six or seven weeks of existence as evidence of its great popularity, the very rarity of such records of visits to the theatres makes them statistically unreliable; their preservation is pure chance. On the other hand, Sir Humphrey Mildmay is, for him, uniquely enthusiastic about the play. In ten years he records attendance at sixty-one plays and masques, but he mentions only twelve by name; *The Lady of Pleasure* is the only play in the ten years which he both names and praises. (See above, ii. 680–1.) Shirley himself said that the play was successful and ranked it among his best in his dedication of the quarto to Lord Lovelace of Hurley in 1637:

> *This Comedy fortunate in the Scene, and one that may challenge a place in the first forme of the Authors compositions. . . .*

The title, though catchy, seems a trifle odd for the play. There is evidence that the phrase was normally used in the time to mean 'prostitute'. In Nabbes's *Microcosmus*, acted at the rival Salisbury Court two years after Shirley's play, there is the following exchange:

Consc[ience]. What are you?

Sens[uality]. A desperate piece of neglected mortality, that have been a Lady of pleasure, and kept an open house where Lords tooke me up at high rates, 'till my bare commons would no longer serve their high feeding.

(Act v, Bullen ed., Works, ii. 212–13.)

John Collop's poem on lust is entitled, '*To a Lady of Pleasure*'. (John Collop, *Poesis Rediviva*, 1656, pp. 41–42.) And Poor Robin in 1681 predicts:

The Planet *Venus* is in her detriment, which shall cause the Suburb

Ladies of pleasure to make great lamentation for want of trading. ('Observations on September', *Poor Robin, 1681, An Almanack of the Old and New Fashion.*)

Now in Shirley's play Aretina is not chaste, but she is no prostitute; she is merely a lady unduly addicted to pleasure who reforms, like the rakes in several of Shirley's other plays. Why did Shirley give the play a title which apparently would have suggested to the audience that it was to see a piece about a prostitute?

No source for the play has been noticed, though Forsythe (op. cit.) calls attention to numerous analogues of the characters and situations in other plays.

At first glance it seems surprising that there are no recorded Restoration performances for this play, which seems to us perhaps the nearest Caroline approach to the Restoration comedy. At least eighteen other plays of Shirley's were performed on the Restoration stage, but not his best comedy of manners. Perhaps the conclusion was too moral and the suggested return to the country unthinkable, but such details are easily altered. The play was used by later dramatists. Langbaine noted that in Aphra Behn's *Lucky Chance,*

... the Incident of *Gayman's* enjoying the Lady *Fulbanck,* and taking her for the Devil, is copied from Mr. *Alexander Kickshaw* and the Lady *Aretina,* in the *Lady of Pleasure.* (*An Account of the English Dramatick Poets* [1691], p. 20.)

William Taverner's *The Artful Husband,* performed at Lincoln's Inn Fields Theatre in 1716/17 and published in 1717, is said to derive one of its plots from *The Lady of Pleasure,* and Charles Johnson's *The Masquerade,* acted at Drury Lane in 1718/19 and published in 1719, is said to be similarly indebted. (Allardyce Nicoll, *A History of Early Eighteenth Century Drama, 1700–1750* [1925], pp. 171 and 358; 156 and 339.)

Whether Richard Brinsley Sheridan studied *The Lady of Pleasure* while writing *The School for Scandal* I do not know, but the situation and dialogue of Sir Peter and Lady Teazle in his play are so similar to those of Sir Thomas and Aretina as to leave only the question, At how many removes from Shirley do they stand?

John Cotgrave used eight quotations from *The Lady of Pleasure* in his collection in 1655. (See G. E. Bentley, ' John Cotgrave's *English Treasury of Wit and Language* and the Elizabethan Drama', *Stud. Phil.* xl [1943], 186–203.)

Though this comedy was printed only once in its own century, it has been a favourite with modern anthologists.

Look to the Lady (?)
(Lost)

Forsythe, Robert Stanley. *The Relations of Shirley's Plays to the Elizabethan Drama* (1914), pp. 379 and 419–29.

Harbage, Alfred. 'The Authorship of the Dramatic *Arcadia*', *Modern Philology*, xxxv (1938), 235–6.

c. 1619–20? The title 'Looke to the Ladye' appears in a list of plays on waste paper of the Revels Office, probably dating about 1619 or 1620. It has been plausibly suggested that the plays of the list were being considered for performance at court. (See Marcham, *Revels*, p. 15, and E. K. Chambers, *R.E.S.* i [1925], 482–4.)

1639/40, 11 Mar. S.R. John Williams and Francis Egglesfield entered for their copies 'two Comedies vizt. The Antiquarie. & Looke to the Ladie by Iames Shirley   xij^d. [*altered from* vj^d.] (Greg, *Bibliography*, i. 52.)

So long as only the Stationers' Register entry of *Look to the Lady* was known, the title was easily accepted as that of a lost Shirley play or an alternative title for an extant play, and numerous attempts have been made to attach it to various comedies now known under other titles. Frank Marcham's publication of the Revels list, however, altered the situation, for that list certainly antedates 1622 and probably belongs to 1619 or 1620, several years before Shirley's first acted play, *Love Tricks, or The School of Compliment*. The *Look to the Lady* of Marcham's list cannot have been unacted, since the plays were apparently proposed for court performance. We are left with two alternatives: either there were two plays called *Look to the Lady*, one in existence in 1619–20 and not by Shirley, and a second written by Shirley some time before March 1639/40; or, alternatively, there was only one play with this title and it was misattributed to Shirley by Williams and Egglesfield. Harbage (op. cit.) argues for the second alternative, but it seems to me that no reasonable choice is possible without further evidence. I find nothing to recommend Forsythe's random conjecture (loc. cit.) that *Look to the Lady* may be the same as *Captain Underwit*.

Love in a Maze

See Shirley, *The Changes*.

Love's Cruelty (1631)

Edition: *James Shirley's Love's Cruelty, edited from the Quarto of 1640 with an Introduction and Notes*, by John Frederick Nims. Unpublished University of Chicago Thesis, 1945.

Bradbrook, M. C. *Themes and Conventions of Elizabethan Tragedy* (1935), pp. 262–4.

Forsythe, Robert Stanley. *The Relations of Shirley's Plays to the Elizabethan Drama* (1914), pp. 164–73.

Nason, Arthur Huntington. *James Shirley, Dramatist* (1915), pp. 224–6.

1631, 14 Nov. '*Love's Cruelty*, by James Shirley, licensed.' (Adams, *Herbert*, p. 33.)

1639, 25 Apr. S.R. Andrew Crooke and William Cooke entered for their copies 'these five playes vidlt Night walters [*sic*], Oportunity. Loues Cruellty, The Coronation witt without money.' (Greg, *Bibliography*, i. 50.)

1639, 10 Aug. Included in the list of plays protected by the Lord Chamberlain for William Beeston and the King and Queen's Young Company against all other companies is 'Loues cruelty'. (See above, i. 330–1.)

1639, 29 Nov. S.R. John Williams and Francis Egglesfield entered as their copies 'Two Playes vizt. A Pastorall called The Arcadia. & a Tragedy called Loues Crueltie. by Iames Shirley xij^d. [*altered from* vj^d] [*in margin* Loues Crueltie is Entered before to m^r Crooke]'. (Greg, *Bibliography*, i. 52.)

1640. Loves Crveltie. A Tragedy, As it was presented by her Majesties Servants, at the private House in *Drury* Lane. Written by *James Shirley* Gent. . . . Printed by *Tho. Cotes*, for *Andrew Crooke*. 1640.

c. 1660. 'Loves Cruelty' is found in a list of the stock plays of Killigrew's company furnished to Sir Henry Herbert, probably shortly after the Restoration, and found among his papers by Malone. (Adams, *Herbert*, p. 82.)

1660, 15 Nov. In a list of performances of plays by 'the Kings Companie at the Red Bull and the new house in Gibbon's Tennis Court near Clare Market', 1660–2, appears the entry, 'Thursday the 15. No. Loues Cruelty'. (Ibid., p. 116.)

1661/2, 6 Feb. Two young Dutchmen visiting London record that they saw on this date a play they called 'Love's Crueality'. (Ethel Seaton, *Literary Relations of England and Scandinavia in the Seventeenth Century* [1935], p. 333.)

1667, 30 Dec. 'Thence with Sir Philip Carteret to the King's play-house, there to see 'Love's Cruelty,' an old play but which I have not seen before. .... So I went out presently, and by coach home. .... I took coach again, and to the King's playhouse again, and come in the fourth act; and it proves to me a very silly play, and to everybody else, as far as I could judge.' (Diary of Samuel Pepys.)

1668, 14 Apr. 'Thence to a play, Love's Cruelty.' (Ibid.)

Three plays of Shirley's were licensed for production in 1631: *The Traitor*, *The Duke or The Humorous Courtier*, and *Love's Cruelty*. The first two were probably prepared in 1630, when the theatres were closed for seven months because of plague (see above, ii. 657–8) and when Sir Henry Herbert is not known to have licensed any plays for production. Since *Love's Cruelty* was the November play, it was probably not a 1630 composition, but the work of the months following the licensing of *The Duke* on 17 May 1631; it was presumably produced at the Phoenix in Drury Lane very shortly after Sir Henry licensed it.

Langbaine said of *Love's Cruelty* that:

The Concealment of *Hyppolito*, and *Chariana*'s [sic] Adultery from her Servant by her Husband *Bellamente*'s Contrivance, is borrow'd from Queen *Margaret*'s Novels, Day 4. Nov 6. The like Story is related in *Cynthio*'s *Heccatomithi, Dec. terza, Novella sesta.*' (*An Account of the English Dramatick Poets* [1691], pp. 480–1.)

Forsythe (op. cit., pp. 164–6) agreed about this particular incident, but asserted that 'the general source' of the tragedy was Heywood's *A Woman Killed with Kindness*. After a careful analysis of all three stories, John Frederick Nims concludes (op. cit., pp. xviii–xx) that the concealment scene is probably based on some version of a story from the *Heptameron*, perhaps from Painter's *Palace of Pleasure*. Nims finds Forsythe's estimate of the influence of *A Woman Killed with Kindness* greatly exaggerated, but sees some influence of Heywood's play on the climactic scene of *Love's Cruelty*. Certain typical attitudes and situations in the love plays of John Ford—a fellow dramatist for Queen Henrietta's company —seem also, according to Nims, to have influenced Shirley in writing this play.

The double entry of *Love's Cruelty* in the Stationers' Register, first to Crooke and Cooke and seven months later to Williams and Egglesfield, has excited various comments, mostly castigations of alleged villains who attempted to victimize poor Shirley during his absence in Ireland, and some have attempted to build up the dishonesty of the firm of Williams and Egglesfield (e.g. Alfred Harbage, 'The Authorship of the Dramatic *Arcadia*', *Mod. Phil.* xxxv [1938], 233–7). Such interpretations ignore the fact that players had better rights to acted plays than playwrights had, and that the theatrical situation of 1637–9 is most likely to have led to the double entry of *Love's Cruelty* in 1639, as Nims points out. (Op. cit., pp. xx–xxvii.) The title-page shows that Queen Henrietta's company had acted the play at the Phoenix, but by 1639 the Queen's men had left the Phoenix, and ownership of the play was vested in Beeston for the King and Queen's Young Company, as the list of 1639 shows. The most likely explanation of the double entry is that Beeston or Shirley gave the play to Cooke and Crooke, and the Queen's men, now at the Salisbury Court theatre, gave it to Williams and Egglesfield. It is almost certain that there were difficulties about their old repertory between the reorganized Queen Henrietta's company at the Salisbury Court and the new King and Queen's Young Company, which kept most of that repertory at the Phoenix. (See above, i. 54–55, 236–41, and 330–1.)

Cornet George Porter and Mr. Charles Porter, to whom the quarto is dedicated by '*W. A.*', were the first and second sons of Endymion Porter. Nims has collected a certain amount of information about them. (Op. cit., pp. 69–76.) The W. A. who signed the dedication may have been the actor William Allen (see above, ii. 344–6), who had long been a member of Queen Henrietta's company and may have been associated with Shirley in Ireland. (See Allan H. Stevenson, 'James Shirley and the Actors at the First Irish Theater', *Mod. Phil.* xl [1942], 151 and 157.) Nims notes (op. cit., p. 79) that Glapthorne's dedication of *The Hollander* (published 1640) to Sir Thomas Fisher seems to have lifted the opening and closing lines of this dedication.

In his detailed investigation of the text of the play John Frederick Nims found (op. cit., pp. xxxix–xli) some evidence that the cast had once included a brother of Eubella, who is satirically described and who may have been the second prisoner indicated by the use of plurals on $F_1{}^v$ and $G_2{}^v$. He suggested the possibility that a character may have been cut out because he was too pointedly satirical, but the greater probability is that the presumed cut indicates simply a casting difficulty.

In Act II Hippolito describes the pleasures of the court, including:

a Maske is prepared, and Musicke to charme *Orpheus* himselfe into a stone, numbers presented to your eare that shall speake the soule of the immortall English *Ionson*, a scene to take your eye with wonder. (D₁.)

Fleay thought that the descriptive passage which follows these lines referred to Jonson's masques of 1630/1 called *Love's Triumph through Callipolis* and *Chloridia* (*Biog. Chron.* ii. 237), and it may well be that these unusually spectacular productions prompted Shirley, but most of the features that Hippolito enumerates occur in many masques. It is true, however, that Nims found nine of the thirteen features described by Hippolito in the two Jonson productions. (Op. cit., pp. 100–5.)

The number of Restoration performances is somewhat surprising in view of the modern neglect of *Love's Cruelty*. There are four quotations from the play in John Cotgrave's *English Treasury of Wit and Language*, 1655. (See G. E. Bentley, *Stud. Phil.* xl [1943], 198.)

Love's Victory

See Shirley, *The Doubtful Heir*.

Love Tricks

See Shirley, *The School of Compliment*.

Love Will Find Out the Way

See Shirley, *The Constant Maid*.

The Maid's Revenge (1625/6)

Edition: *James Shirley's The Maid's Revenge*, edited from the Quarto of 1639, with introduction and notes, by Albert Howard Carter. Unpublished University of Chicago Thesis, 1940.

Forsythe, Robert Stanley. *The Relations of Shirley's Plays to the Elizabethan Drama* (1914), pp. 136–47.
Nason, Arthur Huntington. *James Shirley, Dramatist* (1915), pp. 174–6.
Sloane, Eugene Hulse. *Robert Gould* (1940), pp. 99–105.
Stevenson, Allan H. 'Shirley's Dedications and the Date of His Return to England', *M.L.N.* lxi (1946), 79–83.

1625/6, 9 Feb. '*The Maid's Revenge*, by James Shirley, licensed.' (Adams, *Herbert*, p. 31.)
1639, 12 Apr. S.R. 'Will: Cooke' entered for his copy 'a play called The Maides Revenge. by Ia: Shirley'. (Greg, *Bibliography*, i. 50.)
1639, 10 Aug. 'the Maids reuenge' appears in a list of plays pro-

tected by the Lord Chamberlain for the King and Queen's Young
Company at the Cockpit. (See above, i. 330–1.)

1639. The Maides Revenge. A Tragedy. As it hath beene Acted
with good Applause at the private house in *Drury Lane*, by her
Majesties Servants. Written by Iames Shirley Gent. . . . 1639.

Sir Henry Herbert's licence gives the approximate date of first
production of the play at the Phoenix, and it was probably composed shortly before that date, though it could have been written
in 1625 and its production delayed by plague. In his dedication to
Henry Osborne, Shirley calls the play 'the second birth in this
kinde, which I dedicated to the Scene', which presumably means
that *The Maid's Revenge* was the second tragedy Shirley had
written. The first was probably the lost *Tragedy of St. Albans*
(q.v.). That *The Maid's Revenge* was successful in the theatre is
implied by Shirley's earlier statement in the dedication, 'It is a
Tragedy which received encouragement and grace on the *English
Stage*'; and by the presence of this title in the repertory list of the
Phoenix company in 1639, when the tragedy was thirteen years
old.

The source of *The Maid's Revenge*, as Langbaine noted (*An
Account of the English Dramatick Poets* [1691], p. 481), is the story
of Antonio and Berinthia printed as the seventh history in the
second book of John Reynolds's *The Triumphs of God's Revenge
against Murder*. The first book of Reynolds's collection was printed
in 1621 and the second in 1622, so that Shirley's source had been
available to him for only three years or so before *The Maid's
Revenge* was licensed. There is an excellent analysis of Reynolds's
story and Shirley's adaptation of it in Professor A. H. Carter's unpublished edition of the play. (Op. cit., pp. xxv–xxxv.)

It has frequently been said that Robert Gould's tragedy, *The
Rival Sisters, or The Violence of Love*, acted in October 1695 and
published in 1696 (see Nicoll, *A History of Restoration Drama*,
3rd ed., pp. 143, 364), is an adaptation of Shirley's *The Maid's
Revenge*. It does indeed set forth the same story, but R. S. Forsythe
suggested (op. cit., pp. 32–33) and Professor Carter has pretty well
demonstrated (op. cit., pp. 136–8) that everything in Gould's play
came from Shirley's source, *The Triumphs of God's Revenge against
Murder*, and there is no indication that Gould used *The Maid's
Revenge* at all.

The identity of the Henry Osborne to whom the quarto is dedicated is uncertain. Carter (op. cit., pp. 72–73) suggests, first, a
Henry Osborne, aged twenty-two in 1640, who married Alice

Lewis in that year, and second, the brother of Dorothy Osborne, the letter-writer, a man who was twenty in 1639. Stevenson (op. cit.) adds some material that tends to suggest the latter.

Carter says that *The Maid's Revenge* was reprinted in 1793 as a supplement to *The Thespian Magazine and Literary Repository*, but I do not find it.

The catalogue of Shirley's publications printed with *The Humorous Courtier* (q.v.) is found in copies of *The Maid's Revenge* quarto of 1639. There are minor variations, and *The Humorous Courtier* is omitted.

The Night Walker, or The Little Thief

Revised by Shirley; see John Fletcher.

No Wit No Help Like a Woman's

(Written by Thomas Middleton; revised by James Shirley?)

Since Shirley published in *Poems &c.*, 1646, a prologue that he wrote for a performance in Ireland of this play of Middleton's, there has been some disposition to say that our text of the play—which was not published until 1657—is one revised by Shirley. Since Middleton died in 1627, it is probable that someone else revised his play for the Dublin performance, which took place in 1638 according to the lines of Weatherwise in Act III (E$_7$):

> If I that have proceeded in five and twenty such Books of Astronomy, should not be able to put down a Schollar now in One thousand six hundred thirty and eight, the Dominical Letter being G, I stood for a Goose.

Shirley says of himself in his prologue, 'two yeare / He has liv'd in *Dublin*', and since 1636 is the probable date of his abandonment of London for Dublin, it seems likely enough that he did revise Middleton's play for a Dublin performance in 1638 when he wrote the prologue. (See Allan H. Stevenson, 'Shirley's Years in Ireland', *R.E.S.* xx [1944], 19–22; and F. G. Fleay, *Anglia*, viii [1885], 408.)

I know of no attempt to determine the extent and character of Shirley's revisions.

The Opportunity (1634)

Anon. [Review of a performance of the play at the University of Illinois], *Nation*, lxxxii (1906), 491.

Elson, John James, ed. *The Wits or Sport upon Sport* (1932), pp. 90–97 and 373–4.

Forsythe, Robert Stanley. *The Relations of Shirley's Plays to the Elizabethan Drama* (1914), pp. 297–304.

Nason, Arthur Huntington. *James Shirley, Dramatist* (1915), pp. 263–70.

Schipper, Jakob. *James Shirley: sein Leben und seine Werke* (1911), pp. 147–59.

Stevenson, Allan H. 'Shirley's Publishers: The Partnership of Crooke and Cooke', *Library*, Fourth Series, xxv (1944–45), 140–61.

—— 'Shirley's Years in Ireland', *R.E.S.* xx (1944), 22–28.

Stiefel, Arthur Ludwig. 'Die Nachahmung spanischer Komödien in England unter den ersten Stuarts', *Romanische Forschungen*, v (1890), 193–220.

1634, 29 Nov. '*The Opportunity*, by James Shirley, licensed.' (Adams, *Herbert*, p. 36.)

1639, 25 Apr. S.R. Andrew Crooke and William Cooke entered for their copies 'these five playes vidlt Night walters [*sic*], Oportunity. Loues Cruellty, The Coronation witt without money. ij^s vj^d.' (Greg, *Bibliography*, i. 50.)

1639, 10 Aug. Included in a list of plays protected against other companies by the Lord Chamberlain for the King and Queen's Young Company at the Cockpit is 'The oportunity'. (See above, i. 330–1.)

1640. The Opportvnitie   A Comedy, As it was presented by her Majesties Servants, at the private House in *Drury* Lane. Written by Iames Shirley ... 1640. (One of the two other variant imprints reads, 'Printed for *Andrew Crooke*, and are to be sold at the Castle Gate in *Dublin*. 1640'. See Greg, *Bibliography*, ii. 713.)

1660, 26 Nov. In a list of performances of plays by 'the Kings Companie at the Red Bull and the new house in Gibbon's Tennis Court near Clare Market', 1660–2, appears the entry: 'Monday the 26. No. [1660] The Opertunity'. (Adams, *Herbert*, p. 117.)

1662[–3?]. Edward Browne's 'Memorandum Book, 1662' contains a list of plays and sums which presumably represent plays which Browne saw and the amounts he paid for seats. Under the heading, 'At the Cock Pit in Drewry Lane', he lists. 'The opportunity ... 2 0.' (W. W. Greg, 'Theatrical Repertories of 1662', *Gentleman's Magazine*, ccci [1906], 69–72, from B.M. MS. Sloane 1900.)

<1663. John Downes lists 'The Opportunity' as one of the plays

acted by the King's company after the opening of the new
Drury Lane theatre in 1663. (*Roscius Anglicanus*, ed. Summers,
p. 8.)

The Opportunity was Shirley's autumn play for the Queen's
men at the Cockpit, following *The Example*, which was licensed
the previous June. It was probably first acted about the time of
Sir Henry's licence and largely composed in the five months
following the allowance of *The Example*.

Shirley's source for *The Opportunity* was Tirso de Molina's
El Castigo del penséque. Stiefel (op. cit.) noticed the indebtedness,
and he and Forsythe (loc. cit.) have worked out in some detail
Shirley's use of the Spanish play; Forsythe also notes the usual
analogues to other English plays.

The quarto was dedicated by Shirley to Captain Richard Owen,
whom Dr. Allan H. Stevenson ('Shirley's Years in Ireland') has
identified as a sea captain who, during Shirley's years in Ireland,
commanded the *Ninth Whelp* in the Irish seas and with whom
Shirley returned to England, probably about the middle of
April 1640. Shirley says in the dedication:

> THis Poeme, at my returne with you, from another Kingdome (wherein
> I enjoyd, as your imployments would permit, the happinesse of your
> knowledge, and conversation) emergent from the Presse, and prepar'd to
> seeke entertainment abroad, I tooke boldnesse thus farre to direct to your
> name and acceptance. . . .

The publication of Shirley's plays while he was in Ireland, far
from being the crass betrayal of an absent poet by his publisher—
as has been frequently postulated—has been analysed by Stevenson ('Shirley's Publishers') as more probably the result of a
publishing agreement with Cooke and Crooke, who jointly or
separately published sixteen of Shirley's plays or revisions in the
four years of his absence, 1636–40. The dramatist's words in the
dedication of *The Opportunity*, '*emergent from the Presse*', do not
indicate surprise or annoyance, but simply coincidence. Stevenson also suggests that the existence of one issue of *The Opportunity* with the imprint 'to be sold at the Castle Gate in *Dublin.
1640*' implies that the play had been acted at the St. Werburgh
Street theatre in Dublin. (Ibid., p. 150.)

The play seems to have had some popularity in the first years
of the Restoration, and there is a somewhat unusual record of
one young playgoer's impression of it as it was given at the Red
Bull, probably by the King's company.

On the Fool in the Play

A Gentleman took his son along with him to the *Red Bull* Playhouse in *St. John-street* to see a Comedy, which was very well acted by *Pimponio* in the *Opportunity*: upon their return his father askt him whom amongst all those brave Fellows he most affected ? Truly, replied the Boy, I liked the Fool best, and could have wisht them all Fools for his sake, because he made the most mirth. ([Archibald Armstrong] *A Choice Banquet of Witty Jests, Rare Fancies and Pleasant Novels* [1660], No. 339, p. 110.)

Perhaps a similar appeal led to the making from *The Opportunity* of the jig called *A Prince in Conceit* (see Elson, loc. cit.), which consists mostly of the adventures of Pimponio.

The Opportunity seems to have been in the repertory of some of the English actors playing in Germany in the early seventeenth century. (Lawrence Marsden Price, *The Reception of English Literature in Germany* [1932], pp. 9–16.)

The Patron of Ireland

See *St. Patrick for Ireland.*

The Politic Father

Original title for *The Brothers* [of 1641] (q.v.).

The Politician (c. 1639?)

Edition: *James Shirley's The Polititian*, edited by Edward Huberman. Unpublished Duke University Thesis, 1934.

Forsythe, Robert Stanley. *The Relations of Shirley's Plays to the Elizabethan Drama* (1914), pp. 173–85.

Harbage, Alfred. *Thomas Killigrew, Cavalier Dramatist, 1612–83* (1930), pp. 193 ff.

Huberman, Edward. 'Bibliographical Note on James Shirley's *The Polititian*', *Library*, Fourth Series, xviii (1937), 104–8.

Nason, Arthur Huntington. *James Shirley, Dramatist* (1915), pp. 47–54 and 307–12.

Schipper, Jakob. *James Shirley: sein Leben und seine Werke* (1911), pp. 242–51.

1653, 9 Sept. S.R. Humphrey Moseley entered as his copies a long list of plays, including 'The Polititian, by Iames Shirley'. (Greg, *Bibliography*, i. 60–61.)

1655. The Polititian, A Tragedy, Presented at *Salisbury* Court
By Her *Majesties Servants*; Written By James Shirley . . . 1655.
1655. [Another issue from the same setting of type, but quarto
instead of octavo. See Greg, *Bibliography*, ii. 856–7 and 861,
and Huberman, op. cit.]

The Politician is one of the few Shirley plays about which there
is uncertainty as to date. No licence for a play of this name is to
be found in the extracts from the manuscript of Sir Henry
Herbert's office-book made by Malone and Chalmers. Dyce and
Forsythe (op. cit., pp. 173–7) contended that the play was to be
identified with the piece licensed by Sir Henry 26 May 1641 as
The Politic Father. Fleay (*Biog. Chron.* ii. 242–3) and Nason (op.
cit., pp. 47–54), however, have demolished their arguments and
made what seems to me a convincing case that the play licensed
as *The Politic Father* is the same as that published as *The Brothers*
(q.v.) in *Six New Playes*, 1653. *The Politician*, then, is one of the
few Shirley plays for which we have no performance licence under
any title.

The only suggestions as to the date of *The Politician* are to be
derived from its relation to *The Gentleman of Venice*. The two
plays were issued at the same time by Humphrey Moseley, both
plays in both quarto and octavo formats, and the two octavo
editions are frequently found bound together, sometimes with a
portrait, but no joint title-page. (See Huberman, *Library*, loc.
cit., and Greg, *Bibliography*, ii. 856–7.) Both plays have title-pages
saying that they were acted by the Queen's men at the Salisbury
Court, both have unusual descriptions of the characters, those
for *The Politician* headed 'The names and small Characters of the
Persons', and those for *The Gentleman of Venice* headed 'The
names with some small Characters of the Persons', and both have
dedications signed by Shirley. Now all these similarities may
indicate simply that Moseley with Shirley's help worked up the
similarities to make a little volume more or less uniform with
Shirley's *Six New Playes*, which Moseley had issued two years
before. But presumably Shirley approved the statements about
acting company and theatre on the two title-pages, and this information is enough to offer some slight indication that the two
were written at about the same time for the same company.
Herbert licensed *The Gentleman of Venice* on 30 October 1639,
and it is possible that Shirley sent *The Politician* back from
Ireland for the Queen's company at about the same time; whether
or not it had been produced at the St. Werburgh Street theatre in

Dublin, there is no evidence. This weak case for the date of the play receives a little feeble support from the apparent reference to it in the proeme to Nabbes's *Unfortunate Mother*, which was never acted, but was entered in the Stationers' Register in 1639, perhaps shortly after rejection by the actors.

Langbaine suggested the source in his discussion of the play: 'A story resembling this, I have read in the first Book of the Countess of *Montgomery's Urania*, concerning the King of *Romania*, the Prince *Antissius*, and his Mother-in-Law.' (*An Account of the English Dramatick Poets* [1691], p. 481.) Huberman (ed. cit., pp. 2–15) develops the suggestion and makes Shirley's indebtedness fairly clear. His further proposal of Shirley's use of Sidney's *Arcadia*, Book II, chapter 15, is not so certain. Forsythe (loc. cit.) cites his usual analogues of situations and characters in other plays.

Thomas Killigrew used *The Politician* as a source for his play, *The Pilgrim*. (See Harbage, loc. cit.)

In his dedication of *The Politician* to 'WALTER MOYLE, Esq;' Shirley has some interesting remarks on the closing of the theatres, but nothing on this particular play or its performance.

Rosania

See *The Doubtful Heir*.

The Royal Master (1637)

MS.: The Players Club, New York. (Lost?)

Edition: Sir A. W. Ward, ed., in C. M. Gayley, ed., *Representative English Comedies*, iii (1914), 545–652.

Forsythe, Robert Stanley. *The Relations of Shirley's Plays to the Elizabethan Drama* (1914), pp. 205–13.

Nason, Arthur Huntington. *James Shirley, Dramatist* (1915), pp. 109–14 and 291–303.

Schipper, Jakob. *James Shirley: sein Leben und seine Werke* (1911), pp. 191–200.

Stevenson, Allan H. 'James Shirley and the Actors at the First Irish Theater', *Mod. Phil.* xl (1942), 147–60.

Stiefel, A. L. 'Die Nachahmung spanischer Komödien in England unter den ersten Stuarts', *Romanische Forschungen*, v (1890), 196, n. 1.

1637/8, 13 Mar. S.R. Andrew Crooke, John Crooke, and 'Rich: Searger' entered for their copy 'a Play called The Royall Master. by Ia: Shirley'. (Greg, *Bibliography*, i. 47.)

1638, 23 Apr. '*The Royal Master*, by James Shirley, licensed.' (Adams, *Herbert*, p. 37.)

1638. The Royall Master; As it was Acted in the new Theater in *Dublin*: And Before the Right Honorable the Lord Deputie of *Ireland*, in the Castle. Written by Iames Shirley . . . 1638. (A variant has the imprint 'and are to be sold by *Thomas Allot* and *Edmond Crooke*, neare the Castle in *Dublin*. 1638'. See Greg, *Bibliography*, ii. 676.)

There are several things about the quarto of this play, with its publication in both London and Dublin, its ten sets of commendatory verses apparently all by residents of Dublin, its epilogue 'As it was spoken to the Lord Deputie on Newyeares-day at night, by way of vote, congratulating the New yeare'—which indicate that there must have been something unusual about the production. Dr. Allan H. Stevenson (op. cit., p. 147, n. 3) has made the very apt suggestion that it was the play used for the opening of the new St. Werburgh Street theatre in Dublin, in 1637. The precise date of the opening of this theatre is unknown, but Stevenson thinks it was about Michaelmas 1637. (Ibid., n. 1.) Sir Henry Herbert's licence for an unknown London production evidently followed the Irish performance, since the publishers had already entered their manuscript in the Stationers' Register before Sir Henry allowed it for performance.

Shirley wrote the dedication of the play to the Earl of Kildare when he himself was on the eve of a trip back to England and before the play had been acted:

. . . since my Affaires in *England* hasten my departure, and prevent my personall attendance, that something of me may be honourd to waite upon you in my absence, this Poeme; tis new, and never yet personated, but expected with the first, when the English Stage shall bee recovered from her long silence, and her now languishing scene changed into a welcome returne of wits and men.

Yet the commendatory verses of James Mervyn, T. I., W. Markham, and John Ogilby all show that the play had been performed when they wrote, and the verses of Dru. Cooper and W. Markham speak of Ben Jonson as recently dead. (Jonson was buried in Westminster Abbey 9 August 1637.) It seems, therefore, that Shirley wrote the dedication before his trip to England in the spring of 1637 (see Stevenson, op. cit., p. 151, and *Library*,

Fourth Series, xxv [1944–5], 153–5), but that the verses were written after the play had been successfully performed at 'the new Theater in *Dublin*' and after the news of Jonson's death was widely known there, presumably during the autumn or winter of 1637. The performance before the Lord Deputy in the Castle that is noted on the title-page was evidently the one for which Shirley wrote the epilogue cited above, and the New Year's Day mentioned there must, therefore, have been New Year's Day, 1637/8.

The lost manuscript of *The Royal Master* appears to have come from this performance. This manuscript is noted in a cutting in the extra-illustrated copy of George Alfred Townsend's *The Life, Crime and Capture of John Wilkes Booth*, now in the Theatre Collection at Harvard and called to my attention by William van Lennep, curator of the collection. The clipping in question comes from a periodical of about 1894 or 1895 that I was unable to identify. The article is written by John Malone and is entitled 'The House of the Players'; it recounts the founding of the Players Club in New York and describes their club house. The description of the library contains the statement:

> The library shelves are well filled with rare books of Shakespeareana, and the history of the drama and its actors. Besides the books, the library contains, carefully preserved in chests and cabinets, thousands of old play-bills, engravings of actors, and manuscripts of absorbing interest to students of the drama. I found there one day a part of a prompt-book of Shirley's 'Royal Master', containing in contemporary handwriting the names of the actors in the play as it was performed in Dublin Castle, before the Lord Deputy of Ireland, Strafford, Earl of Wentworth, by the players of his Master of the Revels, John Ogilby, on 'New Year's Day at Night' 1635.

Nothing is known of this manuscript at the Players Club now. With the kind permission of The Players I spent three days searching for it in their collection without success. The description of John Malone, who was long a member of the club and for years its secretary and librarian, is probably accurate, for no casual reader would have known about the performance before the Lord Deputy or that Ogilby was his Master of the Revels. The date 1635—which John Malone did not include in his quotation marks—is surely an inference, however, for Shirley did not go to Ireland until 1636.

The source of *The Royal Master* has been said to be the *Decameron*, x. 7, but Stiefel said (loc. cit.) that the play had a Spanish source, though, so far as I know, he never presented his evidence. Forsythe (loc. cit.) found the play peculiarly related to *The Great Duke of Florence* and *A Maidenhead Well Lost*, as well as analogous in various situations and characters to earlier plays.

Shirley printed the epilogue in his *Poems &c.*, 1646, under the title, '*To the never enough Honoured E. of St. on New-yeares day at night, after other entertainment*'. Gifford and Fleay thought that the prologue in this volume entitled 'A Prologue there to the *Irish Gent.*' was the prologue for *The Royal Master*, but Shirley distinguishes the prologues and epilogues for his own plays in this collection by placing them last and indicating in each title his authorship of the play. The prologue for *The Irish Gentleman* comes early in the group and has no indication of Shirley's authorship of the play.

The Tragedy of St. Albans (> 1625?)
(Lost)

Forsythe, Robert Stanley. *The Relations of Shirley's Plays to the Elizabethan Drama* (1914), pp. 150–2.
1639/40, 14 Feb. S.R. William Cooke entered for his copy 'a Play called The Tragedy of S^t. Albons by Mr Iames Shirley'. (Greg, *Bibliography*, i. 52.)

The only record of the play is the entry in the Stationers' Register. Forsythe notes (loc. cit.) that Shirley said in the dedication to *The Maid's Revenge*, licensed for production 9 February 1625/6 but not printed until 1639, '. . . though it come late to the Impression, it was the second birth in this kinde, which I dedicated to the Scene'. He suggests that Shirley's first 'birth in this kinde', i.e. tragedy, probably was *The Tragedy of St. Albans*, since no other known tragedy of Shirley's could have been 'dedicated to the Scene' before February 1625/6. This is plausible, and the title would seem to relate the piece to Shirley's years at St. Albans about 1617–24. Forsythe approves Nissen's speculation that the play concerned Alban, the first British martyr, and he postulates that it was a sort of miracle play influenced by *The Virgin Martyr*. However speculative these guesses may be, they are more probable than Fleay's (*Biog. Chron.* ii. 243–4) that the piece may have dealt with Bacon's career or that of Clanrickard, Earl of St. Albans. Shirley wrote a short poem on St. Alban. (See R. G. Howarth, *R.E.S.* ix [1933], 29.)

St. Patrick for Ireland (1639?)

Forsythe, Robert Stanley. *The Relations of Shirley's Plays to the Elizabethan Drama* (1914), pp. 220–31.

MacMullan, Hugh. 'The Sources of Shirley's *St. Patrick for Ireland*', *P.M.L.A.* xlviii (1933), 806–14.

Nason, Arthur Huntington. *James Shirley, Dramatist* (1915), pp. 313–14.

Schipper, Jakob. *James Shirley: sein Leben und seine Werke* (1911), pp. 205–13.

Stockwell, La Tourette. *Dublin Theatres and Theatre Customs (1637–1820)* (1938), pp. 12–17.

Wright, Louis B. 'Extraneous Song in Elizabethan Drama after the Advent of Shakespeare', *Stud. Phil.* xxiv (1927), 273.

1640, 28 Apr. S.R. R. Whitaker entered for his copies 'two Playes vizt. S^t. Patrick for Ireland. & The Constant Maide. by Iames Shirley'. (Greg, *Bibliography*, i. 53.)

1640. S^t. Patrick For Ireland. The first Part. Written by *James Shirley* . . . 1640.

In the canon of Shirley's generally sophisticated plays, *St. Patrick for Ireland* is conspicuous for its crudeness; it is more like a Red Bull play than like Shirley's characteristic pieces for the Cockpit and Blackfriars. The prologue suggests that the dramatist despaired of pleasing Irish taste:

> *WE know not what will take, your pallats are*
> *Various, and many of them sick I feare:*
>
> .   .   .   .   .
>
> *We should be very happy, if at last,*
> *We could find out the humour of your taste,*
> *That we might fit, and feast it. . . .*

Here he relies on subject-matter, songs, buffoonery, and raw spectacle, with what success we do not know. Shirley's intention to present further dramatization of the saint's legend is indicated by the phrase, 'The first Part', on the title-page, by the last lines of the prologue saying that the material on St. Patrick is too much for one play and that

> *if ye*
> *First welcome this, you'll grace our Poets art,*
> *And give him Courage for a second part,*

and by the epilogue statement,

Yet this is but a part of what our Muse
Intends, if the first birth you nobly use.

No second part is known.

St. Patrick was obviously written during Shirley's residence in Ireland, 1636–40, and the lines of the prologue indicated that he had had some experience of the Irish audience when he prepared it. W. R. Chetwood published this play first in his *A Select Collection of Old Plays*, 1750, with a separate title-page bearing the statement, 'First Acted By His MAJESTY's Company of Comedians in the Year 1639'. Though Chetwood is a most unreliable authority, the date fits such other information as we have.

Mr. Hugh MacMullan has shown (op. cit.) that Shirley probably took his material for the play from Jocelyn's account of St. Patrick as given by 'Fr. B. B.' in *The Life of the Glorious Bishop S. Patrick*, published at St. Omers in 1625. Other sources for the play given by Ward and Forsythe are dubious, including *Cymbeline*. The fact that modern critics are reminded of *Cymbeline* when they read scenes about men retired to caves is not evidence. A bit more likely as a source for the adventures of the magic bracelet is I. C.'s *The Two Merry Milkmaids*.

The School of Compliment, or Love Tricks (1624/5)

Baskervill, C. R. 'The Source of the Main Plot of Shirley's *Love Tricks*', *M.L.N.* xxiv (1909), 100–1.

Elson, John James, ed. *The Wits or Sport upon Sport* (1932), pp. 60–67 and 370–1.

Forsythe, Robert Stanley. *The Relations of Shirley's Plays to the Elizabethan Drama* (1914), pp. 117–36.

Greg, W. W. *Pastoral Poetry & Pastoral Drama* (1906), p. 408.

Hart, H. C. ' "The Captain" in Fletcher and Ben Jonson', *N. & Q.*, Tenth Series, ii (1904), 184–5.

Nason, Arthur Huntington. *James Shirley, Dramatist* (1915), pp. 170–4.

Schipper, Jakob. *James Shirley: sein Leben und seine Werke* (1911), pp. 11–22.

1624/5, 11 Feb. 'For the Cockpit Company; A new Play, called, *Love-Tricks with Compliments.*' (Adams, *Herbert*, p. 31.)

1624/5, 11 Feb. 'The Cock: comp: A new P. call. Love tricks with comp^{ts}. 11^{++}. Feb: 1624. 1^{li}.' (Folger Shakespeare Library, MS. Scrap-books of J. O. Halliwell-Phillipps, *Lowin*, p. 71.)

1630/1, 25 Feb. S.R. Francis Constable entered for his copy 'vnder the handes of Sr Henry Herbert and mr Kingston warden The Schoole of Compliment by Iames Shirley'. (Greg, *Bibliography*, i. 39.)

1631. The Schoole Of Complement. As It Was Acted by her Maiesties Seruants at the Priuate house in Drury Lane . . . By *J. S.* . . . 1631.

1637. The Schoole Of Complement. As It Was Acted by her Majesties Servants at the Private house in Drury Lane . . . By *I. S.* . . . 1637.

1639, 10 Aug. Included in a list of plays protected against other companies by the Lord Chamberlain for the King and Queen's Young Company is 'The schoole of complement'. (See above, i. 330–1.)

1666. 'The first new Play that was Acted in 1666, was: *The Tragedy of Cambyses* . . . . *After this the Company Reviv'd Three Comedies of* Mr. Sherly's, *viz. The Grateful Servant. The Witty Fair One. The School of Complements. The Woman's a Weather Cock.* These Plays being perfectly well Perform'd . . . prov'd as Beneficial to the Company, as several succeeding new Plays.' (John Downes, *Roscius Anglicanus*, Summers ed., p. 27.)

1667, 9 May. In a warrant for payment for plays given before royalty by the Duke's company is the entry: '[1667, May] 9. The Schoole of Complements at Court . . . 20.' (Nicoll, *A History of Restoration Drama*, 3rd ed., p. 308.)

1667. Love Tricks: Or, The School Of Complements; As it is now Acted by His Royal Highnesse The Duke of *York's* Servants At the Theatre In *Little Lincolns-Inne Fields*. By *J. S.* Licens'd *May* 24. 1667. Roger L'Estrange . . . 1667.

1667, 5 Aug. '. . . to the Duke of York's house, and there saw "Love Trickes, or the School of Compliments;" a silly play, only Miss [Davis's] dancing in a shepherd's clothes did please us mightily.' (Diary of Samuel Pepys.)

1667/8, 7 Jan. '. . . to the Nursery . . . but the house did not act to-day . . . therefore to the other two playhouses into the pit, to gaze up and down . . . and there did by this means, for nothing, see an act in 'The Schoole of Compliments' at the Duke of York's house, and 'Henry the Fourth' at the King's house; but, not . . . liking either of the plays, I took my coach again, and home.' (Ibid.)

1691. 'Of these [Shirley's plays] I have seen four since my Remembrance, two of which were acted at the King's House; and the other two presented at the Duke's Theatre, in Little

Lincolns-Inn Fields: *viz. Court Secret, Chan[g]es, Grateful Servant, School of Compliments*: with what success, I leave it to the Players now in being.' (Langbaine, *An Account of the English Dramatick Poets* [1691], p. 475.)

The approximate date of the first production is indicated by Sir Henry Herbert's allowance. The second version of this licence has been clipped from a transcript of Herbert's entries in a hand apparently of the nineteenth century—perhaps that of Craven Ord—and pasted into one of his scrap-books by Halliwell-Phillipps. It is an interesting confirmation of the transcripts of Malone and Chalmers and adds the fee which the company paid for the licence, the Master of the Revels' usual fee for allowing a new play at this time.

The company performing at the Cockpit or Phoenix theatre in Drury Lane at the time of this licence was the Lady Elizabeth's men (see above, i. 182–8), though their existence as a London company was soon ended by the great plague of 1625. (Ibid. and ii. 654–7.) Evidently their manager, Christopher Beeston, kept the manuscript of *The School of Compliment* in his theatre, and most of the performances of the play were given by the successors of the Lady Elizabeth's company, Queen Henrietta's men (see above, i. 218 ff.), whose name appears on the title-pages of the 1631 and 1637 editions.

The School of Compliment was the first of Shirley's plays to be produced, though not necessarily the first he wrote. The entire prologue is devoted to an apology for the new-fledged dramatist, and it includes the specific statement:

> . . . this Play is
> The first fruits of a Muse, that before this
> Neuer saluted Audience, nor doth meane,
> To sweare himselfe a Factor for the Scene.
> Though he employ some houres he onely prayes
> You take it as first borne. . . .
>
> .   .   .   .   .
>
> Accept then a beginning; all men know,
> He first kist bayes, that wore them on his brow.

Forsythe conjectured (op. cit., p. 117) that the miscellaneous and amateurish character of the play indicated that Shirley had written it while still at St. Albans. The conjecture is not an impossible one, but the precise date of Shirley's removal to London is uncertain, and he may have been in town long enough to write the play before the date of its allowance. Baskervill (loc. cit.)

showed that the source of the Selina–Infortunio–Rufaldo plot was Barnabe Rich's *Riche his farewell to militarie profession,* first published in 1581. Forsythe (loc. cit.) points out numerous analogues to the situations and characters; the newspaper satire of the opening scene is very similar to that in Jonson's *Staple of News* (q.v.) and Fletcher's *Fair Maid of the Inn* (q.v.). Evidently the burlesque in the third act which Shirley called the 'Complement-Schoole' proved popular, for though Herbert licensed the play by the more inclusive title, *Love Tricks,* and Shirley used the same title in the epilogue, it was known as *The School of Compliment* by the time of the Stationers' Register entry in February 1630/1, and this latter title is used on both early quartos and in the Cockpit repertory list of 1639.

From Shirley's scenes about the comic Welshman, a droll called *Jenkins Love-Course, and Perambulation* was made and published in *The Wits.* (See Elson, loc. cit.)

Edward Rimbault in his edition of Purcell's *Bonduca* (p. 11) says that music for this play of Shirley's was written by Thomas Brewer and that 'some of the music is preserved in Playford's various collections'. Presumably this music was written for one of the Restoration performances.

The three editions of Shirley's first acted play and the records of Restoration performances are indications of its rather surprising popularity.

The Sisters (1642)

Forsythe, Robert Stanley. *The Relations of Shirley's Plays to the Elizabethan Drama* (1914), pp. 313–21.

Nason, Arthur Huntington. *James Shirley, Dramatist* (1915), pp. 362–72.

Schipper, Jakob. *James Shirley: sein Leben und seine Werke* (1911), pp. 271–80.

Summers, Montague. 'A Restoration Prompt-Book', *T.L.S.,* 24 June 1920, p. 400; reprinted in the author's *Essays in Petto* [1928?], pp. 103–10.

1642, 26 Apr. '*The Sisters,* by James Shirley, licensed.' (Adams, *Herbert,* p. 39.)

1646, [4] Sept. S.R. Humphrey Moseley and Humphrey Robinson entered as their copies a long list of plays, all apparently from the repertory of the King's company. Included is: 'The Sisters ... by Mr Shirley.' (Greg, *Bibliography,* i. 56–57.)

1652. The Sisters, A Comedie, As It was acted at the private

House In *Black Fryers*, Written By James Shirley. *Never Printed before . . .* 1652. (Separate title-page in *Six New Playes*, 1653.)

1668/9, *c.* 12 Jan. In 'A Catalogue of part of His Ma^tes Servants Playes as they were formerly acted at the Blackfryers & now allowed of to his Ma^tes Servants at ye New Theatre' occurs the title 'The Sisters.' (Nicoll, *A History of Restoration Drama*, 3rd ed., pp. 315–16.)

1672/3, 30 Jan. S.R. In a long list of plays transferred from Humphrey Robinson, executor of Humphrey Robinson, to John Martin and Henry Herringman is '[90] Systers, halfe.' (Greg, *Bibliography*, i. 72.)

1683, 21 Aug. S.R. In a long list of plays transferred from Sarah Martin, executrix of John Martin, to Robert Scott is the title, '[97] Sisters,' in which one-fourth interest was transferred. (Ibid., p. 75.)

The Sisters is the fifth play Shirley prepared for the King's men at Blackfriars, and the last of his pieces to open there before the wars. It was first printed in *Six New Playes*, 1653, with a prologue which shows how difficult the theatrical situation had become, when the plays of Shakespeare, Fletcher, and Jonson, the back-bone of the company's repertory, would no longer draw. (See above, i. 67–68.)

There is a minor problem connected with this prologue, since it appears, with slight alterations and the insertion of eight new lines, in Shirley's *Poems &c.*, 1646, under the title, '*Prologue to his Tragedy call'd* the Cardinall', though another prologue is printed with the first edition of *The Cardinal*, 1652. Both versions of *The Sisters* prologue give as one of the reasons for the small audiences the fact that 'London is gone to York', a line which provides an argument that the prologue was first prepared for *The Sisters*. The King reached York 19 March 1641/2, and many noblemen and gentlemen followed him in April and May (Gardiner, x. 178–96); thus the reference to the Blackfriars patrons absent in York would be appropriate in performances of that spring (note that *The Sisters* was licensed for performance 26 April 1642) but not appropriate for the earlier performances of *The Cardinal* immediately after 25 November 1641. Probably Shirley revised his *Sisters* prologue with the addition of eight new lines for some revival of *The Cardinal* early in the summer of 1642, for one of the new lines says, 'We are to have but little Summer here'.

Sion College in London has a prompt book of *The Sisters* prepared for a performance by Killigrew's company between 1668 and 1671. The prompter has added numerous directions and actors' names in a copy of *Six New Playes*, 1653. This book was first noticed in Gifford and Dyce's *Dramatic Works and Poems of James Shirley*, 1833 (v. 354), in a description presumably written by William Gifford. The Reverend Montague Summers (loc. cit.) examined the prompt book, worked out the cast and the date, and copied many of the stage directions. In the University of Chicago Library is a copy of *Six New Playes* that was once the property of William Gifford. In the text of *The Sisters* in this volume are copious additions and alterations in two different inks. The additions and alterations in brown ink appear to be those proposed by Gifford for his edition of 1833; at any rate, of the 664 brown ink corrections I examined in the first twenty-nine pages of the text, all but thirty-five are made in Gifford's edition, and in these thirty-five instances further changes from the 1652 text have been made in the 1833 text. The additions and altera- tions in black ink in the University of Chicago copy are the same as the prompt notes found in the Sion College copy, and if the page reproduced by Summers (*Restoration Theatre*, p. 142) is a fair example, they are very accurately copied. The interesting thing about this University of Chicago copy is that it gives be- tween three and four times as many prompter's jottings as Summers printed. I have not been able to see the Sion College copy or to get a photostat of it.

No comprehensive source for the action of this light comedy has been found, but it makes use of several familiar situations and character types; Forsythe (loc. cit.) finds the chief parallels with Shirley's own *Gentleman of Venice* and *Young Admiral*, with Fletcher's *Elder Brother*, and with *Twelfth Night*, but there are other parallels with numerous earlier plays.

Genest records (*Some Account of the English Stage*, iii. 142 ff.) an anonymous adaptation of *The Sisters* under the title, *Like to Like, or a Match Well Made Up*, produced at Lincoln's Inn Fields, 28 November 1723, but said to have been acted twenty years before. He says also that the opera *The Fancied Queen*, which was acted in the summer of 1733, is made from *The Sisters*. (Ibid., p. 395.)

The Sophy

John Denham's tragedy, *The Sophy*, was attributed to Shirley in the advertisement of Rogers and Ley in 1656. Apparently this false attribution is the result of the accidental slipping of Shirley's name from the preceding item, *The School of Compliment*. (See W. W. Greg, 'Authorship Attributions in the Early Play-Lists, 1656–1671', *Edinburgh Bibliographical Society Transactions*, ii, Part 4 [1946], 307.) See Denham.

The Toy

See Anon.

The Traitor (1631)

Edition: *James Shirley's The Traitor. Edited from the Quarto of 1635*, with introduction and notes, by John Stewart Carter. Unpublished University of Chicago Thesis, 1941.

Forsythe, Robert Stanley. *The Relations of Shirley's Plays to the Elizabethan Drama* (1914), pp. 152–64.

Gregory, George M. 'Shirley's Authorship of *The Traytor*', in *Two Studies in James Shirley* (1935).

Nason, Arthur Huntington. *James Shirley, Dramatist* (1915), pp. 198–220.

1631, 4 May. '*The Traitor*, by James Shirley, licensed.' (Adams, *Herbert*, p. 33.)

1634, 3 Nov. S.R. William Cooke entered for his copy 'vnder the hands of Sʳ. Henry Herbert & both the wardens a Play called the Traytor &ᶜ. by Iames Shirley'. (Greg, *Bibliography*, i. 44.)

1635. The Traytor. A Tragedie, Written By Iames Shirley. Acted By her Majesties Servants . . . 1635.

1639, 10 Aug. 'The Traytor' appears in a list of plays protected by the Lord Chamberlain for the King and Queen's Young Company at the Cockpit. (See above, i. 330–1.)

c. 1660. 'The Traytor' is found in a list of the stock-plays of Killigrew's company furnished to Sir Henry Herbert, probably shortly after the Restoration, and found among his papers by Malone. (Adams, *Herbert*, p. 82.)

1660, 6 Nov. 'Tusday the 6. No. The Traitor' appears in a list of performances of plays by 'the Kings Companie at the Red Bull and the new house in Gibbon's Tennis Court', 1660–2. (Ibid., p. 116.)

1660, 22 Nov. 'Thursday the 22. No. The Trayter' appears in a list of performances of plays by 'the Kings Companie at the Red

Bull and the new house in Gibbon's Tennis Court', 1660–2. (Ibid.)

1660, 22 Nov. '. . . I to the new playhouse and saw part of the "Traitor," a very good Tragedy; Mr. Moon did act the Traitor very well.' (Diary of Samuel Pepys.)

1661, 10 Oct. '. . . Sir W. Pen and my wife and I to the Theatre . . . where the King came to-day, and there was "The Traytor," most admirably acted; and a most excellent play it is.' (Ibid.)

<1663. John Downes lists 'The Traytor' as one of the plays acted by the King's company after the opening of the new Drury Lane theatre in 1663. (Downes, *Roscius Anglicanus*, Summers ed., pp. 8–9.)

1664/5, 13 Jan. '. . . to the King's house, to a play, "The Traytor," where, unfortunately, I met with Sir. W. Pen, so that I must be forced to confess it to my wife, which troubles me.' (Diary of Samuel Pepys.)

1667, 2 Oct. '. . . and took them to the King's house to see "The Traytour," which still I like as a very good play.' (Ibid.)

1674, 20 Oct. In a warrant for payment for plays acted before royalty at court or at the Theatre Royal appears the item, 'Octo 20 The Traytor . . . [£]10'. (Nicoll, *A History of Restoration Drama*, 3rd ed., pp. 306–7.)

1692. The Traytor. A Tragedy: With Alterations, Amendments, and Additions. As it is now Acted at the Theatre Royal, by their Majesties Servants. Written by Mr. *Rivers*. . . . MDCXCII.

The Traitor probably had its opening performance at the Phoenix about the date of Herbert's licence, but it is likely that it was written some months earlier. During the period of his association with Queen Henrietta's men at the Phoenix it seems to have been Shirley's custom to write two plays a year for the company. In the calendar year 1631, however, Sir Henry Herbert licensed three of Shirley's plays for the Queen's men, and in the calendar year 1632 three, two of them for Queen Henrietta's company. Now when one notes that no plays at all were licensed in the year 1630, when the theatres were closed by plague for much of the year (see above, ii. 657–8), the normal deduction is that the two plays he wrote in 1630 were held by the company and licensed after the theatres reopened, and that the 1631 compositions were spread out a bit to keep from glutting the Phoenix patrons with Shirley openings. If such is the case, *The Traitor* was probably written in 1630.

It has been said that the twelfth novel of the *Heptameron* is the

source of the main plot of *The Traitor*, and it is true that the rudiments of the story are there, but Forsythe (loc. cit.) shows that the
names and many of the events correspond much more closely to
Florentine history than to the *Heptameron*. He could not determine which history Shirley used, nor could Carter. (Op. cit.,
pp. xxvii–xxx.)

The Traitor that was published in 1692 as 'Written by Mr.
Rivers' has led to some confusion because of the statement by
Peter Motteux printed in *The Gentleman's Journal, or the Monthly
Miscellany*, 13 April 1692, p. 21 (cf. Dyce, *Works*, i, p. xv):

> The *Traytor*, an old Tragedy, hath not only been revived the last
> Month, but also been reprinted with Alterations and Amendments;
> It was supposed to be *Shirly*'s, but he only usher'd it into the Stage;
> The Author of it was one Mr. *Rivers* a Jesuite, who wrote it in his Con-
> finement in *Newgate*, where he died. It hath always been esteemed a
> very good Play, by the best Judges of Dramatick Writing.

Greg (*Bibliography*, ii. 643–4) seems to imply that there may be
some connexion between the story of Rivers, the Jesuit, and the
dedication of the 1692 edition to the Earl of Clancarty, a Roman
Catholic peer in the Tower at the time. At any rate, there is no
reason to believe Motteux's story. The play is characteristic of
Shirley, and the Jesuit Rivers who died in Newgate is not known
to have written anything. Most of the alterations in the 1692 text
are clearly acting-cuts for Restoration performance. (See Carter,
op. cit., pp. x–xvii, and notes.)

The number of Restoration performances listed above indicates
that *The Traitor* was one of Shirley's most familiar plays after the
wars. After the seventeenth century the appeal of the material, if
not of Shirley's particular formulation of it, continued. Genest
records performances 19 October 1703 and 10 October 1704 (*Some
Account of the English Stage*, ii. 295 and 316), but in the first
instance the play is called *Traytor, or Tragedy of Amidea*, which
suggests an alteration. Christopher Bullock's adaptation of the
play was printed in 1718. (Genest, ii. 648.) In the nineteenth century Richard Sheil used the first half of *The Traitor* for his popular
Evadne, or The Statue, which was frequently played in both England and America. (See Carter, op. cit., pp. xxxii–xxxvii.)

There seems to have been some disposition in the seventies to
think of *The Traitor* as one of the great English tragedies of the
past. In his preface to *The Women's Conquest*, 1671, Edward
Howard said:

> I do not find but the highest of our English Tragedies (as *Cataline*,

The Maids Tragedy, Rollo, The Cardinal and Traytor) considerable enough to be rank'd with the best of these [Tragi-Comedies].

And Sir Francis Fane in the epilogue to *Love in the Dark, or The Man of Business*, 1675, speaking of poor contemporary actors, says,

> Let them the Traytor *or* Volpone *try,*
> Could they . . .
> Rage like Cethegus, *or like* Cassius *die,*
> They ne'er had sent to Paris *for such Fancies,*

The Traitor was in the repertory of some of the English actors playing in Germany in the early seventeenth century. (See Lawrence Marsden Price, *The Reception of English Literature in Germany* [1932], pp. 9–16.)

The Triumph of Beauty (> 1646)

Forsythe, Robert Stanley. *The Relations of Shirley's Plays to the Elizabethan Drama* (1914), pp. 400–1.

Greg, W. W. *Pastoral Poetry & Pastoral Drama* (1906), p. 386.

1646. The Trivmph Of Beavtie. As it was personated by some young Gentlemen, for whom it was intended, at a private Re-creation. By James Shirley . . . MDCXLVI. (Separate title-page in *Poems &c. By James Shirley*, 1646.)

The subject of the masque is the choice of Paris, but it is introduced by a species of antimasque of seven shepherds. This comic material, as Langbaine noted (*An Account of the English Dramatick Poets* [1691], p. 485), is derived from the first scenes of the Athenian mechanicals in *A Midsummer Night's Dream*: Shirley's shepherds discuss their proposed presentation of the tragedy of the Golden Fleece with the same confusions and malapropisms with which Shakespeare's mechanicals discuss the presentation of Pyramus and Thisbe.

Fleay dated *The Triumph of Beauty* 1640 (*Biog. Chron.* ii. 244–5) because he imagined a feud between Heywood and Shirley, and he thought that Shirley made fun of Heywood's Lord Mayor's pageants in *A Contention for Honour and Riches* and *The Triumph of Beauty*. Lord Mayors' pageants are indeed satirized in *Honour and Riches*, but Heywood's are not singled out, and there was no reason for Heywood to take offence, nor is there any evidence that he did. There is no satire of either pageants or Heywood in *The Triumph of Beauty*, nor do I find any other evidence of date. The title-page reference to performance 'by some young Gentlemen' and 'a private Recreation' could refer to Shirley's schoolboys, but the date is a little too early for us to be sure that Shirley had already returned to pedagogy, and the cast does not show such clear adaptation for boys as does that of *The Contention of Ajax and Ulysses*. The masque could have been written almost any time during Shirley's career, though it seems more characteristic of his activities after the closing of the theatres.

The Triumph of Peace (3 and 13 February 1633/4)

Forsythe, Robert Stanley. *The Relations of Shirley's Plays to the Elizabethan Drama* (1914), pp. 398–9.

Green, A. Wigfall. *The Inns of Court and Early English Drama* (1931), pp. 123–32.

Greg, W. W. '*The Triumph of Peace*: A Bibliographer's Nightmare', *Library*, Fifth Series, i (1946), 113–26.

Nason, Arthur Huntington. *James Shirley, Dramatist* (1915), pp. 79–81.

Reyher, Paul. *Les Masques anglais* (1909), *passim*.

Schipper, Jakob. 'Shirleys Maskenspiel "The Triumph of Peace"', in *Festschrift Wilhelm Viëtor. Die Neueren Sprachen*, Ergänzungsband (1910), pp. 129–45. Reprinted, with minor changes, in *James Shirley: sein Leben und seine Werke* (1911), pp. 122–38.

Simpson, Percy, and C. F. Bell. *Designs by Inigo Jones for Masques & Plays at Court* (1924), pp. 79–82.

Welsford, Enid. *The Court Masque* (1927), pp. 225–8.

Whitelocke, Bulstrode. *Memorials of the English Affairs* (1732), pp. 19–22.

1633, 17 Oct. 'No law studied in the Inns of Court; now all turned dancing schools. There came a desire from the King about a fortnight ago to the Inns of Court by my Lord Keeper that the gentlemen of the several Inns would show themselves at Court by the presentation of a mask, which desire was suddenly accepted, and speedily concluded upon. There are four maskers of every Inn of Court appointed, and 25 gentlemen of every house, in all 100, to attend the maskers to the Court upon light horse out of the King's stable, all in trappings as gallantly accoutred as can be imagined, with plumes, &c., with 2, 4, or 6 men on each side their horse, with torches as they please; the maskers come after them in chariots. This is all the talk of the town, drowns all other news, in the Inns of Court. . . . Who is the poet, or who makes the mask dance, I do not yet understand.' (Letter of Thomas Coke to Sir John Coke [the Younger], MSS. of Earl Cowper, *Hist. MSS. Com.*, Twelfth Report, Appendix II, Part 2, p. 34.)

1633, 25 Oct. 'For a masque to be presented before the King at Court in joyful acknowledgment of the happy birth of his second son, the Duke of York, for which each Inn will contribute 600*l.*, the Benchers have taxed themselves at 3*l.* each, Barristers at 40*s.*, and other gentlemen 20*s.* The collection is to be made by a roll of names according to the pension roll. Every gentleman admitted before the masque is performed, is to contribute.' (C. H. Hopwood, ed., *Middle Temple Records*, 4 vols. [1904–5], ii. 812.)

1633, 12 Nov. ' "Whereas there having been no representation of any mask or other show before the King's Majesty by the four Inns of Court or any of them sithens his Highness' access unto the Crown, a consultation hath been lately had by the several benchers in their several Houses touching the same, whereupon it is unanimously agreed by them that a mask shall be jointly presented in this next Christmas before his Majesty, at the equal charges of the said four Houses . . . every fellow of this House shall be taxed to pay as followeth, viz.:"—Every bencher, 5*li.*; every utter barrister of seven years' standing, 50*s.*; every utter barrister under seven years' standing, 40*s.*; every gentleman under the bar . . . 20*s.*' (F. A. Inderwick, *A Calendar of the Inner Temple Records*, 3 vols. [1896–1901], ii. 210.)

1633, 6 Dec. 'All the Inns of Court are at a common Charge to set out a Masque and Barriers this *Christmas*, which shall be presented at Court on *Twelfth-Night*. It will cost 4 or 5000 *l.* No Man so forward to further this Action as Mr. *Noy.*' (G. Garrard to the Lord Deputy in Ireland, *The Earl of Strafforde's Letters and Dispatches*, i. 167.)

1633, 27 Dec. [i.e. 6 Jan. 1633/4, M.V.] 'Four bodies (universita) of students have joined together to collect a large sum of money to meet the heavy expense of masques and representations to be made a few days hence in a rare display, for the entertainment of the king and queen.' (Venetian Ambassador to the Doge and Senate. *Calendar of State Papers, Venetian, 1632–6*, p. 180.)

1633/4, 9 Jan. 'There are two Masques in Hand, the first of the Inns of Court, which is to be presented on *Candlemas-day*; the other the King presents the Queen with on *Shrove-Tuesday* at Night: High Expences, they speak of 20000 *l.* that it will cost the Men of the Law. Oh that they would once give over these

Things, or lay them aside for a Time, and bend all their En-
deavours to make the King Rich!' (G. Garrard to the Lord
Deputy in Ireland, *The Earl of Strafforde's Letters and Dispatches*,
i. 177.)

1633/4, 24 Jan. S.R. William Cooke entered for his copy 'vnder
the hands of Mr Attorney Sr Iohn ffinch & M^r. weaver warden
The Maske of the four Inns of Co^{rt}. wth the Sceane as it is to be
p^{r}sented before his Ma^{ty}. at white hall the third of ffebr: next'.
(Greg, *Bibliography*, i. 43.)

1633/4, 24 Jan. 'Mr. Thorpe, one of the committees for the masque
of the four Inns of Court before the King, having stated that
600*l.* more was wanted from each House, the Masters of the
Bench order that 600*l.* be borrowed on security.' (C. H. Hopwood, op. cit. ii. 814.)

1633/4, 28 Jan. 'Francis Chafin, Second Butler, is fined 40*s.* for
neglecting to summon personally . . . certain gentlemen whom
the Masters of the Bench wished to attend them to be dealt
withal "touching their attendance of the masquers appointed
to the Court on horseback." ' (Ibid., pp. 814–15.)

1633/4, 29 Jan. 'Whereas the Gent: of the Innes of Court, haue
desired permission to present to their Maties. a Masque, wch his
Matie out of his Roiall favour toward[es] them hath bene gra-
tiously pleased to accept, and it is to be pformed in the beginning
of the next weeke, To the end they may haue the better and fairer
way in their passadge towardes his Ma$^{t[es]}$ Court; and likewise
to prevent all disorders and disturbanc[es], wch in the like cases,
vsually happen by the Concourse of vnruly people. Wee doe
therefore hereby praie and expressely require your Lo^p, to take
present and effectuall order, that the Street[es] through w^{ch}
they are to passe, especially Aldersgate Street, be very well
clensed against monday night next at the farthest. And a very
good and carefull watch kept by the Constables and better sort
of Citizens themselues, aswell wthin the Citie it selfe as wthin that
part of the liberties that lyeth that waie. . . . ffrom the Star-
chamber the 29. Janu: 1633.' (Letter from the Privy Council to
the Lord Mayor. *Mal. Soc. Col.* i. i. 99–100, from *Remembrancia*,
vii. 106.)

1633/4, 3 Feb. 'The Inns of court gentlemen presented their
masque at court, before the kinge and queene, the 2 February,
1633, and performed it very well. Their shew through the streets
was glorious, and in the nature of a triumph.—Mr. Surveyor
Jones invented and made the scene; Mr. Sherley the poett made
the prose and verse.' (Adams, *Herbert*, p. 54. The general agree-

ment on the date of 3 February, or the day *after* Candlemas, shows that Herbert's 2 February is an error for 3.)

1633/4, 3 Feb. 'att nighte in the strande, att the lodgeinge of Monsr: Bobarre where wee supped, & sawe the stately Masque.' (Diary of Sir Humphrey Mildmay. See above, ii. 675.)

N.D. [1633/4, 4–10 Feb.] 'I have sent you a booke of our Masque, which was presented on munday last with much applause and commendation from the K and Queene and all the Spectators. The K and Q supt that night at Salisbury House, and there saw us ride in the streetes, after which they presently went by water to Whitehall, and there saw us again from the long gallery at the upper end of the tilting yard. When the masque was ended, we all kissed the K and Queenes hand, and then were conducted by my Lord Chamberlain and other Lords to a rich banquet, whether the K and Q came, and took a taste, and then graciously smiling upon us, left us to the sole enjoying of that well furnisht table, with strict command that not any should touch a bitt but ourselves. The next day the K sent for our Marshall, Mr.Thomas Dorrell of Lincolns Inn, and Knighted him. And being much pleased and taken with the sight hath sent us to ride againe on Tuesday next to Merchant Taylers Hall, in the same manner as we rode to White-hall, and there to meete his Ma^{ty} at supper, and to present our Masque. Sir Henry Vayne, and other great Travellers say they never saw such a sight in any part of the world.' (Justinian Paget to his 'cousin Tremyll'. J. P. Collier, *History of English Dramatic Poetry* [1831], ii. 60–61.)

1633/4, 7 Feb. [i.e. 17 Feb. 1633, M.V.] 'Some bands of the richest young students in this city have collected a large sum of money and devoted it to presenting representations, music and dancing for the entertainment of the king and queen.

'Their display at the palace with a numerous, stately and glittering cavalcade, by their dresses, liveries and devices, attracted a great crowd, exciting the curiosity and applause of all the people, and afforded particular gratification to their Majesties, so that they had to repeat their procession and representation.' (Venetian Ambassador to the Doge and Senate. *Calendar of State Papers, Venetian, 1632–36*, p. 195.)

1633/4, 9 Feb. 'Forasmuch as the moneys taxed upon all the gentlemen by the act of 12 November last, towards the mask lately presented before his Majesty, will come far short of so great a sum as will be occasioned thereby, as now appears by the relation of Willis, who has been employed and trusted in that service; and forasmuch as the treasurer has already furnished

Willis with some moneys out of the stock of this House for that purpose, and there is occasion for the disbursement of more, it is ordered that the treasurer may deliver to Willis from the stock of the House such further sums as he shall have occasion to spend about the same business.' (Inderwick, op. cit. ii. 212.)

1633/4, 13 Feb. '. . . . this nighte was againe the famous Masque before there Ma^{ts}: att Marchant Taylers hall in London.' (Diary of Sir Humphrey Mildmay. See above, ii. 676.)

1633/4, 14 Feb. 'A great maske or showe presented to ye King.' (*The Diary of Thomas Crosfield*, ed. Frederick S. Boas [1935], p. 70. Boas is clearly mistaken in his note that the masque was Carew's *Coelum Britannicum* [q.v.], for that masque was performed 18 February, and it was not presented *to* the King, but given *by* him.)

1633/4, 14 Feb. 'Letter of news. . . . Account of the Masque performed at Court, on the 4th inst., by the gentlemen of the Inns of Court, here called the young gentlemen of the palace. It is said to have been played in la Cassine [the Casino?] at Whitehall. The writer notices also that on the 13th inst. the King and Queen had supped with the Lord Mayor in Merchant Taylors' Hall, and that after supper the Masque had been again performed.' (Robert Reade to Thomas Windebank [original letter written in French.] *C.S.P., Dom., Charles I, 1633–4*, p. 464.)

1633/4, 27 Feb. 'On *Monday* after *Candlemas-day*, the Gentlemen of the Inns of Court performed their Masque at Court; they were sixteen in Number, who rode through the Streets in four Chariots, and two others to carry their Pages and Musicians, attended by an hundred Gentlemen on great Horses, as well clad as ever I saw any, they far exceeded in Bravery any masque that had formerly been presented by those Societies, and performed the dancing Part with much Applause. In their Company there was one Mr. *Read* of *Gray's-Inn*, whom all the Women and some Men cry'd up for as handsome a Man as the Duke of *Buckingham*. They were well used at Court by the King and Queen, no Disgust given them, only this one Accident fell, Mr. *May* of *Gray's-Inn*, a fine Poet, he who translated *Lucan*, came athwart my Lord Chamberlain in the Banquetting House, and he broke his Staff over his Shoulders, not knowing who he was, the King present, who knew him, for he calls him his Poet, and told the Chamberlain of it, who sent for him the next Morning, and fairly excused himself to him, and gave him fifty Pounds in Pieces. I believe he was the more indulgent for his Names sake. This riding Shew took so well, that both King and Queen desired to see it again, so that they invited themselves to Supper at my Lord Mayor's within a Week after, and the Masquers came in a more glorious Show with all the Riders, which were increased twenty, to *Merchant-Taylors* Hall, and there performed it again.' (Mr. Garrard to the Lord Deputy of Ireland, *Strafforde Letters*, i. 207.)

N.D. 'The manner of the progression of the Masque. (6½ pp.)

Thomas Basset, the Lancashire Bagpipe, and John Seywell, the Shalme, riding abreast together, and two men to lead their horses and two torch bearers. *Fancy*, riding single, *Opinion and Confidence*, riding together, and a pair of torch bearers to each. *The Jews harp*, *the Tongs*, and *the Byad*, with three men to lead their horses, and two torch bearers. Projectors, viz. the jocky, the countryman, the lamp-man, the case, the Carrot man, the seaman, John Morton the Byad, each with two torch bearers. The Magpie, the Crow, the Jay, and the Kite riding in a quadrangle with the Owl in the middle; these have five men to lead their horses and four torch bearers. Three satyrs have four torch bearers. Two dotterells have two men to lead their horses and two torch bearers, and a single dotterell has a horse leader and two torch bearers. The Myne [Wynd?] Mill, a Fantastique and the Dancer have each two torch bearers, and the dancer has a horse leader. Seven pair of trumpeters, each pair having two torch bearers. One hundred gentlemen riding two and two together, each gentleman having two of his own men torch bearers and a groom. The marshal and his 40 men. The first chariot for Musicke, Sir Henry Fane's coachman is charioteer; it carries eight persons and has three flambeaux bearers on the right and three on the left. The second chariot for Musicke, the Earl of Northumberland's coachman is charioteer; of this chariot are the Genies, Amphilucke, Irene (Mr. John Lanier), Eunomia, Diche, and five Constellacions (the fourth is Mr. Henry Lawes); it has three flambeaux bearers on the right and three on the left; two pair of gentlemen riding together and two torch bearers for each pair; a chariot of orange and silver with four masques in it, with two horse leaders, and four flambeaux bearers on the right and four on the left; two pair of gentlemen riding together, and two torch bearers for each pair; a chariot of blue and silver with four masks in it, with two horse leaders, and four torchbearers on the right and four on the left; two pair of gentlemen riding together, and wo torchbearers for each pair; a chariot of crimson and silver with four masks in it, two horse leaders, and four flambeaux bearers on the right and four on the left;

two pair of gentlemen riding together, with two torch bearers for each pair; a chariot of white and silver with four masks in it, two horse leaders and four flambeaux bearers on the right and four on the left. The two Marshals of London and a guard of 200 halberdiers.' (*Hist. MSS. Com.*, Fifth Report, Part I [1876], MSS. of Richard Cholmondeley of Condover Hall, Shropshire, p. 355.)

1633/4. The Trivmph Of Peace. A Masque, presented by the Foure Honourable Houses, Or *Jnnes of Court*. Before the *King* and *Queenes* Majesties, in the *Banquetting-house* at *White Hall*, February the third, 1633. Invented and Written, By *James Shirley*, of *Grayes Inne*, Gent. . . . 1633.

1633/4. [Another edition set up simultaneously. The sheets of the two editions are indiscriminately bound together. See W. W. Greg, *Library*, Fifth Series, i (1946), 113–26.]

1633/4. [Another edition. 'Invented and Written, By *James Shirley*, of *Grayes-Inne*, Gent. The third Impression . . . 1633.']

1633/4. [Another issue with an added leaf containing a speech by Gen⟨ius⟩.]

1633, 3 Nov.–3 Nov. 1635. Various records of late bills and of collections for the presentation of the masque. (F. A. Inderwick, op. cit., ii. 213–26.)

1646, 12 Dec. S.R. William Cooke transferred to Humphrey Moseley all his rights 'in these two playes or masques vizt. Contention for honor & Riches. & The Triumph of peace. by Mr Iames Shirley'. (Greg, *Bibliography*, i. 58.)

The spectacular display of the Inns of Court's masque, *The Triumph of Peace*, was in the nature of an assertion of loyalty and a repudiation of the villainies of William Prynne, member of Lincoln's Inn and author of that anathema, *Histriomastix*, which he had tactlessly dedicated 'To his mvch Honovred Friends, The Right Worshipfvll Masters of the Bench of the Honourable flourishing Law-Society of Lincolnes-Inne.'

Bulstrode Whitelocke, who was a member of the committee in charge of the preparations for the masque, recounts the initiation of the project (loc. cit.):

About *Allholantide*, several of the principal Members of the Societies of the four Inns of Court, amongst whom some were Servants to the King, had a design that the Inns of Court should present their Service to the King and Queen, and testify their affections to them, by the outward and splendid visible testimony of a Royal Masque of all the four Societies joining together, to be by them brought to the

Court, as an expression of their Love, and Duty to their Majesties.

This was hinted at in the Court and by them intimated to the chief of those Societies, that it would be well taken from them, and some held it the more seasonable, because this action would manifest the difference of their opinion, from Mr. *Prynne's* new learning, and serve to confute his *Histrio Mastix* against Interludes.

Whitelocke goes on to give a very long and detailed account of the preparations for and performance of the masque (loc. cit.), but he says nothing of the selection of the poet or of his activities.

Shirley may have recommended himself to the lawyers by his condemnation of Prynne in his verses for Ford's *Love's Sacrifice* (S.R., 21 January 1632/3) and by his ironic dedication of *The Bird in a Cage* (S.R., 19 March 1632/3) to Prynne in the Tower. He must have been known to many of them, at least to the members of Gray's Inn, for he lived in or near that institution, and he was made a member during the preparations for the production of his masque. (See Life.)

The Triumph of Peace was one of the famous spectacles of its time. It is frequently alluded to and described, and the number of issues of the printed text suggests that more people bought copies of it than of any other Jacobean or Caroline masque. It was not Shirley's genius that led to the acclaim, for the masque is far inferior to a number of Jonson's. Part of the popularity no doubt derived from the unusually large number of people involved in a production sponsored and performed by all four of the Inns of Court, but more was due to the dazzling parade through the streets of London. Various accounts mention this parade, and the *Calendar of State Papers* notes a poem on the subject, entitled 'A brief expression of the delight apprehended by the author, at seeing of the solemn triumphs of the gentlemen of the Inns of Court riding with the masque presented before his Majesty'. Only the opening and closing lines are quoted:

> Now did Heaven's charioteer, the great day's star,
> In western ocean lave his weary car
>
> .   .   .   .   .
>
> And be as valiant in the midst of fight
> As they seemed glorious in the masque of Night.
>   (*C.S.P., Dom., Charles I, 1633–4*, p. 450.)

A copy of the poem with the date 'Feb. 3rd 1633' added to the title is also preserved among the papers of Evelyn P. Shirley at Ettington Hall in Warwickshire. (*Hist. MSS. Com., Fifth Report* [1876], Appendix, p. 365.) The brilliant parade is also described by Bulstrode Whitelocke (loc. cit.) and by Shirley in his text of the masque.

A third description of the procession is quoted above from the report by the Historical Manuscripts Commission of the manuscripts of Mr. Richard Cholmondeley. The Commissioners have assigned the undated paper to 'Temp. James I', but they are plainly wrong about the date, for all the details clearly describe the procession of the masquers and individual characters of *The Triumph of Peace*. This description is much too precise and detailed to have been written by an ordinary spectator; it must be some order of march prepared for the lawyers. It gives many details not found in Bulstrode Whitelocke's account and seems to order the procession differently. Shirley's own account of the procession in the edition of his masque gives the same order as the anonymous list; Shirley records more about the costumes, but he gives no names, and he is less specific about the arrangement of horsemen, footmen, torches, and flambeaux. The three accounts dovetail beautifully and together give an unusually vivid and detailed picture of the famous procession.

There must have been much talk of the preparations for the great show, for the printers, in anticipation of a large sale, seem to have set up the description and text of the masque in duplicate in order to have approximately 3,000 copies ready for sale. (See *The Carl H. Pforzheimer Library: English Literature 1475–1700*, No. 935, pp. 960–1, and W. W. Greg, loc. cit.)

Shirley asserts at the end of the text that his masque was 'for the variety of the Shewes, and richnesse of the Habits, the most magnificent that hath beene brought to Court in our time'. He also records that:

THE Scene and Ornament, was the act of *Inigo Iones* Esquire, Surueyer of his Maiesties workes.

The Composition of the Musicke, was perform'd by Mr. *William Lawes*, and Mr. *Simon Ives*, whose Art gaue an Harmonious soule to the otherwise languishing Numbers.

The names of the masquers are given in Francis Lenton's *The Inns of Court Anagrammatist; or The Masquers Masqued in Anagrammes*, 1634.

As various contemporaries indicate, the masque was repeated by royal request at Merchant Taylors' Hall in the city. For this performance Shirley wrote an additional speech, an address by *Genius* to be spoken to the King and Queen. This speech, printed on an added leaf, is the distinguishing characteristic of the final issue of the masque. (See Greg, *Bibliography*, ii. 634.)

Several of the sketches and designs for costumes and sets for the masque are preserved in the collection at Chatsworth. (See Simpson and Bell, loc. cit.)

Edward F. Rimbault says in his edition of Purcell's music for *Bonduca* (Musical Antiquarian Society, vii [1842], 11) that all the music of Lawes and Ives for the masque is preserved in the Music School at Oxford.

The Wedding (May 1626?)

Forsythe, Robert Stanley. *The Relations of Shirley's Plays to the Elizabethan Drama* (1914), pp. 322–31.

Harbage, Alfred. 'Shirley's *The Wedding* and the Marriage of Sir Kenelm Digby', *Phil. Quart.* xvi (1937), 35–40.

Nason, Arthur Huntington. *James Shirley, Dramatist* (1915), pp. 40–42 and 177–82.

Schipper, Jakob. *James Shirley: sein Leben und seine Werke* (1911), pp. 32–37.

1629. The Wedding. As it was lately Acted by her Majesties *Seruants, at the Phenix in Drury Lane. Written By* Iames Shirley, *Gent. . . .* 1629.

1633. [Another edition.]

1637, 25 Sept. S.R. John Grove assigned to William Leake all his rights in 'these ffour Playes following (vizt.) The Wedding. The Tragedie of Hoffman The gratefull Servant. Hollands Leaguer'. (Greg, *Bibliography*, i. 46.)

1639, 10 Aug. The Lord Chamberlain forbade all other London companies to act any of a list of plays belonging to the King and Queen's Young Company at the Cockpit in Drury Lane. Included in the list is 'The wedding'. (See above, i. 330–1.)

1660. [Another edition.]

c. 1660. 'The Weddinge' is found in a list of the stock-plays of Killigrew's company furnished to Sir Henry Herbert, probably shortly after the Restoration, and found among his papers by Malone. (Adams, *Herbert*, p. 82.)

1660/1, 9 Jan. 'Monday the 9. Jan. [1660/1] The weddinge' appears in a list of performances of plays by 'the Kings Companie at the Red Bull and the new house in Gibbon's Tennis Court near Clare Market,' 1660–2. (Ibid., p. 117.)

1664/5, 13 Jan. '13 Jan., F. [i.e., Friday], "The Wedding" acted at University College.' (Andrew Clark, *The Life and Times of Anthony Wood*, ii. 28.)

The status of *The Wedding* is rather unusual among Shirley's plays in that neither Herbert's licence for acting nor the original Stationers' Register entry for the printing of the comedy has been preserved. (Ward [*D.N.B.* iii. 130] is in error in asserting that there was an acting licence, and Fleay [*Biog. Chron.* ii. 233] has no evidence for saying that it was originally licensed to John Grove, though Grove did transfer it in 1637.) A passage which does seem to indicate the date of the original performance was pointed out by Fleay, however. (*Biog. Chron.* ii. 236.) Rawbone, the comic citizen-miser (played by William Robbins), in the second scene of the third act (F₃) reads to Jane his contract, concluding,

> In witnesse whereof, I haue here-vnto put my hand and seale ... the last day of the first merry moneth, and in the second yeare of the raigne of King *Cupid*.

To allude to King Charles as King Cupid would be a not unusual form of compliment, and Rawbone's date would then become 31 May 1626. Such a date would be compatible with performance by Queen Henrietta's men at the Phoenix and the date of publication, and it would fit plausibly into the series of Shirley's known compositions for the Queen's men in 1625 and 1626—*The School of Compliment* and *The Maid's Revenge* (if delayed by plague) in 1625; *The Wedding* and *The Brothers* (a lost play) in 1626.

Professor Harbage has suggested, somewhat tentatively (op. cit.), that *The Brothers* which Sir Henry Herbert licensed 4 November 1626—and which, it is generally agreed, is not Shirley's *Brothers* (q.v.), published in *Six New Playes* in 1653—may have been *The Wedding* under another title. Since there are no brothers in *The Wedding*, the identification has little to support it, as Professor Harbage realizes. He is more interested in his suggestion that *The Wedding* is intended to reflect the affair of Sir Kenelm Digby and Venetia Stanley as related in *Private Memoirs of Sir Kenelm Digby ... Written by Himself*, which was published in 1827. There are indeed parallels between the affair and the play, but most of them are fairly common romantic episodes, and it seems to me doubtful that Shirley would have dared to meddle with such material. Moreover, several of the divergences between the adventures of Sir Kenelm and the play require the assumption of revisions of which I see no evidence.

Professor Arthur Ludwig Stiefel asserted flatly that *The Wedding* has a Spanish source. (' Die Nachahmung spanischer Komödien in England unter den ersten Stuarts ', *Romanische Forschungen*, v [1890], 196, n. 1), but so far as I know he never presented his evidence. The thoroughness with which he made his case for *The Opportunity* and *The Young Admiral*, however, tend to persuade one that he probably did have the evidence. Forsythe (loc. cit.) finds the usual analogues to characters and situations in earlier plays, especially *Much Ado, Twelfth Night*, and Shakespeare's Falstaff plays.

The most unusual feature of the quarto of 1629 is the cast given for the play, which is headed 'The Actors names', and which is complete for all save the minor roles, assigning parts to ten adult and four boy actors. (See above, i. 246.) Such casts are exceedingly rare in Elizabethan and Jacobean play quartos, but in 1629 there was a striking coincidence when casts were printed in three publications, Massinger's *Roman Actor*, Carlell's *Deserving Favourite*, and *The Wedding*, and an actor list was given in Ford's *Lover's Melancholy The Roman Actor* (q.v.) may have been intended as a defence of the actors, and there is a strong suggestion of co-operation between Massinger, Ford, and Shirley. Not only did all three in the same year use the very unusual device of printing a cast or an actor list, but John Ford wrote commendatory verses for the plays of both Massinger and Shirley, and two other authors of commendatory verses for *The Wedding*—Thomas May and Robert Harvey —also wrote commendatory verses for *The Roman Actor*. In the following year, 1630, Shirley wrote verses for Massinger's *Renegado*, and Massinger wrote verses for Shirley's *Grateful Servant*. The evidence suggests, therefore, that these coincidences in cast publication were arranged by the three playwrights. They do not appear to have been arranged by the actors or the printers, for the plays are all printed and published by different men, and *The Roman Actor* and *The Lover's Melancholy* were performed by the King's men, while *The Wedding* belonged to Queen Henrietta's men.

Shirley's dedication of the play to William Gowre indicates a summer publication in the line, 'This Comedy comming forth to take the ayre in Summer', and mentions performance in the theatre, though claiming no great success: 'It hath passed the Stage.' None of the writers of commendatory verses—Edmond Colles, Robert Harvey, Thomas May, John Ford, or William Habington—mentions success in the theatre, but the piece was still thought worth protecting from other London companies in the Cockpit repertory list of 1639, and it evidently had some appeal in the early years of the Restoration.

The Witty Fair One (1628)

Edition: *James Shirley's The Wittie Fair One*, a Critical Edition of the 1633 Quarto, with Introduction and Notes, by Esther Melvina Power. Unpublished University of Chicago Thesis, 1942.

Forsythe, Robert Stanley. *The Relations of Shirley's Plays to the Elizabethan Drama* (1914), pp. 331–42.

Nason, Arthur Huntington. *James Shirley, Dramatist* (1915), pp. 184–91.

Schipper, Jakob. *James Shirley: sein Leben und seine Werke* (1911), pp. 29–32.

1628, 3 Oct. 'The Witty Fair One, by James Shirley, licensed.' (Adams, *Herbert*, p. 32.)

1632/3, 15 Jan. S.R. William Cooke entered for his copy 'vnder the hands of S^r. Henry Herbert & m^r Aspley warden a Play called The witty faire one by Ia: Shirley'. (Greg, *Bibliography*, i. 42.)

1633. The Wittie Faire One. *A Comedie*. As it was presented at the Private House in Drvry Lane. *By her Maiesties Servants*. By Iames Shirley. . . . 1633. [Sir Henry Herbert's licence is printed on K$_2$: 'This Play, called The Witty Faire One, as it was Acted on the Stage, may be Printed, this 14. of *Ianuary*. 1632. Henry Herbert.']

1639, 10 Aug. 'A witty fayre one' appears in a list of plays protected by the Lord Chamberlain for the King and Queen's Young Company at the Cockpit. (See above, i. 330–1.)

1666. 'The first new Play that was Acted in 1666, was: *The Tragedy of* Cambyses. . . . *After this the Company Reviv'd Three Comedies of* Mr. Sherly's, viz. *The Grateful Servant*. *The Witty Fair One*. *The School of Complements*. *The Woman's a Weather Cock*. These Plays being perfectly well Perform'd . . . prov'd as Beneficial to the Company, as several succeeding new Plays.' (John Downes, *Roscius Anglicanus*, ed. Montague Summers, p. 27.)

The play was probably given its first performance by Queen Henrietta's men at the Phoenix shortly after Sir Henry Herbert licensed it on 3 October 1628. Composition in the immediately preceding months would have been normal for a playwright like Shirley, who was turning out plays in a fairly regular sequence for Queen Henrietta's men. (See above, i. 226–7.) Miss Power notes (op. cit., pp. xliv–xlv) that in the geography lesson in the first scene of the second act Sir Nicholas Treedle says, 'Is't so? An Iland then is, no matter let it goe, 'tis not the first Iland wee ha lost.' This sounds like an allusion to the widely discussed fiasco of the English expedition to the island of Rhé, June to November 1627 (see Gardiner, vi. 167–200), especially in the light of Treedle's remark a few lines later, 'We haue had too many *French* cuts already.'

No comprehensive source for the play has been noted, and Miss Power thinks it unlikely that there was one. Forsythe notes several parallels to *The Witty Fair One* (op. cit., pp. 331 ff.), all of which, except *Bartholomew Fair* and Fletcher's *Monsieur Thomas*, Miss Power doubts that Shirley used. She does suggest, however, that Shirley may have used *Los cigarrales de Toledo* by Tirso de Molina, an author whose *El Castigo del penséque* Shirley adapted for his *Opportunity*, licensed in 1634. The novela called *Los tres maridos burlados* in Tirso's collection is rather close to Shirley's scenes of Penelope's plot involving the pretended death of Fowler. (Power, op. cit., pp. xlvi–lii.)

The quarto is dedicated to Sir Edward [Edmund in some copies] Bushell, who, Miss Power thinks, was probably the Sir Edward Bushell whose earlier career Leslie Hotson traces at some length in *I, William Shakespeare*. The dedication says nothing significant about the play except that '*It wanted no grace on the Stage*', a statement which presumably indicates Shirley's satisfaction with the production and at least implies that the play did not fail in the theatre. Its inclusion in the Phoenix repertory list of 1639 is a further indication that it pleased audiences.

Miss Power found an unusual number of variants (about 150) in the fourteen copies of the quarto which she examined. (Op. cit., pp. iii–xvi.) She suggests a variety of reasons for the many changes: 'the state of the press materials, the presence of alterations and revisions in a not too clearly written manuscript, and the rush of activities with the author'. (Ibid., pp. xvii–xxx.)

If the performance of the play in 1666 was as successful as John Downes indicates, it seems likely that there would have been other Restoration performances, but no other record is known.

Genest says (*Some Account of the English Stage*, ii. 569–70) that Newburgh Hamilton's *The Doating Lovers or The Libertine Tamed*, which was acted at Lincoln's Inn Fields 23 June 1714, is largely derived from Shirley's *The Witty Fair One*; Oulton's musical farce, *Frightened to Death*, given at Drury Lane 27 February 1817, is also based on part of Shirley's play. (Ibid. viii. 589.)

The Young Admiral (1633)

Bowers, Fredson Thayer, ed. *The Fary Knight* (1942), pp. xxxiv–xli and 65–83.

Forsythe, Robert Stanley. *The Relations of Shirley's Plays to the Elizabethan Drama* (1914), pp. 190–9.

Nason, Arthur Huntington. *James Shirley, Dramatist* (1915), pp. 247–52.

Schipper, Jakob. *James Shirley: sein Leben und seine Werke* (1911), pp. 107–12.

Stiefel, A. L. 'Die Nachahmung spanischer Komödien in England unter den ersten Stuarts', *Archiv für das Studium der neueren Sprachen und Literaturen*, cxix (1907), 309–50.

1633, 3 July. '*The Young Admiral*, by James Shirley, licensed. (Adams, *Herbert*, p. 35.)

1633, 3 July. 'The comedy called *The Yonge Admirall*, being free from oaths, prophaness, or obsceanes, hath given mee much delight and satisfaction in the readinge, and may serve for a patterne to other poetts, not only for the bettring of maners and language, but for the improvement of the quality, which hath received some brushings of late.

'When Mr. Sherley hath read this approbation, I know it will encourage him to pursue this beneficial and cleanly way of poetry, and when other poetts heare and see his good success, I am confident they will imitate the original for their own credit, and make such copies in this harmless way, as shall speak them masters in their art, at the first sight, to all judicious spectators. It may be acted this 3 July, 1633.

'I have entered this allowance, for direction to my successor, and for example to all poetts, that shall write after the date hereof.' (Ibid., pp. 19–20.)

1633, 19 Nov. 'On tusday, the 19th of November, being the king's birth-day, *The Yong Admirall* was acted at St. James by the queen's players, and likt by the K. and Queen.' (Ibid., p. 53.)

1637, 13 Apr. S.R. Andrew Crooke and William Cooke entered for their copies 'vnder the hands of Tho: Herbert Deputy to Sr. Hen: Herbert & Mr. Downes warden two Playes called. The Lady of pleasure. & The young Admirall. by Iames Shirley.' (Greg, *Bibliography*, i. 46.)

1637. The Yovng Admirall. As It Was Presented By her Majesties Servants, at the private house in *Drury* Lane. Written by *James Shirly* . . . 1637.

1639, 10 Aug. The Lord Chamberlain forbade all other London companies to act any of a list of plays belonging to the King and Queen's Young Company at the Cockpit in Drury Lane. Included in the list is 'The young Admirall:' (See above, i. 330–1.)

1661, 4 July. 'In the afternoone the same day a tragedy called "The Yong Admirall", 6d.' At Oxford. (Accounts of Anthony à Wood, in Andrew Clark, *The Life and Times of Anthony Wood*, i. 405.)

1661, 8 July. 'July 8, M., "Yong Admirall," and "The Rape of Lucrece" a tragedy.' (Ibid.)

1661, 13 July. 'July 13, S., in the afternoone "the Rump" and "Yong Admirall," 1s.' (Ibid., p. 406.)

1662, 20 Nov. 'Dined with the Comptroller, Sir Hugh Pollard; afterwards, saw "The Young Admiral" acted before the King.' (William Bray, ed., *The Diary of John Evelyn* [1870], i. 393.)

As a source for *The Young Admiral*, Shirley has used Lope de Vega's *Don Lope de Cardona*, as Professor Stiefel has demonstrated. (Loc. cit.) Shirley has omitted much of Lope's material and developed and modified most of the rest. The play exhibits the usual analogues to characters and situations in earlier English plays, as Forsythe notes (loc. cit.), but there is no clear evidence that Shirley has had recourse to the text of any of them, except possibly *The Alchemist* for the gulling of Pazzorello.

Sir Henry Herbert's very unusual commendation of the play may be an indication of his taste for this type of highly contrived, almost ludicrous, tragicomedy. The wording of Herbert's praise, however, is more suggestive of the satisfaction of a harassed public official over a play which would cause him no trouble. In *The Young Admiral* he liked the 'cleanly way of poetry', 'this harmless way', and he hoped the play would become a model 'for the bettring of maners and language'. In the last two years poor Sir Henry had had censorship troubles with Massinger's *Believe as You List*, Jonson's *Magnetic Lady* and *Tale of a Tub*, and Shirley's *The Ball*; and the local satire of Marmion's *Holland's Leaguer*, Brome's *Weeding of the Covent Garden*, and Nabbes's *Covent Garden* probably did not please him. 'The quality' had indeed 'received some brushings of late', and to the censor inoffensive plays would seem more admirable than they would to the actors or the playwrights.

In his dedication of the quarto to George, Lord Berkeley, Shirley says that the play '*hath beene gratefull to the stage, and graciously entertain'd at Court by their Majesties*'. Sir Henry Herbert's

comment on the court performance of 1633 verifies the statement
about the royal reception and suggests that a later court performance might have been acceptable, but no evidence of any other
is extant. Crooke and Cooke, Shirley's regular publishers (see
Allan H. Stevenson, 'Shirley's Publishers: The Partnership of
Crooke and Cooke', *Library*, Fourth Series, xxv [1944–5], 140–
61), probably brought out *The Young Admiral*, *The Lady of
Pleasure*, and *Hyde Park* at the same time, for not only were all
three plays licensed on the same day, but Greg has pointed
out that the imprint in all three, and possibly the line containing
the author's name, are from the same setting of type. (*Bibliography*,
ii. 663.)

The number of Oxford and London performances of *The Young
Admiral* immediately following the Restoration is a little surpris-
ing, especially the three presentations at Oxford. An enthusiastic
spectator at the Oxford performances was Richard Walden, of
Queen's College, who notes that the role of Rosinda in *The Young
Admiral* was performed by Mrs. Anne Gibbs. (Montague Summers,
The Playhouse of Pepys [1935], pp. 126–7, from Richard Walden,
Io Ruminans, 1662, A₃.) The first three acts of George Powell's
Alphonso, King of Naples, produced at Drury Lane theatre in
1691, are said to be derived from *The Young Admiral*. (Forsythe,
op. cit., p. 33.)

The enthusiasm of one anonymous admirer is recorded before
the closing of the theatres in an epigram '*To Mr. James Shirly on
his Comedy* viz. *the yong Admirall*':

> How all our votes are for thee (*Shirly*) come
> Conduct our troops, strike up Apollo's drum,
> We wait upon thy summons and do all,
> Intend to choose thee our yong Admirall:
>   (*Wit's Recreations* [1640], B₇ᵛ.)

Possibly admiration for *The Young Admiral* is also indicated by
the detailed borrowings from the play which Professor Bowers has
pointed out in *The Fairy Knight* (loc. cit.), but plagiarism is more
often inspired by desperation than by admiration.

JONATHAN SIDNAM
fl. 1630

Jonathan Sidnam was not a dramatist but a translator from the
Italian. It seems unlikely that either of his translations was ever
intended for production. Of the man I know nothing. There were

various Sydenhams at both universities in the sixteenth and seventeenth centuries, but no Jonathan is recorded.

Filli di Sciro

Greg, W. W. *Pastoral Poetry & Pastoral Drama* (1906), pp. 247–50.

1655. *Filli Di Sciro*. Or Phillis of Scyros. An Excellent Pastorall. Written in Italian By *C. Guidubaldo de' Bonarelli*. And Translated into English, By *J. S.* Gent. . . . 1655.
1655. [Another issue.]

No expansion of the initials J. S. appears in the quarto, but Greg noted (loc. cit.) that a marginal note to the commendatory verses of I. H. reads:

This Comedy was Translated long ago by M. I. S. and layd by, as also was Paster Fido, *which was since Translated and set forth by Mr. Rich. Fanshaw.*

and that a note to another set of verses says that both translations were made '*neer twenty years agone*'. The titles, the dates, and the initials fit so neatly the manuscript translation of *Pastor Fido* by Jonathan Sidnam dated 1630 that it can scarcely be doubted that the J. S. of *Filli di Sciro* was Jonathan Sidnam.

Sidnam's translation is a purely literary production; there is no indication that it ever had or was intended to have any connexion with the theatre.

Il Pastor Fido or The Faithful Shepherd

MS.: B.M. Add. MS. 29493.

Greg, W. W. *Pastoral Poetry & Pastoral Drama* (1906), pp. 243–4.

The title-page of the folio manuscript in the British Museum reads:

Il / Pastor Fido / Or / The Faithfull Sheapheard / An Excellent Pastorall / Written / In Italian by Battista Guarini / And translated into English / By / Jonathan Sidnam Esq / Anno 1630

Greg pointed out (op. cit., pp. 247–8) that the marginal notes of Sidnam's translation of *Filli di Sciro* indicate that the appearance of Fanshaw's translation of *Pastor Fido* caused Sidnam to withhold his own from print. There is no indication that the translation was ever intended to have any connexion with the English stage.

JOSEPH SIMONS (Simeon)
1594–1671

Simons was not an English dramatist within the definition applied for this volume, but since a number of his continental Latin plays are extant and have caused some confusion, a cursory account of the man and his plays is included.

He was born Emmanuel Lobb in Portsmouth in 1594 and sent at the age of eleven to Portugal, where he was converted to Roman Catholicism. He was sent to the Jesuit College of St. Omers and later to the English College at Rome. From 1623 to 1631 he was a master in the Jesuit College for English boys at St. Omers, where he wrote and produced his plays. (William H. McCabe, *Phil. Quart.* xvii [1938], 236, n. 44.) In 1647 he was appointed rector of the English College at Rome, and in 1650 rector of the Theologate at Liége. In 1667 he became English provincial of the Jesuits. He died in London 24 July 1671.

Five of Simons's plays were issued together under the title *Josephi Simonis, Tragœdiæ quinque*, 1656, 1657, 1680, and 1697. Manuscripts of two of these and two or three others are extant. Father McCabe said in 1937 that he had in preparation 'a detailed study of Simons' work as illustrating the widespread Jesuit theatre of the seventeenth century'.

Mercia seu Pietas Coronata, Tragœdia (7 February 1623/4)

McCabe, William H. 'Notes on the St. Omers College Theatre', *Phil. Quart.* xvii (1938), 225–39.
—— 'The Play-List of the English College of St. Omers 1592–1762', *Revue de littérature comparée*, xvii (1937), 355–75.

1648. *Mercia Tragœdia Josephi Simonis Angli e Societate Jesu* (Romae, 1648).
1649. [A reported Antwerp edition of this date.]
1657. *Josephi Simonis Angli E Societate Jesu Tragœdiæ Quinque Quarum duæ postremæ nunc primùm lucem vident* (Liége, 1657). (Second play.)
1680. [Another edition.]
1697. [Another edition.]

The tragedy was performed in the Jesuit College for English boys at St. Omers, 7 February 1623/4. Father McCabe notes that the subject is 'the murder by King Wulfere of Mercia . . . of his two sons, Wulfade and Rufin, who had been converted by St. Chad', and that the cast includes sixty-two persons. ('Play-List', p. 363.)

S. Damianus Episcopus Ticinensis Turbas Italiæ Divinitus Prædicit (13 February 1625/6)

MSS.: Cambridge, St. John's College MS. 504; Stonyhurst B. VI. 25.

McCabe, William H. 'Notes on the St. Omers College Theatre', *Phil. Quart.* xvii (1938), 225–39.
—— 'The Play-List of the English College of St. Omers 1592–1762', *Revue de littérature comparée*, xvii (1937), 355–75.

The play was performed in the Jesuit College for English boys at St. Omers, 13 February 1625/6. Father McCabe conjectures that it was written by Simons because both manuscripts of the play are associated with other manuscripts of his and because it resembles his other plays. He notes that it consists of three acts and about 1,000 lines of verse. ('Play-List', p. 365.)

Theoctistus sive Constans in Aula Virtus, Tragœdia (8 August 1624)

McCabe, William H. 'Notes on the St. Omers College Theatre,' *Phil. Quart.* xvii (1938), 225–39.
—— 'The Play-List of the English College of St. Omers 1592–1762,' *Revue de littérature comparée*, xvii (1937), 355–75.

1653 *Theoctistus sive Constans in Aula Virtus, Tragoedia Josephi Simonis Angli, e Societate Jesu* (Liége, 1653).
1657. *Josephi Simonis Angli E Societate Jesu Tragœdiæ Quinque Quarum duæ postremæ nunc primùm lucem vident* (Liége, 1657). (Third play.)
1680. [Another edition.]
1697. [Another edition.]

The tragedy was performed in the Jesuit College for English boys at St. Omers, 8 August 1624. ('Play-List', p. 364.)

Ultio Divina sive Leo Armenus, Tragœdia (1624–9?)

MSS.: Cambridge, St. John's College MS. 504; Cambridge University Library MS. Ii. vi. 35; Stonyhurst B. VI. 25.

McCabe, William H. 'Notes on the St. Omers College Theatre', *Phil. Quart.* xvii (1938), 225–39.

—— 'The Play-List of the English College of St. Omers 1592–1762', *Revue de littérature comparée*, xvii (1937), 355–75.

1657. *Josephi Simonis Angli E Societate Tragœdiæ Quinque Quarum duæ postremæ nunc primùm lucem vident* (Liége, 1657). (Last play.)

1680. [Another edition.]

1697. [Another edition.]

The tragedy was acted at the Jesuit College for English boys at St. Omers. Father McCabe suggests that its date of performance was 1624–9 because the St. Omers records were not well kept in this period and the play evidently belongs to the group Simons wrote there. He notes that though the Cambridge MS. divides the play into three acts and the printed text into five, the texts are the same. ('Play-List', p. 364.)

Vitus sive Christiana Fortitudo, Tragœdia (13 May 1623)

McCabe, William H. 'Notes on the St. Omers College Theatre', *Phil. Quart.* xvii (1938), 225–39.

—— 'The Play-List of the English College of St. Omers 1592–1762,' *Revue de littérature comparée*, xvii (1937), 355–75.

1657. *Josephi Simonis Angli E Societate Jesu Tragœdiæ Quinque Quarum duæ postremæ nunc primùm lucem vident* (Liége, 1657). (Fourth play.)

1680. [Another edition.]

1697. [Another edition.]

The play was performed in the Jesuit College for English boys at St. Omers, 13 May 1623. Father McCabe notes that the cast includes '18 persons besides a Chorus of Angels and a cast of 10 for a play-within-the-play about St. Genesius the Comedian, converted while playing before Diocletian and martyred'. ('Play-List', p. 361.)

Zeno sive Ambitio Infelix, Tragœdia (7 August 1631)

MSS.: Cambridge, St. John's College MS. 504; Cambridge University Library MS. Ii. 6. 35; Stonyhurst B. VI. 25; B.M. MS. Harl. 5024.

McCabe, William H. 'Notes on the St. Omers College Theatre', *Phil. Quart.* xvii (1938), 225–39.

McCabe,William H. 'The Play-List of the English College of St. Omers 1592–1762', *Revue de littérature comparée*, xvii (1937), 355–75.

1648. *Zeno Tragoedia Josephi Simonis Angli e Societate Jesu.* Rome, 1648.
1649. [A reported Antwerp edition of this date.]
1657. *Josephi Simonis Angli E Societate Jesu Tragœdiæ Quinque Quarum duæ postremæ nunc primùm lucem vident* (Liége, 1657). (First play.)
1680. [Another edition.]
1697. [Another edition.]

The play, the last Simons wrote for the students, was performed at the Jesuit College for English boys at St. Omers, 7 August 1631. Father McCabe notes that the play involves dancing, songs, three dumb shows, a masque, and music between the acts, and that its subject is the fall of Zeno of Byzantium, buried alive by Anastasius. ('Play-List', p. 366.)

Unnamed Tragedy (19 June 1623)
(Lost)

McCabe, William H. 'Notes on the St. Omers College Theatre', *Phil. Quart.* xvii (1938), 225–39.
—— 'The Play-List of the English College of St. Omers 1592–1762', *Revue de littérature comparée*, xvii (1937), 355–75.

In the Jesuit College for English boys at St. Omers there was acted on 19 June 1623 a tragedy 'superbi Imperatoris qui verba illa (deposuit potentes) ex Sacris litteris audaciore animo deleverat'. The tragedy was acted by the Grammar class, and Father McCabe points out that since Joseph Simons was then master of Grammar, the play was probably written by him. ('Play-List', p. 362.)

THOMAS SINGLETON
1621–<88/89

Thomas Singleton was a schoolmaster, the author of one Latin play that was possibly written before the closing of the theatres. He matriculated at Oxford from Queen's College 19 May 1637; the entry says that he was 's. of Thomas of Basildon Berks, sac. . . . aged 16'. (*Alumni Oxon.* iv. 1360.) There seems to be no record that he took a degree.

Singleton next appears as headmaster of Eton during the Protectorate. In his list of headmasters at Eton H. C. Maxwell-Lyte gives '1655 Thomas Singleton Queen's College, Oxford', and in his running account he notes a few details:

Thomas Horne . . . Dying in August 1654, he was succeeded by John Boncle or Bunkley, who, after one years service, was promoted to a Fellowship, by order of Oliver Cromwell. After him came Thomas Singleton. (*A History of Eton College, 1440–1910*, 4th ed. [1911], pp. 241 and 599.)

Apparently Singleton retained his post for five years, but lost it in the changes at the Restoration. Maxwell-Lyte records that:

The new Provost and Fellowes lost no time in manifesting their antipathy to the late *regime*. . . . A similar policy led to the dismissal of Thomas Singleton from the post of Schoolmaster, notwithstanding his protests and entreaties. He was succeeded by Thomas Montague. (Ibid., p. 251.)

The record of a petition in the *Calendar of State Papers, Domestic, 1660–1* (p. 119), shows that Singleton tried to recover his post:

109. John Price to Sec. Nicholas. Mr. Singleton, who held the place of Schoolmaster at Eton, under the late pretended provosts, Mr. Rous and Mr. Lockier, is now displaced in favour of Mr. Montague, a worthy gentleman, nineteen years usher. Requests that the petition of the former for restoration may not be hastily acceded to.

Singleton is next known as the schoolmaster who taught Richard Mead, the physician. Matthew Maty says that when Richard Mead's father fled to Holland in 1683, he placed his son

in a school under the direction of an excellent master (c) [(c). Mr. *Thomas Singleton*, who had been second master of *Eton* school which he was obliged to quit in 1662, on account of his non-conformity.] who was of the same principles with himself: here in a few years, the youth distinguished himself to such advantage . . . that at the latter end of the year 1689, at the age of sixteen, he was sent to *Utrecht*. ([Matthew Maty] *Authentic Memoirs of the Life of Richard Mead, M.D.* [1755], pp. 3–4.)

I have found nothing further of the man. His play, *Talpae*, which was copied out by his pupil Richard Mead in 1688/9, was evidently written for boys, but for what school, or when, is unknown.

Talpae, sive Conjuratis Papistica (?)

MS.: Bodleian MS. Rawlinson D. 288.

The Bodleian manuscript is headed:

Talpæ / sive / Conjuratio Papistica / Tragico-Comœdia / Autore Dom^no. Singleton. / Scripta Febr: 7:^imo / 168$\frac{8}{9}$ / Richard Mead

Richard Mead's name is found again at the end of the transcript. The fact that Mead calls the author of the play 'Dom^no. Singleton' and dates the transcript during his attendance at Singleton's school identifies the playwright as the former Eton schoolmaster. When Singleton wrote the play that young Mead copied I do not know, but since the author was only twenty-one when the theatres closed and seems to have had a long career as a schoolmaster, a date after 1642 would seem much more probable than one before.

The fact that the dramatis personae includes characters like Rex Jacobus, Catsbeius, Perseius, Faukius (the last three Conjurati), as well as Chorus Protestantiũ and Cho: Catholicorum indicates that the play deals with the Gunpowder Plot. I have not read it.

SMITH

Nothing is known of a Jacobean or Caroline dramatist named Smith save that in 1623 Sir Henry Herbert licensed a play 'Written by Smith', and that Warburton said that a lost manuscript play was written by Will. Smith, though there is no evidence that the manuscript was Jacobean or Caroline rather than Elizabethan. Whether this Smith, or these Smiths, had any connexion with the Wentworth Smith who appears several times in Henslowe's Diary, or with the W. Smith whose *Hector of Germany* was published in 1615, is unknown.

The Fair Foul One, or The Baiting of the Jealous Knight
(1623)
(Lost)

1623, 28 Nov. 'For a Strange Company at the Red Bull; *The Faiyre fowle one, or The bayting of the Jealous Knight*: Written by Smith.' (Adams, *Herbert*, p. 26.)

Play, playwright, and company are all unknown. Herbert's designation of 'Strange Company' means that the players at the

Red Bull were not one of the regular London companies. Probably they were the same troupe for which he had allowed *Come See a Wonder* by John Day two months before. (See Adams, *Herbert*, p. 25.)

St. George for England (?)
(Lost)

c. 1710–50. 'S^t. Geõ. for England by Will. Smithe' appears in Warburton's list of manuscript plays. (See W. W. Greg, *Library*, Third Series, ii [1911], 231.)

Most of the titles in Warburton's famous list of manuscripts that he says his cook destroyed appear also in other lists, especially long entries in the Stationers' Register. And for them there is a strong suspicion that Warburton never owned them at all, but simply copied the entries as desiderata. (See W. W. Greg, 'The Bakings of Betsy', *Library*, Third Series, ii. 225–59.) But *St. George for England* and seventeen other plays Warburton claims to have had (Greg, op. cit., p. 248) do not appear in other lists, and it seems possible that he may really have owned the manuscripts, some of which his cook may have destroyed.

In any case, nothing now is known of *St. George for England* or its author.

THOMAS SNELLING
1614–<48

According to the registers of the Merchant Taylors' School, which he entered in 1626, Snelling was born 23 December 1614. (Robinson, *Merchant Taylors*, i. 116.) The Oxford records show that he was the son of William Snelling of Bushey, Herts., and that he matriculated 27 June 1634, aged nineteen, and was granted degrees of B.A. 3 May 1636 and M.A. 28 March 1640. His college was St. John's, of which he was a Fellow 1635–48. (*Alumni Oxon.* iv. 1387.) A man of these names was beneficed in Kent. (Ibid.)

Wood says (*Athenæ Oxon.*, ed. 1721, ii. 135) that when Snelling took his M.A. 'he was esteem'd an excellent *Latin* Poet, as his Poems printed occasionally in several Books before the Rebellion broke out in 1642, shew. Afterwards he suffered for the Royal cause, and published *Pharamus, sive Libido Vindex, Hispanica Tragoedia. Lond.* 1650. *oct.* . . . Various Poems—some of which are printed in several Books occasionally written.'

*Thibaldus sive Vindictæ Ingenium, or Pharamus sive
Libido Vindex, Hispanica Tragœdia* (1636?–40)

Bolte, Johannes. 'Die Oxforder Tragödie Thibaldus (1640)',
Shakespeare Jahrbuch, xxvii (1892), 228–9.

Madan, Falconer. *The Early Oxford Press. A Bibliography of
Printing and Publishing at Oxford '1468'–1640* (1895), p. 223.

Morgan, Louise B. 'The Latin University Drama', *Shakespeare
Jahrbuch*, xlvii (1911), 87–88.

1640. Thibaldvs Sive Vindictæ Ingenivm. Tragoedia . . . Oxoniæ
. . . 1640. (With six sets of Latin commendatory verses.)

1650 Pharamus siue Libido vindex, Hispanica tragoedia. Oxford
. . . 1650.

The issues of 1640 and 1650 have frequently been treated as
two separate plays, but Falconer Madan noted that *Pharamus* is
simply the sheets of the 1640 *Thibaldus* with a new title-page.
Vindictæ Ingenium is the running-title and the one most frequently
used in the commendatory verses.

The name of the author is not recorded on either title-page,
but Madan noted that Bishop Barlow had written it on the title-
page of his copy, and Wood records it. Since each of the six
writers of commendatory verses for the play was a St. John's
contemporary of Snelling, and since three of them were also
exact contemporaries of his at the Merchant Taylors' School, the
attribution seems plausible.

There is a brief synopsis of the play and cursory comments on
its analogues in Johannes Bolte's article, but so far as I know its
relationship to *The Spanish Tragedy* has never been fully examined.

The play was probably intended for production at St. John's
College, Oxford, since its author and the writers of the six sets
of commendatory verses were all St. John's men. The date of
production has been given as 1640, but I find no evidence for this
date beyond the title-page of the first edition, which makes 1640
only a *terminus ad quem*. Any date between Snelling's matriculation and publication would square with the evidence, but a date
after the granting of his B.A. seems somewhat more likely.

THOMAS SPARROW
c. 1614–?

There were no Thomas Sparrows at Oxford in the sixteenth and
seventeenth centuries, and only three at Cambridge. The first of

the Cambridge men is known only from his matriculation in 1549; the second matriculated in 1629/30; and the third in 1670. The third is eliminated because the Bodleian MS. of the play, *Confessor*, was owned by Richard Walden in 1666; the first is too early.

The remaining Thomas Sparrow, a native of Essex, was apparently at Westminster School (though there are no school records of his attendance) as a Bishop's Boy, that is, on the foundation of Bishop Williams, Lord Keeper and later Archbishop of York, a foundation established in 1623 and 1624. (*Record of Old Westminsters*, ii. 871 and 1109.) Sparrow was admitted as a pensioner and Bishop Williams Scholar at St. John's College, Cambridge, 4 November 1629, and he matriculated from that college in the Lent term, 1629/30. He commenced B.A. in 1632/3. This is the last certain record of the man, but there was a Thomas Sparrow, 's. and h. of Thomas, of St. Botolph's, Aldersgate, Esq.', admitted to Gray's Inn 14 August 1635. (*Alumni Cantab*. iv. 128.)

That this Thomas Sparrow was the author of *Confessor* seems likely because the play is dedicated in the Bodleian MS., 'Vestris manibus, (tanquam Asylo) Episcope Reverende Patrone. Nullis nominibus colende satis. Confessorem suum, dedicat consecrat*que* Humillimus vester Alumnus Thom: Sparrowe.' Though the name of the bishop is never mentioned, these lines would be quite appropriate if addressed to Bishop Williams by the Thomas Sparrow who had been a Bishop's Boy at Westminster and had entered St. John's College as a Bishop Williams Scholar. The neatness of the manuscript and the use of occasional outlining in red suggest that the Bodleian MS. is the one prepared for presentation to the patron.

Confessor, utinam feliciter nata comœdia (1628–40 ?)

MS.: Bodleian MS. Rawl. Poet. 77 (formerly 14571).

The Bodleian MS. is inscribed on the fly-leaf, ' Johannes Ludovicus. 1675. Ex libris Rici Walden Ex Inter Templi in sub urbañ Londiñ V. 1666. E.' The character of the manuscript suggests that it may be the copy prepared for presentation to the unnamed bishop to whom it is dedicated. The facts of Sparrow's career and the terms of the dedication suggest that the bishop may have been John Williams, who was made Bishop of Lincoln and Lord Keeper in 1621. If so, the dedication must have been written before he was made Archbishop of York in 1641. Moore Smith suggests about 1634 as the date, but he offers no evidence beyond the dates of

Sparrow's matriculation and B.A. (*M.L.R.* iii [1908], 155.) Since so little is known of Sparrow's career, and since there is no evidence whatever of the performance of the play, its dating is extremely hazardous. Sparrow would have been 'Humillimus vester alumnus' while he was on the Bishop's foundation at Westminster as well as during his Cambridge career, though perhaps composition not far from the date of his B.A. is the least questionable guess. Halliwell-Phillipps's date of 'about 1666' is evidently based on the date of Richard Walden's ownership and has nothing to recommend it. (*Dictionary of Old English Plays,* p. 55.)

It is possible, as has been several times suggested, that the play was performed at St. John's College, but the only evidence is the fact that St. John's was Sparrow's college; there are no records of plays at St. John's in the reign of Charles I.

JOHN SPEED
1594/5–1640

John Speed, son of the chronologer, was born in January 1594/5. In January 1603/4 he entered the Merchant Taylors' School from Middlesex. He went to St. John's College, Oxford, as a Merchant Taylor scholar and matriculated 30 October 1612. (Simmonds, *Merchant Taylor Fellows,* pp. 16–17.) From Oxford he received degrees of B.A. 19 June 1616; M.A. 5 May 1620 (incorporated Cambridge 1629); and M.B. and M.D., and he was licensed to practise medicine 20 June 1628. In 1633 he was admitted to Gray's Inn. (*Alumni Oxon.* iv. 1396.) He had married a daughter of Bartholomew Warner of Oxford and practised medicine in Oxford. (Simmonds, loc. cit.) Wood says, 'In which last faculty [i.e., doctor of physic] he became eminent (especially for the practic part) among the academians.' (*Athenæ Oxon.,* Bliss ed., ii. 660–1.) He died in May 1640.

Simmonds (loc. cit.) says there is a manuscript treatise on anatomy written by Speed in St. John's College library. Wood (op. cit.) is the only authority for his dramatic activity.

The Converted Robber [Stonehenge (?)] (1635 or 1637)

MS.: B.M. Add. MS. 14047, fols. 44^v–59^v.

Greg, W. W. *Pastoral Poetry & Pastoral Drama* (1906), pp. 382–4.
Laidler, Josephine. 'A History of Pastoral Drama in England until 1700', *Englische Studien,* xxxv (1905), 234–6.

The only authority for John Speed as a playwright is Anthony à Wood. In his account of Speed in *Athenæ Oxonienses* he lists:

> *Stonehenge*, a Pastoral—Acted before Dr. Rich. Baylie the president and fellows of the said coll. in their common refectory, at what time the said doctor was returned from Salisbury, after he had been installed dean thereof an. 1635. The said *Pastoral* is not printed, but goes about in MS. from hand to hand. (Bliss ed. ii. 660.)

No play called *Stonehenge* has ever been recorded elsewhere, but W. W. Greg made a suggestion about its identity in *Pastoral Poetry & Pastoral Drama*, pp. 382–3 and n. 1:

> Another of these miniature pastorals is preserved in a British Museum manuscript, where it bears the title of *The Converted Robber*. No author's name appears, but a plausible conjecture may be advanced. The scene of the piece, namely, is Stonehenge, and it is evident that the occasion on which it was first performed had some connexion with Salisbury, for there is obviously a topical allusion in the final words:
>
> > Lett us that do noe envy beare um
> > Wish all felicity to Sarum.
>
> Now in 1636, according to Anthony à Wood, there was acted at St. John's College, Oxford, a play by John Speed, entitled *Stonehenge*, the occasion being the return of Dr. Richard Baylie after his installation as Dean of Salisbury. We can hardly be far wrong in identifying the two pieces. The only difficulty is that in the manuscript the play is dated 1637. This, however, may either be a mere slip of the scribe, or may possibly imply that the piece was produced in 1636–7, the scribe adopting the popular and modern, whereas Wood always adhered to the old or legal reckoning. . . . The piece [*The Converted Robber*] has hitherto been ascribed to George Wilde, on the authority of Halliwell. There appears to be no reason for this ascription, beyond the fact that the same volume also contains two pieces by Wilde. His name, however, does not occur in connexion with the present play, and the volume, which is in a variety of hands, certainly includes work not by him.

In considering Greg's suggestion it is well to begin with the B.M. MS. Add. 14047, in which the play is found. This is a small quarto volume of 159 folios, containing as its first three items *Love's Hospital*, 1–39^r, *The Converted Robber*, 44^v–59^v, and *Eumorphus*, 60–96^v. The title-page of *Love's Hospital* says, 'Authore GEORGJO WJLDE. LL: Bac:'; that of *Eumorphus*, 'Authore Georgio Wilde ejusd^m Coll. Soc. et L. L. Bacc.' There is no ascription of authorship in any part of *The Converted Robber*. Scattered through the volume and at the back, reversed, are numerous sets of verses, epitaphs, epigrams, epilogues, and prologues 'spoken to the University by the Duke's house' or the King's house, and a pastoral on the death of the Duchess of Southampton; most of the verses are of the Restoration period, though there is also a copy of 'Randolph to his adopted father Ben: Johnson', and others of undetermined date, including several recited by named scholars at Winchester or about Winchester figures. This rough description is enough to indicate that the volume is not a simple collection of Wilde's plays, as has sometimes been implied. Indeed, the designation of Wilde, including his degree, on the title-pages of *Love's Hospital* and *Eumorphus* would suggest that the omission of his name from the title-page of the intervening play, *The Converted Robber*, indicates that the transcriber did not know who wrote it, or at least that he did not think Wilde did. The three plays are all designated on the title-pages as St. John's plays and carefully dated 1636, 1637, and 1634[/5?], and it is this common association with St. John's, not common authorship, which seems to be the reason for their being brought together. Probably they were all copied by the same man, for the general character of the transcripts—stage directions, dramatis personae, speech titles, and spacings—are quite similar, though *Love's Hospital* is more formally prepared than the others. The hands and inks are also very like, though I am not prepared to say that they are identical.

All in all, then, there is no evidence in the manuscript for Wilde's authorship of *The Converted Robber*, and some indication that the transcriber of the only known text of the play thought that he was not. No external evidence for Wilde's authorship has ever been presented.

With Wilde eliminated, what evidence is there that the play is the *Stonehenge* which Wood says Speed wrote? Greg notes that *The Converted Robber* ends with a topical allusion to Sarum and that Wood says Speed's play was presented to celebrate Baylie's return from his installation as Dean of Salisbury, and that the setting of *The Converted Robber* is Stonehenge. This setting is unusually conspicuous for a Caroline piece: early in the play, fol. 46^v, occurs the stage direction: 'The sceane is opend and it is shew⟨ne⟩ to be like stoña⟨ge⟩ ye wonder y^t is vpon that Play⟨ne⟩ of Sarum. Soft Musicke play 2 boys sing'; several times thereafter the dialogue refers to the stones; and three or four explanations of their presence are offered at different times. *Stonehenge* would, therefore, be a good popular title for the play; in fact, if the set were as well painted as it is unusual, an inevitable one. Greg does not point out that there are two or three dramatically unnecessary allusions to Salisbury Cathedral, or stress the fact that *The*

Converted Robber is a St. John's pastoral, as Wood said *Stonehenge* was, or note that the brevity of the play (800 to 900 lines) would make it especially suitable for a private performance on a special St. John's occasion before the President and Fellows.

There remains to be considered the discrepancy in dates. The play in Add. MS. 14047 is headed:

The converted Robber   A
Pastorall Acted by s^t. Johns. Collg.
1637

Wood says *Stonehenge* was acted 'at what time the said doctor was returned from Salisbury, after he had been installed dean thereof an. 1635'. Greg has misread Wood's date and then tried to reconcile 1636 and 1637 by the new and old calendars. Unfortunately Wood said 1635, and Le Neve says in his list of deans of Salisbury that Baylie 'was presented 10th April 1635'. (*Fasti Ecclesiæ Anglicanæ*, Hardy ed. [1854], ii. 618.) There are many possible explanations of this discrepancy between Wood's 1635 and the 1637 of the manuscript, but I see no very plausible one with the evidence now at hand. In any event, the evidence for the identification of *Stonehenge* and *The Converted Robber* seems to me too strong to be disturbed by the discrepancy in dates.

It is possible that this is the play which Marriott entered in the Stationers' Register with twenty others in 1653 under the title 'Salisbury Plaine a comedy'. No play with the title *Salisbury Plain* is otherwise known, and the title would be appropriate for this comedy with its setting on Salisbury Plain and its several references to Salisbury.

Miss Josephine Laidler remarks that the author of the play 'must have known his Spenser, for the play has more of an eclogue character than most of its kind'. (Op. cit., p. 236.) She gives a full synopsis.

In a letter to *The Times Literary Supplement* of 29 August 1936, p. 697, Mr. R. H. Bowers announced his intention of preparing an edition of *The Converted Robber*, but so far as I know it has not appeared.

Stonehenge

See *The Converted Robber*.

JOHN SQUIRE
fl. 1620

Nothing is known of the John Squire who wrote the Lord Mayor's pageant for 1620. In the *S.T.C.* this pageant and several sermons printed 1618–37 are all listed under one John Squire, but it does not seem likely that a lord mayor's pageant would have been written by a clergyman. There were several men of the name at Oxford and Cambridge in the years when an author of 1620 might have been a youth, but all of them took orders except one, John Squyrs of St. Alban Hall, who received a B.A. at Oxford in 1593 and concerning whom no other fact is recorded.

Tes Irenes Trophœa, or The Triumphs of Peace (1620)

Reprint: John Nichols, *The Progresses, Processions, and Magnificent Festivities of James the First* (1828), iv. 619–27.

Fairholt, Frederick W. *Lord Mayors' Pageants* (Percy Society, vol. x), pp. 46–48.

1620. Tes Irenes Trophæa. Or, The Tryumphs of Peace. *That Celebrated the Solemnity of the* right Honorable Sr *Francis Iones* Knight, at his Inauguration into the Maioraltie *of London, on Monday being the* 30. *of* October, 1620. At the particular cost and charge of the right *worshipfull and ancient Society of* the Haberdashers. With explication of the seuerall shewes and deuices by *I. S.* . . . 1620.

Though only the initials of the author appear on the title-page, his name is signed, ' Jo. Squire', to the dedication to the new Lord Mayor. The show consists of two water pageants, followed by three on land. The pageant concludes with the statement:

The credit of this workmanship (curiously exceeding many former Shewes, and far more ritch then any, in regard no mettall was used to adorne it but gold and silver,) I impose on Francis Tipsley, Cittizen and Haberdasher of London.

THOMAS STANLEY
1625–78

Bentley, G. E. ' James Shirley and a Group of Unnoted Poems on the Wedding of Thomas Stanley', *Huntington Library Quarterly*, ii (1938–9), 219–31.
D.N.B.

Thomas Stanley, the classics scholar, was not a dramatist, but he translated a number of Greek plays, all of which, however, appeared after the closing of the theatres. He was a patron of playwrights and other poets. Several Caroline dramatists wrote verses or dedicated plays to him—Richard Brome, James Shirley, Thomas Jordan, Richard Lovelace.

SIR ROBERT STAPLETON (Stapylton)
c. 1600?–69

Summers, Montague. *The Playhouse of Pepys* (1935), pp. 196–205.

There is no direct evidence that Sir Robert Stapleton, the Restoration playwright, wrote any of his plays before the closing of the theatres, but there is a possibility that one of them may have been written then.

The man, whose date of birth is unknown, was the son of Richard Stapleton, of Carlton by Snaith, Yorkshire. He was educated in the Benedictine monastery of the English Congregation at Douay, and there became a professed monk of the order, 30 March 1625. Later, as Montague Summers phrases it, 'he proved so capricious and infatuate as even to break his vows', became a Protestant, and returned to England. He became a Gentleman of the Privy Chamber to Prince Charles and was knighted at Nottingham, 13 September 1642. He was with the King at Oxford and remained there until the surrender to Fairfax in 1645. Thereafter he is said to have lived in retirement until the Restoration. (*D.N.B.* and Summers, op. cit., p. 196.) His career after the Restoration is better known, but is irrelevant here.

It is not known when he wrote *The Royal Choice*, though Summers says it was while he was in seclusion after the surrender of Oxford. It seems a little odd that a man attached to the play-writing court of Charles I and who wrote at least four plays in his life should have waited until he was nearly fifty to begin. That he had some interest in the drama before his first play was licensed is indicated by his commendatory verses for Shirley's *Grateful Servant*, 1630, Harding's *Sicily and Naples*, 1640, the Beaumont and Fletcher Folio, 1647, and Cartwright's *Comedies*, 1651.

Stapleton also published a number of translations, all before the Restoration.

Pastor Stapilton (?)
(Lost)

Pastor Stapilton is one of the titles listed by Rogers and Ley in their 'exact and perfect Catalogue of all *Playes* that are Printed' which they included A₂–A₄ᵛ in their edition of Goffe's *Careless Shepherdess*, 1656. No such title is known from any other source, and it has an odd sound. Greg suggests in Appendix ii of his *List of Masques, Pageants, &c.* (p. xcvii) that the title may represent an unknown translation of *Pastor Fido* ascribed to Sir Robert Stapleton. Though the suggestion is not entirely convincing, I know of no better one. At any rate, the inclusion of the title in the list indicates that Rogers and Ley thought it was a play.

The Royal Choice (> 1653)

1653, 29 Nov. [Dec.?] S.R. Richard Marriott entered twenty-one plays, of which the ninth is 'The Royall Choice by Sʳ Robᵗ. Stapleton.' (Greg, *Bibliography*, i. 62.)

The only evidence for the existence of a play of this name is Marriott's entry in the Stationers' Register. Two-thirds of the twenty-one titles in this list of plays occur nowhere else, and only three were published later under the titles given there, though four others are known from previous references. (See Anon., *The Woman's Law*, for the entire list.)

Though Sir Robert's extant plays are all of the Restoration period, the events of his life make it not unlikely that he should have written a play before the closing of the theatres.

WILLIAM STRODE
1602/3–44/45

Dobell, Bertram, ed. *The Poetical Works of William Strode* (1907), pp. xiii–lv.

He was the son of Philip Strode, born in or near Plympton, Devonshire, and baptized 11 January 1602/3. At an unknown date he was sent to Westminster School, where he held a King's scholarship and was elected to Christ Church, Oxford, in 1617. He must have gone up to Oxford shortly thereafter, for he had the female role of Tarentilla in Burton's *Philosophaster* (q.v.), performed at Christ Church by the students of the college 16 February 1617/18; he did not matriculate, however, until 1 June 1621.

From the University he received the degrees of B.A. 6 December 1621, M.A. 17 June 1624, B.D. 10 December 1631, and D.D. 6 July 1638. (*Athenæ Oxon.*, Bliss, ed., iii. 151–2; *Alumni Oxon.* iv. 1438; *Record of Old Westminsters*, ii. 892.)

At Oxford he was a well-known figure. He contributed to a number of the university collections of verse, beginning with *Annæ Funebria Sacra* in 1619, and his verse is commonly found in the commonplace books of university men from 1625 to the Restoration. Wood says, 'As for Strode, he was a person of great parts, but not equal to those of Cartwright, a pithy and sententious preacher, exquisite orator and an eminent poet.' (*Athenæ Oxon.*, Bliss ed., iii. 151–2.) He is called 'that renowned wit *W. Strode*' in the advertisement for his *Floating Island* appended to Samuel Austin's *Naps upon Parnassus*, 1658 (G₇).

In 1629 Strode was appointed proctor with Thomas Atkinson, the first in the new cycle of proctors after the scandals of 1628. Also in 1629 he was made Public Orator, being, according to Anthony à Wood, 'a most florid preacher in the university'. In 1633 he became rector of East Bradenham, Norfolk, in 1638 canon of Christ Church and vicar of Blackbourton, Oxford, and in 1639 vicar of Bradby, Northamptonshire. He died 10 March 1644/5 and was buried in the Divinity Chapel of Christ Church Cathedral. (*Athenæ Oxon.* iii. 151–2; *Alumni Oxon.* iv. 1438; *Record of Old Westminsters*, ii. 892; *D.N.B.*; Dobell, ed., *Works*, pp. xiii–lv.)

In addition to his published works, *The Floating Island*, and sermons, Wood adds:

Orations, Speeches, Epistles, Sermons, &c.—They were left behind him fairly written in several volumes; which coming into the hands of Dr. Rich. Gardiner canon of Ch. Ch. came after, or before his death, into those of Rich. Davies of Oxon bookseller. . . . I have seen several of his poems that have had musical compositions of two and three parts set to be sung, by the incomparable Mr. Hen. Lawes; as also certain anthems, particularly one to be sung on Good Friday, which had a composition also set thereunto by Rich. Gibbs organist of Ch. Ch. in Norwich. (*Athenæ Oxon.* iii. 152.)

Collected Edition

The Poetical Works of William Strode (*1600–1645*), edited by Bertram Dobell with a memoir of the author (1907).

The Floating Island (Passions Calmed, Prudentius)
(29 August and 3 September 1636)

MS.: Bodleian MS. Malone 21 contains Henry Lawes's music for the play.

Edition: *The Poetical Works of William Strode (1600–1645) Now First Collected from Manuscript and Printed Sources: to which is added The Floating Island a Tragi-comedy now first reprinted from the original edition of 1655*, edited by Bertram Dobell (1907), pp. 137–240.

Evans, Willa McClung. *Henry Lawes, Musician and Friend of Poets* (1941), pp. 122–35.

Russell, H. K. 'Tudor and Stuart Dramatizations of the Doctrines of Natural and Moral Philosophy', *Stud. Phil.* xxxi (1934), 1–27.

1655. The Floating Island: A Tragi-Comedy, Acted before his Majesty at Oxford, *Aug*. 29. 1636. By the Students of Christ-Church. Written by William Strode, late *Orator* of the University of Oxford. The *Aires* and *Songs* set by Mr. Henry Lawes, servant to his late Majesty in his publick and private Musick . . . 1655.

When Charles and Henrietta Maria visited Oxford with their two nephews, the Princes of the Palatinate, 29–31 August 1636, *The Floating Island* was the play with which they were entertained on the first night, Wilde's *Love's Hospital* (q.v.) following on the afternoon of the 30th, and Cartwright's *Royal Slave* the night of the 30th. The visit had been arranged by Archbishop Laud, then Chancellor of Oxford, who was writing to the Vice-Chancellor about the plays six weeks in advance of the visit:

Since I writ last to you, the Dean of Christ Church came to me, and acquainted me with two things, which are very necessary you should both know and remedy.

The one is, that the University seems to be unwilling to contribute to the charge of the Plays, which are to be at Christ Church. Now this charge, as by reason of their building, they are not able to bear alone; so I must needs acknowledge, there is no reason that they should, whatever their ability be: for the King is to be entertained by Oxford, not by Christ Church. And that he lies there, is but for the conveniency of the place, where there are so many fair lodgings for the great men to be about him. Indeed, if Christ Church men will say, they will have no actors but of their own House, let them bear the charge of their own Plays, in God's name: but if they will take any good actors from any other College or Hall, upon trial of their sufficiency to be as good, or better than their own; then I see no reason in the world, but that the whole University should contribute to the charge. . . .

The other is, that since the University must contribute to this charge, (for so it was done when King James came, and at the last coming of Queen Elizabeth, both within my own memory,) I hold it very fit, that all the materials of that stage, which are now to be made new, and the proscenium, and such apparel, whatever it be, as is wholly made new, shall be laid up in some place fit for it; to which the Vice-Chancellor for the time being shall have one key, and the Dean of Christ Church the other, that it may not be lost, as things of like nature and use have formerly been. (*Autobiography*, 1839 ed., pp. 195–7.)

The visit was a great success, and Laud himself describes it at some length. After noting their entrance into Oxford on the morning of Monday, 29 August, their welcome a mile outside the town with a speech by the Vice-Chancellor, and the speech at St. John's by Thomas Atkinson, Laud continues:

Within Christ Church gate, Mr. William Strode, the University Orator, entertained them with another speech, which was well approved. Thence the King accompanied his Queen to her lodging, and instantly returned, and went with all the Lords to the Cathedral. There after his private devotions ended, at the west door, Dr. Morris, one of the Prebendaries, entertained him with another short speech, which was well liked. And thence his Majesty proceeded into the quire, and heard service. After supper, they were entertained with a Play at Christ Church, which was very well penned, but yet did not take the Court so well. (Ibid., pp. 200–1.)

Such a great occasion was, of course, recorded by various Oxford men. George Evelyn, brother of the diarist, wrote to his father on 26 September 1636 a long description of the festivities in which he spoke of the play:

Then, retiring himself a little, he went to prayers; they being ended, soon after to supper, and then to the play, whose subject was the Calming of the Passions; but it was generally misliked of the Court, because it was so grave; but especially because they understood it not. (William Bray, ed., *Diary and Correspondence of John Evelyn* [1870], i. 424.)

George Garrard wrote to Viscount Conway 4 September 1636 that 'That night there was a play at Christchurch "fitter for scholars than a court." Lord Carnarvon said it was the worst that ever he saw but one that he saw at Cambridge.' (*C.S.P., Dom., 1636–7*, pp. 113–14.) Thomas Crosfield, a Fellow of Queen's

College, gives a fairly detailed account of the whole visit and says of Monday's activities at Christ Church:

6. When ye King & *Queen* & *Palsgrave* were lighted out of their Coach within Ch*rist* Ch*urch* the Orator made a speech & ye ViceChancelo*ur* delivered ye bookes *ut supra*.

7. After Supper ye Play, Prudentius, wth intellectus agens & ye re[be]llious passions was acted from 7. aclocke till 9. or 10 at night: all this upo*n* Munday. (*Crosfield Diary*, p. 91.)

The best account, including a very unusual description of staging, is Anthony à Wood's:

That night, after the King, Queen, and two Princes had supped, they saw a Comedy acted in Christ Church Hall, but such an one it was, that it had more of the Moralist than Poet in it. And though it was well penned, yet it did not take with the Courtiers so well, as it did with the togated crew. It was intituled, ' Passions calmed,' or 'The Setling of the floating Island,' made by Strode the Orator, and performed by the Scholars beyond expectation. It was acted on a goodly stage, reaching from the upper end of the Hall almost to the hearth place, and had on it three or four openings on each side thereof, and partitions between them, much resembling the desks or studies in a Library, out of which the Actors issued forth. The said partitions they could draw in and out at their pleasure upon a sudden, and thrust out new in their places according to the nature of the Screen, whereon were represented Churches, Dwelling-houses, Palaces, &c. which for its variety bred very great admiration. Over all was delicate painting, resembling the Sky, Clouds, &c. At the upper end a great fair shut of two leaves that opened and shut without any visible help. Within which was set forth the emblem of the whole Play in a very sumptuous manner. Therein was the perfect resemblance of the billows of the Sea rolling, and an artificial Island, with Churches and Houses waving up and down and floating, as also rocks, trees and hills. Many other fine pieces of work and Landscapes did also appear at sundry openings thereof, and a Chair also seen to come gliding on the Stage without any visible help. All these representations, being the first (as I have been informed) that were used on the English stage, and therefore giving great content, I have been therefore the more punctual in describing them, to the end that posterity might know that what is now seen in the Play-houses at London belonging to his Majesty, and the Duke of York, is originally due to the invention of Oxford Scholars. (*History and Antiquities of the University of Oxford*, ii, Book i. 408-9.)

Whatever one may think of Wood's theatrical history, his account of the staging of Strode's play is a great service. Would that someone had done as much for a contemporary commercial performance in London! Various stage directions in the text

(Dobell, ed., *Works*) help to particularize his account: 'After The Appearance Of A *Floating Island*, Enter The *Prologue*, As Coming Out Of The Sea'; I. I, '*The Scene turns to the Court of Prudentius*'; II. I, '*The Scene turns to Fancies Court*'; III. 5, '*The Scene turns to feilds, walkes & scattered houses*'; V. I, '*The Scene turnes to the house of Despair. A Table there laid*'; V. 9, '*The Scene returns to* Prudentius *his Court*'; and between the tableau and the epilogue, 'After the musick ended, the Island appearing Setled'. The devices must have been interesting, even though they cannot be expected to have greatly impressed the courtiers of Charles and Henrietta Maria, accustomed to the scenic spectacles of Inigo Jones.

The music for the play—there are half a dozen songs, several dances and shows, and several notations of incidental music—was composed by Henry Lawes, as the title-page indicates. Miss Willa McClung Evans (loc. cit.) discusses the music for this play and for the others in the Oxford series.

There was a second performance for the university community, most of whom would have been crowded out by the court at the first performance. The first edition has a second prologue '*To The Vniversity Before whom it was afterwards acted*'. Wood records this performance:

On Friday in the afternoon (Sept. 2) was acted according to the Chancellor's appointment, 'The Royall Slave,' in Christ Church Hall, before the University and Strangers, and the next day in the after-noon, 'Passions calmed.' Both which were acted very quietly and gave great content. (*History and Antiquities of Oxford*, ii, Book i. 412.)

'Very quietly' evidently does not mean without scenery, for the prologue to the University refers to the set.

The play itself is more of a moral masque than a tragi-comedy. It is clearly allusive, and though the identifications cannot be carried very far with assurance, one or two of them seem in-escapable. Prudentius, the King who retires to give his rebellious subjects a chance to entangle themselves in their own unre-strained folly, is evidently intended to make the audience think of the Royal Spectator himself. The epilogue 'To His Majesty' has the lines:

Our Scene which was but Fiction now is true;
No King so much Prudentius as you:
(Dobell, ed., p. 239.)

In I. 4, when the conspirators are planning to murder Prudentius, he walks in, and they are so awed by his presence that they cannot strike. Audax says, 'O his brow! I turn to feare.' After he has left, Malevolo, the Puritan conspirator, says:

> His flaming Temples
> Strike with such charming Power, such secret Spells,
> That if you see the Light upon his Face,
> Your spirits quaile; it must be done by night.
> (Dobell, ed., p. 155.)

At the end of the play, after the quarrelling conspirators have given his crown back to him, Prudentius talks of their disposal:

> But *Melancolico* and *Concupiscence*
> Shall keep their state; i' th' suburbs, or new-England.
> (Ibid., p. 238.)

In the same way Malevolo, the seditious and malevolent Puritan, acknowledges too many of the sentiments and deeds of William Prynne not to have been identified in Oxford only twenty-eight months after Prynne had been publicly expelled from the University and degraded at a Convocation of the entire University specially called for the purpose. (Wood, op. cit., pp. 393–5.) Moreover, *The Floating Island* was acted before an audience which included Prynne's principal opponent (Laud) and his principal victim (allegedly the Queen).

Early in the play, when the conspirators are enumerating their grievances (I. 2), Malevolo says:

> For my part, if I broach
> Some biting libel, venomous word or Book
> Against some prosprous Object which I hate,
> My Eares are questioned. Locks which I have scorn'd
> Must hide my Eare stumps.
> (Dobell, ed., p. 148.)

Other people had noted Prynne's unshorn hair, grown long, contrary to Puritan practice, in order to hide his ears, which had been mutilated in 1634; at his trial in 1637 Justice Finch ordered his long hair held back to reveal his former punishment. (Gardiner, viii. 228.) In III. 8 of *The Floating Island* Malevolo says to Irato:

> Sir you and we were acted at the Court.
> We loosers are made laughing-stocks, and sport
> For open Stages.
> (Dobell, ed., p. 196.)

And a few lines later in the scene, Memor says to him:

> This trick *Malevolo*
> Was chiefly meant to you, because your pen
> Hath scourged the Stage.   (Ibid.)

That Malevolo presents Anglican Oxford's conception of William Prynne is most strikingly illustrated by Anthony à Wood. Some thirty-odd years after the performance of *The Floating Island*, Wood wrote his account of the University's expulsion and degradation of the author of *Histriomastix*, in the course of which he writes a short description of Prynne. As a characterization of Prynne it is notably inadequate, but it might easily be taken for a description of Malevolo:

As for this person, he was one of a hot fiery spirit and eager of any thing that was put into his head, but afterwards growing weary of himself when he had no enemy in a manner to encounter with, became more moderate and mild. (Op. cit., p. 395.)

The attack on Prynne in *The Floating Island* seems to have been recognized by the enemies of Laud. That sturdy Puritan, Henry Burton, clearly refers to the Oxford plays in the sermon that he preached at St. Matthews, Friday Street, two months later on 5 November 1636 and published under the title *For God and the King*—a publication for which he was pilloried and mutilated with Prynne and Bastwick, 30 June 1637. (Gardiner, viii. 231–2.) In this sermon he inveighs against those who have attacked the Puritans and continues:

Nor are they content, to abuse our pious Princes eares in the Pulpit, but also on the Stage. O pyous, holy, reverend, grave, gracious Prelates, whose Academicall Entertainment of pious and religious Kings and Princes (in stead of learned and Scholasticall disputations or exercises intable [*sic*] to the condition of a learned Academy) is a scurrilous Enterlude, and this in disgrace of that, which is the greatest beauty of our religion, to wit, true piety and vertue! O blush at this ye Prelates, and in your shrift confesse how unseemly this was for YOV, that pretend to succeede the Apostles. . . . Nay, as if this had not been sufficient, this is done, in the very heat and height of Gods Tragedy, still Acting in the Imperiall City, when we were all mourning, yea, and every moment as dying men. Was this a time then of Entertaining the Court, and poysoning their eares with Enterludes, and thereby provoking the Lord further to plague the Kings good people, . . . And was that a time of Enterludes ? Why did you not feare some Plague to grow in such a mighty assembly ? When notwithstanding Preaching is made dangerous by you, for feare of the plague; which should be a meanes (as it hath beene formerly) to drive away the plague, by bringing the people to true humiliation and reformation. Whereas your guelded Fast-book (contrary to the Proclamation) I am sure brought us for a hansell, a double increase of the Plague that weeke, to any weeke since the Plague began: (Henry Burton, *For God and the King. The Summe of two Sermons* [1636], pp. 49–50 (G$_1$–G$_1$^{v}].)

Burton's reference to the prelates' 'Academicall Entertainment of pious and religious Kings and Princes' with an interlude clearly refers to Laud's entertainment of the King and the two Princes of the Palatinate at Oxford with one of the three plays, *The Floating Island, Love's Hospital,* and *The Royal Slave,* the preceding 29 and 30 August. The occasion is confirmed by his plague reference: 'your guelded Fast-book . . . brought us for a hansell, a double increase of the Plague that weeke'. The recorded weekly deaths from the plague in London were: 4 August, 181; 11th, 244; 18th, 284; 25th, 380; and the week of the plays, 1 September, 536. (See above, ii. 669.)

The play which Burton singled out for his attack was *The Floating Island,* for though the other two plays were equally Laud's academic entertainment for the King and the Princes, and equally plague-time assemblies, only *The Floating Island* contained extended ridicule of Puritans, and might be called a 'scurrilous Enterlude . . . in disgrace of that, which is the greatest beauty of our religion, to wit, true piety and vertue!' The important characters of Malevolo, Melancholico, and Fuga are used largely to set forth Puritan hypocrisy and malice; Malevolo must have been especially objectionable to Burton in its unsympathetic presentation of his fellow sufferer, the stalwart Prynne. Since the trial and punishment of Burton, Prynne, and Bastwick are so significant in the rush of events towards civil war, *The Floating Island* ought, perhaps, to have somewhat more consideration than has been accorded it.

EDMUND STUBBE (Stub, Stubbs)
c. 1595?–1659

Stubbe matriculated from Trinity at Easter 1611, as the son of Francis Stubbe of Scottowe, Norfolk. He had come to Trinity as a Scholar from Westminster School. He received the degrees of B.A. 1614/5, M.A. 1618, and B.D. 1631. (*Alumni Cantab.* iv. 178.) In 1616 he became a minor Fellow of Trinity, in 1617 a major Fellow, and payments were made to him as Fellow beginning in 1618 and ending in 1621. (Innes, *Fellows of Trinity College, Cambridge,* p. 30.) Stubbe must have been well known in college dramatics, for he played Sulpitia in the Trinity College production of *Adelphe* in 1611/12, Alcinus in the Trinity College production of *Melanthe* in 1614/15, and Callidamus in his own *Fraus Honesta.* (G. C. Moore Smith, *College Plays,* pp. 76–81.)

On 24 January 1622/3 William Beale, Fellow of Jesus College, wrote to William Boswell, Secretary to the Lord Keeper in London, 'Gemina Comœdia in fieri est; næquidem et in Agere, apud Trinitarios: Autoribus Hacket, et Stubs: lepidis Jupiter, et comicissimis.' (See Ward, *Fucus Histriomastix*, and Hacket, *Loyola*.) This would suggest that Hacket's play of *Loyola*, apparently first written in 1616, was revised or adapted by Stubbe for the performances of February and March 1622/3, as Moore Smith has suggested. (Ed., *Fucus Histriomastix*, p. xii, n. 2.)

From 1621 to 1659 Stubbe was rector of Huntingfield in Suffolk. The coincidence of his appointment and the cessation of payments to him as Fellow of Trinity suggest that he may have left Cambridge in 1621, but this is too conjectural to eliminate him as the probable reviser of *Loyola*. In 1630 he was rector of Longford, Derbyshire, and 'still there, 1650' (*Alumni Cantab.* iv. 178). In 1635 he became rector of Cookley, Suffolk. At some unknown date he married Margaret, daughter of Wolfran Smith of Lackfield, Suffolk. He died 9 April 1659. (Ibid.)

Fraus Honesta (10 February 1618/19 and 24 September 1629)

MSS.: Emmanuel College, Cambridge, 3. 1. 17; Trinity College, Cambridge, R. 17. 9 and R. 17. 10; B.M. Harleian MS. 2296, fol. 151. (The play in this last manuscript is called *Callidamus et Callanthia* in *Cambridge History of English Literature*, vi. 483, and 'A Latin Comedy without a Title or the Author's Name' in the *Catalogue of Harleian Manuscripts*, ii. 644, but Moore Smith says in *College Plays*, p. 96, that it is *Fraus Honesta*.)

1631, 28 Sept. S.R. Richard Thrale entered for his copy under the hands of 'Sʳ. Henry Herbert & mʳ. Smethwicke warden a Play called ffraus honesta'. (Greg, *Bibliography*, i. 40.)

1632. *Fravs Honesta* Comœdia Cantabrigiæ Olim Acta. Authore Mʳᵒ. Stvbbe Collegii Trinitatis Socio . . . 1632.

The date of the first performance has several times been given as 1616 (*Retrospective Review*, xii [1825], 34; Cooper, *Annals of Cambridge*, iii. 105; Fleay, *Biog. Chron.* ii. 254) because of a note in the Emmanuel College MS. where, beside the dramatis personae, is written, apparently in the same hand but a different ink, 'Scæna est fflorentiæ decimo die ffebruarij. 1616'. This statement, however, must refer to the date of the action, not of performance, for two of the manuscripts of the play designate Stubbe as 'Mᵒ'

or 'M^{ro}' and he did not become Master of Arts until 1618. Moreover, two of the members of the cast did not matriculate until
1618 and two others not until 1617, while four others did not
receive the degrees by which they are designated until 1617,
1618, and 1618/19. Finally, Trinity College MS. R. 17. 10 carries
the statement, 'Acta erat haec Comedia decimo die Febr. A^{no}
D^{ni} 1618.' The evidence indicates that the first performance was
10 February 1618/19, as Moore Smith concluded, though he cited
no evidence. (*College Plays*, pp. 68, 81, 96.) He gives the cast from
the Emmanuel College MS. and from Trinity R. 17. 10.

There was a revival of the play at Trinity on 24 September
1629 on the occasion of a visit of Lord Holland, who was Chancellor of the University, and the French ambassador. Joseph
Mead tells of the occasion in a letter to Sir Martin Stuteville,
dated from Christ's College, 26 September 1629:

The French ambassador came hither on Wednesday, about three
o'clock, and our chancellor with him, and was lodged at Trinity
College. That night came also my Lord of Warwick, with very many
horse. On Thursday morning, they had an act at the schools well performed; went thence to our Regent House, to be incorporated, where
the orator entertained him with a speech, then dined at Trinity College, where were great provisions sent in before by our chancellor, and
a gentleman of his also with them to order that part of the entertainment. At three o'clock they went to the comedy, which was '*Fraus
Honesta*', acted some years since; the actors now were not all so perfect as might have been wished, yet came off handsomely. The music
was not so well supplied as heretofore, said those who have skill that
way.' (Birch, *Charles I*, ii. 29.)

A much fuller account of the visit, with an extract from the
play and a full dramatis personae, is given by Masson (*Life of
John Milton*, i. 187–90), who contends that John Milton was one
of the spectators at this performance.

SIR JOHN SUCKLING
1608/9–42

Anon. 'The Singing Cavalier', *T.L.S.*, 9 May 1942, p. 236.
Clarke, Andrew (ed.) '*Brief Lives*,' *chiefly of Contemporaries, set
    down by John Aubrey, between the Years 1669 & 1696*, 2 vols.
    (1898), ii. 240–5.
D.N.B.
Harbage, Alfred. *Cavalier Drama* (1936), pp. 109–15.

Hazlitt, W. C. *The Poems, Plays, and Other Remains of Sir John Suckling* (1874), i. pp. vii–lxxi.

Lynch, Kathleen M. *The Social Mode of Restoration Comedy*, University of Michigan Publications, Language and Literature, vol. iii (1926), pp. 69–79.

Suckling, Alfred. *Selections from the Works of Sir John Suckling* (1836), pp. 1–62.

Thompson, A. Hamilton. *The Works of Sir John Suckling in Prose and Verse* (1910), pp. ix–xvii.

Sir John Suckling, who so nearly approximated to the Cavalier ideal—at least in the eyes of the Puritans—and was called by John Aubrey 'the greatest gallant of his time, and the greatest gamester, both for bowling and cards' (*Brief Lives*, ii. 240–1), was less of a dramatist than a lyric poet, but for more than half a century his plays were widely admired.

The poet was baptized at Whitton, near Twickenham, Middlesex, on 10 February 1608/9, the grandson of a mayor of Norwich and the son of John Suckling, later Sir John, Master of Requests and comptroller of the Royal Household. (Alfred Suckling, op. cit., pp. 1–3.) His mother was Martha, sister of Lionel Cranfield, later the first Earl of Middlesex. (Ibid.) Aubrey (op. cit., p. 240) thought the boy might have been sent to Westminster School, but his name does not appear in the printed records, and it is not known where he got his pre-university schooling.

In the Easter term, 1623, young Suckling matriculated at Cambridge as a Fellow-Commoner from Trinity College, but he apparently left without a degree. (*Alumni Cantab.* iv. 183.) On 23 February 1626/7 he was admitted to Gray's Inn (Joseph Foster, *The Register of Admissions to Gray's Inn 1521–1889* [1889], p. 180), and about one month later the death of his father left him the master of a large estate. (Alfred Suckling, op. cit., pp. 8–9.)

In 1628 the young heir began his continental travels (ibid., p. 10); their precise duration is unknown, but they must have been at least interrupted in November 1629, for there is extant a letter concerning his return dated 18 November 1629 from Suckling to William Davenant. (See Hazlitt edition, ii. 177–9.) In the next year Suckling was knighted at Theobalds, 19 September [or December?] 1630. (W. A. Shaw, *The Knights of England* [1906], ii. 198.)

At the end of July 1631 Suckling left England with the Marquis of Hamilton and his command of 6,000 men to serve with Gustavus Adolphus. Alfred Suckling (op. cit., pp. 10–11) names several

actions in the war—including Leipzig—at which he says the poet
was present, but he offers no evidence. Suckling was back at
Whitehall on 2 May 1632, presumably as a messenger, for his
letter of this date to Sir Henry Vane describes his reception at
court, the reception of his 'packet', and the attitude of the King
and court towards his news of the wars in Germany. (*C.S.P. Dom.*,
1631–3, pp. 322–3.)

It was after his return from Germany that Suckling's notorious
career as a prodigal court figure developed. He was widely known
as a gambler for high stakes, especially at bowls and cards, he is
said to have invented the game of cribbage (Aubrey, *Brief Lives*,
ii. 240–1 and 245), and there are contemporary stories of the great
sums he won and lost. His reputation as a roisterer and philanderer
is found mostly in Puritan accounts, though his own poetry invites
it, as in his characterization of himself in his 'Sessions of the
Poets'. In 1634 there was a sensational affair in which Suckling
was beaten by Sir John Digby, younger brother of Sir Kenelm,
in connexion with Suckling's addresses to the daughter of Sir
Henry Willoughby. (See Alfred Suckling, op. cit., pp. 19–23;
Strafforde Letters, i. 336–7; and Aubrey, *Brief Lives*, ii. 241.)
Perhaps the affair was a simple assault, but Suckling's reputation
suffered because of his submission.

Suckling's great court success, *Aglaura*, appeared in 1637 and
soon after was printed in folio, an ostentatious display which
greatly annoyed Richard Brome (see above, i. 58–60) and others.
Suckling's extravagance in buying spectacular costumes for the
King's men to use in the performance simply added another to
the current stories of his prodigality. (Ibid.)

Similar to his extravagance in outfitting the players was his
provision in 1639 of a troop of 100 horse for service with the King
against the Scots in the Bishops' War. The spectacular white and
scarlet uniforms of his men are said to have cost the poet £12,000,
and they attracted the greatest attention when the troopers
paraded through London. (Aubrey, *Brief Lives*, ii. 242; Alfred
Suckling, op. cit., p. 30.) Of course the rout of the King's forces
in the north laid Suckling and his gaudy troop especially open to
ridicule. (See '*Vpon Sir* John Sucklings *most warlike preparations
for the Scotish Warre*', *Musarum Deliciae*, by Sir J. M. and Ja:
S. [1655], pp. 82–83.)

In February 1639/40 Sir John was commissioned captain of a
troop of carabineers (*C.S.P. Dom.*, *1639–40*, p. 481), and his new
absorption in political affairs is seen in his election to the Long
Parliament in the autumn of 1640 (Alfred Suckling, op. cit., p. 37)

and in his letter of political advice for the King, printed in 1641 as a pamphlet entitled *A Coppy of a Letter found in the Privy Lodgeings at Whitehall* and reprinted in *Fragmenta Aurea*, 1646, pp. 91–96. Soon after he was one of the principal conspirators in the first army plot (see Gardiner, *History of England*, ix. 348–64, and Alfred Suckling, op. cit., pp. 42–47), which was designed to release the Earl of Strafford from the Tower and to bring an army into London. Suckling did not answer the summons of Parliament, and was charged with treason, and on 8 May 1641 a proclamation was issued against him, Henry Percy, Henry Jermyn, William Davenant, and Captain Billingsley. (Ibid.) Suckling had fled, however, and he was never caught and never returned to England.

Nothing precise is known of the rest of his life. Various pamphlets about him, or allegedly written by him, appeared in 1641 and 1642. Most of these pamphlets concur in asserting that Sir John was in Paris at least part of the time after his flight. He must have died, presumably at Paris, in 1642, for *An Elegie Vpon The Death Of The Renowned Sir John Svtlin* appeared in 1642 and was dated February by George Thomason on his copy, and in 1643 there was published *A copy of two remonstrances, brought over the River Stix in Carons Ferry-boate, by the Ghost of Sir Iohn Sucklin.* Aubrey says that Suckling, while lodging with an apothecary in Paris, 'tooke poyson, which killed him miserably with vomiting. He was buryed in the Protestants church-yard.' (*Brief Lives*, ii. 242.) Alfred Suckling (op. cit., pp. 48–49), who had access to family papers, accepted this account (though Aubrey gives the date as 1646 in error), and he cast doubt on the more sensational— but to him less shocking—story that the poet was killed by a valet who placed an open razor, or pen-knife, in his boot.

Allusions to Sir John Suckling are fairly common in the seventeenth century—I have collected about fifty—though a number of them refer to his courtly rather than his literary accomplishments. A good example of the Puritan animosity towards Suckling may be seen in the broadside entitled *The Sucklington Faction or Suckling's Roaring Boys*, with its large engraving of roistering cavaliers. (See W. C. Hazlitt, op. cit. ii. 275–6.)

Suckling's admiration for Shakespeare is obvious in much of his work and is several times recorded. Noteworthy is a revealing reference to *Henry IV, Part I* in a letter written from the Tweed during the Bishops' War (see Alfred Suckling, op. cit., p. 31) and Van Dyke's portrait of Suckling, now in the Frick Gallery, New York, in which the poet holds in his hand a Shakespeare folio opened at *Hamlet*.

Collected Editions

1646. Fragmenta Aurea. A Collection of all The Incomparable Peeces, Written By Sir John Svckling. *And published by a Friend to perpetuate his memory.* Printed by his owne Copies . . . MDCXLVI.

1648. [Another edition.]

1658. [Another edition: 'The Third Edition, with some New Additionals.']

1659. The Last Remains of Sr John Suckling. Being a Full Collection Of all his Poems and Letters which have been so long expected, and never till now Published. With *License* and *Approbation* of his Noble and Dearest Friends . . . 1659. [Contains *The Sad One*.]

1672? [Another edition of *Fragmenta Aurea* and *The Last Remains*, falsely dated 1648 and 1659. See *Library*, Fifth Series, i (1946–7), 85.]

1676. [Another issue. See ibid.]

1676. Letters, &c. Published by His Friends (from his own Copies) to perpetuate his Memory . . . 1676.

1696. The Works of Sir John Suckling, containing All his Poems, Love-Verses, Songs, Letters, and his Tragedies and Comedies. *Never before Printed in One Volume* . . . 1696.

1709. The Works of Sir John Suckling. Containing his Poems, Letters, and Plays . . . 1709.

1719. [Another edition.]

1770. The Works of Sir John Suckling. Containing his Poems, Letters, Plays, 2 vols. (1770).

1836. Alfred Suckling, ed. *Selections from the Works of Sir John Suckling* (1836). Includes the four plays.

1874. W. C. Hazlitt, ed. *The Poems, Plays, and Other Remains of Sir John Suckling*, 2 vols. (1874).

1892. [Another edition.]

1910. A. Hamilton Thompson, ed. *The Works of Sir John Suckling in Prose and Verse* (1910).

Aglaura (1637)

MS.: B.M. MS. Royal 18 C. xxv.

Harbage, Alfred. *Cavalier Drama* (1936), pp. 110–12.
McGinn, Donald Joseph. *Shakespeare's Influence on the Drama of His Age* (1938), pp. 48–51.

1637, 24 July. 'I pray send hither Sir Jhon Suckling's play, and I begin with this request that you may the better remember it.

(Viscount Conway from the *Triumph* in the Downs to George Garrard in London. *Hist. MSS. Com.*, Fourteenth Report, Appendix, Part ii, MSS. of the Duke of Portland at Welbeck, iii [1894], 46.)

1637/8, 7 Feb. 'Two of the King's Servants, Privy-Chamber Men both, have writ each of them a Play, Sir *John Sutlin* and *Will. Barclay*, which have been acted in Court, and at the *Black Friars*, with much Applause. *Sutlin's* Play cost three or four hundred Pounds setting out, eight or ten Suits of new Cloaths he gave the Players; an unheard of Prodigality.' (George Garrard to the Earl of Strafford. *Strafforde's Letters*, ii. 150.)

1638, 3 Apr. '[Plays acted] before the king & queene this [present] yeare of our lord 1638. . . . At the Cockpit the 3ᵈ of Aprill . . . Aglaura.' (Adams, *Herbert*, p. 76; see also G. E. Bentley, *T.L.S.*, 8 December 1932, p. 943.)

1638, 18 Apr. S.R. Thomas Walkley entered for his copy 'a Play called Aglaura by Sʳ. Io: Sucklin knight'. (Greg, *Bibliography*, i. 48.)

1638, 18 Apr. '*Aprilis* 18. 1638. Imprimatur, Matth. Clay.' (Folio of 1638, A₁ᵛ.)

1638. Aglaura . . . 1638.

1640. 'Scorning all glory that is not her owne,
    Nor needing a *Blacke-Fryers* shaven crowne,
    (As some,) to wispe her temples, though put forth
    So poore, that *six-pence* charge buyes all she's worth;
      She'le out-blaze bright *Aglaura's* shining robe:
      Her scene shall never change, the world's her *Globe*.'
(From commendatory verses by S. Hall to Samuel Harding's *Sicily and Naples*, 1640.)

1640. 'If learning will beseem a Courtier well,
    If honour waite on those who dare excell,
    Then let not Poets envy but admire,
    The eager flames of thy poetique fire;
    For whilst the world loves wit, Aglaura shall,
    Phoenix-like live after her funerall.'
('*To Sr. John Suckling*', Anon., *Wits Recreations*, 1640, B₃ᵛ.)

1641. '14 Could not the plot, By which I got
      Such credit in the play-a
    Aglaura bright that Persian wight,
      My roving fancie stay-a,
    15 But I must flie at things so high,
      Above me not allow'd-a
      And I Sir John, like Ixion,

For Juno kisse a cloud-a?
   16 Would I had burn'd it, when I turn'd it
Out of a Comedie-a:
   There was an omen in the nomen
(I feare of Tragedie-a,
   17 Which is at last upon me cast
And I proclaim'd a sott-a
   For thinking to with English doe
As with a Persian plot-a
   18 But now I finde with griefe of minde
What will not me availe-a,
   That plots in iest are ever best,
When plots in earnest faile-a.'

(From a Parliamentary ballad entitled *A Letter Sent By Sir Iohn Svckling from France, deploring his said Estate and flight*, 1641, p. 3.)

1642.   'To Sir Iohn Svtlin upon his *Aglaura*:
   First, a bloody Tragædy, then by the said
      Sir Iohn, turn'd to a *Comedie*.

When first I read thy Book, me thought each word
Seem'd a short Dagger, and each line a Sword.
Where Women, Men, Good, Bad, Rich, Poore, all dy;
That needs must prove a fatall Tragedy.
But when I finde, whom I so late saw slaine,
In thy first Booke, in this revive againe:
I cannot but with others much admire,
In humane shape a more then earthly Fire.
So when *Prometheus* did informe this Clay,
He stole his Fire from heaven. What shall I say?
First for to kill, and then to life restore,
This *Sutlin* did, the Gods can doe no more.'

(Appended to the anonymous pamphlet, *An Elegie vpon the Death of the Renowned Sir Iohn Svtlin*, 1642.)

1646. Aglaura. Presented At the Private House in *Black-Fryers*, by his Majesties Servants. Written by Sir John Svckling . . . 1646. (Separate title-page in *Fragmenta Aurea*, 1646.)

1646. Aglaura. Represented At the Court, by his Majesties Servants. Written by Sir John Svckling . . . 1646. (Separate title-page for alternative ending in *Fragmenta Aurea*, 1646.)

1647/8, 22 Feb. S.R. Humphrey Moseley had assigned over to him by Thomas Walkley three books, including 'Aglaura a play by Sr Iohn Suckling'. (Greg, *Bibliography*, i. 59.)

1648. [Another edition, with two title-pages, as above, in *Fragmenta Aurea*, 1648.]

1656. In his poem, 'The Impartial Doom,' John Phillips sets forth a series of suggested bequests for Fortune, including:

> Lest the Players should grow poor,
> Send them Aglauras more and more.

(*Sportive Wit*, 1656, p. 40 [F₄ᵛ].)

1658–9 [Another edition with two title-pages, as above, in *Fragmenta Aurea*, 1658–9.]

1659. Prefixed to *The Weeding of Covent-Garden* is a sarcastic poem by Brome entitled 'Upon AGLAURA printed in Folio'. (Richard Brome, *Five New Playes*, 1659.)

1659–60. In a list of plays in the repertory of Rhodes' company acting at the Cockpit, John Downes lists '*Aglaura*'. (*Roscius Anglicanus*, Summers ed., pp. 17–18.)

1661, 28 Dec. In a list of performances of plays by 'the Kings Companie at the Red Bull and the new house in Gibbon's Tennis Court near Clare Market' Sir Henry Herbert lists 'Aglaura. 28. De.' (Adams, *Herbert*, pp. 116–18.)

1661/2, 27 Feb. In the same list Sir Henry notes, 'Aglavara the Tragicall way 27. Febr.' (Ibid.)

1662, 24 Sept. '. . . he told me how Bird [Theophilus Bird] hath lately broke his leg, while he was fencing in "Aglaura" upon the stage.' (Diary of Samuel Pepys.)

1664, 5 Sept. '. . . and then to Deptford, and so home, all the way reading Sir J. Suck[l]ing's "Aglaura", which, methinks, is but a mean play; nothing of design in it.' (Ibid.)

1667, 16 May. '16 Auglaura at Court' in a warrant for payment for plays presented at court by the Theatre Royal company. (Allardyce Nicoll, *A History of Restoration Drama*, 3rd ed., pp. 305–6.)

1667/8, 10 Jan. '. . . to the King's house, to see "Aglaura", which hath been always mightily cried up; and so I went with mighty expectation, but do find nothing extraordinary in it at all, and but hardly good in any degree.' (Diary of Samuel Pepys.)

1668/9, *c*. 12 Jan. In 'A Catalogue of part of His Maᵗᵉˢ Servants Playes as they were formerly acted at the Blackfryers & now allowed of to his Maᵗᵉˢ Servants at yᵉ New Theatre' occurs the title 'Aglaura.' (Allardyce Nicoll, op. cit., pp. 315–16.)

1672 (?) [Another edition with two title-pages, as above, in *Fragmenta Aurea*, falsely (?) dated 1658.]

1674, 16 Nov. In a warrant for payment for plays presented at court by the Theatre Royal company is the entry, 'Nouember

16 Aglaura the King & Queene 20.' (Allardyce Nicoll, op. cit., p. 307.)

1676. [Another issue in *The Works of John Suckling*, 1676.]

1669–96. 'When his *Aglaura* was ⟨acted⟩, he bought all the cloathes himselfe, which were very rich; no tinsill, all the lace pure gold and silver, which cost him . . . I have now forgott. He had some scaenes to it, which in those dayes were only used at masques. . . . Sir Francis Cornwallis made his *Aglaura*, except the end.' (Aubrey, *Brief Lives*, ii. 244–5.)

1694. [Another edition, with alternative title-pages, each dated 1694, in *The Works of Sir John Suckling*, 1696.]

The numerous references cited show what a sensation *Aglaura* created when it first appeared, but it seems likely that more of the talk was engendered by the notoriety of the author and the prodigality of his production than by any suggestion that his play was a dramatic masterpiece. Perhaps, however, Richard Flecknoe's statement, in spite of its appended reservation, expresses an opinion that was common at court:

> *Beaumont* and *Fletcher* first writ in the Heroick way, upon whom *Suckling* and others endeavoured to refine agen; one saying wittily of his *Aglaura*, that 'twas full of fine flowers, but they seem'd rather stuck, then growing there. (*A Short Discourse of the English Stage*, appended to *Love's Kingdom*, 1664.)

Viscount Conway's letter of 24 July 1637 shows that he had heard about the play by then, but not necessarily that it had been produced; indeed, it is most unlikely that a play of this character, obviously intended for the court, should have been tried out in a public theatre so long before the court performance about which Garrard was writing—as news—on 7 February 1637/8. One would guess that Garrard had seen the manuscript of the play—or possibly only heard of it from London gossip—and that Viscount Conway had understood, mistakenly, that a text was available. As a matter of fact, a second letter from Conway to Garrard suggests this interpretation, but it is too vague to allow of certainty. In this letter, also sent from the *Triumph* in the Downs, dated 31 July 1637, Conway writes, after several sentences of bantering:

> But if you would have gone any farther then wishes the play booke would have endured cariadge, and allthough it be none of yours, you might have stollen it; both your conscience and ours would have endured it; a seaman, an usurer, and a thiefe put into a bagge when they comme out, a thiefe commes first; but if it be not a se[c]ond play we

neede it not. (*Hist. MSS. Com.*, Fourteenth Report, Appendix, Part II, MSS. of the Duke of Portland, iii [1894], 47.)

Though no author or title is named, Conway was probably writing about the play mentioned in his letter of the week before and replying to Garrard's protest that he had only seen a manuscript by admonishing him—jocosely—that he should have stolen Suckling's 'play booke' and sent it along. Thus, though one could wish that the correspondents had been more explicit, they indicate that a manuscript of *Aglaura* was in existence by the end of July 1637. Probably the King's men tried out the play at Blackfriars in the autumn before the Christmas production about which Garrard wrote on 7 February 1637/8.

After the first performance of the play at court Suckling was evidently persuaded to alter his tragedy into a tragi-comedy by writing a new fifth act. Both fifth acts are printed in the edition of 1638, the second version with a repeated title-page, and the prologue to the second, or tragi-comic, version indicates that it was first presented before the King during the Easter season. The prologue begins:

> *'Tis strange, perchance (you'll thinke) that shee that di'de*
> *At Christmas, should at Easter be a Bride:*
>
> .   .   .   .   .   .
>
> *That can be done onely by Gods and Kings.*
> *Of this wild guilt hee faine would bee thought free,*
> *That writ this Play, and therefore (Sir) by mee,*
> *Hee humbly begs, you would be pleas'd to know,*
> *Aglaura's but repreiv'd this night, and though*
> *Shee now appeares upon a Poets call,*
> *Shee's not to live, unlesse you say shee shall.*

The Christmas performance was apparently the one Garrard referred to in his letter of 7 February 1637/8, and the Easter performance the one Sir Henry recorded on 3 April 1638.

Garrard's letter of 7 February 1637/8 and statements in the later editions of the play show that the actors who performed *Aglaura* were members of the King's company, as one would have expected. According to contemporary accounts, Suckling gave the play to the King's men instead of selling it, like a good workaday playwright, and he paid for special costumes and, according to Aubrey, scenery as well. Richard Brome could not forget this unfair competition with the poor professionals and grumbled about it repeatedly. (See above, i. 58–60.)

The B.M. MS. of the play in a handsome contemporary binding presents the original tragic version. It is almost certainly, according to Greg (*Dramatic Documents*, pp. 332–3), the copy prepared by a professional scribe for presentation to King Charles at the first court performance. All the alterations and additions in the manuscript appear in the printed version, and a number of others as well.

The fact that the first edition of the play appeared pretentiously in a folio, rather than a quarto format, evidently annoyed some of Suckling's contemporaries. See Richard Brome's verses 'Upon AGLAURA printed in folio', which were published with his play, *The Weeding of Covent Garden*, in *Five New Playes*, 1659.

John Aubrey's assertion that 'Sir Francis Cornwallis made his *Aglaura*, except the end' is probably only another example of Aubrey's baseless gossip. Not that Sir John was above suspicion, but, considering the very large number of contemporary allusions to the play and the amount of hostility to Suckling, the charge would certainly have been made by others had there been any truth in it.

Many of the allusions to the play before the Restoration may be attributed to the notoriety of the author, but the wish of John Phillips in 1656 seems to imply that the play was a profitable item in the Blackfriars repertory. Certainly the number of references to *Aglaura* after 1660 indicates that it was performed oftener before Restoration audiences than one would think it deserved. Miss Lynch (*The Social Mode of Restoration Comedy* [1926], pp. 135–6) notes that Dryden in *The Wild Gallant*, v. 3, even quotes from Suckling's play, and that as late as 1691 Langbaine said, 'This Play is much priz'd at this Day.' (Ibid., p. 69, n., from *An Account of the English Dramatick Poets* [1691], p. 497.)

The setting of two songs in the play by Henry and William Lawes is discussed by Miss Willa McClung Evans. (*Henry Lawes Musician and Friend of Poets* [1941], pp. 145–7.)

Brennoralt, or The Discontented Colonel (1639–41)

Harbage, Alfred. *Cavalier Drama* (1936), pp. 112-15.

Henderson, Fletcher. 'Camus' "Iphigene" as a Source for Suckling's *Brennoralt*', *T.L.S.*, 4 February 1939, pp. 73–74.

Krzyzanowski, Julius. 'Source of Suckling's *Brennoralt*', *T.L.S.*, 9 April 1938, p. 252.

1641, 7 Aug. 'The discontented Colonell' appears in a list of plays belonging to the King's men which the Lord Chamberlain forbade the printers to publish without the company's consent. (See above, i. 65–66.)

1642, 5 Apr. S.R. Francis Egglesfield entered for his copy 'a booke called The discontented Colonell. by Sr Iohn Sucklyn kn^t.' (Greg, *Bibliography*, i. 54.)

N.D. The Discontented Colonell. Written by Sir Iohn Sucklin.

1646, 1 Aug. S.R. Humphrey Moseley recorded the assignment to him by Francis Egglesfield and Henry Twiford of 'ye Play called The Discontented Colonell &ᵭ. by S^r. Io: Sucklin'. (Greg, *Bibliography*, i. 56.)

1646. Brennoralt. A Tragedy. Presented at the Private House in Black-Fryers, by His *Majesties* servants. Written By Sir John Suckling ... MDCXLVI. (Separate title-page in *Fragmenta Aurea*, 1646.)

1648. [Another edition with separate title-page in *Fragmenta Aurea*, 1648.]

1658-9. [Another edition with separate title-page in *Fragmenta Aurea*, 1658-9.]

1661, 23 July. '. . . I went to the Theatre, and saw "Brenoralt", I never saw before. It seemed a good play, but ill acted.' (Diary of Samuel Pepys.)

1661, 26 Oct. <>1 June 1662. In a list of performances of plays by the King's company at the Red Bull and the new house in Gibbon's Tennis Court near Clare Market, Sir Henry Herbert lists an undated performance of 'Contented [*sic*] Collinell' after 26 October 1661 but before 1 June 1662. (Adams, *Herbert*, pp. 116–18.)

1662, 12 May. Later in the same list Sir Henry Herbert has 'Sir J. Sucklings Brenoralt 12. May'. (Ibid.)

1667, 12 Aug. '. . . to the King's playhouse, and there . . . The play is "Brenoralt," which I do find but little in, for my part.' (Diary of Samuel Pepys.)

1667, 18 Oct. '. . . to the King's house, and saw "Brenoralt," which is a good tragedy that I like well.' (Ibid.)

1667/8, 5 Mar. '. . . to the King's house, and there saw part of "The Discontented Colonel," but could take no great pleasure in it, because of our coming in in the middle of it.' (Ibid.)

1668/9, c. 12 Jan. In 'A Catalogue of part of His Ma^tes Servants Playes as they were formerly acted at the Blackfryers & now allowed of to his Ma^tes Servants at ye New Theatre' occurs the title, 'Brenoralt'. (Allardyce Nicoll, *A History of Restoration Drama*, 3rd ed., pp. 315–16.)

1672 (?) [Another edition with separate title-page in *Fragmenta Aurea*, falsely (?) dated 1658.]

1676. [Another issue in *The Works of Sir John Suckling*, 1676.]

1694. [Another edition with separate title-page dated 1694 in *The Works of Sir John Suckling*, 1696.]

Though the first edition of the play is undated, the fact that it was printed for '*Francis Eagles-field*', who had entered it in the Stationers' Register on 5 April 1642, makes it probable that the quarto was printed in 1642. The King's men had included the play in their repertory that the Lord Chamberlain protected for them 7 August 1641, and presumably they had produced it before this date. The fairly obvious discussion of King Charles's troubles with his Scottish subjects, which takes place in the conference of the King of Poland and his Lords in Act IV, indicates that the play must have been written after the Bishops' Wars of 1638–9, in which Suckling was directly concerned. A date of first production for the play between summer 1639 and summer 1641 thus seems fairly certain.

Several scholars have noted (A. H. Upham, *The French Influence in English Literature* [1908], pp. 378–9 and 390; Krzyzanowski, loc. cit.; and Fletcher Henderson, loc. cit.) that the source for Suckling's tragedy is the French novel *Iphigene* by J. P. Camus. Henderson notes, however, that there is no discontented colonel named Brennoralt in the novel and suggests that Suckling invented him to facilitate comment on the Scottish troubles. He further suggests that the close historical parallels between the affairs of Poland and Lithuania in 1569—which Camus followed accurately in his novel—and those of England and Scotland in 1639 were what drew Suckling to the French story.

Suckling's success with *Aglaura* and his standing at court lead one to think that *Brennoralt* must have had a court performance by the same company that had made so much of *Aglaura*. Yet none of the editions of the play alludes to a production at court, and no prologues or epilogues are published with any edition. Perhaps the King's men were not ready for a court performance before the Army Plot was revealed in May 1641, and thereafter it was thought indiscreet to produce Suckling at court.

The popularity of the play on the Restoration stage is notable and less disillusioning than the similar records of success of the preposterous *Aglaura*. Perhaps no one should be so quixotic as to try to defend the Restoration taste in tragedy.

The Discontented Colonel

See *Brennoralt*.

Francelia

In several of the editions of *The Goblins* 'Francelia' appears as
the head-title. There is no reason to think that this was ever an
alternative title for the play; 'Francelia' is the scene and must
have crept in as a head-title in error. (See W. W. Greg, *Bibliography*, ii. 757–8.) Perhaps the fact that Francelia is a principal
character in Suckling's *Brennoralt, or the Discontented Colonel*
contributed to the confusion.

The Goblins (1637 ?–41)

Harbage, Alfred. *Cavalier Drama* (1936), p. 112.
Lynch, Kathleen M. *The Social Mode of Restoration Comedy*,
University of Michigan Publications, Language and Literature,
iii (1926), pp. 90–94.
Wallerstein, Ruth. 'Suckling's Imitation of Shakespeare', *R.E.S.*
xix (1943), 290–5.

1641, 7 Aug. 'The Goblins' appears in a list of King's men's plays
which the Lord Chamberlain forbade the printers to publish
without the company's consent. (See above, i. 65–66.)
1646, 24 July. S.R. Humphrey Moseley entered for his copy
'vnder the hands of Sʳ. Nathaniell Brent & Mʳ Seale warden a
[Play *interlined above* booke *deleted*] called The Goblins &ↄ. by
Sʳ. Iohn Sucklyn'. (Greg, *Bibliography*, i. 56.)
1646. The Goblins A Comedy. Presented at the Private House in
Black-Fryers, by His *Majesties* servants. Written By Sir John
Suckling . . . MDCXLVI. (Separate title-page in *Fragmenta Aurea*,
1646.)
1648. [Another edition with a separate title-page in *Fragmenta
Aurea*, 1648.]
1658–9. [Another edition, with a separate title-page in *Fragmenta
Aurea*, 1658–9.]
1666/7, 23 Jan. After a performance of *The Humorous Lieutenant*
at the King's house, 'Knipp made us stay in a box and see the
dancing preparatory to to-morrow for "The Goblins," a play
of Suckling's, not acted these twenty-five years.' (Diary of
Samuel Pepys.)
1666/7, 24 Jan. 'And, anon, at about seven or eight o'clock, comes
Mr. Harris, of the Duke's playhouse, and brings Mrs. Pierce
with him, and also one dressed like a country-mayde with a
straw hat on; which, at first, I could not tell who it was, though

I expected Knipp; but it was she coming off the stage just as she acted this day in "The Goblins," a merry jade.' (Ibid.)

1667, 22 May. '... to the King's house, where I did give 18*d*., and saw the two last acts of "The Goblins," a play I could not make any thing of by these two acts, but here Knipp spied me out of the tiring-room, and come to the pit door ... being in a country-dress, she and others having, it seemed, had a country-dance in the play, but she no other part.' (Ibid.)

1667, 21 Nov. In a warrant for payment for plays presented at court by the Theatre Royal company, appears the entry, 'Nov. 21   The Goblins at ye Theatre . . . 10.' (Allardyce Nicoll, *A History of Restoration Drama*, 3rd ed., pp. 305–6.)

1668/9, *c*. 12 Jan. In 'A Catalogue of part of His Ma^tes Servants Playes as they were formerly acted at the Blackfryers & now allowed of to His Ma^tes Servants at ye New Theatre' is the title, 'The Goblins'. (Ibid., pp. 315–16.)

1672 (?) [Another edition with separate title-page dated 1658 in *Fragmenta Aurea*, falsely (?) dated 1658.]

1676. [Another issue in *The Works of Sir John Suckling*, 1676.]

1694. [Another edition with separate title-page dated 1694 in *The Works of Sir John Suckling*, 1696.]

The Goblins, Suckling's only comedy, was a Blackfriars play, like his others, and protected in the repertory of the King's men in August 1641. It must have been written before this date, and one would guess that it followed *Aglaura*, but the evidence is distressingly slight. A. H. Thompson pointed out (*Works of Sir John Suckling*, p. 389) that when *Poet* thinks he is in the lower world he asks about literary figures there:

> *Po*. Carer per so lo carer,
>   Or he that made the fairie Queene.
> I *Th*. No, none of these:
>   They are by themselves in some other place;
> But here's he that writ *Tamerlane*.
>   (*Fragmenta Aurea, Goblins*, p. 45.)

Thompson asserted that all the figures mentioned must be dead, like Spenser and Marlowe, that Antonio de Mendoza, author of *Querer por solo Querer*, died in 1639, and that, consequently, the passage must have been written after 1639. But Angel Valbuena Prat (*Historia de la Literatura Española* [1946], p. 102) and Fitzmaurice-Kelly (*A History of Spanish Literature* [1926], p. 316) give Mendoza's death date as 1644. I see no evidence in this passage to date the play.

There is no evidence that *The Goblins* was ever performed at court, though it might seem good business for the King's men to include all Suckling's plays in their court list; it must also be remembered that they performed at court many times during 1638–42 when the titles of the productions are unknown. (See above, i. 100.) Miss Kathleen M. Lynch (loc. cit.) has pointed out, however, how much mild satire of the Platonic cult the play contains, and this feature could have been a reason for withholding the comedy from a court performance at which Queen Henrietta Maria might have been displeased.

Suckling's interest in Shakespeare is almost obtrusive in the play. He says in the prologue:

> *When* Shakespeare, Beamont, Fletcher rul'd the Stage,
> *There scarce were ten good pallats in the age.*

He quotes from *Othello* in Act IV; in the same act he has the Poet praise *'Englands Joy'* as like Shakespeare; and there are other Shakespearian echoes, most of them noted in A. H. Thompson's notes. (Ed. *Works*, pp. 383–92.) Miss Ruth Wallerstein (loc. cit.) goes much farther and asserts that *The Goblins* was 'written with Shakespeare's *Tempest* in mind'. She has a number of very suggestive observations, but a more detailed presentation of the evidence would be required to make them entirely convincing.

A musical setting for the song 'A health to the nut-brown lass' by Henry or William Lawes is preserved in a manuscript in the New York Public Library. (Willa McClung Evans, *Henry Lawes* . . . [1941], p. 147.)

The Masque at Witten (> 1641)
(Lost)

Published in *The Last Remains of Sir John Suckling*, 1659 (C₆, p. 37), is:

> *A Prologue of the Author's to a*
> *Masque at* Witten.

> Expect not here a curious River fine,
> Our wits are short of that: alas the time!
> The neat refined language of the Court
> We know not; if we did, our Country sport
> Must not be too ambitious; 'tis for Kings,
> Not for their Subjects, to have such rare things.
> Besides though, I confess, *Parnassus* hardly,
> Yet *Helicon* this Summer-time is dry.

The lost masque was not necessarily written by Suckling, though it may have been. Witten, or Whitton, near Twickenham, was the place of Suckling's birth. His father's house there was left to him, but his uncle, Lionel Cranfield, Earl of Middlesex, also had a house at Whitton, and the masque could have been written for either place.

The first line of the prologue might be an allusion to the engineering feat of Sir John Lawrence, the subject of Suckling's poem in the same volume, '*Vpon Sir* John Laurence's *bringing Water over the hills to my L.* Middlesex *his House at* Witten'. The third and fourth lines suggest a bucolic production of the household; the eighth line shows that the masque was performed in the summer.

The Sad One (> 1637?)

1659. The Sad One. A Tragedy. By Sʳ *John Svckling* . . . 1659. (Separate title-page in *The Last Remains of Sir John Suckling*, 1659.)

1672 (?) [Another edition with a separate title-page dated 1659 in *Fragmenta Aurea*, falsely (?) dated 1658. See *Library*, Fifth Series, i (1946–7), 85.]

1676. [Another issue in *The Works of Sir John Suckling*, 1676.]

1694. [Another edition with separate title-page dated 1694 in *The Works of Sir John Suckling*, 1696.]

The Sad One consists of five acts with two to five scenes in each, but every scene is short, and the play breaks off in the midst of v. 2. It is not easy to tell just what Suckling intended to do with it; as it stands, it is half to two-thirds the length of his other plays. There are several long descriptive stage directions in the text which almost suggest a scenario that was to have been developed later. Professor Harbage noted (*Cavalier Drama* [1936], p. 111) that *The Sad One* contains plot materials 'identical with those of *Aglaura*', but he thinks the treatment and dialogue better. Nevertheless, the great success of *Aglaura* makes it unlikely that Suckling should have started in *The Sad One* to rework part of it.

Hazlitt (ed., *The Poems, Plays, etc.*, ii. 162, n.) thought the lines in ɪv. 2, 'A man shall have his ears cut off for speaking / A truth', might be an allusion to Prynne, but surely Suckling was no man to speak a good word for William Prynne. Less implausible is Thompson's statement (ed., *The Works*, pp. 400–1) that the poet Multecarni in ɪv. 4 is intended for Jonson. The treatment accorded Multecarni is not unlike that Suckling accorded Jonson in 'A

Sessions of the Poets'. Several items would fit the laureate, and Suckling had written a sort of parody of Jonson's lines to Charis in IV. 3. Thompson implies that Suckling would not have so treated Jonson after his death, and therefore he dated *The Sad One* before August 1637. The case is not flawless, but there is nothing to contradict it.

The Last Remains of Sir John Suckling has an address to the reader by the publisher which justifies the publication of a fragment by the precedent of

an Author, who confessedly is reputed the Glory of the English Stage (whereby you'll know I mean *Ben: Johnson*), and in a Play also of somewhat a resembling name, *The Sad Shepherd*.

The play proper is introduced by a synopsis of the antecedent action in the Sicilian civil wars, which might be thought the product of Suckling's pen, but the last sentence reads: 'Thus far the Author drew the curtain; the rest of the Plot is wrapt up in the following Scenes.'

GILBERT SWINHOE
fl. 1658

Nothing is known of Gilbert Swinhoe save what can be derived from the front matter of his play. The three sets of commendatory verses all remark upon his youth. The verses of F. S., who says he is the author's 'Countreyman', begin:

> So young! and yet so good a Tragedy,
> If I'de not seen't, I'de sworn 'tad been a Lye:
> But since I see't, Sir, give me leave to tell
> *Northumberland* can boast a Miracle
> Of Wit and Worth.

Another set of verses addressed '*To the hopeful Youth of his much honoured Kinsman*' is signed by Eldred Revett, presumably the Eldred 'Revet' who was admitted pensioner at Clare College, Cambridge, 29 June 1650. (*Alumni Cantab.* iii. 463.) His emphasis on Swinhoe's youth would suggest that the author of *The Unhappy Fair Irene* was younger than he.

Several Swinnows and Swinscos are recorded at Cambridge, but no Gilbert, and none from Northumberland.

The Tragedy of the Unhappy Fair Irene (c. 1658?)

1658. The Tragedy Of The unhappy Fair Irene. By *Gilbert Swinhoe*, Esq; *London* . . . M. DC. LVIII.

Swinhoe's tragedy is another dramatization of the popular story of the Sultan Mahomet and his sacrifice of his beloved Irene. Professor G. Warner Rice says that the source is Richard Knolles's *General History of the Turks*, and that Swinhoe's only innovation, the lover Pæologus, is derived from the account in Knolles immediately preceding the Irene story. (*Turk, Moor, and Persian in English Literature 1550–1660*, Unpublished Harvard Dissertation, 1926, p. 347.) Harbage suggests (*Cavalier Drama* [1936], p. 219) that the idea of Pæologus may have come from Lodowick Carlell's play, *Osmond the Great Turk* (q.v.).

It is unlikely that *The Unhappy Fair Irene* was ever acted or even written before the closing of the theatres. The writers of commendatory verses for the 1658 edition, 'Ja.' Swinhoe, the author's brother, Eldred Revett, his kinsman, and F. S., his 'Countreyman', all remark on the author's youth, so that presumably sixteen years before, in 1642, when the theatres were closed, he was not beyond infancy. That the tragedy is only closet drama is also suggested by the fact that several stage directions are not only literary in type but indicative of the writer's inability to dramatize, e.g. '*Enter Mahomet, and his Bashaws, as in open Councel, about settlement of their new Conquests.*' (A₄ᵛ.) The untheatrical character of the prologue, which is signed 'Gilb. Swinhoe', also suggests closet drama.

Only the first four scenes are marked off. Several marginal additions have been printed as stage directions. After the last speech of the play is printed the couplet:

> This is a Spectacle of like Woe
> To that of *Juliet* and her *Romeo*.

A copy of the play in the British Museum has Thomason's addition to the title-page date, '8 ᵇer 29:'

JOHN TATHAM (Tatam, Tateham)
c. 1610?–<64

John Tatham's extant work dates mostly from the Interregnum and the Restoration, but he wrote one play before the closing of the theatres, and there are indications of other Caroline dramatic activities.

Nothing is known of his birth or education, and his parentage is known only from the title to one of his poems in *Ostella*, 1650, p. 112: '*To my Mother, Mʳⁱˢ· Dorothy Tatham, one of the Daughters of Christopher Percy of Manson in the County of Dorset, Esquire, then Iustice of Peace and Quorum, and High Sheriff of that County.*'

The same volume contains (p. 113) an uninformative poem '*Vpon the Death of my* Father'.

Tatham's short pastoral play, *Love Crowns the End*, published in his collection called *Fancies Theatre*, 1640, was, according to the separate title-page, 'Presented By The Schollees Of Bingham in the County of *Notingham*, in the yeare 1632'. If Tatham had been a scholar at the school when he wrote the play, it seems likely that either he or some of the thirteen writers of commendatory verses for *Fancies Theatre* would have boasted of his youthful precocity; since no one does, a better guess would be that in 1632 Tatham was a schoolmaster at Bingham.

It is not known when he came to London, but by the time he published *Fancies Theatre* in 1640 he had several acquaintances among the dramatists, four of whom wrote commendatory verses for his book—R[ichard?] Brome, Thomas Nabbes, Robert Chamberlain, and Thomas Rawlins. Tatham, in turn, wrote commendatory verses for the dramatists Thomas Rawlins (*The Rebellion*, 1640) and Richard Brome (*The Jovial Crew*, 1652), and for the actors Theophilus Bird and Andrew Pennycuicke, who published Dekker and Ford's *The Sun's Darling* in 1656 after both authors were dead.

The most direct statement of friendship for Tatham by a dramatic figure is the forty-line poem, 'To *his faithful ingenuous friend and old acquaintance*, JOHN TATHAM, *Gent.*', written by Thomas Jordan, Tatham's successor as writer of Lord Mayors' pageants. Jordan says in part:

> The Sun hath twenty Summers strew'd the earth
> With flowers, since our Acquaintance first took birth:
> It was a season when our Drums and Flutes
> Did give precedency to *Love* and *Lutes*:
>
> .   .   .   .
>
> Ere *Austin* was put down and *Burton* Sainted.

The volume in which the poem appears, *Wit in a Wildernesse of Promiscuous Poesie*, is not dated, but a number of lines in the poem about the good old days before Parliamentary restraints indicate clearly that it was written before the Restoration; one line refers to the arraignment of the King. Another poem in the volume is an elegy for 'Sir Nath. Brent', who died in 1653. It seems not unlikely that Jordan knew Tatham in the mid-thirties, presumably in London.

One piece published in *Fancies Theatre*, 1640, and three in Tatham's later collection, *Ostella*, 1650, suggest that he was connected with a theatre. In *Fancies Theatre* is '*A Prologue spoken upon removing of the late Fortune Players to the Bull'.* (See above, i. 315–16.) In *Ostella* are several songs for a masque (see below, *A Masque*), '*A Prologue spoken at the* Red-Bull *to a Play called the* Whisperer, *or what you please*', and '*A Prologue spoken at the* Cock-pit, *at the coming of the* Red Bull *Players thither*'. All three of these prologues, with their emphasis on the ideas and interests of the players, not of the dramatist, suggest that Tatham was attached to a troupe of Red Bull players, as Richard Brome (q.v.) was attached for several years to the Salisbury Court company, and that he wrote regular prologues for them.

The first prologue can be dated Easter 1640, from other records of the exchange of theatres by the companies at the Fortune and the Red Bull. (See above, i. 315–16.) The third prologue may well belong to May of the same year, but one cannot be sure that it does not belong to the Interregnum period, for both the Red Bull and the Cockpit were used for surreptitious playing after the closing of the theatres. (See Leslie Hotson, *The Commonwealth and Restoration Stage* [1928], pp. 28–58.) Certain lines in this '*Prologue spoken at the* Cock-pit, *at the coming of the* Red Bull *Players thither*' might apply to a performance at the Cockpit after the closing of the theatres, following a raid on a previous company at the Cockpit by Parliamentary soldiers. Or the lines might apply to a Red Bull troupe performing temporarily at the Cockpit in May 1640, after the King and Queen's Young Company had been suppressed and their leaders, William Beeston, Stutville, and Mohun, sent to jail, and before the company was restored under the new direction of William Davenant. (See above, i. 332–5.) The suggestive lines are as follows:

> . . . 'Tis long since *here*
> So many *Glorious bodies* did appear,
> Whose *Beams* gave *Life* to *Action*, as the *Sun*
> Gives *growth* to th' Infant *Plants* he *Smiles* upon.
> Then *flourisht* here those *Roscio's* of the *Age*,
> That *trod* the perfect *measure* of the *Stage*,
> Who from your *eys* took *Motion*; such as *drew*
> *Encouragement* to *them*, *Content* to *you*.
> Yet those so exquisite in *Comedies*,
> Have *Acted* since their own sad *Tragedies*.
> Who could have di'd more bravely? Yet we must
> Leave to *Opinion* that; our onely *Trust*
> Is in your *Favours*: Nor think cause your *share*
> Of *Sweets* are gone, that all things *bitter* are.
> If you'l *shoot* equal *Beams* on us wee'l strive
> To make you *think* that *They* in *Vs* survive.

On the whole, the allusions in this prologue seem to suggest too settled a course of performances for an Interregnum occasion, and the 'Infant *Plants*' of the fourth line suggest a troupe like Beeston's Boys, for which reasons the 1640 date appears the more plausible. Yet there is no other indication that any company came to the Cockpit to replace the King and Queen's Young Company when they were suppressed.

In any case, the evidence remains that Tatham was for a time in 1640, and perhaps both earlier and later, a regular theatre poet at the Red Bull. All three of the prologues exhibit a man performing the functions of a theatre poet, not those of an independent dramatist introducing his own plays. All three show him associated with the Red Bull, and one indicates that he was working for a company at that theatre in Easter 1640; another may show him working in May 1640 for the same troupe; and the third is undated, but still written for players at the Red Bull. If Tatham was a regular poet for the Red Bull, he probably wrote plays for the company acting there, but none of his extant plays seems to belong to this period. Possibly Red Bull plays by Tatham are lost.

Nothing is known of Tatham's private life in London, but a baptismal entry of 11 March 1638/9 in the registers of St. Giles in the Fields—the parish of the Cockpit theatre—may well refer to his daughter; the entry reads 'Amey Daughter of John & Joanna Tateham'. (See G. E. Bentley, *R.E.S.* vi [1930], 165.) The place is a likely one for actors and dramatists (ibid., pp. 149–50), and the date is compatible with what little we know of Tatham's life.

The sometimes repeated statement of Maidment and Logan (*The Dramatic Works of John Tatham* [1879], p. 117), 'It is very probable that Tatham had served under the Earl of Carnarvon in the civil wars', is only a guess based on Tatham's dislike of the Scots.

Tatham's later publications, besides non-dramatic verse, are city shows and anti-Puritan pieces showing a strong bias against the Scots—*The Distracted State*, 1651, *The Character of the Rump*, 1660, *The Rump*, 1660, and *The Scots Figgaries*, 1652. He wrote a series of city pageants for Lord Mayors' shows and other occasions, 1657–64, several of which contain remarks about the City which suggest that he was official City Poet. After his pageant of 1664 nothing further is heard of him. A portrait is prefixed to *Ostella*, 1650.

Samuel Sheppard wrote an epigram on Tatham before any of

his city pageants had appeared. It is much less enthusiastic than
Sheppard's usual literary opinions.

To Tatam.

Tatam makes Verses of all sorts, and sizes,
And Playes, and Songs, and Ballads he comprizes:
In keene *Iambicks* a Lymphatick Lyrick
He is, and playes, and sings, sweeter then *Derick*,
For which, amongst *Broakers* and *Broomcriers*,
Amongst *Watermen*, 'mongst *Dolts*, and *Driers*,
Hee's cri'd up for a *Bards* and he is one,
For he writes *Welsh*, or in some stranger tone.
(*Epigrams Theological, Philosophical and Romantic* [1651], L$_5$^{v}–L$_6$,
pp. 142–3.)

Collected Edition

1879. [James Maidment and W. H. Logan, eds.] *The Dramatic
Works of John Tatham.*

Aqua Triumphalis (1662)

Tatham's pageant for London's welcome for the King and
Queen on the Thames, 23 August 1662.

The Distracted State (written 1641?)

1650, 23 Nov. S.R. John Tey entered for his copy 'a Tragedy
called the distracted State written in the yeere 1641 by Iohn
Tatham'. (Greg, *Bibliography*, i. 59.)
1651. The Distracted State, A Tragedy. Written in the Yeer, 1641.
By *J. T.* Gent. . . . 1651.

The Distracted State was certainly not acted in the Caroline
theatre, and even the title-page statement that it was written in
1641 seems very dubious. The analogy between characters and
events in Sicily—the locale of the tragedy—and those in England
in the later forties may have been prophetic, but it seems rather
more likely that Tatham predated the composition of his play as
a precautionary measure. Some support for this hypothesis may
be found in the fact that the publisher took the most unusual step
of having the date of composition recorded in the Stationers'
Register entry.

Though Tatham's name does not appear on the title-page, it is
found in the Stationers' Register entry, and the dedication to

Sir John (in some copies Sir William) Sidley is signed ' J: Tatham'. There are three sets of commendatory verses signed 'I. R.', 'R. D.', and 'G. Lynn'. In George Thomason's copy of the play in the British Museum he has altered the date on the title-page from 1651 to 'Nou. 29 1650'.

Knavery in All Trades (1664)

1664. Knavery in All Trades: Or, The Coffee-House. A Comedy, As it was acted in the Christmas Holidays by several Apprentices With great Applause . . . 1664.

The play has been ascribed to Tatham, but there seems to be no very reliable evidence that it was his. In any case, it was performed long after the closing of the theatres, though the dialogue contains a discussion of Caroline theatrical affairs. (See above, i. 318.)

Londinium Triumphans (1663)

Tatham's Lord Mayor's pageant for Anthony Bateman, Skinner, 1663.

London's Glory, Represented by Time, Truth, and Fame (1660)

Tatham's entertainment for the King, the Duke of York, the Duke of Gloucester, and Parliament at the Guildhall, 5 July 1660.

London's Triumph for John Robinson (1662)

Tatham's Lord Mayor's pageant for John Robinson, Clothworker, 1662.

London's Triumph for Thomas Allen (1659)

Tatham's Lord Mayor's pageant for Thomas Allen, Grocer, 1659.

London's Triumph, Presented by Industry and Honour (1658)

Tatham's Lord Mayor's pageant for Sir John Ireton, Clothworker, 1658. See Frederick W. Fairholt, The Lord Mayors' Pageants, Percy Society Publications (1843), i. 66–67.

London's Triumphs for John Fredrick (1661)

Tatham's Lord Mayor's pageant for John Fredrick, Grocer, 1661. See ibid., pp. 68–70.

London's Triumphs for John Lawrence (1664)

Tatham's Lord Mayor's pageant for John Lawrence, Haberdasher, 1664. See ibid., pp. 71–73.

London's Triumphs for Richard Chiverton (1657)

Tatham's Lord Mayor's pageant for Richard Chiverton, Skinner, 1657. See ibid., pp. 64–65.

Love Crowns the End (1632)

Greg, W. W. *Pastoral Poetry & Pastoral Drama* (1906), pp. 380–2.

1640, 21 Apr. '21 *Aprilis*, 1640. *Imprimatur*, Johannes Hansley.' (Imprimatur for *Fancies Theatre*, printed on A$_4$^{v}.)

1640, 15 Oct. S.R. Richard Best entered for his copy 'a booke called The ffancies Theater. by Iohn Tatham'. (Greg, *Bibliography*, i. 53.)

1640. Love Crownes The End. *A Pastorall* Presented By The Schollees Of Bingham in the County of *Notingham*, in the yeare 1632. Written by *Io. Tatham* Gent. . . . 1640. (Separate title-page in *Fancies Theatre*, 1640.)

1657. Love Crowns The End: A Tragicomedy; Acted by the Schollars of *Bingham* in the County of *Nottingham*. By *Jo. Tatham*, Gent. (Cancel title-leaf in reissue of *Fancies Theatre* as *The Mirrour of Fancies*, 1657.)

Nothing is known of the circumstances of production of this school play beyond the information given by the author on the title-page. The prologue seems to indicate that it was the third part of some special celebration at the school:

> You *starres* of Honour, brighter than the *day*
>   .   .   .   .   .
> Accept the choicest *dish* our *wits* prepare,
> As a *third* course to please your eye, which still
> Covets to haue of *novelties* its fill.

The play is short, and its confused character is due in part, as Greg pointed out (loc. cit.), to the fact that the author has tried to develop a full romantic-pastoral plot in a small compass.

Presumably Tatham was a schoolmaster at Bingham when the play was written, for it seems likely that had he been a school-boy when he wrote *Love Crowns the End* the title-page or the prologue of the play, or the dedication or commendatory verses of the volume would have mentioned the fact. Such boasting would have been especially likely in 1640, just two years after the publication of *Love's Riddle*, Abraham Cowley's similar schoolboy effort at Westminster School.

Dr. Greg (loc. cit.) saw in the play the influence of Fletcher's *Faithful Shepherdess* and, less convincingly, of the anonymous *Maid's Metamorphosis*, *As You Like It*, and Goffe's *Careless Shepherdess*. The influence of Goffe's play seems particularly dubious, though Greg suggests several examples, since Tatham's play was produced twenty-four years before Goffe's was printed. Nothing we know of Tatham suggests that he might have been familiar with the London performance of a play in or before 1632.

A Masque (> 1650 ?)
(Lost)

There is no certain evidence that John Tatham ever wrote a masque, but several of the poems printed in his *Ostella*, 1650, suggest that he did. On pages 106-9 (P_1^v–P_3) is a series of poems headed 'Songs in a Masque'. The compositions which follow are called: '1 *Song*: Fortune Descending', '2 *The poor Schollers Song*', '3. *Song. The Country-life*', '4. *Song. Ambition*', '5. Song'.

These verses may have been contributions to some unknown masque written by another, but it is just as likely that the masque was written by Tatham, and the songs were all that he thought worth preserving. I know no evidence as to the date of this un-known masque save that it must have antedated the publication of *Ostella*, 1650. Surely it was not a court piece, since the later court masques were written by men of some association with the court—Townshend, Carew, Davenant. A private masque like those of Salusbury, Milton, Mildmay Fane, or Aston Cokayne is a possibility, or even a theatre masque like Ford and Dekker's *The Sun's Darling*, for which Tatham wrote verses, or his friend Thomas Nabbe's *The Spring's Glory*.

Neptune's Address (1661)

Tatham's description of the water pageant, with one speech congratulating Charles II on his coronation, 22 April 1661.

The Royal Oak (1660)

Tatham's Lord Mayor's pageant for Sir Richard Brown, Merchant Taylor, 1660. See R. T. D. Sayle, *Lord Mayors' Pageants of the Merchant Taylors' Company in the 15th, 16th & 17th Centuries* (privately printed, 1931), pp. 128 ff.

The Rump, or The Mirror of the Late Times (1660)

1660. The Rump: Or The Mirrour Of The late Times, A New Comedy, Written by J. Tatham, Gent. Acted Many Times with Great Applause, At the Private House in *Dorset*-Court . . . 1660.
1661. The Rump: Or The Mirrour Of The late Times. A New Comedy, Written by J. Tatham, Gent. Acted many times with Great Applause, At the Private House in *Dorset* Court. *The Second Impression, Corrected, with many Additions* . . . 1661.

The play is a lively satire of persons and events in the last two or three years before the Restoration.

The Scots Figgaries, or A Knot of Knaves (1652)

1652. The Scots Figgaries: Or, A Knot of Knaves. A Comedy . . . 1652.
1652-3. [Another edition, some copies dated 1652, some 1653.]

The dedication to Robert Dormer is signed 'Jo. Tatham'. The piece was surely not intended for production; it is an anti-Scottish political satire reflecting events of the forties. Thomason's copy in the British Museum is dated 'Nouemb. 14'.

The Whisperer, or What You Please
(Lost)

In Tatham's collection of verse called *Ostella, or The Faction of Love and Beauty Reconcil'd*, 1650, is a prologue (p. 111) entitled 'A Prologue spoken at the Red-Bull to a Play called the Whisperer, or what you please'.

No play of this name is known. It may have been written by Tatham himself, but it was common enough for a dramatist connected with a theatre to write prologues for the plays of other men. (See above, Richard Brome.) When prologues were published separately it appears to have been usual for the author to cite the occasion, or, if the play rather than the occasion was identified, to have indicated when the play was his own. (See James Shirley, *Poems &c.*, 1646, and Thomas Heywood, *Pleasant Dialogues and Dramas*, 1637.) On the whole, it seems likely that John Tatham was not the author of *The Whisperer*. See Anon.

JOHN TAYLOR
1580–1653

D.N.B.

John Taylor, the Water Poet, was a most prolific writer, but he was not a dramatist. His only semi-dramatic composition was *The Triumphs of Fame and Honour*, the Lord Mayor's pageant written in 1634 for the inauguration of Robert Parkhurst, Clothworker. His *England's Comfort and London's Joy*, 1641, has several times been listed as a dramatic composition, but there are no dramatic features to the pamphlet.

Taylor was born in Gloucester in August 1580, and for a time went to a grammar school there, but he left and was apprenticed to a London waterman. He spent several years, he says, on the Queen's ships and then returned to London as a waterman again. He became a most prolific pamphleteer and rhymster. Many of his travels, adventures, and quarrels are recounted in his numerous short pieces. When the wars began Taylor went to Oxford, where he kept a public house until the city fell, after which he returned to London and opened another. He was buried at St. Martin's-in-the-Fields in December 1653.

England's Comfort and London's Joy (1641)

This eight-page pamphlet of John Taylor has several times been listed as a dramatic piece, but it is not. It is a description, with illustrations, of the meeting of Charles I and his train by the city officials when the King returned to London from Scotland, 25 November 1641. According to Taylor, the occasion was splendid, and he reprints verses given to the King and a speech made to him. But there is no impersonation at all; *England's Comfort and London's Joy* is a simple piece of descriptive journalism.

The Triumphs of Fame and Honour (1634)

1634. The Trivmphs Of Fame and Honovr: Or The Noble Accomplish'd solemnity, full of Cost, Art and state, at the Inauguration and Establishment of the true worthy and right nobly minded Robert Parkhvrst, into the Right Honourable office of Lord *Maior* of London. The particulars of every Invention in all the Pageants, Shewes and Triumphs both by Water and Land, are here following fully set downe, being all performed by the Loves, Liberall Costs, and charges of the Right Worshipfull and worthy Brother-hood of the Cloth-workers the 29 of October 1634. Written by *Iohn Taylor* . . . 1634. (Greg, *Bibliography*, ii. 639.)

Only one copy of Taylor's pageant for the Lord Mayor's show in 1634 is recorded, that in the John Rylands Library. (See E. Gordon Duff, *A Catalogue of Books in the John Rylands Library Manchester Printed . . . to . . . 1640* [1895], p. 83.) I have not seen it.

WILLIAM TAYLOR
c. 1630-?

Though William Taylor is a common Oxford name, there is only one who was contemporary with Roger Shipman (q.v.) at St. John's, as Ernst Rühl pointed out (*Grobianus in England*, pp. lii–liii), and is therefore presumably the William Taylor whose name is connected with Shipman's on the manuscript of *Grobiana's Nuptials*. This man was a son of William Taylor, a physician of Oxford, who had also been a St. John's man. He matriculated 16 December 1636 at the age of sixteen and was granted his B.A. 24 July 1641. (*Alumni Oxon.* iv. 1464.)

THOMAS TOMKIS
c. 1580–1634

Pathomachia, or the Battle of Affections, or Love's Loadstone has several times been attributed to Thomas Tomkis, but Hugh G. Dick, in the best discussion of Tomkis (in his edition of *Albumazar: A Comedy*, University of California Publications in English, vol. xiii [1944], pp. 1–9 and 11), points out that Tomkis lived until 1634, while the author of *Pathomachia* was said to be dead in 1630.

There is no evidence that Tomkis wrote any plays after 1616. (Op. cit., pp. 1–16.)

See Anon., for *Pathomachia*.

CYRIL TOURNEUR
?–1625/6

Though Cyril Tourneur did not die until February 1625/6, there is no evidence that he wrote any plays after *The Nobleman*. It is true that this piece was still in the repertory of the King's company in 1641 (see above, i. 65–66), but it had been acted at court by the company in February 1611/12, and entered in the Stationers' Register in the same month.

See *The Elizabethan Stage*, iii. 499–500.

AURELIAN TOWNSHEND (Tounesend, Tounshend, Townsend)
1583><1643

Chambers, E. K. *Aurelian Townshend's Poems and Masques* (1912), pp. ix–xlvii.

Smith, G. C. Moore. 'Aurelian Townsend', *T.L.S.*, 23 October 1924, p. 667.

Aurelian Townshend was the son of John Townshend of West Dereham, Norfolk. The date of his birth is unknown, but it must have been in or before 1583, for in December of that year a legacy was left him and his sister. (Chambers, op. cit., p. xii.) As a young man he was sent abroad for study by Sir Robert Cecil in order to prepare him for attendance on Cecil's son. Townshend reached Paris in April 1600, and remained abroad for three years, often in financial straits. It is obvious that he cannot have been— as is often asserted—the Townsend upon whose bounty John Manningham said Ben Jonson was living in 1603. (Ibid., pp. xii–xiv and xxxvii–xlvii.)

In 1608–9 Townshend was again abroad, this time with Sir Edward Herbert, and Chambers thinks that after his return he may have been again attached to the household of the Earl of Salisbury—formerly Sir Robert Cecil—until the Earl's death in 1612. (Ibid., pp. xv–xvi.)

From this time until his appearance as a masque-writer in 1631/2 little is known of Townshend save that he had married Anne Wythies and had had several children baptized at St. Giles',

Cripplegate. His datable verse belongs mostly to the period after 1632 (ibid., pp. xvi–xviii), and Chambers thinks that the masques, the first of which Townshend says was written in obedience to the King's command, gave him 'his place in the world of letters'. He was admitted to Gray's Inn in August 1633. (Joseph Foster, *The Register of Admissions to Gray's Inn, 1521–1889* [1889], p. 200.)

Townshend's last years seem to have been poverty-stricken (see Chambers, p. xxiv). He is not certainly traceable after 1643, but Chambers thinks he may have been the 'Mr Townshend, Gent.' who left England with Prince Rupert and Prince Maurice after the fall of Oxford. (Ibid., pp. xxix–xxx.) G. C. Moore Smith, noting (loc. cit.) that according to Miss V. Sackville-West (*Knole and the Sackvilles* [1922], p. 106) there are at Knole manuscript poems by Townshend on the death of Charles I and on the death of Edward Sackville in 1651, suggests that during the wars Townshend enjoyed the protection of the Earl of Dorset at Knole. It would be desirable to have some confirmation that the A. Townsend of the Knole papers and the writer of the masques were the same man.

Except for the masques, Townshend published none of his work. It was collected for the edition of 1912 from manuscript copies.

Albion's Triumph (8 January 1631/2)

Edition: E. K. Chambers, ed., *Aurelian Townshend's Poems and Masks* (1912), pp. 55–78 and 116–18.

Reyher, Paul. *Les Masques anglais* (1909), pp. 200–2 *et passim*.
Simpson, Percy, and C. F. Bell, eds. *Designs by Inigo Jones for Masques & Plays at Court* (1924), pp. 61–69.
Welsford, Enid. *The Court Masque* (1927), pp. 220–4.

1631, 20 Dec. 'The Duke de Vendosme, having obtained permission to return into France, will not stay to see either the King's or the Queen's masques, which are to be acted on Twelfth Day and at Shrovetide.' (Sir Thomas Edmondes to Henry Vane, quoted Chambers ed., p. 116, from *S.P., Dom., Charles I*, cciv. 80.)

1631, 29 Dec. 'A Warr^t for A priuy seale of 1000^{li} to bee payd vnto Edmund Tauerner Esq to bee imployed towardes the expence of A Masque to bee p^{r}sented before his Matie on twelfth day next . . . Dec. 29. 1631.' In margin, 'Masque money

Tauerner Edmund'. (*Malone Society Collections*, ii, Part iii [1931], 356. Reyher says, op. cit., p. 530, that there was a supplementary grant of £400 to George Kirke, but I have not seen it.)

1631[/2]. Albions Trivmph. Personated In A Maske at Court. *By the Kings Maiestie and his Lords*. The Sunday after Twelfe Night. 1631. . . . 1631.

1631/2. [Another issue. The Huntington Library copy has manuscript corrections and minor additions.]

1631/2, 12 Jan. 'The last Sunday at night the Kinges masque was acted in the banquetting house, the Queens being suspended till another time, by reason of a sorenes which fell into one of her delicate eyes. The Inventor or Poet of this masque was Mr. Aurelian Townshend sometimes towards the lord Treasurer Salisbury, Ben Jonson being for this time discarded, by reason of the predominant power of his Antagonist, Innigo Jones, who this time tweluemoneth was angry with him for putting his owne name before his in the title-page, which Ben Jonson made the subject of a bitter Satyr or twoe against Innigo.' (John Pory to Sir Thomas Puckering, quoted Chambers ed., p. 117, from B.M. MS. Harl. 7000, fol. 318ᵛ.)

1631/2, 15 Feb. 'At Shrovetide this King and Queen intend going to Newmarket, which together with this years double masques still increases the charge.' (Sir Thomas Edmondes to Henry Vane, quoted Chambers ed., p. 117, from *S.P.*, *Dom.*, *Charles I*, ccxi. 45.)

Townshend evidently took warning from the fate of Ben Jonson in his quarrel with Inigo Jones, as noted in John Pory's letter. No name appears on the title-page of *Albion's Triumph*, and Townshend opens his account with a modest statement that, the King and Queen having signified their pleasure to have a new masque, 'Master *Ingio Iones* and I were employed in the Invention'. At the close he is properly admiring of scenes, music, and dancing, but modest about the writing.

The masquers, listed at the end of the text, include the King and fourteen gentlemen of the court.

Thirty-one drawings and sketches by Inigo Jones of scenes, machines, costumes, &c., for the masque are described by Simpson and Bell, and Miss Welsford suggests (op. cit., p. 224, n. 2) that four others probably belong to *Albion's Triumph*. She also notes that in this masque Jones has made use of two or three designs of Parigi.

Tempe Restored (14 February 1631/2)

Edition: E. K. Chambers, ed., *Aurelian Townshend's Poems and Masks* (1912), pp. 79–100 and 118–22.

Dunlap, Rhodes, ed., *The Poems of Thomas Carew with His Masque Coelum Britannicum* (1949), pp. 74–77 and 251–2.

Reyher, Paul. *Les Masques anglais* (1909), pp. 200–2 *et passim*.

Simpson, Percy, and C. F. Bell, eds. *Designs by Inigo Jones for Masques & Plays at Court* (1924), pp. 69–75.

Welsford, Enid. *The Court Masque* (1927), pp. 224–5.

1631, 20 Dec. 'The Duke de Vendosme, having obtained permission to return into France, will not stay to see either the King's or the Queen's masques, which are to be acted on Twelfth Day and at Shrovetide.' (Sir Thomas Edmondes to Henry Vane, quoted Chambers ed., p. 116, from *S.P., Dom., Charles I*, cciv. 80.)

1631/2, 23 Jan. 'A warrant for a priuy seale of 800^{li} to bee payd vnto Edmund Tauerner Esq to bee imployed towardes the expence of a maske to bee p^{r}sented before ye Queene at Shrouetide next . . . Ian. 23th 1631.' In margin: 'Masque money shrouetide 1631.' (*Malone Society Collections*, ii, Part iii [1931], p. 356.)

1631/2, 2 Feb. 'The queen and her ladies do practise the masque, which they intend to perform at Shrovetide twice a-week.' (Sir George Gresley to ——, Birch, *Court and Times of Charles the First* [1849], ii. 95. The letter is dated 'Essex House, February 2, 1632', but it must be 1631/2, not 1632/3, as Williams thought, for the letter refers to the reception of the new Venetian ambassador, which took place in January 1631/2. See *C.S.P., Venetian* [1629–32], pp. 581 ff.)

1631/2, 8 Feb.

'A warr^t for A Habitt for Mr Tho: Killegrew.　A Warraunt for ye great Wardrobe for ye providing of these parcells following for a masqueing habit for Mr Thomas Killegrew one of His M^{tes} Pages of Hono^r who is to p^{r}sent the person of an enamoured Courtier in the Masque p^{r}sented by the Queenes Matie at Shrouetide next & that you cause them to bee compleatly fitted & furnished (vizt) A doublet of white Satin, Breeches of Carnation Satin Cloake Masqueing habit. of the same coloured Satin lined wth Carnation coloured Plush trimmed wth siluer lace: silke stockins of pearle colour white shooes Roses and Garters of Carnation, A Hatt & a feather A falling Band wth lace of the newest fashion Gloues Girdle & pointes sutable & such other thinges as shall bee requisite for that purpose. Febr. 8. 1631.' (*Malone Society Collections*, ii, Part iii [1931], pp. 357-8, from a Lord Chamberlain's Warrant Book.)

1631/2. Tempe Restord. A Masque Presented by the Qveene, and foureteene Ladies, to the Kings Maiestie at *Whitehall* on Shrove-Tuesday. 1631 . . . 1631.

1631/2, 17 Feb. [i.e. 27 Feb. M.V.] 'The queen celebrated the end of the carnival by a sumptuous masque, performed with wonderfully rich decorations before a numerous assembly in the great hall of the royal palace. The king himself, by gaily taking part in the dancing, proved the pleasure which he took in it.' (Viscenzo Gussoni and Giovanni Soranzo to the Doge and Senate, *C.S.P.*, *Venetian* [1629-32], pp. 592-3.)

1632-40. Carew's verse letter entitled '*In answer of an Elegiacall Letter upon the death of the King of* Sweden *from* Aurelian Townsend, *inviting me to write on that subject*', first published in his *Poems*, 1640, contains a long description of the performance of *Tempe Restored*. (See Rhodes Dunlap, loc. cit.)

At the end of his second and rather feeble masque Townshend is even more discreetly self-effacing than in his first, crediting Jones with the subject, the allegory, the description, and the apparatus of the scenes. Of himself he says, 'All the Verses were written by M^r. *Aurelian Townesend*.' Chambers noted that the style of the descriptions differed from those in *Albion's Triumph*, and concluded that Jones had written them and that only the verses of *Tempe Restored* were by Townshend. (Op. cit., p. 119.)

Reyher, who praises the designs of Inigo Jones, notes that the literary idea is derived from the *Ballet comique* called *Circe* by Baltasar de Beaujoyeulx. (Op. cit., pp. 201, 374.)

The text notices the singing of '*Madam Coniacke*' and '*M^ris Sheperd*', and the singing or playing of '*M^r. Laneere*'. At the end are recorded the names of the seven ladies and seven gentlemen who represented the 'Influences' and of the Queen and the fourteen ladies who were the masquers.

Twenty-three drawings and sketches of scenes, figures, and costumes by Inigo Jones for the masque are described and a few reproduced by Simpson and Bell.

Unknown Masque (?)

At the Huntington Library is an unidentified fragment of a masque by Aurelian Townshend which consists of five unnumbered pages. At the top of the first page is an ornamental headpiece, and below it 'The Ante-Masques'. Then follow four stanzas headed, respectively, 'The first that enters is A Man of Canada', 'The second are 2. Ægyptians', 'The third are 3. Pantaloones', 'The fourth are 4. Spaniards'. Then comes a twelve-line song, followed by 'The Subiect of the Masque'. At the end is a sort of epilogue headed 'A Pigmees Speech', followed by:

My owne Excuse
To the most Magnanimous and Vnanimous
KING and QVEENE.

So many are the faults J make,
Jn this loose Paper; that J feare,
Onely for this poore Poëms sake,
J may hereafter loose your eare:
J would, by your Two bounties live,
But now; Jf yee forgive, yee give.
AVRELIAN TOVNSHEND.

In the margin of the first page is the remains of some sort of correction or addition in a contemporary hand. All that remains is 'faire Franc'.

It may be that the Huntington fragment is all that was ever printed, since it begins with a headpiece and ends with Townshend's apology. The fact that he calls his work '*this loose Paper*' also suggests something incomplete, but why should such a fragment have been printed?

Miss Willa McClung Evans notes (*Henry Lawes* [1941], pp. 120–1 and 235–6) that on page 79 of Henry Lawes's manuscript book of his own compositions is a setting for a song of Townshend's which Lawes has labelled in a marginal note 'A Baccanall Songe in A maske before their Majestyes, 1636'. The masque is unknown, and she suggests that it may have been the lost masque presented by Lady Hatton to 'the King, Queen, Palsgrave, and his brother' on Shrove Tuesday, 1635/6. (Letter of 8 March 1635/6, Papers of the Gawdy family, *Hist. MSS. Com.*, Tenth Report, Appendix, Part II [1885], p. 157.) It is also possible that 'A Baccanall Songe' was another part of the masque represented by the Huntington fragment. Indeed both could have been parts of Lady Hatton's masque.

THOMAS VINCENT
c. 1603?–33

Thomas Vincent, a King's Scholar at Westminster School, was elected to Trinity College, Cambridge, in 1617. He matriculated in Easter term 1618, and received the degrees of B.A. 1621/2, M.A. 1625, and B.D. in 1632. He became a junior Fellow of Trinity in 1624 and a senior Fellow in 1625, but there are no recorded payments to him as Fellow. He was minister at St. Edward's, Cambridge, in 1631 and vicar of Blyth in Nottinghamshire in 1633. He was buried at Blyth 28 September 1633. (*Alumni Cantab.* iv. 304; Innes, *Fellows of Trinity College, Cambridge,* p. 31; *The Records of Old Westminsters,* ii. 952.)

Paria (3 March 1627/8)

MSS.: Emmanuel College, Cambridge, MS. 1. 3. 16 (item 4); Folger Shakespeare Library MS. 420411.

1627/8, 4 Feb. 'The 4th in Febr. aforesayd [1627/8] for six Labourers six dayes imployed in furnishing Trinity Colledge in Cambridge where his Maty then heard A Comedy.' (One of the bills signed by the Lord Chamberlain 1 March 1628/9. Lord Chamberlain's Warrant Books, *Malone Society Collections,* ii, Part iii [1931], 349.)

1627/8, 22 Feb. 'We have two or three Comedies at Trinity this Shrovetide, and the stage there built to that purpose. But of the king's coming, it was not talked of, when I wrote last, and if it be, it is but private and accidental. Some say, he will be here on the Monday; and my Lord of Durham, that was, is now in town, as is thought, for some direction to that purpose. Yet others doubt whether he will come or not.' (Joseph Mead of Christ's College, Cambridge, to Sir Martin Stuteville. Birch, *Court and Times of Charles I,* i. 325.)

1627/8, 15 Mar. 'Of our comedies I hear little one way or other, only some actors extraordinarily commended. I was not there—I could not endure to sit and wait so long.' (The same to the same, ibid., p. 329.)

1648. Paria. *Acta coram sereniss. Rege* Carolo: *Authore* Tho. Vincent, *Trin. Colleg. Socio.* . . . 1648. (Separate title-page in the 1648 edition of *Loyola, Stoicus Vapulans, Cancer,* and *Paria.* There is no general title.)

The precise date and even the hour of the performance of *Paria* are given on the Emmanuel College MS.: 'Acta coram

Serenis: Rege Caro. Martij 3°. 1627. Ab horâ vndecimâ ad quintam.' But nothing is known of the other comedies that Joseph Mead says were performed on the occasion of the same visit. The Lord Chamberlain's warrant mentions only one, but perhaps the same structures in the hall could have served for several.

The Emmanuel College MS. gives a cast, which is printed by G. C. Moore Smith, *College Plays*, p. 84.

On the following page is 'Proloquitur / m^r Suckline' (the poet?), followed by an address to the audience and another to King Charles, and on the next page 'Argumentum m^r Driwood'.

An anonymous writer in *The Retrospective Review* (xii [1825], 40) says that

Upon March the 12th, 1641, Prince Charles passed through Cambridge, on his way to York, when he was entertained by the representation of *Paria*, written by Thomas Vincent.

He is almost certainly mistaken, since Joseph Beaumont's letter of 21 March 1641/2 from Cambridge, giving a rather full account of the visit of the Prince, mentions only one comedy, and that in English. (Cooper, *Annals of Cambridge*, iii. 321–2.) That comedy was Cowley's *Guardian* (q.v.).

The 1648 edition of *Paria* contains a scene-by-scene synopsis in English, as well as an argument, prologue, epilogue, and an address 'Ad Regem Carolum'. Moore Smith points out that 'The play is based on Eusebio Luchetti's *Le due Sorelle Rivali*'. (*College Plays*, p. 97.)

The Folger MS. of the play (see Mewe, *Pseudomagia*) differs in a number of minor respects from the printed text of 1648. It lacks the argument and the synopsis by scenes and the address to Charles, as well as a song, v. 2, and most of v. 6 and v. 7.

J. W.
fl. > 1637

Nothing is known of the J. W. who is named as author on the title-page of *The Valiant Scot*. The only known Jacobean or Caroline dramatist with these initials was John Webster.

The Valiant Scot (> 1637)

Carver, John Linton. '*The Valiant Scot*, By "J. W."', in Allison Gaw, ed., *Studies in English Drama*, First Series, University of Pennsylvania (1917), pp. 75–104.

Hach, T. *Uber das Drama The Valiant Scot* (1901). (I have not seen this book.)

1637, 26 Apr. S.R. Mr. Waterson entered for his copy 'vnder the hands of M^r. Tho: Herbert deputy to S^r. Hen: Herbert & m^r. Downes warden a Tragedy called the Valiant Scott'. (Greg, *Bibliography*, i. 46.)

1637. The Valiant Scot. By *J. W.* Gent . . . 1637.

1640/1 (?) After telling how the players at the Fortune were arrested for church satire in *The Cardinal's Conspiracy* (q.v., Anon.) the writer continues: 'And having nothing left them but a few old Swords and Bucklers, they fell to Act the *Valiant Scot*, which they Played five dayes with great applause, which vext the Bishops worse then the other, insomuch, as they were forbidden Playing it any more; and some of them prohibited ever Playing againe.' (*Vox Borealis, or The Northern Discoverie*, 'the yeare coming on, 1641'. See above, i. 277–8.)

There have been two suggestions about the authorship of the play, neither very persuasive. A number of scholars have noted that the initials given on the title-page as the author's are also those of the publisher, John Waterson, and they have suggested or asserted that Waterson was the author. This idea is most fully developed by John Linton Carver (op. cit., pp. 86–92). There is nothing to encourage this identification beyond the accident of the initials. John Webster had the same initials and the further advantage of established experience as a playwright, but there are no grounds for thinking that he wrote the play. Another suggested author is William Bowyer, who says in his dedication to the Marquis of Hamilton:

. . . . *I would use the application to my selfe, having been one amongst your meanest followers in your Lordships practicall life of a Souldier: what I haue I bestow upon you, and doe hope though it be clothed in the light dressing of a Play, it will not be denied your Lordships acceptance since it contains the Character which History hath left to Posterity of your own truly valiant Countriman.* . . .

> Your Lordships most humble
> servant and Souldier,
> William Bowyer.

Nothing is known of William Bowyer beyond what he says in this dedication (see Carver, op. cit., pp. 92–93), and the dedication seems to me to suggest the owner of a manuscript, rather than a proud—or even a modest—author. There is precedence for such sponsorship, for manuscript owners, rather than authors, wrote dedications for Heminges's *The Fatal Contract*, Ford and Dekker's *The Sun's Darling*, Hawkins's *Apollo Shroving*, Henry Shirley's *The Martyred Soldier*, Fletcher's *Monsieur Thomas* (see life of Richard Brome), and others. The only evidence as to the authorship of *The Valiant Scot* at present available is that it was written by an unknown J. W.

The title-page of the play lacks the usual statement about the producing company, but the author of *Vox Borealis* says that it was revived at the Fortune, apparently in 1639 or 1640. There are dubious elements in his statement, however. The play which he says was suppressed at the Fortune was 'a new old Play' called *The Cardinal's Conspiracy*, which *Vox Borealis* says was produced with '*Altars, Images, Crosses, Crucifixes*, and the like' and therefore offended the bishops and landed the players in the Court of High Commission. Now this offensive play was evidently the same as that reported to Viscount Conway by Edmund Rossingham:

> Thursday last the players of the Fortune were fined 1,000*l.* for setting up an altar, a bason, and two candlesticks, and bowing down before it upon the stage, and although they allege it was an old play revived. . . . (See above, i. 277.)

But Rossingham's letter is dated 8 May 1639, and *Vox Borealis* writes as if his news were fresh 'the yeare coming on, 1641'. If he were so slippery about his dates, can he be relied upon in his statement about *The Valiant Scot*, especially when the title (taken as referring to the noble Scottish Presbyterians and the salutary drubbing they gave the enforcers of episcopal tyranny in the Bishops' Wars) is such a magnificent and unindictable jeer at the bishops who called the players before the Court of High Commission for their alleged anti-episcopal propaganda in *The Cardinal's* [Laud's] *Conspiracy*? Certainly the Puritan writers did make use of this story for propaganda purposes, for the *Vox Borealis* account is reprinted verbatim in *A Second Discovery by the Northern Scout*, 1642. (See Leslie Hotson, *The Commonwealth and Restoration Stage* [1928], pp. 3–4.) It may be, then, that *The Valiant Scot* was the property of the Fortune company and that they revived it for a very successful five-day run in 1639, but it would be comfortable to have testimony more reliable than that of a slippery Parliamentarian news-writer for whom it made such pat propaganda.

The play, which is an old-fashioned chronicle history, suitable enough for the Fortune in the late thirties, offers no evidence of its date. Belated examples of the form, like Ford's *Perkin Warbeck*, Glapthorne's *Albertus Wallenstein*, Davenport's *King John and Matilda*, and presumably his lost *Henry I* and *Henry II*, had appeared in the decade or so before *The Valiant Scot* was published. The source of the play, Mr. Carver has shown (op. cit., pp. 77–85), is Henry the minstrel's old Scottish poem about Wallace, in its later editions called *The Lyfe and Actis of W. Wallace*. It had appeared in seventeenth-century editions of 1611, N.D., 1618, 1620, and 1630. (*S.T.C.* Nos. 13151–4) before *The Valiant Scot* was published, but Carver makes no attempt to show which edition was used. J. W.'s derivation of his incidents from *Wallace* seems clear enough, but the verbal parallels are much less noteworthy than Mr. Carver thinks.

A notable feature of the play is the Scots dialect which is used regularly in the part of Peggie and sometimes in that of Wallace. Carver finds (op. cit., pp. 97–101) that it shows knowledge of the Scots tongue but not perfect familiarity.

ROBERT WARD (Warde)
c. 1595–<1642

Ward is known only from Professor Moore Smith's investigations in connexion with his presumptive authorship of *Fucus Histrio-mastix*. He entered Queens' College, Cambridge, from Westmorland and was granted his B.A. in 1615/6, his M.A. in 1619, and his B.D. in 1628. He was made a Fellow of Queens' in 1617, and Proctor in 1625. (*Alumni Cantab.* iv. 334.) Moore Smith notes that 'He was still Fellow on Aug. 3, 1642, when he signed the order for sending the College plate to the King, but had ceased to be so before the general ejection of April 1644.'

In his extracts from the Ely episcopal records A. Gibbons gives in his section, 'Notes on the Bishops' Transcripts', under the parish of Oakington, or Hockington, in Cambridge: '1629. Rob. Ward, *vicar*. 1640. Daniel Chaundler, *vicar*', apparently indicating that Chaundler succeeded Ward in 1640. (*Ely Episcopal Registers*, printed for private circulation [1891], p. 343.) W. G. Searle says (*The History of the Queens' College of St. Margaret and St. Bernard in the University of Cambridge* [1867], p. 465) that Ward was nominated by the college to the vicarage of Hockington, 29 October 1630.

Fucus Histriomastix or Fucus sive Histriomastix (1622/3)

MSS.: Lambeth Palace MS. 828; Bodleian MS. Rawl. Poet. 21.

Edition: *Fucus Histriomastix. A Comedy probably written by Robert Ward and acted at Queens' College, Cambridge, in Lent, 1623. Now first printed with an Introduction and Notes by G. C. Moore Smith* (1909).

Moore Smith says that of the two manuscripts of the play, the Oxford one, in which the play is called *Fucus sive Histriomastix*, is the more carefully written, 'but the Lambeth MS represents apparently the text as revised for the performance before the King, and in spite of its gross errors, due apparently to the ignorance of the scribe and necessitating a long list of corrections, has been taken as the basis of the present edition'. (Op. cit., p. vii.)

Ward's authorship is inferred from three pieces of evidence not wholly conclusive but strongly suggestive. Moore Smith, who had more experience with Cambridge plays than any other scholar, thought that Ward's appearance in the title-role in the cast given in the Lambeth MS. was presumptive evidence of his authorship, strongly supported by the last four lines of *Prologus Prior*:

> Date veniam atque ignoscite nostro Fuco:
> Quem vobis ecce vltro detegimus ipsi:
> Per hunc enim vnicum si non stetisset Fucum,
> Difficilis Histriomastix nunquam prodiret hodie.
> (Ibid., pp. ix and 3.)

A third indication of Ward's authorship of this play is furnished by a letter of William Beale, Fellow of Jesus, to William Boswell, Secretary to the Lord Keeper, endorsed 24 January 1622[/23]:

> Comœdia habenda est nouissimè a nostratibus Jesuanis, et iam scenæ omnes in Actu sunt quotidiano. Gemina Comœdia in fieri est; næ quidem et in Agere, apud Trinitarios: Autoribus Hacket, et Stubs: lepidis Jupiter, et comicissimis. Altera pol, excudenda excludenda a Wardo quodam Reginali Artium magistro, et quidem lepidarum [.] Deus faxit bonus, bene vt habeant istæc: melius multo vt Tu et (si quis*quam*). (Ibid., pp. xi–xii.)

The Trinity College play by Hacket and Stubbe was evidently *Loyola* (q.v.), which was acted before the University 28 February 1622/3 and before the King 12 March 1622/3, and presumably Ward's play was *Fucus Histriomastix* and belongs to the same season, a presumption supported, as Moore Smith points out, by the phrase, 'Hac venit quadregesima', of I. I, 49, in the text. At

this season the references in the prologue and in I. I to the state
of academic comedy would refer to the difficulties about *Loyola*.
This date is also compatible with the residence of the sixteen
Queens' men named in the cast, though the designation of their
degrees presents one or two inconsistencies. (Ibid., pp. viii–xi.)

That the play was presented before the University and a second
time before the King is known from the two prologues and two
epilogues, the second of which is headed 'Epilogus Posterior
Coram Rege'. The date of the second performance before the
King is somewhat uncertain, but Moore Smith inclines to think
that it took place at Newmarket in March 1622/3. (Ibid., pp.
xiii–xv.)

The extensive satire of Puritan hypocrisy in the play may
have been prompted by the affair of *Loyola*, but it has much in
common with *Bartholomew Fair*. Moore Smith notes that Ward
draws on Plautus, Terence, Juvenal, Horace, Vergil, Martial, and
Seneca, and that a number of lines seem to derive from *Lælia*.
(Ibid., p. xx and notes.) The dozen or so song fragments which
Villanus sings have their tunes indicated in the Lambeth MS.

At the end of the beautiful Oxford MS., just below the 'Finis',
the date '1610' has been written in a hand quite different from
that of the rest of the manuscript. This date has sometimes been
read 1616, but it seems to me clearly 1610. In any case it cannot
refer to the production of the play, since only two or three
members of the cast had matriculated in the University even by
1616. It may refer to the anonymous *Histriomastix*, published
in 1610, which some uninformed owner has confused with the
Latin play.

A set of verses on the play by H. Molle (presumably Henry
Molle, Fellow of King's, B.A. 1616/17; M.A. 1620) are found in
Rawlinson MS. Poet. 147; they were copied by Halliwell-Phillipps
into one of his scrap-books (Lowin, p. 121) now at the Folger
Shakespeare Library.

> On Fucus, a comedy acted before the King by some of
> Queens Colledge in Cambridge.
>
> > Now honour befall those merry boyes all
> >   To see the good chance of thinges
> > For they that while ere but the Queenes players were
> >   Are now become the Kinges
> > The players of London will surely be undone
> >   They have little cause to thank 'um
> > For Lowin, nor Towley, nor Tayler, nor Rowley
> >   Could ever dance Prinkum prankum.

If the author was informed about the King's company in London, his verses are a rough confirmation of Moore Smith's dates for the play. The verses must have been written before Tooley's death, between 3 and 5 June 1623, and after Rowley's transfer from the Prince's company to the King's, between 1619 and August 1623. (See above, ii. 556–7 and 601–2.)

DAVID WATERHOUSE
c. 1680–1758

Waterhouse has been listed as a Caroline dramatist in error. He was admitted a sizar at Christ's College, Cambridge, 9 May 1698, aged eighteen. He received his B.A. in 1701-2 and his M.A. in 1705. After serving two parishes, he died 4 November 1758. (*Alumni Cantab*. iv. 344.)

Cleophilus

So far as I can find, there was no 1650 edition of this play, as has been asserted, and therefore no suggestion of Caroline composition. The only edition I can find is that of 1700. On the title-page of the 1700 edition in the Folger Shakespeare Library is written in an old hand 'author D. Waterhouse X^{ti} Coll Can^t hunc (?) temp. Junr Sophista'. At the top of the title-page is written, apparently in the same hand, '[?] Robt Warren X^{ti} Coll Can^t.' Since the only D. Waterhouse listed in the seventeenth century at either Cambridge or Oxford is the David Waterhouse noted above, and since a Robert Warren aged seventeen was admitted sizar at Christ's, Cambridge, 7 June 1697, B.A. 1700–1, M.A. 1704 (*Alumni Cantab*. iv. 342), the evidence suggests that the Robert Warren and D. Waterhouse of the notes on the Folger title-page were contemporaries at Christ's and that the latter wrote *Cleophilus*, while he was an undergraduate, very shortly before it was published in 1700.

JOHN WEBSTER
c. 1580–>1634

Crawford, Charles. 'John Webster and Sir Philip Sidney', in *Collectanea*, First Series (1906), pp. 20–46.
—— 'Montaigne, Webster, and Marston: Donne and Webster', in *Collectanea*, Second Series (1907), pp. 1–63.

Howarth, R. G. 'John Webster', *T.L.S.*, 2 November 1933, p. 751.
Lucas, F. L., ed. *The Complete Works of John Webster* (1927), i. 49–56.
Morgan, F. C. 'A Deed of Gift (1624) and John Webster', *N. & Q.* cxcii (1947), 496.
Pierce, F. E. *The Collaboration of Webster and Dekker* (Yale Studies in English, No. XXXVII) (1909).
Wagner, Bernard. 'New Verses by John Webster', *M.L.N.* xlvi (1931), 403–5.

(Mr. R. G. Howarth reported in 1948 that he was at work on a study of the life and works of John Webster, 'Research in Progress', *P.M.L.A.*, lxiii [1948], Supplement, p. 192, No. 1140.)

The biographical records of John Webster are astonishingly meagre. There is no record of his birth or of his age at any point in his career; the commonly conjectured birth-date of *circa* 1580 can be supported only by the lame observation that twenty-two would have been a good age for him when he first appears in Henslowe's Diary in May 1602, as collaborating with Munday, Middleton, and Drayton on 'sesers ffalle'. (*Henslowe's Diary*, i. 166.) Though his plays exhibit learning, there is no likely record of a John Webster at Oxford or Cambridge, unless he could be the man of that name who matriculated at St. John's, Cambridge, in Easter term 1585, but took no degrees. (*Alumni Cantab.* iv. 356.) Perhaps this record has too lightly been assumed to be too early.

Monuments of Honour, the Lord Mayor's pageant written for the inauguration of John Gore, merchant-tailor, in 1624, was published in the same year with the title-page statement, '*Invented and Written* by Iohn Webster Merchant-Taylor', and, in his dedication to Gore, Webster speaks of himself as 'one borne free of your Company'. This has generally been taken as indicating that Webster's father was a merchant-tailor, and various Websters have been suggested (see *Elizabethan Stage*, iii. 507), but no evidence to associate any of them with the dramatist has been forthcoming.

Lucas (op. cit. i. 50) is inclined to identify the dramatist with the John Webster, son and heir of John Webster of London, who was admitted to the Middle Temple 1 August 1598. The environment would seem a suitable one, and Webster had associates at the Middle Temple, but again there is no evidence for identification.

Chambers (*Elizabethan Stage*, iii. 507) notes that there was an

English actor named John Webster in Germany in 1596 and suggests that the dramatist may have had a player's career before he became a dramatist. Lucas (op. cit. i. 51) notes other suggestions indicating a player's career, but is not much impressed by them, since Webster, in the epilogue to *The White Devil*, speaks of the actors of the Queen's company and of the testimony of 'some of their owne quality'. His plays would seem to me to display much of the scholar and little or nothing of the actor.

Webster's earliest known dramatic work was done for Henslowe—collaborations with Munday, Drayton, Middleton, Dekker, Heywood, Chettle, and Wentworth Smith in 1602 on *Caesar's Fall* (probably the same as *Two Shapes*) and *Lady Jane* (generally thought to have been incorporated in part in *Sir Thomas Wyatt*, published in 1607 as by Dekker and Webster).

In 1604 he wrote an Induction for Marston's *Malcontent* when it was acted by the King's company, and in this and the following year he collaborated with Dekker on *Westward Ho!* and *Northward Ho!* for the Children of Paul's. No dramatic composition has heretofore been definitely attributed to him in the next five years, though *Appius and Virginia*, not always accepted as Webster's, is assigned by Fleay, Brooke, and Chambers to 1608 or a little later, and I think *The Devil's Law-Case* probably belongs to the year 1610. *The White Devil* was written for Queen Anne's men between 1609 and 1612—Lucas favours 1611–12. (Op. cit., i. 67–69.) For the King's company Webster wrote *The Duchess of Malfi* in 1613 or 1614.

The verses which Webster wrote for the 1612 edition of Thomas Heywood's *Apology for Actors* suggest a friendship somewhat deeper than those ordinarily recorded in commendatory verses, since these stanzas are headed, 'To his beloued friend Maister Thomas Heywood' and are signed, 'By your friend Iohn Webster'.

The most significant of Webster's non-dramatic work was also done about the time of his two great tragedies. His *Monumental Column*, on the death of Prince Henry, appeared in 1613. The group of thirty-two new characters, which first Baron A.F. Bourgeois and later F. L. Lucas (op. cit. iv. 6–14) attributed to Webster, appeared in the sixth edition of Overbury's *Characters* in 1615.

Thus not only Webster's best work but the majority of all his writing was accomplished before 1616. After that date his only certain dramatic compositions were the Lord Mayor's show entitled *Monuments of Honour* and the collaboration *The Late Murder of the Son upon the Mother, or Keep the Widow Waking*. Five other plays have been inconclusively attributed to Webster, or are of uncertain date.

Besides these five there is *The Thracian Wonder*, which was published in 1661 as by Webster and Rowley, but it has been almost universally rejected from the Webster canon. (See *Elizabethan Stage*, iv. 49.) *The Weakest Goeth to the Wall* was published anonymously in 1600 and 1618 and only assigned to Webster by Phillips and Winstanly. (*Theatrum Poetarum*, p. 116, and *Lives of the Most Famous English Poets*, p. 137.) No one else has accepted the attribution. (See *Elizabethan Stage*, iv. 52–53.)

Allusions to Webster in his lifetime are uninformative or cryptic. The only commendatory verses published with his works are those contributed by Thomas Middleton, William Rowley, and John Ford for the 1623 edition of *The Duchess of Malfi*. These verses reveal rather more than the usual respect for the dramatist, but neither personalia nor particular affection. Quite different are the allusions in H[enry] F[itzgeffrey's] *Satyres and Satyricall Epigrams*, 1617, and William Heminges's manuscript *Elegy on Randolph's Finger*, c. 1632. The former occurs in the section of the book called 'THE Third Booke of *Humours*: Intituled *Notes from* BLACK-FRYERS'. This section is a long verse monologue spoken by a member of the audience at a Blackfriars play in which he comments on the scene and particularly on members of the audience. Towards the end he exclaims when a new patron enters the theatre:

> Bvt h'st! with him Crabbed (*Websterio*)
> The *Play-wright, Cart-wright:* whether? either! *ho*—
> No further. Looke as yee'd bee look't into:
> Sit as ye woo'd be *Read: Lord!* who woo'd know him?
> Was euer man so mangl'd with a *Poem*?
> See how he drawes his mouth awry of late,
> How he scrubs: wrings his wrests: scratches his Pate.
> A *Midwife*! helpe! By his *Braines coitus*,
> Some *Centaure* strange: some huge *Bucephalus*,
> Or *Pallas* (sure) ingendred in his *Braine*,
> Strike *Vulcan* with thy hammer once againe.

> This is the *Crittick* that (of all the rest)
> I'de not haue view mee, yet I feare him least,
> Heer's not a word *cursiuely* I haue *Writ*,
> But hee'l *Industriously* examine it.
> And in some 12. monthes hence (or there *about*)
> Set in a shamefull sheete, my errors *out*.
> But what care I it *will* be so obscure,
> That none shall vnderstand him (**I** am sure.)

$$(F_6{}^v-F_7.)$$

Lucas implies that this attack on Webster by Fitzgeffrey may have been a retaliation for the attack by Webster (?) in the character, 'An Excellent Actor', on Fitzgeffrey's friend J. Stephens. (Op. cit. i. 54–55, and iv. 8–10.) Whatever the motive, the attack is clear enough. Webster is pictured as a carping critic and a laborious and obscure poet. The charge of slow and painful composition had evidently been made before against Webster, as against Jonson, for Webster replies to it in the address in the 1612 edition of *The White Devil*. The line, 'The *Play-wright, Cart-wright:* whether? either! *ho*—', is perhaps a clumsy thrust at Webster's laboriousness, but R. G. Howarth pointed out (loc. cit.) that it relates curiously to a passage in Heminges's *Elegy on Randolph's Finger*. In this amusing burlesque elegy on the poets escorting to the River Styx the cortège of the finger which Thomas Randolph had lost in a tavern fray, lines 33–42 read:

> that wch soe ofte has toumbled ore a Verse
> Is toumbled now ytt selfe Into a hearse,
> Borne to yttes graue, by Art Inuention
> Thrice blessed Nature, Imitation.
> Ytt had byn drawne and wee In state aproche
> but websters brother would nott lend a Coach:
> hee swore thay all weare hired to Conuey
> the Malfy dutches sadly on her way,
> And wittye fortune ytt seemes thought ytt more meett
> to haue our Poettes quayntly vse thayr feett.
> (G. C. Moore Smith, ed., p. 12.)

Heminges here seems to say that a brother of John Webster was in some way connected with the hire of coaches, and Fitzgeffrey's line may have been intended to play on this association as well as on Webster's methods of composition. Perhaps it is relevant to note, in connexion with Fitzgeffrey's odd 'Cart-wright' epithet, that Webster, according to the Company accounts for the production of his Lord Mayor's pageant, *Monuments of Honour* (q.v.), seems to have been one of the producers as well as the author of this show. Could Webster, like Anthony Munday, have had previous pageant-producing experience before 1617 at which Fitzgeffrey was sneering?

These brief and cryptic comments by Fitzgeffrey and Heminges tell us little about Webster, but that little is nearly all we have. The facts connected with the publication and performance of his later plays are listed below with the plays. Even in the notorious affair of *Keep the Widow Waking* in 1624 we know only that

Webster collaborated hastily with Dekker, Ford, and Rowley. There is no record that he testified in the ensuing suit.

The date of Webster's death is inferred to be before November 1634, when Heywood's *Hierarchie of the Blessed Angels* was licensed, because in his verses about his contemporary poets Heywood seems to use his tenses carefully to distinguish the living from the dead (Lucas, op. cit. i. 52, n.), and he uses the past tense for Webster. C. J. Sisson has doubted the significance of these tenses (*Lost Plays of Shakespeare's Age*, p. 102, n. 1) and suggests that an entry in the burial registers of St. James's, Clerkenwell, of a John Webster on 3 March 1637/8 refers to the poet. Since John Webster was such a common London name, and since there is nothing to connect the dramatist with this parish, the weight of the evidence seems to me to indicate that Webster's friend Heywood meant to speak of him as dead in 1634 and that the Clerkenwell parishioner was not the poet.

Later allusions to Webster are not numerous except in John Cotgrave's *English Treasury of Wit and Language*, 1655. This interesting dramatic anthology prints some 1,686 quotations, nearly all of them from Jacobean and Caroline plays. (See G. E. Bentley, *Stud. Phil.* xl [1943], 186–203.) Of the forty-nine dramatists quoted, Cotgrave used only five more often than he did Webster; and of the 246 plays drawn upon, only Greville's *Alaham* and *Mustapha* are quoted more frequently than *The White Devil* and *The Duchess of Malfi*. (Ibid., pp. 199–202.)

Cotgrave, however, was more aware of Webster's distinction than most of his contemporaries. Howes listed him with twenty-six other great Elizabethan and Jacobean poets in his continuation of Stow's *Annals of England* (ed. 1615, p. 811; ed. 1631, pp. 811–12), but most of the other chroniclers ignored him. Heywood noted in *The Hierarchie of the Blessed Angels* that he had been called ‘ Jack ’ (p. 206); the author of *A City Dog in a Saint's Doublet*, 1648, quoted *The White Devil* by ‘ the excellent Tragedian Webster ’ (p. 4). He was listed in small groups of famous poets by Mercurius Pragmaticus (*The Second Part of Crafty Cromwell*, 1648, *Address*) and by Samuel Holland (*Wit and Fancy in a Maze* [*Don Zara del Fogo*], 1656, p. 102). E. M. noted Webster's reference to Perkins in *The White Devil* (*Wit and Drollery*, 1661, A_4), and James Wright quoted *The Duchess of Malfi* (*Country Conversations*, 1694, pp. 54–55). The most notable praise of Webster is Samuel Sheppard's in his *Fairy King* (Bodleian MS. Rawlinson Poet. 28, stanza 70):

WEBSTER the next, though not so much of note
Nor's name attended with such noise & crowd
yet by the Nine & by Apollo's vote
whole Groves of Bay are for his head allow'd,
most Sacred Spirrit (some may say J Doate)
of thy three noble Tragedies, bee as proud
as great voluminous Johnson, thou shallt bee
read longer, & with more Applause then hee.
(Quoted by H. E. Rollins, *Stud. Phil.* xxiv [1927], 554.

Collected Editions

1830. *The Works of John Webster*, edited by Alexander Dyce, 4 vols.
1857. [Another edition in one volume.]
1857. *The Dramatic Works of John Webster*, edited by William Hazlitt, 4 vols.
1897. [Another issue.]
1927. *The Complete Works of John Webster*, edited by F. L. Lucas, 4 vols.

Anything for a Quiet Life

The play was first published in 1662 as by Thomas Middleton, and Webster's collaboration was not suggested until Dugdale Sykes contended in 1921 that Webster had had a preponderant share in it. Lucas (op. cit. iv. 66–68) accepts his conclusions and reprints the play in his edition of Webster. The evidence is not convincing to me. (See Middleton.)

Appius and Virginia (1624–34?)

Edition: *The Complete Works of John Webster*, edited by F. L. Lucas (1927), iii. 121–254.

Brooke, Rupert. 'The Authorship of the Later "Appius and Virginia"', *M.L.R.* viii (1913), 433–53.
Clark, A. M. 'The Authorship of "Appius and Virginia"', *M.L.R.* xvi (1921), 1–17.
—— *Thomas Heywood, Playwright and Miscellanist* (1931), pp. 252–75.
Gray, H. D. '*Appius and Virginia*: by Webster and Heywood', *Stud. Phil.* xxiv (1927), 275–89.
Lauschke, Johannes. *John Websters Tragödie Appius and Virginia, eine Quellenstudie* (1899).

Sykes, H. Dugdale. *Sidelights on Elizabethan Drama* (1924). [Contains an essay which brings together material on Webster's authorship of *Appius and Virginia* that had previously appeared in *N. & Q.* for 24 and 31 May, 14 June, and 26 July 1913.]

1639, 10 Aug. 'Appius & Virginia' is last in a list of plays belonging to William Beeston and the King and Queen's Young Company and forbidden to all other companies by the Lord Chamberlain. (See above, i. 330–1.)

1654, 13 May. S.R. Richard Marriott entered for his copy 'A Play called Appeus and Virginia Tragedy written by Iohn Webster'. (Greg, *Bibliography*, i. 62.)

1654. Appius And Virginia. A Tragedy. By *John Webster* . . . 1654.

1654. [Another issue with a cancel title-leaf.]

1655. [Another issue with another cancel title-leaf.]

1659, 11 June. S.R. Humphrey Moseley entered twenty-one copies which had been transferred to him from Richard Marriott. Included is 'Appeus & Virginia a Tragedy by Iohn Webster'. (Greg, *Bibliography*, i. 67.)

1659. [Another issue with a third cancel title-leaf.]

1669, 12 May. 'After dinner, my wife and I to the Duke of York's playhouse, and there, in the side balcony, over against the musick, did hear, but not see, a new play, the first day acted, "The Roman Virgin," an old play, and but ordinary, I thought.' (Diary of Samuel Pepys.)

1679. Appius and Virginia, Acted at the Dukes Theater under the name of The Roman Virgin Or Unjust Judge, A Tragedy. By *John Webster* . . . 1679. [Another issue with a fourth and completely changed title-leaf.]

The attempts to date this play of Webster's have been chaotic. H. D. Gray selected 1603–4; Brooke and Chambers, *c.* 1608; Fleay, *c.* 1609; Sir Sidney Lee, >1619; Stoll, <1623; Sykes, 1626–34 or <1630; and Lucas, 1625–7. In each case the evidence presented seems to me at best inadequate, often absurd, and frequently tied to arguments for hypothetical collaborators. Lucas (ed. cit., pp. 121–30) summarizes the arguments of his predecessors. For his own dating he places far too much weight on his metrical tables. Complete metrical analyses have been found to be none too reliable; what reliance can be placed on Lucas's analysis of 890 lines out of about 2,600? Parallel passages and situations are presented by all the commentators, but none is very distinctive, and they range in date from 1599 to 1635.

Perhaps most considerable is Lucas's observation that the scenes of starvation in the camp are not found in the source, as most of the other incidents are, and that the starvation of English troops on the Continent was a subject of comment and concern in 1624–6. There were, of course, other periods of such concern, but this one is at least suggestive. Lucas also notes a possible allusion in v. 1, lines 163–6, to a flax warehouse fire 12 November 1623 that was spectacular enough to be recorded in Chamberlain's letters and in the continuation of Stow's *Chronicle*. His further argument based on his version of Webster's development as an artist is as dubious as most such arguments. Thus the evidence for the date of the play is inconclusive, but the period from 1624 to Webster's death seems to have slightly more to be said for it than have the other dates offered.

Brooke and Lucas (ed. cit., pp. 131–3) have shown that the sources of the play are Dionysius of Halicarnassus, edition or translation unascertained, and Livy in Philemon Holland's translation.

Most recent students of Webster and Heywood have refused to accept the simple attribution of this play to Webster and have assigned varying portions of it to Thomas Heywood. Brooke thought it was almost all Heywood; Gray, mostly Heywood; Sykes, all Webster; Clark, Heywood, superficially revised by Webster; and Lucas, with commendable hesitancy, that it is predominantly Webster with various bits unaccountably by Heywood. Nearly all the arguments are simple impressionism rationalized by dubious parallel passages, bold statements about vocabulary based on grossly inadequate evidence, and sage pronunciamentos about Webster's artistic development, doubly ludicrous in this case because there is only the flimsiest evidence of the date of the play. I see no grounds for any dogmatic assertions about the authorship of the play. The number of passages which have sounded like Heywood to several students is worth noting, though their presence could indicate original authorship, collaboration, revision, imitation, or only the suggestibility of the students. Without more reliable evidence one can only accept the statement of the publisher.

The presence of the play in the repertory of the King and Queen's Young Company at the Cockpit in 1639 indicates only that the company owned the manuscript and presumably thought the piece still worth acting in that year. Other plays in this list had once been the property of Prince Charles's (I) company, Lady Elizabeth's company, Queen Anne's company, or Queen

Henrietta's company, so that nothing of the play's date or original company can be deduced from this list.

Pepys's contradictory designations of the play he saw—'a new play, the first day acted, "The Roman Virgin," an old play'— indicate that the piece was probably the one noted by John Downes:

The Unjust Judge, or *Appius Virginia*, done by the same Author [Betterton]. *Virginius Acted* by *Mr. Betterton, Appius*, the Unjust Judge, by *Mr. Harris: Virginia*, by *Mrs. Betterton*. And all the other Parts *Exactly* perform'd, it lasted Successively 8 Days, and very frequently *Acted* afterwards. (*Roscius Anglicanus*, ed. Summers, p. 30.)

Betterton must have done a revision, not a new play. The text is not extant, but the title-page of the 1679 issue of Webster's play evidently attempts to capitalize on the popularity of Betterton's adaptation. Gerard Langbaine implies that Betterton's version was printed:

And Appius *and* Virginia, *written by* Webster, *is afterwards ascrib'd to* T. B. *though as the deceased Comedian Mr.* Cartwright, *a Bookseller by Profession, told me, 'twas onely the old Play Reprinted, and Corrected by the above-mentioned Mr.* Batterton; *with several others.* (*Momus Triumphans*, 1688, Preface A₂ᵛ.)

Caesar's Fall, or The Two Shapes
with Dekker, Drayton, Middleton, and Munday
(Lost)

See W. W. Greg, *Henslowe's Diary*, i. 166–7.

Christmas Comes but Once a Year
with Chettle, Dekker, and Heywood
(Lost)

See W. W. Greg, *Henslowe's Diary*, i. 184 and 186.

A Cure for a Cuckold (1624–5)
with William Rowley

Edition: *The Complete Works of John Webster*, edited by F. L. Lucas (1927), iii. 3–118.

Gray, H. D. ' "A Cure for a Cuckold" by Heywood, Rowley and Webster', *M.L.R.* xxii (1927), 389–97.

Lucas, F. L. 'An Unexplained Allusion in Webster and Rowley',
  T.L.S., 15 April 1926, p. 283.
Sykes, H. D. 'Webster's Share in "A Cure for a Cuckold"',
  N. & Q., Eleventh Series, ix (1914), 382–4, 404–5, 443–5, 463–4.

1661. A Cure For A Cuckold. A Pleasant Comedy, As it hath been
  several times Acted with great Applause. *Written by* John
  Webster *and* William Rowley . . . 1661 [Some copies of this
  edition were issued with *The Thracian Wonder* in the same
  year with a joint title-page.]
1661. [Another issue.]

The late date of the first edition of the play and the general
reputation of its publisher, Francis Kirkman, have led various
scholars to question the title-page ascription of authorship. Lucas,
however, finds satisfactory evidence of the work of Rowley and
Webster, though he is impressed by H. D. Gray's case for
evidence of Heywood's work. (*M.L.R.* xxii [1927], 389–97.) He
thinks the play a collaboration by the three, divides the scenes,
and presents the evidence for Webster. (Ed. cit. iii. 10–18.) The
traces of Heywood do not seem to me entirely convincing, but
the investigations serve more to confirm than to contradict
Kirkman's attribution to Webster and Rowley.

Lucas points out that the description of the sea-fight with
Spanish ships in III. 3, lines 66–114, probably was written after
the beginning of the hostilities with Spain; that the line, 'Will
not the Ballad of *Flood* that was prest, make them leave their
knavery?' (IV. 1, lines 118–19), refers to a ballad about an event
of January 1623/4; and that the reference to a twelvepenny fine
for swearing (V. 1, lines 208–9) refers to the statute of 1623–4.
He would date the play 1625. Additional evidence unknown to
him is the record of Rowley's burial 11 February 1625/6, which
furnishes a definite *terminus ad quem*. A date of 1624–5 would
seem to me well supported.

Lucas follows Rupert Brooke and Stoll in declaring that the
main plot of *A Cure for a Cuckold* was suggested by Massinger's
Parliament of Love, a play that was licensed for the Cockpit
company by Sir Henry Herbert, 3 November 1624, but that was
never published in the seventeenth century and is extant only in
a manuscript of the last four acts. The relationship seems to me
fairly clear, but it is not quite so certain that Webster and Rowley
took their play from Massinger and had it on the boards in a few
months with no available quarto. Various events to account for

the relationship could be imagined, but I see no adequate evidence for any of them.

Hazlitt pointed out (*Manual*, p. 41) that Joseph Harris's *The City Bride, or the Merry Cuckold*, published in 1696, is an adaptation of *A Cure for a Cuckold*.

Love's Graduate, published by S. E. Spring-Rice in 1885, is the part of *A Cure for a Cuckold* that the editor assumes to be by Webster, published separately.

The Devil's Law-Case, or When Women Go to Law the Devil is Full of Business (1610?)

Edition: *The Complete Works of John Webster*, edited by F. L. Lucas (1927), ii. 213–372.

1623. The Deuils Law-case. Or, When Women goe to Law, the Deuill is full of Businesse. *A new Tragecomœdy. The true and perfect Copie from the Originall.* As it was approouedly well Acted by her Maiesties Seruants. *Written by* Iohn Webster . . . 1623.

The various dates which have been suggested for the play, all of them dependent upon internal evidence, are reviewed by Lucas (op. cit. ii. 213–16). Lucas favours a date after 1616 because two passages in the play, I. 2, lines 193 ff., and II. 1, lines 164 ff., are similar to, and therefore supposedly derived from, passages in Jonson's *Devil Is an Ass*. He thinks the date must be before the summer of 1622, when he supposes Queen Anne's company, named on the title-page as performers of the play, was broken up. Because of various suggested allusions—all of which seem dubious to me—he favours 1620, next 1619, and next 1621.

But Queen Anne's company did not break in 1622; it broke in 1619, after the death of the Queen. (See above, i. 164–6.) This fact makes most of the dubious allusions either impossible or later insertions. The best evidence for the date of the play seems to me that offered by Fleay (*Biog. Chron.* ii. 272–3), who noted that Romelio, said to be thirty-eight, was born in 1572. Lucas brushes this aside, but it seems to me that neither Fleay nor Lucas gave sufficient weight to the insistence on dates in IV. 2. This is the big scene, in which Romelio's mother, Leonora, asserts that he is the bastard son of a Spaniard, and the circumstances of his conception are recounted for the court by the maid, Winifred. There is unusual insistence on the dates: Romelio is said to have been in Naples thirty-eight years (line 128); the lawyer says his mother conceived him thirty-nine years ago (ll. 197 ff.); the judge says that it is odd that Leonora confesses her sin some forty years after the event (l. 269); the judge asks when Romelio was begot, and the attorney says, 'In *Anno* seventie one, my Lord'(l. 375); the judge repeats, 'Very well, seventie one', and notes that it was the year of the Battle of Lepanto (ll. 376–7); Winifred says she is forty-six, and the judge notes that this would make her eight in '71 (ll. 435–9); the judge repeats that Romelio is thirty-eight (l. 438); the judge pins Winifred to the admission that the Spaniard lay with Leonora only in '71 (ll. 453–62); the judge—who is really the accused Spaniard—has his picture brought in and says he looked like that forty years ago (ll. 518–19); the judge says he, the real Spaniard, is accused of adultery in '71 (ll. 525–6). It has been often observed that when the events of a play are dated by Elizabethan dramatists, they tend to make the present of the action the date of production. When dates are so frequently reiterated as in this scene, it seems impossible that the entire audience would not have been aware that the trial was held in 1610. That was presumably, therefore, the year in which Webster expected it to be produced by Queen Anne's company, for whom he wrote *The White Devil* about the same time. This date would place the play before our period; it is included because it is not discussed in *The Elizabethan Stage*.

No source is known for the plot of the play, but various parallels have been pointed out, especially the similarity of Romelio and his development to Marlowe's Barabas. (See O. Schröder, *Marlowe und Webster* [1907], and Lucas, op. cit. ii. 217–18.) There is the faintest suggestion that the actor Richard Perkins (see above, ii. 525–8) may have had something to do with this relationship, for Webster praised him at the end of the 1612 edition of *The White Devil*, and Webster's friend Heywood called attention to his performance of Barabas in his prologue and epilogue in the 1633 edition of *The Jew of Malta*, published as acted by Queen Henrietta's men, a company which derived part of its actors and repertory from the old Queen Anne's troupe. (See above, i. 218–20 and 250–9.) Now Romelio's lines, III. 2. 1–17, when he is disguised as a Jew, not only clearly refer to Barabas, as has been noted, but lines 1–3:

> . . . why me thinks,
> That I could play with mine owne shaddow now,
> And be a rare Italienated Jew;

sound as if Perkins might be titillating an audience by making himself up as he did in *The Jew of Malta* and coyly referring to his own acting in another play.

Langbaine noted that the attempted assassination which becomes a successful piece of surgery might be derived from Goulart's *Histoires admirables*. (*An Account of the English Dramatick Poets*, p. 509.) The story of the mother who falsely admits her son's bastardy is found in various places noted by Lucas (op. cit. ii. 218–21), though he oddly omits *A Fair Quarrel*. None is close enough to Webster's version to be a certain source, and such a good melodramatic episode is sure to have been used in other stories and plays not noted or lost.

I have found no records of later performances of the play or allusions to it in the seventeenth century, except the twenty-three quotations in Cotgrave's *English Treasury of Wit and Language*, 1655. (See G. E. Bentley, *Stud. Phil.* xl [1943], 186–203.)

The Duchess of Malfi (1613–14; revised 1617–23?)

See *The Elizabethan Stage*, iii. 510–11.

The first edition of *The Duchess of Malfi* was published in 1623 with two casts of King's men. The first, which includes William Ostler, must date before his death on 16 December 1614; the second, in which Richard Burbage's role of Ferdinand is taken by Joseph Taylor, presumably dates after the death of Burbage, who was buried 16 March 1618/19. (See above, ii. 396.)

This double cast, unique among Jacobean and Caroline records, might suggest a complete revision of the play, and it is true that the first scene contains an allusion to the murder of the Maréchal d'Ancre, which occurred 24 April 1617, but the passage may well be an isolated insertion for a revival, as Lucas suggests. (Op. cit. ii. 4–5.) There is no adequate evidence of a complete revision, and the appearance of the second cast remains something of a mystery.

The Fair Maid of the Inn (1625/6)

The play was licensed by Sir Henry Herbert 22 January 1625/6 as by John Fletcher (q.v.) and acted at the Blackfriars; it was first published in the Beaumont and Fletcher Folio of 1647. Webster was first suggested as a collaborating author, with several others, by Sykes on the basis of the usual parallel passages, and Lucas accepts Webster's part (op. cit., iv. 148–52) and reprints the play in his complete Webster. He divides the play among Webster, Massinger, and Ford, allowing Fletcher no part in it at all. This seems to me arrant wilfulness. The Master of the Revels was not an irresponsible advertising agent, and the King's men knew their business and were directly involved in the preparation of the 1647 Folio. (See Fletcher.)

Guise (> 1623)
(Lost)

Our only reliable information about this play comes from Webster's statement in his dedication of *The Devil's Law-Case*, 1623, to Sir Thomas Finch: 'Some of my other Works, as *The white Devill, The Dutchesse of Malfi, Guise*, and others, you have formerly seene; I present this humbly to kisse your hands, and to find your allowance.'

In Rogers and Ley's 1656 list 'of all Playes that are Printed' appears 'Guise, *Marstone*'; in Archer's 'Exact and perfect CATALOGUE of all the PLAIES that were ever printed', 1656, is 'Guise. C. *Iohn Webster*'; in Kirkman's 1661 list of printed plays is 'Guise', and in his 1671 list, 'Guise. T.' (Greg, *List of Masques, Pageants, &c.*, App. II, p. lxxii.) These listings suggest the existence of an anonymous edition of the play, for there is a suggestive variety in the attributions and classifications. It is possible that the listings indicate only a reading of the dedication of *The Devil's Law-Case*, but the lists in general contain so many easily corrected errors that one hesitates to suggest that any of these publishers ever read the plays they advertised. It is true that Marlowe's *Massacre at Paris* is sometimes called *The Guise* in *Henslowe's Diary*, but these publishers were not referring to Marlowe's play, for it is listed under its proper title by each publisher, and Archer and Kirkman attribute it to Marlowe.

John Payne Collier tried to create an early history for the play by adding 'Webster' to one of Henslowe's manuscript entries about purchase of 'a clocke for the gwisse', and then concluding (*H.E.D.P.*, ed. 1831, iii. 101–2) that Webster revised Marlowe's play. Though the forgery is one of Collier's cruder efforts and has been universally rejected, the hypothesis that Webster's *Guise* was a revision of Marlowe's *Massacre at Paris* has attracted Webster's editors. (Hazlitt, i, pp. viii–ix; Lucas, ii. 321.) Such a conclusion is the purest speculation.

There is no evidence of the date of the play, save that it must have appeared before Webster referred to it in his dedication of 1623. Lucas (op. cit. ii. 321) suggests that Webster named the plays in chronological order in the dedication and that *Guise* would therefore date 1613<>1623. Perhaps this is the best hypothesis offered, but it is very shaky.

Sheppard's reference in his *Fairy King* to Webster's 'three noble Tragedies' (see above, Webster's life) is arresting. Could he have seen *Guise*? Or did he think *Appius and Virginia* great, or *The Devil's Law-Case* a tragedy?

Lady Jane

with Chettle, Dekker, Heywood, and Wentworth Smith

(Lost?)

See *The Elizabethan Stage*, iii. 293–4.

The Late Murder of the Son upon the Mother, or Keep the Widow Waking

(Lost)

A collaboration of Webster, Ford, Rowley, and Dekker (q.v.).

Love's Graduate

See *A Cure for a Cuckold*.

The Malcontent

For Webster's additions to Marston's play, see *The Elizabethan Stage*, iii. 431–2.

Monuments of Honour (1624)

Editions: *The Complete Works of John Webster*, edited by F. L. Lucas (1927), iii. 313–39. R. T. D. Sayle, *Lord Mayors' Pageants of the Merchant Taylors' Company in the 15th, 16th, and 17th Centuries* (privately printed, 1931), pp. 106–16. (Contains text and extensive company accounts.)

1624. Monuments of Honor. Deriued from remarkable Antiquity, and Celebrated in the Honorable City of *London*, at the sole Munificent charge and expences of the Right Worthy and Worshipfull Fraternity, of the Eminent MERCHANT-TAYLORS. Directed in their most affectionate Loue, at the *Confirmation of their right Worthy Brother* IOHN GORE in the High Office of His *Maiesties Liuetenant ouer this His Royall* Chamber. Expressing in a Magnificent Tryumph, all the Pageants, *Chariots of Glory, Temples of Honor, besides a* specious and goodly Sea Tryumph, as well particularly to the Honor of the City, as generally to the Glory of this our Kingdome. *Invented and Written by* Iohn Webster Merchant-Taylor . . . 1624.

Webster wrote this typical Lord Mayor's Pageant for the inauguration of John Gore, Merchant-Taylor, as Lord Mayor in 1624. The title-page says that the piece was '*Invented and Written by* Iohn Webster Merchant-Taylor', and in his dedication to Gore Webster speaks of himself as 'one borne free of your Company'; in the description of the scene in Paul's Churchyard he speaks of Merchant-Taylors' Hall as 'our Hall' and later of Sir John Hawkwood as 'Free of our Company', and twice later of 'our company'. The prominence of references to Prince Henry is notable in view of Webster's poem, *A Monumental Column.*

Mr. Sayle notes that the pageant cost the company more than £1,000, a sum unequalled by the costs of any other Merchant-Taylors' show in the three centuries he considers. The accounts of the company that he publishes seem to show that Webster was not only the writer but one of the producers of the elaborate pageant.

Itm̃, paid to John Webster, ye Poet, and to John Terry painter and William Patten and George Lovett, for ye device making and painting and guilding all the land and water shewes, pageantes, chariott greene men and theire ffire-workes, apparell porters to carry them, and for all other necessaries belonging unto them, the some of two hundred three score and tenn pounds, as by the agreem^t in writing made between ye Company and ye parties above named, more at large appeareth, wee said paid the some of ⎫
⎬ cclxx^{li}.
⎭

Itm̃, paid more unto them over and above the agreem^t wch the Company gave them by way of gratuity the some of tenn pounds ⎫
⎬ x^{li}
⎭

(Op. cit., pp. 110–11.)

Northward Ho!

with Thomas Dekker

See *The Elizabethan Stage*, iii. 295–6.

Sir Thomas Wyatt

with Thomas Dekker

See *The Elizabethan Stage*, iii. 293–4.

The Thracian Wonder

See *The Elizabethan Stage*, iv. 49.

The Weakest Goeth to the Wall

See Anon.

Westward Ho!

with Thomas Dekker

See *The Elizabethan Stage*, iii. 295.

The White Devil

See *The Elizabethan Stage*, iii. 509–10.

FRANCIS WHITE
c. 1589–<1643

White was born in London and matriculated at Magdalen Hall,
27 November 1607, aged eighteen. He was a demy of Magdalen
College from 1610 to 1614, receiving his B.A. 10 June 1611 and
M.A. 5 July 1614. From 1614 to 1617 he was master of the college
school, and he was Fellow of the college 1623–6. He was rector
of Compton Beauchamp 1616–43 and vicar of Ashbury, Berks.,
1622–31. (*Alumni Oxon.* iv. 1613.)

White has not before been recognized as a playwright, but an
entry of Peter Heylyn in 'Heylyn's Own Memoranda' indicates
that he probably was one:

1616[/17] March 8. My English Tragedy cal'd Spurius was acted
privatly (as Mr White's and Mr Bernard's plaies were) in the president's lodgings. (Bloxam, ed., *Memorial of Bishop Waynflete*, p. xiv.)

There is independent evidence that Samuel Bernard's *Julius et
Gonzaga* (q.v.) was acted at the President's house, as Heylyn says,
five weeks before; presumably, therefore, his statement may be
accepted about White's play. That 'Mr White' refers to Francis
White is suggested by the fact that he was a Magdalen man, like
Bernard, Heylyn, and the President, William Langton. Moreover,
Bernard became Master of the Magdalen School in succession to
Francis White in this year, and it is not unlikely that both men
wrote their plays for the boys of the Magdalen School and brought
them to entertain the President of the college.

There is no indication of the character or date of White's play, but Heylyn's association of the three plays suggests that it was acted not long before the other two.

ROBERT WHITE
fl. 1617

Robert White was the author of a masque called *Cupid's Banishment* performed before Queen Anne at Greenwich by the young ladies of Ladies' Hall at Deptford in May 1617. In the dedication of his manuscript to Lucy, Countess of Bedford, White speaks of the encouragement she 'gave us in presentinge our Maske to hir Majesty', and in the course of the masque notes that a dance was prepared by '*Mr. Ounslo, Tutor to the Ladies' Hall*'. The pronouns in the first quotation and the information in the second suggest that White was connected with the school, perhaps as master. Intimate association with the school is also suggested by the fact that in the course of the masque Diana presents to Queen Anne '*two of the Queene's Godaughters*', with references to their distinction. The young ladies make gifts of their needlework to the Queen.

Presumably it was the implied social standing of these two girls which led John Nichols to say that Ladies' Hall 'was probably one of the principal Schools of the period'. (*The Progresses . . . of King James I* [1828], iii. 282.) Nothing more seems to be known of the school or of Robert White.

Cupid's Banishment (4 May 1617)

MS.: John Nichols said that he printed the masque 'by the kind permission of Mr. William Upcott, of the London Institution, from the original MS. in his possession, purchased from the Library of the learned and amiable John Evelyn, of Wotton'. (Ed. cit. iii. 283, n. 1.) Hazlitt said that the manuscript was sold 'among Mr. R. S. Turner's books in 1881'. (*A Manual for the Collector and Amateur of Old English Plays* [1892], p. 55.) Its present whereabouts is unknown.

Edition: John Nichols, *The Progresses . . . of James I* (1828), iii. 283–96.

The heading for the masque as reprinted by Nichols is presumably a transcription of the heading of the manuscript, though he does not say so. It is 'Cupid's Banishment, / A Masque Presented

To Her Majesty, / By Younge Gentlewomen Of The Ladies' Hall, / In Deptford At Greennwich, / The 4th Of May 1617. / By Robert White'. Nichols noted that opposite the title-page was a note in the handwriting of John Evelyn, former owner of the manuscript: 'twelve yeare old, Richard Browne, 1617, acted herein before Queene Anne.' (Op. cit., p. 283, n. 1.) This was evidently the actor listed among the performers: 'Mr. Rich. Browne acted Diana'; presumably he was the Richard Browne, son of Christopher Browne of Deptford, who later became an ambassador and whose daughter and heir married John Evelyn.

The masque seems rather elaborate for the school. Thirty-one performers are named, including six young men, and there were nine Bacchanalians whose names are not given. The presenter and general supervisor of the action is Occasion, who reads the prologue and epilogue and appears to remain on stage throughout the performance. Occasion was played by 'Mr. R. W.', obviously the author, since all other names are given in full. This prominent supervising function of Robert White in the production is a further reason for thinking that he was probably master at the school.

The rather peculiar action of the masque is accounted for by certain lines in the dedication and others in the prologue. In his address to the Countess of Bedford, White says:

The ground of our plott is choosinge of a Kinge and Queene by Fortune's doome; which is a sporte our litle Ladies use on Candlemasse night . . . it was no marriage, but a forme of unitinge chaste harts, to shew a defiance to Cupid and his contracts, and that there could bee a chast combination without his powers.

In the prologue to the Queen, Occasion says:

Againe shee [Occasion] is summon'd by that lovely crew
Of Ladies' Hall, an academy
Where Modesty doth onely sway as Governesse.
These pretty Nimphs, devoted to your Excellence,
Present a sport which they yearely celebrate
On Candlemas-night, with due solemnity
And with great applause.
They have a Kinge and a Queene of Fortune's choice;
These bee the revells they intend.

Other lines in both the dedication and the prologue alluding to envy, spite, and detraction, and to the protection of both the Countess and the Queen, suggest that White had been attacked for the activities of his young ladies, as one would expect.

GEORGE WILDE (Wild)
1609/10–65

George Wilde, son of Henry Wilde of London, was born 9 January 1609/10 and admitted to the Merchant Taylors' School in 1619. He was elected a Merchant Taylor Scholar in 1628, matriculated at Oxford from St. John's College 13 November 1629, and became a Fellow in 1631. At Oxford he was granted degrees of B.C.L. 7 February 1634/5 (incorporated at Cambridge 1635) and D.C.L. 23 November 1647. (Mark J. Simmonds, *Merchant Taylor Fellows of St. John's College, Oxford*, p. 21; *Alumni Oxon.* iv. 1631.) Wood says that 'In his younger years he was accounted a person of great ingenuity' (*Athenæ Oxon.*, Bliss, ed., iii. 720), and this reputation no doubt accounts for his selection to write the play for the entertainment of the King and Queen at St. John's in August 1636. The selection must have had the personal approval of Archbishop Laud, who proposed to pay all the expenses for the performance himself—and did. (*Autobiography* [1839], pp. 199 and 211.) Wilde became one of Laud's chaplains, and at the archbishop's death he was bequeathed a ring. (M. J. Simmonds, loc. cit.) In 1640 Wilde became rector of Biddenden in Kent. (*Alumni Oxon.* iv. 1631.)

Wilde preached before the King and Parliament when they were at Oxford during the wars. Partly in consequence, no doubt, he was sequestered from his living at an unspecified date, and on 17 October 1648 he was expelled from his fellowship by the Parliamentary Visitors. (Simmonds, op. cit., p. 21.)

During the Commonwealth Wilde is said to have fitted up a room and held services in Fleet Street. (*Athenæ Oxon.*, Bliss, ed., iii. 720.) After the Restoration he was consecrated Bishop of Londonderry 27 January 1660/1. He died 29 December 1665. (*Alumni Oxon.* iv. 1631.)

The Converted Robber

There is no good evidence for the attribution of this play to Wilde. It is probably the same as John Speed's *Stonehenge* (q.v.).

Eumorphus sive Cupido-Adultus (1634/5)

MS.: B.M. Add. MS. 14047, fols. 60–96ᵛ.

The B.M. MS. in which the play is found has been described

elsewhere. (See Speed, *Stonehenge, or The Converted Robber*.) The title-page for this play in the volume reads:

> *Sequit*^r
> Eumorphus
> sive
> Cupido—Adultus
> Comœdia Acta A Joañensis
> Oxoñ Feb. 5° 1634
> Authore Georgio Wilde
> ejusd^m. Coll. Soc. et L. L. Bacc.

There follow a dramatis personae and prologue, both given by Miss Louise B. Morgan, together with a scene-by-scene synopsis of the play, in *Shakespeare Jahrbuch*, xlvii (1911), 84–87.

Wood lists the play in his account of Wilde as '*Hermophus, a Com.*—written in Lat. and several times acted, but not printed' (*Athenæ Oxon.* iii. 720), but there is no other evidence of repeated performances. The play has been variously referred to as *Hermophus, Kermophus,* and *Euphormus,* but the title and the frequently repeated name of the title-character in the unique manuscript should leave no doubt about Wilde's title. The dramatic bibliographers are responsible for the variants; there is no contemporary evidence for the existence of two (Fleay) or three (Hazlitt) different Latin plays covered by these titles.

Euphormus

Inaccurate title for *Eumorphus* (q.v.).

Hermophus

Inaccurate title for *Eumorphus* (q.v.).

Kermophus

Inaccurate title for *Eumorphus* (q.v.).

Love's Hospital [Lovers' Hospital] (30 August 1636)

MSS.: B.M. Add. MS. 14047, fols. 1–39^r; Folger Shakespeare Library MS. 1487.2 (Lambarde volume), fragment.

Evans, Willa McClung. *Henry Lawes, Musician and Friend of Poets* (1941), pp. 122–35.

1636, 30 Aug. '2ᵃ post meridiem. Then comeing out of yᵉ Library, the Queene met him at yᵉ gate & so they went to dinner at St. Johns, a Comedy after dinner till 7. a clocke, then returned to Chr*ist* Ch*urch* to supper, & after supper a Comedy viz*t* yᵉ Royall Slave was acted wᵗʰ good applause of King & Queene./' (F. S. Boas, ed., *The Diary of Thomas Crosfield*, p. 92.)

1655, 17 Nov. S.R. John Grismond entered as his copy 'a comedy entituled *Lovers hospitall*, presented to the King and Queen at Sᵗ Johns Colledge in Oxon, August 29ᵗʰ 1636 by the fellowes of the said Colledge'. (G. E. B. Eyre, *Transcript of the Registers of the Worshipful Company of Stationers, 1640–1708*, ii. 19.)

The title-page of the play in the B.M. MS. reads:

LOVES HOSPITALL

as it was acted before
the Kinge & Queens
Majestyes a by [*sic*]
the students
of
Sᵗ. Jo. Baptists Coℓℓ.
in Oxon: Augustij
29° 1636

Authore
GEORGJO WILDE LL: BAC:

There is a dramatis personae but neither prologue nor epilogue. The manuscript, though not a particularly beautiful one, may have been prepared as a presentation copy, for there is a running title on nearly every page, and the text has been boxed with red rules.

The second page of the manuscript gives the dramatis personae:

The Sceane
Napells
Dramātis Personæ

Lepidus ⌠ A merry humorouse old Lord father to Facetia ⌡ ⌠ Olimpa
Cæcilius │ A rich blinde Gentelmã, Father to │ │ &
Ægidius │ A Rich lame vserer ⌠ │ ⌡ Comastes
Piscinus │ A dumbe Gentelman ⌡ Suitors to │
Suzdato ⌊ A deafe Spaniarde ⌊ Facetia ⌋

Comastes sonn to Cæcilius & lover of Facetia

Lysander   A Gent: nephew to Ægidius, & married to Olimpa
Columella Friende and interp^{r}ter to Piscinus
Macilento Servante to Suzdato

    Facetia   daughter to Lepidus
    Olympa   daughter to Cæcilius
    disguised like A blackamoore
        caled Nigella
Seirgeants 2
Boy   Himen the p^{r}senter of y^e
           Antemaske and maske

The Folger MS. of the play is a two-page fragment, entitled
'Lovers Hospitall' in the Lambarde collection of plays, consisting
of the first scene and the first line of the second scene. Aside from
minor spelling variations, the Folger text differs from the British
Museum one in the stage directions and in the omission, probably
through oversight, of two and one-half lines in the last speech of
Lepidus in Act I, Scene I. The stage directions in the B.M. MS.
are fuller, more accurate, and better placed than those in the
Folger fragment.

The variant in the title shown in the Folger MS. has been used
as often in referring to the play as has the title of the B.M. MS.,
'Love's Hospital'. The confusion evidently dates from the time
of the first performance, for the last line of the play reads, 'And
stile my howse ye LOVERS HOSPITALL'. 'Lovers' Hospital' would
be appropriate in a double sense, since the united lovers are
expected to attend upon the company invited into the house,
and since four of the rejected lovers of the play were blind, dumb,
deaf, and lame. In spite of this appropriateness, the only complete manuscript of the play clearly has 'LOVES HOSPITALL' on
the title-page and as the running head at the top of every page
except two, which have no running titles. Presumably, then, this
title was Wilde's choice.

The occasion for the play was the visit of King Charles, Queen
Henrietta Maria, and their nephews, the two Princes of the Palatinate, to Oxford at the end of the summer progress, on Monday,
Tuesday, and Wednesday, the 29th, 30th, and 31st of August
1636. Oxford entertained them with the usual speeches, gifts,
honorary degrees, tours of inspection, banquets, and with three
plays, Strode's *Floating Island* at Christ Church on the 29th,
Wilde's *Love's Hospital* at St. John's on the afternoon of Tuesday
the 30th, and Cartwright's *Royal Slave* at Christ Church on the
night of the 30th. (*Autobiography of Archbishop Laud* [1839], pp.
200–9; Wood, *History and Antiquities of Oxford*, ii, Book i. 407–12;

and *Crosfield's Diary*, pp. 90–93.) This date for the performance of *Love's Hospital* contradicts the one on the title-page of the manuscript, but there can be no doubt that the manuscript is wrong. Laud's account is precise and official, and it is corroborated by Wood, Crosfield, and the title-pages of the early editions of both *The Floating Island* and *The Royal Slave*.

Archbishop Laud, at this time Chancellor of Oxford, was directly concerned with the visit and particularly with the presentation of *Love's Hospital*. Six weeks in advance of the visit he wrote to the Vice-Chancellor in a letter of 15 July 1636:

> For the Play, which I intend shall be at St. John's, I will neither put the University nor the College to any charge, but take it wholly upon myself. And in regard of the great trouble and inconvenience I shall thereby put upon that House, as also in regard it shall set out one of the Plays by itself, I think there is great reason in it, and do therefore expect it, that no contribution should be required from St. John's towards the Plays at Christ Church. (*Autobiography*, p. 199.)

This intention he apparently carried out, for he later wrote:

> There was great store of provision in all kinds sent me in towards this entertainment; and yet (for I bare all the charge of that Play, which was at St. John's, and suffered not that poor College to be at a penny loss or charge in any thing). . . . (Ibid., pp. 210–11.)

Since he bore the cost, Laud, who was not accustomed to neglect his prerogatives, presumably had a hand in the selection of Wilde's play for the great occasion, possibly the beginning of his patronage of the author. His account of the place of the play in the festivities is probably the most reliable:

> This year his Majesty and the Queen invited themselves to me to Oxford, and brought with them Charles, Prince Elector Palatine, and his brother Prince Rupert, being both then in England. They came into Oxford at the end of this summer's progress, on Monday, August 29. . . . The next day being Tuesday, the King came to service soon after eight in the morning. . . . When dinner was ended, I attended the King and the Queen together with the Nobles into several withdrawing chambers, where they entertained themselves for the space of an hour. And in the mean time I caused the windows of the Hall to be shut, the candles lighted, and all things made ready for the Play [Wood interpolates, 'called "The Hospitall of Lovers," made for the most part (as 'tis said) by Mr. George Wild, Fellow of St. John's College.'] to begin. When these things were fitted, I gave notice to the King and the Queen, and attended them into the Hall, whither I had the happiness to bring them by a way prepared from the President's lodging to the Hall, without any the least disturbance; and had the

Hall kept as fresh and cool, that there was not any one person when the King and Queen came into it. The Princes, Nobles, and Ladies entered the same way with the King, and then presently another door was opened below to fill the Hall with the better sort of company; which being done, the Play was begun and acted. The plot was very good, and the action. It was merry, and without offence, and so gave a great deal of content. In the middle of the Play, I ordered a short banquet for the King, the Queen, and the Lords. And the College was at that time so well furnished, as that they did not borrow any one actor from any College in town. The Play ended, the King and the Queen went to Christ Church, retired and supped privately, and about eight o'clock, went into the Hall to see another Play, which was upon a piece of Persian story. (*Autobiography*, pp. 200–7.)

Wood's account of the occasion (*History and Antiquities of Oxford*, ii, Book i. 407–12) is clearly taken from Laud's, with a few minor additions; Crosfield adds only the fact that the performance of the St. John's play was over at seven o'clock.

It was evidently intended that all three plays presented to the royal visitors should be repeated for the University, but apparently the undergraduates got out of control, and the performance of *Love's Hospital* had to be abandoned. Wood records the occasion:

Upon Thursday [after the departure of the royal party on Wednesday morning] after dinner the Chancellor departed from St. John's to the Bishop of Oxford's new House at Cudesdon, and then the Play which was acted before the King on Tuesday in the afternoon should have been represented again at the same place to the University, and Strangers that were remaining in the City, but such was the unruliness of the young Scholars in breaking in and depriving the Strangers of their places, that nothing at all was done in it. (Op. cit., p. 412.)

The other two plays were repeated on Friday and Saturday. (Ibid.)

In 1911 Miss Louise B. Morgan said that she intended shortly to bring out an edition of the play (*Shakespeare Jahrbuch*, xlvii [1911], 87), but so far as I know it has never appeared.

Miss Willa McClung Evans discusses (loc. cit.) the music of the Lawes brothers written for this play and for the other plays of the Oxford series.

ROBERT WILD (Wilde, Wylde)
1615 or 1616–1679

Hunt, John, ed. *Poems by Robert Wilde, D.D., One of the Ejected Ministers of 1662* (1870).

The Presbyterian wit and poet was the son of Robert Wild, shoemaker, of St. Ives, Huntingdon. He was admitted sizar at St. John's College, Cambridge, 26 January 1631/2, 'aet. 16' (*Admissions . . . St. John*, i. 9), elected Scholar in 1634, and granted degrees of B.A. 1635/6 and M.A. 1639. He was ordained deacon in 1637/8 and priest in 1639. In November 1642 he became B.D. of Oxford and D.D. 9 November 1660. (*Alumni Cantab.* iv. 407; *Alumni Oxon.* iv. 1631.) On 22 July 1646 he was inducted into the living of Aynhoe, Northamptonshire, by order of the House of Commons. Though he was Royalist in politics, he was ejected from his living by the Act of Uniformity in 1662, and later he was indicted for keeping a conventicle. He was buried at Oundle, Northamptonshire, 30 July 1679.

Wild's career between the granting of his M.A. and his induction at Aynhoe is obscure, but Miss C. Fell Smith pointed out (*D.N.B.*) that Wild's well-known ballad, 'Alas! poor scholar, whither wilt thou go?' apparently written in February or March 1640/1, seems to allude to a period when he was usher in a free school.

Wild's verse of the Commonwealth and Restoration elicited many imitations and answers, one writer saying that 'every unfathered sheet that's thrown abroad' had been attributed to him. (See *D.N.B.*) But his career after the outbreak of the wars is not a primary concern here.

The Benefice (1641?)

MSS.: B.M. MS. Lansdowne 807.4, fols. 78–88. (Fragment beginning III. 4.) Folger Shakespeare Library MS. 7042.

Greg, W. W. *Dramatic Documents from the Elizabethan Playhouses* (1931), pp. 365–6.
Summers, Montague. *The Playhouse of Pepys* (1935), pp. 345–6.

1689. The Benefice. A Comedy. By *R. W.* D. D. Author of Iter
    Boreale. Written in his Younger Days . . . M.DC.LXXXIX.
1689. [Another issue.]

The '*R. W.* D. D.' of the quarto title-page is more precisely identified in the address 'To The Reader', which begins, "*'Tis now several Years since these* Papers, *of the most Ingenious Dr.* R. Wild's *first fell into my Hands'*.

The B.M. MS., which is a fragment beginning III. 4, with an old pagination 25 to 45, has on the last page, 'ffinis actus Q^{ti} / Robert Wild', and Greg says the hand of the signature and of the text are the same and that certain corrections may be those of an author.

(Op. cit., p. 365.) He notes that the corrections in the manuscript are incorporated in the quarto.

The Folger MS. has a great many minor variations from the quarto, in most of which the manuscript is inferior. A number of the manuscript stage directions are in Latin, whereas—except for the conventional forms—they are all in English in the quarto. Twice the manuscript has 'Cambridge' where the quarto has 'Oxford', an odd change, presumably for the purpose of disguising the provenance of the play.

The play is larded with references to events of 1639, 1640, and especially 1641 (see Gardiner, vol. ix, *passim*): J. D.'s *The Knave in Grain* (quarto, p. 18), the payments to the Scottish army (p. 6), the suppression of monopolies and projections (p. 5), the censured clergymen, Finch and Lamb (in the MS., not the quarto), the beheading of Strafford (p. 7), the City petition for the exclusion of the bishops (p. 12), the flight of Windebank (p. 38), the suppression of the Star Chamber (p. 38), the imprisonment of Laud (p. 43), the abolition of the Court of High Commission and of Ship Money (pp. 44–45), and the invasion of the Scots (p. 49). There are a number of others, some of which I cannot identify. In such a highly allusive play as this, the number of references to events of the first half of 1641, and the absence of allusions to anything in the last half of 1641 or in 1642, when equally sensational events were taking place, strongly suggests a composition date about the third quarter of 1641.

Though this date presumably falls within the period of Wild's Cambridge residence, and though *The Benefice* has the satiric and irregular character of some college plays, there are odd things about it. In the first scene, Invention, describing the assembly to Ceres, says:

> They'r no Rebellious Rout.
> But here they'r set to see Children play Men,
> And Boys wear Beards.

The dialogue of the first act seems to indicate that the performance takes place in a barn. Perhaps Wild prepared the piece for a zealous schoolmaster.

Montague Summers thinks that *The Benefice* is largely derived from Hausted's *Rival Friends* (*Playhouse of Pepys*, p. 346), and Langbaine noted resemblances to *The Return from Parnassus*. These resemblances are suggestive, for both were Cambridge plays.

ARTHUR WILSON
1595–1652

Manuscript autobiography: Cambridge University MS. Add. 33.

[Bliss, Philip, ed.] *The Inconstant Lady, A Play. The Author Arthur Wilson, Esq. Sometime of Trinity College, Oxford* (1814), pp. 108–60.

Feuillerat, Albert. (ed.) *Arthur Wilson, The Swisser* (1904), pp. xiii–cxxii.

Wagner, Bernard M. 'Manuscript Plays of the Seventeenth Century', *T.L.S.*, 4 October 1934, p. 675.

Wilson, Arthur. 'Observations of God's Providence, in the Tract of my Life', in Francis Peck, ed., *Desiderata Curiosa* (1732), Lib. xii, No. v (1779), pp. 460–82; reprinted in Bliss's edition of *The Inconstant Lady*, pp. 109–51.

Nearly all the facts of Wilson's life are derived from an account which he was prompted to write by a sermon preached by 'Mr. Beadle of Banston' on 21 July 1644. (Bliss, ed., p. 137.) The preacher said that every Christian for the greater glory of God ought to keep a record of the dangers and hazards he had escaped. Wilson wrote up such a record of his life, properly giving greatest attention to his narrow escapes. The basic facts of his career are really set down only as a necessary background for these examples of God's providence. Apparently he began his account shortly after he heard the sermon and continued it for five years. It was appropriately entitled 'Observations of God's Providence, in the Tract of my Life', and first published from the manuscript, now in the Cambridge University Library (MS. Add. 33), by the Reverend Francis Peck in his collection called *Desiderata Curiosa* in 1732.

Arthur Wilson, 'Sonne of John and Suzan', was baptized at Yarmouth in Norfolk 14 December 1595. (Bliss, ed., p. 108.) Nothing is known of his earliest youth, but he says in his autobiography that when he was fourteen 'and fit for Cambridge' he was sent instead to France, where he stayed for nearly two years. (Ibid., pp. 109–10 and 170, and Feuillerat, p. xviii, n. 4. The manuscript clearly says '14 yeares'.) After his return he spent six months with Mr. John Davis in Fleet Street (John Davies of Hereford), learning the Court and Chancery hands, and then was taken by Sir Henry Spiller as one of his clerks in the Exchequer office. (Bliss, ed., p. 110.) After two years with Sir Henry he was discharged because, he says, of the malice of Lady Spiller. About a year later, in 1614, he became at the age of nineteen a retainer of the Earl of Essex who, according to Wilson, 'intrusted mee with keeping his private purse'. (Bliss, ed., pp. 112–13.)

In 1620 Wilson went with the Earl to fight in the Palatinate. They returned that winter, but returned again each of the three following summers, apparently campaigning in the good weather and going home in the bad. (Ibid., pp. 116–19.) Wilson says:

The winters wee spent in England. Either at Draiton, my Lord's grandmother's; Chartley, his owne house; or some of his brother, the Earle of Hertford's, houses. Our private sports abroad, hunting; at home, chesse or catastrophe. Our publique sports (and sometimes with great charge and expence) were masks or playes. Wherein I was a contriver both of words and matter. For as long as the good old Countesse of Leicester lived (the grandmother to theise noble families,) her hospitable entertainment was garnisht with such, then harmeles, recreations. (Ibid., p. 119.)

Wilson gives no further particulars of these plays and masques, and one must wonder if his three extant plays produced at Blackfriars eight or ten years later did not have their origin in these winter interludes between campaigns.

Wilson seems to say that he campaigned on the Continent with Essex every summer from 1620 to 1627. (Ibid., pp. 119–24.) After sixteen years with the Earl, Wilson left his service, a separation that he attributes to the jealousy and malice of the new Lady Essex, and went to Trinity College, Oxford, where he lived on an allowance from his former master. Wilson says this separation took place in July 1630, but it must have been 1631, for Essex and Elizabeth Paulet were not married until 1631, and Wilson matriculated at Oxford from Trinity 25 November 1631. (Ibid., pp. 124–6; Feuillerat, ed., pp. xxxi–xxxv, and *Alumni Oxon.* iv. 1654.) After less than two years at Oxford he entered the service of Robert Rich, second Earl of Warwick.

Wilson's *Inconstant Lady* was produced by the King's men before he went to Oxford, for the company acted it at court in September 1630 (see below), but his two other plays, *The Swisser* and *The Corporal*, were performed at Blackfriars while he was at Trinity. (See below.) Perhaps it was Wilson's presence at Oxford which led the King's men to choose his plays for performance there when they were on the road. Edward Bathurst, who was at Trinity with Wilson, says:

He made some Comedies, which were acted at Black-Friers in London, by the King's players, and in the Act time at Oxon, with good applause, himself being present. (Bliss, ed., p. 156.)

It was customary for the King's company to appear at Oxford at this time of year (July), as the diary of Thomas Crosfield shows. (Frederick S. Boas, ed., *The Diary of Thomas Crosfield, M.A., B.D., Fellow of Queen's College, Oxford* [1935], *passim.*)

While in the service of the Earl of Warwick, Wilson was married to Susan Spitty, 13 November 1634. (Feuillerat, ed., p. xlvii.) He acted as Warwick's steward, and in February 1636/7 Sir Humphrey Mildmay records his collections of ship money:

To Westminster and Whitehall and with my Lord of good Warwick. He had his full money, viz. £3 13s 2d sol., in good money; 30s of his man Arthur Wilson. (Philip Lee Ralph, *Sir Humphrey Mildmay: Royalist Gentleman* [1947], p. 83.)

Professor Feuillerat notes a letter in the Record Office in which Warwick advises the Lord Mayor that Wilson will receive in his name an enormous sum, and the letter carries Wilson's receipt for £10,000 dated 30 July 1641. (Feuillerat, ed., p. li.)

Wilson's autobiography gives no indication that he served with Warwick in the field during the wars, but several anecdotes of his actions suggest that he was often in charge of Warwick's house. His will, proved 16 October 1652, disposes of a good deal of property. (See Feuillerat, ed., pp. cvi–cx.) He was buried in the chancel of Felsted Church, in Essex. His wife had died between the making of the will 1 August 1651, and the signing of the codicil, 28 September 1652.

In addition to his plays, Wilson wrote *The History of Great Britain, Being the Life and Reign of King James the First, relating what passed from his first Access to the Crown, till his Death,* 1653. He also wrote several poems, three of which are reprinted by Feuillerat (ed. cit., pp. cxi–cxviii). An elegy by Wilson on the death of the Lady Ann Rich in an unpublished manuscript collection of such elegies, by John Gauden, Bishop of Worcester, and dated 22 October 1638, is noted in a catalogue of Percy Dobell and Son, Tunbridge Wells. (Catalogue No. 106, January 1949.) His autobiography, 'Observations of God's Providence', was not published until the eighteenth century.

Cambridge University MS. Add. 33 is a miscellaneous volume apparently kept by Wilson. It contains his autobiography, religious essays and notes, and several didactic letters, a few dated or signed 'A. W.'

Better Late than Never

See Wilson, *The Inconstant Lady.*

The Corporal (1632/3 ?)
(Fragment)

MSS.: Bodleian MS. Rawl. Poet. 9, fol. 45^r (fragment, title, and dramatis personae only) ; Bodleian MS. Douce C. 2 (fragment, Act I and 125 lines of Act II in a late-seventeenth- or early-eighteenth-century transcript) ; Victoria and Albert Museum, Forster Collection, MS. 638 (fragment of two odd pages).

Feuillerat, Albert (ed.). *Arthur Wilson. The Swisser* (1904), pp. lxiv–lxv.

Wagner, Bernard M. 'Manuscript Plays of the Seventeenth Century', *T.L.S.*, 4 October 1934, p. 675.

1632/3, 14 Jan. 'In Sir Henry Herbert's Office Book, under date of January 14, 1632, there is an entry of a payment of £2, or 40s., to the King's Company, for allowing the performance of it [Wilson's *The Corporal*] by my Lord of Essex his servants.' (W. C. Hazlitt, *A Manual for the Collector and Amateur of Old English Plays* [1892], p. 50. Not in Adams, *Herbert*.)

1641, 7 Aug. In a list of King's men's plays which the Lord Chamberlain forbade the printers to publish without the consent of the company is the title 'The Corporall'. (See above, i. 65–66.)

1646, [4] Sept. S.R. Humphrey Robinson and Humphrey Moseley entered for their copies a long list of plays, all apparently from the repertory of the King's company. Included are:

> Switzer   } Mr Wilson.
> The Corporall

(Greg, *Bibliography*, i. 56–57.)

1672/3, 30 Jan. S.R. John Martin and Henry Herringman entered for their copies by virtue of an assignment from Humphrey Robinson, executor of Humphrey Robinson, a long list of titles, including '[95] The Corporall. halfe'. (Ibid., pp. 72–73.)

1683, 21 Aug. S.R. Robert Scott entered for his copies by virtue of an assignment from Sarah Martin, executrix of John Martin, a long list of titles, including '[102] Corporall'. (Ibid., pp. 75–76.)

The single page of *The Corporal* in MS. Rawl. Poet. 9 follows directly after Wilson's *The Inconstant Lady*. According to Professor Bald (*Library*, Fourth Series, xviii [1937–8], 292), it is in Wilson's own hand and was apparently prepared by him as the title-page for a transcript. After the title come the lines, 'Acted at the Blackfriars' and 'The Scæne Lorraine', and then a dramatis personae of twelve name parts, from which Professor Feuillerat suggests the action. (Ibid.)

Hazlitt's note from Sir Henry Herbert's office-book is quite puzzling. In the first place, no such record is found in the transcripts of Professor J. Q. Adams, and R. C. Bald says that he could not find it in Adams's sources (ibid., pp. 290–1), but some such record must exist, for Fleay published a note of it the year before Hazlitt did, though in quite a different form. (*Biog. Chron.* ii. 278.) Fleay's form is a normal one for a Herbert entry: '1633, Jan. 14. *The Corporal* was licensed for acting at Blackfriars by the King's men', but the entry as Hazlitt records it is quite unusual. The ordinary fee charged by Herbert in the 1630's for licensing a new play was indeed £2, but it was paid *by* the acting company, not *to* it. Hazlitt's statement, unlike Fleay's, seems to indicate that the King's men had already licensed the play and were leasing rights to perform it to the servants of the Earl of Essex. Though this would be an unusual transaction, I see nothing improbable about it, but why should Sir Henry Herbert have recorded it? That the servants of the Earl of Essex should have been interested in a Wilson play is likely enough, for Wilson had himself been a servant of the Earl of Essex from 1614 to 1630. (See Life.) If Herbert's record, wherever it is, means that the King's men were leasing the play to Essex's servants, and not, as Fleay has it, licensing it for themselves, then 14 January 1632/3 is not an approximate production date for *The Corporal*, but only a *terminus ad quem*.

The Victoria and Albert fragment consists of two non-consecutive leaves. One is the beginning of 'Scena Secunda', but of what act there is no indication. Characters are Eurick, Jogalon, Theo., Erf., Rod., and Clod. There are three or four corrections on the first leaf. The second leaf consists of a dialogue between 'Feli:' and 'Theo:'.

The Inconstant Lady, or Better Late Than Never (> 1630)

MSS.: Bodleian Rawlinson Poet. 9; Bodleian Rawlinson Poet. 128; Folger Shakespeare Library, Lambarde volume, MS. 1487.2.

Edition: [Philip Bliss, ed.] *The Inconstant Lady, A Play. The Author Arthur Wilson, Esq., Sometime of Trinity College, Oxford* (1814).

Bald, R. C. 'Arthur Wilson's *The Inconstant Lady*', *Library*, Fourth Series, xviii (1937–8), 287–313.

1630, 3 Sept. 'At [H]ampton Court . . . The 30th of September, The Inconstant Ladye' appears in a bill of the King's company for plays presented at court in 1630 and 1630/1. (See above, i. 27–28.)

1634/5, Mar. 'In March [1634/5] he saw *The Changeling* and *The Inconstant Lady*.' (E. M. Symonds, 'The Diary of John Greene (1635–57)', *English Historical Review*, xliii [1928], 386.)

1641, 7 Aug. 'The inconstant Lady' appears in a list of King's men's plays which the Lord Chamberlain forbade the printers to publish without the company's consent. (See above, i. 65–66.)

1653. In a letter to the *T.L.S.*, Bernard Wagner says that *The Inconstant Lady* was 'revived during the Commonwealth at Wilson's own college, Trinity, Oxford, in 1653'. I do not know the source of his information. (*T.L.S.*, 4 October 1934, p. 675.)

1653, 9 Sept. S.R. At the end of a long list of plays entered for his copies by Humphrey Moseley is 'The Inconstant Lady by Mʳ. Arth. Wilson'. (Greg, *Bibliography*, i. 60–61.)

c. 1710–50. 'The Inconstant Lady Wᵐ. Wilson' appears in Warburton's list of manuscript plays. (W. W. Greg, *Library*, Third Series, ii [1911], 231.)

The three manuscripts of the play are described by Professor Bald (op. cit.), who notes that Rawlinson Poet. 9 (the text Bliss printed in 1814) and the Folger MSS. are holograph, while Rawlinson Poet. 128 is an early-eighteenth-century transcript. The Folger MS. in the Lambarde volume is clearly the earliest version of the three, and it includes numerous revisions, excisions, and additions by the author. Many of these revisions are stylistic, but others seem to be changes made in anticipation of censorship, and Bald surmises that Wilson may have made them at the suggestion of the King's men. (Op. cit., p. 297.) He says:

The Lambarde manuscript is clearly the manuscript on which the author worked for a while before the production of the play, and MS. Rawl. Poet. 9, with its ruled pages and its calligraphy, is equally clearly a copy made after it had been performed for presentation to some friend or patron. (Op. cit., p. 300.)

The third manuscript of the play—Rawlinson Poet. 128— though written in an eighteenth-century hand, exhibits evidence of having been transcribed from a manuscript in Wilson's autograph. (Ibid., pp. 300–3.) In it a quarter to a third of the play has been cut, and Professor Bald suggests (ibid., pp. 303–4) that it may be a copy of Wilson's shortening of his play for the court production. Perhaps he is right, but one wonders if the King's men would not have assigned such an important task to their regular theatre poet—Massinger?—rather than to an amateur like Wilson.

The appearance of the title in Warburton's list of plays is not necessarily an indication that Warburton ever owned a manuscript of the play, or indeed that he had ever seen any more than the Stationers' Register entry. (See W. W. Greg, 'The Bakings of Betsy', *Library*, Third Series, ii [1911], 225–59.)

Though *The Inconstant Lady* is in no way a remarkable production, the King's company seems to have done well enough with it, for they presented it at court in 1630, they were still performing it when John Greene saw the play in March 1634/5, and in 1641, when it was more than ten years old, they thought it still worth keeping out of the hands of the printers.

Though the sub-title, 'Better Late Than Never', appears at the head of the Folger MS. only, the use of the phrase as the closing words in all three versions of the play shows that the subtitle may have continued in use.

The Swisser (1631)

MS.: B.M. MS. Add. 36759.

Edition: Albert Feuillerat, ed. *Arthur Wilson. The Swisser* (1904).

1641, 7 Aug. In a list of King's men's plays which the Lord Chamberlain forbade the printers to publish without the consent of the company is the title 'The Switzar'. (See above, i. 65–66.)

1646, [4] Sept. S.R. Humphrey Moseley and Humphrey Robinson entered for their copies a long list of plays, all apparently from the repertory of the King's company. Included in the list are:

> Switzer   ⎫ Mr Wilson.
> The Corporall ⎭

(Greg, *Bibliography*, i. 56–57.)

1672/3, 30 Jan. S.R. John Martin and Henry Herringman entered for their copies by virtue of an assignment from Humphrey Robinson, executor of Humphrey Robinson, a long list of titles, including '[94] the Switzer. halfe'. (Ibid., pp. 72–73.)

1683, 21 Aug. Robert Scott entered for his copies by virtue of an assignment from Sarah Martin, executrix of John Martin, a long list of titles, including '[101] the Switzer'. (Ibid., pp. 75–76.)

The date and place of performance of the play are recorded on the title-page of the careful transcript in Wilson's hand, now in the

British Museum: 'The Swisser Acted at the Blackfriers 1631.' On the following page Wilson gives the names of the twelve members of the King's company who performed the name parts. (See above, i. 84–85.) Ten years later, in 1641, the King's men still thought enough of the play to have it protected from the printers as part of their repertory. (See above, i. 65–66.)

The bits of history of Lombardy which Wilson uses might have come from various sources, but Professor Feuillerat makes a good case that Wilson has made some use of the *De Gestis Langobardorum* of Paulus Diaconus and of William Thomas's *The Historye of Italy*, and he notes certain resemblances between Wilson's play and Davenant's Lombardian play, *Albovine*, which was published two years before *The Swisser* was acted at Blackfriars. (Ed. cit., pp. lxv–lxviii.) He finds the Alcidonus–Selina plot of the play influenced by *Romeo and Juliet*. (Ibid., pp. lxxiii–lxxvi.) It may have been, for certain of the romantic incidents in the affair of the two lovers are roughly analogous to others in Shakespeare's tragedy, but they are also analogous to those in other romantic plays. Indeed, one is most reminded in reading *The Swisser* of the incidents, character types, and techniques of the tragedies and tragi-comedies of John Fletcher, of which there are many performance records during the fifteen years before *The Swisser*, though there are none for *Romeo and Juliet*.

Far more dubious is Feuillerat's notion (ibid., pp. lxix–lxxiii) that *The Swisser* sets forth the anti-royalist sentiments which Wilson's autobiography and especially his *History of Great Britain* show that he held in the forties. In the first place, all the examples of anti-royalist feeling which Feuillerat found in *The Swisser* can be duplicated in the plays of Beaumont and Fletcher, those darlings of the court and the aristocracy, whose plays were produced at court in Wilson's time far oftener than those of any other dramatist. (See above, i. 29 and 94–100.) In the second place, if the hostility to the Crown which Professor Feuillerat sees in the play had been apparent to Caroline readers, the play would never have been licensed by Sir Henry Herbert, or even submitted to him by those special protégés of royalty, the King's players. It is not unusual to find subjects of King Charles I whose sentiments about the King or the institution of monarchy as expressed in 1644–52 were not the same as those they had expressed in 1630 or 1631.

RALPH WOOD
?–?

Ralph Wood is only a name attached to two lost plays in the list of manuscript plays which John Warburton owned—or says he owned—before they were burned by his cook. (See W. W. Greg, 'The Bakings of Betsy', *Library*, Third Series, ii [1911], 225–59.)

The Flying Voice (?)
(Lost)

'The Flying Voice by Ra. Wood' is the twelfth item in Warburton's list. (See Greg, op. cit., p. 230.) Since it does not appear in the Stationers' Register, where Warburton appears to have found a number of his titles, it may be that he did own such a manuscript at one time. There is no other record of such a play.

An Interlude (?)
(Lost)

'An Interlude by Ra. Wood worth Nothing' is the twenty-eighth item in Warburton's list. (See Greg, op. cit., p. 231.) Like *The Flying Voice*, the title is not recorded elsewhere, not even in the Stationers' Register, but 'worth Nothing' is presumably Warburton's comment on the literary value of the play—an indication that he really did possess such a manuscript at one time.

ABRAHAM WRIGHT
1611–90

Abraham Wright, the preacher and anthologist, was born in London in 1611 and admitted to the Merchant Taylors' School in 1626. He went on to St. John's College, Oxford, in 1629, received his B.A. in 1633 and his M.A. in 1637. (Mark J. Simmonds, *Merchant Taylor Fellows of St. John's College, Oxford* [1930], p. 22.) When the King and Queen visited Oxford in August 1636, Wright wrote and spoke the verses of welcome at St. John's (Thorn-Drury, ed., *Parnassus Biceps*, pp. 121–2, and *Athenæ Oxon.*, Bliss, ed., iv. 275), and he acted that night in Wilde's play, *Love's Hospital* (q.v.). Wood says that before this time he had composed a comedy, *The Reformation*. (Op. cit., iv. 277.) In 1637 Wright was ordained deacon, and in December 1639, priest. (Ibid., p. 275.) He was a popular preacher for several years at court and in London.

During much of the Interregnum he was tutor in the family of Sir James Grime or Graham at Peckham. (Wood, op. cit. iv. 275–6.) After the Restoration he settled into his vicarage of Oakham, Rutland, and lived quietly there until his death in 1690. He is principally known for his edition of the anthology called *Parnassus Biceps*, 1656.

The Reformation (c. 1631?)

(Lost)

In his account of Abraham Wright, Anthony à Wood says:

He hath also compleated other books, which are not yet printed, as (1) *A comical Entertainment called The Reformation*, presented before the university at S. John's coll. Written while he was an undergraduate. (*Athenæ Oxon.*, Bliss, ed., iv. 277.)

Wood seems to indicate that the manuscript was known to him. G. Thorn-Drury (ed. *Parnassus Biceps* [1927], p. v) suggested that Wood got his information from Wright's son and that the manuscript may have been destroyed in the fire at the Temple in 1679.

Since Wood says only that the play was performed at St. John's but not for what occasion, and that it was written when Wright was an undergraduate, i.e. 1629 to 1633, it can properly be dated within that span. Thomas Warton narrowed this to about 1631 (*Poems upon Several Occasions . . . by John Milton* [1785], pp. 602–3), but he offered no authority and may have been guessing.

RICHARD ZOUCHE (Zouch)

1590–1660/1

Richard Zouche was born at Ansty, Wiltshire, in 1590, son of Francis Zouche, lord of the manor and sometime M.P. He was elected Scholar of Winchester in 1601, Scholar of New College, Oxford, in 1607, and Fellow in 1609. He received the degrees of B.C.L. in 1614 and D.C.L. in 1619. In 1617 (*Alumni Oxon.* says 1618) he was admitted an advocate of Doctors' Commons, and in 1620 succeeded John Budden as Regius Professor of Civil Law at Oxford. In 1621 he was M.P. for Hythe and again in 1624. In 1622, apparently, he married Sarah Harte, resigned his fellowship, and settled at Brill, Oxfordshire. He was a proctor in Doctors' Commons and became a Fellow-Commoner at Wadham College, which he remained until he was made Principal of St. Alban Hall in 1625, an office he held until 1641. After becoming Principal, according to the *D.N.B.*, he seems to have divided his time between academic engagements and London practice. At Oxford he took a leading part in the codification of the University statutes under Laud. In 1641 he was appointed Judge of the High Court of Admiralty. (*Alumni Oxon.* iv. 1706, and *D.N.B.*)

During the wars Zouche was a Royalist and helped negotiate the surrender of Oxford to Fairfax. In 1646 he compounded for his estates and retained his academic preferments, though he had lost his judgeship. In 1657 he was engaged in a sensational contest, recounted at length by Wood (*Athenæ Oxon.*, Bliss, ed., iii. 1073–6), with John Wallis for the University office of *custos archivorum*. As Aubrey says, 'Dr. ⟨Richard⟩ Zouch had the majority of voyces, but because Dr. Zouch was a malignant (as Dr. Wallis openly protested, and that he had talked against Oliver), he was putt aside'. (Clark, ed., *Brief Lives*, ii. 281.) After the Restoration he was restored to his judgeship. He died in his house at Doctors' Commons, 1 March 1660/1.

Zouche seems to have been widely esteemed. Wood says: 'He was an exact artist, a subtile logician, expert historian, and for the knowledge in, and practice of, the civil law, the chief person of his time, as his works much esteemed beyond the seas (where several of them are reprinted) partly testify.' (*Athenæ Oxon.*, Bliss, ed., iii. 511.)

His published works are rather numerous, but the ones which seem most appropriate for the author of *The Sophister* are a descriptive geographical poem, *The Dove: or Passages of Cosmography*, 1613, and three handbooks for university disputations, published in 1652, 1653, and 1660. (*D.N.B.*)

Fallacy, or the Troubles of Great Hermenia

Title of the manuscript version of *The Sophister* (q.v.).

The Sophister (1610–31)

MS.: B.M. MS. Harleian 6869. 2, fols. 24ᵛ–56ᵛ, 'R: Z. Fallacy: or The Troubles of great Hermenia'.

1638, 7 Nov. S.R. Humphrey Moseley entered for his copies 'Two bookes vizᵗ. The Academy of Complemᵗ[es] &c. and a Comedy called The Sophister'. (Greg, *Bibliography*, i. 49.)

1639. The Sophister. A Comedy ... 1639. [The quarto contains the notation: 'Imprimatur *Mathew Clay*, 3. *Novemb.* 1638.']

The attribution of *The Sophister* to Richard Zouche has not been finally established, but the evidence makes it appear highly probable. Miss Louise B. Morgan noted that the published *Sophister* and the manuscript *Fallacy* are different versions of the same play (*Shakespeare Jahrbuch*, xlvii [1911], 87, n. 1), and the manuscript play is headed: 'R: Z. Fallacy: or The Troubles of great Hermenia.' Before she made the identification, David Erskine Baker had said of *The Sophister*, 'At the end of a book, this play is said to be written by Dr. Z. (probably Dr. Zouch).' (*Biographia Dramatica*, 1782 ed., ii. 349.) Dr. Greg notes that in the advertisement lists of plays which Humphrey Moseley issued with various of his publications from 1650 to 1660, *The Sophister* appears twice anonymously, five times as 'by Dr. S.', and twice—in the lists of latest date—as 'by Dr. Z.' (*Bibliography*, ii. 696.) Perhaps it was one of these later advertisements of Moseley's that Baker intended to designate by 'At the end of a book'.

Since *The Sophister, or Fallacy, or The Troubles of Great Hermenia* is clearly an academic play (see below) and written between 1610 and 1631, we may assume that the author was an R. Z. who was at Oxford or Cambridge at some time in that period and who was awarded a Doctor's degree before 1650. Richard Zouche is almost the only candidate, and the legal material in the play would seem to make the identification almost certain.

That the play was written for an academic audience is clear from its concentration upon matters of the schools, from the prologue of the quarto 'spoken by *Mercury* to the Academicall Auditors', and from the concluding couplets of the prologue, whose academic puns are advertised by the typography:

> But here the Sophister, how to commence,
> Or take's Degree, as yet is in suspence:
> By keeping of his Acts, he now will try
> To get your Placet by his Fallacy.

The opening lines of the epilogue suggest actual performance, or at least anticipated performance, before an academic audience:

> Should this our Play on Common Stage appeare,
> Some of the ignorant multitude would sweare
> That we chopt Logick; for such strains of Wit
> They still like worse, the better they are writ.
> But you, that fill this Orbe. . . .

Some confirmation of Zouche's authorship of *The Sophister* may be seen in the elaborate allegorical consideration of academic discourse, as well as the concern with legal matters in such passages as:

> Our Civill Law doth seeme a royall thing,
> It hath more Titles than the *Spanish* King:
> But yet the Common Law quite puts it downe,
> In getting, like the Pope, so many a Crowne.

Harleian MS. 6869 contains three plays, *Love's Loadstone*, *Fallacy*, and *Ignoramus*, the first two written in the same hand. *Fallacy, or The Troubles of Great Hermenia* is a version of *The Sophister* which seems to be earlier than the quarto version. A note in the Harleian MS. signed by G. C. Moore Smith and dated 16 September 1914 says:

> The second play 'Fallacy' (f. 24ᵦ) is an earlier and fuller form of the play, '*The Sophister, a Comedy*', London, 1639. *The Sophister* has been attributed to Richard Zouche (v. D.N.B.) and the initials 'R. Z.' appear above the title of 'Fallacy'. There are considerable differences between the two forms of the play—the printed form being much abridged and containing errors which the MS corrects. 'Paralogismus' of the MS appears apparently as 'Ignoratio Elenchi' in the printed book. The printed book has a new Epilogue.

My examination of the manuscript confirms these observations. I note also that though a number of the minor alterations in the quarto may well indicate misreadings, others are corrections tending to regularize the verse. Many of the cuts appear to be for the purpose of shortening the play, but others suggest censorship, or fear of censorship, such as III. 3, through IV. 1, of the quarto, which has been substituted for 45^r–46^v of the manuscript; other cuts in IV. 2; the thirty-five lines omitted from the end of IV. 3; the fifteen lines from V. 1; and the omission of fol. 54 of the manuscript. A characteristic cut suggesting fear of censorship is the quarto's omission of these lines from 43^r of the manuscript.

> I know the enuious & malicious sort
> Who haue beene held chiefe Nobility
> ffinde it distastfull to their tender palates;
> But I shall teach their wanton appetites
> Better to rellish this our gouernment.

The conclusion of the prologue in the manuscript suggests that political applications were expected:

> what yee may expect
> In this—yee see; if ought else yee conceive
> Your kinder thoughts to fallacy I leaue.

These lines of the manuscript prologue, as well as all others except the four printed as 13–16, are dropped from the quarto, and a new prologue substituted.

The date of the play must, of course, be before the quarto imprimatur, 3 November 1638. At the end of the manuscript appears the line, 'Aug: 13: 1631 C$_R$'. This line has been interpreted as indicating date of performance, which it may, but it might equally well indicate the date of transcription of the manuscript. It seems to me that we can safely accept this only as a *terminus ad quem*. An obvious *terminus a quo* of 1610 has been noted in the lines:

> But yesterday an Herauld was with me, who, as I lov'd to save blood-shed, intreated me to helpe him to pacifie two incensed Citizens, who since the yeare 1610, when all Artificers and Tradesmen became Gentlemen, fortuned to light both upon the same Coate-armour, and now were ready to fight, who should have it most proper. (II. i, C$_2$.)

These lines, however, seem to suggest that the year 1610 is some time in the past, not the immediate past.

A possible clue to the date and provenance of the manuscript may be found in the direction written on the blank first leaf of the manuscript and addressed 'For Sr Robert Filmer in Westminster'. This is written in the hand of the scribe of *Love's Loadstone* and *Fallacy*. Sir Robert was presumably the political writer who matriculated at Cambridge in 1604, was knighted by King James in 1618/19, and died in 1653. He seems to have lived at one time in Westminster. (Peter Laslett, ed. *Patriarcha* [1949], p. 2.)

I can find no definite evidence to date the play more precisely than 1610–31, with a slight preference for the years 1614–20. After he became Regius Professor Dr. Zouche seems to have been too busy and full of honours to have been concerned with playmaking.

ANONYMOUS PLAYS

Aleumista (?)
(Lost)

This title—marked 'Latin'—is fifty-first in the list of manuscript plays found among the papers of Abraham Hill. (See Middleton, *The Conqueror's Custom*.) The list seems to have been Hill's record of the stock of some bookseller, set down between 1677 and 1703, but it is notable that nearly all the identifiable plays and playwrights of the list are Jacobean or Caroline.

The title is not known from any other record. It may well have been an academic play.

Alexander et Aristobulus (24 July 1642)
(Lost)

McCabe, William H. 'The Play-List of the English College of St. Omers 1592–1762', *Revue de littérature comparée*, xvii (1937), 355–75.
—— 'Notes on the St. Omers College Theatre', *Phil. Quart.* xvii (1938), 225–39.

This tragedy was performed at the Jesuit College for English boys at St. Omers, 24 July 1642. Father McCabe notes that the subject was 'the twin sons of Herod the Great executed by him on a false charge'. ('Play-List', p. 367.)

Alfonso

See Anon., *Alphonsus, Emperor of Germany*.

[Alice and Alexis] (?)
(Fragment)

MS.: Bodleian MS. Douce 171, fols. 48*b*–70.

The play in the Douce MS. has no title, but it has several times been referred to by scholars as *Alice and Alexis* because these two are the principal characters in the argument. It would only be confusing to invent a new title now, even though in the play as it stands the heroine is called Stella and not Alice.

The fragment begins with a dramatis personae:

Anthony: a m^rchant ye father
Critus his brother
Alexis. ye yonge gallant
Tanto ye Italionated Lord
Alice, ye daughter of Anthony
Simper: her maid
Mumble ye nurse

fatuus, ye rich heire
blinkes, his man
dic: Alexis footman
yonge bonyface Tantoes page
3 theeues in ye habitt of furies

There follows the argument:

Criticus had one daughter named [*blank*] who was deepely in loue wth yonge [Amintas *deleted*] Alexis [All these first two lines are deleted, and he begins again.] Anthony a Cytysen in London had one onely daughter [daughter *deleted*] named Alice who was deepely in loue wth a gallant youth Alexis A man of answeareable fortunes, but he by ye perswasions of Tanto a wicked Italionated English, & vsually nicke namd ye hater of women who spent his time [vsually *deleted*] wholy in inueigheinge against [women *deleted*] y^t sex vterly refust her loue, though she were faire & vertuous, wherevppon she falls in a deepe consumption Critus her vncle hopinge to diuert her loue frō ye other bringes in Fatuus a rich cytisens sonne & heire as a sutor to her but she vtterly disdaines ye fond yonge man, & her Made by cunninge daliance wth him, so intangled y^e [fond yonge man *deleted*] foole in her loue as he priuately marries her. & so it happend y^t tanto dotinge most vnnaturally of ye faire Alexis & by a whisper discoueringe his base thoughtes to ye yonge man, he all in collor hauinge first by a sleight wonne ye vilaines pistoll frō him kills him wth ye same, he [*overwritten with* &] flies but hauinge his pardon bought by Anthony in gratuity thereof returnes a sutor to his daughter who intertaines ye motion & they are most ioyfully conioind in matrimony.

In the two acts and one scene which follow, neither the dramatis personae nor the argument is precisely followed. Alice is called Stella and her maid is called Lucy, not Simper; the rich heir seems to be Abraham, for no Fatuus has appeared yet when the play breaks off. Mumble, Blinks, Dick, Bonyface, and the three thieves are not found in the extant scenes, but several characters unnoted in the dramatis personae have appeared—Gregory; his son Abraham; Cranke; Promus, the butler; Tany, Alexis' serving-man; and Sara, Gregory's mistress for thirty years. Nevertheless the play half written is that of the argument with minor changes and probably the addition of a sub-plot that accounts for most of the new characters. The number of changes shown in the argument and the changes in the text made on the blank verso opposite each page indicate that the hand is probably that of the author.

I see little evidence to date *Alice and Alexis*. The pages in the manuscript preceding the play are accounts of the household of the Earl of Essex 1576–85, but the play is in a different and apparently later hand. The setting is London, there are several references to the King and the King's palace, and there are Puritan references that appear to be pre-Restoration. A very childish hand has scribbled in the manuscript, and once the date 1604 is scrawled, but this does not seem to be related to the play.

All Is Not Gold That Glisters (?)
(Lost)

The title occurs sixth in Abraham Hill's list of plays in manuscript. (See Middleton, *The Conqueror's Custom.*) This list seems to have been Hill's record of some bookseller's stock, set down between 1677 and 1703, but it is notable that nearly all the identifiable plays and playwrights in the list are Jacobean or Caroline.

J. Q. Adams points out in his discussion of the list (*Library*, Fourth Series, xx [1939], 82) that Henslowe was paying Henry Chettle for a play with this proverbial title in the spring of 1601. (*Henslowe's Diary*, i. 135.) The manuscript that Hill saw might have been Chettle's, or a revision of Chettle's play, or an entirely different piece.

Aloysius sive Saeculi Fuga (April 1640)
(Lost)

McCabe, William H. 'The Play-List of the English College of St. Omers, 1592–1762', *Revue de littérature comparée*, xvii (1937), 355–75.
—— 'Notes on the St. Omers College Theatre', *Phil. Quart.* xvii (1938), 225–39.

The play was performed at the Jesuit College for English boys at St. Omers, in April 1640. Father McCabe identifies the subject as St. Aloysius Gonzaga. ('Play-List', p. 367.)

Alphonsus, Emperor of Germany (> 1604?; revised > 1630?)

Editions: Herbert F. Schwarz, ed., *Alphonsus, Emperor of Germany* (1913); Thomas Marc Parrott, ed., *The Plays and Poems of George Chapman. The Tragedies* (1910), pp. 401–71 and 683–711; Karl Elze, ed., *George Chapman's Tragedy of Alphonsus, Emperor of Germany* (1867).

Bowers, F. T. '*Alphonsus, Emperor of Germany* and the *Ur-Hamlet*', *Modern Language Notes*, xlviii (1933), 101–8.

—— 'The Date and Composition of *Alphonsus*', *Harvard Studies and Notes in Philology and Literature*, xv (1933), 165–90.

Chambers, E. K. *The Elizabethan Stage* (1923), iv. 2–3.

Dowling, Harold M. 'Peele and Some Doubtful Plays. 1. "Alphonsus, Emperor of Germany"', *N. & Q.* clxiv (1933), 366–7.

Greg, W. W. 'Authorship and Attributions in the Early English Play-Lists', *Edinburgh Bibliographical Society Transactions*, ii, Part 4 (1946), 323.

Koeppel, Emil. *Quellen-Studien zu den Dramen George Chapman's, Philip Massinger's und John Ford's* (1897), pp. 73–79.

Starck, Taylor. 'The German Dialogue in *Alphonsus, Emperor of Germany* and the Question of Authorship', *Harvard Studies and Notes in Philology and Literature*, xv (1933), 147–64.

Sykes, H. D. 'Peele's Authorship of "Alphonsus Emperor of Germany"', *N. & Q.*, Twelfth Series, ii (1916), 464–7, 484–6, 503–5. Reprinted as 'Peele's "Alphonsus, Emperor of Germany"', in *Sidelights on the Elizabethan Drama* (1924), pp. 79–98.

Van Dam, B. A. P. 'Robert Greene's "Alphonsus"', *English Studies*, xiii (1931), 129–42.

Wellek, René. 'Bohemia in Early English Literature', *The Slavonic and Eastern European Review*, xxi (1943), 134–5.

Wells, William. '"Alphonsus, Emperor of Germany"', *N. & Q.* clxxix (1940), 218–23 and 236–40.

1630, 3 Oct. 'At [H]ampton Court . . . The 3 of October. Alfonso' appears in a bill of the King's company for plays presented at court in 1630 and 1630/1. (See above, i. 27–28.)

1636, 5 May. 'The 5th: of May at the Blackfryers for the Queene and the prince Elector . . . Alfonso' appears in a bill of the King's company for plays presented before the King and Queen in 1636 and 1636/7. (Adams, *Herbert*, pp. 75–76.)

1641, 7 Aug. 'Alfonso Emperor of Germany' appears in a list of King's men's plays which the Lord Chamberlain forbade the printers to publish without the company's consent. (See above, i. 65–66.)

1653, 9 Sept. S.R. Humphrey Moseley entered for his copy 'a Play called Alphonso, Emperor. of Germany, by Iohn [*sic*] Peele'. (Greg, *Bibliography*, i. 60.)

1654. The Tragedy Of Alphonsus *Emperour* Of Germany As it hath been very often Acted (with great applause) at the Privat house in Black-Friers by his late Maiesties Servants. By *George Chapman* Gent. . . . 1654.

Most of the numerous discussions of *Alphonsus, Emperor of Germany* are concerned with the authorship of the play, which was licensed as by John Peele—not Poole, as sometimes stated—and published as by George Chapman. The Chapman attribution has been generally doubted for reasons best summarized by Parrott. (Ed. cit., pp. 683–92.) Whether George Peele wrote it or not is an unsettled question, but there is fairly general agreement that the play published as Chapman's in 1654 is at least basically an Elizabethan play.

Is this Elizabethan play the same as the one produced by the King's men in the thirties? The evidence seems to me to indicate that it is, Bowers and Starck (op. cit.) to the contrary notwithstanding. The 1654 title-page makes the explicit statement that the play belonged to this company and was produced in their principal theatre, and the assertion is repeated in the address to the reader:

I Shall not need to bespeak thee Courteous, if thou hast seen this Piece presented with all the Elegance of Life and Action on the *Black-Friers* Stage; But if it be a Stranger to thee, give me leave to prepare thy acceptation, by telling thee, it was receiv'd with general applause.

Moreover, the fact that in the records of performance at court in 1630 and 1636 the play is called 'Alfonso' cannot be said to suggest a different play, for when the King's men listed the plays of their repertory for the Lord Chamberlain in August 1641, they gave the full title, 'Alfonso Emper^or of Germany', showing that they made no distinction between Alfonso and Alphonsus. As if to reiterate the identity of the two, Humphrey Moseley called the play 'Alphonso' when he entered it in the Stationers' Register on 9 September 1653 and 'Alphonsus' when he printed it two months later (Thomason's copy of the quarto is dated 'Nouemb 29, 1653'). The available evidence seems to me, therefore, to show that the play Moseley printed in 1653 and dated 1654 is the one belonging to the King's men's repertory at Blackfriars and produced by that company at court in 1630 and before the Queen and the visiting Elector Palatine at Blackfriars in May 1636.

Had this old play been revised for presentation before the Elector? The evidence on this question has been confused by the debate over Chapman's authorship and by the presence in the play of an unusual amount of better-than-usual German, which is printed in black-letter in the quarto. On the old assumption that

Chapman was the author but could not have written the German, a German reviser, possibly George Rudolph Weckherlin, has been postulated for the performance before the King's German nephew in 1636. Now that Chapman is abandoned as author, and Professor Starck has shown (op. cit.) that Weckherlin is not likely to have been the writer of the German, and a court performance of 1630 before that at Blackfriars of 1636 is known, all the old structure collapses. Starck thought that the German was more probably written by an Englishman well acquainted with Germany—possibly an English actor in Germany. Bowers contended (loc. cit.) that the play is all of a piece and all written early, at least before Marston's *Malcontent* in 1604, and he and Starck both contend that *Alphonsus, Emperor of Germany* was unsuitable for presentation before the Elector and therefore probably not the play of 1636. The evidence seems to me to be all against them on the last point, but I cannot be confident about the others. Since the King's men repeatedly used the play in the thirties and thought it still worth protecting in 1641, it seems to me undeniable that they and their fashionable Blackfriars audiences must have seen more in it than an old-fashioned Elizabethan production. Such an interest might well have been provided by revisions especially prepared for this audience. Beyond this I cannot go, and I am none too confident of even so much.

[*The Masque of Amazons, or The Ladies' Masque*] (January 1617/18; not performed)

(Lost)

1617, 30 Dec. 'Lord Clifton is sent to the Tower for saying he would kill the Lord Keeper. Ladies' masque at Lord Hay's deferred; performers in it enumerated, &c.' (Sir Gerard Herbert to Sir Dudley Carleton, *C.S.P., Dom., James I* [1611–18], p. 505.)

1617/18, 2 Jan. 'The Qu: hath caused ye La: maske to be put of wch my Ld Hay should have made at ye robes last night.' (Nathanael Brent [to Sir Dudley Carleton], *S.P. Dom., James I,* xcv. 3, quoted Mary Sullivan, *Court Masques of James I* [1913], p. 106, n. 3. This sentence is ignored in the summary of the letter, *C.S.P., Dom., James I,* 1611–18, p. 511.)

1617/18, 3 Jan. 'The Muscovie ambassadors shalbe feasted at court to morow, and on Twelfth Night is the Princes maske [Jonson's *Pleasure Reconciled to Virtue*]. There was a maske of nine Ladies in hand at theyre owne cost, wherof the principall was the Lady Haye as Quene of the Amazons accompanied by her sister the Lady Dorothie, Sir Robert and Sir Harry Riches Ladies, Mistris Isabella Rich, Mistris West the Lord Delawares daughter, Mistris Barbara Sidney, Sir Humfrie Mayes Lady, and the Lady Cave daughter to Sir Harbert Crofts: they had taken great paines in continuall practising, and were almost perfet and all theyre implements provided, but whatsoever the cause was, neither the Quene nor King did like or allow of yt and so all is dasht.' (John Chamberlain to Sir Dudley Carleton, *The Letters of John Chamberlain*, ii. 125–6.)

1617/18, 12 Jan. 'The Masque of Ladies at Lord Hay's given up, from some remark of the King or Queen, &c.' (Sir Gerard Herbert to Sir Dudley Carleton, *C.S.P., Dom., James I* [1611–18], p. 512.)

Apparently this masque of the court ladies was never performed, the author is unknown, and the text is lost. Hazlitt refers to:

The Ladies' Masque: The Masque of Ladies, in three parts, conducted by Lady Hay.
This masque was performed at Court early in the year 1618. See Add. MS. B.M. 10,444. (*Manual*, p. 127.)

The B.M. MS. he refers to is a collection of music with many short airs, a large number of them with the word 'masque' in the title. (See above, John Adson.) So far as is known, the only masque sponsored by the Lady Hay is the one which was cancelled and in which Chamberlain says she was to play the Queen of the Amazons. According to Nathanael Brent, it was prepared for production on New Year's Day, 1618, but apparently it was never given. I do not know why Hazlitt thought the masque was in three parts, unless he misunderstood the three tunes in the B.M. MS. He also seems to imply that *The Amazonians' Masque* or *The Masque of Amazons* and *The Ladies Masque* 'conducted by Lady Hay' were two separate productions. It is true that in the British Museum catalogue description of Add. MS. 10444 there appear the titles 'Amazonians Masque', as well as 'The Ladies' Masque [? 1617–1618] three tunes', but the names for the tunes in this book are not necessarily masque names. In a brief examination of the manuscript I noted such titles as 'The first of the Lords', 'The first witches dance', and 'The first of the Ladyes after the Cuckolds'.

Although no one of the early authorities seems to give an exact title for the masque prepared by Lady Hay and the other court ladies, I know of no reason for Hazlitt to think that there was more than one masque sponsored by her. Fleay gives it (facetiously?) an additional title of *The Masque of Disappointed Ladies*.

(*Biog. Chron.* ii. 343–4.) There was a 'Maske of Amasones' given at the court of Queen Elizabeth in 1579 (Welsford, *The Court Masque*, p. 151), but if known to Lady Hay it would surely have seemed too old-fashioned.

Ambitio Infelix sive Absalom tragoedia (28 November 1622)

MS.: Stonyhurst MS. A. VII. 50 (2).

McCabe, William H. 'The Play-List of the English College of St. Omers 1592–1762', *Revue de littérature comparée*, xvii (1937), 355–75.
—— 'Notes on the St. Omers College Theatre,' *Phil. Quart.* xvii (1938), 225–39.

The play consists of about 500 lines of verse in three short acts. Father McCabe reports that the cast consists of seventeen persons, besides Angels, Messengers, Soldiers, and Pages. ('Play-List', pp. 360–1.)

The performance took place in the English College at St. Omers on 28 November 1622. The author was probably a teacher or student at the school.

The Tragedy of Amurath, Third Tyrant of the Turks

See Thomas Goffe, *The Courageous Turk*.

The Angel King (1624)
(Lost)

1624, 15 Oct. 'For the Palsgrave's Company; A new Play, called, *The Angell King.*' (Adams, *Herbert*, p. 29.)
1624, 15 Oct. 'For the Palsg: comp:—A new P. Call: The Angell King 15 Oct. 1624—1^{li}.' (Folger Shakespeare Library, Halliwell-Phillipps's Scrap-books, *Fortune*, p. 149.)

The Angel King is known only from Sir Henry Herbert's record of his licence to the Palsgrave's men to perform it at the Fortune in 1624. At that time the Palsgrave's company was engaged in a desperate attempt at survival after the destruction of their repertory in the Fortune fire of 9 December 1621. (See above, i. 141–2 and 149–51.) Most of the phenomenal number of plays licensed to the company in this period are now lost, probably an indication of their inferior quality.

The first version of Sir Henry Herbert's licence is the familiar one printed by J. Q. Adams from George Chalmers's printing of extracts from his transcription. The second version comes from an independent transcript in a nineteenth-century hand—perhaps Craven Ord's—which has been cut up and pasted into appropriate volumes of Halliwell-Phillipps's scrap-books now at the Folger Shakespeare Library. It adds only the information that the company paid Herbert a fee of £1 for his licence—the usual fee for allowing a new play at this time. (See Adams, *Herbert*, pp. 17-18.)

Fleay says of the play, 'The story of Robert, King of Sicily, I suppose'. (*Biog. Chron.* ii. 327.)

Antoninus Bassianus Caracalla (?)

MS.: Bodleian MS. Rawlinson C. 590.

Churchill, G. B., and W. Keller. 'Die lateinischen Universitäts-Dramen Englands in der Zeit der Königin Elisabeth', *Shakespeare Jahrbuch*, xxxiv (1898), 264-7.

The manuscript is a vellum-bound notebook in which miscellaneous material has been entered in a variety of hands and inks. The play is found at the back of the book, reversed. It begins abruptly with the title, 'Antoninus Bassianus Caracalla', 'Actus i^{us}', and the entrance from two sides of the stage of more than a dozen characters, including Antoninus, Geta, Julia, Pompeius, Julius Asper, &c. Numerous corrections have been made by the writer, and several lines have been added or deleted. Though there are nearly two pages of Act v, Scene 5, the play appears to be not quite finished. There is a note at the end in a much later hand, but so badly smeared as to be almost illegible. It reads in part, 'the End (?) . . . Reason (?) why . . . this did write no moe'.

The date of the play is uncertain, but the hand would be compatible with a date in the middle third of the seventeenth century. Certain notes in the volume concern the career of Thomas Iles, Canon of Christ Church and Principal of Hart Hall at Oxford, who matriculated in 1604 and died in 1649, and of his son, who was admitted to Gray's Inn 18 November 1646. (*Alumni Oxon.* ii. 785, and Joseph Foster, *The Register of Admissions to Gray's Inn, 1521-1889* [1889], p. 242.)

Churchill and Keller (loc. cit.) list the dramatis personae, give the first few lines, synopsize the play, and note the Senecan influence.

The Arcadian Lovers, or the Metamorphosis of Princes

See Thomas Moore.

Astraea (9 and 12 October 1625)

(Lost)

McCabe, William H. 'The Play-List of the English College of St. Omers 1592–1762', *Revue de littérature comparée*, xvii (1937), 355–75.
—— 'Notes on the St. Omers College Theatre', *Phil. Quart.* xvii (1938), 225–39.

A masque which probably had this title was acted by almost the entire student body of the Jesuit College for English boys at St. Omers on the 9th and 12th of October 1625. The occasion was the visit of the Princess Isabella of Belgium to the school. Father McCabe gives a synopsis of the action, and notes that it was an allegory of the pacification of Belgium under Albert and Isabella. ('Play-List', p. 365.)

A Bad Beginning Makes a Good Ending

See Ford, *An Ill Beginning Has a Good End.*

Baggs Seneca

(Lost?)

In 'An Exact and perfect Catalogue of all the Plaies that were ever printed', published with his edition of Massinger, Middleton, and Rowley's *The Old Law* in 1656, Edward Archer lists 'Baggs Seneca. T.' It is impossible to determine now what he meant by this entry; some translation of a Senecan tragedy seems most likely.

The Bastard

See Thomas Goffe.

The Battle of Affections

Sub-title of the anonymous *Pathomachia* (q.v.).

The Battle of Afflictions

A misprint for *The Battle of Affections*, the sub-title of the anonymous *Pathomachia* (q.v.).

The Battle of the Vices against the Virtues
(Lost?)

In his list of '*Plays extant in MS., of which I, not having seen them, can give no further account*', F. G. Fleay lists (*Biog. Chron.* ii. 337) '337. Battle of the Vices against the Virtues. Moral. MS., *temp*. Charles I, in Thorpe's *Catalogue*, 1835, p. 11.'

I know of no manuscript on which just this title is used. The anonymous *Pathomachia* (q.v.) was entered in the Stationers' Register as 'The Battell of The affections' and published as *Pathomachia: Or, The Battell of Affections*, and the play is extant in two manuscripts. Or possibly Thorpe had the manuscript of Mildmay Fane's Φ[Ψ?]*yxomaxia id est de pugna animi* (q.v.), now in the British Museum.

Bays
(Lost?)

Richard Rogers and William Ley published 'An exact and perfect Catalogue of all Playes that are Printed' and appended it to their edition of Thomas Goffe's *The Careless Shepherdess*, 1656. One item in this list is 'Bays'. No such play is known, and the title sounds like an error of some sort. Greg suggested (*Bibliography*, ii. 994) that it might conceivably be the same as 'Baggs Seneca. T.' in the similar list of William Archer, but nothing is known about that title either.

The Bear

See Anon., *The Lover's Holiday, or The Bear*.

The Beggars

1641, 7 Aug. In a list of King's men's plays which the Lord Chamberlain forbade the printers to publish without the consent of the company appears the title 'Beggars'. (See above, i. 65–66.)

No play of just this title is known, but at the time the Lord Chamberlain protected these plays in the active repertory of the King's company, Fletcher's play, *The Beggars' Bush*, was still unpublished, and there are several records of its production by the King's men at court in the thirties. It is fairly certain that it was still a popular play in 1641, but it does not appear in the Lord Chamberlain's list. It seems very likely, therefore, that 'Beggars' is a short title for Fletcher's *The Beggars' Bush* (q.v.).

The Black Lady (1622)
(Lost)

1622, 10 May, 'A new Play, called, *The Blacke Ladye*, was allowed to be acted by the Lady Elizabeth's Servants.' (Adams, *Herbert*, p. 23.)

The play is known only from Sir Henry Herbert's licence for the Lady Elizabeth's men to act it. (On a suggested error in the licence date, see above, i. 205, n. 5, and Anon., *The Dutch Painter and the French Branke*.)

The metropolitan Lady Elizabeth's company was new and apparently prosperous in the months following this entry. (See above, i. 176–84.) Of the thirteen plays known to have been licensed for them by Sir Henry Herbert in the first thirty-three months of their London existence, only this play, Bonen's *The Cra . . . Merchant, or Come to My Country House*, and the anonymous *Valiant Scholar* are lost. (See above, i. 185–6.)

The Black Wedding (> 1653)
(Lost)

1653, 29 [Dec.?] S.R. Richard Marriott entered as his copies twenty-one play titles, including 'The Blacke Wedding'. (Greg, *Bibliography*, i. 62.)

The only evidence for the existence of a play of this name is Marriott's entry in the Stationers' Register. Two-thirds of the twenty-one titles in this list of plays occur nowhere else, and only three were published later under these titles, though four others are known from other references. See below, Anon., *The Woman's Law*, for the entire list.

The Bond Woman (> 1653)
(Lost)

1653, 29 [Dec.?] S.R. Richard Marriott entered as his copies twenty-one play titles, including 'The Bond Woman'. (Greg, *Bibliography*, i. 62.)

The only evidence for the existence of a play of this name is Marriott's entry in the Stationers' Register. Two-thirds of the twenty-one titles in this list occur nowhere else, and only three were published later under these titles, though four others are known from other references. See below, Anon., *The Woman's Law*, for the entire list.

Boot and Spur (1611–20?)

MS.: Folger Shakespeare Library MS. 2203.1, fols. 19–23.

This little 'show' of about 300 lines occupies fols. 19–23 in a Jacobean (?) commonplace book at the Folger Shakespeare Library. The similarity in length, general character, and punning dialogue of *Boot and Spur* to *A Christmas Messe* (q.v.) in the same commonplace book might lead one to guess that *Boot and Spur* was near the date of *A Christmas Messe*—1619—and that it was a college show of some sort, but *Boot and Spur* does not have the clear college and university allusions of the other piece. Both have something of the informal, intimate character of Thomas Randolph's *Salting* (q.v.).

At the beginning of the little play is the dramatis personae:

Prologus) Epilogus) a Shoemaker	Pumpe / Bootes ffooteman
Boote / a Trauelor	Shooe / a Citizen,
Spurre / Bootes man	Shootie Shooes page
	Slipper a Chamberlaine

The dialogue which follows is largely a series of puns on the functions of the characters and their names. There is a clue to the date in the dialogue of Shoe and Boot on travel and travellers. Boot says:

As greate as any y^t goes vpon earth for trauell Coriat could neuer come neere me. . . .

Such a remark must have been made after the publication of Thomas Coryate's first travel book, *Coryat's Crudities*, in 1611, and one would think that it would have lost its effectiveness within a few years of Coryate's death at the end of 1617.

In the epilogue to the play, two lines of Shoemaker suggest that the occasion of performance of *Boot and Spur* may have been a recurrent one:

Next tyme I hope my worke shall be more meet
Now I haue learnd ye lenght [*sic*] of all your feet

The play as originally written was given no title. The title 'Boot & Spurr: &c.' has been added in another hand at the head of the text.

The Bridegroom and the Madman (> 1620?)
(Lost)

Oliphant, E. H. C. *The Plays of Beaumont and Fletcher* (1927), pp. 439–40.

c. 1619–20. 'the Bridegr' appears in a list of plays on waste paper of the Revels Office, probably dating about 1619 or 1620. It has been plausibly suggested that the plays of the list were being considered for performance at court. (See Marcham, *Revels*, p. 15, and Chambers, *R.E.S.* i [1925], 484.)

1641, 7 Aug. 'The Bridegroome & ye Madmã' appears in a list of King's men's plays which the Lord Chamberlain forbade the printers to publish without the company's consent. (See above, i. 65–66.)

It is not certain that 'the Bridegr' suggested for performance at court and 'The Bridegroome & ye Madmã' which was part of the repertory of the King's company in 1641 are the same play, but it seems likely because the part of the Revels list containing 'the Bridegr' is in the handwriting of the scribe and book-keeper of the King's company, according to R. C. Bald and W. W. Greg (R. C. Bald, ed., *Hengist, King of Kent; or The Mayor of Queenborough. By Thomas Middleton* [1938], p. xxi, n. 1), and 'the Bridegr' may, therefore, have been part of the repertory of this company in or before 1620. But this suggestion cannot be pressed very far, because other plays in the list in this hand—like *A Fair Quarrel* and *All 's Lost by Lust*—appear to have been in the repertory of other companies. The King's company certainly owned *The Bridegroom and the Madman* of the 1641 list. No other play title beginning with the letters of the Revels entry is known in the Elizabethan, Jacobean, or Caroline periods.

It has several times been suggested that *The Bridegroom and the Madman* was the play published in the Beaumont and Fletcher Folio of 1647 under the title, *The Nice Valour, or the Passionate Madman* (see above, under John Fletcher), but I see nothing to recommend the identification. *The Bridegroom* would not be an appropriate title for the folio play, and there is no evidence that the King's men owned that play as they did *The Bridegroom and the Madman.*

Britanniae Primitiae, sive S. Albanus protomartyr (?)
(Fragment)

MS.: Bodleian MS. Rawlinson Poet. 215.

McCabe, William H. 'Notes on the St. Omers College Theatre', *Phil. Quart.* xvii (1938), 225–39.
—— 'The Play-List of the English College of St. Omers 1592–1762', *Revue de littérature comparée*, xvii (1937), 355–75.

The play is found in a manuscript book of Latin exercises in verse on religious and classical subjects which Madan says were 'made by Roman Catholic students in about A.D. 1600, written out in a foreign hand'. (*A Summary Catalogue of the Western MSS. in the Bodleian Library*, iii. 331, No. 14706.) They look very much like a product of the Jesuit College for English boys at St. Omer, and the manuscript contains also *Sanguis Sanguinem, siue Constans fratricida tragoedia* (see under Anon.), which may be the play produced there 14 April 1640. ('Play-List', pp. 366–7.) Father McCabe does not list *Britanniae Primitiae*, but he does list a number of recorded performances where the name of the play is not known.

The play in the Bodleian MS. is incomplete, breaking off after twenty lines of II. 3.

The Buck Is a Thief (> 1623)
(Lost)

1623, 28 Dec. 'Upon Innocents night, falling out upon a Sonday, *The Buck is a Thief*, the king and prince being there. By the king's company. At Whitehall.' (Adams, *Herbert*, p. 51.)

The play is known only from Sir Henry Herbert's record that the King's men performed it at court on Innocents' Day in 1623. Though it was good enough for performance at court in 1623, it must have lost its appeal in the next eighteen years, for it is not included in the repertory of the company protected by the Lord Chamberlain in 1641. (See above, i. 65–66.) Fleay's conjecture that it was Fletcher's *Devil of Dowgate* and his *Wit at Several Weapons* (*Biog. Chron.* i. 218) has nothing to recommend it.

Callidamus et Callanthia

The manuscript play in B.M. MS. Harl. 2296 which is called *Callidamus et Callanthia* in the *Cambridge History of English*

Literature vi. (1910), 483, is Edmund Stubbe's *Fraus Honesta* (q.v.), according to G. C. Moore Smith. (*College Plays*, p. 96.)

Cancer (1611–13)

MS.: Folger Shakespeare Library MS. 2203.2.

1648. Cancer. Comoedia. Londini, Typis *R. C.* sumptibus *Andr. Crooke.* 1648. (Printed with *Loyola, Stoicus Vapulans, and Paria,* paged continuously.)

Moore Smith points out that the play is 'based on Lionardo Salviati's *Il Granchio* of which a second edition appeared with the same author's *La Spina* at Florence in 1606'. (*College Plays*, p. 99.) He assumes it to be a Cambridge play because of its publication with three others which were, and in his chronological table he dates it '? *c.* 1625.' (Ibid., p. 69.) Hazlitt, for unknown reasons, called it 'a Latin play supposed to have been acted before James I in 1622'. (*Manual*, p. 34), and Harbage, also for unknown reasons, dated it *c.* 1618–28. (*Annals*, p. 92.)

The Folger MS. of *Cancer* is found in a commonplace book of about 1614–25, and since all the rest of the items in the manuscript seem to be from Cambridge, the conjecture that this play is a Cambridge one is strengthened. The text differs in a number of minor ways from the printed one, especially in stage directions, a number of which have been added, seven or eight of them in English. The most notable feature of the manuscript is the cast, which has been added to the dramatis personae in a different ink.

Dramatis personæ

Rodericus senex. Sr Faulcon.	Albertus. Monachus. Mr Coote
Lucilius Adolescens. Mr Coote.	Carpinius Fur. Mr Hickes.
Corbus seruus. Sr Goolfinch	Pyrachmus faber ser. Sr Wilson.
Fortunius. adolescens. Mr Chappell	Bargello cum Sr Filmore.
	4 lictoribus
Granchio. Mr Blaxston.	
Sempronius senex. Sr Dorington.	
Fannius servus. Mr Thopham,	De his fit mentio
Fantichus. puer. Greeke.	
Balia. nutrix claricia. Mr Sleepe.	Constantia.
Vrsilia vidua. Pears.	Lysa.
Erminia. virgo. Mr Walpole.	Claritia.
Gallus puer. Mr Rimmington.	Manlianus

This cast gives a good approximation of the date of the play. It is noteworthy that seven, or possibly nine, of the *Cancer* actors appear also in the cast for Brooke's *Adelphe*, acted at Trinity in 1611/12 and 1612/13 (Moore Smith, *College Plays*, pp. 76–77); six of them in his *Scyros*, Trinity, 1612/13 (ibid., p. 77); and three in his *Melanthe*, Trinity, 1614/15 (ibid., p. 78). This is enough to suggest that *Cancer* is a Trinity College play acted about the same time as *Adelphe*, with which it shares so many actors. Of the common names, seven of them are given the same academic designation in both *Adelphe* and *Cancer*; Greeke is given no title in *Cancer*, indicating that he had no degree yet, whereas in *Adelphe* his bachelor's degree is indicated by the designation 'D^s'. This would suggest that *Cancer* antedated *Adelphe* were it not for the fact that there were two Greekes at Trinity: John, who matriculated 1612, graduated B.A. in 1616/17 and M.A. in 1620, and Thomas, who matriculated 1609 and graduated B.A. 1612/13 and M.A. 1616. Evidently Thomas appeared in *Adelphe*, but it may have been John in *Cancer*. Three of the men in the *Cancer* cast received the degrees by which they are designated in 1610/11 or 1611; Dorington and Goolfinch, who are both designated 'S^r', received their M.A. degrees in 1613 and 1614 respectively. If we can rely on the cast in the Folger MS., then, the play was performed at Trinity College, Cambridge, between 1611 and 1613, a date which is confirmed by the very similar cast of *Adelphe*, acted in 1611/12 and 1612/13.

Canterbury His Change of Diet (1641)

1641. A new Play Called Canterburie His Change of Diot. Which sheweth variety of wit and mirth: privately acted neare the *Palace-yard* at Westminster.

In the {
1 Act, the Bishop of Canterbury having variety of dainties, is not satisfied till he be fed with tippets of mens eares.
2 Act, he hath his nose held to the Grinde-stone.
3 Act, he is put into a bird Cage with the Confessor.
4 Act, The Jester tells the King the Story.
}

Printed Anno Domini, 1641.

The performance statement on the title-page is clearly an indication of the locale of the satiric action, not a record of a dramatic performance, as it has sometimes been taken to be. The piece is closet drama, really a part of the pamphlet war of the period, a political skit, not a play prepared for production. It consists of four very short acts whose action is outlined on the

title-page and is an obvious attack on the Archbishop of Canterbury. The cage into which the Archbishop is put must represent
the Tower of London, and the piece would therefore date after
Laud's imprisonment, 1 March 1640/1. (Gardiner, ix. 297.)

Caracalla

See Anon., *Antoninus Bassianus Caracalla.*

The Cardinal's Conspiracy (> 1639)
(Lost)

1639, 8 May. 'Thursday last [2 May] the players of the Fortune
were fined 1,000*l.* for setting up an altar, a bason, and two
candlesticks, and bowing down before it upon the stage, and
although they allege it was an old play revived, and an altar
to the heathen gods, yet it was apparent that this play was
revived on purpose in contempt of the ceremonies of the Church;
if my paper were not at an end I would enlarge myself upon this
subject, to show what was said of altars.' (*C.S.P., Dom., 1639*,
pp. 140–1, from a letter of Edmund Rossingham to Viscount
Conway.)

1640/1. 'In the meane time let me tell ye a lamentable Tragedie,
acted by the Prelacie, against the poore Players of the *Fortune*
Playhouse, which made them sing

> *Fortune my foe, why dost thou frown on me?* &c.

[f]or they having gotten a new old Play, called *The Cardinalls
conspiraie*, whom they brought upon the *stage* in as great *state*
as they could, with *Altars, Images, Crosses, Crucifixes*, and the
like, to set forth his pomp and pride. But wofull was the
sight to see how in the middest of all their *mirth*, the Pursevants
came and seazed upon the poore Cardinall, and all his Consorts,
and carryed them away. And when they were questioned for it,
in the High Commission Court, they pleaded *Ignorance* and
told the Archbishop, *that they tooke those examples of their Altars,
Images*, and the like, *from Heathen Authors*. This did somewhat
asswage his anger, that they did not bring him on the Stage:
But yet they were fined for it, and after a *little Imprisonment*
gat their *liberty.*' (*Vox Borealis, or The Northern Discoverie,*
'the yeare coming on, 1641', B₂–B₂ᵛ.)

The play is known only from the allusion in *Vox Borealis*, an
allusion which corresponds so closely to the facts mentioned about

the play of the Fortune players in Edmund Rossingham's letter of 8 May 1639 that it seems clear that the two accounts must refer to the suppression of the same Fortune play, in spite of the fact that *Vox Borealis* seems to be trying to make the event appear more recent than it really was. Both accounts agree that the play was an old one revived, but the words 'new old Play' in the second account seem intended to show that the play had also been revised.

Perhaps the fine mentioned in Rossingham's letter was exaggerated; surely no Fortune players of the time were successful enough to have been able to pay such a large sum.

The Carwidgeon
(Ghost title)

In Act v, Scene 1, of Middleton's *The Mayor of Quinborough, or Hengist King of Kent* (q.v.), the rascals pretending to be a troupe of players give to the mayor a list of plays from which he may choose. One of these titles is *The Carwidgeon*, and it has several times been listed as a lost play. It is fairly clear, however, that all the titles are fictitious, mostly puns on the situation of the rascals and the gullible mayor. Even *The Wild Goose Chase* probably refers to the proverbial expression and not to Fletcher's play of the name.

Castara, or Cruelty without Hate (> 1653)
(Lost)

1653, 29 [Dec.?] S.R. Richard Marriott entered as his copies twenty-one play titles, including 'Castara or Cruelty without hate'. (Greg, *Bibliography*, i. 62.)

The play is known only from the Stationers' Register entry of 1653. Two-thirds of the titles in this list of twenty-one plays licensed for Marriott occur nowhere else, and only three were later published under these titles, though four are known from other references. (See below, Anon., *The Woman's Law*, for the entire list.)

Castara is the title of William Habington's popular collection of poems first issued in 1634, and since Habington did write one play, *The Queen of Aragon*, it is conceivable that he wrote *Castara, or Cruelty without Hate*, but there is no evidence whatever, and Allott (ed., *Poems of William Habington* [1948], p. xlvii) ignores the possibility.

It might be argued that the title of the play derives from Habington and that it was therefore written after 1634. In the absence of other evidence, however, there is no sufficient reason for any date beyond the terminal one of Marriott's entry.

The Catchpole

See Anon., *The Roaring Girl.*

Catilina Triumphans (?)
(Lost?)

W. C. Hazlitt listed *Catilina Triumphans* as 'A Latin comedy of the seventeenth century, of which two copies, one imperfect, are among the MSS. of Trinity College, Cambridge'. (*A Manual for the Collector and Amateur of Old English Plays* [1892], p. 36.) No such play was known to the historian of the Cambridge drama, G. C. Moore Smith (*College Plays Performed at the University of Cambridge* [1923]), or to the cataloguer of the manuscripts at Trinity (M. R. James, *Western Manuscripts in the Library of Trinity College, Cambridge*, 4 vols. [1900–4]), both of whom wrote well after Hazlitt had published. No such manuscripts are in the Trinity catalogues now or known to the librarian. I do not believe that Hazlitt invented the manuscripts, and I doubt if they have been lost since his time. Probably his entry is the result of some confusion in titles, but I cannot now resolve it.

Charles, Duke of Bourbon (?)
(Lost)

1641, 15 Apr. S.R. John Nicholson entered for his copies 'three playes, vizt. *A Tragedy called Charles, Duke of Burbon, The Parroiall of Princes & Englands first happines, or, the Life of St. Austin* . . . xviii^d.' (G. E. B. Eyre, *A Transcript of the Registers of the Worshipful Company of Stationers from 1640–1708 A.D.*, i. 20. Inadvertently omitted in Greg, *Bibliography*, i. 54, but summarized in ii. 977.)

The tragedy of *Charles, Duke of Bourbon* is known only from Nicholson's entry of his manuscript in the Stationers' Register. Dr. Greg points out that the Duke's career (1489–1527) provided excellent tragic material and that Pembroke's men had a play called *Bourbon* in 1597. (*Bibliography*, ii. 977.) Nicholson's manuscript could have been the play of 1597, but plays newly licensed in the forties—as opposed to transfers—were very rarely so old.

The Chaste Woman against Her Will (?)
(Lost)

'The chaste woman against her will: a Comedy' appears in a list of 'Books in the Press and now printing' which were advertised by Nathaniel Brook of the Angel in Cornhill, in E. Phillips, *The New World of English Words*, 1658. Under similar headings the title also appeared in other such lists 1558–1662. (See Greg, *Bibliography*, ii. 1000.) The advertisement must have been at least premature, for there is no evidence that the play was ever printed, though one would assume that Brook had a manuscript. Nothing else is known of a play of this title.

The Cheater and the Clown
(Ghost title)

In Act v, Scene 1, of Middleton's *The Mayor of Quinborough, or Hengist King of Kent* (q.v.), the rascals pretending to be a troupe of players give the mayor a list of plays from which he may choose. One of the titles is *The Cheater and the Clown*, and it has several times been listed as a lost play. It is fairly clear, however, that all the titles are fictitious, mostly puns on the situation of the rascals and the gullible mayor. Even *The Wild Goose Chase* probably refers to the proverbial expression and not to Fletcher's play of the name.

Entertainment at Chirke Castle (*Entertainment at Sir Thomas Middleton's*) (*Masque of the Four Seasons*) (1634?)

MS.: B.M. MS. Egerton 2623, fols. 20–23.

Edition: 'The Mask of the Four Seasons', Peter Cunningham and J. P. Collier, eds., *Inigo Jones, a Life; and Five Court Masques*, The Shakespeare Society (1848), pp. 143–8.

The anonymous, untitled, short banquet entertainment of less than 200 lines was once the property of John Payne Collier, who gave it the title, 'The Masque of the Four Seasons', and tried to associate it with the work of Inigo Jones, the subject of the biography published in the same volume. Collier says in his introduction:

> Our volume closes with a fifth hitherto unprinted Masque, or, more properly, Show, which is rather of a peculiar character, since it was written for the sake of introducing and terminating a supper, upon some occasion which has not been recorded. It is called 'The Masque

of the Four Seasons;' and among the finished drawings from the rough designs of Inigo Jones, in the possession of the Duke of Devonshire, are representations of the four Seasons, which perhaps were used for this very exhibition. In this piece, also, it is possible that Nicholas Lanier played Orpheus, and that the sketch of him, with his harp, upon which we have already remarked, belongs to it. This consideration may give it especial claims to notice; and as the manuscript was in this instance also the property of the editor, he did not hesitate to insert it. . . . From p. 143, &c., it is evident that James I., his Queen, the Princes Henry and Charles, and Princess Elizabeth, were present, and hence we may be sure that the performance occurred before 1612. (Ed. cit., pp. xx–xxi.)

Most of Collier's suggestions are either mistaken or deliberately misleading, as is shown by the note accompanying the manuscript in the British Museum and by the entry in the Museum's catalogue of manuscripts 1882–7. The note says:

Court Entertainment Temp. James I. Anonymous and unprinted. With Introductory Speeches by Genius and Songs in various lyrical measures by Orpheus, Winter, Summer, Spring, &c.
Printed by J. P. Collier as an appendix to P. Cunningham's Life of Inigo Jones Shakespeare Soc, 1848.

The catalogue entry corrects and supplements this information:

13. Poetical addresses by 'Genius,' 'Orpheus,' and 'Winter,' delivered at an entertainment 'at Chirke Castle [the seat of Sir Thomas Middleton], 1634.' The endorsement, giving the place and date, has been carefully erased, but may still be read. (*Catalogue of Additions to the Manuscripts in the British Museum, 1882–87* [1889], p. 352.)

I see no reason to doubt the endorsement of the manuscript (erased by Collier?), for several passages refer to the fact that the produce for the banquet came from local fields and meadows, indicating a country production, and repeated references to the nearby mountains are quite compatible with a Welsh provenance. If the endorsement is correct, the entertainment was certainly not presented in the presence of James I and his family before 1612 or at any other time. As for the sketches of Inigo Jones and Collier's deductions therefrom, the four seasons and Orpheus are not uncommon as masque figures, and it is somewhat unlikely that Jones and Lanier should have been at such a remote place as Chirke Castle in Wales, though it is not impossible.

The lines which, as Collier noted, indicate the presence of royalty are spoken by the presenter, Genius, near the beginning of the entertainment:

But soft! what doo I see?
Beuty join'd hand in hand with Majesty?
Mars and ye Queen of Love? Sure, tis not they.
I see noe wanton glances, but a raye
like bright Diana's smiles; and in his face
a grave aspect, like Jove's, taking his place
amidst heavns counsellors: nor are those twayn
yonge Cupids: they have eys, and I in vayne
guesse at yon fresher beauty then ye Spring,
or smooth-fac't Hebe.   (Lines 13–22)

It is true that these lines would be appropriate for an actor gazing at James, Anne, the Princes Henry and Charles, and Princess Elizabeth, but the date on the endorsement of the manuscript rules them out. They could with equal appropriateness refer to King Charles, Queen Henrietta Maria, the Princes Charles and James, and the infant Princess Mary. Indeed, the lines 'nor are those twayn / yonge Cupids: they have eys' are much more appropriate for Charles and James (aged about three and four in 1634) than they would have been for the Princes Henry and Charles, who were eighteen and twelve respectively by 1612.

That the entertainment was written for summer production is indicated by the lines in the welcoming speech of Genius: 'the parching heat / that lately chapt out feilds', and 'the earth in robes of a new Spring arrayde, / seems proude of some late gueste'.

The internal evidence, then, seems compatible with the manuscript endorsement, which Collier ignored or erased, in showing that the entertainment was prepared for a visit of the royal family to Chirke Castle in the summer of 1634. One is given pause, however, by the fact that the royal children seem too young to have been taken to Wales in 1634. And the summer progress of the King and Queen in that year seems to have been too far east to allow a visit to Chirke Castle. (See the list of journeys for the progress, *C.S.P., Dom., Charles I, 1634-5*, p. 149.) Perhaps other facts about the royal progress of 1634 could be found to confirm or disprove the visit to Chirke Castle. Certainly the words of the entertainment assume a royal audience.

A Christmas Messe (Christmas 1619)

MS.: Folger Shakespeare Library MS. 2203.1, fols. 105–15.

This little show is divided into five full acts of three to five scenes each, but it is only five or six hundred lines in total length. The playlet is preserved in a Jacobean (?) commonplace book, now at the Folger Shakespeare Library, and it is similar in general character to *Boot and Spur* (q.v.), which is preserved in the same volume. Various allusions show that *A Christmas Messe* must be a college entertainment of some sort. In I. 4 Cushion says:

> Your fellow quothe? how can you bee fellowes,
> That puff out anger like our Colledge bellowes?

And Cook, at the end of IV. 2:

> Lett's hast, mee thinkes J heare the scollers say
> Where is this Cooke, this, knaue? hee's runne away.

There are numerous jeers at the freshmen.

The tone of the piece, its length, and the general device of impersonating items at a banquet are so much like Thomas Randolph's *Salting* (q.v.) that the occasion of its production must have been a similar college banquet, and a Cambridge college is therefore suggested.

The action of the playlet consists of boasting dialogue, debate style, by the various accessories of the feast, and a battle between King Beef, Sir Vinegar, and Sir Pepper on one side, and King Brawn, Lord Sauce, and Mustard on the other. The characters in the order of appearance are:

Belly	Cushion	King Brawn
Trencher	King Beef	Lord Sauce
Tablecloth	Sir Vinegar	Mustard
Bread	Sir Pepper	Cook
Salt	Queen Mincepy	

The Christmas Ordinary (1633 < > 1642)

1660, 29 June. S.R. The tenth in a list of eleven plays entered to Humphrey Moseley is 'The Christmas Ordinary. a Comedy by Trinity Coll. Oxford'. (Greg, *Bibliography*, i. 69.)

1682. The Christmas Ordinary, A Private Show; Wherein is expressed the *Jovial Freedom* of that *Festival. As it was Acted at a Gentleman's House among other* Revels. By *W. R.* Master of Arts . . . 1682.

The 1682 title-page must be wrong in assigning the play to 'W. R. Master of Arts'. These are the initials signed to the preface, which is dated 'Helmdon, Octob. 18 1682'. They are probably those of William Richards (q.v.), who was rector of that parish in 1682, was a man of some literary interests, and a former student and Fellow of Trinity College, Oxford, which the Stationers' Register entry says was the provenance of *The Christmas Ordinary*.

But the writer of the preface was not the author of the play. He says:

'Tis the First-Born of a young Academick Head, which since hath been Deliver'd of most excellent Productions. It hath lain Dormant almost half an Age, and hath only crawl'd out in Manuscript into some few hands.

Not only do these words verify Moseley's statement in the Stationers' Register as to the academic origin of the play, but the tone indicates that the play was not written by the author of the preface, but by a young man '*half an Age*' before, presumably fifty years. (The *O.E.D.* gives examples of 'age' used to mean 'century' in 1594, 1635, and 1749.)

The text of the play confirms W. R.'s assertion that it was an academic piece by a young author. The prologue speaks of his '*Cradle Muse*' and calls him '*our Infant-Cook*'. It ends,

> *We'll joy our Ordinary with such Resort,*
> *Will both be made a College, and a Court.*

Roger bequeaths 'my Poverty, to a College of Scholars' (Scene 9.) The entire character of the short piece has the tone of an undergraduate rag, like *A Christmas Messe* or Randolph's *Salting*. The immediate occasion of performance was evidently a Christmas celebration, as is suggested by the title and by the preliminary statement, 'The Time from Christmas till Twelfth-night'.

That the play is an Oxford rather than a Cambridge piece is suggested by the lines:

I have been lately reputed a most renowned Cheater, and indeed I borrow'd that Art of a certain City-Major, who was properly married to his Trade; for his Wives Petty-coat was his best Warehouse; whence he grew to be the Frontis-piece of the Town; for the Ford he maintain'd in his Cellar, and the Ox in his Head. (Scene 1)

A date of some time after 1632 is indicated by the statement in the preface of 1682 that '*It hath lain Dormant almost half an Age*'. The prologue line, '*We bar those Histrio-masticks of the Age*', seems to be an allusion to the publication of Prynne's *Histriomastix* in 1633, and there might possibly be an allusion to the mutilation of his ears in May 1634, in the satiric statement in Scene 7:

I have seen the *Terra Incognita*, where . . . the Usurers lend *Gratis*, and the Prodigals build Hospitals: Nay, the very Scriveners have long Ears.

The description of the dwarf in Scene 7 seems to refer to Ben Jonson (d. 1637) as still alive.

> *His Ears, and Shoulders kiss'd, his Waste did shun*
> *All Smiles b'ing swoln beyond* Ben-John-Sons-*Tun.*

There are various slurs at Puritans in the play, but no references to war, and in Scene 8 Shab-Quack laments that surgeons starve because there is no fighting in England. This would suggest a date before 1642. Altogether the allusions seem to me to point to a date not earlier than 1633 and not later than 1642, but see W. W. Greg, *Bibliography*, ii. 1007–8.

The title-page statement, '*As it was Acted at a Gentleman's House among other* Revels', could record a revival of the piece, but the collegiate character of the little play makes it seem unlikely that it was originally intended for performance outside college walls.

The Christmas Prince

The Christmas Prince has once or twice been listed as a late Jacobean production. The title covers a lord-of-misrule series of entertainments at St. John's College, Oxford, in 1607–8. See *The Elizabethan Stage*, iv. 71.

The City (> 1620)
(Lost)

c. 1619–20. 'the Cittye: . . . ' appears in a list of plays on waste paper of the Revels Office, probably dating about 1619 or 1620. It has been plausibly suggested that the plays of the list were being considered for court performance. (See Marcham, *Revels*, p. 15, and Chambers, *R.E.S.* i [1925], 484.)

This title is known only from the Revels list which may well have been notes of plays proposed for court performance. The fact that it is followed by a colon might suggest an abbreviated title, but two other apparently complete titles on the page are also followed by colons. Other titles which begin with these words are *The City Gallant*, a sub-title for *Greene's Tu Quoque*, acted in 1611 (see *The Elizabethan Stage*, iii. 269–70); Massinger's *The City Madam* (q.v.), not licensed until 1632; Jasper Mayne's *The City Match* (q.v.), which was written for performance at Oxford in 1636; Robert Davenport's *The City Nightcap* (q.v.), which was licensed for production in 1624; the anonymous *Second Part of*

The City Shuffler (q.v.), which was suppressed—apparently when new—in 1633; and Richard Brome's *The City Wit, or the Woman Wears the Breeches* (q.v.), which seems to date from about 1629. None of these seems very likely to have been the play suggested for court production in 1619 or 1620.

The part of the list in which this title occurs is in the hand of the book-keeper of the King's company (see R. C. Bald, ed., *Hengist, King of Kent; or The Mayor of Queenborough by Thomas Middleton* [1938], p. xxi, n. 1), and this fact seems to suggest that it was the property of that troupe, but at least two other titles in this hand, *A Fair Quarrel* and *All 's Lost by Lust*, belonged to other companies.

The City Shuffler, Part I (> 1633)
(Lost)

The only evidence that Part I of *The City Shuffler* ever existed is Sir Henry Herbert's reference to 'the second part of *The Citty Shuffler.*' Assuming that he referred to the second of two plays, Part I was presumably acted before Part II, but how long before one can only guess. One would also guess that it was performed at the Salisbury Court theatre, like Part II.

The City Shuffler, Part II (1633?)
(Lost)

1633—Oct. 'Octob, 1633. Exception was taken by Mr. Sewster to the second part of *The Citty Shuffler*, which gave me occasion to stay the play, till the company [of Salisbury Court] had given him satisfaction; which was done the next day, and under his hande he did certifye mee that he was satisfyed.' (Adams, *Herbert*, p. 20.)

c. 1610–50. 'Citty Shuffler' appears in Warburton's list of manuscript plays. (W. W. Greg, *Library*, Third Series, ii [1911], 230.)

Usually the appearance of a title in Warburton's famous list of plays allegedly burned by his cook is no good evidence that he ever owned a manuscript of the play or had even seen one, for most of his entries in form and in order are suspiciously like those in the Stationers' Register. (See Greg, op. cit., pp. 252–9.) *The City Shuffler*, however, does not appear in the Stationers' Register, and there is reason, therefore, for thinking that Warburton may have owned a manuscript once, as he did in the case of a few of the other plays on his list. (Ibid., p. 250.)

Sir Henry Herbert does not indicate how old the play was when Mr. Sewster objected to it—presumably because of personal satire, as in the case of Jonson's *Tale of a Tub* (q.v.), Shirley's *The Ball* (q.v.), and the anonymous *The Whore New Vamped* (q.v.). It was probably a new play at the time the objections were registered, as the Shirley play was, but there is a possibility that Jonson's *Tale of a Tub* and *The Whore New Vamped* were revisions with new material, and *The City Shuffler* may have been too.

Sir Henry inconsiderately omits to tell what satisfaction the players offered Mr. Sewster, but one would guess that they cut the offensive material and then continued to act the play.

Cleopatra (?)
(Lost ?)

Richard Rogers and William Ley published in 1656 'An exact and perfect Catalogue of all Playes that are Printed', and they appended the list to their edition of Thomas Goffe's *The Careless Shepherdess*, 1656. One title in this list is 'Cleopatra'. Since Samuel Daniel's play of the name (see *The Elizabethan Stage*, iii. 275) and Thomas May's (see above) are both listed elsewhere in the Rogers and Ley catalogue, this title does not appear to be intended for either of them. Dr. Greg points out that in Edward Archer's similar list of the same year, which appears to derive from that of Rogers and Ley, Archer has added to this entry 'T. Samuell Daniel', though he had listed Daniel's play elsewhere and labelled it a comedy. (Greg, *Bibliography*, ii. 994 and 996.)

One suspects confusion with an extant play on the part of the publishers, but there may have been another *Cleopatra*, now lost.

The Cloudy Queen and Singing Moor (?)
(Lost)

This title is thirty-second in the list of manuscript plays found among the papers of Abraham Hill. (See Middleton, *The Conqueror's Custom*.) The list seems to have been Hill's record of the stock of some bookseller, set down between 1677 and 1703, but it is notable that nearly all the identifiable plays and playwrights of the list are Jacobean and Caroline.

In his list Hill comments on this title, '(2 Copies)', the only one so marked. No other record of the title is known. It seems hard that both manuscripts of a play with such a catchy title should have disappeared.

Masque at Coleoverton (2 February 1617/18 ?)

MS.: Victoria and Albert Museum, Dyce MS. No. 36.

Edition: Rudolf Brotanek. *Die Englischen Maskenspiele* (1902), pp. 328–37. See also pp. 218–19, 353–4.

The masque, printed by Brotanek from the Dyce MS., is entitled:

A maske presented on Candlemas nighte at Coleoverton, by the earle of Esex, the lorde Willobie, Sr Tho. Beaumont, Sr Walter Devereux, Mr Christopher Denham, Mr Walter T-------, Mrs Ann R-------, M^{rs} An Burnebye, Mrs Susann Burnebye, Mrs Elizabeth Beaumont, Mrs Katherine Beaumont, Mrs Susann Pilkingetun, to Sr William Semer and the ladie Francis Semer.

By an analysis of the biographies of the persons named, Brotanek deduced that the performance could have taken place only on Candlemas 1617/18. (Op. cit., p. 354.) His argument that the masque is the work of Ben Jonson has not been generally accepted. An author who comes to mind because of his associations with Seymour is Richard Brome, who dedicated an undated manuscript of his comedy, *The English Moor*, now in Lichfield Cathedral Library, to 'William Lord Seamor Earle of Hertford Lord Beauchampe &c' and signed himself 'amongst the faithfullest of your Seruants'. But if Brotanek is right about the date, the Coleoverton masque is too early to fit into Brome's career as we know it now.

The masque is simpler than the great court masques, though there is one provision that '*Here the scene opens*'. It is, however, rather gracefully managed.

The Combat of Caps

See John Mason.

The Conceited Duke (> 1639)
(Lost)

1639, 10 Aug. 'The conceited Duke' is included in a list of plays which the Lord Chamberlain protected as the property of the King and Queen's Young Company at the Cockpit. (See above, i. 330–1.)

No play of the name is known now. J. O. Halliwell[-Phillipps] (*A Dictionary of Old English Plays* [1860], p. 55) thought it probably was Fletcher's *The Noble Gentleman* (q.v.), but he was surely wrong, for that play belonged to the King's men at Blackfriars in February 1625/6, according to Sir Henry Herbert, and the Lord Chamberlain himself verified their ownership in 1641. Fleay's identification of the play with Shirley's *The Humorous Courtier* (*Biog. Chron.* ii. 237) is adequately refuted by A. H. Nason. (*James Shirley, Dramatist* [1915], pp. 102–3.)

Most of the plays in the repertory list of 1639 had formerly belonged to Queen Henrietta's men when they were performing at this theatre before 1637 (see above, i. 236–8 and 250–9), and *The Conceited Duke* may have belonged to them too, but it could be that William Beeston or his father, Christopher, had acquired it for his new company at the Cockpit in the two years before the Lord Chamberlain certified it as part of the Cockpit repertory.

The Conceits (> 1653)
(Lost)

1653, 29 [Dec.?] S.R. Richard Marriott entered as his copies twenty-one play titles, including 'The Conceits.' (Greg, *Bibliography*, i. 62.)

The only evidence of the existence of a play of this name is Marriott's entry in the Stationers' Register. Two-thirds of the titles in this list of twenty-one plays occur nowhere else, and only three were published later under these titles, though four are known from other references. (See below, Anon., *The Woman's Law*, for the entire list.)

Cornelianum Dolium

See T. R.

Corona Minervae

See Francis Kynaston.

The Costly Whore (> 1632)

Edition: A. H. Bullen, ed. *A Collection of Old English Plays*, iv (1885), 219–98.

Koeppel, Emil. *Quellen-Studien zu den Dramen George Chapman's, Philip Massinger's und John Ford's* (1897), pp. 200–9.

Lawrence, W. J. 'The Authorship of "The Costelie Whore"', *Modern Language Review*, xvii (1922), 167–8.
Worral, Walter. 'The Authorship of "The Costelie Whore"', ibid., p. 411.

1632, 2 Nov. S.R. William Sheares entered for his copy 'vnder the hands of S^r. Henry Herbert & m^r Aspley warden a Comedy called The costly whore.' (Greg, *Bibliography*, i. 41.)
1633. The Costlie Whore. A Comicall Historie, Acted by the companie of *the Revels*. 1633.

I know of no clue to the authorship of the play save that the frequent references to German customs suggest that the writer had some experience of that country, and the verse and structure suggest that he had very little experience of play-writing. W. J. Lawrence contended (loc. cit.) that the author was Henry Martin, because one of a series of queries in a pamphlet of 1660 called *Free-Parliament Quaeres* is:

23. Whether that Comedie, called *The Costly Whore*, was not intended for the life of the Lady *Sands*, and was written by *Henry Martin*?

Walter Worral (loc. cit.) had no difficulty in demonstrating the absurdity of the ascription by simply quoting from the pamphlet a few of the other queries, which are all gibes at the men of 'the late Rump', several of the gibes—like this one—made by punning on the titles of plays and poems.

The 'companie of *the Revels*' of the title-page has often been taken as referring to the King's Revels company, which played at the Salisbury Court theatre and elsewhere for several years after 1629. (See above, i. 283–96.) To me the play seems much too crude for this troupe and more characteristic of the repertory of the Red Bull Revels company of 1619–23. (See above, i. 165–70 and 174–5.) In the year that *The Costly Whore* was published, its printer, Augustine Matthews, printed another play, Thomas May's *The Heir*, undoubtedly a Red Bull Revels play, and he used precisely the same designation of company on each title-page, 'Acted by the Company of the Reuels', varying only spelling and typography.

F. G. Fleay (*Biog. Chron.* ii. 339) said that he found a number of allusions in the play to events of the period 1631–2, but A. H. Bullen (ed. cit., pp. 219–21) thought that several of the same allusions referred to events of 1613. Most of the allusions, such as those to the exportation of corn, inclosure, export licences, and letters of Mart, seem to be applicable to too many different years.

Koeppel (loc. cit.) shows the unknown dramatist's use of Robert Greene's prose narrative as a source.

The Countryman (> 1653)
(Lost)

1653, 9 Sept. S.R. 'The Countrey man' entered with forty-odd other plays to Humphrey Moseley. (Greg, *Bibliography*, i. 60–61.)

1657, [5 Nov.?] 'To the music for 5 November, 1657, and their yearly fee, and acting "The Countrieman." 3*li*. 6*s*. 8*d*.' (Hyder Rollins, *Stud. Phil.* xx [1923], 63, quoting F. A. Inderwick, *A Calendar of the Inner Temple Records*, ii. [1898], 328.)

Nothing is known of the play save the two records noted. The list of plays licensed by the great dramatic publisher Moseley on 9 September 1653 is a puzzling one, since more than half of them are now lost and several, like *Believe as You List*, *The Soddered Citizen*, and *The Inconstant Lady*, were never printed in the seventeenth century. Moseley names authors for all but three of the plays, of which *The Countryman* is one. It follows two by Lodowick Carlell and precedes Davenant's *Siege*. This juxtaposition may be the reason for Harbage's conjecture that '*The Countryman* was probably a droll fashioned from Davenant's *The Wits*'. (*Cavalier Drama*, p. 213, n. 32.) I know of no evidence that it was a droll or that it should be associated with Davenant.

A Court Purge (?)
(Lost)

This title is thirty-first in the list of manuscript plays found among the papers of Abraham Hill. (See Middleton, *The Conqueror's Custom*.) The list seems to have been Hill's record of some bookseller's stock, set down between 1677 and 1703, but it is notable that nearly all the identifiable plays and playwrights of the list are Jacobean and Caroline.

The title is not known from any other source. J. Q. Adams points out in his discussion of Hill's list that 'In Dekker's *Match Me in London*, the King says, near the end of the play, "I purge my Court", but the phrase is not conspicuous enough to warrant an identification'. (*Library*, Fourth Series, xx [1939], 93.)

Crafty Cromwell, or Oliver Ordering Our New State (1648)

A political pamphlet in the form of two short plays of five acts each, attacking Cromwell.

The Cruel War
(Lost? Ghost title?)

F. G. Fleay (*Biog. Chron.* ii. 340) notes a tragedy of this name which he says was published in 1643. I find no other evidence of the existence of such a play, and I suspect some sort of confusion in Fleay's notes, but I cannot guess what it was.

The Cuckolds' Masque

Not a masque or play, as sometimes indicated, but a short musical composition in B.M. MS. 10444.

Cupid's Festival (1614–18?)
(Lost)

Bald, R. C. 'A Revels Office Entry', *T.L.S.*, 17 March 1927, p. 193.

A holograph manuscript of Sir George Buc's 'A Commentary Vpon the New Roulle of Winchester', written 1614–18 and now in the possession of Major G. Halswell of Wylmington Hayes, Honiton, Devonshire, has in it a number of inserted slips, possibly added later by Sir George. One of these slips has been written on the back of a scrap of paper from the Revels Office. The Revels entry reads:

> Cupid's festivall comed
> Intrat in off. Rev
> 18 Deceb p Histr. Dausse Rob

Presumably this is a note of the licence of a comedy called *Cupid's Festival*, the manuscript of which was brought to Sir George by the actor Robert Dawes. The piece is otherwise unknown. Dawes, who was an actor with the Duke of York's company in 1610 and with the Lady Elizabeth's company in 1614 (see above, ii. 422), has left no later records. It is possible that the slip of discarded paper Buc used had been lying about for a number of years before he used it for his corrections, or that it records an entry made between the completion of his first draft of the 'Commentary' and his death. It seems slightly more plausible, however, that the slip dates from the years of composition of his 'Commentary'.

The Cyprian Conqueror, or The Faithless Relict (> 1642)

MS.: B.M. MS. Sloane 3709.

Adams, J. Q. 'The Cyprian Conqueror, or The Faithless Relict', M.L.N. xxiii (1908), 65–67.

Harbage, Alfred. 'Elizabethan Acting', P.M.L.A. liv (1939), 698.

Dr. Greg describes the manuscript as 'written in "printed" letters by an illiterate scribe (one would almost suppose a child)' and finds the composition almost as naïve as the writing. (*Dramatic Documents* [1931], pp. 364–5.) He tentatively dates the manuscript c. 1640?, but such a hand reveals little, and I see no datable allusions in the play, though the use of the present tense in the preface statement—'I conceive is well performed in our english Theatres'—suggests that it was written not later than 1642. Professor Harbage (loc. cit.) suggests that the play dates not long after 1633 because of allusions to the animosity against plays, which he takes to refer to Prynne's *Histriomastix*, but I can see nothing sufficiently specific in these allusions to suggest Prynne rather than any of the other enemies of the theatre who were articulate for more than a century.

The epilogue begins with the statement that 'Our author is a country man', but reveals nothing more about him. Both prologue and epilogue are intended for performance, but there is no evidence that there ever was one. Professor Adams's assertion in his youthful article (loc. cit.) that the stage directions indicate performance is very naïve when one notes the directions he quotes. His evidence for thinking that the play was 'performed in one of the regular London playhouses' is negligible. It is difficult to imagine a London or university audience listening to the play—at least in the mood the author intended. For example, in his dying speech in the first scene Philander delivers the lines:

> A dyer distemper mee doth take
> My head, back, & bones doe ake.

Professor Adams (loc. cit.) synopsizes the plot and the sub-plot of the play and notes that the former is the popular story of the 'Matron of Ephesus' which Chapman had used in *The Widow's Tears*. There is no similarity to Chapman's treatment, however, and Adams suggests that the author of *The Cyprian Conqueror* used Petronius Arbiter. The sub-plot comes from the *Decameron*, xii. 2.

Between the dramatis personae and the prologue in the manuscript is a long preface by the author defending his choice of subject, and plays in general. He also has remarks on gestures and acting which interested Professor Harbage. (Loc. cit.) The playwright's comments seem to me as naïve as his verse, and I should hesitate to accept them as reflections of the technique current in the sophisticated London theatres.

The Death of the Black Prince (?)
(Lost?)

W. C. Hazlitt listed in *A Manual for the Collector and Amateur of Old English Plays* (1892), p. 59, 'The Death of the Black Prince: A tragedy. *Heber's MSS.*' I know nothing of a play of the name or of the manuscript.

Demetrius and Marina [Marsina], or The Imperial Impostor and Unhappy Heroine (?)
(Lost)

In the catalogue for the sale of the manuscripts of John Warburton in 1759 was listed a manuscript entitled 'Demetrius and Marina, or the Imperial Impostor and Unhappy Heroine, a Tragedy. Fol.' (See W. W. Greg, 'The Bakings of Betsy', *Library*, Third Series, ii [1911], 227–8, 257.) The title does not appear in the list of plays which Warburton says his cook destroyed (ibid.), but nothing is known of it now. It could, of course, have been a play of the Restoration or early eighteenth century. Fleay gives the title as *Demetrius and Marsina*. (*Biog. Chron.* ii. 337.)

Diana's Grove, or The Faithful Genius (?)
(Lost?)

W. C. Hazlitt lists in *A Manual for the Collector and Amateur of Old English Plays* (1892), p. 63, 'Diana's Grove; or, the Faithful Genius: A tragi-comedy, never acted. A MS. in private hands.' Presumably F. G. Fleay was following Hazlitt when he recorded '*Diana's Grove, or The Faithful Genius.* T. C. In private hands' under the heading '*Plays extant in MS., of which I, not having seen them, can give no further account.*'(*Biog. Chron.* ii. 337.)

I know nothing of the play or the present location of the manuscript.

Dick of Devonshire (1626?)

MS.: B.M. MS. Egerton 1994, fols. 30–51.

Edition: A. H. Bullen, ed., 'The Play of *Dicke of Devonshire.*
A Tragi-Comedy', in *A Collection of Old English Plays*, ii (1883),
1–99.

Boas, F. S. 'A Seventeenth Century Theatrical Repertoire',
Library, Third Series, viii (1917), 225–39. Reprinted in *Shakespeare and the Universities.*

Clark, A. M. *Thomas Heywood, Playwright and Miscellanist* (1931),
pp. 103 and 276–86.

Greg, W. W. *Dramatic Documents from the Elizabethan Playhouses*
(1931), pp. 329–32.

McManaway, J. G. 'Latin Title-Page Mottoes as a Clue to Dramatic Authorship', *Library*, Fourth Series, xxvi (1945), 28–36.

Nason, Arthur Huntington. *James Shirley, Dramatist* (1915), pp.
62–68.

Rowe, J. Brooking, ed. *Richard Peeke of Tavistock His Three to
One, The Commendatory Verses, and the Play of Dick of Devonshire* (1905).

Velte, Mowbray. *The Bourgeois Elements in the Dramas of Thomas
Heywood* (1922), pp. 92–96.

The manuscript has a fly-leaf title reading 'The Play of Dicke of
Devonshire. A Tragi Comedy. Hector adest secumq[ue] Deos
in prælia ducit.' (See Greg, op. cit., pp. 329–30.) The play was
first printed by Bullen.

The play called *Dick of Devonshire* in Egerton 1994 was first
printed by Bullen in the second volume of his *Collection of Old
English Plays*. Dr. Greg says that the manuscript has the general
appearance of a scribal one, though some alterations and corrections suggest an author. He thinks it shows no evidence of playhouse use or censorship or even of preparation for the theatre,
and that the continuous writing and the Latin motto 'suggest a
purely literary intention.' (Op. cit., p. 330.) This conclusion is
questioned by Dr. McManaway (loc. cit.), who thinks the manuscript is a playhouse text because a photostat of Egerton 1994,
fols. 30–51, shows faintly the familiar folded lines for margins
and because there is one clearly anticipatory stage direction on
fol. 46. Both these points do suggest theatrical intentions, but they
are slight. Far more anticipatory directions would have been required for production, and the faint lines from folding do not seem

conclusive proof. The balance of the evidence seems to me in favour of Greg's conclusion that the manuscript is a literary one. Dr. McManaway notes that the manuscript additions to the Folger copy of Middleton's *Blurt, Master Constable*, 1602, inserted to supply the text of the missing leaves H₂ and H₃, are in the same hand as *Dick of Devonshire* in Egerton 1994. This unknown scribe may have been a regular theatre employee, but not necessarily. The conclusion that *Blurt, Master Constable*, and *Dick of Devonshire* were once in the same repertory is possible, but by no means certain, and the suggestion that this repertory was that of Queen Henrietta's men is no more than a guess. (McManaway, op. cit., pp. 31–33.)

   The main plot of *Dick of Devonshire* is based on a pamphlet by Richard Peeke (or Pike), the hero of the play. The pamphlet was entered to J. Trundle, 18 July 1626, and published in the same year with the title, *Three to One: Being, An English-Spanish Combat, Performed by a Western Gentleman, of Tavistock in Devonshire with an English Quarter-Staff, against Three Spanish Rapiers and Poniards, at [Xeres] in Spain, The fifteenth day of November, 1625. In the Presence of Dukes, Condes, Marquesses, and other Great Dons of Spain, being the Council of War.* Pike's exploit was no doubt a short-lived wonder, and the play would presumably have been prepared as soon as possible, i.e. in 1626 or 1627. That it was intended to be acted in 1626 is indicated by the interruption of the second Devonshire Merchant to the first Devonshire Merchant's patriotic account of the defeat of the Spanish Armada. A few lines after the first Merchant has mentioned the date of the Armada, the second says:

> Stay; Eighty Eight,—
> Thirty eight yeares agoe: much about then
> Came I into the world.—Well, sir, this fleete?
>
> (i. 2. Bullen ed., p. 16.)

   James Shirley, Robert Davenport, and Thomas Heywood have each been advocated as the author of *Dick of Devonshire*. Fleay asserted (*Biog. Chron.* ii. 236–7) that it was Shirley's play, *The Brothers*, licensed for performance 4 November 1626, because a few lines before the end of the play the Duke of Macada says:

> Letters shall forthwith fly into *Madrid*
> To tell the King the storyes of Two Brothers,
> Worthy the Courtiers reading.
>
> (Bullen ed., p. 99.)

According to Fleay, in this passage, 'This play is expressly called (near the end) "the story of Two Brothers."' This exercise in Fleay's favourite game has caused more than the usual confusion, for Shirley published in his *Six New Playes*, 1653, a play which he called *The Brothers, A Comedie*, and which he dedicated to Thomas Stanley. Fleay then argues that *The Brothers* of the 1653 collection is not *The Brothers* licensed in 1626, but is instead *The Politique Father*, licensed for performance by Sir Henry Herbert on 26 May 1641. (Adams, *Herbert*, p. 39.) The identification of *The Brothers* of 1653 with *The Politique Father*, licensed in May 1641, is accepted by Nason on what appear to be very good grounds (*James Shirley, Dramatist*, pp. 54–62), but he rejects Fleay's identification of the manuscript *Dick of Devonshire* with Shirley's *Brothers* of November 1626. (Ibid., pp. 62–68.) This rejection seems to me well grounded, for the constantly reiterated anti-Catholic sentiments of *Dick of Devonshire* are surely impossible for the Catholic Shirley, and the occasional and jingoistic character of the Richard Pike material is quite unlike him.

Robert Davenport was claimed by Fleay as the author of *Dick of Devonshire* before Bullen's publication of the play in 1883 (Bullen ed., p. 4, n.), but Bullen rejected the attribution, and Fleay himself abandoned it before he published his *Biographical Chronicle of English Drama*, for he espoused Shirley there, as we have seen. Dr. McManaway has taken up the case for Davenport (loc. cit.), but his evidence—that the Latin motto on the manuscript is the same as that on the 1639 title-page of *The Bloody Banquet* by T. D., which he attributes to Davenport, and that he finds 'considerable internal evidence that it [*Bloody Banquet*] and *Dick of Devonshire* are from the same pen, and that the writer was indeed Robert Davenport' (op. cit., p. 35)—seems to me quite inadequate.

Thomas Heywood was suggested as the author of the play by Bullen in his original edition, and he has been accepted as the author by Clark and Velte. The attitudes in the play towards England, Catholicism, bourgeois sentiments, and English adventurers abroad, as well as the structural characteristics of the piece, seem to me very like Heywood. Clark has made by far the best case for attribution of the play (loc. cit.), and only the warning of the chaos created by Fleay's attributions restrains me from listing *Dick of Devonshire* as a Heywood play without more ado.

The Disappointed Ladies
(Ghost title?)

W. C. Hazlitt lists in his *Manual for the Collector and Amateur of Old English Plays* (1892), p. 64, 'The Disappointed Ladies. A Court masque, produced in the reign of James I'. No such masque is known to have been produced, but we may have a clue to it in a masque planned by Lady Hay and other ladies for 1 January 1617/18 but cancelled at the last moment and never performed. The masque is lost, and its writer is unknown, but, from what is known of its subject and performers, it has generally been called *The Masque of Amazons, or The Ladies Masque* (q.v.). F. G. Fleay (*Biog. Chron.* ii. 343–4) also called it, presumably out of pity for the fruitless rehearsals, *The Masque of Disappointed Ladies*, and Hazlitt, through some confusion, must have thought it another masque.

The Divorce (> 1653)
(Lost)

1653, 29 [Dec.?] S.R. Richard Marriott entered as his copies a list of twenty-one play titles, including 'The Diuorse'. (Greg, *Bibliography*, i. 62.)

The only evidence for the existence of a play of this name is Marriott's entry of the play in the Stationers' Register. Two-thirds of the twenty-one titles in this list of plays occur nowhere else, and only three were published later under these titles, though four more are known from other references. (See below, Anon., *The Woman's Law*, for the entire list.)

The Doge and the Dragon (1641)
(Lost)

1641, 23 June '23ᵈ. Iune 1641 Recēd for the licensinge a booke for the Fortune comp. called the Doge & the Dragon. 2ˡⁱ'
Herbert MS. (Folger Shakespeare Library, MS. Scrap-books of J. O. Halliwell-Phillipps, *Fortune*, p. 48.)

The above item is one of a number that have been cut out of a manuscript and pasted into one of his many voluminous scrap-books by J. O. Halliwell-Phillipps. The original manuscript was a transcript (or partial transcript) of Sir Henry Herbert's office-book made in a nineteenth-century hand, possibly that of Craven

Ord. Most of the items pasted into the scrap-books duplicate entries copied by Malone or Chalmers and collected by Dr. J. Q. Adams in his *The Dramatic Records of Sir Henry Herbert* (1917), though they generally differ in spelling and punctuation and often add the fee paid and occasionally another bit ignored by Malone or Chalmers. The entry above is one of the very few not found in the extracts of Malone or Chalmers in any form.

The fee of £2 was Sir Henry's regular charge for licensing a new play at this time and indicates that *The Doge and the Dragon* was not an old piece with new scenes. The troupe playing at the Fortune when this play was licensed was probably Prince Charles's (II) men. (See above, i. 316–20.) The company was not distinguished, and the theatre at this time had a reputation for noise and vulgarity. (Ibid. and ii. 690–1.)

Don Manuel

See James Shirley, *The Court Secret.*

[Don Pedro] (?)

At a sale at Sotheby's on 13 December 1938 the following item was sold:

482 Play, in Latin, founded on the history of Don Pedro, the Cruel King of Castille (1334–69) MS *on paper*, 34 *ll. limp vellum. early XVIIth cent.*

The British Museum copy of the sale catalogue says that the manuscript was sold to Maggs for ten shillings.

I know nothing more of the play; it may have been earlier than 1616 or later than 1642. I take it from the entry that there was no title on the manuscript. Could it be *The Spanish Tragedy of Petrus Crudelis*? See under Anon.

The History of Don Quixote, or the Knight of the Ill-Favoured Face (?)
(Lost)

'The History of Donquixiot, or the Knight of the illfavoured face: a Comedy', appears in a list of 'Books in the Press and now printing' which were advertised by Nathaniel Brook of the Angel in Cornhill, in E. Phillips, *The New World of English Words*, 1658. Under similar headings the title also appears in other such lists 1658–62. In Kirkman's list of 1661 it is called 'Don Quixot, or the Knight of the ill-favoured countenance. C.' (See Greg, *Bibliography*, ii. 1000–1.) The advertisements must have been at least premature, for there is no evidence that the play was ever printed, though one would assume that Brook had a manuscript.

This lost play is ascribed to the ubiquitous Robert Baron by Edward Phillips in *Theatrum Poetarum*, 1671 (Part ii, p. 160), and by William Winstanley in his *Lives of the Most Famous English Poets*, 1687 (p. 113). Dr. Greg (loc. cit.) says that the ascription of Phillips was made through a misunderstanding and that Winstanley simply followed him. Gerard Langbaine pointed out their error in his *Account of the English Dramatick Poets*, 1691, p. 13.

Duke Humphrey (?)
(Lost)

1660, 29 June. S.R. Humphrey Moseley entered as his copies a
  long list of plays, including:
    The History of King Stephen. ⎫
    Duke Humphrey. a Tragedy ⎬ by Will: Shakspeare.
    Iphis & Iantha, Or a marriage ⎪
      without a man. a Comedy. ⎭
  (Greg, *Bibliography*, i. 68–69.)
c. 1710–50. 'Duke Humphery Will. Shakespear' appears in Warburton's list of manuscript plays. (W. W. Greg, *Library*, Third
  Series, ii [1911], 243.)

The occurrence of Moseley's title in Warburton's list of plays that were allegedly burned by his cook is no evidence that Warburton ever owned the manuscript, or had even seen it. (See Greg, op. cit., pp. 225–59.)

It is quite unlikely that Shakespeare wrote the tragedy of Duke Humphrey, for no other reference to the title has been found. I know of no evidence as to the date or authorship of the manuscript Moseley had in 1660.

Duke of Lerma

See Henry Shirley, *The Spanish Duke of Lerma*.

Durance Masque
(Ghost title)

J. O. Halliwell[-Phillipps] in *A Dictionary of Old English Plays* (1860), p. 80, followed by F. G. Fleay (*Biog. Chron.* ii. 345), lists a piece called *Durance Mask* or *The Masque of Durance*, of the time of Charles I, but he took the title from the B.M. Add. MS. 10444. This manuscript is a collection of short musical compositions, many of them possibly composed for masques, and some, perhaps, having the name of the masque, but the titles refer to the airs. (See John Adson, above.) Incidentally, Augustus Hughes-Hughes in his *Catalogue of Manuscript Music in the British Museum*, iii (1909), 174, questions whether this title is not intended for 'G. Durant's Masque'.

The Dutch Painter and the French Branke [*Brawle, Branle*?] (1622)

1622, 10 June. 'A new Play, called, *The Duche Painter, and the French Branke*, was allowed to be acted by the Princes Servants at the Curtayne.' (Adams, *Herbert*, p. 24.)

1622, 10 June. '10⁺⁺ Iune for allow: of a new P. conteyn: 13 sheetes 2 [pages ½ called the] Duche painter & the French brank acted by the [Princes players at] the Curtayne—20.ˢ [Herbert MS. 1622]' (Halliwell-Phillipps's Scrap-books, *Fortune*, p. 85, Folger Shakespeare Library.)

c. 1677–1703. 'the Dutch painter & the french brawle.' ('Hill's List of Early Plays in Manuscript', *Library*, Fourth Series, xx [1939], 74. This title is No. 26 in Hill's list.)

There are two slightly different versions of Herbert's licence for performance of the play. The first is the well-known one in J. Q. Adams's *Herbert* which was taken from the extracts from Herbert's manuscript published by George Chalmers in his *Supplemental Apology for the Believers in the Shakespeare-Papers*. The second comes from an independent transcript of Herbert's office-book in a nineteenth-century hand. This transcript, perhaps that of Craven Ord, has been cut up and pasted into appropriate sections of Halliwell-Phillipps's scrap-books, now preserved in the Folger Shakespeare Library. The bracketed sections in the above quotation of this transcript indicate passages in a different hand. The first two are replacements of parts of the original transcript inadvertently clipped off before pasting; the third is Halliwell-Phillipps's citation of the source. The two transcripts differ only in minor details and in the addition of information about the length of the manuscript and the allowance fee in the Halliwell-Phillipps scrap-book transcript. Presumably Chalmers omitted this information as irrelevant for his purposes.

Two matters of controversy are affected by the second transcript. Fleay (*History of the Stage*, p. 301), followed by other scholars, altered Chalmers's date of this and three adjacent entries to 1623 because they thought 1622 incompatible with other facts in theatrical history of the time. The evidence was poor (see above, i. 205, n. 5) and the confirmation of 1622 by an independent transcript would seem to me to eliminate any reason for questioning Chalmers's date.

The second uncertainty is the last word of the title. 'Branke' is an unfamiliar word, though the *O.E.D.*, in addition to defining it as a verb, cites sixteenth-century usage of the word as a noun to mean buckwheat and—though rarely in the singular—a scold's bridle or gag. Since the title occurs in Hill's list (see below) as 'the Dutch painter & the french brawle', J. Q. Adams (*Library*, Fourth Series, xx [1939], 92) suggested quite plausibly that 'branke' was a misreading or a mistake for 'brawle'. This seemed convincing to me (see above, i. 216) until I saw the second transcript from Herbert's office-book. It now appears that Herbert wrote 'branke'—at least, two independent transcribers read the word that way. To confuse the issue still further, Grove (*Dictionary of Music*, ed. 1904–10) defines 'BRANLE . . . A French dance popular in England during the 16th century. . . . It is identical with the Bransle or "Brangill," and probably also with the "Brawl," supposed to be so named from its similitude to an altercation.' What the title of the play that Herbert licensed really was or what it means I do not know, but a fine lot of material for guesses is herewith offered.

This title, with the last word spelled 'brawle', is the twenty-sixth in the list of manuscript plays found among the papers of Abraham Hill. (See Middleton, *The Conqueror's Custom*.) The list seems to have been Hill's record of some bookseller's stock, set down between 1677 and 1703, but it is notable that nearly all the identifiable plays and playwrights in the list are Jacobean or Caroline. Evidently a manuscript of the play Herbert licensed for the Prince's men in 1622 was still extant towards the end of the century.

Fleay's suggestion (*Biog. Chron.* ii. 156) that this play was the same as *The Painter, or The Wandering Lovers* (actually it was *The Wandering Lovers or the Painter*), which was entered in the Stationers' Register as Massinger's in 1653, seems to me one of his more irresponsible suggestions. It has to recommend it only the facts that both plays are lost and both titles contain the word 'painter'.

England's First Happiness, or the Life of St. Augustine (?)
(Lost)

1641, 15 Apr. S.R. John Nicholson entered for his copies 'three playes, vizt. *A Tragedy called Charles, Duke of Burbon, The Parroiall of Princes & Englands first happines, or, the Life of St. Austin* . . . xviii^d.' (G. E. B. Eyre, *A Transcript of the Registers of the Worshipful Company of Stationers from 1640–1708 A.D.*, i. 20. Inadvertently omitted in Greg, *Bibliography*, i. 54, but summarized, ii. 977.)

Nothing is known of a play with this title, or, Dr. Greg asserts (*Bibliography*, ii. 977), of any play on the life of St. Augustine of Canterbury. It might have been of any date before the Stationers' Register entry, but very few plays earlier than the times of James I were entered in the Stationers' Register for the first time in the 1640's.

The English Arcadia (?)
(Play? Lost?)

Edward Archer published 'An Exact and perfect Catalogue of all the Plaies that were ever printed; together, with all the Authors names; and what are Comedies, Histories, Interludes, Masks, Pastorels, Tragedies'. This catalogue was appended to his edition of Massinger, Middleton, and Rowley's *The Old Law*, 1656. Dr. Greg shows that this catalogue of Archer's is derived from the similar list of Rogers and Ley published in the same year. (*Bibliography*, ii. 996.) One title in Archer's list is 'English Arcadia C.' It seems probable, Dr. Greg notes (op. cit., p. 997), that the title refers to Markham's romance, published in 1607 and 1613, and included here by mistake; Shirley's play of the name is listed elsewhere by Archer.

Entertainment at or of ——

See the next word in such titles.

The Essex Antic Masque
(Ghost)

J. O. Halliwell[-Phillipps] lists a number of masques as 'c. 1620' or 'temp. Jac I', including 'Essex Antic Masque'. (*A Dictionary of Old English Plays* [1860], p. 88.) All the titles come from the

B.M. MS. Add. 10444. This manuscript is not a collection of masques, but a collection of short musical compositions, many of which use the word 'masque' in the title. (See above, John Adson.) There is no assurance that these tunes were even attached to masques, much less that the name of the tune was the name of a masque.

The Eunuch

See William Heminges, *The Fatal Contract*.

The Fair Captive

See Anon., *The Fair Spanish Captive*.

The Fair Spanish Captive (?)
(Lost)

'The fair Spanish Captive: a Trage-Comedy' appears in a list of 'Books in the Press and now printing' which were advertised by Nathaniel Brook of the Angel in Cornhill in E. Phillips, *The New World of English Words*, 1658. Under similar headings the title also appears in other such lists, 1658–62. (See Greg, *Bibliography*, ii. 1000–1.) The advertisements must have been at least premature, for there is no evidence that the play was ever printed, though one would assume that Brook had a manuscript. Nothing else is known of a play of the title.

Dr. Greg notes (ibid.) that one of the plays in Abraham Hill's list is called 'The Conquerors custome or the fair prisoner Tho Middleton' (q.v.). Though this sub-title is similar to the one Brook advertised, there is no reason to assume that they represent the same play.

The Fair Star of Antwerp (1624)
(Lost)

1624, 15 Sept. 'For the Palsgrave's Company; A Tragedy, called, *The Faire Star of Antwerp*.' (Adams, *Herbert*, p. 29.)

1624, 15 Sept. 'For the Palsg: comp:—A Trag: called the Faire Star of Antwerp 15^{++} Sept. 1624 1^{li}' (Folger Shakespeare Library, MS. Scrap-books of Halliwell-Phillipps, *Fortune*, p. 149.)

The play is known only from Sir Henry Herbert's record of his licence to the Palsgrave's men to perform it at the Fortune in 1624. At that time the Palsgrave's company were engaged in a desperate attempt at survival after the destruction of their repertory in the Fortune fire of 9 December 1621. (See above, i. 141–2 and 149–51.) Most of the phenomenal number of plays licensed to the company in this period are now lost, probably an indication of the inferior quality of the plays.

The first version of Sir Henry Herbert's licence entry is the familiar one printed by J. Q. Adams from George Chalmers's printing of extracts from his transcription. The second version comes from an independent transcript in a nineteenth-century hand—perhaps Craven Ord's—which has been cut up and pasted into appropriate volumes of Halliwell-Phillipps's scrap-books, now at the Folger Shakespeare Library. It adds only the information that the company paid Herbert a fee of £1 for his licence—the usual fee for allowing a new play at this time. (See Adams, *Herbert*, pp. 17–18.)

The Fairy Knight, or Oberon the Second (1637 ?–58 ?)

MS.: Folger Shakespeare Library MS. 46.1.

Edition: Fredson Thayer Bowers, ed., *The Fary Knight or Oberon the Second* (1942).

Bowers, F. T. 'Ben Jonson, Thomas Randolph, and The Drinking Academy', *N. & Q.* clxxiii (1937), 166–8.

The existence of this play was first generally commented upon (though its existence had been noted by De Ricci and Wilson in *Census of Medieval and Renaissance Manuscripts in the United States and Canada*, i. 278) by Professor Bowers at a meeting of the Modern Language Association of America in 1936, and first printed by him in 1942. The manuscript had been purchased by Mr. Folger from the London bookseller, Pearson, who had bought it shortly before at a Puttick and Simpson auction of 11 July 1900. Apparently it had formerly been bound with miscellaneous material and with *The Drinking Academy* (q.v.), which has been transcribed and corrected in the same hand.

The attribution of *The Fairy Knight* to Thomas Randolph is much more dubious than that of *The Drinking Academy*, with which it is associated, because of their similar character, their discovery at about the same time, their former inclusion in the same manuscript, and their transcription in the same hand. None of these associations is evidence of common authorship. The play is cruder than *The Drinking Academy*. The verse especially seems much too crude for a clever versifier like Randolph, even in his Westminster days.

Professor Bowers is convinced (ed. cit., pp. xxii–xlii, *et passim*) that the play is Randolph's, but his evidence is weak. The passages which he cites are much less Randolphian than those Day noted in arguing the case of *The Drinking Academy*, and the parallels fewer and less exact. It is true that the parallels of situation and character are close, but this seems to me evidence *against* Randolph's authorship. Randolph often repeats his own phrases—they might pass unnoticed in a performance—and apparently he did lift some situations from his obscure school play *The Drinking Academy* for his *Jealous Lovers*, produced for a royal visit to Cambridge, but this is quite a different thing from repeating plot and characters for the same audience at the same place and, if Bowers's dates are accepted, after an interval of not more than three years. Furthermore, the imitations in *The Fairy Knight* of *The Alchemist* (1610), *The Masque of Queens* (1608/9), *The Traitor* (1631), and *The Young Admiral* (1633) are even closer than the parallels to Randolph's own work. Professor Bowers would have these later imitations, especially the ones of *The Young Admiral*, which are so close as to have required the use of the first quarto of 1637, the work of a reviser. The manuscript does show evidence of revision, but minor revision of words and phrases, not major ones. I can see no difference between the way the Randolph material is worked into the play and the way the Jonson and Shirley material is worked in.

Professor Bowers's dating of the play (1623–4) derives from his conviction that Randolph wrote it before he went up to Cambridge. (Ed. cit., p. xxxiii.) Internal evidence for a Jacobean date is negligible. The proverbial 'ten in the hundred' for usurers would not be changed by the passage of a law in 1624; vintners in the city broke at various times; the burgomaster of Amsterdam newly arrived to 'bribe the new states' sounds more like a Commonwealth than a Jacobean allusion, and Bowers himself cites visits of Amsterdam burgomasters in 1651 and 1660 as well as 1621–3. Bowers's elaborate contention that the First and Third Intermeans of *The Staple of News* refer to the gulling in *The Fairy Knight* and that Randolph replied in the prologue to *The Drinking Academy* (*N. & Q.*, loc. cit.) seems to me quite fantastic. I see nothing notably anti-Spanish in the play, let alone satire of a sort which would date the play about the time of the Spanish marriage proposals. In short, the only reason I can see for dating the play in the early twenties is the conviction that it is a play written by Thomas Randolph for Westminster boys. For Randolph's authorship I see little evidence, but much against it; for Westminster

School there is only the evidence of the simple character of the cast and setting and the clear references to child actors, e.g. 'ffalts merit pardon when as children play'. These features would be equally suitable to many other groups of boys, and at any time in the seventeenth century.

If the date is not 1623–4, what is it? Since, to my mind, the play shows no evidence of large-scale revision, it must date after the composition of *The Traitor* (licensed 4 May 1631) and *The Young Admiral* (licensed 3 July 1633), to both of which Bowers shows specific and detailed indebtedness. (Ed. cit., pp. 65–86.) The imitation seems too close to be accounted for by memory of a performance, so that the author must have had before him either Shirley's manuscripts or printed copies of the plays (1635 and 1637), as well as editions of *The Masque of Queens* (1609) and *The Alchemist* (1612). Other internal evidence of date seems to me too weak for consideration. The best would be the allusion in lines 60–63 to the visit of the 'burgar master of Amsterdame', but reference to the visit of Gerard Schaep in 1651–2 would be no more probable than Bowers's suggestion of the visit of Dirck Bas, 1621–3. The latest possible date for the play would appear to be the upper limit date set by Bowers for the manuscript—1658, the date of the death of Frances Monson, whose epitaph was at one time part of the manuscript which included *The Fairy Knight*. Even this date is none too secure, for since the manuscript has been broken up, we cannot say with assurance that the epitaph was written after the play.

There remains for consideration Sir Henry Herbert's licence of 11 June 1624 of 'A new play, called, *The Fairy Knight*: Written by Forde, and Decker'. (See under Dekker.) All the evidence cited above against an early date for the Folger MS. play applies equally against its identification with the unknown play of Sir Henry Herbert's licence. Moreover, nothing in the manuscript sounds like Ford or Dekker, or, for that matter, like any experienced or talented writer for the stage. In spite of the tempting identity of titles, there is no discernible reason to make a connexion between the lost Ford and Dekker play and the Folger MS.

The Fairy Masque
(Ghost title)

J. O. Halliwell[-Phillipps] lists a number of masques as 'c. 1620' or 'temp. Jac I', including 'The Fairy Masque'. (*A Dictionary of Old English Plays* [1860], p. 91.) All the titles come from the B.M.

MS. Add. 10444. This manuscript is not a collection of masques, but a collection of short musical compositions, many of which use the word 'masque' in the title. (See above, John Adson.) There is no assurance that these tunes were even attached to masques, much less that the name of the tune was the name of a masque.

The Fairy Queen (?)
(Lost)

c. 1710–50. 'Farry [sic] Queen' appears in Warburton's list of manuscript plays. (See W. W. Greg, *Library*, Third Series, ii [1911], 232.)

No sixteenth- or early-seventeenth-century play called *The Fairy Queen* is known except from John Warburton's list of the manuscripts he said he once owned. Most of Warburton's titles are suspiciously similar to entries in the Stationers' Register, and it is doubtful if he ever owned the manuscripts (see Greg, op. cit., pp. 252–9), but he did own some of the plays he listed, and *The Fairy Queen* does not appear in the Stationers' Register.

The False Friend (?)
(Lost?)

This title is forty-eighth in the list of manuscript plays found among the papers of Abraham Hill. (See Middleton, *The Conqueror's Custom.*) The list seems to have been Hill's record of the stock of some bookseller, set down between 1677 and 1703, but it is notable that nearly all the identifiable plays and playwrights of the list are Jacobean and Caroline.

The title also appears as 'The Falce Frend' in a list of plays on waste paper of the Revels Office, probably dating about 1619 or 1620. It has been plausibly suggested that the plays of this list, most of them the property of the King's company, were being considered for court performance. (See Marcham, *Revels*, p. 11, and E. K. Chambers, *R.E.S.* i [1925], 481 and 484.) Chambers suggested (ibid.) that this title might indicate *The False One* of the Beaumont and Fletcher Folio, but I hesitate to identify them. J. Q. Adams notes in his discussion of Hill's list (*Library*, Fourth Series, xx [1939], 98) Mrs. Pix's *The False Friend, or The Fate of Disobedience*, published in 1699, and Vanbrugh's *The False Friend*, acted in 1701/2 and published in 1702. Considering the late date of these two plays and the general character of the list, it seems a little more likely that the play Hill saw was the one considered in the Revels Office in Jacobean times.

The Famous History (or Tragedy or Comedy) of ——

See under next noun in such titles.

The Fatal Banquet (?)
(Lost)

This title occurs twentieth in Abraham Hill's list of manuscript plays. (See Middleton, *The Conqueror's Custom*.) The list seems to have been Hill's record of the stock of some bookseller, set down between 1677 and 1703, but it is notable that nearly all the identifiable plays and playwrights of the list are Jacobean and Caroline.

There is no record of this title elsewhere, though as J. Q. Adams points out in his discussion of Hill's list (*Library*, Fourth Series, xx [1939], 90), plays involving slaughter or poisonings at banquets are not uncommon.

The Fatal Marriage, or a Modern Lucretia (?)

MS.: B.M. MS. Egerton 1994[7].

Boas, F. S. 'A Seventeenth Century Theatrical Repertoire', *Shakespeare and the Universities* (1923), pp. 96–110.
Bullen, A. H. *A Collection of Old English Plays* (1883), ii. 425–7.
Greg, W. W. *Dramatic Documents from the Elizabethan Playhouses* (1931), pp. 337–9.
Harbage, Alfred. 'Notes on Manuscript Plays', *T.L.S.*, 20 June 1936, p. 523.

The Fatal Marriage is the seventh play in the collection brought together in Egerton 1994. Dr. Boas (loc. cit.) noted Warner's conjecture that this collection might have been one of the volumes of manuscript plays bequeathed to Dulwich College by the actor William Cartwright, Junior (see above, ii. 404–5), and Boas found a certain amount of evidence to support the conjecture.

The Fatal Marriage is one of the least revealing plays of the lot. At the head of the text is the title, 'The ffatall maryage or A second Lucreatya:', but there is no dramatis personae, no prologue, epilogue, or sign of authorship, no indication of censorship or of playhouse use. Professor Harbage suggests very tentatively (loc. cit.) that the extracts given by Bullen sound like work of the nineties, and he wonders if the name of the character 'Galeas' identifies the play with the lost *Galiaso*, whose production Henslowe records in 1594. Dr. Greg (loc. cit.) dated the hand 'c. 1630–40?'

The Florentine Friend (> 1653)
(Lost)

1653, 29 [Dec.] S.R. Richard Marriott entered as his copies a number of play titles, including 'The fflorentine freind'. (Greg, *Bibliography*, i. 62.)

The only evidence for the existence of a play of this name is Marriott's entry in the Stationers' Register. Two-thirds of the twenty-one titles in this list of plays occur nowhere else, and only three were published later under these titles, though four are known from other references. (See below, Anon., *The Woman's Law*, for the entire list.)

I see no reason for identifying this title with that of *The Florentine Ladies*, for which Thomas Jordan (q.v.) wrote a prologue.

The Florentine Ladies (?)
(Lost)

The play is known only from Thomas Jordan's publication in his *A Royal Arbor of Loyal Poesie* (1663), reissued as *A Nursery of Novelties in a Variety of Poetry* [1665?], of 'A Prologue to a Play Call'd "The Florentine Ladies", played in the night by gentlemen' and 'The Epilogue on New-Years-Day at Night'. These titles would suggest an occasional piece by amateurs, but lines 4–8 of the epilogue seem to be more appropriate for professional players:

> But if you grant us License, and appear
> Each day to see us thorow the whole year,
> Come to our Wedding, to requite your loves,
> Shew us your hands, we'l fit you all with gloves.

There seems to be no reason to identify *The Florentine Ladies* with *The Florentine Friend*, an anonymous play which Richard Marriott entered in the Stationers' Register with a number of other plays on 29 December 1653.

Florimene (> 1635)
(Lost)

Harbage, Alfred. *Cavalier Drama* (1936), pp. 18, 119.

Nicoll, Allardyce. *Stuart Masques and the Renaissance Stage* (1937), pp. 79–80, 112–13, *et passim*.

Simpson, Percy, and C. F. Bell, eds. *Designs by Inigo Jones for Masques & Plays at Court* (1924), pp. 98–101 and Plates xxviii–xxxii.

1635, 14 Dec. 'The pastorall of *Florimene*, (says Sir Henry) with the description of the sceanes and interludes, as it was sent mee by Mr. Inigo Jones, I allowed for the press, this 14 of Decemb. 1635. The pastorall is in French, and 'tis the argument only, put into English, that I have allowed to be printed.' (Adams, *Herbert*, p. 41.)

1635, 21 Dec. 'Le pastorale de *Florimene* fust representé devant le roy et la royne, le prince Charles, et le prince Palatin le 21 Decem. jour de St. Thomas, par les filles Françoise de la royne, et firent tres bien, dans la grande sale de Whitehall, aux depens de la royne.' (Adams, *Herbert*, p. 55.)

1635, 25 Dec. [i.e. 4 Jan. 1635/6 M.V.] 'On Monday evening the queen presented a most beautiful pastoral to her maids in French. She has now withdrawn to Somerset House for the devotions of Christmas. When these are over she will proceed to St. Gems to await the hour of her delivery, which should take place in a few days.' (Venetian Ambassador to the Doge and Senate, *C.S.P., Venetian, 1632–6*, p. 499.)

1635. The Argvment Of the Pastorall of *Florimene* with the Discription of the Scœnes and Intermedij. Presented By The Queenes Maiesties Commandment, before the Kings Maiesty in the Hall at White-hall, on S. Thomas day the 21. of *December M.DC.XXXV. . . . 1635.*

Florimene is not extant, and the author is unknown. Professor Harbage (*Cavalier Drama* [1936], p. 18) suggests that the Queen may have written the play herself, and this is an interesting possibility, but it does not seem to me a very likely one. Surely Herbert or the Venetian ambassador or some court gossip would have left a comment on such an unusual royal activity.

The argument of the play gives a synopsis of every scene in the five acts. At the end of each of the first four acts there is an intermedium, with a new set showing Winter, Spring, Summer, and Autumn, and appropriate symbolic action. At the end of the fifth act,

the Heavens open, and there appeare many deities, who in their songs expresse their agreements to these marriages.

The designs for the sets for this play are among the most illuminating for the layman of those left by Jones and Webb. They are described and some are reproduced by Professor Nicoll (loc. cit.) and in the catalogue of Simpson and Bell.

A Fool and Her Maidenhead Soon Parted (> 1639)
(Lost)

1639, 10 Aug. The Lord Chamberlain issued an order that no London company should presume to act any of a list of plays belonging to William Beeston and the King and Queen's Young Company (Beeston's Boys). Included in the list is 'A foole & her maydenhead soone parted'. (See above, i. 330–1.)

1653, 29 [Dec.] S.R. Richard Marriott entered a number of plays as his copies, including 'A Foole & her maiden head soone Parted'. (Greg, *Bibliography*, i. 62.)

There are only two known references to this play: in William Beeston's repertory list of 1639 and Richard Marriott's list of plays licensed for publication in 1653.

Most of the plays of Beeston's list are well known and found their way into print, but two-thirds of the twenty-one titles in Marriott's list occur nowhere else, and only three were later published under his titles, though four are known from other references. (See below, Anon., *The Women's Law*, for a discussion of Marriott's entire list.) The presence of *A Fool and Her Maidenhead Soon Parted* in Beeston's list means that the play presumably was in active repertory at the Cockpit, for Beeston was getting the plays forbidden to other London companies by the Lord Chamberlain. Unfortunately Beeston's list suggests little about date; few of the plays could have been composed for Beeston's Boys, and though most of them are compositions of the twenty years previous, one is a sixteenth-century play.

Fleay's deduction (*Biog. Chron.* ii. 336) that the play was written by Davenport because the title came between two others of Davenport's in Beeston's list is not very well supported by an analysis of the list. It is true that the plays of Beaumont and Fletcher, of Massinger, and of Shirley, which compose half the repertory, are grouped together at the beginning, but thirteen plays come between Rowley's collaborations with Middleton and his *Cupid's Vagaries* (or *Hymen's Holiday*), and A. Brome's *Cunning Lovers* comes between the only two Heywood plays in the list. R. Brome's two plays are separated by ten others. The five anonymous plays are scattered through the list, and at least one of them is not likely to have been written by either of the play-wrights to whose acknowledged titles it is adjacent.

The Fool's Masque
(Ghost title)

J. O. Halliwell[-Phillipps] lists a number of masques as 'c. 1620' or 'temp. Jac I', including 'The Fools' Masque'. (*A Dictionary of Old English Plays* [1860], p. 100.) All the titles come from the B.M. MS. Add. 10444. This manuscript is not a collection of masques, but a collection of short musical compositions, many of which use the word 'masque' in the title. (See above, under John Adson.) There is no assurance that these tunes were even attached to masques, much less that the name of the tune was the name of a masque.

The Fool Transformed (?)
(Lost)

'The Fool transformed: a Comedy' appears in a list of 'Books in the Press and now printing' which were advertised by Nathaniel Brook of the Angel in Cornhill, in E. Phillips, *The New World of English Words*, 1658. Under similar headings the title also appeared in other such lists 1658–1662. (See Greg, *Bibliography*, ii. 1000.) The advertisement must have been at least premature, for there is no evidence that the play was ever printed, though one would assume that Brook had a manuscript. Nothing else is known of a play of the title. Fleay's rather coy suggestion that it was Sir Aston Cokayne's *Trappolin Supposed a Prince* (q.v.) has nothing to recommend it.

The Fortunate Isles (?)
(Ghost title?)

Edward Archer published 'An Exact and perfect Catalogue of all the Plaies that were ever printed: together, with all the Authors names; and what are Comedies, Histories, Interludes, Masks, Pastorels, Tragedies'. This catalogue was appended to his edition of Massinger, Middleton, and Rowley's *The Old Law*, 1656. Dr. Greg shows that this catalogue of Archer's is derived from the similar list of Rogers and Ley published in the same year. (*Bibliography*, ii. 996.) One title in Archer's list is 'Fortunate Isles C.' It seems

likely that this entry is a confused duplication of the entry for
Jonson's masque of the name. (See Greg, *Bibliography*, ii. 997.)

Masque of the Four Seasons

See Anon., *Entertainment at Chirke Castle.*

The Four Sons of Amon (> 1603)
(Lost)

1623/4, 6 Jan. 'For the Prince's Company; *The Four Sons of Amon*;
being an Old Playe, and *not of a legible hand.*' (Adams, *Herbert*,
p. 27.)

The play was in existence long before 1616 and therefore does
not properly belong in this volume. It is included because of its
use in the repertory of a late Jacobean company and because the
material is not available in *The Elizabethan Stage.*

Henslowe advanced money for a play of the name—probably
the one the Prince's company had in 1623/4—to Robert Shaw in
1602/3. Shaw seems to have been acting as agent for the company
and not receiving money for his own composition. (See Greg, ed.,
Henslowe's Diary, i. 173, 176, and ii. 227.)

Dr. Greg also notes that Heywood (*An Apology for Actors*, 1612,
Shakespeare Society ed., pp. 58–59) has an anecdote about a
performance of the play by English comedians in Amsterdam.

It was probably this play which Prince Charles's (I) company
took to Sir Henry Herbert for licensing in 1623/4. Sir Henry
does not say that the play had been revised. It might have been
brought to him because it was not a part of the regular repertory
of the Prince's company (which did not derive from the troupe for
which Henslowe bought the play), but had recently been secured
from some unknown source.

Fratrum Discordia Felix sive Stanislaus Fuga Victor
(May 1640)
(Lost)

McCabe, William H. 'Notes on the St. Omers College Theatre',
Phil. Quart. xvii (1938), 225–39.
—— 'The Play-List of the English College of St. Omers 1592–
1762', *Revue de littérature comparée*, xvii (1937), 355–75.

The play was performed at the Jesuit College for English boys
at St. Omers in May 1640. Father McCabe notes that the subject is

'the boy St. Stanislaus Kostka, S.J. (1550–1568) and his persecution by his brother in Vienna'. ('Play-List', p. 367.)

Fraus Pia (< 1640)

MS.: B.M. Sloane 1855.

Smith, G. C. Moore. 'Notes on Some English University Plays', *Mod. Lang. Rev.* iii (1907–8), 155–6.

Professor Moore Smith thought the play clearly a university production, but he could not be sure whether it belonged to Oxford or Cambridge. He noted a reference to Smectymnuus in the prologue which established a date not earlier than 1640, and near the end of the play a reference to an amnesty that he thought might indicate a date in or after 1660.

The French Schoolmaster (?)
(Lost)

Nothing is known of a play of this name save its advertisement. In the edition of *The Wits*, Part I, 1662, a number of books sold by Henry Marsh are advertised. In the list of 'Comedies, and Tragedies' is 'The French School-master, a Comedy. 4'. (See Greg, *Bibliography*, ii. 1008.) The play may not belong to the period before 1642.

Fucus Histriomastix

See Robert Ward.

Fuimus Troes, or The True Trojans

See Jasper Fisher.

The Furies' Masque
(Ghost title)

J. O. Halliwell[-Phillipps] lists a number of masques as 'c. 1620' or 'temp. Jac I', or 'about 1624', including 'The Furies' Masque'. (*A Dictionary of Old English Plays* [1860], p. 105.) All the titles come from the B.M. MS. Add. 10444. This manuscript is not a collection of masques, but a collection of short musical compositions, many of which use the word 'masque' in the title. (See above, under John Adson.) There is no assurance that these tunes were even attached to masques, much less that the name of the tune was the name of a masque.

Geminus Alcides (7 February 1639/40)
(Lost)

McCabe, William H. 'Notes on the St. Omers College Theatre', *Philol. Quart.* xvii (1938), 225–39.

—— 'The Play-List of the English College of St. Omers, 1592–1762', *Revue de littérature comparée*, xvii (1937), 355–75.

A play of this name concerned with Loyola and Xavier, 'monstrorum per orbem terrae renascentium domitores ac christianae pietatis vindices', was acted at the Jesuit College for English boys at St. Omers on 7 February 1639/40. Father McCabe says that it was 'the first of a series of seven plays for the centenary of the Society of Jesus, all based on its history'. ('Play-List', p. 366.)

The General (1636–40 ?)
(Lost?)

Part of James Shirley's duties while he was attached to Ogilby's Dublin theatre (1636–40) was evidently the writing of prologues and epilogues for the company's productions—his own plays as well as those of others. Eight of these prologues for other men's plays he published with ten prologues and epilogues for his own plays in *Poems &c.*, 1646. One prologue is entitled '*To a Play there*, [i.e., in Ireland] *called the* Generall'. Whether this play is a lost anonymous piece or an early form of Roger Boyle's tragi-comedy *The General* (q.v.) is a matter of dispute.

A Gentleman, No Gentleman, A Metamorphosed Courtier (?)
(Lost)

This title is twenty-seventh in the list of manuscript plays found among the papers of Abraham Hill. (See Middleton, *The Conqueror's Custom*.) The list seems to have been Hill's record of some bookseller's stock, set down between 1677 and 1703, but it is notable that nearly all the identifiable plays and playwrights of the list are Jacobean or Caroline.

The listing of this title differs from all but two others in Hill's list of fifty-one, for here he mentions the names of certain characters in the play:

> a Gentleman no Gentleman a metamorphosed Courtier
> Actors Eustace, frampole, friswood &c

As J. Q. Adams points out in his discussion of the list (*Library*, Fourth Series xx [1939], 92), Hill's recording of the names of certain characters suggests that he examined the manuscript of this play with some additional care. Unfortunately his extra facts do not indicate the date or identity of the play.

Presumably *A Metamorphosed Courtier* was the sub-title of the play.

George a Greene (> 1593)

Chambers, E. K. *The Elizabethan Stage*, iv. 14–15.

1639, 10 Aug. 'George a greene' is included in a list of plays protected by the Lord Chamberlain for the King and Queen's Young Company at the Cockpit. (See above, i. 330–1.)

The play was already old in 1593. It is included here because of the evidence of its currency in 1639 which does not appear in Chambers's account. *George a Greene* seems a very old-fashioned play for the smart young company at the Phoenix or Cockpit in 1639.

Gesta Graiorum

See Anon., *Mountebanks, The First Antimasque of.*

[Ghismonda, or Tancred and Ghismonda] (< 1623)

MS.: B.M. MS. Add. 34312.

Edition: Herbert G. Wright, ed., *Ghismonda, A Seventeenth-Century Tragedy* (1944).

Bentley, G. E. [Review of Wright ed. *Ghismonda*] *J.E.G.P.* xlvi (1947), 109–12.
Brooks, Harold F. [Review of Wright ed. *Ghismonda*] *R.E.S.* xxiii (1947), 174–5.
Greg, W. W. *Dramatic Documents from the Elizabethan Playhouses* (1931), p. 356.
Orsini, Napoleone. *Studii sul Rinascimento italiano in Inghilterra* (1937), pp. 60–73.
Wright, Herbert G. 'The Date and Authorship of *Ghismonda*', *R.E.S.* xxiii (1947), 358.

The play in the B.M. MS. is without title; it has been called variously *Ghismonda* and *Tancred and Ghismonda*, from the principal characters. The epilogue indicates that the author contemplated performance, but there is no evidence of production, and the play has the character of closet drama: the stage directions are of the literary type, and the management of the action is very awkward.

The source of the play is the story of Guiscardo and Ghismonda, the first told on the fourth day in the *Decameron*, and Mr. Wright treats at length the use of the story in European drama. (Ed. cit., pp. 8–113.) He cites evidence that the unknown author used the English translation of 1620, and he found further evidence of the date of the play in the description of Glausamond in the dramatis personae as 'a chronomasticall courtier'. Chronomastix is Jonson's name for George Wither in *Time Vindicated* (q.v.), which was produced at court in 1622/3 and published immediately.

In his edition Mr. Wright assumes that the play is of the Restoration period because he thinks a reference to Indians as sun-worshippers must derive from *The Indian Emperor* or *The Queen*; he wisely abandoned this position in his note in *The Review of English Studies*. He notes several apparent borrowings from *Othello*.

The other manuscripts in the volume of which the play is a part furnish clues to date and authorship which could be followed up more rigorously than Mr. Wright did. The volume carries the book-plate of Sir John Dolben, Bt., of Northamptonshire. The first four items (the play is eighth and last) are dated, or closely related to material so dated, 1642, 1595, 1628, and 1644, and the seventh, 1621. The fifth item is part of a sermon which the B.M. MS. catalogue says was preached in Northamptonshire by John Dolben, who was Bishop of Rochester, 1666, and Archbishop of York, 1683–6. Another member of the Dolben family, David Dolben, was Bishop of Bangor, 1631–3. (Wright ed., pp. 3–4.)

These episcopal Dolbens are interesting because the verso of the last leaf of the play, which carries the epilogue on the recto, bears the inscription, 'Scriptum p Capellanum tuum deuinct—& deuot-issimum'. This chaplain could have been either the author or the copyer of the play, but Mr. Wright did not get far with his investigation of hands. He noted that David Dolben had a chaplain named Hugh Williams and that John Dolben had one named Leonard Welsted. Wright notes that the ideas and interests in the play would seem to be compatible with those of an ecclesiastic, but, unfortunately for such reasoning, so would the ideas and interests in many plays not written by chaplains. And several seventeenth-century academic plays written by men who became chaplains could scarcely be called 'fitting' to their later calling.

The hand of the manuscript is a rough one which Dr. Greg dated 'c. 1600?' while Dr. Robin Flower thought that 'the script is of the latter part of the century'.

The Ghost, or the Woman Wears the Breeches (1640?)

1653. The Ghost Or The Woman wears the Breeches. A Comedy Written in the Year MDCXL . . . 1653.

The title-page statement of the date of the play may be true, but one hesitates to accept it as proof of a regular theatre production of 1640. The play seems too crude for private theatres, yet the line in the prologue, ' *You are welcome Gallants to a merry Ghost*', and those in the epilogue:

> *We*
> *Will dress our Scenes with various novelty,*
> *And teach you wit enough for eighteen pence*
> *Above the reach of the Common Councils sense.*

surely do not apply to performances at a public theatre. One wonders if it could have been prepared for surreptitious performance after the closing of the theatres and published with a careful disclaimer on the title-page? The opening lines of the epilogue might fit such a performance:

> *Tis done without* Amen, *or superstition,*
> *Popes* Bull, *or the Committees inquisition:*
> *What think ye now of Plays? Abominable:*
> *Or is't 'cause you want wit to unfold a Fable,*
> *Pick out the Allegory, drive the sense*
> *Where the Plot aims it: that your benevolence*
> *Should clap us, and our mouths up. Confess, confess;*
> *You would be something, and 'gainst Plays you press,*
> *To be prickt down as States-men, not because*
> *You do conceive um hurtfull, but will make Laws,*
> *To undo the Gallants pastime of the Land:*
> *Beats down because you cannot understand.*

Yet these lines might also be apt at the Blackfrairs or Salisbury Court in 1640/1, after the inhabitants of the parishes of St. Anne's, Blackfriars, St. Martin's, Ludgate, and St. Bride's—in the first and last of which the two private theatres were situated—had petitioned the House of Commons against the playhouses in their parishes. (See above, i. 64.) The anti-Scots propaganda in the play would have found sympathetic hearers either in 1640/1 or after the closing of the theatres.

Gigantomachia, or Work for Jupiter (1600–20?)

MS.: Folger Shakespeare Library MS. 2203.1, fols. 186–200.

This short play of 400 or 500 lines in ten scenes is preserved in
the same commonplace book—dated *c.* 1600–20 by the Folger
staff—as *A Christmas Messe* (q.v.), and it is similar in character
to that piece. *A Christmas Messe* is dated 1619, and various
allusions show that it was prepared for a college celebration (at
Cambridge?).

Gigantomachia is also a celebration of the Christmas season, as
the opening speech of the Knave of Clubs, acting as chorus, shows:

> What are ye sate soe close? 'tis wel done, wel done;
> Yet J could wish, your cardinge still had held on:
> Christmas once past, you scorne the knaue of Clubs,
> J am thrust out of dores, those churlish Chubs
> The boyes within there, bid me seeke my fate,
> Tel me that cardes are almost out of date;
> Jndeed the first three knaues are, J confesse,
> But J, know, J, the chiefest of the messe,
> Doe purpose for to shew yee one more boute,
> Or two, yfayth, ere christmas once goe out:

The action of the play is broad farce, recounting the fight of the
gods against the giants 'Bounc-bigge', 'Thunder-thwart', 'Bumb-
crack', 'Thumpapace', &c. In the battle the giants carry their
hills, 'Olympus', 'Pelion', 'Ossa', &c., apparently for throwing.

The burlesque spirit of all this is similar to that of other exube-
rant undergraduate shows like the anonymous *Christmas Messe*
and *The Christmas Ordinary*, and Thomas Randolph's *Aristippus*
and his *Salting* (qq.v.), but there are no recognizable college
allusions, unless 'The boyes within there' of the Knave of Clubs'
opening speech be one. One would guess this Christmas celebration,
then, to be a college show, perhaps a Cambridge product, as other
items in the commonplace book are. Since there seem to be no
datable allusions in the piece, one must fall back on the approximate dating of the whole commonplace book—*c.* 1600–20.

The Gypsy

The play called '*The Gipsye*', which Sir Henry Herbert recorded
as performed at court by the Cockpit company in 1623, was
evidently Middleton and Rowley's *The Spanish Gypsy* (q.v.)

Gonsalvus Sylveira (1640)
(Lost)

McCabe, William H. 'Notes on the St. Omers College Theatre',
Phil. Quart. xvii (1938), 225–39.
—— 'The Play-List of the English College of St. Omers 1592–
1762', *Revue de littérature comparée*, xvii (1937), 355–75.

The play was performed in the Jesuit College for English boys
at St. Omers on an unspecified day in 1640. Father McCabe
identifies Sylveira as 'a Jesuit missionary martyred in South
Africa in 1561'. ('Play-List', p. 367.)

The Gossips' Brawl, or The Women Wear the Breeches
(c. 1654)

1655. The Gossips Braule, Or, The Women weare the Breeches. A
Mock Comedy . . . 1655.

Because of the almost identical sub-titles, *The Gossips' Brawl*
and the anonymous *The Ghost* (q.v.) have been sometimes identified. They are quite distinct. *The Gossips' Brawl* is a short one-
scene piece of six pages, a scolding match between whores in an
ale-house.

The Governor

See Cornelius Formido.

Grammercy Wit (> 1621)
(Lost)

1621, 30 Dec. '2º Marcii. A warrant for allowance of xx^tie nobles
for one play acted by Ellisworth and his fellowes late servaunts
to Queene Anne and now the Companie of the Revells the play
called gramarcie witt on of 30th of December *1621* and 3^li 6^s 8^d
by way of reward.' (MS. 515, Inner Temple Library, as reprinted
by J. T. Murray, *English Dramatic Companies* [1910], ii. 192–3.)

The play is known only from the payment for a court performance recorded in the Lord Chamberlain's book preserved in the
Inner Temple Library. The acting company was the remnant of
the old Queen Anne's men, who were acting at the Red Bull in
1621 as the Company of the Revels. (See above, i. 165–7.) This
troupe continued to act some—probably many—of the plays
formerly belonging to Queen Anne's men. (See above, i. 174–5.)
Consequently *Grammercy Wit* may have been written long before
1621.

The Great Cham (?)

MS.: Folger Shakespeare Library MS. 5.28.45 (temporary number).

This manuscript fragment is entitled:

A stately Tragedy contayninge the ambitious life and death of the great Cham The inchantments of Bagous the Brachman wth the straunge fortunes of Roxen the Captiuity release and death of his brother Manzoc the Turchestan King and happy Fortunes of the Sophy of Persia with the loue of Bargandell his sonne.

The manuscript consists of two leaves only. In the Sotheby sale of Sir Israel Gollancz's manuscripts on 24 April 1945 it was catalogued as '270 JACOBEAN DRAMA . . . contains a reference to tobacco'. So far as I can see, the tobacco reference is the only reason for calling *The Great Cham* Jacobean, for it could be earlier or later than the time of James I.

It had been catalogued for the earlier Sotheby sale of 12 April 1927 as 'the fragment of an unusual burlesque masque', and that catalogue suggests that the collection of which it is a part may well have been assembled by James Wright (1642–1713). *The Great Cham* is certainly not a masque. As for burlesque, the style is inflated and the tone of the prologue ambiguous, but there is not enough in these sixty-one lines to demonstrate that the attitude of the author was mocking rather than naïvely solemn.

The manuscript consists of only the first sixty-one lines of the tragedy. There is no dramatis personae, but the piece begins with a prologue which is literary rather than theatrical in character.

One odd characteristic of the manuscript is the number at the bottom of each page that records the total number of lines from the beginning. Character names are written in the left-hand margin, and the stage directions are boxed.

The Greeks and Trojans (?)
(Lost?)

No play of the name is known, but Edmund Gayton refers to it twice:

Our *Don* is not so much transported with *Belianis* his Blowes as a passionate Butcher of our Nation was, who being at the Play, called *the Greeks and Trojans*, and seeing *Hector* over-powred by *Mirmydons*, got upon the Stage, and with his good Battoone tooke over the true *Trojans* part so stoutly, that he routed the *Greeks*, and rayled upon them loudly for a company of cowardly slaves to assault one man with

so much odds. He strooke moreover such an especiall acquaintance
with *Hector*, that for a long time *Hector* could not obtaine leave of him
to be kill'd, that the Play might go on; and the cudgelled *Mirmydons*
durst not enter againe, till *Hector*, having prevailed upon his unexpected second, return'd him over the Stage againe into the yard from
whence he came. (*Pleasant Notes upon Don Quixot* [1654], p. 3.)

And in a later passage (see above, ii. 690–1) Gayton recommends
plays which are suitable on holidays when the crowd may get out
of hand if they are not pleased:

some tearing Tragædy full of fights and skirmishes: As the *Guelphs*
and *Guiblins*, *Greeks* and *Trojans*, or the three *London Apprentices*.
(*Pleasant Notes*, p. 271.)

Professor G. F. Reynolds suggested that *The Greeks and Trojans*
might have been Heywood's play, *The Iron Age* (*The Staging of
Elizabethan Plays at the Red Bull Theater, 1605–1625* [1940], p. 10),
in which Hector's death is staged, which Heywood says was very
popular, and which might be expected to please a holiday crowd.

Even though Gayton did not write until 1654, there is no
assurance that *The Greeks and Trojans* was a late play, for other
pieces which he recommends for holiday productions are *Tamburlaine* and *The Jew of Malta*. (See above, ii. 690–1.)

Grobiana's Nuptials

See Roger Shipman.

Guelphs and Ghibellines (?)
(Lost?)

The title is known only from Edmund Gayton's recommenda-
tion of plays that are suitable for performance in the theatres on
holidays when the crowd may get out of hand:

some tearing Tragædy full of fights and skirmishes: As the *Guelphs*
and *Guiblins*, *Greeks* and *Trojans*, or the three *London Apprentices*.
(*Pleasant Notes upon Don Quixot* [1654], p. 271. See above, ii. 690–1,
for more of the passage.)

The title may be invented, or it may be another name for some
extant play, but most of the titles in this passage are recognizable.

Guido Varvicensis (9 February 1622/3)
(Lost)

McCabe, William H. 'Notes on the St. Omers College Theatre',
   Phil. Quart. xvii (1938), 225–39.

McCabe, William H. 'The Play-List of the English College of St. Omers, 1592–1762', *Revue de littérature comparée*, xvii (1937), 355–75.

The play was performed in the English College at St. Omers on 9 February 1622/3. ('Play-List', p. 361.) Father McCabe says that it dealt with Guy of Warwick's contest with the giant Colbrand.

Gull upon Gull
(Ghost title)

In Act v, Scene 1, of Middleton's *The Mayor of Quinborough, or Hengist, King of Kent* (q.v.), the rascals, pretending to be a troupe of players, give to the mayor a list of plays from which he may choose. One of these titles is *Gull upon Gull*, and it has several times been listed as a lost play. It is fairly clear, however, that all the titles are fictitious, mostly puns on the situation of the rascals and the gullible mayor. Even *The Wild Goose Chase* probably refers to the proverbial expression and not to Fletcher's play of the name.

The Tragical History, Admirable Achievements, and Various Events of Guy of Warwick (?)

Crane, R. S. 'The Vogue of *Guy of Warwick*', *P.M.L.A.* xxx (1915), 125–94.

1618, 14 Oct. 'The next day I came to *London*, and obscurely coming within Moregate, I went to a house and borrowed money: And so I stole backe againe to *Islington*, to the signe of the Maydenhead, staying till Wednesday, than my friends came to meete me, who knew no other, but that Wednesday was my first comming: where with all loue I was entertained with much good cheere: and after Supper we had a play of the life and death of *Guy of Warwicke*, played by the Right Honourable the Earle of *Darbie* his men. And so on the Thursday morning being the fifteenth of October, I came home to my house in *London*. (*The Pennyles Pilgrimage*, 1618, in *All the Workes of John Taylor the Water Poet*, N₄ᵛ; the account describes his journey to Scotland in 1618.)

1619/20, 15 Jan. S.R. 'Iohn Trundle Entred for his copie . . . A Play Called the life and Death of Guy of Warwicke written by Iohn Day and Tho: Decker.' (Greg, *Bibliography*, i. 31.)

1620, 13 Dec. S.R. 'Tho: Langley Assigned ouer vnto him by Iohn

Trundle . . . [1] The Play of Guy of warwicke.' Greg, *Bibliography*, i. 32.)
1661. The Tragical History, Admirable Atchievments and various events of Guy Earl of Warwick. A Tragedy Acted very Frequently with great Applause, By his late Majesties Servants. Written by B. J. . . . 1661.

There is no certainty as to how many different plays about Guy of Warwick are involved in the entries above. The only extant text is that of 1661. Certainly this play was not written by Ben Jonson, as the initials on the title-page were probably intended to imply, and Bullen thought it too bad to be the one written by Dekker and Day. (*The Works of John Day* [1881], i. 11.) Either the Day and Dekker play, or the play of 1661, or still a third piece about the popular Guy of Warwick, could have been the one John Taylor saw.

The play published in 1661 is a crude piece which probably was never acted by the King's company, as the title-page says. Since all the material on which it is based was available before the end of the sixteenth century (see Crane, op. cit., pp. 162–5), it seems to me more likely to be an Elizabethan or early Jacobean play than a later Jacobean or Caroline one. It is not considered, however, in *The Elizabethan Stage*.

Great confusion about the date of *The Tragical History of Guy of Warwick* has been caused by the imprimatur found in one copy of the play: 'Imprimatur. April. 6. 1639. Math. Clay', on the basis of which various scholars have asserted that there was an edition of 1639 and that the play was entered in the Stationers' Register in that year, neither of which conclusions is true. Greg has now found (*Bibliography*, ii. 916–17) that this imprimatur leaf has been bound in with the Dyce copy of the play in error, and that it really belongs in the 1640 quarto of Thomas Nabbes's *The Bride*.

Dr. Greg thinks (ibid.) that the Stationers' Register entry to Trundle and the transfer to Langley probably refer to the play John Taylor saw fifteen months earlier in 1618. His further suggestion that the *Guy of Warwick* referred to by a character in Nabbes's *Covent Garden* was probably also the 1618 play is compatible with the country setting for that play, but the allusion is such that almost any kind of entertainment involving Guy of Warwick could be intended. (See above, i. 227–8.)

Professor Crane said in his article in 1915 (op. cit., p. 162, n. 70) that an edition of the play was to be published shortly in *Materialien*, but so far as I can find it has never appeared.

Haeresis Triumphata sive B. Ignatius Societatis Jesu Fundator (? August 1640)

(Lost)

McCabe, William H. 'Notes on the St. Omers College Theatre', *Phil. Quart.* xvii (1938), 225–39.

—— 'The Play-List of the English College of St. Omers, 1592–1762', *Revue de littérature comparée*, xvii (1937), 355–75.

The play was performed at the Jesuit College for English boys at St. Omers. Father McCabe notes that it was the climax of the series of seven plays for the centenary of the Society of Jesus. ('Play-List', pp. 366–7.)

[*Hannibal*] (?)

MS.: Bodleian Library, Malone 531.

Bodleian MS. Malone 531 contains a fragment of a Latin comedy, an English bidding prayer that Madan thought was used before the University of Oxford by a Magdalen man about 1610–20, and a sermon in the same hand as the bidding prayer. (F. Madan, *A Summary Catalogue of Western Manuscripts in the Bodleian Library at Oxford* [1897], iv. 432.) The play has no title, but was dubbed Hannibal', after the chief character, by Madan. It consists of one act, one scene of the second act, and two lines of the next scene. At this point the scribe has simply broken off. Madan said that the piece was 'of the latter part of the sixteenth century?', but he offered no evidence.

The Haymakers' Masque

(Ghost title)

J. O. Halliwell[-Phillipps] lists a number of masques as 'c. 1620' or 'temp. Jac I', including 'The Haymaker's Masque'. (*A Dictionary of Old English Plays* [1860], p. 114.) All the titles come from the B.M. MS. Add. 10444. This manuscript is not a collection of masques, but a collection of short musical compositions, many of which use the word 'masque' in the title. (See above, under John Adson.) There is no assurance that these tunes were even attached to masques, much less that the name of the tune was the name of the masque.)

The Tragedy of Heildebrand (?)
(Lost?)

The title is known only from its occurrence in Edmond Malone's long list of plays not known to have been printed. His sources for many of the titles are known, but not for this one; it is not found in Greg's list of plays that were advertised but are not known to have been printed. (See Malone, *Variorum* [1821], ii. 438–9.)

Henry the Una . . . (> 1620)
(Lost)

c. 1619–20. 'Henrye the vna. . . .' appears in a list of plays on waste paper of the Revels Office, probably dating about 1619 or 1620. It has been plausibly suggested that the plays of the list were being considered for court performance. (See Marcham, *Revels*, p. 15, and Chambers, *R.E.S.* i [1925], 484.)

This mutilated title—whatever it may have been in its perfect form, the last three letters are doubtful—is known only from the Revels list. The particular list in which it occurs seems to be in the hand of a copyist and book-keeper of the King's company (see R. C. Bald, ed., *Hengist, King of Kent; or The Mayor of Queenborough by Thomas Middleton* [1938], p. xxi, n. 1), and this fact might suggest that *Henry the Una . . .* was a King's men's play, but unfortunately other plays in the list in his hand, like *All's Lost by Lust* and *A Fair Quarrel*, belonged to other companies.

Hermophus
(Ghost title)

See George Wilde, *Eumorphus*.

Heteroclitanomalonomia (1613)

MS.: Folger Shakespeare Library MS. 2203.1, fols. 118–33.

The play is dated 1613 in the manuscript and therefore does not belong in the period treated in these volumes; it is briefly noted here because it does not appear in *The Elizabethan Stage*.

Heteroclitanomalonomia is a short play in the same Folger MS. as *Boot and Spur*, *A Christmas Messe*, and *Gigantomachia* (qq.v.). The general character of the piece is indicated in the prologue:

> Wee purpose to p[re]sent vpon o^r Stage
> A Battaile wch was fought before o^r age:

> The Grammer kings both greedie of commaunde
> Each in the cheefest place of speech would stand
> Till Lillie setts betweene them both a barr, *etc.*

The college environment is established by the lines in the epilogue:

> ffor when we tooke in hand this toy, we ment
> By the defectives freshmen to p[re]sent,
> wch daylie like irregulers rebell
> Ageinst vs seniors, pray Sirs marke me well.

The History of ——

See the next word in such titles.

Honour in the End (1624)
(Lost)

1624, 21 May. 'For the Palsgrave's Company; a Playe, called, *Honour in the End.*' (Adams, *Herbert*, p. 28.)

1658–61. In certain publications of these years, e.g., *The Mysteries of Love and Eloquence* and *Naps upon Parnassus*, this title is listed in advertisements of books ready for printing. See discussion below.

When Sir Henry Herbert licensed *Honour in the End* for the Palsgrave's company, that troupe was engaged in a desperate attempt at survival after the destruction of their repertory in the Fortune fire of 9 December 1621. (See above, i. 141–2 and 149–51.) Most of the phenomenal number of plays licensed for them in this period are now lost, probably an indication of the inferior quality of the plays.

Honour in the End did not disappear quite so promptly as some of the others, however, for the publisher, Nathaniel Brook, advertised it in a list of '*Books in the Presse, and ready for Printing*' at the end of his edition of Edward Phillips's *New World of English Words*, 1658: '8. Honour in the end: a Comedy.' Brook inserted this list again at the end of his edition of Phillips's *Mysteries of Love and Eloquence*, 1658, and of *Naps upon Parnassus*, 1658, and in the 1660 supplement to William London's *Catalogue of the Most Vendible Books in England*, 1658, the title, apparently copied from Brook's list, appears as 'Honour in the end 4°.' As Halliwell noticed (*A Dictionary of Old English Plays*,

p. 122), the play, '8 Honour in the end, a Comedy', is also advertised as in the press at the end of *Wit and Drollery*, 1661.

These advertisements must indicate at least that a manuscript
of the play was still extant in 1658. How serious the intentions to
print were is problematical. William London's '4°', for instance,
is the usual advertiser's fraud; he lists eight consecutive plays
this way, all in the order they had appeared in Brook's list, and
none ever known to have been printed. If the intention to print
was serious, it is odd that the play was not licensed in the Stationers' Register.

The House Is Haunted (> 1620)
(Lost)

c. 1619–20. 'the House is Haunte . . .' appears in a list of plays on
   waste paper of the Revels Office, probably dating about 1619 or
   1620. It has been plausibly suggested that the plays of the list
   were being considered for court performance. (See Marcham,
   Revels, p. 15, and Chambers, *R.E.S.* i [1925], 484.)

This slightly mutilated title—presumably only the 'd' of the
last word is missing—is known only from the Revels list. The
particular list in which it occurs seems to be in the hand of a
copyist and book-keeper of the King's company (see R. C. Bald,
ed., *Hengist, King of Kent; or The Mayor of Queenborough by Thomas
Middleton* [1938], p. xxi, n. 1), and this fact might suggest that
The House Is Haunted was a King's men's play, but unfortunately
other plays in this list in his hand, like *All's Lost by Lust* and *A
Fair Quarrel*, belonged to other companies.

Humour in the End

A ghost title from Fleay's misreading (*Biog. Chron.* ii. 326) of
Honour in the End (q.v.).

The Hypochondriac, or The Turmoil of Love (?)
(Fragment)

MS.: B.M. Sloane 1863, fols. 44ᵃ–69ᵇ.

The manuscript book of which *The Hypochondriac* is a part is a
miscellaneous notebook. The first part consists of chemical notes
and recipes; the second part, mostly in the book reversed, is
chiefly arithmetic. *The Hypochondriac* is written on scattered
pages and half-pages in the arithmetic section. It is confused, and
the hand is often difficult, but *The Hypochondriac* appears to be

notes for a play and odd speeches, rather than fragments of a once complete play. One note on 49[a] reads: 'This to be his Mans plot. S[r] T is persuaded to faine a resolu[ti]on of kil himself w[ch] may win his M[rs] fauour.' The title appears in the margin of 44[b] turned lengthwise: 'The Hypochondriake / or / The Turmoyles of Love.'

Though I saw no clear indication of date, the hand could be mid-seventeenth century, and certain notes would be compatible with such a date, i.e. reference to 'some 300[1] in old Jacobuses', on 54[a]. Some accounts dated 'Lond: March y 1st 59' are in a hand similar to, if not identical with, that of the play scraps.

Impatient Grissell (?)
(Ghost title?)

Edward Archer published 'An Exact and perfect Catalogue of all the Plaies that were ever printed; together, with all the Authors names; and what are Comedies, Histories, Interludes, Masks, Pastorels, Tragedies'. This catalogue was appended to his edition of Massinger, Middleton, and Rowley's *The Old Law*, 1656. Dr. Greg shows that this catalogue of Archer's is derived from the similar list of Rogers and Ley published in the same year. (*Bibliography*, ii. 996.) One title in Archer's list is 'Impatient Grissell C.' No such play is known, and the entry is probably the result of another confusion by Archer, but one cannot be sure.

In Duc Reducem, or A Welcome from the Isle of Rhé

This title has sometimes been listed as that of an entertainment or play. The piece, now in the Huntington Library, is not dramatic, but consists of a set of satiric verses on Buckingham. The same verses, under the title 'The Duke Return'd Againe', have been printed from a B.M. MS. by Frederick W. Fairholt, *Poems and Songs Relating to George Villiers, Duke of Buckingham; and His Assassination by John Felton August 23, 1628*, 1850 (Percy Society Publications, vol. xxix), pp. 19–24. Besides the ones at the Huntington and the British Museum, there are several manuscript copies in the Bodleian Library.

An Induction for the House (November 1630)
(Lost)

This title is known only from its occurrence in a bill presented by the King's men for performances at court in 1630 and 1630/1.

The fifth item is: 'The 5 of November, An Induction for the Howse, And The Madd Louer.' (See above, i. 27–28.)

The entry is unlike others in this bill, or in any of the other known bills for performances at court before 1642. I have suggested (see above, i. 28, n. 1) that *An Induction for the House* was probably a short house-warming piece of some kind for the newly opened royal Cockpit theatre attached to the palace in Whitehall. The first four plays listed in the bill are marked 'At [H]ampton Court', but this one and the fifteen following are marked 'At the [Co]ck-pitt'. Though the opening of that theatre has been variously dated, the King's men's bill seems to me to offer the only considerable evidence of date. (See ibid.)

The only other Jacobean or Caroline example of such a curtain-raiser that I know is Randolph's *Praeludium* (q.v.), but one would assume that there must have been others.

The Invisible Knight
(Ghost title?)

A play of this name is mentioned in the dialogue of Act II of James Shirley's *The Bird in a Cage*, published in 1633 and acted shortly before.

> Don[dolo]. Sir if you can assure vs this invisible walking, for wee are not so ignorant as wee seeme, wee ha seene the Play of the *Jnvisible Knight*, and—
> Bon[amico]. That of the Ring too, ha ye not.
> Don. Yes.
> Bon. The one was Magick, and t'other an imposture, what I doe is by Art faire and naturall. (D₃ᵛ.)

No play of this title is now known; it may be that the titles are fictitious, like those in v. 1 of Middleton's *Mayor of Quinborough*, but the situation here does not suggest it so strongly.

Iphis and Iantha, or A Marriage without a Man (?)
(Lost)

1660, 29 June. S.R. Humphrey Moseley entered as his copies a long list of plays, including:

The History of King Stephen.
Duke Humphrey. a Tragedy
Iphis & Iantha, Or a marriage without a man. a Comedy. } by Will: Shakspeare.

(Greg, *Bibliography*, i. 68–69.)

It is quite unlikely that this comedy was written by Shakespeare, for no other reference to the title is known. Presumably the story came from Ovid, but I know of no evidence of the date or authorship of the manuscript Moseley had in 1660.

The Irish Gentleman (1636–40 ?)
(Lost)

The title is known only from the prologue which James Shirley published in his *Poems &c.*, 1646, entitled 'A Prologue there [i.e. Ireland] to the *Irish Gent.*' The play clearly was not written by Shirley, as has occasionally been assumed, for the distinction between the prologues for Shirley's own plays and those for the plays of other men is clear in *Poems &c.*: the first eight prologues given there are for the plays of others, and all but one are assigned to a title or an author; the last six (four with epilogues attached) are for Shirley's own plays, and each is identified as Shirley's in the heading: 'To his own Comedy', 'to his Comedy', 'to his Tragedy', &c. Presumably *The Irish Gentleman* was produced during the period of Shirley's incumbency at the St. Werburgh Street Theatre in Dublin.

The prologue indicates nothing of the character of the play; it merely chides the audience for its failure to patronize good plays.

I know of nothing to support the suggestion (Harbage, *Annals of English Drama, 975–1700*, p. 112) that the play may have been written by Henry Burnell, except the fact that the prologue to *Landgartha* says that Burnell had written an earlier play and that nothing is known of it now.

The Irish Rebellion (1642)
(Lost)

1642, 8 June. 'Received of Mr. Kirke for another new play called *The Irishe Rebellion*, the 8 June, 1642, 2*l*.o.o.' (Adams, *Herbert*, p. 39.)

Nothing besides this entry is known of the play. It is often said to be by John Kirke, but such an assertion shows slight knowledge of Sir Henry Herbert's procedures. Plays were brought to him not by their authors, but by the managers of, or an agent for, the company that was to act the play. Kirke was apparently manager of Prince Charles's (II) company at this time. (See above, ii. 492–3.)

One would have thought the bloody outburst in Ireland too dangerous a subject for a play at this time. Perhaps Sir Henry was compensating for earlier harshness, for on the same day he records that he had burned another play which Kirke brought him to license. (See Kirke, Untitled Play, 1642.)

The Italian Night-Piece [or Night-Masque]

See Philip Massinger.

John a Green
(Ghost title?)

The title is known only from a passage in Edmund Gayton's *Pleasant Notes upon Don Quixot* [1654], p. 129:

> Behold and view the very Picture of the Salutation-Taverne re-form'd; an *Andaluzian*, and a *Manchegan* in the Spanish mode, passing Punctilios upon one another. I wonder it scap'd our Pencill men, especially when they had so many Signes to alter. A *Knight-Errant* and a Bedlam exactly drawn, in the livliest postures of the *Madrid Salutados*, would have been as magnetick and beneficiall to the house, as the Renouned pieces of *John a Green*, or *Mul-sack*.

No play of the title is now known. Gayton must have had some particular play in mind, since the whole point of his remark would seem to depend upon recognition by the reader of a popular play. It seems likely that *Mul-sack* was J. D.'s *The Knave in Grain New Vampt* (q.v.), and I should guess that *John a Green* was a title for some play of which we have records under another name, but I do not know what it is. Could Gayton have meant *George a Greene*? See *Elizabethan Stage*, iv. 14–15.

Joseph's Afflictions
(Ghost title?)

'Josephs afflictions I' appears in the list of plays advertised by Edward Archer in 1656 as 'An Exact and perfect Catalogue of all the Plaies that ever were printed', and it was taken over by Kirkman in his similar list in 1661. It is probably a misprint for another title, such as *Job's Afflictions*. (See Greg, *Bibliography*, ii. 998.) In any case, the 'I' (Interlude) probably indicates that the piece belonged to the sixteenth century.

Jovis et Junonis nuptiæ

See below, p. 1452.

Jugurtha, or The Faithless Cousin German

See William Boyle.

Jugurth, King of Numidia

See William Boyle.

Juno in Arcadia

See Anon., *Time's Triumph.*

Juno's Pastoral, or The Bonds of Peace

See Anon., *Time's Triumph.*

Kermophus
(Ghost title)

See George Wilde, *Eumorphus.*

The King and Queen's Entertainment at Richmond
(12 Sept. 1636)

Edition: W. Bang and R. Brotanek, eds., *The King and Queenes Entertainment at Richmond nach der Q 1636 in Neudruck herausgegeben (Materialien),* 1903.

Brotanek, Rudolph. *Die englischen Maskenspiele* (1902), pp. 201–2.

Elson, J. J., ed. *The Wits or Sport upon Sport* (1932), pp. 297–304 and 408–9.

Harbage, Alfred. *Cavalier Drama* (1936), pp. 195–6.

1636. The King *And* Qveenes Entertainment at *Richmond.* After Their Departvre from Oxford: In a Masque, presented by the most Illustrious Prince, *Prince* Charles Sept. 12. 1636. Oxford . . . M. DC. XXXVI.

1672. 'Wiltshire Tom, An Entertainment at Court', extracted from *The King and Queen's Entertainment at Richmond,* appears in Kirkman's collection of drolls entitled *The Wits or Sport upon Sport,* Part II, 1672. See J. J. Elson, ed., pp. 297–304.

The place and date of presentation of this masque are recorded on the title-page. The visit to Oxford mentioned there had taken place a fortnight before, at the end of August, and had been the occasion for the performance of three plays (see above, William Cartwright, *The Royal Slave*)—evidently not enough to satisfy the appetite of the Queen. The foreword of the quarto describes the genesis and character of the entertainment:

Her Majestie signifying her plesure that she would see her Sonne the most illustrious Prince in a dance; His seruants and others in the family thought it not amisse to entertain her a while with a Country dance, and some other rude ones, that might the better set off the Princes, which were made by *Simon Hopper*, and perform'd by those that undertooke them, but all this while, the disposition of them was the thing last in their thoughts; so that now of necessity a body was to be fitted to their garment, which made one in the company to shew them, that the country dance might be introduc'd by some Clownes speaking; And because most of the Interlocutors were *Wilshire* men, that country Dialect was chosen, and thus every man fitted his part to his owne fancy, and the constitution of the whole tending to a greater bulke, it came to be what it is, without any designe, but rather out of a kind of necessity vrging it.

This foreword seems to assert that the entertainment had no author in the ordinary sense, and the same suggestion of composite improvisation is found in the dedication to the Queen—especially in the word 'compacted':

> See, Madam, here, what for your sole delight
> Is rais'd of nothing to wast out this night.
> Scarse is the Author: what he meanes lesse knowne
> None will the words, none will the Musique owne.
> Yet here it is; and as o' th' world some thought
> That it by Atomes of it selfe was wrought:
> So this concurring with your high commands
> Came to be thus compacted, as it stands;
> For Princes like to Gods with vs on earth
> Project on nothing, yet produce a birth.

The foreword and the dedication taken together indicate that first the dance of the masquers was prepared to show off Prince Charles (aged six years three months), that then a country dance was added as antimasque, and that finally the dialogue of Tom, Richard, Madge, and Dorothy was added to introduce the country dances, and that this dialogue was written in dialect because the dancers were Wiltshire men. The Wiltshire men who spoke were, according to the text, 'Tho. Chefinch, Tho. Steeling. Iohn Quinne,

Iohn Foxe'. One of them, according to the stage directions, *'hauing discouer'd M. Edward Sackvile standing neere the Queene, as looking on, calls to him'*. Quite a little dialogue ensues between Tom and 'Mʳ Yedward'. Surely Master Yedward, who is usually designated as *'M. Sa.'* in the speech tags, was not Edward Sackville, fourth Earl of Dorset and Lord Chamberlain to the Queen, as has been suggested, but his second son, Edward Sackville, who would more properly be addressed as Master Edward and who could be called Master Sackville in the speech tags. The age of this boy is unknown (see Charles J. Phillips, *History of the Sackville Family* [1930], i. 379), but his elder brother, Lord Buckhurst, who became the fifth Earl, was born 16 September 1622, and in the portrait of the two boys painted in 1637, the year after the masque took place, and now at Knole, Edward is almost exactly the size of Lord Buckhurst, and the identical costumes might allow them to be taken for twins. (Ibid. i. 384 and ii. 434.) We can reasonably conjecture that Edward was close in age to his elder brother and that he could have been thirteen. Both boys took part in the masque, for the comment at the end praises them, and not for their dancing—though they were among the five masquers who appeared with the young prince—but for their acting:

> The speaking and action (*which grac'd the words*) *perform'd by my* Lord *of* Buckhurst, *and* M. Edward Sackvile, *shew'd that genuine action, was not so much confin'd to the stage, but a Gentleman might reach it, if not transcend it.*

It may be that the two young Sackvilles were also the British Captain and the Druid, the next largest parts. If so, Edward had a very large evening.

In all this I see no reason, however, for concluding, as has several times been done, that Edward Sackville, fourth Earl of Dorset, or even his second son, Edward, wrote the entertainment. Since the Earl's two sons had such a large part in the entertainment, one might conjecture that Joseph Rutter (q.v.), who was their tutor the next year and perhaps earlier, may have had a hand in writing it.

Probably the Sackvilles were very active in the preparations, for in addition to the dancing and acting of the two sons, their father, as Lord Chamberlain to the Queen, may well have made advance arrangements, and his Countess, as Governess to Prince Charles, could well have had something to do with the rehearsals of the young prince, but our only evidence as to the authorship of the words is that it was 'without any designe' and composite.

The dances, as the text states, were arranged by Simon Hopper, and the music, according to the last line of the text, and contrary to the dedication statement, '*was excellently compos'd by Master Charles Coleman*'. According to Edward F. Rimbault (ed. of Purcell's music for *Bonduca* [1842], p. 11), some of this music is preserved in the manuscripts of the Music School at Oxford.

The text records that there were six masquers: Prince Charles as Britomart, and five supporting knights: the Duke of Buckingham, Lord Francis Villiers, Lord Buckhurst, Lord Carr, and Mr. (i.e. Edward) Sackville.

Elson notes (op. cit., pp. 408–9) the similarity of the antimasque of the four Wiltshire rustics to that in Shirley's *Triumph of Peace*, published two and a half years before.

Entertainment of King Charles at Edinburgh

See William Drummond.

The Famous Tragedy of King Charles I (1649)

The play was written after the execution of the King on 30 January 1648/9. It is closet drama and not intended for production. (See Greg, *Bibliography*, ii. 799–800, and Alfred Harbage, *Cavalier Drama* [1936], pp. 179–80.)

The King's Mistress (?)
(Lost)

1653, 9 Sept. S.R. In a long list of plays which Humphrey Moseley entered as his copies occurs the title, 'The Kings Mistresse'. (Greg, *Bibliography*, i. 61.)

Nothing is known of the play save the entry in the Stationers' Register. This list of plays licensed by the great dramatic publisher Humphrey Moseley on 9 September 1653 is a puzzling one, since more than half the plays are now lost, and several others, like *Believe as You List*, *The Soddered Citizen*, and *The Inconstant Lady*, were never printed in the seventeenth century. Many of the plays in the list have alternative titles, and in some cases the alternative titles cover two plays. (See Greg, *Bibliography*, ii. 979–80.) Moseley names authors for all the plays in the list except *The Countryman*, *The King's Mistress*, and *The Politic Bankrupt, or Which Is the Best Girl*. *The King's Mistress* stands between plays by John Ford and Sir Cornelius Formido, but there seems no good reason to connect it with either author.

Dr. Greg notes (*Bibliography*, ii. 981) that there is a tune in B.M. MS. Add. 10444 called 'The King's Mistress'. Though a number of the tunes in this manuscript book have the word 'masque' in the title (see above, John Adson), I do not know that all of them should be thought to be dramatic.

The History of King Stephen (?)
(Lost)

1660, 29 June. S.R. Humphrey Moseley entered as his copies a long list of plays, including:

> The History of King Stephen. ⎫
> Duke Humphrey. a Tragedy ⎪
> Iphis & Iantha, Or a marriage ⎬ by Will: Shakspeare.
>   without a man. a Comedy. ⎭

(Greg, *Bibliography*, i. 68–69.)

It is most unlikely that *The History of King Stephen* was written by Shakespeare, for no other reference to the title is known. I know of no evidence as to the date or authorship of the manuscript that Moseley had in 1660.

The Knave in Grain New Vampt

See J. D.

The Ladies' Masque

See Anon., *The Masque of Amazons*.

Lady Alimony, or The Alimony Lady (c. 1640?; revised 1659)

Edition: *A Select Collection of Old English Plays* (Hazlitt's Dodsley), xiv (1875), 274–367.

Harbage, Alfred. *Cavalier Drama* (1936), pp. 232–3.
Nethercot, Arthur H. *Sir William D'avenant. Poet Laureate and Playwright-Manager* (1938), pp. 328, 339–40.

1659. Lady Alimony; Or, The Alimony Lady. An Excellent Pleasant New Comedy Duly Authorized, daily Acted, and frequently Followed . . . 1659.

The very odd structure of *Lady Alimony* as it is printed in the quarto of 1659 is arresting. Acts III, IV, and V are of approximately equal length; Act II is two to three times the length of any of the last three; Act I is shorter than any other, about one-fourth the length of Act II. There is no prologue at the beginning of the play, but there is a prologue before Act II which refers to the rest of the play but has no reference to Act I. The subject of Act I is quite different from that of the rest of the play, and the principal characters in it do not appear in any of the later acts. Act I, in fact, is really an induction about the London theatrical situation and has very little to do with the rest of the play.

It seems to me fairly clear that, as Dr. Greg suggested (*Bibliography*, ii. 903), the piece really consists of an induction, a prologue, and five acts, but that Acts I and II (mistakenly or deliberately) have been run together as Act II and the Induction printed as Act I, to make *Lady Alimony* look like an ordinary play without an induction.

In the induction—i.e. Act I as printed in 1659—a current London theatrical situation is set out, though not all the allusions and allegations can be fully understood now. Professor Nethercot has shown (loc. cit.) that there are obvious references to William Davenant as poet laureate, author of *Madagascar*, and traveller, and that there are allusions to special features in Davenant's production of his play, *The Cruelty of the Spaniards in Peru*, in 1658, and apparently to his use of actresses on his stage. Other allusions are clearly intended as references to individuals and episodes in a contemporary theatrical feud, though more information is needed for precise identification. Professor Nethercot suggests that Davenant's opponents, the company producing the play, may have been John Rhodes's young company at the Cockpit.

These allusions (most inescapably the clear references to *The Cruelty of the Spaniards in Peru*) show that the lines were written in the year of publication, 1659, or possibly late in the preceding year. It is notable, however, that all these allusions occur in the Induction, the printing of which as Act I in the 1659 edition distorts the play. Was *Lady Alimony* a Caroline play with a new induction written in 1658 or 1659 for a revival, perhaps by Rhodes's company?

The evidence is not conclusive, but there is enough to indicate that the play may have had some such history. First, the odd mishandling of the Induction by the printer suggests that the state of the manuscript was confusing and that he did not see how to handle the new material. Then the frequent allusions in the Induction to theatrical affairs just before the Restoration and the total absence of such allusions in the body of the play suggest different dates or different hands, or both. Again, the whole subject of the play, which is not mentioned in the Induction, is the Platonic love-fad, a courtly interest of the thirties. In iv. 2 there are also references to the popular resorts of the thirties, the Spring Garden and the Sparagus Garden; the latter is possibly also an allusion to Richard Brome's popular play of the name (q.v.) in 1635. Finally the number of boy actors required for production of the piece—six ladies and two boys all prominent on stage in the same scenes, and later a countrywoman and a vintress—suggests a boy company with the make-up of the King and Queen's Young Company, sometimes called Beeston's Boys, of 1636/7-42. (See above, i. 324-35.) The two choral songs, one in iii. 3 and one in iv. 3, also suggest boys and a resemblance to Brome's semi-musical, *The Jovial Crew* (q.v.), which was produced by this company in 1641.

All this falls far short of proof that *Lady Alimony* was a production of the late thirties or early forties, perhaps for Beeston's Boys, with an induction, and perhaps revisions, in 1658 or 1659, but that interpretation of the evidence seems to me the least unsatisfactory one. The designation of Benhadad as ' a Quaker' at the head of iii. 3 could be a late addition or an earlier use of the word for the foreign sect. (See *O.E.D.*) Benhadad has only one speech, he does not appear in the dramatis personae, and he seems to act like a Puritan.

Fleay's assignment of the entire play to 1640 or 1641 (*A Chronicle History of the London Stage* [1890], pp. 357-8) is confused because he did not see that the Induction contains allusions to *The Cruelty of the Spaniards in Peru* and is probably later than the rest of the play, but he did recognize allusions to Davenant. (Ibid., p. 348.)

Edward Phillips's absurd attribution of the play to Greene and Lodge (*Theatrum Poetarum* [1675], Part ii, pp. 161-2) scarcely needs any refutation in view of the subject and the allusions in the play, but it has been carelessly repeated once or twice in the twentieth century.

The Law Case (> 1653)
(Lost)

1653, 29 [Dec.] S.R. Richard Marriott entered a number of plays as his copies, including 'The Law Case'. (Greg, *Bibliography*, i. 62.)

The only evidence for the existence of a play of this name is Marriott's entry in the Stationers' Register. Two-thirds of the twenty-one titles in this list of plays occur nowhere else, and only three were published later under the names there given, though four of the titles are known from other references. (See below, Anon., *The Woman's Law*, for the entire list.)

The title brings to mind Webster's *The Devil's Law Case* (q.v.), but that play had been printed for John Grismand in 1623, and it does not seem likely that Marriott would have entered it in the Stationers' Register in 1653.

The History of Lewis II, King of France
(Ghost title)

A ghost title from Fleay's misprint (*Biog. Chron.* ii. 338) for *The History of Louis the Eleventh, King of France* (q.v.).

The Life and Death of Guy of Warwick

See Anon., *Guy of Warwick*.

Lisander and Calista

See Fletcher, *The Lovers' Progress*.

The London Chanticleers (?)

Edition: *A Select Collection of Old English Plays* (Hazlitt's Dodsley), xii (1875), 319–60.

Walker, Andrew Jackson. *Popular Songs and Broadside Ballads in the English Drama 1559–1642.* Unpublished Harvard Thesis, 1934, pp. 128–32.

Wright, Louis B. 'Extraneous Song in Elizabethan Drama after the Advent of Shakespeare', *Stud. Phil.* xxiv (1927), 261–74.

1658/9, 28 Jan. S.R. Simon Miller entered for his copy 'a booke called The London Chaunticleres a Witty Comedy &c.' (Greg, *Bibliography*, i. 67.)

1659. The London Chaunticleres. A Witty Comoedy, Full of Various and Delightfull Mirth. Often Acted with Great Applause And never before Published . . . 1659.

The London Chanticleers is an odd play, about half the length of a standard five-act comedy, but longer than the short interregnum pieces like *The Gossips' Brawl*. It is a show in fourteen scenes with enough popular songs to suggest that it is moving in the direction of ballad opera. The assumption of literacy in the prologue might suggest an academic audience, but if the play was written for a university performance, the occasion must have been a public one, for the epilogue is addressed to '*Gentlemen and Lady's*'. The lines in the prologue,

> *You're welcome then to* London, *which our show*
> *Since you mayn't go to that, has brought to you,*

have prompted various speculations. They certainly indicate that the play was performed in the provinces, but not necessarily that the time was the period of plague closing in 1636 (Fleay, *Biog. Chron.* ii. 340, on the basis of dubious allusions) or a Commonwealth date when the Royalist audience could not get to London. (Harbage, *Cavalier Drama*, pp. 210, 214.) Harbage finds further evidence of a Commonwealth date in the title of one of the ballads offered by the character Ditty, '*The second part of Mother Shiptons Prophecies*'. 'The prophesie of Mother Shipton' was published in 1641, several other pamphlets of her prophecies in 1642, 1643, and 1648, and an undated pamphlet, said to be 1651, entitled 'The second part of Mother Shiptons prophecies'. This evidence carries more weight, though Dr. Walker, who has examined the ballads most carefully, still dates the play *c.* 1636.

Look on Me and Love Me, or Marriage in the Dark (?)
(Lost)

The title occurs seventh in Abraham Hill's list of plays in manuscript. (See Middleton, *The Conqueror's Custom*.) This list seems to have been Hill's record of some bookseller's stock, set down between 1677 and 1703, but it is notable that nearly all the identifiable plays and playwrights in the list are Jacobean or Caroline.

There is no other record of this title.

Look to the Lady (?)
(Lost)

It is not clear whether there were two plays of this name, an anonymous one written not later than 1620 and another written by James Shirley, or only the anonymous play which was later misattributed to Shirley. See James Shirley.

Louis the Eleventh, King of France (?)
(Lost)

'The History of Lewis the eleventh King of France: a Trage-Comedy' appears in a list of 'Books in the Presse and ready for Printing' that were advertised by Nathaniel Brook of the Angel in Cornhill, in E. Phillips, *The New World of English Words*, 1658. Under similar headings the title also appears in other such lists, 1658–62. (See Greg, *Bibliography*, ii. 1000–1.) The advertisements must have been at least premature, for there is no evidence that the play was ever printed, though one would assume that Brook had a manuscript. Nothing else is known of a play of the title.

The Lovers Holiday or The Bear (?)
(Lost)

This title, 'The Lovers holiday or the Beare', is fifth in the list of manuscript plays found among the papers of Abraham Hill. (See Middleton, *The Conqueror's Custom*.) The list seems to have been Hill's record of some bookseller's stock, set down between 1677 and 1703, but it is notable that nearly all the identifiable plays and playwrights of the list are Jacobean and Caroline.

The only other occurrence of the title is in the forty-fourth entry in the same list: 'the Lovers holyday'. Possibly Hill saw duplicate manuscripts of the same play, but in the absence of all other evidence only speculation is possible. It may be that the double entry of the title indicates that *The Bear* and *The Lovers Holiday* were really two separate plays. Both *Lovers* and *Holiday* are favourite words in the titles of seventeenth-century plays, but *Bear* is unusual.

Since neither entry uses an apostrophe, it is impossible to tell how many lovers had a holiday, but one would guess more than one.

The Lovers of Ludgate (?)
(Lost)

The title, 'The Lovers of Loodgate', is known only from John Warburton's list of manuscript plays which he says he once owned but which his cook destroyed. Many of the titles in Warburton's list are suspiciously like entries in the Stationers'

Register, and it is by no means certain that he ever owned the manuscripts at all. (See W. W. Greg, *Library*, Third Series, ii [1911], 225–59.) But 'The Lovers of Loodgate' does not occur in the Stationers' Register, and it may be that Warburton once owned a manuscript with this title. Nothing more is known of it.

Love's Aftergame

See Anon., *The Proxy, or Love's Aftergame*.

Love's Changelings' Change (c. 1630–40?)

MS.: B.M. MS. Egerton 1994[14].

Boas, F. S. 'A Seventeenth Century Theatrical Repertoire', *Shakespeare and the Universities* (1923), pp. 96–110.
Greg, W. W. *Dramatic Documents from the Elizabethan Playhouses* (1931), pp. 342–4.
—— *Pastoral Poetry & Pastoral Drama* (1906), p. 326.

Love's Changelings' Change (not *Changed* as sometimes quoted) is the fourteenth in the collection of manuscript plays brought together in Egerton 1994. Dr. Boas (loc. cit.) noted Warner's conjecture that the collection might have been one of the volumes of manuscript plays bequeathed to Dulwich College by the seventeenth-century actor William Cartwright, Junior (see above, ii. 404–5), and Boas found evidence to support the conjecture.

The play is a pastoral founded on the *Arcadia*, written in a literary hand which Dr. Greg dated 'c. 1630–40?' (*Dramatic Documents*, p. 342.) He found no evidence that the manuscript had been censored or used in the playhouse, though the stage directions were written with production in mind. No evidence to date the play has been adduced, save the very tentative dating of the hand, which, on the evidence of the alterations, Dr. Greg thought might be that of the author.

Love's Infancy (?)
(Lost)

The title is forty-fifth in the list of manuscript plays found among the papers of Abraham Hill. (See Middleton, *Conqueror's Custom*.) The list seems to have been Hill's record of some bookseller's stock, set down between 1677 and 1703, but it is notable that nearly all the identifiable plays and playwrights of the list are Jacobean and Caroline.

There is no other record of a play of precisely this title, but J. Q. Adams in his discussion of Hill's list (*Library*, Fourth Series, xx [1939], 96–97) notes that a play of Richard Flecknoe's, which was published as *Love's Dominion* and later as *Love's Kingdom*, was performed on the Continent about 1650 as *Love in Its Infancy*. He can, however, find no justification for a title of *Love's Infancy* in *Love's Kingdom* and discounts the possibility that Hill had seen a manuscript of Flecknoe's play.

Love's Lodestone

An alternative title for the anonymous *Pathomachia* (q.v.).

The Loves of Alice and Alexis

See Anon., *Alice and Alexis*.

Love's Victory (?)

MS.: Henry E. Huntington Library HM 600.

Edition: Edited by Helena Maxwell, unpublished thesis, Stanford University, 1933; J. O. Halliwell[-Phillipps], *A Brief Description of the Ancient and Modern Manuscripts Preserved in the Public Library, Plymouth* (1853), pp. 212–36 (long extracts comprising nearly one-third of the play).

Greg, W. W. *Pastoral Poetry & Pastoral Drama* (1906), pp. 367–8.

There has been some confusion about this play because of its popular title. It is quite distinct from *Love's Victory* by William Chamberlaine (q.v.), published in 1658, and distinct from James Shirley's *The Doubtful Heir, or Rosania, or Love's Victory* (q.v.), published in 1652.

The manuscript from which Halliwell-Phillipps published extracts, amounting to about 500 lines, at that time belonged to Sir E. Dering, Bt.; it was apparently the manuscript now owned by the Huntington Library. The play in the Huntington MS. is incomplete, about 1,900 lines, beginning somewhere in the first act and breaking off in v. 1. The author seems to have had little understanding of the theatre and perhaps did not intend his play for production; the stage directions are very meagre, and some seem to be omitted. The manuscript is in two hands, one of which writes most of the regular acts and the other the interludes between the acts. Miss Maxwell thinks that the second hand is that of the author. She found little evidence of date, but thought the piece 'not early' and noted a strong similarity between the rustic in *Love's Victory* and Jonson's Lorel in *The Sad Shepherd*.

One of the odd features of the play is an interlude at the end of the first, second, and fourth acts in which Venus or Cupid or both speak about love. There was to have been another at the end of the third act, and 'Venus' has been written at the head of the page, but the rest of the page is blank.

Halliwell-Phillipps's extracts from the play are somewhat confusing, for Miss Maxwell notes that he has several times taken speech titles for the names of characters in the dialogue, and thus run two speeches together.

The play is in rhyme, mostly couplets.

Love Yields to Honour (?)
(Lost ?)

The title is known only from its occurrence in Edmond Malone's long list of plays not known to have been printed. His sources for many of the titles are known, but not for this one; it is not found in Greg's list of plays that were advertised but are not known to have been printed. (See Malone, *Variorum* [1821], ii. 438–9.)

Luminalia, or The Festival of Light

See William Davenant.

Lusiuncula (?)
(Lost ?)

The only record I can find of a play with this title is Hazlitt's statement: 'A Latin play, which is said to be constructed on the same story as that used in the tragedy of *Macbeth*.' (*A Manual for the Collector and Amateur of Old English Plays* [1892], p. 145.)

Man and Wisdom

See Anon., *Manhood and Misrule*.

Manhood and Misrule (?)
(Lost)

Richard Rogers and William Ley published in 1656 'An exact and perfect Catalogue of all Playes that are Printed', and they appended the list to their edition of Thomas Goffe's *The Careless Shepherdess*, 1656. One title in this list is 'Manhood and misrule'. Dr. Greg says that this title is probably the same as the 'Manhood and wisdom C.' of Edward Archer's derivative list appended to his edition of *The Old Law* in the same year, and also the same as 'Man & Wisdome' in Kirkman's similar derivative list. (*Bibliography*, ii. 994–5.) The title sounds like that of a morality play, but nothing is known of it.

Manhood and Wisdom

See Anon., *Manhood and Misrule*.

The Man in the Moon Drinks Claret (> 1621)
(Lost)

1621, 27 Dec. '6º Marcii. A warrant for allowance of xx^tie Marks for two plaies to the Princes Servaunts [for presenting plays at court] the one 27º Decembris 1621, called the man in the moone drinks Clarett.' (From a Lord Chamberlain's Warrant Book, now Inner Temple Library MS. 515, No. 7, printed by J. T. Murray, *English Dramatic Companies 1558–1642* [1910], ii. 193.)

Nothing is known of the play save the record of its performance by Prince Charles's (I) men at court in 1621. It was not necessarily a recent play when acted at court. The company was performing in London as early as 1610 (see above, i. 198), and it may be that this was one of their earlier plays of which we have no record until 1621.

Marcus Tullius Cicero (> 1651)

1651. The Tragedy Of *That Famovs* Roman Oratovr Marcus Tullius Cicero . . . 1651.

Langbaine observed, 'I know not whether ever this Play was acted; but it seems to me to be written in Imitation of *Ben. Johnson's Cataline*. For the Plot, see *Plutarch* in his Life: See likewise his own Works, *Hist. Ciceroniana Lambin*; as also *Dion, Appian, &c.*' (*An Account of the English Dramatick Poets* [1691], p. 540.)

Probably the play was never acted, and it is not unlikely that it is a closet drama written not long before it was published, but I know of no evidence as to the date of composition.

Edward Phillips (*Theatrum Poetarum* [1675], Part ii, p. 47)
followed by Winstanley, attributed the play to Fulke Greville,
Lord Brooke, and G. C. Moore Smith notes that Aldis Wright
attributed it with little reason to Samuel Brooke. (*College Plays*,
p. 108.)

[*The Marquesse d'Ancre*] (1617 ?)
(Lost)

The play is known only from an order of the Privy Council
directing its suppression. At the sitting of 22 June 1617 a letter
was sent to Sir George Buc, Master of the Revels, saying:

Wee are informed that there are certeyne Players or Comedians wee
knowe not of what Company, that goe about to play some enterlude
concerning the late Marquesse d'Ancre, wch for many respect[es] wee
thincke not fitt to be suffered: Wee doe therefore require yo^w vpon
yor pill to take order that the same be not represented or played in
any place about this Citty or ellswhere, where yo^w haue authoritie.
(*Dramatic Records from the Privy Council Register*, Malone Society
Collections, i, Parts 4 and 5 [1911], 376.)

Presumably the play was new when the Privy Council ordered
it suppressed. It is noteworthy that the Council does not say that
'Marquis d'Ancre' was the title of the play, but only that it concerned him. As Sir Edmund Chambers points out (*Elizabethan
Stage*, iii. 511), it is not likely that the allusion to the Marquis in
Webster's *Duchess of Malfi* identifies that tragedy as the play the
Council had in mind, for Webster's masterpiece is certainly not an
'enterlude concerning the late Marquesse d'Ancre'. It may be
that the play is to be identified with one of the many other lost
pieces known to us only by some unrevealing title.

The Marriage Night (?)
(Lost?)

This title is forty-sixth in the list of manuscript plays found
among the papers of Abraham Hill. (See Middleton, *The Conqueror's Custom*.) The list seems to have been Hill's record of
some bookseller's stock, set down between 1677 and 1703, but
it is notable that nearly all the identifiable plays and playwrights
of the list are Jacobean and Caroline.

What Hill saw was probably a manuscript of the play of this
name written by Henry Cary, fourth Viscount Falkland, died
1663 (not written, as so often said, by his famous father, Lucius,
who was killed at Newbury in 1643), and published in 1664.

J. Q. Adams notes in his discussion of Hill's list (*Library*, Fourth Series, xx [1939], 97) Sir A. W. Ward's contention that Cary's play was a reworking of a much earlier lost play. I do not know where Ward said this, for in his main account of *The Marriage Night* (*History of English Dramatic Literature* [1899], iii. 335–6) he goes only so far as to note evidence of 'its author's familiarity with the pre-Revolution drama', and imitations of *Julius Caesar*, and to state that 'I much mistake unless the lurid colouring of the action together with certain suggestions in the plot, notwithstanding the difference in issue, is partly due to reminiscences of *The Revenger's Tragedy*'. If Cary's play was a reworking of an earlier tragedy, it is of course possible that Hill's manuscript was that play.

[*The Marriage of the Farmer's Son*] (1617/18)
(Lost)

1617/18, 12 Jan. 'Early in 1618, however, the Gentlemen gave two productions of a masque representing the marriage of the son of a farmer, the first at "Enfielde" where "Sr George Goringe vpon sentinge a farmer's sonne & apparrell thereafter the rest, weare come to daunce at his weddinge wth many pleasant speeches, & much mirth dree the ende. Which the kinge hearinge, desired to see them performe the same at Tibbalds the night ere he pted, wch he did and was much contented & very merry therewth." ' (Mary Sullivan, *Court Masques of James I* [1913], pp. 107–8, quoting Gerrard Herbert to Sir Dudley Carleton, *State Papers, Domestic, James I*, xcv, No. 14.)

Nothing is known of the masque beyond Herbert's letter. It has been thought to be the same as the anonymous *Tom of Bedlam*, produced at Theobalds by the gentlemen at the same time, but since *The Marriage of the Farmer's Son* is called a masque and is said to have pleased the King, whereas *Tom of Bedlam* is called a play or interlude and is said to have displeased the King, it seems to me rather more likely that the two were distinct productions.

The Masculine Bride

See Anon., *The Whimzies of Señor Hidalgo, or The Masculine Bride*.

The Masque

See above, Richard Gunnell.

Masque of ——, Masque at ——

See the next word in the title.

A Match without Money, or The Wives' Prize (?)
(Lost)

This title occurs twenty-second in Abraham Hill's list of plays in manuscript. (See Middleton, *The Conqueror's Custom*.) The list seems to have been Hill's record of some bookseller's stock, set down between 1677 and 1703, but it is notable that nearly all the identifiable plays and playwrights in the list are Jacobean and Caroline.

Though the word *Match*, variously qualified, is popular in Jacobean and Caroline play-titles, this particular title is not found elsewhere. J. Q. Adams, in his discussion of Hill's list (*Library*, Fourth Series, xx [1939], 90), notes the somewhat similar titles of Fletcher's *Wit without Money* and his *Woman's Prize*, but there is no reason to associate either with this title.

Medea

MS.: B.M. Sloane 911, fols. 100–15.

An anonymous translation of Seneca's *Medea*; not Studley's or Sherburne's.

The Merchant's Sacrifice (?)
(Ghost title?)

In John Warburton's list of manuscript plays, which he says he once owned but which were burned by his cook, occurs the title, 'The [Marchants Sacrifice] Crafty Marchant (sic) C. Shack. Marmio[n]'. The first two bracketed words have been deleted in the manuscript. (W. W. Greg, 'The Bakings of Betsy', *Library*, Third Series, ii [1911], 231.) *The Merchant's Sacrifice* is probably only an error in copying, but it is conceivable that it is the title of an unknown play, deleted for an unknown reason. (See also William Bonen, *The Cra . . . Merchant*.)

Mercurius Rusticans (?)

MS.: Bodleian MS. Wood D. 18.

The manuscript of this Latin play is headed 'Mercurius Rusticans/Scena Hyneksey vel Hincksie'. Various references and the familiar use of the neighbouring village of Hinksey show that it is an Oxford play, and the prologue and epilogue are delivered by 'Genius Academiae'. Scrawled at the end of the play in another hand is:

Mr Sellar of C C C in jeere
of this play
Of old leather thongs
And other mens songs
They patcht us up a play
Th' were so often out
We began to doubt
Whether th' were Hynkesie men or they

The tunes to which several of the songs are to be sung are written in the margin: 'The hunt is up', 'Whoop doe me noe harme', and 'Bonny nell'.

Falconer Madan says (*A Summary Catalogue of Western Manuscripts in the Bodleian Library at Oxford* [1937], ii, Part ii, p. 1183) that the manuscript was 'written in 1663', but I do not know what his evidence is.

[*Microcosmus*] (< 1612 ?)

MS.: Trinity College, Cambridge, MS. R–10–4 (item 4).

Smith, G. C. Moore. *College Plays* (1923), pp. 108–9.

The text of the play is preceded in the manuscript by a blank page which may have been the title-page, but a piece has been torn out that is large enough to have contained a title and even an author's name. The verso of this page bears the single word, 'Prologus', but no prologue follows. There is no dramatis personae or epilogue. The play has five full acts, but the scenes are short. The characters in order of appearance are: Arterio, Spiritus, Psyche, Chærinus, Venulus, Jecorino, Neruus, Encephalus, Memoria, Communis sensus, Abdomen, Nasus, and Phusis. There are numerous corrections, deletions, and additions in the text. The entire first scene and almost two full pages in III. 4 have been marked for deletion. Moore Smith, who called the play *Microcosmus*, noted references in the text which he thought indicated that it had been written for a Cambridge audience. He also thought that 'Its references to the abundance of food in Virginia and the absence of fasts points to a date later than 1612'.

Entertainment at Sir Thomas Middleton's

See Anon., *Chirke Castle.*

Monsieur Perrolis

See John Fletcher.

The Moor's Masque (1636?)
(Lost?)

In his list of University plays acted in the time of Charles I, F. G. Fleay has the entry:

Acted near Eastgate. Anon. 8. 1636. *Moore's Mask.* Mr. Moore was one of the six Moors in the Anti-Mask. MS. Exhibited twice in public; once in private for gentlewomen. (*Biog. Chron.* ii. 358.)

I find no other record of this masque. Presumably Fleay's information was derived from the manuscript, but I do not know where it is.

More Than Nine Days Wonder, Two Constant Women (?)
(Lost)

This title occurs nineteenth in Abraham Hill's list of manuscript plays. (See Middleton, *The Conqueror's Custom.*) The list seems to have been Hill's record of some bookseller's stock, set down between 1677 and 1703, but it is notable that nearly all the identifiable plays and playwrights in the list are Jacobean and Caroline.

There is no other record of such a title, though J. Q. Adams points out in his discussion of Hill's list (*Library*, Fourth Series, xx [1939], 90) that the *Wonder* titles are common in the first three or four decades of the seventeenth century.

Mors Valentiniani Imperatoris (16 December 1642)
(Lost)

McCabe, William H. 'Notes on the St. Omers College Theatre', *Phil. Quart.* xvii (1938), 225–39.
—— 'The Play-List of the English College of St. Omers 1592–1762', *Revue de littérature comparée*, xvii (1937), 355–75.

The play was performed at the Jesuit College for English boys at St. Omers, 16 December 1642. Father McCabe notes that the subject was 'the death of Valentinian II, murdered at Vienne, Dauphiny (392) before he could be baptized by St. Ambrose' ('Play-List', p. 368), and that on 31 August 1667 there was a performance of a play called *Valentinianus*, which he thinks was 'probably a revival of 1642c [i.e. *Mors Valentiniani Imperatoris*]'. (Ibid., p. 372.)

Mother Rumming
(Ghost title?)

Edward Archer published 'An Exact and perfect Catalogue of all the Plaies that were ever printed; together, with all the Authors names; and what are Comedies, Histories, Interludes, Masks, Pastorels, Tragedies'. This catalogue was appended to his edition of Massinger, Middleton, and Rowley's *The Old Law*, 1656. Dr. Greg shows that this catalogue of Archer's is derived from the similar list of Rogers and Ley published in the same year. (*Bibliography*, ii. 996.) One title in Archer's list is 'Mother Rumming C.' The title is probably the result of some confusion on Archer's part (see ibid., p. 998), but one can never be sure.

The First Antimasque of Mountebanks (2 and 19 February 1617–18)

MSS.: B.M. Add. MS. 5956, fols. 72–84^v; Bodleian MS. Rawlinson D. 1021; Huntington Library MS. H.M. 21; B.M. Add. MS. 10444, fol. 44^v, 'The Mountebanks Dance at Grayes Inne' (music only).

Editions: Peter Cunningham and J. Payne Collier, *Inigo Jones . . . and Five Court Masques*, The Shakespeare Society (1848), pp. 111–30; A. H. Bullen, *The Works of John Marston* (1887), iii. 418–43; J. Nichols, *The Progresses and Public Processions of Queen Elizabeth* (1823), iii. 332–48.

Brotanek, Rudolf. *Die englischen Maskenspiele* (1902), pp. 355–6.

1617/18, 2 Feb. 'On the 2d, which was Candelmas-day, the Students of Gray's Inn performed the Tilt of Henry Prince of Purpool, and the Masque of Mountebanks, concluding with a 'Song for the Entertainment of the Lord Chancellor [Sir Francis Bacon] at Gray's Inn, on Candlemas-day, and of other Lords.' (John Nichols, *The Progresses of . . . King James the First* [1828], iii. 466.)

1617/18, 7 Feb. 'The Lord Chauncellor hath ben absent from

Westminster Hall three dayes this weeke . . . and yet on Monday (beeing Candlemas Day) he dined at Grayes Ynne to geve countenance to theyre Lord or Prince of Purpoole, and see theyre revells.' (John Chamberlain to Sir Dudley Carleton, *The Letters of John Chamberlain*, McClure ed., ii. 136.)

1617/18, 21 Feb. 'On Shrovetewsday the Princes maske for Twelf Night was represented again with some few alterations and additions, but little bettered: on Thursday night the gentlemen of Grayes Ynne came to the court with theyre shew, (for I cannot call yt a maske seeing they were not disguised nor had visards). For the rest, theyre fashion and devise was well approved, though yt were thought to be somewhat out of season to revell in Lent, the cause wherof was that they wold not be turned into the hall as was apointed on Shrovemonday, by reason that the Princes shewes and devises could not be set up and orderly placed in so short time, yf they shold possesse the banquetting roome the night before: but seeing no reasons for perswasions wold serve the turne, they must of necessitie be put of till Thursday, or some longer time. The Quene was not present at either of them but kepes close at Denmarke House.' (Ibid., p. 142.)

1617/18, 21 Feb. 'On thursday night the maske of Grayes Inne pleased tolerably wel . . . there was in it som wittie ribalderie that made the companie merrie.' (Nathaniel Brent to Sir Dudley Carleton, *State Papers*, xcvi, Art. 24, as quoted by Brotanek, op. cit., p. 356.)

1617/18, 22 Feb. 'Grayes Inn maske was . . . thursday night . . . one called Paradox . . . was much comended.' (Gerrard Herbert to Sir Dudley Carleton, ibid., Art. 27, quoted by Brotanek, loc. cit.)

The show which the gentlemen of Gray's Inn presented at court was not a masque, as John Chamberlain makes clear, but a part of their traditional Christmas entertainment for the Prince of Purpoole. The entire entertainment for 1617/18, of which this is a part, is printed by Nichols (op. cit., pp. 320–48) under the title, *Gesta Grayorum*, Part II. It was the whole entertainment which Francis Bacon, a member of Gray's Inn who had been created Lord Chancellor only a month before, witnessed at the Gray's Inn feast on Candlemas (2 February 1617/18). John Chamberlain records in his letter of 21 February 1617/18 that it was intended that the Gray's Inn performance, or rather the Mountebanks' part of it, should be repeated at court on Shrove

Monday (16 February 1617/18). This is obviously the reason for
the date of 16 February 1617/18 in one of the manuscripts. But
as the rest of Chamberlain's letter shows, the performance was
postponed from Monday to Thursday, and the letters of Nathaniel
Brent and Gerrard Herbert agree that it was actually performed
at court on Thursday, i.e. 19 February 1617/18.

It was only the Mountebanks' part of the entertainment that
was given at court, and even this needed some modification, for
on fol. 83 of the B.M. MS. appears the statement: 'The followinge
paradoxes wer read at Grayes Jnn but left out at Aul[?] to avoyd
tedioussnes.'

Brotanek (loc. cit.), following Hazlitt (*A Manual for the Collector* [1892], p. 161), notes that the fourteenth impression of
Sir Thomas Overbury His Wife, 1630, reprints 'Paradoxes, as they
were spoken in a Maske, and presented *before his Maiesty* at White-
Hall' and 'The Mountebankes Receipts', V_2–V_8v.

In the collection of tunes in the B.M. MS. Add. 10444 (see
above, John Adson) there is one entitled 'The Mountebanks
Dance at Grayes Inne'.

Collier in the introduction to his edition of the *Antimasque of
Mountebanks* from the Duke of Devonshire's manuscript attributed it to John Marston, because he said Marston's name was
written in pencil on the manuscript he saw, and because he said
corrections in the text were in Marston's hand. (Op. cit., pp.
xviii–xix.) For these reasons Bullen, 'with some diffidence', published the piece in his edition of Marston, though he had not seen
the manuscript. As Sir Edmund Chambers pointed out, 'the
known dates of Marston's career render [Collier's ascription]
extremely improbable' (*Elizabethan Stage*, iii. 435), and he might
have added that neither Collier's allegations of pencilled notes
nor his identification of contemporary hands commands much
respect any more.

At the end of the B.M. MS. are two poems by Thomas Campion,
and he has consequently been suggested as author of the antimasque. Though he would be a better candidate than John
Marston, the evidence seems inadequate for ascription.

Mull Sack, or The Looking-Glass, the Bachelor or the Hawk (?)

(Lost)

c. 1677–1703. 'mull sack or the looking glass the Bachelor or the
     Hawk' is the twelfth title in Hill's list of plays. (J. Q. Adams,

'Hill's List of Early Plays in Manuscript', *Library*, Fourth Series, xx [1939], 71–99. See Middleton, *The Conqueror's Custom.*)

The title would seem to indicate two plays, but Professor Adams points out that Hill customarily kept the titles separate in his list. The identifiable plays of the list are Jacobean and Caroline, and the presumption is that *Mull Sack* was. 'Mull Sack' was an alias for the pickpocket and highwayman, Jack Cottington, and Professor Adams suggests that *Mull Sack, or The Looking-Glass, the Bachelor or the Hawk* was a play about that highwayman, and that it was revised and printed as *The Knave in Grain New Vampt* (q.v., under J. D.).

Mustapha (?)

This title is fortieth in the list of manuscript plays found among the papers of Abraham Hill. (See Middleton, *The Conqueror's Custom.*) The list seems to have been Hill's record of some bookseller's stock, set down between 1677 and 1703, but it is notable that nearly all the identifiable plays and playwrights of the list are Jacobean and Caroline.

As J. Q. Adams points out in his discussion of Hill's list (*Library*, Fourth Series, xx [1939], 95), the play is likely to have been either Fulke Greville's play of the name published in 1609, or Roger Boyle's *Mustapha, the Son of Solyman the Magnificent*, published in 1668 and extant in a number of manuscripts. It could, however, have been still another, and otherwise unknown, play.

The Tragedy of Nero (Piso's Conspiracy) (> 1623?)

MS.: B.M. Egerton MS. 1994[12].

Edition: A. H. Bullen, ed., *A Collection of Old English Plays*, i (1882), 3–98.

Boas, F. S. 'A Seventeenth Century Theatrical Repertoire', *Shakespeare and the Universities* (1923), pp. 96–110.

Briggs, W. D. 'The Influence of Jonson's Tragedy in the Seventeenth Century', *Anglia*, xxxv (1912), 284–7.

Chester, Alan Griffith. *Thomas May* (1932).

Evans, G. Blakemore. 'Note on Fletcher and Massinger's *Little French Lawyer*', *Modern Language Notes*, lii (1937), 406–7.

Forsythe, R. S. 'An Indebtedness of *Nero* to the Third Part of *King Henry VI*', ibid. xxv (1910), 211–12.

Greg, W. W. *Dramatic Documents from the Elizabethan Play-houses* (1931), pp. 314–18.

Mustard, Wilfred P. 'Notes on the Tragedy of Nero', *Phil. Quart.* i (1922), 173–8.

Quintana, Ricardo. 'Samuel Butler: A Restoration Figure in a Modern Light', *E.L.H.* xviii (1951), 9, n. 3.

Rutherford, W. G. 'The Anonymous Play of *Nero*', *Athenaeum*, No. 4123 (3 November 1906), pp. 559–60.

Schmid, F. E. *Thomas May's Tragedy of Julia Aggripina, Materialien*, xliii (1914), 155–217.

1624, 15 May. 'The Tragedy of *Nero* was allowed to be printed.' (Adams, *Herbert*, p. 28.)

1624. The Tragedy Of Nero, *Newly Written* . . . 1624.

1633. The Tragedy of Nero. *Newly written* . . . 1633.

1633, 24 Oct. S.R. All the rights of Thomas Jones in a series of titles were assigned to Augustine Mathews. Included in the series is '[6] Tragedy of Nero'. (Greg, *Bibliography*, i. 43.)

1641, 28 July. S.R. Augustine Mathews assigned over to William Sheeres his rights in four titles, including '[3] Tragedy of Næro'. (Ibid., p. 54.)

1676. Piso's Conspiracy, A Tragedy Acted at the Duke's *Theatre.* . . . 1676. (Dr. Greg has pointed out, ibid., p. 562, that this is *Nero* with minor alterations and omissions in Act IV.)

1689, 13 June. S.R. Francis Saunders entered by virtue of an assignment from the executors of William Cadman a long list of titles, including '[29] Pizoes Conspiracy'. (Ibid., p. 76.)

An allusion to a speech in *Nero* by a character in Fletcher's *Little French Lawyer* (IV. 4) has been pointed out by Mr. G. Blakemore Evans (loc. cit.):

> *La.-Writ.*   I love a dire revenge
>   Give me the man that will all others kill,
>   And last himself.
> *Cler.* You stole that resolution.
> *La.-Writ.* I had it in a play, but that's all one:
>   I would see it done.

They are referring to the lines of Nero in this play, III. 2 (E_1):

> What may I easily doe? kill thee, or him,
> How may I rid you all? where is the Man
> That will all others end, and last himselfe?

This reference indicates a surprising assumption of the audience's familiarity with *Nero*, and it probably shows that the play had been performed before *The Little French Lawyer* was written, May 1619<>May 1623 (see under John Fletcher), though it is always possible that the lines are a later insertion in a play which the King's men withheld from publication for about a quarter of a century. The assumption of familiarity also suggests either that *Nero*, like *The Little French Lawyer*, was performed by the King's company, or—considering the absurdity of La Writ—that it was notorious for its absurdities. The play seems too good for the latter and the title-page of the quartos too reticent for the former.

Nero, which is not always easily distinguished in the records from Matthew Gwinne's Latin tragedy of the name (see *Elizabethan Stage*, iii. 332) and the anonymous *Claudius Tiberius Nero* (ibid. iv. 5), has sometimes been attributed to Thomas May. The scholarly competence of the author of *Nero* has reminded critics of May's tragedies on closely related classic subjects, and Fleay pointed out (*Biog. Chron.* ii. 84) that the rights in the play were transferred in the Stationers' Register in 1633 along with rights to May's *Heir* and his translation of Lucan. Neither of these reasons should carry much weight in considering an age of Latin scholars and of wholesale publishing transfers. Attributions to Massinger based on an alleged manuscript attribution in an old hand and on a binder's grouping of old plays are equally dubious. (See Schmid, loc. cit., and Chester, loc. cit.)

The author of *Nero* has used a wide variety of classic sources, most of which are discussed by Schmid, with some additions by Wilfred Mustard. Forsythe makes a good case that the author of *Nero* planned III. 4 of his play with II. 5 of *Henry VI, Part 3* in mind, and Dean Briggs presents evidence showing respectful consideration if not imitation of Jonson's *Sejanus*.

It has been noticed that thirty-one lines of the play on G_4^v use some of the same figures and sequences as Carew's 'Rapture'. Rhodes Dunlap (*The Poems of Thomas Carew* [1949], pp. 236–7) thinks that Carew was the originator, and it is true that his use of the material is the more effective. I am not entirely convinced that either poet need necessarily have seen the work of the other.

The manuscript of the play in the British Museum is part of the collection discussed by Boas. Dr. Greg notes that *Nero* is written in six different scribal hands, perhaps dividing up the copy page for page among them, and that a seventh has made some corrections. Two leaves of the manuscript have been lost, and others have been bound in the wrong order. The text of the manuscript is very similar to that of the quarto, but it adds a number of quotations not found there, and there are numerous differences in the stage directions. The manuscript shows no evidence of censorship or of playhouse use, and Dr. Greg suggests a purely literary origin.

Professor Quintana notes that Samuel Butler's commonplace book has a number of extracts from the play, extracts which at one time led to assertions that Butler had written an unfinished tragedy.

The Play of the Netherlands (?)
(Lost)

Richard Rogers and William Ley published in 1656 'An exact and perfect Catalogue of all Playes that are Printed', and they appended the list to their edition of Thomas Goffe's *The Careless Shepherdess*, 1656. One title in this list is 'Play of the Netherlands'. Dr. Greg suggests that it might have been the same as *The Life and Death of Sir Martin Skink, with the Wars of the Low Countries* (see Richard Brome), which Humphrey Moseley entered in the Stationers' Register in 1654. (*Bibliography*, ii. 995.) That play is lost, but the titles do not seem very similar to me.

Nineveh's Repentance (?)
(Lost?)

Richard Rogers and William Ley published in 1656 'An exact and perfect Catalogue of all Playes that are Printed', and they appended the list to their edition of Thomas Goffe's *The Careless Shepherdess*, 1656. One title in this list is 'Nineves repentance'. Edward Archer's similar derivative list published with his edition of *The Old Law*, 1656, includes 'Niniveehs repentance I'. Dr. Greg notes that Niniveh's repentance at the preaching of Jonah is the theme of *A Looking-Glass for London and England*, published in 1594, but that play is listed separately in the catalogues. (*Bibliography*, ii. 995.) Nothing is now known of such a play.

The Noble Friend (?)
(Lost?)

The title is known only from its occurrence in Edmond Malone's long list of plays not known to have been printed. His sources for many of the titles are known, but not for this one; it is not found in Greg's list of plays that were advertised but are not known to have been printed. (See Malone, *Variorum* [1821], ii. 438–9.)

The Noble Ravishers (> 1653)
(Lost)

1653, 29 [Dec.] S.R. Richard Marriott entered as his copies a number of plays, including 'The Noble Rauishers'. (Greg, *Bibliography*, i. 62.)

The only evidence for the existence of a play of this name is Marriott's entry in the Stationers' Register. Two-thirds of the twenty-one titles in this list of plays occur nowhere else, and only three were published later under these titles, though four are known from other references. (See below, Anon., *The Woman's Law*, for the entire list.)

Nottola (?)

MS.: Bodleian MS. Douce 47 (formerly Bodleian MS. 21621).

Morgan, Louise B. 'The Latin University Drama', *Shakespeare Jahrbuch*, xlvii (1911), 88–91. Includes synopsis.

The beautifully prepared manuscript of this Latin comedy offers to a hasty examination no clue as to date, authorship, or provenance except the binder's stamp: 'Nottola / Comædia / M.S. / 1648.'

The pages have double-ruled borders, and the character names are in red, features which, with the careful and uncorrected hand, suggest a presentation copy. There is, however, no title-page, dedication, prologue, epilogue, or other extraneous matter except a dramatis personae, which gives twenty-three characters, and 'Scena Ferraria'. The volume carries the book-plates of Peter Hall and Francis Douce. The play runs to 130 folios, but there is very little on a page.

Odoardus Varvici Comes (27 February 1641/2)
(Lost)

McCabe, William H. 'Notes on the St. Omers College Theatre', *Phil. Quart.* xvii (1938), 225–39.
—— 'The Play-List of the English College of St. Omers 1592–1762', *Revue de littérature comparée*, xvii (1937), 355–75.

The play was performed at the Jesuit College for English boys at St. Omers, 27 February 1641/2. Father McCabe notes that the subject was 'the Earl of Warwick executed with Perkin Warbeck under Henry VII'. ('Play-List', p. 367.)

Orpheus (?)
(Lost)

The title, 'Orpheus C.', is known only from its appearance in
John Warburton's list of play manuscripts which he says he once
owned but which his cook burned. Most of the titles in Warburton's list are suspiciously like certain entries in the Stationers'
Register, and it can by no means be assumed that he ever owned
these manuscripts. (See W. W. Greg, *Library*, Third Series, ii
[1911], 225–59.) But 'Orpheus' does nor occur in the Stationers'
Register, and it may be that Warburton once owned a play
manuscript with this title.

According to *Biographia Dramatica* (1812 ed., iii. 107), followed
by Hazlitt and Fleay, there was a fragment of a drama on the same
subject, 'perhaps far more ancient', in the British Museum, but
Dr. Greg (op. cit., p. 252) said that he was unable to find it.

Ortenus or Ortenas
(Ghost title?)

Edward Archer published 'An Exact and perfect Catalogue
of all the Plaies that were ever printed; together, with all the
Authors names; and what are Comedies, Histories, Interludes,
Masks, Pastorels, Tragedies'. This catalogue was appended to his
edition of Massinger, Middleton, and Rowley's *The Old Law*, 1656.
Dr. Greg shows that this catalogue of Archer's is derived from the
similar list of Rogers and Ley published in the same year. (*Bibliography*, ii. 996.) In Archer's list appear two consecutive titles,
'Ortenus C' and 'Ortenas T'. As Dr. Greg points out (ibid.,
p. 998), it seems likely that only one play, and not both a comedy
and a tragedy with almost identical titles, was intended. Even so,
the title is probably the result of some confusion and not evidence
of another lost play.

Osman the Turk, or the Ottoman Custom (?)
(Lost?)

This title occurs eighteenth in Abraham Hill's list of manuscript plays. (See Middleton, *The Conqueror's Custom.*) The list
seems to have been Hill's record of some bookseller's stock, set
down between 1677 and 1703, but it is notable that nearly all the
identifiable plays and playwrights in the list are Jacobean and
Caroline.

J. Q. Adams suggests (*Library*, Fourth Series, xx [1939], 89) that Hill's play may have been Lodowick Carlell's *Osmond the Great Turk, or the Noble Servant* (q.v.), but one of the odd things about that play is that Osmond, in spite of the title, is not *the Great Turk* or even *the Turk*, though he is *the Noble Servant*. Though Carlell's title is inappropriate for his play, this one would seem to be more so.

Ovo Frisius (11 July 1624)
(Lost)

McCabe, William H. 'Notes on the St. Omers College Theatre', *Phil. Quart.* xvii (1938), 225–39.
—— 'The Play-List of the English College of St. Omers 1592–1762', *Revue de littérature comparée*, xvii (1937), 355–75.

The play was acted at the Jesuit College for English boys at St. Omers, 11 July 1624. Father McCabe notes that the probable subject was a Benedictine of Fontenelle who died in 749. ('Play-List', p. 363.)

The Owl
(Ghost title?)

The evidence concerning an allegedly printed play called *The Owl* is set forth by Dr. Greg. (*Bibliography*, ii. 976.) On 8 February 1603/4 White and Lynge entered in the Stationers' Register 'A Booke called the Owle', apparently Drayton's poem of the name, which they published. On 29 June 1624 their rights to 'The Owle' were transferred to Edward Aldee, but sixteen years later the copy that was transferred from Mrs. Aldee to Oulton was called 'The Owle a play'. In 1655 'The Owle, a Play' was advertised among 'Bookes Printed; and . . . Sold by Jane Bell', who, according to Dr. Greg, 'is known to have come somehow into possession of a number of Oulton's copies', and in 1656 'Owle C.' appeared in Edward Archer's 'Exact and perfect Catalogue of all the Plaies that were ever printed'.

All this sounds very much like the accidental transformation of a poem into a play, and it may be that nothing more is involved. Jane Bell may, however, have had something more than Drayton's poem; there was a play called 'the Oule' delivered to Henslowe by Robert Daborne in 1614, but there is no evidence that it was ever printed.

Whether the various records indicate a simple confused

designation of a poem as a play, or a survival of Daborne's manuscript, it does not seem likely that there is any evidence here of
a play written after 1616 called *The Owl*.

The Painted Lady (?)
(Lost)

The title occurs ninth in Abraham Hill's list of plays in manuscript. (See Middleton, *The Conqueror's Custom*.) This list seems
to have been Hill's record of some bookseller's stock, set down
between 1677 and 1703, but it is notable that nearly all the identifiable plays and playwrights in the list are Jacobean or Caroline.

There is no other record of this title. In his discussion of Hill's
list (*Library*, Fourth Series, xx [1939], 83) J. Q. Adams points out
that the title would apply to Milicent of Brome's *English Moor*
(q.v.), whose husband paints her, that the term is used in the
stage directions, and that a manuscript of the play is extant. The
evidence seems to me quite inadequate for identifying Hill's play
with *The English Moor*. That play already has the sub-title *The
Mock Marriage*; Bernard Wagner's report of the manuscript
(*T.L.S.*, 4 October 1943, p. 675) says nothing of another title used
there; the prologue and epilogue do not use the term 'painted lady'
or refer to that action in the play; the last scene of the play does
not refer to 'painted lady', though just before the end one character
says, 'Though Mr. *Quicksands* made a *Mock-marriage* with his
English Moor, Ile not mock thee'. Such evidence as we have,
therefore, indicates only that *The Painted Lady* is an otherwise
unknown play.

Pandoræ Pyxis (?)
(Lost)

This title—marked 'Latin'—occurs fiftieth in the list of manuscript plays found among the papers of Abraham Hill. (See
Middleton, *The Conqueror's Custom*.) The list seems to have been
Hill's record of the stock of some bookseller, set down between
1677 and 1703, but it is notable that nearly all the identifiable
plays and playwrights of the list are Jacobean or Caroline.

As J. Q. Adams points out in his discussion of Hill's list (*Library*,
Fourth Series, xx [1939], 98), the play may well have been an
academic drama, though we have no record of the treatment of
the theme. William Killigrew's *Pandora, or The Converts*, published in 1664, is in English.

The Parricide (1624)
(Lost)

1624, 27 May. 'For the Prince's Company; A Play, called, *The Parracide.*' (Adams, *Herbert*, p. 28.)

The very tempting conclusion that this play was the same as, or an earlier form of, 'The Paraside or Revenge for hono^r by Henry Glapthorne', entered in the Stationers' Register by Richard Marriott 29 December [?] 1653 (see Greg, *Bibliography*, i. 62), and published the next year as *Revenge for Honour* 'By George Chapman', is almost certainly to be rejected. (See above, Glapthorne, *Revenge for Honour.*)

Nothing is known of the play licensed for the Prince's company.

The Parroiall of Princes (?)
(Lost)

1641, 15 Apr. S.R. John Nicholson entered for his copies 'three playes, vizt. A Tragedy called Charles, Duke of Burbon, The Parroiall of Princes & Englands first happines, or, the Life of St. Austin . . . xviii^d'. (G. E. B. Eyre, *A Transcript of the Registers of the Worshipful Company of Stationers from 1640–1708 A.D.*, i. 20. Inadvertently omitted in Greg, *Bibliography*, i. 54, but summarized ii. 977.)

The play is known only from Nicholson's entry of his manuscript. Even the title is uncertain: Dr. Greg points out that 'Parroill' could equally well have been a miswriting of '"Parail" (apparel),"Pareil" (equal, mate),"Parol" (utterance),or"Parole" (word of honour)'. (*Bibliography*, ii. 977.)

Parthenia (c. 1625–30?)

MS.: Emmanuel College, Cambridge, 1. 3. 16 (item 5).

Churchill, George B., and Wolfgang Keller. 'Die lateinischen Universitäts-Dramen Englands in der Zeit der Königin Elisabeth', *Shakespeare Jahrbuch*, xxxiv (1898), 319–22.

Greg, W. W. *Pastoral Poetry & Pastoral Drama* (1906), p. 368, n. 1.

This Latin play follows the *Pseudomagia* of Mewes of Emmanuel and the *Paria* of Vincent of Trinity in the Emmanuel College MS. Since both the others were Cambridge plays, there is a suggestion that *Parthenia* was too, a suggestion made more tempting by the fact that all three plays are transcribed in very similar —possibly identical—hands. Unlike the others, *Parthenia* begins abruptly without any indication of authorship, dramatis personae, or prologue; it does have an epilogue. The association with the other plays suggests a date in the middle twenties, but this is extremely weak evidence.

Churchill and Keller, who give a synopsis of the play, note that its source is Luigi Groto's *Il Pentimento Amoroso*, published at Venice in 1576 (1586?). Greg's observation that the names of the principal characters were the pastoral titles of Sidney and Watson is, in the light of the source, as he suspected, probably a coincidence. Greg and Churchill and Keller say that the play was probably acted at Cambridge, but they offer nothing beyond the provenance of the manuscript as evidence.

The Partial Law (?)

MS.: Folger Shakespeare Library MS. 553.1.
Edition: Edited by Bertram Dobell, 1908.

Greg, W. W. [Review of *The Partial Law*, Dobell ed.] *Modern Language Review*, iv (1908–9), 118–19.
Parrott, T. M. 'Two Late Dramatic Versions of the Slandered Bride Theme', *Joseph Quincy Adams Memorial Studies* (1948), pp. 537–51. (Includes synopsis.)

The source of the play is the Ariodante and Ginevra story from the fifth canto of *Orlando Furioso*, which, according to Dobell, has been followed all too closely. Professor Parrott considers various versions of the tale. There seems to be no evidence that the author of *The Partial Law* was influenced by Shakespeare's handling of the story in *Much Ado about Nothing*.

No clue to the authorship of the play has been found. Dobell considers and rejects Glapthorne and Massinger; Dr. Greg, in his review of the edition, concurred in the rejection and noted that it sounds rather like the work of some courtly amateur of the reign of Charles I.

Dobell dates the manuscript, from the hand, 1615–30. Though I know nothing to contradict such a conclusion, dating of this sort is hazardous in the extreme, for the play itself yields no specific evidence of date; though it sounds Caroline, a few plays written both before and after the reign of Charles I sound so too.

If the tragi-comedy was ever produced, the text shows no sign of it. The stage directions are literary in type, and some of them suggest that the author did not have stage practicability very clearly in mind. Probably *The Partial Law* is closet drama.

Passions Calmed

An alternative title for Strode's *Floating Island* (q.v.).

The Pastoral (> 1634)
(Ghost title?)

1633/4, 6 Feb. 'For a booke & the play of pastorell [?] . . . 00–02–00.' (Account book of Sir Humphrey Mildmay. See above, ii. 675.)

1634, 8 Apr. 'The Pastorall was playd by the king's players on Easter-tusday night, at the Cockpitt in court.' (Adams, *Herbert*, p. 55.)

It is not unlikely that both the above entries refer to Fletcher's pastoral, *The Faithful Shepherdess*, but one cannot be sure. That play had been reprinted in 1629 and 1634 (see Greg, *Bibliography*, i. 424–5), and there was a court performance by the King's men on 6 January 1633/4, which must have been widely noted, since the company acted in the costumes that had been made for the Queen and her ladies the year before. (See above, i. 38–39 and n. 1.) Mildmay's entry seems to record the purchase of a printed play; the 1629 edition of *The Faithful Shepherdess* was available, and the 1634 edition may have been already off the press. It is noteworthy that the company which performed 'The Pastorall' at court was the one which owned *The Faithful Shepherdess* and had performed it there successfully three months before.

A lost play called *The Pastoral* could have been performed by the King's men at court. It is not likely that Sir Humphrey could have bought a printed play of which there is no other record, but his entry is oddly stated. It might possibly be construed to mean that his two shillings covered the cost of a book and admission to a performance of 'the play of pastorell', though it is not in the form customarily used by Mildmay for expenses at the theatre. Such an interpretation seems to me extremely dubious on other grounds, however, since his diary entry for that day records his attendance at a play at court which he does not name, but which other records show to have been Shirley's *Gamester* (q.v.). I doubt if he would have gone to one play in the afternoon and another at court at night.

The Mildmay entries are sadly confused in Philip Lee Ralph's *Sir Humphrey Mildmay, Royalist Gentleman* (1947), p. 48. He has scrambled the diary and account records for two different days, assumed the account above to indicate a theatre admission and not a book purchase, and combined Mildmay's companions on two different occasions.

Pastor Stapilton

See Sir Robert Stapleton.

Pathomachia, or The Battle of the Affections, or Love's Loadstone (1615–17??)

MSS.: Bodleian MS. Eng. Misc. e. 5; B.M. MS. Harl. 6869, Article 1.
Edition: Edited by Paul Edward Smith, 1942.

Boas, F. S. 'University Plays', *Cambridge History of English Literature* (ed. 1910), vi. 323–4.
Russell, H. K. 'Tudor and Stuart Dramatizations of the Doctrines of Natural and Moral Philosophy', *Stud. Phil.* xxxi (1934), 1–27.

1630, 16 Apr. S.R. Mr. Constable entered for his copy 'vnder the hand[es] of Sr Hen: Herbert and Mr Bill warden A play Called The Battell of The affections or Loues. Loadstone'. (Greg, *Bibliography*, i. 38.)
1630. Pathomachia: *Or*, The Battell Of *Affections*. Shadowed By A Faigned Siedge Oe The Citie *Pathopolis*. Written some yeeres since, and now first published by a Friend of the deceassed Avthor . . . 1630.

The alternative titles of this play have several times been treated as separate pieces, but all three are used in the first edition; the first two appear on the title-page, and the third is used as the running title. '*Battel of Affliction*', which appears in Archer's list of 1656 and has sometimes been copied elsewhere, is probably a misprint or a misreading of the sub-title of this play.

Pathomachia has been variously assigned to Anthony Brewer, H. More, and Thomas Tomkis. The Brewer assignment, like several others to this overworked dramatist, is due to a misreading of Kirkman's list in which many plays that he treated as anonymous have been taken as assigned to the dramatist last mentioned in his list. (See Smith ed., *Pathomachia*, pp. 4–6.) The attribution to H. More was made without reason or comment by

Lowndes: 'a drama attributed to H. More'. Nothing further
about this man has ever appeared. Smith succeeds in eliminating
all the H. Mores discoverable at Cambridge, including the Cambridge Platonist, except one. He finds nothing at all about this
man except the record of his entrance at Trinity in 1611, not
enough to verify Lowndes's statement. (Ibid., p. 8.) The attribution to Thomas Tomkis, author of *Lingua* and *Albumazar*, has had
many supporters since Moore Smith pointed out *Pathomachia*'s
resemblances in type, method, and subject-matter to *Lingua*, as
well as two direct references to 'Madame Lingua'. (*M.L.R.* iii
[1908], 149–50.) Smith (ed. cit., pp. 10–23) develops these resemblances and points out that *Pathomachia* is complementary to
Lingua, since the latter deals with 'the outward senses which
initiate the process of transmitting "phantasms" to the brain' and
the former 'with the "sensitive appetite" which consists of the
affections'. His case for Tomkis's authorship is interesting, but
it seems to be demolished by Hugh Dick (ed. *Albumazar*, pp.
7–9 and 11), who has succeeded in tracing Tomkis's later career
to his burial at Wolverhampton on 30 September 1634. This burial
date destroys his candidacy, for the author of *Pathomachia* is
called the 'deceassed Avthor' on the title-page of the 1630
edition, and the publisher of the play confirms the description
in his dedication: 'The Author (being dead).' In any case, the
similarities between the two plays do not, as Professor Dick
points out, 'constitute proof of identical authorship, because they
do not exclude the possibility of deliberate imitation'.

Pathomachia appears to be a university play: probably no
other Jacobean audience would have listened to such an involved
allegorical presentation of psychology; for no other audience
would an author write, 'I could sing, I thinke, as well as the
Florentine Nunne, if I might see Mules tread vpon the Altars;
or Stables of Asses, or Kennels of Hounds in the Colledges of the
Vniuersities' (I. 2. 35–38), or 'This is a fresh question indeed, as
if one should aske how many Colledges, or Halles there be in the
Vniuersities' (I. 3. 13–15), or 'you would haue Fellowes in Colledges
to haue Wiues' (IV. 3. 27–28), as pointed out by Moore Smith
(*M.L.R.* iii [1908], 149) and Hanford (*Anniversary Papers* . . .
Kittredge, p. 455). Cambridge rather than Oxford is indicated by
the fact that the three plays referred to in the text, *Lingua*,
Albumazar, and *Ignoramus*, are all productions of Trinity College,
Cambridge. In the B.M. MS. of the play, two pages before the
beginning of the text of *Pathomachia*, 'For Sr Robert Filmer in
Westminster' is written across the page; Moore Smith notes

(*College Plays*, p. 100) that Filmer matriculated at Trinity 5 July 1604 and was knighted 24 January 1618/19. These facts all imply that *Pathomachia* was written by a Trinity man for performance at that college.

Various allusions in the play noted by Moore Smith suggest a date in 1615 or not long after. The play contains allusions to the Gunpowder Plot (1605), *Lingua* (1607), the assassination of Henry IV (1610), Coryat (presumably to his first publications of 1611), and to *Ignoramus* and *Albumazar* (both performed at Trinity in March 1614/15). Moore Smith thinks that 'Sir Octaviana-opobalsama-owennist', one of the additional names of Pride added in the Bodleian MS. of the play, may refer to John Owen, a Catholic of Godstow who achieved some notoriety in 1615. In the light of these allusions Moore Smith suggests 'that *Lingua* was revived in 1616 or 1617 and *Pathomachia* acted at the same time or a year later'. (*M.L.R.* iii [1908], 150.) This date accords well enough with the statement on the title-page of the 1630 quarto, 'Written some yeeres since', but better evidence for a *terminus ad quem* would be welcome. P. E. Smith has nothing new on the problem of date.

I have not seen the Bodleian MS. of the play, which contains a number of additional titles for Pride (quoted Smith ed., p. 158), several of which probably incorporate allusions that escape me. The B.M. MS. (P. E. Smith collates neither of the manuscripts) is written in a hand at least very similar to that of *The Fallacy* (q.v.), which immediately follows in the manuscript. A sampling collation suggests that the B.M. MS. is a better text than the quarto and somewhat fuller.

Paulus Japonensis (11 June 1624)
(Lost)

McCabe, William H. 'Notes on the St. Omers College Theatre', *Phil. Quart.* xvii (1938), 225–39.
—— 'The Play-List of the English College of St. Omers 1592–1762', *Revue de littérature comparée*, xvii (1937), 355–75.

The play, a tragedy, was acted at the Jesuit College for English boys at St. Omers 11 June 1624. Father McCabe suggests that the subject was probably 'one of several Pauls martyred at Nagasaki with the Jesuit Charles Spinola in 1622'. ('Play-List', p. 363.)

The Peaceable King or the Lord Mendall (1606–22)
(Lost)

1623, 19 Aug. 'For the Prince's Servants of the Red Bull; an Oulde Playe, called, *The Peaceable King; or the Lord Mendall*, which was formerly allowed by Sir George Bucke, and likewise by me.' (Adams, *Herbert*, pp. 24–25.)

1623, 19 Aug. 'For the Princes servants of the Rede Bull—An oulde [playe called the] Peacable Kinge or the lord Mendall former[ly allowed of by Sir] George Bucke & likewise by mee & because [itt was free from adition] or reformation I tooke no fee this 19‡ Aug! [1623].' (Folger Shakespeare Library, Scrapbook of J. O. Halliwell-Phillipps, *Theatres of Shakespeare's Time*, p. 53.)

The second version of Sir Henry Herbert's licence comes from an independent transcript of his office-book in a nineteenth-century hand. This transcript, perhaps that of Craven Ord, has been cut up and pasted into appropriate sections of Halliwell-Phillipps's scrap-books now in the Folger Shakespeare Library. The bracketed words seem to have been inadvertently cut off before the pasting and have been added in a different hand. This transcript adds the information that no revisions of the play had been made, and Herbert took no fee.

If Sir George Buc licensed the play in its original form, it must have been first produced during his period of activity in the Revels Office, 1606–22. (See 'Sir George Buc, Master of the Revels', in C. J. Sisson, ed., *Thomas Lodge and Other Elizabethans* [1933], pp. 432–5, 459–64, 481–2.) I know of no evidence to restrict the period more narrowly, though one might assume that 'Oulde Playe' did not mean one of the last year or so. The company had been active in London since 1610 (see above, i. 198), but that date will not do for a *terminus a quo*, since the Prince's men could have got it from an earlier company.

Nothing is known of the subject or the later history of the play.

Pelopidarum Secunda (?)

MS.: B.M. MS. Harleian 5110, fols. 27–81ᵛ.

The manuscript of this rather long play in English is simply headed 'Pelopidar̄u Secunda' and begins without further ado. Under the title is written in a different hand the date '16 October 1725', and this might be thought significant for the play, until it is noted that the same date in the same hand appears at the head of several other manuscripts in the volume, one of which is internally dated 1593 and another 1645. The eighteenth-century date may be a date of purchase or assembly, but it is not the date of *Pelopidarum Secunda*. There appear to be several hands in the play, apparently taking over a copying task seriatim; they are all sixteenth or early seventeenth century in character. The action seems to get a good part of the story of the house of Atreus crowded into five acts.

The association of the piece with Winchester is indicated by several lines in the epilogue:

> We might alleadge our youth and discipline
> the want of imitatio͞ of lives
> Of famous me in this retired place
>
> .   .   .   .
>
> Know this that our [most?] thankfull recompense
> can but account yᵘ founders (?) of our merit (?)
> and   you wᵗʰ good willi͞a of Wickam
> Thincke this (?) is no small magnificence
> to be the founders of a colledge praise

Composition in the reign of Queen Elizabeth seems to be indicated in the epilogue line, 'And many helps that god oʳ Queene and founder / yealds'.

Perfidus Hetruscus (?)

MS.: Bodleian MS. Rawlinson C. 787.

Churchill, George B., and Wolfgang Keller. 'Die lateinischen Universitäts-Dramen Englands in der Zeit der Königin Elisabeth', *Shakespeare Jahrbuch*, xxxiv (1898), 250–2.

Churchill and Keller quote the dramatis personae of the play, part of the prologue, and the last speech, and they give a synopsis. They have nothing to offer concerning place of production or date, except a general classification of the tragedy as seventeenth century.

Petrus Crudelis

See Anon., *A Spanish Tragedy of Petrus Crudelis*.

[*Philander, King of Thrace*] (< 1627)
(Lost? Unwritten?)

Adams, J. Q. 'The Author-Plot of an Early Seventeenth Century Play', *Library*, Fourth Series, xxvi (1945–6), 17–27.

In the Folger Shakespeare Library (MS. 1137.5) there is an author's scenario and miscellaneous notes for three acts of a tragi-comedy without title, which was called *Philander, King of Thrace* in a Maggs catalogue of 1923. (Adams, loc. cit.) Dr. Adams found references to and quotations from a publication of 1627 in the plot and notes, thus establishing a *terminus a quo*. In his article Dr. Adams reprints the entire author-plot; there is no evidence that the play planned was ever written.

Philip of Macedon (?)
(Lost)

This title is twenty-eighth in the list of manuscript plays found among the papers of Abraham Hill. (See Middleton, *The Conqueror's Custom*.) The list seems to have been Hill's record of some bookseller's stock, set down between 1677 and 1703, but it is notable that nearly all the identifiable plays and playwrights of the list are Jacobean or Caroline.

There is no other record of a seventeenth-century play of this title.

Pity the Maid (> 1653)
(Lost)

1653, 29 [Dec.] S.R. Richard Marriott entered as his copies a number of plays, including 'Pitty the Maid'. (Greg, *Bibliography*, i. 62.)

The only evidence for the existence of a play of this name is Marriott's entry in the Stationers' Register. Two-thirds of the twenty-one titles in this list of plays occur nowhere else, and only three were published later under these titles, though four are known from other references. (See below, Anon., *The Woman's Law*, for the entire list.)

A Tragedy of the Plantation of Virginia (1623)
(Lost)

1623, Aug. 'For the Company at the Curtain; A Tragedy of *the*

Plantation of Virginia; *the profaneness to be left out*, otherwise not tolerated.' (Adams, *Herbert*, p. 24.)

1623, Aug. 'August [1623] `A Tragedy of the Plantation of Virginia, the [prophaness left out] contayninge 16 sheets & one   May be acted [els not for the] companye at the Curtune Founde fault with the length of this playe & [commanded a] reformation in all their other playes.' (Folger Shakespeare Library, Scrap-books of J. O. Halliwell-Phillipps, *Fortune*, p. 85.)

The second version of Sir Henry Herbert's licence comes from an independent transcript of his office-book in a nineteenth-century hand. This transcript, perhaps that of Craven Ord, has been cut up and pasted into appropriate sections of Halliwell-Phillipps's scrap-books, now in the Folger Shakespeare Library. The bracketed words seem to have been inadvertently cut off before the pasting and have been added in a different hand. The incoherence of the statement suggests that part of it may have been undecipherable or mutilated in the original. This transcript adds the information about the length of the play and Herbert's objection to it. Herbert seems to mean that the reformation he demanded in the rest of the company's plays was in their length, but a reformation of profaneness would be a more usual request, especially if the company were a provincial one with an unfamiliar repertory.

It is not clear what company was acting at the Curtain in August 1623. (See above, i. 205–9.) Prince Charles's (I) company had recently been there, but they appear to have moved to the Red Bull by this date and left the Curtain to some troupe that was not one of the regular London companies. (Ibid.) Such a troupe could have been one of those which normally played in the provinces but which was trying a London season.

Nothing of the tragedy is known; the title is highly suggestive, especially to those interested in colonial American history, for a play devoted largely to the American colonies would be unique at this time.

Plenum Reconciled to Kulum

The manuscript described under this title in the Historical Manuscripts Commission, Third Report, 1872, Appendix, p. 43, and so listed elsewhere, is Jonson's masque, *Pleasure Reconciled to Virtue*. See Herford and Simpson, *Ben Jonson*, vii [1941], 475–8.

The Politic Bankrupt, or Which Is the Best Girl (?)

(Lost)

1653, 9 Sept. S.R. In a long list of plays which Humphrey Moseley entered as his copies occurs the title, 'The Politique Bankrupt, or which is yᵉ Best Girle'. (See Greg, *Bibliography*, i. 61.)

Nothing is known of the play save the entry in the Stationers' Register. This list of plays licensed by the great dramatic publisher Humphrey Moseley on 9 September 1653 is a puzzling one, since more than half the plays are now lost, and several others, like *Believe as You List*, *The Soddered Citizen*, and *The Inconstant Lady*, were never printed in the seventeenth century. Many of the plays in the list have alternative titles, and in some cases the alternative titles cover two plays. (See Greg, *Bibliography*, ii. 979–80.) Moseley names authors for all the plays in the list except *The Countryman*, *The King's Mistress*, and *The Politic Bankrupt, or Which Is the Best Girl*. This title stands between plays by William Rowley and Shakerley Marmion, but I know no reason to connect it with either man.

The Prince of Prigs' Revels

See J. S.

Priscianus Vapulans (> 1622)

(Lost?)

W. C. Hazlitt listed *Priscianus Vapulans* as a lost play (*A Manual for the Amateur and Collector of Old English Plays* [1892], p. 185), on the basis of an extract from Peacham's *The Compleat Gentleman*, printed by John Fry in his *Bibliographical Memoranda in Illustration of Early English Drama* (1816), p. 193. Hazlitt said that the play was entered in the Stationers' Register 'Feb. 9, 1630[-1]', but here he confused Fry's note to Peacham, which says that *Pedantius*, not *Priscianus Vapulans*, was entered on that date, as indeed it was, and duly published in 1631. What Peacham said was:

Hence it comes to passe, that in many places, especially in *Italy*, of all professions that of *Pedanteria* is held in basest repute; the Schoole-master almost in euery Comedy being brought vpon the Stage, to paralell the *Zani*, or *Pantaloun*. He made vs good sport in that excellent Comedy of *Pedantius*, acted in our Trinitie Colledge in

Cambridge: and if I bee not deceiued, in *Priscianus vapulans*, and many of our English Playes. (*The Compleat Gentleman*, [1622], pp. 26–27. Fry quoted from the 1627 edition.)

I have not been able to find any other record of a *Priscianus Vapulans*. Hazlitt understood Peacham to mean that it was a Latin play written in England, like the Elizabethan *Pedantius*. (See the edition by G. C. Moore Smith, *Materialien*, viii [1905].) Peacham might, however, have been referring to a continental Latin play and might have expected his statement to be understood as meaning 'in *Priscianus vapulans*, as well as in many of our own English Playes'. The title and the context suggest that the play made a butt of Priscianus Caesariensis.

A Projector Lately Dead (1634–6)
(Ghost title?)

A pamphlet of 1636, sometimes said to have been written by William Prynne and sometimes by Henry Burton, notes a play which is otherwise entirely unknown:

His [Attorney-General Noy's, d. 1634] clients the Players, for whom he had done knight-service, to requite his kindnesse, the next Terme following make him the subject of a merry Comedy, stiled, *A Projector lately dead*; wherein they bring him in his Lawyers robes upon the Stage, and openly dissecting him, find 100 Proclamations in his head, a bundle of motheaten records in his maw, halfe a barrell of new white sope in his belly, which made him to scoure so much, and yet, say they, he is still very blacke and foule within. (*A Divine Tragedie Lately Acted, Or A Collection of Sundry Memorable Examples of Gods Judgements upon Sabbath-Breakers* [1636], p. 45.)

The account of the play in Robert Ryece's letter of 1 March 1636/7 from London to John Winthrop in Massachusetts is not an independent record, but a summary and quotation of the pamphlet. (*Winthrop Papers*, Massachusetts Historical Society, iii [1943], 361.)

It may be that there was such a play, but it seems to me equally likely that it was invented by the pamphleteer for propaganda purposes. It is a relevant consideration here that Noy as Attorney-General had prosecuted William Prynne with great vigour, and much of the pamphlet is a vilification of him; the Puritan author betrays great satisfaction in the painful circumstances of Noy's last illness and death.

The Proxy, or Love's Aftergame (1634)
(Lost)

1634, 24 Nov. '*The Proxy, or Love's Aftergame*, was produced at the theatre at Salisbury Court, November 24, 1634.' (Adams, *Herbert*, p. 36.)

1635/6, 24 Feb. '*Loves Aftergame*, played at St. James by the Salisbury Court players, the 24 of Feb. 1635.' (Ibid., p. 56.)

1636/7, 18 Feb. 'A Warrant for payment of 50^{li} vnto Richard Heton for himselfe and the rest of ye company of ye Players at Salisbury Court for playes Acted by them before his Ma^{ty} in Octob. & Feb. 1635 (vizt) 2 at 20^{li} a peece at Hampton, the other at 10^{li} being at St Iames. Febr. 18. 1636.' The marginal entry is 'Players of Salisbury Court'. (*Malone Society Collections*, ii. 381–2, from a book of Lord Chamberlain's warrants at the Public Record Office, L.C. 5/134.)

1653, 29 [Dec.] S.R. Richard Marriott entered as his copies a number of plays, including 'The Proxe or Loues after Game'. (Greg, *Bibliography*, i. 62.)

The play is not extant, and there is no hint as to its author, though we have several records of its existence. Since the King's Revels company seems to have been performing at the Salisbury Court theatre at the time Sir Henry Herbert says that the play was acted there (see above, i. 291–4), the play must have been the property of that company. The fact that they presented it at court in one of their few known performances there (see above, i. 299) suggests that it was one of their better plays, and as such one would have expected it to get into print, but not even Fleay (*Biog. Chron.* ii. 336) has suggested an identification with an extant play, and Marriott's licence ought to indicate that it had not been printed before 1653. Of the twenty-one titles that Marriott licensed in this entry, two-thirds are otherwise unknown, only three were published later under these titles, and only three besides *The Proxy* are known from other sources, though unpublished. (See Anon., *The Woman's Law*, for the entire list.)

Presumably *The Proxy* is the play for whose performance at St. James's Richard Heton, manager of the Salisbury Court theatre, was paid 18 February 1636/7. (*M.S.C.* ii. 381–2.)

Prudentius

An alternative title for Strode's *Floating Island* (q.v.).

Publius Cornelius Scipio Sui Victor (?)

MS.: Folger Shakespeare Library MS. 1. 27. 42.

This is a very short—500 to 800 lines—Latin play in five acts. The hand seems to be a seventeenth-century one, but I saw no signs of provenance or date. The characters are Publius Cornelius Scipio, Eucharis, Allucius, Spartus, Lucius, Mago, &c., and a large collection of gods and heroes, mostly in the choruses.

Pygmalion (?)

MS.: Bodleian Library MS. Rawl. D. 317, fols. 190–5.

Bowers, R. H. 'An Anonymous Renaissance Pygmalion Playlet', *Mod. Phil.* xlvii (1949–50), 73–81.

The manuscript volume, formerly belonging to Thomas Hearne, which includes *Pygmalion* contains a large number of miscellaneous items, more than a score of them dated variously from 1609 to 1707 and three-fourths of these from 1620 to 1670. The play is very short, 260 lines, without title-page, dramatis personae, or prologue. The hand looks like a mid-seventeenth-century one.

Professor Bowers (loc. cit.) reprints the text. He dates it 1630–50, and though this seems a reasonable guess, there is little to support it, certainly not the evidence he cites.

The Queen

See John Ford.

Revenge for Honour

See Henry Glapthorne.

The Ring
(Ghost title?)

A play of this name is mentioned in the dialogue of Act II of James Shirley's *The Bird in a Cage*, published in 1633 and acted shortly before.

> *Don[dolo]*. Sir if you can assure vs this invisible walking, for wee are not so ignorant as wee seeme, wee ha seene the Play of the *Jnvisible Knight*, and—

Bon[amico]. That of the Ring too, ha ye not.
Don. Yes.
Bon. The one was Magick, and t'other an imposture, what I doe is
by Art faire and naturall. (D₃ᵛ.)

No play of the title is now known. Robert Dodsley said in his
notes on the passage (*A Select Collection of Old Plays* [1780], viii.
232, n. 8) that *The Ring* is 'the comedy of *The two merry Milkmaids, or, The best Words weare the Garland.* By J. C. 1620.' This
seems to me highly dubious, but I cannot say that it is impossible.
It may be that the two titles are fictitious, like those used by
Middleton in *The Mayor of Quinborough,* Act v. Scene 1, but the
situation here does not suggest it so strongly.

Risus Anglicanus (< 1608)

MS.: Folger Shakespeare Library MS. 2203.1, fols. 24–43.

This anti-Catholic Latin play is concerned with the quarrel
between James I and the Jesuits. A papal document at the end of
II. I is dated 'Kal: Sept: 1608'. Among the characters are 'Igna-
tius Loiola', 'Lucifer', 'Paulus PP Quintus', 'Matthæus Tortus',
'Gaspar Scioppius', 'Martinus Becanus', 'Andræas Eudæmon
Joannes', 'Bartolus Pacenius I. C.ᵗᵘˢ', 'Leonardus Coquæus',
'Franciscus Soarez', 'Thomas Fitz-herbert', and 'Typographus
Politanus'. FitzHerbert always speaks English.

Several of the characters could probably be identified and the
play more closely dated by a study of the pamphlet literature of
the controversy.

The Roaring Girl or the Catchpole (c. 1640?)
(Lost?)

In Act III, Scene 3, of Thomas Jordan's popular success, *The
Walks of Islington and Hogsdon* (q.v.), Tripes, a Sergeant, says:

> If scurvy usage will make them quarrel they shal not want it, I hope
> *Tripes* is not to learn to use a man scurvily, I'm sure I have practiz'd
> these 20. years, and there's never a one that ever I arrested yet can
> give me a good word; The Players brought me oth' Stage once I
> thank them in a Play call'd the *Roaring Girle,* or *The Catchpole,* he
> was a pretty fellow that acted me, but he came short of the rogueries
> I have done. (Ed. 1657, E₂ᵛ–E₃.)

Tripes seems to allude to Middleton and Dekker's comedy, *The
Roaring Girl, or Moll Cut-Purse,* which was printed in 1611 and

probably acted not long before. (See *The Elizabethan Stage*, iii. 296–7.) But allusions in plays are generally timely, and there is no record that the Middleton–Dekker comedy—itself a timely piece—had been acted for over a quarter of a century when Jordan's play was produced in 1641. Moreover, the sub-title of *The Roaring Girl* is not *The Catchpole* but *Moll Cut-Purse*, after the notorious London figure. There is a sergeant, Curtleax, in the Middleton–Dekker play, but he appears in only one scene and has few lines, surely not enough for an audience to remember and appreciate Tripes's remark, as Jordan evidently expected them to.

In the circumstances one can only conjecture that in 1641 the old Middleton–Dekker comedy had been recently revived with the part of Curtleax expanded enough to make it memorable, and perhaps with a new sub-title, or else that Jordan was referring to another play called *The Roaring Girl or The Catchpole*, which had been produced in 1640 or 1641 and is now lost.

Incidentally, it would be in accord with comic repertory tradition if the actor in the role of Tripes at the Red Bull in 1641 were the same as the one who had played the other sergeant recently in *The Roaring Girl*—whichever play it was—at this same theatre before the same audience.

Robin Conscience (?)
(Ghost title?)

Richard Rogers and William Ley published in 1656 'An exact and perfect Catalogue of all Playes that are Printed', and they appended the list to their edition of Thomas Goffe's *The Careless Shepherdess*, 1656. One title in this list is 'Robin conscience'. The title also appears in several other seventeenth-century play-lists. (See Greg, *Bibliography*, ii. 995.) Dr. Greg points out that it probably refers to 'The Booke in Meeter of Robin Conscience', twice published in the sixteenth century, which is a dialogue, not a play.

Robin Hood, Parts I and II
(Ghost title?)

Edward Archer appended to his edition of Massinger, Middleton, and Rowley's *The Old Law*, 1656, 'An Exact and perfect Catalogue of all Plaies that were ever printed; together, with all the Authors names; and what are Comedies, Histories, Interludes, Masks, Pastorels, Tragedies'. Dr. Greg shows that this catalogue of Archer's is derived from the similar list of Rogers and Ley published in the same year. (*Bibliography*, ii. 996.) One title in Archer's list is 'Robin Hood, both parts C'. It seems likely that this unidentifiable title is the result of another of Archer's confusions (see ibid., p. 999), and in any case it is not likely to refer to a play of the period 1616–42. But one cannot be certain.

[*Romanus*] (?)
(Fragment)

MS.: B.M. Harleian MS. 4628, Article 14, fols. 272–82ᵛ.

This manuscript is a synopsis and a fragment of a titleless play whose chief character is Romanus. The fragment consists of two scenes of the first act, ending:

Rom: This was not all for when

Apparently no more was written—or copied—for the fragment breaks off about an inch higher on the page than the writer was accustomed to stop. The synopsis begins:

The first act contaynes
1 Romanus returns to Sardinia after victory over the scithians

and continues for five acts of several scenes each. At the end Romanus and Eudoria die of grief.

A number of papers in the miscellaneous collection of which this play-fragment is a part pertained to a man named James Cobbes whose name appears in various places and is scribbled several times at the end. One document is endorsed 'To my very woorthy Vncle Mʳ James Cobbs at Mʳˢ Bashfords howse ouer agᵗ the blew bore in Holbourne'. There is no indication that James Cobbes was the author of the play or even any certain evidence that he was the owner of the manuscript.

Roxolana, or the Ambitious Stepdame (?)
(Lost?)

This title occurs seventeenth in Abraham Hill's list of plays in manuscript. (See Middleton, *The Conqueror's Custom*.) The list seems to have been Hill's record of some bookseller's stock, set down between 1677 and 1703, but it is notable that nearly all the identifiable plays and playwrights in the list are Jacobean or Caroline.

J. Q. Adams points out (*Library*, Fourth Series, xx [1939], 89) that this title could well apply to Roger Boyle's *Mustapha, Son of Solyman the Magnificent*, produced in 1665, in which a principal character is Roxolana, who is an ambitious stepmother. Furthermore, several manuscripts of the play are extant. On the other hand, the story was well known, and Turkish history had been repeatedly used for plots since Elizabethan times; a later manuscript in Hill's list is called *Mustapha* and could be either Boyle's or Greville's play. The stepmother in Greville's play is called Rossa. Adams notes (loc. cit.) several other plays with 'stepmother' in the title, but none is very suggestive.

'Running Masque'

This name does not refer to a particular masque, but a type. On 12 February 1619/20 John Chamberlain wrote to Sir Dudley Carleton:

they passe the time merrilie at Newmarket and the running maske raunges all over the countrie, where there be fit subjects to entertain yt, as lately they have ben at Sir John Crofts neere Berrie. (McClure ed., *Letters of John Chamberlain*, ii. 288.)

And on 2 January 1627/8 Rowland Woodward wrote to Francis Windebank:

A thin court and a dead Christmas, only there will be a running masque on Sunday, which is not of above six days' conception. (*C.S.P., Dom., 1627–8*, p. 502.)

This type of masque is defined in a manuscript letter of Richard Sackville, written probably to Lady Temple and dated 3 January 1619/20:

They speake of three maskes this Christmass, but two certien the running maske and the Princes, the first soe called because they meane to runn from one howse to another some few of their selected frendes, where it shall be daunced, J humbly thanke them they wowlde haue don me the Honor to haue brought it to my howse, but my wiues being out of towne is a lawfull impedimente, and J showlde be out of countenaunce to entertaine soe many Ladyes alone as J knowe will come. (Folger Shakespeare Library, MS. 991 (1).)

The Sailors' Masque
(Ghost title)

J. O. Halliwell[-Phillipps] lists a number of masques as 'c. 1620' or 'temp. Jac I', including 'The Sailors' Masque'. (*A*

Dictionary of Old English Plays [1860], p. 218.) All the titles come from the B.M. MS. Add. 10444. This manuscript is not a collection of masques, but a collection of short musical compositions, many of which use the word 'masque' in the title. (See above, under John Adson.) There is no assurance that these tunes were even attached to masques, much less that the name of the tune was the name of a masque.

S. Damianus Episcopus Ticinensis turbas Italiae divinitus praedicit

See Joseph Simons.

S. Pelagius Martyr, tragoedia (27 July 1623)

MS.: Stonyhurst MS. B. VI. 10, No. 3.

McCabe, William H. 'Notes on the St. Omers College Theatre', *Phil. Quart.* xvii (1938), 225–39.
—— 'The Play-List of the English College of St. Omers 1592–1762', *Revue de littérature comparée*, xvii (1937), 355–75.

The play was performed at the Jesuit College for English boys at St. Omers on 27 July 1623. Father McCabe says that it consists of about 1,200 lines in verse in three acts on the subject of the boy martyr of Cordova. ('Play-List', p. 362.)

Salisbury Plain (> 1653)
(Lost?)

1653, 29 [Dec.] S.R. Richard Marriott entered as his copies a number of plays, including 'Salisbury Plaine a comedy'. (Greg, *Bibliography*, i. 62.)

The only certain evidence of the existence of a play of this name is Marriott's entry in the Stationers' Register. (See below, Anon., *The Woman's Law*, for the entire list.) It is possible that the manuscript which Marriott had was a copy of John Speed's *Stonehenge* (q.v.) with a different title.

Sanguis Sanguinem, tragoedia (14 April 1640)
(Lost?)

MS.: Bodleian MS. Rawlinson Poet. 215. (Probably not the St. Omers play.)

McCabe, William H. 'Notes on the St. Omers College Theatre',
Phil. Quart. xvii (1938), 225–39.

—— 'The Play-List of the English College of St. Omers 1592–
1762', *Revue de littérature comparée*, xvii (1937), 355–75.

A play called *Sanguis Sanguinem, tragoedia* was acted at the
Jesuit College for English boys at St. Omers 14 April 1640. Father
McCabe says that it concerned 'contemporary Jesuit martyrs in
England'. ('Play-List', pp. 366–7.) The play in the Bodleian MS.
is entitled *Sanguis Sanguinem, siue Constans fratricida tragœdia*,
and Madan says it is 'about the Emperor Constans ii, who killed
his brother Theodosius'. (*A Summary Catalogue of Western MSS.
in the Bodleian Library*, iii. 331, No. 14706.) The Bodleian MS. in
which *Sanguis Sanguinem* is found and which Madan dates about
1600 contains other Latin exercises of a religious nature by Roman
Catholic students and may well be a product of St. Omers. In
spite of the titles these plays are probably not the same; it is
somewhat more likely that the Bodleian play is the same as
Furor impius sive Constans fratricida in Stonyhurst MS. A. VII.
50 (2).

At the end of the Bodleian MS. of *Sanguis Sanguinem* after
'finis' appears the name, 'P. Couf'. Madan suggests that the
English version of the name would be Cuff, but there is no indication whether the name is that of the author of the play or not.

The Scholar Turned to School Again (> 1620)
(Lost)

c. 1619–20. '[T]he Scholler turnd to schoole againe' appears in a
list of plays on waste paper of the Revels Office, probably
dating about 1619 or 1620. It has been plausibly suggested that
the plays of the list were being considered for court performance.
(See Marcham, *Revels*, p. 11, and Chambers, *R.E.S.* i [1925],
484.)

The title is known only from the list of the Revels Office,
apparently prepared for consideration for performance at court.
Most of the plays on this page belonged to the King's company,
and none certainly belonged to any other company. Probably *The
Scholar Turned to School Again* belonged to the King's men.

The School Moderator

See John Mason.

Senilis Amor (1635 or 1635/6)

MS.: Bodleian MS. Rawlinson 9, fols. 46–81.

Mills, Laurens J. *Peter Hausted, Playwright, Poet, and Preacher.* Indiana University Publications, Humanities Series No. 12 (1944), p. 57.

Morgan, Louise B. 'The Latin University Drama', *Shakespeare Jahrbuch*, xlvii (1911), 81–82.

The play has several times been assigned to Peter Hausted (q.v.), with little more reason, apparently, than the similarity of the title to his *Senile Odium* (q.v.). The most extended presentation of evidence is Miss Louise Morgan's:

This play is usually accredited, although doubtfully, to Peter Hausted . . . or else is called anonymous. I think it is highly probable, from certain resemblances in title, *dramatis personae*, and general local atmosphere, (one play being located at Amsterdam, and the other at Frankfort-am-Main where an Antwerp merchant is staying temporarily) between this play and Hausted's known Latin play *Senile Odium*, that he is also the author of *Senilis Amor*. (*Shakespeare Jahrbuch*, xlvii [1911], 82.)

As evidence, this leaves something to be desired, and one is inclined to accept on faith Professor Mills's promise that 'the evidence, as I shall show in another paper, is altogether against such an attribution'. (*Hausted*, p. 57.)

The manuscript of the play is confused and incomplete. Miss Morgan notes, 'The ms is a very poor one, written on only one side of folios 46–80, in a large and clear, but careless script. The first act stands in good shape, with its seven scenes in due course, but the acts and scenes through the rest of the play are in the utmost disorder. Act III. sc. 5 for example follows an unnumbered scene of Act V.' (Op. cit., p. 81.) G. C. Moore Smith agrees as to the state of the manuscript and adds: 'A missing scene is sketched in another hand, with the note, "this sceane full of sport was basely torne out of this place".' (*College Plays*, p. 109.)

The date '1635' is written at the head of the manuscript itself, and Cooper suggests that it may have been one of the plays acted when the Elector Palatine, the Chancellor, and other nobles were entertained with feasting and comedies at the University in 1635/6. (*Annals of Cambridge*, iii. 273.) It is apparently from this suggestion that Moore Smith gets his date of 'c. Feb. 4 or 5' 1635/6 in his table of Cambridge performances. (Op. cit., p. 70.) The only reason for his queried assignment of the play to Queens'

College (ibid., p. 109) is that that was Hausted's college—a negligible reason, with no more evidence of Hausted's authorship than we have. There is somewhat better reason for thinking that *Senilis Amor* may have been presented at Trinity. Sir Simonds D'Ewes wrote in his autobiography:

> The next morning [i.e. 4 February 1635/6] . . . I came, with my brother Richard D'Ewes, pretty early to Newmarket . . . and had some general discourse with his Highness [the Prince Elector]. He was preparing for his departure for Cambridge; and I, intending to have been there some time before him, departed from Newmarket with the said Mr. Stone, and two others that had some relation to his Highness, about ten of the clock in the morning towards the University. But by an unfortunate mistake of the way, my coach came thither some half an hour after the Prince Elector was alighted at Trinity College. His Highness having seen St. John's College, King's College Chapel, (and having been welcomed with a Latin oration in each of those two places,) went into the Regent House about three of the clock in the afternoon, where he was made a Master of Arts, which degree also I took with him, as did many of the nobility and others. There was afterwards a Latin comedy acted at Trinity College, the hearing and sight of which I purposely avoided, because of women's apparel worn in it by boys and youths. (J. O. Halliwell, *The Autobiography and Correspondence of Sir Simonds D'Ewes*, ii. 139–40.)

There is, of course, no proof that the Trinity play for the Prince Elector which D'Ewes so sanctimoniously avoided was *Senilis Amor*, but at least there is evidence that a play was presented at Trinity on this occasion, and none that a play was presented at Queens'. The only Cambridge play that we have dated 1635 is *Senilis Amor*.

The Shepherds' Masque
(Ghost title)

J. O. Halliwell[-Phillipps] lists a number of masques as 'c. 1620' or 'temp. Jac I', including 'The Shepherd's Masque'. (*A Dictionary of Old English Plays* [1860], p. 225.) All the titles come from the B.M. MS. Add. 10444. This manuscript is not a collection of masques, but a collection of short musical compositions, many of which use the word 'masque' in the title. (See above, under John Adson.) There is no assurance that these tunes were even attached to masques, much less that the name of the tune was the name of a masque.

Sight and Search

See Anon., *Time's Triumph*.

Simo
(Ghost title?)

W. C. Hazlitt lists 'Simo: A Latin comedy. 4to, 1652'. (*A Manual for the Collector and Amateur of Old English Plays* [1892], p. 211.) Though his entry has been copied once or twice, I can find no evidence that a play with this title was printed in 1652, or at any other time in the sixteenth or seventeenth centuries.

Sisigambis, Queen of Syracuse (?)
(Fragment)

MS.: Bodleian Library MS. Rawlinson Poet. 167.

The Bodleian MS. is a fragment of the play, consisting of the first act and three scenes of the second. The front matter has been lost, and the page on which the text of the tragedy begins has been numbered 7 by the scribe. The hand is a late one, which Falconer Madan dated about 1700. (*A Summary Catalogue of Western Manuscripts in the Bodleian Library at Oxford* iii. [1895], 319.) It may be that the tragedy is a Restoration composition.

Sophomorus (1620?)
(Lost?)

The only direct evidence that a play of this name ever existed is Halliwell's statement: 'SOPHOMORUS. A Latin comedy, of the seventeenth century, formerly in Dr. Bliss's collection. It is dated 1620.' (*A Dictionary of Old English Plays*, p. 233.) This statement was repeated with slight revision by Hazlitt. (*Manual*, p. 215.)

Moore Smith says: 'It is not now in the Bliss collection at the Bodleian. . . . That it was a Cambridge play seems evident, as the term 'sophomore' was only used at Cambridge.' (*College Plays*, p. 109.) He alters the date to 1620/1, presumably because more plays were presented at Cambridge in January, February, and March than at any other season. Many plays were, however, acted there at other times, and it seems unnecessary to add a conjectural date to a dubious play.

The Spanish Preferment (?)

(Lost)

The title occurs tenth in Abraham Hill's list of plays in manuscript. (See Middleton, *The Conqueror's Custom*.) This list seems
to have been Hill's record of some bookseller's stock, set down between 1677 and 1703, but it is notable that nearly all the identifiable plays and playwrights in the list are Jacobean and Caroline.
There is no other record of the title. J. Q. Adams points out
in his discussion of Hill's list (*Library*, Fourth Series, xx [1939],
83) that similar titles for lost plays are *The Spanish Purchase* and
The Spanish Viceroy. This seems to me irrelevant. *Spanish* was a
popular word in play-titles—sixteen or seventeen examples could
be named in the seventeenth century—and there is no good reason
for identifying any of them with this play.

The Spanish Puecas

(Ghost title)

The title, *The Spanish Purchase* (q.v.), in John Warburton's
list of play manuscripts which he says were burned should read
'*The Spanish Puecas*', according to F. G. Fleay. (*Biog. Chron.* ii.
336.) There seems to be no reason for this change except Fleay's
reading of the hand. In such matters Fleay's authority will not
stand against that of Dr. Greg, who reads 'Purchas'. (*Library*,
Third Series, ii [1911], 232.)

The Spanish Purchase (?)

(Lost)

The title, 'The Spanish Purchas C.', is known only from John
Warburton's list of plays which he says he once owned, but which
his cook destroyed. (See W. W. Greg, *Library*, Third Series,
ii [1911], 232.) Many of the titles in Warburton's list are suspiciously like entries in the Stationers' Register, and it is by no means
certain that he ever owned the manuscripts at all. (Ibid., pp.
225–59.) But 'The Spanish Purchase' does not occur in the
Stationers' Register, and it may be that Warburton once owned a
manuscript with this title. Nothing more is known of a comedy
called *The Spanish Purchase*.

[*A Spanish Tragedy of Petrus Crudelis*] (1626–48?)
(Lost)

This play is known only from an anecdote told by Edmund
Gayton in his *Pleasant Notes upon Don Quixot*:

In a Tragedie (that was prepar'd for the publike view of the University,) the Actors were privately to be tried upon the Stage, that upon
the insufficiency of the persons, or unfittednesse, the men might be
chang'd. But two Scholars were there in this Spanish Tragedy (which
was the story of *Petrus Crudelis*) whose parts were two Ghosts or
Apparitions of some Noble Personages, which that Bloody Prince
had Murder'd. These two at the Repetitions spoke their lines very
confidently, insomuch, that the Judges thought they would be very
good Ghosts; but when the tryall night came, that the Play was to be
presented to some few friends before the publick exhibit, and then
these two Scholars were put out of their black into white long robes,
their Faces meal'd, and Torches in their hands, and some flashes of
Sulphur made at their entrance, just as they put their heads through
the hangings of the Scene, comming out at two severall sides of the
Stage, they shook so, and were so horribly affrighted at one anothers
gashly lookes, that no force of those behind them, could get them to
advance a foot forward toward the stage, or speak a word of their
Parts; but there as they first stood, they stood for halfe an houre
shaking, quaking, and staring one upon another, Insomuch, that they
put the Auditory into such a shaking with laughing, that they had
almost died with the excessive motions of the *Diaphragme*. In *fine*, the
Ghosts retreated, and two other Persons of better hearts were pitched
upon. (*Pleasant Notes upon Don Quixot* [1654], pp. 94–95.)

One would guess that Gayton's story is an account of an occurrence of his time at St. John's College, Oxford, i.e. 1626–48.
(*Athenæ Oxon.*, Bliss ed., iii. 756–8.) He himself performed in
George Wilde's *Love's Hospital* (q.v.) when it was acted before the
King and Queen at St. John's in 1636 (ibid. iv. 275), and the re-
hearsal story could well refer to a St. John's episode of about this
time.

The subject of the play was Peter the Cruel, King of Castile,
1350–69. (See Prosper Mérimée, *The History of Peter the Cruel,
King of Castile and Leon*, English translation, 2 vols., 1849.)
Gayton seems to me to be using the phrase 'This Spanish Tragedy'
facetiously, for a man with his knowledge of popular performances
at the Fortune and Red Bull (see above, ii. 690–1) must have been
familiar with Kyd's play. A chronicle history of the reign of Peter
the Cruel could easily have provided enough horrors to remind
Gayton of the melodramatics of *The Spanish Tragedy*. *Petrus*

Crudelis would therefore probably be nearer the title of the college play, but since it has been called *The Spanish Tragedy* before, I have only cross-indexed it under *Petrus Crudelis*. Could this play be the one sold at Sotheby's in 1938? See Anon., *Don Pedro*.

The Spanish Viceroy (1624)

(Lost)

Phelan, James. 'Philip Massinger', *Anglia*, ii (1879), 55–56.

1624, 20 Dec. 'To Sir Henry Herbert, Kᵗ. master of his Ma.ᵗⁱᵉˢ Revels.

After our humble servise remembered unto your good worship, Whereas not long since we acted a play called *The Spanishe Viceroy*, not being licensed under your worships hande, nor allowd of: wee doe confess and herby acknowledge that wee have offended, and that it is in your power to punishe this offense, and are very sorry for it; and doe likewise promise herby that wee will not act any play without your hand or substituts hereafter, nor doe any thinge that may prejudice the authority of your office: So hoping that this humble submission of ours may bee accepted, wee have therunto sett our hands. This twentiethe of Decemb. 1624.

Joseph Taylor.	John Lowen.
Richard Robinson.	John Shancke.
Elyard Swanston.	John Rice.
Thomas Pollard.	Will. Rowley.
Robert Benfeilde.	Richard Sharpe.'
George Burght.	

(Adams, *Herbert*, p. 21. Sir Henry copied the letter into his office-book in connexion with a controversy in 1633 with the note, "Tis entered here for a rememberance against their disorders'.)

1653, 9 Sept. S.R. Humphrey Moseley entered as his copies a long list of plays, including 'The Spãnish ViceRoy, or the Honoʳ: of Women . . . by Phill: Massinger'. (Greg, *Bibliography*, i. 60–61.)

About four months before they acted *The Spanish Viceroy* without Sir Henry Herbert's licence, the King's company had had the greatest success of their history with Thomas Middleton's *Game at Chess* (q.v.; also above, i. 9–14). Though that play had been duly licensed by he tMaster of the Revels, the uproar which it aroused would undoubtedly have made him very chary about future plays concerned with Spanish political figures, and probably knowledge of this fact prompted the company to act the play without submitting it to him—though such foolhardiness was by no means characteristic of the premier London company. The very humble letter of submission shows that the company had been badly caught out. Every patented member of the troupe except John Heminges and Henry Condell signed the letter. One wonders if these veteran leaders of the company had dissociated themselves in some way from the risky actions of their fellows.

Probably one can assume that *The Spanish Viceroy* was a play with political reflections, for such a play would provide the most obvious reason for fearing Herbert's censorship. It has been asserted that it probably concerned Gondomar, as *A Game at Chess* had, but there is no evidence.

Humphrey Moseley's listing of Philip Massinger's *The Honour of Women* (q.v.) as a sub-title for *The Spanish Viceroy* is pretty surely a fraudulent identification to save a licensing fee, as in several other instances in this list. (See Greg, *Bibliography*, ii. 979–80.) In 1660 Moseley again entered *The Honour of Women*, this time as a single title and as by Massinger, and it may be that *The Spanish Viceroy* was written by him too, but the evidence is too slight for an ascription.

The coupling of *The Spanish Viceroy* with *A Very Woman* and *The Maid of Honour* is only an accidental result of attempts—unjustifiable, I think—to identify *The Honour of Women* with those two plays.

Phelan's discussion (loc. cit.) of the title collects a number of unwarranted assertions about *The Spanish Viceroy* and makes others.

Stoicus Vapulans (1618 or 1618/19)

1648. Stoicvs Vapvlans. *Olim Cantabrigiæ actus In Collegio* S. Johannis Evangelistæ *Ab ejusdem Collegii Iuventute* . . . 1648. (Separate title in Andrew Crooke's edition of four Latin plays, *Loyola, Stoicus Vapulans, Cancer,* and *Paria.* There is no general title-page.)

Fleay dated the play 1627 (*Biog. Chron.* ii. 364), but his only reason was that it was published with *Loyola, Cancer,* and *Paria.* Such evidence might have merited consideration had the other three plays approximated to this date, but only Vincent's *Paria* (q.v.) does.

The title-page assertion that *Stoicus Vapulans* was a St. John's College, Cambridge, play is confirmed and the date set by the diary of Sir Simonds D'Ewes. This part of the diaries has not been printed, and there is nothing of the play in Halliwell's *Autobiography and Correspondence of Sir Simonds D'Ewes*, but the anonymously edited *College Life in the Time of James the First as Illustrated by an Unpublished Diary of Sir Symonds D'Ewes* (1851) extracts the relevant information, though one could wish for fuller quotation. The information is recorded under the date 1618, D'Ewes's first year at St. John's:

> According to ancient custom the festival of Christmas was kept with much state and hospitality for the period of twelve days; but the only part of it to which we find special allusion made in this Diary, is the Latin play entitled '*Stoicus vapulans*,' which 'was very well acted in the hall of our house.' . . . Symonds does not mention his having been present at the representation of this comedy. (p. 61.)

Neither D'Ewes nor any other source that I know offers any suggestion about the author of the play, but he was presumably a St. John's man resident at the college in 1618. It is tempting to suggest that he was John Barrett (q.v.), whom D'Ewes mentions as his friend and as author of the St. John's Christmas Latin comedy for 1619. But D'Ewes, if the extracts in *College Life in the Time of James the First* can be trusted, speaks of two different Christmas plays at St. John's: the play for Christmas 1618, which was *Stoicus Vapulans*, and the play for Christmas 1619, which was written by his friend Barrett. It would not be surprising for St. John's to have had an annual Christmas play, but the extracts could be confused. The complete diary of Sir Symonds would be welcome.

Stonyhurst Pageants (1610–25)

MS.: Stonyhurst College MS. A. VI. 33.

Edition: Carleton Brown, ed., *The Stonyhurst Pageants, Hesperia* (1920).

This little-known cycle of seventeenth-century Old Testament plays exists in an imperfect manuscript at Stonyhurst College in Lancashire. The manuscript, a paper book, has lost, since the leaves were numbered, the first fifty-five leaves, six leaves in the middle, and an unknown number of leaves at the end, but 8,740 lines of text are still left. (Brown ed., pp. 7 and 13.) Several names are written at various places in the margins of the manuscript, one with the date 1686; none is certainly identifiable, though all are Lancashire names, and Professor Brown thinks it likely that the manuscript was owned in Lancashire before the end of the seventeenth century. (Ibid., pp. 8–10.)

The manuscript is written throughout in a single Italian hand of the first half of the seventeenth century, and various corrections and alterations suggested to the editor that it is probably the hand of the author. (Ibid., pp. 7 and 10–13.) The language of the text is northern, but it is early seventeenth-century rather than medieval. (Ibid., pp. 13–16.) A further help in dating the pageants is Professor Brown's demonstration that the author used as his source the English translation of the Vulgate, published at Douay 1609–10, often taking over the phraseology and the spelling of proper names, and frequently making use of the marginal annotations. (Ibid., pp. 16–19.) On the evidence of the source and the characteristics of the language, the editor dates the plays 1610–25. (Ibid., p. 19.)

There are various indications that the author of the plays was a Roman Catholic, and Professor Brown suggests that he may have been a priest in training, possibly a Jesuit. (Ibid., pp. 19–21.) Some slight evidence exists that the pageants were intended to be divided into three groups, I–VII, VIII–XII, and XIII–XVIII, perhaps for performance on separate days, but there are no stage directions, and the evidence for grouping is very slight. (Ibid., pp. 26–27.)

The last of the extant plays, *The Pageant of Naaman*, is much superior to the others, though apparently by the same author, and shows the influence of Plautus. Although there are numerous minor indications that the author had production in mind, there is no evidence that the plays ever were produced. (Ibid., pp. 26–30.)

The Stonyhurst MS. at present contains the following plays: 6, *The Pageant of Jacob*; 7, *The Pageant of Joseph*; 8, *The Pageant of 'Moyses'*; 9, *The Pageant of 'Iosue'*; 10, *The Pageant of Gideon*; 11, *The Pageant of 'Iepthe'*; 12, *The Pageant of Sampson*; 14, *The Pageant of Saul*; 15, *The Pageant of David*; 16, *The Pageant of Solomon*; 17, *The Pageant of Elias*; 18, *The Pageant of Naaman*.

The Supposed Inconstancy (> 1653)

(Lost)

1653, 29 [Dec.] S.R. Richard Marriott entered as his copies a number of plays, including 'Supposed Inconstancy'. (Greg, *Bibliography*, i. 62.)

The only evidence for the existence of a play of this name is Marriott's entry in the Stationers' Register. Two-thirds of the twenty-one titles in this list of plays occur nowhere else, and only three were published later under these titles, though four are known from other references. (See below, *The Woman's Law*, for the entire list.)

Susanna's Tears
(Ghost title?)

Edward Archer appended to his edition of Massinger, Middleton, and Rowley's *The Old Law*, 1656, 'An Exact and perfect Catalogue of all Plaies that were ever printed; together, with all the Authors names; and what are Comedies, Histories, Interludes, Masks, Pastorels, Tragedies'. Dr. Greg shows that this catalogue of Archer's is derived from the similar list of Rogers and Ley published in the same year. (*Bibliography*, ii. 996.) One title in Archer's list is 'Susanna's tears I', and the title is repeated later in similar lists. No doubt it is a result of some confusion (see ibid., p. 999), but one cannot be sure. In any case, the designation 'I[nterlude]' suggests a date much too early for the Jacobean and Caroline theatre.

Swetnam the Woman-Hater Arraigned by Women (1617–18?)

Edition: Edited by A. B. Grosart (1880).

Reynolds, George Fullmer. *The Staging of Elizabethan Plays at the Red Bull Theater, 1605–1625* (1940), pp. 44–46.
Schelling, Felix E. *Elizabethan Drama 1558–1642* (1908), ii. 237–8.

1619, 17 Oct. S.R. Richard Meighen entered for his copy 'vnder the hand[es] of Sʳ. George Bucke and Mʳ Iaggard warden, A Comedy called Swetnam the woemen hater, Arraign'd by woemen'. (Greg, *Bibliography*, i. 31.)
1620. Swetnam, The Woman-hater, Arraigned By Women. *A new Comedie*, Acted at the *Red Bull*, by the late Queenes Seruants ... 1620.

Langbaine long ago noted (*An Account of the English Dramatick Poets* [1691], p. 551) that the main plot of the play is derived from the sixteenth-century *Historia da Aurelia y Isabella hija del Rey Escotia*, attributed to Juan de Flores. Schelling thought (loc. cit.) that Fletcher was probably independent in his use of the same

source for his *Women Pleased*. The name of the play, the most
sensational part of the action, and no doubt its principal appeal
were derived from Joseph Swetnam's notorious pamphlet, *The
Arraignment of Lewd, Idle, Froward, and Unconstant Women*, to
which there are many direct references in the play. This diatribe
was first published in 1615 and reissued four times before 1620
and five times in the period 1622–37. In the play Swetnam, often
called Mysogynos, is tried, as the title indicates, by women, and
the popularity of this part of the play is indicated not only by the
prologue and the epilogue, but by the preparation of a cut of the
scene for the title-page, a contemporary stage picture of which
Professor Reynolds (loc. cit. *et passim*) makes much.

There were at least four pamphlets published in reply to
Swetnam, one in 1616 and three in 1617 (see Grosart edition,
pp. xxix–xxxiv, and *D.N.B.*), and since the players were not men to
disdain profits from public squabbles it seems likely that the play
was prepared to exploit the public interest at this time. The numerous references in the comedy to Swetnam as a fencer suggest a
knowledge of his *School of the Noble and Worthy Science of Defence*,
published in 1617.

In the trial scene Swash gives an account of the career of his
master, Swetnam, up to their presence in Sicily, the scene of the
play. He concludes his account:

> And then we came to London: there forsooth,
> He put his Booke i' the Presse, and publisht it,
> And made a thousand men and wiues fall out.
> Till two or three good wenches, in meere spight,
> Laid their heads together, and rail'd him out of th' Land,
> Then we came hither: this is all forsooth.   (K₁ᵛ.)

The lines about the two or three wenches who put their heads
together and railed Swetnam out of the land is evidently a
reference to the three railing replies to Swetnam's pamphlet,
which were published in 1617 under three feminine pseudonyms,
Constantia Munda, Esther Sowerman, and Rachael Speght (see
S.T.C. 18,257, 22,974, and 23,058), and they show that the play
could not have appeared before late 1617. (The last of the three
pamphlets to be entered in the Stationers' Register appears there
under date of 29 April 1617. It may be that the fourth line
quoted from Swash's speech is intended as a pun on the name
Rachael Speght.)

The play was not immediately forgotten. About fifteen years
after it was first performed Thomas Nabbes referred to it in his
Tottenham Court (q.v.), acted at the Salisbury Court theatre in

1633. In this play the Wife makes a clear reference in II. 2 to the women's big arraignment scene in *Swetnam the Woman-Hater*:

Let's get him arraign'd, as one was in a play. Let me alone to aggravate his indictment to the Jury; which shall be twelve Midwives of my acquaintance.

Her later mention of Swetnam in III. 3 could refer to the pamphlet rather than to the play, but her previous allusion to the comedy suggests that the audience might have been expected to remember the character on the stage rather than the author of the pamphlet. She says:

He is one into whom the spirit of *Swetnam's* crept. I hope sir you are of a kinder disposition to our sexe.

These allusions, one of which certainly depends upon the familiarity of the Salisbury Court audience with the play, suggest that in 1633 it may have been recently performed, perhaps at the Salisbury Court.

Syrgiannes, tragoedia (16 August 1630)
(Lost)

McCabe, William H. 'Notes on the St. Omers College Theatre', *Phil. Quart.* xvii (1938), 225–39.
—— 'The Play-List of the English College of St. Omers, 1592–1762', *Revue de littérature comparée*, xvii (1937), 355–75.

A play of this name was acted in the Jesuit College for English boys at St. Omers 16 August 1630. ('Play-List', p. 366.)

Tancred and Ghismonda

See Anon., *Ghismonda*.

The Telltale (c. 1630–40?)

MS.: Dulwich College MS. xx.

The Dulwich College MS. is written in a literary hand which Dr. Greg seems to think is that of a scribe of about 1630–40 (?), rather than that of the author, in spite of the corrections. He finds no evidence of playhouse use or censorship. (*Dramatic Documents*, pp. 339–41.) Warner, who prints a brief synopsis of the five-act comedy, says that the manuscript 'appears to have belonged to the actor who played the leading part of the Duke, the word "mine" being written opposite his first speech'. (George F. Warner, *Catalogue of the Manuscripts and Muniments . . . at Dulwich* [1881], pp. 342–3.) Two and a half pages in the fourth act have been left blank. Dr. Greg notes that at the end of the play there is a 'monogram of the letters "Nicholas" '. (*Bibliography*, ii. 1001.) This monogram suggests that the manuscript might repay analysis to see if it could be the lost unnamed comedy by John Nichols or Nicholas (q.v.) that was performed at Trinity College, Cambridge, in 1639 or 1640.

Apparently the comedy was at one time intended for publication, for the title, 'Tell Tale: a Comedy', appears in a list of 'Books in the Presse, and ready for Printing' that were advertised by Nathaniel Brook of the Angel in Cornhill in E. Phillips, *The New World of English Words*, 1658. Under similar headings the title also appears in other such lists, 1658–62. (See Greg, *Bibliography*, ii. 1000–1.) There is no evidence that *The Telltale* ever was printed as announced.

The Theatre of Apollo

See Sir John Beaumont.

Thibaldus sive Vindictæ Ingenium

See Thomas Snelling.

[Time's Triumph] [Juno in Arcadia] [Juno's Pastoral, or The Bonds of Peace] [Sight and Search] (1643)

MS.: B.M. MS. Egerton 1994[9].

Edition: Edited by R. C. Elsaly as *Juno in Arcadia*, Unpublished Thesis, University of Birmingham, 1950.

Boas, F. S. 'A Seventeenth Century Theatrical Repertoire', *Shakespeare and the Universities* (1923), pp. 96–110.
Bullen, A. H. *A Collection of Old English Plays*, ii (1883), 428–30.
Harbage, Alfred. 'An Unnoted Caroline Dramatist', *Stud. Phil.* xxxi (1934), 28–36. (Condensed in his *Cavalier Drama* [1936], p. 201.)
Jump, J. D. 'The Anonymous Masque in Egerton 1994', *R.E.S.* xi (1935), 186–91.
Leech, Clifford, ed. *Mildmay Fane's Raguaillo D'Oceano 1640 and Candy Restored 1641, Materials for the Study of Old English Drama* (1938), p. 22.

The ninth dramatic piece in Egerton 1994, an anonymous, titleless 'masque', which is really not a masque but an allegorical show with songs and dances, has been variously called *Time's Triumph*, *Juno in Arcadia*, and *Juno's Pastoral, or The Bonds of Peace*. Since the first title has been used most often, I have elected to use it; it is good enough to serve, but one should bear in mind that it is a modern convenience; there is no evidence as to what the author intended his show to be called. He has headed Act 1 'Sight and Search', and this has once or twice been given as the title of the masque. Actually Sight and Search are only the names of the speakers in the first scene; nearly the same form is used at the beginning of the second act.

In the manuscript the piece is dated 'August 5th: 1643:' and it is not unlike the allegorical entertainments which were written about this time by Mildmay Fane, second Earl of Westmorland (q.v.). This similarity prompted Professor Harbage (loc. cit.) to suggest that Fane may have been the author. Dr. Leech (loc. cit.), who has had most experience with Fane's manuscripts, had no hesitation in saying that the hand is not his; he recognized a certain resemblance to Mildmay Fane's work in the structure and in the use of contemporary allusions, but he concluded that there was 'not sufficient evidence for us to include it in the Westmorland canon. The Egerton "masque" might have been written by almost any talented amateur of the period, and is indeed a little too skilfully handled for Fane.'

Bullen (loc. cit.) pointed out a long passage in the piece which is clearly derived from Chapman's *Byron's Tragedy*. J. D. Jump cites a number of lines and phrases in the manuscript which are like those of Chapman, but most of them are common figures. Since the manuscript is dated 5 August 1643 and uses 'weekly Intelligences' in a sense not known before 1641, Jump concludes that though it must date 1641–3 'it is evident that the piece is either the revision by an unknown hand of a masque by Chapman, or a work, substantially original, containing important borrowings from the earlier poet'. The evidence seems to me to show only that one long passage from *Byron's Tragedy* was adapted.

Hazlitt's suggestion (*A Manual for the Collector and Amateur of Old English Plays*, p. 228) that this allegorical piece may have some connexion with the lost play called *Time's Triumph* which was acted for Henslowe (*Henslowe's Diary*, i. 52 and ii. 183–4) is as irresponsible as Fleay's guess about the same title. (See above, Thomas Heywood, *Misanthropus*.) Only the title of Henslowe's play is known, and this piece has no title.

I have not seen the manuscript edition of the show at the University of Birmingham.

Titus and Vespatian (> 1620)
(Lost)

c. 1619–20. 'Titus, and Vespatian' appears in a list of plays on waste paper of the Revels Office, probably dating about 1619 or 1620. It has been plausibly suggested that the plays of the list were being considered for court performance. (See Marcham, *Revels*, p. 15, and Chambers, *R.E.S.* i [1925], 484.)

Philip Henslowe recorded his receipts in 1591 and 1592 for a play called *Titus and Vespatian* (see W. W. Greg, ed. *Henslowe's Diary*, i. 14–15 and ii. 155). Various scholars have thought this lost play was revised by Shakespeare as *Titus Andronicus*. (See Chambers, *William Shakespeare*, i. 316–22.) The play listed for possible performance at court in 1619 or 1620 could have been the old unrevised play, but it seems unlikely that such an antiquated piece would be proposed for the delectation of the court when it was nearly thirty years old. It could have been Shakespeare's play under the old title, but this also seems most unlikely after *Titus Andronicus* had already been published three times under that title. Or it could have been another play not recorded elsewhere.

The part of the Revels list in which *Titus and Vespatian* is found is in the hand of the copyist and book-keeper of the King's company. (See R. C. Bald, ed., *Hengist, King of Kent; or The Mayor of Queenborough By Thomas Middleton* [1938], p. xxi, n. 1.) This fact seems to suggest that *Titus and Vespatian* was the property of the King's company when the list was made, but unfortunately at least two other titles in this hand, *A Fair Quarrel* and *All's Lost by Lust*, are known to have belonged to other companies.

The Tragedy of Tomerania (?)
(Lost)

This title is forty-seventh in the list of manuscript plays found among the papers of Abraham Hill. (See Middleton's *The Conqueror's Custom.*) The list seems to have been Hill's record of the stock of some bookseller, set down between 1677 and 1703, but it is notable that nearly all the identifiable plays and playwrights of the list are Jacobean and Caroline.

No other record of such a title is known, and the name 'Tomerania' is strange. J. Q. Adams suggests in his discussion of Hill's list (*Library*, Fourth Series, xx [1939], 97–98) that Tomerania may be a misreading of Pomerania, or, alternatively, Tamercam; if the latter, it might have been a manuscript of I or II *Tamar Cam* of Henslowe's Diary. Adams does not, however, fancy either of these conjectures, and neither do I.

Tom of Bedlam (1617/18)
(Lost)

1617/18, 10 Jan. 'He [Sir Robert Naunton] is gon this morning after the King who removes to Roiston from Tiballs, where he was to have yesternight a play acted by Sir Tho: Dutton, Sir Tho: Badger, Sir George Goring, Sir Tho: Tirringham, Sir Ed: Zouch, Sir Robert Yaxeley, and the like: of Tom of Bedlem, the Tincker and such other mad stuffe.' (John Chamberlain to Sir Dudley Carleton, *Letters of John Chamberlain*, ii. 129.)

1617/18, 17 Jan. 'I have litle to adde to what I wrote the last weeke, more then the knighting of Sir John Bingley at Tiballs, where the play or enterlude did not *riuscire* to the expectation, but rather fell out the wronge way, specially by reason of a certain song sunge by Sir John Finet, (wherin the rest bare the bourdon) of such scurrilous and base stuffe that yt put the King out of his goode humor, and all the rest that heard yt.' (The same to the same, ibid., p. 131.)

Nothing is known of the play save John Chamberlain's remarks. It may be that *Tom of Bedlam* is the same as the anonymous *Marriage of a Farmer's Son* (q.v.), which was acted at Theobalds at the same time, but since that piece is called a masque and *Tom of Bedlam* is called a play or interlude, and since the King is said to have been pleased with *The Marriage of a Farmer's Son* and displeased with *Tom of Bedlam*, it seems to me somewhat more likely that the two were distinct.

The Tooth-Drawer (?)
(Lost)

'The Tooth-Drawer: a Comedy' appears in a list of 'Books in the Presse, and ready for Printing' which were advertised by Nathaniel Brook of the Angel in Cornhill, in E. Phillips, *The New World of English Words*, 1658. Under similar headings the title also appeared in other such lists 1658-62. (See Greg, *Bibliography*, ii. 1000.) The advertisement must have been at least premature, for there is no evidence that the play was ever printed, though one would assume that Brook had a manuscript. Nothing else is known of a play of the title.

The Toy (1636-40)
(Lost)

The title is known only from the prologue which James Shirley published in his *Poems &c*, 1646 (Part ii, D₇ᵛ-D₈), entitled 'A Prologue to a play there [i.e. Ireland]; Call'd THE TOY'. The prologue reveals nothing about the play except to imply that it was a rather trivial one offered by the company because superior plays had recently been ill received by the audience. Presumably the play was written during the period of Shirley's incumbency at the St. Werburgh Street Theatre in Dublin.

I know of nothing to support Harbage's suggestion (*Annals of English Drama, 975-1700*, p. 112) that the play may have been written by Henry Burnell, except the fact that the prologue to *Landgartha* says Burnell had written an earlier play and that nothing is known of it now.

Fleay's suggestions, (1) that *The Toy* may have been *A Toy to Please Chaste Ladies*, and (2) that the reference to a bracelet as 'a pretty toy' in *Saint Patrick for Ireland*, Act IV (F4ᵛ), is a reference to this play (*Biog. Chron.* ii. 304, 339, 242), are simply wild guesses.

Tradeway's Tragedy (?)
(Lost)

This title is forty-ninth in the list of manuscript plays found among the papers of Abraham Hill. (See Middleton, *The Conqueror's Custom.*) The list seems to have been Hill's record of the stock of some bookseller, set down between 1677 and 1703, but it is notable that nearly all the identifiable plays and playwrights of the list are Jacobean and Caroline.

Though the title does not occur elsewhere, J. Q. Adams points out in his discussion of Hill's list (*Library*, Fourth Series, xx [1939], 98) that it suggests the contemporary murder plays popular in the early seventeenth century.

The Tragical History, Admirable Achievements, and Various Events of Guy of Warwick

See Anon., *Guy of Warwick.*

Trebellius Bulgarorum Rex (2 May 1624)
(Lost)

McCabe, William H. 'Notes on the St. Omers College Theatre', *Phil. Quart.* xvii (1938), 225–39.
—— 'The Play-List of the English College of St. Omers 1592–1762', *Revue de littérature comparée*, xvii (1937), 355–75.

The play was acted in the Jesuit College for English boys at St. Omers 2 May 1624. Father McCabe ('Play-List', p. 363) gives a one-sentence summary of the story of Trebellius.

The Triumph of Innocence (?)
(Lost)

This title is twenty-ninth in the list of manuscript plays found among the papers of Abraham Hill. (See Middleton, *The Conqueror's Custom.*) The list seems to have been Hill's record of some booksellers's stock, set down between 1677 and 1703, but it is notable that nearly all the identifiable plays and playwrights of the list are Jacobean and Caroline.

The title does not occur elsewhere in records of seventeenth-century plays. J. Q. Adams says in his discussion of Hill's list (*Library*, Fourth Series, xx [1939], 92–93), 'If it is to be found among extant plays I would suggest Heywood's *The Captives*, in which the word "Innocence" is not infrequent, and the title would be applicable to both the main plot and sub-plot.' Unfortunately the triumph of the innocent and unjustly accused is too hackneyed a dramatic subject to give *The Captives* any distinction in this respect.

The True Tragi-Comedy Formerly Acted at Court . . .
(< 1654)

MS.: B.M. Add. MS. 25348.

Wagner, Bernard M. 'A Jonson Allusion, and Others', *Phil. Quart.* vii (1928), 306–8.

This play, whose full title reads 'The True tragi-Comedie

formarly acted at court & now reui[v]ed by ane Eie witnes before which ar drawn the Liuely pictures or caracters of the most considarable parsons Represented', was evidently not intended for performance or for publication. It is an account of the notorious Countess of Essex and the development of her affair with Somerset. Mrs. Turner is a principal character, and there is much retailing of London scandals, often made more specific in the marginal notes. The play is preceded by long 'characters' of all the principal figures of rank.

The piece has been dated after September 1634 in the British Museum catalogue because of references to the Earl of Northumberland as dead. Professor Wagner would date the composition shortly after 1654 because of the reference in the last of the 'characters', that of 'Sr Edward Cook', to a letter in 'a late booke, Entitaled the Cabala', which refers to the second part of *Cabala, sive Scrinia Sacra: Mysteries of State*, entered in the Stationers' Register and published in that year. He said that he proposed to discuss the play in detail at a later date, but I have not seen such a discussion.

The True Trojans

See Jasper Fisher, *Fuimus Troes or The True Trojans.*

Truth's Triumphs (> 1634/5)

(Lost?)

The play is known only from John Greene's record in his diary that he saw it performed in February 1634/5. Miss E. M. Symonds summarizes the facts, though, unfortunately, she does not quote the diary directly:

> Thus . . . we hear . . . in February [1634/5] of visits to Blackfriars Theatre or the Cockpit where John saw *Rule a Wife and have a Wife, The Elder Brother, Truth's Triumphs*, and the *Malcontent*. ('The Diary of John Greene (1635–57)', *The English Historical Review*, xliii [1928], 386.)

Two of these plays, Fletcher's *The Elder Brother* and *Rule a Wife and Have a Wife*, belonged to the King's company and were therefore plays Greene saw at Blackfriars. A third, Marston's *Malcontent*, was published in one of its three 1604 editions as performed by the King's men (see *The Elizabethan Stage*, iii. 431–2), and this play may, therefore, also have been seen by Greene at Blackfriars. If so, *Truth's Triumph* is the only one left that might have been performed at the Cockpit and would, accordingly, have been the property of Queen Henrietta's company. It is unfortunate that Greene's words were not transcribed from the diary, which is in private hands.

It may be that *Truth's Triumph* is an unknown sub-title to a known play. It is surely not Middleton's *The Triumphs of Truth* (see *The Elizabethan Stage*, iii. 443), however, for that is a Lord Mayor's show unlikely ever to have been performed in a theatre, least of all an exclusive private theatre like the Cockpit or Blackfriars.

A Turk's Too Good for [Him?] (> 1620)
(Lost)

c. 1619–20. '. . . age—Turkes too good for [hi?] . . .' appears in a list of plays on waste paper of the Revels Office, probably dating about 1619 or 1620. It has been plausibly suggested that the plays of the list were being considered for court performance. (See Marcham, *Revels*, p. 15, and Chambers, *R.E.S.* i [1925], 484.)

This title, apparently only slightly mutilated, is known only from the Revels list, which seems to have been notes of plays proposed for court performance. The 'age' before the title was 'Trage', for Tragedy, as a later entry shows. I am not at all sure that the last two letters of the title are 'hi', as Marcham read them.

The part of the list in which *A Turk's Too Good for [Him?]* appears is in the hand of a copyist and book-keeper of the King's company. (See R. C. Bald, ed., *Hengist, King of Kent; or The Mayor of Queenborough By Thomas Middleton* [1938], p. xxi, n. 1.) This fact seems to suggest that the play was the property of the King's company, but unfortunately at least two other titles in this hand, *All's Lost by Lust* and *A Fair Quarrel*, are known to have belonged to other companies.

The Two Noble Ladies and the Converted Conjurer
(1619–23)

MS.: B.M. Egerton MS. 1994[11].

Edition: Edited by Rebecca G. Rhoads (Malone Society Reprints, 1930).

Boas, F. S. 'A Seventeenth Century Theatrical Repertoire', *Shakespeare and the Universities* (1923), pp. 96–110.

Greg, W. W. *Dramatic Documents from the Elizabethan Play-houses* (1931), pp. 274–9.

Reynolds, George Fullmer. *The Staging of Elizabethan Plays at the Red Bull Theater, 1605–1625* (1940), pp. 23–24 and 42–43.

The manuscript of the play carries the statement on fol. 224[b]:

The two noble Ladies: A Trage-comicall Historie often tymes acted w'h approbation At the Red Bull in S': Iohns Streete By the Company of y⁰ Reuells

This company was formed from the remnant of Queen Anne's men after her death in 1619 and seems to have begun acting at the Red Bull immediately and to have continued there until some time in the first half of 1623. (See above, i. 165–70.) The performances by the Revels company at the Red Bull, which the manuscript notes, must therefore have taken place 1619–23.

The B.M. MS., Dr. Greg found, 'is evidently an author's fair copy containing numerous alterations and corrections, often made *currente calamo*'. The appearance of six actors' names inserted in a different hand at various points in the text shows that the manuscript was used as a prompt copy. Miss Rhoads points out evidence at two points in the text which seems to indicate that the author and the prompter who prepared the piece for production were working on the manuscript at the same time. (Ed. cit., pp. viii–ix.) If so, the performances at the Red Bull were presumably the first the play had, and it therefore dates 1619–23.

F. G. Fleay said (*Biog. Chron.* ii. 334) that the play 'is founded on Calderon's *Magico Prodigioso*', and W. C. Hazlitt echoed that it is 'From the Spanish of Calderon'. (*A Manual for the Collector and Amateur of Old English Plays*, p. 241.) A hasty comparison of the two plays shows that this is at best an exaggeration. Ciprian's attempt on Justina and some of the magic scenes, as well as the names of these two characters, are closely related, but most of the scenes in *The Two Noble Ladies and the Converted Conjurer* show no similarity to those in the Spanish play. Moreover, since Calderón's play was written in 1637, the unknown author of *The Two Noble Ladies and the Converted Conjurer* could scarcely have used it; he must have got his story of Cyprian and Justina elsewhere.

The Two Spanish Gentlemen (?)

(Lost)

This title is thirty-fifth in a list of manuscript plays found among the papers of Abraham Hill. (See Middleton, *The Conqueror's*

Custom.) The list seems to have been Hill's record of some book-seller's stock, set down between 1677 and 1703, but it is notable that nearly all the identifiable plays and playwrights of the list are Jacobean and Caroline.

All three of the principal words in this title are favourites with Elizabethan and seventeenth-century dramatists, but this particular combination occurs nowhere else so far as I know.

Two Wise Men and All the Rest Fools (> 1619)

Edition: John S. Farmer, ed., Tudor Facsimile Texts (1913).

1619. Two Wise Men And All The *Rest Fooles*: Or A Comicall Morall, Censuring the follies of this age, as it hath *beene diverse times acted*. Anno. 1619.

This anonymous piece was advertised as by George Chapman in Kirkman's list of plays for sale in 1661, and he was followed by Winstanley (*The Lives of the Most Famous English Poets*, 1687, p. 113), and by Langbaine, who did have the grace to say, 'tho' I am led only by Tradition to believe this Play to be his'. (*An Account of the English Dramatick Poets* [1691], p. 64.) It has accordingly been reprinted in some editions of Chapman, but there is no good reason for thinking that Chapman wrote it.

Though there is a prologue and epilogue which seem intended for a performance, it is difficult to imagine an audience sitting through *Two Wise Men and All the Rest Fools*. There is almost no plot or action, for it is little more than a series of dialogues. Possibly the obscure satire might be clear enough to entertain an unusually homogeneous audience, such as a college group, and the repeated direction, '*Turnes to the people*', or '*speakes thus to the people*', suggests such a group. The reference in the epilogue to '*the King, and his families enduring happinesse*' indicates a Jacobean date, and the statement in III. 2 that someone 'went ouer with Sir *Robert Sherley* into *Persia*' suggests a reference to Sir Robert's return to Persia in 1612/13, though he had first gone in Elizabeth's reign.

Since there is no entry of the piece in the Stationers' Register and no imprint on the title-page of the first edition, Dr. Greg suggests (*Bibliography*, ii. 509) that it may have been privately printed. It may also have been privately acted.

Fleay (*Biog. Chron.* ii. 333–4) argued that the character Antonio stands for Anthony Munday, but in the light of more recent knowledge of Munday, his case will not stand. (See Celeste Turner,

Anthony Mundy An Elizabethan Man of Letters [1928], *passim*.)
The text of 1619 is very oddly divided to make seven acts, and
Fleay suggested that Acts III and IV had been intended for a single
act, as had Acts VI and VII.

Tyrannical Government Anatomized, or A Discourse Concerning Evil Councellors, Being the Life and Death of John the Baptist

This closet drama, published in 1642, is not a new piece, but a
translation of George Buchanan's *Baptistes siue Calumnia tragedia*,
first printed in 1577.

The Unfaithful Wife (?)
(Lost)

This title is thirty-seventh in a list of manuscript plays found
among the papers of Abraham Hill. (See Middleton, *The Conqueror's Custom*.) The list seems to have been Hill's record of some
bookseller's stock, set down between 1677 and 1703, but it is
notable that nearly all the identifiable plays and playwrights of
the list are Jacobean and Caroline.

The title does not appear elsewhere, though the subject is
common enough in seventeenth-century plays.

Valentinian, or Rape's Revenge (?)
(Lost?)

This title occurs twenty-first in Abraham Hill's list of plays in
manuscript. (See Middleton, *The Conqueror's Custom*.) This list
seems to have been Hill's record of some bookseller's stock, set
down between 1677 and 1703, but it is notable that nearly all the
identifiable plays and playwrights in the list are Jacobean or
Caroline.

The title of Hill's manuscript is apt for Fletcher's *The Tragedy
of Valentinian*, for the Earl of Rochester's revision of it as *Luci-
nia's Rape, or The Tragedy of Valentinian*, or for his further revision of it as *Valentinian, a Tragedy*. (See Montague Summers, *The
Playhouse of Pepys*, pp. 290–2.) Since Fletcher had derived his
play largely from D'Urfé's *Astrée*, one of the most popular sources
for Jacobean and Caroline plays, the title may also indicate an
otherwise unknown play from the same sensational story.

The Valiant Scholar (1622)
(Lost)

1622, 3 June. 'A new Play, called, *The Valiant Scholler,* allowed to be acted by the Lady Elizabeth's Servants.' (Adams, *Herbert,* p. 24.)

The Valiant Scholar is known only from Sir Henry Herbert's licence for the Lady Elizabeth's men to act it. (On a suggested error in the licence date, see above, i. 205, n. 5, and Anon., *The Dutch Painter and the French Branke.*)

In the months following the licence of *The Valiant Scholar,* the metropolitan Lady Elizabeth's company was new and apparently prosperous. (See above, i. 176–84.) Of the thirteen plays known to have been licensed for them in the first thirty-three months of their London existence, only this play, Bonen's *The Cra— Merchant, or Come to My Country House,* and the anonymous *Black Lady* are lost. (Ibid., pp. 185–6.)

The Valiant Scot

See J. W.

The Masque of Vices
(Fragment? Lost?)

There is much confusion about this title. Edward F. Rimbault prefixed to his edition of Purcell's music for *Bonduca* an historical sketch of early English dramatic music in which he said that Henry Lawes's music for the 'Masque of Vices' was 'Preserved entire in MS Addit. Brit. Mus. 10338. I cannot discover any record of the performance of this masque.' (*Musical Antiquarian Society Publications,* vii [1842], 11.) Conjecturally Rimbault dated the music about 1635, presumably because the following music in the manuscript contains several songs for comedies produced in the thirties. His notation of a masque called 'The Masque of Vices' was taken up by Rudolf Brotanek (*Die englischen Maskenspiele* [1902], p. 339) and Miss Gertrude Sibley (*The Lost Plays and Masques* [1933], p. 194).

An examination of the manuscript puzzles one as to what Rimbault meant by 'Preserved entire'. So far as I can make out, only the three songs on fols. 24^v–29^v could possibly be associated with the title 'The Masque of Vices', and three songs would not be the 'entire' music for a masque. Moreover, the association of these three songs with the masque title is only conjectural, for the title is written, not before the group of songs, but after the last one, and it is followed by blank pages which have been ruled for music but on which nothing has been written. 'The Masque of Vices', then, might apply to the three preceding songs, or it might apply to music which the owner of the manuscript intended to write into his book following the title but never actually copied.

The three songs in the manuscript are entitled 'Musicke thou Queene of Soules', 'Coy Cælia', and 'Say Daunce' from the first words of the songs. Mr. John P. Cutts noticed ('The Masque of Vices', *N. & Q.* cxcvii [8 November 1952], 492) that the words of the song 'Say Daunce' are those of the song in i. 4 of Thomas Randolph's *The Muses' Looking Glass* (q.v.) where it is introduced as part of 'a rude Dance / Presented by the seven deadly sinnes', and he concluded that 'The Masque of Vices' was the title of the moral entertainment that was given at this point in Randolph's play and that it balanced the Masque of the Virtues in v. 1 and v. 2 of the same play.

Mr. Cutts did not notice, however, that the words of the other two songs in the group are also Randolph's. 'Musicke thou Queene of Soules' was published in his *Poems with The Muses Looking-Glass and Amyntas*, 1638, under the title '*A Song*', and Henry Lawes's setting of it was printed in Lawes's *Ayres & Dialogues*, 1653, The First Book, p. 14. 'Coy Cælia' was also printed in the Randolph collection of 1638 under the title '*A Pastorall Ode*'.

It is possible that these two songs once also belonged to the text of *The Muses' Looking Glass* and were omitted from the editions of the play. Their words surely were not appropriate to 'a rude Dance / Presented by the seven deadly sinnes' and perhaps sometimes called 'The Masque of Vices', but they could conceivably have been appropriate to the Masque of the Virtues in v. 1 and v. 2 of the play, from which at least one song is omitted in the printed text.

One must conclude from this scattered and somewhat contradictory evidence that: (*a*) there is certainly no complete music for a masque called 'The Masque of Vices' in the B.M. MS.; (*b*) all three songs which have been grouped together were written by Thomas Randolph, at least one of them for his *Muses' Looking Glass*; (*c*) the title 'The Masque of Vices' may apply to the interlude in i. 4 of the play, or it may apply to music quite different and never written into MS. 10338 at all, but it certainly does not apply to all three of the Randolph songs that precede it in the manuscript; (*d*) possibly all three of the Randolph songs belong together, the first two for the Masque of the Virtues in v. 1 and 2 of *The Muses' Looking Glass*, and the third for 'the rude Dance' in I. 4.

Virgil's Eclogues
(Lost play?)

Edward Archer appended to his edition of Massinger, Middleton, and Rowley's *The Old Law*, 1656, 'An Exact and perfect Catalogue of all Plaies that were ever printed; together, with all the Authors names; and what are Comedies, Histories, Interludes, Masks, Pastorels, Tragedies'. Dr. Greg shows that this catalogue of Archer's is derived from the similar list of Rogers and Ley published in the same year. (*Bibliography*, ii. 996.) One title in Archer's list is 'Virgils Eclogs T.' It must surely be the result of some sort of confusion (see Greg, *Bibliography*, ii. 1000), but one cannot be sure.

Virtue and Beauty Reconciled
(Ghost title?)

Fleay (*Biog. Chron.* ii. 345) listed this title under the heading of masques by anonymous authors with the description, 'c. 1625, May 11. In honor of the marriage of the King and Queen; n.d.' Hazlitt (*Manual*, p. 247) listed the same title with the same description, but attributed it to Ben Jonson. It seems likely that both entries refer to Jonson's *Fortunate Isles* (q.v.).

The Vision of Lethe
(Ghost title)

The Vision of Lethe is W. C. Hazlitt's title (*Manual*, p. 247) for the masque 'presented by the Lord Hay at the Wardrobe to the French Ambassador, the Baron de Tour, February 22, 1617'. The masque presented on this occasion was Ben Jonson's *Lovers Made Men* (q.v.). Why Hazlitt listed it as anonymous I do not know.

A Vow and a Good One (> 1622/3)
(Lost?)

1622/3, 6 Jan. In his list of court performances for the season 1622–3, Sir Henry Herbert recorded, 'Upon Twelfe night, the Masque being put off, *A Vowe and a Good One* was acted by the princes servants'. (Adams, *Herbert*, p. 50.)

Nothing is known of the play save the record of the court performance set down by the Master of the Revels. Fleay at one point
(*Biog. Chron.* i. 200) tentatively identified the play with Fletcher's
The Chances; a very dubious identification, since *The Chances* be-
longed to the King's company. Later (ibid. ii. 98 and 328) he
asked whether the title should not be identified with Middleton and
Rowley's *A Fair Quarrel*. This second guess is a better one, since
the Middleton–Rowley play did belong to the right company, but
A Vow and a Good One is not so apt a title as *A Fair Quarrel* for the
play. Moreover, at the time of the court performance of 1622/3 *A
Fair Quarrel* had already been used as the title in the Stationers'
Register, on three title-pages and in the list of about 1619–20 on
waste paper of the Revels Office. The title-pages say that it had
been acted at court before. Since *A Fair Quarrel* had already been
used so many times for the Middleton–Rowley play, including
at least one time in the records of his own office, it seems very
unlikely that Sir Henry would have used in 1622/3 another title
that never appears again. It seems to me almost certain that *A
Vow and a Good One* is lost, like more than half of the known
repertory of Prince Charles's (I) company after 1615. (See above,
i. 214–17.)

The Wandering Jew (?)
(Lost)

This title occurs fifteenth in Abraham Hill's list of plays in
manuscript. (See Middleton, *The Conqueror's Custom*.) The list
seems to have been Hill's record of some bookseller's stock, set
down between 1677 and 1703, but it is notable that nearly all
the identifiable plays and playwrights in the list are Jacobean or
Caroline.

The play is not known from any other source. Presumably it
dramatized one of the various versions of the legend of the Jew
condemned by Jesus to wander until the Second Coming.

The Wasp (c. 1630–38?)

MS.: Alnwick Castle, Northumberland, MS. 507.

Gourlay, James J. 'Caroline Play, "The Wasp"', *T.L.S.*, 5
June 1943, p. 271.
—— 'Thomas Jordan', ibid., 17 August 1933, p. 549.
Greg, W. W. *Dramatic Documents from the Elizabethan Play-
houses* (1931), pp. 360–1.

In 1931 Dr. Greg said that an edition of this manuscript, which

I have not seen, was in preparation, and in 1933 Mr. Gourlay said that he had been for some time engaged in transcribing it, but in his letter of 5 June 1943 he said nothing of proposed publication, though he announced some of his conclusions. I know of no edition of the play.

In both his letters Mr. Gourlay says that he thinks the play is the work of Thomas Jordan, and in the first letter, but not the second, he records his belief that it is a Jordan autograph. Perhaps he is right, but he has presented no evidence whatever yet, and in the meantime it is much safer to classify the play as anonymous until a good case for ascription has been made.

Assuming, in his later letter, that the play is by Thomas Jordan, and assuming—also without presenting any evidence—that it was written about 1638, Mr. Gourlay concludes that:

> It was therefore presumably acted by the amalgamated King's Revels-Queen Henrietta's Company at Salisbury Court in Fleet Street, since the manuscript contains the names of several King's Revels actors (Barrett, Jordan, Morris).

Accepting for the moment the reasoning from conjecture, there is still no good reason to think that a play written by Jordan in 1638 was written for Queen Henrietta's men at the Salisbury Court. No evidence has been produced that Jordan was ever a member of this company (see above, ii. 487–90), and no evidence that any of his plays was written for them. (See above, Thomas Jordan.) Dr. Greg mentions only 'Ellis' and 'Ambros' as actors' names appearing in the manuscript. If the names of [John?] Barrett, [Thomas] Jordan, and [Mathias] Morris are there also, there is good reason to associate the play with the King's Revels company, for four of the five actors probably indicated by the names appear in other records of the company (see above, i. 297), but not after March 1634/5. The actor named 'Noble' whom Mr. Gourlay reports as also appearing in the manuscript is not otherwise known.

Dr. Greg pointed out (loc. cit.) that the manuscript had been used in the playhouse for performance, and he noted that the prompt notes, including those involving the names of actors, had been added in another hand. He dated the play—presumably on the character of the principal hand—as c. 1630? If the names which Mr. Gourlay read and Dr. Greg did not are correct, a date of c. 1634–6 would better fit what is known of the actors; no evidence for Mr. Gourlay's conjecture of 1638 has appeared, but there may be some. In the absence of assembled facts about *The Wasp*, one can only conjecture the date limits as c. 1630–8.

A Way to Make a Knave Honest (?)
(Lost)

This title is thirty-eighth in a list of manuscript plays found among the papers of Abraham Hill. (See Middleton, *The Conqueror's Custom*.) The list seems to have been Hill's record of some bookseller's stock, set down between 1677 and 1703, but it is notable that nearly all the identifiable plays and playwrights of the list are Jacobean and Caroline.

The title does not appear elsewhere.

A Welcome from the Isle of Rhé

Not a play. See Anon., *In Duc Reducem*.

The Welsh Ambassador

See Dekker.

The Welsh Traveller (1622)
(Lost)

1622, 10 May. 'A new Play, called, *The Welsh Traveller*, was allowed to be acted by the players of the Revels.' (Adams, *Herbert*, p. 23.)

The only record of *The Welsh Traveller* is Sir Henry Herbert's entry of his allowance of the play to the company of the Revels on 10 May 1622. It has several times been asserted that this date is a mistake for 1623, but 1622 seems to be correct. (See above, i. 205, n. 5. and Anon., *The Dutch Painter and the French Branke*.)

The players of the Revels were the remnants of Queen Anne's men who continued to play at the Red Bull after her death in 1619 and the defection of certain members of the troupe to other London companies. (See above, i. 165–70.) It was not a very distinguished organization.

Several historians and bibliographers have suggested that *The Welsh Traveller* may have been the same as *The Welsh Ambassador*, which is extant in a manuscript in the Cardiff Public Library. There was never much beyond the similar titles to prompt the identification, and after the publication of *The Welsh Ambassador* in 1920 it became clear that it could scarcely have been called *The Welsh Traveller*. (See Thomas Dekker.) The title, *The Witch*

Traveller, is only a typographical error for *The Welsh Traveller*.
On 5 April 1655 William Gilbertson entered in the Stationers'
Register eight titles, including '4. *The Welsh Traveller, or the
unfortunate Welshman*, by H. C.', and on 18 April 1666 '*The
Welch Traveller*' was entered with a long list of other titles
assigned to Robert White by the executors of William Gilbertson.
(G. E. B. Eyre, *A Transcript of the Registers of the Worshipful
Company of Stationers from 1640–1708 A.D.*, i. 471 and ii. 364.)
In spite of the identical titles, this piece was not the play of 1622,
but a satirical verse account of a Welsh booby by Humphrey
Crouch, the first extant edition of which was published in 1671. It
was reprinted by J. O. Halliwell[-Phillipps] in a limited edition in
1860. It seems to have no connexion with the play.

The Whibble
(Ghost title)

In Act v, Scene 1, of Middleton's *The Mayor of Quinborough or
Hengist, King of Kent* (q.v.), the rascals pretending to be a troupe
of players give to the mayor a list of plays from which he may
choose. One of these titles is *The Whibble*, and it has several times
been listed as a lost play. It is fairly clear, however, that all the
titles are fictitious, mostly puns on the situation of the rascals
and the gullible mayor. Even *The Wild Goose Chase* probably
refers to the proverbial expression and not to Fletcher's play of
the name.

Which Is the Best Girl
(Lost)

See Anon., *The Politic Bankrupt*.

The Whimsies of Señor Hidalgo or The Masculine Bride
(1649–65 ?)

MS.: B.M. MS. Harleian 5152.

This manuscript play in the Harleian collection has a title-page
which reads 'A New Comedy Calld The Whimseyes of Señor
Hidalgo Or the Masculine Bride'. The prologue says of the author
that:

> His learning is not great; but yet hee thinkes
> The wisdome of ye best at small faults winkes;

> 'Tis much against his temper to betray
> His Customers; who ready mony pay;
> And then Apologize for doing wrong;

and later seems to include him among 'ffresh beginners'. In the
epilogue the author speaks frankly in his own person:

> J pump'd noe books;
> nor yet have turn'd invention wth sowre looks
> my library was hunger, & my plott
> in raysing recknings where J pd noe shott.
> Jf J bee recompenc'd for this, you may
> expect Jll make you S^{rs}: another play
> if not J nere intend to feed on bayes

These lines from the prologue and epilogue suggest an inexper-
ienced writer—as the verse does—and a commercial theatre where
financial rewards are anticipated.

Several lines in the play imply a late Commonwealth or early
Restoration rather than a Caroline composition. In III. 8 BotiJa
rails at his wife for taking a barrel and a hogshead to her religious
meetings. In I. 6 Sabroso says to his servant, Creado, 'Now you
looke like a good Commonwealthsman & not a Courtier Creado.
—Oh a new coat! what cost it?' In II. 3 Creado says of his master
that

all trades curse him & yet they can hardly live w^{th}out him, hee is a
good Commonwealth man hee furnishes every one wth mony, but the
Devill has not witt enough to cheat him of one odde halfepenny.

And in II. 8 Punctilla says:

but Good S^{r}: come not at her for then J shall have such a Lecture &
of that length that it woud reach beyond the patience of a mortifi'd
quaker to heare.

The characters are middle class, and most of the action takes
place at an inn. The principal characters are Señor Redondo,
Señor Hidalgo, Pandolpho, BotiJa, the Innkeeper, Sabroso, 'a
carking wretch', Creado, Domingilla, Palabresa, Punctilla, and
Susiada, 'a whore, belonging to the [house *deleted*] Jnne'.
The play is written with very few corrections in a clear hand
on lines ruled in pencil. The hand might well be of the Restoration
period.

The Whirligig
(Ghost title)

In Act v, Scene 1, of Middleton's *The Mayor of Quinborough, or
Hengist, King of Kent* (q.v.), the rascals pretending to be a troupe

of players give to the mayor a list of plays from which he may choose. One of these titles is *The Whirligig*, and it has several times been listed as a lost play. It is fairly clear, however, that all the titles the rascals use are fictitious, mostly puns on the situation of the scheming rogues and the gullible mayor. Even *The Wild Goose Chase* probably refers to the proverbial expression and not to Fletcher's play of the name.

It does not seem likely that the pretending players were referring to Edward Sharpham's play, *Cupid's Whirligig*, published in 1607 (see *The Elizabethan Stage*, iii. 491) as *The Whirligig*.

The Whisperer, or What You Please (> 1650)
(Lost)

A prologue for a performance of this play is printed in John Tatham's collection of verse entitled *Ostella, or The Faction of Love and Beauty Reconcil'd*, 1650:

> *A Prologue spoken at the* Red-Bull *to a Play*
> *called the* Whisperer, or what you please.
>
> Now bless my *eye-sight*! what! the house so thin,
> And we upon preparing to begin!
> Whence comes this strange *Neglect*? have you injoy'd
> Of late so much variety y'are *cloi'd*?
> Or do you think you pay too dear for *Wit*,
> And so would grossly take your leave of it.
> Grossly indeed; for hither you do come,
> Like so many *Churls*, and leave your *Wives* at home,
> Our *Author* likes the *Women* well, and says,
> You do 'em wrong to hinder 'em from *Plays*.
> And therefore wishes you to be more kind,
> And on *his Day* to leave them not behind.
> The more the merrier, rather than come alone
> For *once* make *use* of what is not your own,
> And bring your *Neighbours Wife*, which if you do
> 'Tis *ten* to *one* hee'l do as *much* for you;
> And if our *Mirth* cannot your *Anger* smother,
> You may go home, and *Laugh* at one another.
> If what *we* fancy, *you* like in the *Play*,
> 'Tis a good sign that *good Wits* jump, you'l say.
> But though *Detraction's* become a *Disease*,
> In spight of *It*, you shall have what you please.
>
> (*Ostella*, p. 111 [P₄].)

The prologue seems to indicate that the play was a comedy, and it may have been written by Tatham himself, but it seems more

likely—since Tatham published the prologue without any reference to authorship—that it was written by someone else and that
Tatham furnished only a prologue for the players.

Normally one would assume that such a play was performed
before the closing of the theatres, but it is known that the Red
Bull was used for surreptitious performances after 1642 (see
Hotson, *The Commonwealth and Restoration Stage* [1928], pp.
34–58), and certain lines of the prologue, if taken ironically, might
be suitable for an interregnum performance. Though one might
guess that the prologue was written for a performance 1640–2, the
evidence shows only that it was performed before 1650.

The White Ethiopian (?)

MS: B.M. MS. Harleian 7313.

Harbage, Alfred. *Cavalier Drama* (1936), pp. 63–64, 220–1.

On the first page of the B.M. MS. the title of the play, 'The
white Ethiopian', is given, followed by two Latin quotations, each
translated into English couplets. The prologue which follows the
dramatis personae was obviously intended for a production, and
so was the epilogue on fol. 131; the prologue ends with the stage
direction, 'pointing at ye Ladys'. But the stage directions in the
acts that follow are literary and innocent of theatrical experience.
On fol. 5 is the direction, 'he museth, scratcheth his head, &
walks two turnes rownd ye stage'. And on fol. 17^v there is an
amusing abandonment of the dramatic for the narrative method
in the direction,

they goe as to ye other side of ye sea and as they goe Cnemon steales
Theagenes sword out of his scabard and as they descend as it were to
ye mouth of a caue, Cnemon espies a dead body lying wth. its mouth
downwards.

Such directions are eloquent of closet drama, whatever intentions
the author may have had when he wrote the prologue.

The story is that of Theagenes and Chariclia from the *Aethiopica*
of Heliodorus. As Hazlitt pointed out (*A Manual for the Collector
and Amateur of Old English Plays*, p. 251), a metrical version of
Heliodorus called *The Fair Œthiopian* by William Lisle was printed
in 1631, and it might be interesting to compare the poem and the
play.

Harbage thought *The White Ethiopian* a Commonwealth production because in the verse the 'Enjambment and end-stopping
side by side' were very similar to this mingling in Mildmay Fane's

interregnum plays. (Op. cit., p. 63.) Though I know of nothing in the play to contradict such a date, general similarities of verse are notoriously weak grounds for dating plays, especially when there is no reason to think they are by the same poet. As Harbage notes elsewhere (ibid., p. 220), the play 'impregnates with *précieuse* sensibilities material which on a previous occasion (in Gough's *Strange Discovery*) had been utilized in a play of mere intrigue and adventure'. Though this characteristic is equally general, it could just as well suggest composition in the thirties under the influence of Queen Henrietta Maria's cult.

The play is written in a large, somewhat childish hand which looks late. There are many corrections, apparently in the same hand. Though there is an epilogue on fol. 131, the text goes on to fol. 139, where it breaks off, at, or near, the end of Act IV, Scene 18 [*sic*].

The White Witch of Westminster, or Love in a Lunacy (?)
(Lost)

This title is the twenty-fifth in the list of manuscript plays found among the papers of Abraham Hill. (See Middleton, *The Conqueror's Custom*.) The list seems to have been Hill's record of some bookseller's stock, set down between 1677 and 1703, but it is notable that nearly all the identifiable plays and playwrights in the list are Jacobean or Caroline.

No other record of a play of this title exists, so far as I know. J. Q. Adams, in his discussion of Hill's list (*Library*, Fourth Series, xx [1939], 91), notes the lost play of *Long Meg of Westminster*, recorded in Henslowe's Diary, but observes that the pamphlet of the same name discloses no features which would make the above title applicable.

The Whore in Grain (1623/4)
(Lost)

1623/4, 26 Jan. 'For the Palsgrave's Company; A Tragedy, called, *The whore in grain.*' (Adams, *Herbert*, p. 27.)

The Whore in Grain is one of fourteen plays licensed for the Palsgrave's company in the fifteen months between the end of July 1623 and the beginning of November 1624, by far the largest number of plays known to have been licensed for performance by any Jacobean or Caroline company in so short a period. This phenomenon is part of the evidence of the desperate attempt of the company to keep going after the destruction of their repertory in the Fortune fire of 9 December 1621. (See above, i. 141–2 and 149–51.) All but one of the plays have disappeared—probably an indication of their inferior quality.

Fleay's identification of *The Whore New Vamped* (q.v.) as a revision of this play (*A Chronicle History of the London Stage, 1559–1642*, p. 358) cannot be proved or disproved, since both plays are lost. It seems to me to have little to recommend it save the common word of the two titles and the fact that Andrew Cane, who had a part in *The Whore New Vamped* (see above, i. 314–15), was a member of the Palsgrave's company when *The Whore in Grain* was licensed. (See above, ii. 398–400.) Whores are not so rare in Jacobean and Caroline drama as Fleay's identification would imply. Moreover, the Palsgrave's play was licensed as a tragedy, and the quotations from the later play suggest a comedy.

There is no indication of the authorship of *The Whore in Grain*. Most of the other plays of the Palsgrave's men at this time are anonymous or by little-known authors.

The Whore New Vamped (1639)
(Lost)

The only records of this play come from the accounts of its suppression in the *Calendar of State Papers, Domestic*, under date of 29 September 1639:

> Order of the King in Council. Complaint was this day made that the stage-players of the Red Bull [have for] many days together acted a scandalous and libellous [play in which] they have audaciously reproached and in a libel [represented] and personated not only some of the aldermen of the [city of London] and some other persons of quality, but also scandalized and libelled the whole profession of proctors belonging to the Court of [Probate], and reflected upon the present Government. Ordered that the Attorney-General be hereby prayed forthwith to call before him, not only the poet who made the play and the actors that played the same, but also the person that licensed it, and having diligently examined the truth of the said complaint, to proceed roundly against such of them as he shall find have been faulty, and to use such effectual ex[pedition] to bring them to sentence, as that their exemplary punishment may [check] such insolencies betimes. (*C.S.P., Dom., Charles I, 1639*, p. 529. A more accurate but slightly less complete version is reprinted *M.S.C.* i. 394–5, from the Privy Council Register.)

Exceptions taken to the play above referred to. In the play called

'The Whore New Vamped,' where there was mention of the new duty on wines, one personating a justice of the peace, says to Cain. 'Sirrah, I'll have you before the alderman;' whereto Cain replies, 'The alderman, the alderman is a base, drunken, sottish knave, I care not for the alderman, I say the alderman is a base, drunken, sottish knave.' Another says, 'How now Sirrah, what alderman do you speak of?' Then Cain says, 'I mean alderman [William Abell], the blacksmith in Holborn;' says the other, 'Was he not a Vintner?' Cain answers, 'I know no other.' In another part of the play one speaking of projects and patents that he had got, mentions among others 'a patent for 12d. a piece upon every proctor and proctor's man who was not a knave.' Said another, 'Was there ever known any proctor but he was an arrant knave?' (*C.S.P., Dom., Charles I, 1639*, pp. 529–30.)

These records indicate the great popularity of the piece, for 'many days together' was a most unusual run for a play of the time. (See above, i. 13, n. 2.) The topical nature of the 'scandalous and libellous play' is enough to account for its run, for the Red Bull had a popular reputation for noise and vulgarity at this time, and the company—Prince Charles's (II) men—seem to have made the most of it. (See above, i. 313–20.)

Nothing is known of the authorship or even the original date of the play. Fleay (*A Chronicle History of the London Stage, 1559–1642*, p. 358) assumed that it was a revision of *The Whore in Grain* (q.v.), but the evidence is inadequate, unless one reads his own interpretation into the documents, as Fleay did.

The Widow Captain (?)
(Lost)

The title occurs twenty-fourth in Abraham Hill's list of plays in manuscript. (See Middleton, *The Conqueror's Custom.*) The list seems to have been Hill's record of some bookseller's stock, set down between 1677 and 1703, but it is notable that nearly all the identifiable plays and playwrights in the list are Jacobean or Caroline.

The title is not found elsewhere, and it does not suggest to me any known play.

Wine, Beer, and Ale [and Tobacco] (1624–6?)

MS.: University of Edinburgh MS. Laing, iii. 493.

Edition: James Holly Hanford, ed., *Stud. Phil.* xii (1915), 1–54.

Wagner, Bernard M. 'Manuscript Plays of the Seventeenth Century', *T.L.S.*, 4 October 1934, p. 675.

1629. Wine, Beere, *And* Ale, Together By The Eares. *A Dialogue*, Written first in *Dutch* by *Gallobelgicus*, and faithfully translated out of the originall Copies, by *Mercurius Brittannicus*, for the benefite of his Nation . . . 1629.

1630. Wine, Beere, Ale, *And* Tobacco. Contending for Superiority. *A Dialogue*. The second Edition, much enlarged . . . 1630.

1658. Wine, Beer, Ale, *And* Tobacco, Contending for superiority. *A Dialogue* . . . 1658.

1662, 15 July. S.R. James Cottrell entered for his copy by virtue of an assignment from John Grove 'a Booke entituled Wyne Beere Ale & Tobaccoe, [&ĉ. *deleted*] Contending for Superiority.' (Greg, *Bibliography*, i. 70.)

Professor Hanford notes that the first edition title-page references to a Dutch original and a translator are not intended to be taken seriously. There is no trace of a Dutch original, the names of author and translator are those of contemporary newsbooks, and the piece is full of English, not Dutch allusions. Several of these allusions, Professor Hanford notes, suggest a date of 1624–6, though not with the finality one might like. The address of the Stationer to the reader is unrevealing.

This short play is of the same debate type as several Cambridge plays, *Lingua*, *Work for Cutlers*, and *Exchange Ware, or Band, Cuff and Ruff*, all published in or before 1615. Professor Hanford finds also a similarity to another Cambridge play, Randolph's *Aristippus* (q.v.), which he did not know was acted in 1625 or 1626, but which he thought probably indebted to *Wine, Beer, and Ale*. Nor did he know that there is a connexion of a sort between it and Randolph's *Conceited Pedlar* (q.v.), acted at Cambridge on All Saints Day, 1627, and found with *Wine, Beer, and Ale* in the University of Edinburgh MS. Laing, iii. 493, both pieces, according to Professor Wagner, probably written in the same hand. These numerous connexions do not prove that *Wine, Beer, and Ale* was a Cambridge show, but they make it seem likely. One is given pause by the absence of recognizable Cambridge allusions in the piece.

The character, date, and associations of *Wine, Beer, and Ale* all suggest Randolph, but Professor Hanford does not think the play clever enough for him, and I should agree.

The second edition, as the title-page indicates, is enlarged by the addition of Tobacco to the dialogue. This edition, which runs to 684 lines, is the one Professor Hanford reprints. According to his notes, it drops early in the play about thirteen lines of the first edition which refer to tobacco, and at a later point adds 176 new lines treating tobacco more favourably. This new material has not been fully integrated, however, for the symbolic dance with which the play ends makes full use of Wine, Beer, and Ale and their servants, but does not mention Tobacco at all.

In a list of ballads entered to Francis Coules, 24 June 1630, is one called 'Wyne Beer and ale'. As Hanford points out (op. cit., p. 5, n. 3), this can scarcely refer to the second edition of the play, which had a different title. A transfer of rights in the first edition of the play in the midst of a ballad list would be very odd. Perhaps the identical titles are just a coincidence, for it does not seem likely that such an academic piece as the anonymous show of 1629 could have prompted a ballad.

The Witch Traveller
(Ghost title)

This title, listed by J. O. Halliwell[-Phillipps] in *A Dictionary of Old English Plays* (1860), p. 274, is presumably an error for the anonymous play, *The Welsh Traveller* (q.v.).

The Woman Is Too Hard for Him (> 1621)
(Lost?)

1621, 26 Nov. In a book that is probably a copy of some part of the books of the Lord Chamberlain of the Household is a series of licences and warrants for payments to players. One, dated 27 March 1622, is 'A warrant for allowance of lx^{li} to John Hemmings and his fellowes the Kings Ma^{ts} Players for 6 plaies vizt ... The Woman is to Hard for him 26° of the same Monethe [i.e., November].' (John Tucker Murray, *English Dramatic Companies*, ii. 193, from Inner Temple MS. 515, No. 7.)

The play is known only from the single record of payment for its performance at court by the King's men. The title, it has been suggested, may be intended for John Fletcher's *The Wild Goose Chase*, which belonged to the same company. It is true that the title would be appropriate for Fletcher's comedy, but since that play was acted at court under its familiar name only two months later, and indeed the record of payment for the two performances is found in the same document, it seems unlikely that a single play would be given two different titles, one of them not otherwise known, in the same record.

Sir Edmund Chambers suggested (*Elizabethan Stage*, iii. 222) that *The Woman Is Too Hard for Him* might be the same as Fletcher's *The Woman's Prize, or The Tamer Tamed*.

The Woman's Law (> 1653)
(Lost)

The only evidence for the existence of a play of this name is its occurrence in an entry in the Stationers' Register. The entry reads as follows:

29th Novemb [December ?] 1653

[This heading appears between others of 22 and 30 December and is probably misdated.]

Rich: Marriott Entred for his copies the severall playes following (vizt)

The Paraside or Revenge for hono^r. by Henry Glapthorne	A Foole & her maiden head soone Parted
The fflorentine freind	Supposed Inconstancy.
The Proxe or Loues after Game	The Womans Law.
The Eunuch a Tragedy	The Diuorse
The Conceits	The Bond Woman
Salisbury Plaine a comedy.	Castara or Cruelty without hate
The Womans Master Peice	The Thracian Wonder
Pitty the Maid	The Blacke Wedding.
The Royall Choice by Sr Robt. Stapleton.	The Law Case
	The Younger Brother
The Noble Rauishers	The Noble Triall x^s vj^d

(Greg, *Bibliography*, i. 62; and ii. 990–3.)

The list is an odd one. There is no other known record of fourteen of the titles: *The Florentine Friend, The Conceits, Salisbury Plain, The Woman's Masterpiece, Pity the Maid, The Royal Choice, The Noble Ravishers, Supposed Inconstancy, The Woman's Law, The Divorce, The Bond Woman, Castara, The Black Wedding,* and *The Law Case.* Several of them might describe known plays published under other titles, but Fleay's example has demonstrated the folly of such identifications without evidence. Most tempting is the title 'Salisbury Plaine a comedy'. This would describe very well the manuscript play in the British Museum, a comedy set at Stonehenge on Salisbury Plain, and including frequent references to Salisbury. (See above, John Speed, *Stonehenge.*) Several other items in the list are similar to known titles: *The Law Case* to

The Devil's Law Case; The Noble Trial to *The Lady's Trial*; and *Pity the Maid* to *'Tis Pity She's a Whore*. But all three had been printed fourteen to thirty years before by other publishers, and it does not seem likely that Marriott would have chosen this method of appropriating them.

Three of the plays in Marriott's list were published later: 'The Paraside or Revenge for honoᵣ' in 1654 by Marriott himself; 'The Thracian Wonder' in 1661 by Kirkman; 'The Eunuch a Tragedy' probably as *The Fatal Contract* by J. M. in 1653 and as *The Eunuch, a Tragedy* by Dorman Newman in 1687. (But see Greg, *Bibliography*, ii. 830–1.)

Four of the plays are known from other sources, though they are lost: *The Proxy, or Love's Aftergame* is noted by Sir Henry Herbert to have been acted at the Salisbury Court theatre 24 November 1634 and at court 24 February 1635/6. *A Fool and Her Maidenhead Soon Parted* was listed by William Beeston as part of the Cockpit repertory in 1639. *The Younger Brother*, according to Edward Alleyn, was the property of the company at the Red Bull in 1617, and the title *The Younger Brother, or The Male Courtesan* appears in Hill's list of manuscript plays towards the end of the century. *The Noble Trial* is in a list of plays entered in the Stationers' Register by Humphrey Moseley 29 June 1660, but there it is ascribed to Henry Glapthorne.

All in all, the list is an odd one which, taken as a whole, throws no light on any of the individual titles. One would like to guess that the list represents part of the repertory of some company, but the evidence is against it, for *The Parricide* (q.v.) belonged to Prince Charles's (I) company, *The Eunuch* under the title of *The Fatal Contract* (q.v. under Heminges) to Queen Henrietta's company, *The Proxy* (q.v.) to the King's Revels, and if *Salisbury Plain* was *Stonehenge* (q.v.) it was a university play. In the absence of evidence one can only assume that Marriott had assembled a miscellaneous group of play manuscripts which he intended to publish, but that he later abandoned nearly all of them.

The Woman's Masterpiece (> 1653)
(Lost)

1653, 29 [Dec.] S.R. Richard Marriott entered as his copies a number of plays, including 'The Womans Master Peice'. (Greg, *Bibliography*, i. 62.)

The only evidence for the existence of a play of this name is

Marriott's entry in the Stationers' Register. Two-thirds of the twenty-one titles in this list of plays occur nowhere else, and only three plays were published later under these titles, though four are known from some other reference. (See Anon., *The Woman's Law*, for the entire list.)

Woodcock of Our Side
(Ghost title)

In Act v, Scene 1, of Middleton's *The Mayor of Quinborough, or Hengist, King of Kent* (q.v.), the rascals pretending to be a troupe of players give to the mayor a list of plays from which he may choose. One of the titles in their list is *Woodcock of Our Side*, and it has several times been listed as a lost play. It is fairly clear, however, that all the titles the rascals use are fictitious, mostly puns on the situation of the scheming rogues and the gullible mayor. Even *The Wild Goose Chase* probably refers to the proverbial expression and not to Fletcher's play of the name.

A. H. Bullen in a note in his edition of *The Mayor of Quinborough* (*Works of Thomas Middleton*, ii. 93) reprints Dyce's observation that in the preface to his *Sir Gregory Nonsense* John Taylor, the Water Poet, mentioned a book with the title *A Woodcock of Our Side*. Taylor's use of the title, however, is similar to Middleton's. At the end of a preface of nonsense he lists a mock-bibliography of such titles as *Boe to a Goose*, *Gammon of Westphallia*, *Quinborough Oysters*, *Shooters Hill*, *Yard of Ale*, and *Zany on tumbling*.

The World

On 10 August 1639 the Lord Chamberlain sent out a list of plays belonging to the repertory of the King and Queen's Young Company at the Phoenix and forbade all other London companies to act them. (See above, i. 330–1.) One play in the list is 'The World'. Since this title immediately follows three other titles of plays written by the collaborators Thomas Middleton and William Rowley, it seems likely that 'The World' stands for *The World Tossed at Tennis*, which was written by them. See under Middleton.

The Wronged Widow's Tragedy (?)
(Lost)

This title occurs fourth in Abraham Hill's list of plays in manuscript. (See Middleton, *The Conqueror's Custom*.) The list seems

to have been Hill's record of some bookseller's stock, set down
between 1677 and 1703, but it is notable that nearly all the
identifiable plays and playwrights in the list are Jacobean or
Caroline.

Professor Adams, who first printed the list, seems to have been
tempted by the applicability of this title to what we know of the
sub-plot of *The Late Murder of the Son upon the Mother, or Keep
the Widow Waking*. (*Library*, Fourth Series, xx [1939], 81–82. See
also my discussion of the play, above under Dekker.) But the
whole point of the suit which gives us our knowledge of this play
is that the dramatists treated the widow hilariously, not tragically.

The Yorkshire Gentleman (?)
(Lost ?)

W. C. Hazlitt listed in *A Manual for the Collector and Amateur
of Old English Plays* (1892), p. 260: 'The Yorkshire Gentleman:
A Tragedy. *Heber's MSS.*' I know nothing of a play of the name
or of the manuscript.

The Younger Brother (> 1617)
(Lost)

1617, 3 Oct. 'I went to yᵉ red bull & R/ for yᵉ younger brother,
   but 3. 6. 4.' (The Diary of Edward Alleyn, quoted in William
   Young, *The History of Dulwich College* [1889], ii. 51.)
1653, 29 [Dec.] S.R. Richard Marriott entered as his copies a
   number of plays, including 'The Younger Brother'. (Greg,
   Bibliography, i. 62.)
1677–1703. In Abraham Hill's list of manuscript plays the twenty-
   third title is 'The younger Brother or male Curtesan'. (See
   above under Middleton, *The Conqueror's Custom*.)

Alleyn's account-book entry is a bit cryptic, but I have suggested
in the light of its context and of the theatrical situation of 1617
that it records the payment of an instalment on their debt by
Prince Charles's (I) company, who seem to have been playing at
the Red Bull at the time. (See above, i. 201–3.) In this case the
payment would have been derived from the take at a performance
of *The Younger Brother*. It is alternately possible that Alleyn was
recording the sale of the manuscript of the play to the company,
but such a transaction would be more unusual for him. In either
case we know only that the play was the property of the company

at the Red Bull on 3 October 1617, and nothing of how long before
it had been written, or by whom. Red Bull plays of the period were
not generally very distinguished.

The second occurrence of the title tells us nothing more. Marriott's list of plays is an odd one. Two-thirds of the twenty-one
titles occur nowhere else; only three were published later under
these titles; four, including *The Younger Brother*, are known from
some other reference but are not extant. (See Anon., *The Woman's
Law*, for the entire list.)

The title in Hill's list of manuscript plays—which J. Q. Adams
dated 1677–1703, preferably around 1678 (*Library*, Fourth Series,
xx [1939], 71–99)—presumably refers to this play in spite of the
addition of a sub-title. If Adams's suggestion that the manuscripts
of Hill's list were the property of some London bookseller is
valid, Hill may have seen the same manuscript that Marriott had
licensed.

Aphra Behn's play, *The Younger Brother, or the Amorous Jilt*,
first acted posthumously and printed in 1696, is not the same as
Hill's play, since it contains no male courtesan. Since her play
does not suggest a revised Elizabethan drama, there is probably
no connexion between *The Younger Brother, or the Amorous Jilt*
and either the Red Bull play or *The Younger Brother, or the Male
Courtesan*—if those two are not to be identified.

PLAYS AND MASQUES WITHOUT TITLE
OR AUTHOR

This section is intended as a guide to extant plays not classifiable
by the usual indices of authors and titles, or associated only with
conjectural titles not generally known or accepted. The many lost
plays and masques whose performance or preparations are referred
to vaguely by contemporaries are not included, except for the
three St. Omers productions in the period that are listed by
Father McCabe. I have listed them so far as possible chronologically.

Unnamed Play (< 1612)

MS.: Trinity College, Cambridge, MS. R. 10. 4 (item 4).

See Anon., *Microcosmus*.

Unnamed Play (1624)

McCabe, William H. 'Notes on the St. Omers College Theatre',
  Phil. Quart. xvii (1938), 225–39.
—— 'The Play-List of the English College of St. Omers, 1592–
  1762', *Revue de littérature comparée*, xvii (1937), 355–75.

Father McCabe notes that in the Jesuit College for English boys
at St. Omers there was given, apparently in 1624, 'A play, no
title, day or description recorded, for the Prince-Governor of
Artois at the College, requested by the town magistrates, as part of
his civic reception . . . composed by the boys'. ('Play-List', p. 364.)

Unnamed Play (August 1634)

McCabe, William H. 'Notes on the St. Omers College Theatre',
  Phil. Quart. xvii (1938), 225–39.
—— 'The Play-List of the English College of St. Omers, 1592–
  1762', *Revue de littérature comparée*, xvii (1937), 355–75.

Father McCabe notes a possible allusion to a play at the Jesuit
College for English boys at St. Omers in August 1634 in the record
in B.M. MS. Add. 9354, fol. 49ᵛ, 'Virgineque Magna Matre saltus
insolentiaeque barbarae aeternum victrice'. He thinks the subject
was possibly Don Juan's victory over the Turks at Lepanto. ('Play-
List', p. 366.)

A Design for a Masque (1638)

The piece in Harleian MS. 4931 at the British Museum headed
'An: 1638. The Designe' is really a synopsis of Thomas Carew's
Coelum Britannicum (q.v.).

Unnamed Play (11 June 1640)

McCabe, William H. 'Notes on the St. Omers College Theatre',
  Phil. Quart. xvii (1938), 225–39.
—— 'The Play-List of the English College of St. Omers, 1592–
  1762', *Revue de littérature comparée*, xvii (1937), 355–75.

Father McCabe finds that on 11 June 1640 a tragedy, 'egregia
tragoedia', was performed at the Jesuit College for English boys at
St. Omers. Neither the name of the tragedy nor its subject is
given. ('Play-List', p. 363.)

ADDENDA

Doctor Lamb and the Witches (?; revised 1634)
(Lost)

1634, 20 July. 'A peticõn of the Kings Players complayning of intermingleing some passages of witches in old playes to ye p^riudice of their designed Comedy of the Lancashire witches, & desiring a prohibition of any other till theirs bee allowed & Acted. Answered p[er] Reference to Blagraue in absence of Sr H. Herbert./Iuly 20. 1634.' [Marginal entry: 'Players peticon about ye Witches.'] (From the Lord Chamberlain's Petition Book, L.C. 5/183, *Malone Society Collections*, ii. 410.)

1634, 16 Aug. 'An ould play, with some new scenes, Doctor Lambe and the Witches, to Salisbury Court, the 16th August, 1634,— £1. 0. 0.' (Adams, *Herbert*, p. 36.)

The old play refurbished to compete with the play of the King's men about the Lancashire witch sensation (Brome and Heywood's *The Late Lancashire Witches*, q.v.) was not necessarily *Doctor Lamb and the Witches*, but the title, the admitted revisions, and the proximity in date of Sir Henry's licence suggest that it probably was.

The revisions made for the players at the Salisbury Court (the King's Revels company) probably consisted of insertions of scenes about witches and were intended to exploit the London interest in the Lancashire witch scare. (See Wallace Notestein, *A History of Witchcraft in England from 1558 to 1718* [1911], pp. 146–60, and the Brome and Heywood play.) If Dr. Lambe was the principal subject of the original play, as the title suggests, it may well have been written at the time of the sensational death of this hated London character in the early summer of 1628. (See above, i. 266–8.)

The Spanish Contract (> 1624)
(Lost)

1624, 26 Apr. 'This day wakefield haueinge brought to Mr Maior a note wch he found fastened vpon the gate of the house of Thomas Marcon beinge the Signe of the white horse nere Tomeland in Norw^ch wherein was written these words, Here w^thin this place at one of the clocke shalbe acted an excelent new Comedy called the Spanishe Contract By the Princesse servants/vivat Rex/.

'. . . the said ffrauncis Wambus . . . onely appeared, and saide confidently that he & his Company would play the Comedy aforesaid And beinge demanded whether the bill nowe shewed vnto him conteining the words aforesaid was his hand wrightinge or not, he said yt was his hand writinge & that he caused yt to be set vp this day And the Counsells order beinge againe redd vnto him hee sayde he would play whatsoeu[r] had bene said to the contrary.' (Mayor's Court Books, Norwich, transcribed by J. T. Murray, *English Dramatic Companies*, ii. 348–9.)

This title is known only from the bill which Francis Wambus, one of the actors in the Lady Elizabeth's provincial company, posted on the gate of the White Horse at Norwich, in defiance of the orders of the mayor and council. (See above, ii. 614–15.) It is possible that *The Spanish Contract* is an alternative title for some play now known by another name. Since Wambus's playbill was an advertisement prepared for a provincial audience—for which the players seem never to have had any great respect—not much reliance should be placed on his assertion that the play was new.

One wonders if the title was intended to make the Norwich audience think the play concerned Prince Charles's proposed Spanish marriage contract, which had been causing such national excitement in 1623 and 1624, and which the King's company exploited with such great profit in London three and a half months later. (See above, i. 9–15, and Middleton, *A Game at Chess*.)

The Three London Apprentices

In his comments on the rowdy activities at the Red Bull and the Fortune theatres, Edmund Gayton mentions among several favourites of holiday audiences 'the three *London Apprentises*, which commonly ends in six acts, the spectators frequently mounting the stage, and making a more bloody Catastrophe amongst themselves, then the Players did'. (See above, ii. 690–1.)

Since several of the other plays he mentions in this context are very old ones, like *Tamburlaine, Jugurth,* and *The Jew of Malta,* I assume that under the guise of *The Three London Apprentices* Gayton was referring to Heywood's *The Four Prentices of London,* a play which seems to have had some popularity and which was well qualified to please the Red Bull audience. Sir Edmund Chambers thought it probably first appeared about 1592. (*Eliz. Stage*, iii. 340–1.)